Employee Training and Development

Third Edition

Raymond A. Noe
The Ohio State University

 Irwin

Boston   Burr Ridge, IL   Dubuque, IA   Madison, WI   New York   San Francisco   St. Louis
Bangkok   Bogotá   Caracas   Kuala Lumpur   Lisbon   London   Madrid   Mexico City
Milan   Montreal   New Delhi   Santiago   Seoul   Singapore   Sydney   Taipei   Toronto

Irwin

EMPLOYEE TRAINING AND DEVELOPMENT

Published by McGraw-Hill/Irwin, a business unit of The McGraw-Hill Companies, Inc. 1221 Avenue of the Americas, New York, NY, 10020. Copyright © 2005, 2002, 1999 by The McGraw-Hill Companies, Inc. All rights reserved. No part of this publication may be reproduced or distributed in any form or by any means, or stored in a database or retrieval system, without the prior written consent of The McGraw-Hill Companies, Inc., including, but not limited to, in any network or other electronic storage or transmission, or broadcast for distance learning. Some ancillaries, including electronic and print components, may not be available to customers outside the United States.

This book is printed on acid-free paper.

1 2 3 4 5 6 7 8 9 0 DOC/DOC 0 9 8 7 6 5 4

ISBN 0-07-287550-X

Vice president and editor-in-chief: *Robin J. Zwettler*
Editorial director: *John E. Biernat*
Executive editor: *John Weimeister*
Editorial coordinator: *Trina Hauger*
Executive marketing manager: *Ellen Cleary*
Producer, Media technology: *Mark Molsky*
Project manager: *Marlena Pechan*
Production supervisor: *Gina Hangos*
Designer: *Adam Rooke*
Cover design: *Jenny EL-Shamy*
Cover image: *© 2003 Getty Images*
Supplement producer: *Betty Hadala*
Senior digital content specialist: *Brian Nacik*
Typeface: *10/12 Times New Roman*
Compositor: *Electronic Publishing Services, Inc., TN*
Printer: *R. R. Donnelley*

Library of Congress Cataloging-in Publication Data

Noe, Raymond A.
    Employee training and development / Raymond A. Noe.—3rd ed.
      p. cm.
    Includes bibliographical references and index.
    ISBN 0-07-287550-X
    1. Employees—Training of. I. Title.
  HF5549.5.T7N59 2005
  658.3'124—dc22

                                   2003067151

www.mhhe.com

This book is dedicated to the many who have helped to train and develop me along the way, including

My wife: Caroline

My kids: Ray, Tim, and Melissa

My parents: Raymond J. and Mildred Noe

The many close friends who have touched my heart and made me laugh

The teachers who have shared their wisdom

The graduate students who have worked with me over the years

Preface

Traditionally, training and development was not viewed as an activity that could help companies create "value" and successfully deal with competitive challenges. Today, that view has changed. Companies that use innovative training and development practices are likely to report better financial performance than their competitors that do not. Training and development also helps a company to meet competitive challenges. For example, as companies attempt to bring new products to market and adjust services just-in-time, employees need knowledge and training to be delivered quickly as needed.

Customers are demanding high-quality products and services. As a result, employees must understand how to monitor and improve the quality of goods and services (a quality challenge). Many companies have decentralized operations and have employees working at home, as they travel, and at different hours. Companies are also trying to better utilize employees' talents through new work designs (such as work teams) and new technologies such as computer-assisted manufacturing processes (a high-performance work system challenge). Although many companies are interested in using high-performance work system practices, including teams and computers, employees may not possess the skill levels for these systems to be effective. For example, they may not have interpersonal skills to work in teams. Or they may lack math skills to use even the most basic quality control methods!

Training and development plays a key role in helping companies meet these challenges. To do so, companies need to train employees to work with persons from different cultures both in the United States and abroad. New technologies such as Web-based training and multimedia reduce the costs associated with bringing employees to a central location for training. At the same time, these training methods include the necessary conditions (practice, feedback, self-pacing, etc.) for learning to occur. Due to growth of the Internet, e-commerce has exploded on the business scene. Companies have recognized that training and development activities can be adapted for the Internet, reducing costs and increasing their effectiveness, resulting in the development of e-learning.

The role of training has broadened beyond training program design. Effective instructional training remains important, but training managers, human resource experts, and trainers are increasingly being asked to create systems to motivate employees to learn, create knowledge, and share that knowledge with other employees in the company. Training has moved from an emphasis on a one-time event to the creation of conditions for learning that can occur through collaboration, online learning, traditional classroom training, or a combination of methods. There is increased recognition that learning occurs without a formal training course.

Also, the employee–employer relationship has changed. Due to rapidly changing business environments and competition that can quickly cause profits to shrink and skill needs to change, companies are reluctant to provide job security to employees. At the same time, as employees see downsizing take place (or experience it themselves!), they are reluctant to be fully committed to company goals and values. As a result, both employees and companies are concerned with developing future skills and managing careers. Companies want a work force that is motivated and productive, has up-to-date skills, and can quickly learn new skills to meet changing customer needs. Employees want to develop skills that not only are useful for their current jobs but also are congruent with their personal interests and values. Employees are interested in developing skills that can help them remain employable with either their current employer or a future one. Given the increasing time demands of work, employees are also interested in maintaining balance between work and nonwork interests.

The chapter coverage of *Employee Training and Development* reflects the traditional as well as broadening role of training and development in organizations. Chapter 1 introduces the student to the role of training and development in companies. Chapter 2, "Strategic Training," discusses how training practices and the organization of the training function can support business goals. Because companies are interested in reducing costs, the amount of resources allocated to training is likely to be determined by how much training and development activities help the company reach business goals. Topics related to designing training programs are covered in Chapters 3 through 6. Chapter 3, "Needs Assessment," discusses how to identify when training is appropriate. Chapter 4, "Learning: Theories and Program Design," addresses the learning process and characteristics of a learning environment, and it provides practical suggestions for designing training to ensure that learning occurs. Chapter 5, "Transfer of Training," emphasizes what should be done in the design of training and the work environment to ensure that training is used on the job. Chapter 6, "Training Evaluation," discusses how to evaluate training programs. Here the student is introduced to the concepts of identifying cost-effective training; evaluating the return on investment of training and learning; and determining if training outcomes related to learning, behavior, or performance were reached. Chapters 7 and 8 cover training methods. Chapter 7, "Traditional Training Methods," discusses presentational methods (e.g., lecture), hands-on methods (e.g., on-the-job training, behavior modeling), and group methods (e.g., adventure learning). Chapter 8, "E-Learning and Use of Technology in Training," introduces the student to new technologies that are increasingly being used in training. These technology-based training methods include Web-based instruction, multimedia, distance learning, e-learning, and blended learning. Chapters 7 and 8 both conclude by comparing training methods on the basis of costs, benefits, and learning characteristics.

Chapter 9, "Employee Development," introduces the student to developmental methods (assessment, relationships, job experiences, and formal courses). Topics such as 360-degree feedback and mentoring are discussed. Chapter 10, "Special Issues in Training and Employee Development," discusses cross-cultural training, diversity training, school-to-work programs, and skill-based pay. Chapters 11 and 12 deal with careers and career management. Chapter 11, "Careers and Career Management," emphasizes the protean career and the career management process. Chapter 12, "Special Challenges in Career Management," deals with special issues that trainers, employees, and managers face. These issues include skills obsolescence, plateauing, employee orientation and socialization, work-life balance, downsizing, outplacement, and retirement. Last, Chapter 13, "The Future of Training and Development," looks at how training and development might be different 10 or 20 years from now.

Employee Training and Development is based on my more than fifteen years of teaching training and development courses to both graduate and undergraduate students. From this experience, I realized that managers, consultants, trainers, and faculty working in a variety of disciplines (including education, psychology, business, and industrial relations) have contributed to research and practice of training and development. As a result, the book is based on research conducted in several disciplines while offering a practical perspective. The book is appropriate for students in a number of programs. It suits both undergraduate and master's-level training courses in a variety of disciplines.

DISTINCTIVE FEATURES

There are several distinctive features of the book. First, my teaching experience taught me that students become frustrated if they do not see research and theory in practice. As a result, one distinctive feature of the book is that each chapter begins with a vignette of a company practice that relates to the material covered in the chapter. More examples of company practices are provided throughout the chapters.

A second distinctive feature of the book relates to the topical coverage. Some chapters relate to what I call instructional design (needs assessment, training methods, learning environment, transfer of training, and evaluation), employee development, and career management. Instructional design is still the "meat and potatoes" of training. But as the role of managers and trainers broadens, they are increasingly involved in developing employees and career management. For example, managers and trainers need to be concerned with knowledge management, cross-cultural training, diversity, outplacement, skills obsolescence, and 360-degree feedback systems—topics that fall outside the realm of instructional design.

The book begins with a discussion of strategic training. Why? Successful training efforts relate to business goals and strategy. In successful, effective training, all aspects of training—including training objectives, methods, evaluation, and even who conducts the training—relate to the business strategy. More and more companies are demanding that the training function and training practices support business goals; otherwise training may be outsourced or face funding cuts. Although students in business schools are exposed to strategic thinking, students in psychology and education who go on to become trainers need to understand the strategic perspective and how it relates to the organization of the training function and the type of training conducted.

Not only has technology changed the way we live and the way work is performed, but it also has influenced training practice. As a result, one chapter is devoted entirely to the use of new technologies in training, such as Web-based instruction, multimedia, and e-learning.

The book reflects the latest "hot topics" in the training area. For example, topics such as corporate universities, competencies, continuous learning, knowledge management, and e-learning are discussed. Each chapter contains the most recent academic research findings and company practices.

FEATURES DESIGNED TO AID LEARNING

Employee Training and Development provides several features to aid learning:

1. Each chapter lists objectives that highlight what the student is expected to learn in that chapter.
2. In-text examples feature companies from all industries including service, manufacturing, and retail.
3. Discussion questions at the end of each chapter help students learn the concepts presented in the chapter and understand potential applications of the material.
4. Important terms and concepts used in training and development are boldfaced in each chapter. Key terms are identified at the end of each chapter. These key terms are important to help the student understand the language of training.

5. Application assignments are useful for the students to put chapter content into practice. Most chapters include application assignments that require the student to use the World Wide Web.
6. Name and subject indexes at the end of the book help in finding key people and topics.

WHAT'S NEW IN THE THIRD EDITION

I want to personally thank all of you who have adopted this book! Based on the comments of the reviewers of the second edition and training research and practice, I have made several improvements. Some important changes in the third edition of *Employee Training and Development* stand out:

- Each chapter has been updated to include the most recent research findings and new best company practices. New examples have been added in each chapter's text.
- All of the chapter opening vignettes are new. For example, the opening vignette for Chapter 5, "Transfer of Training," highlights how KLA-Tencor expects both employees and managers to be accountable for training.
- This edition offers new and expanded coverage of such topics as lesson design, competencies, knowledge management, blended learning, work-life balance, and succession planning.
- New and updated Web-based application assignments are included at the end of each chapter. These assignments are also found on the book's website, where they can be updated and new Web exercises can be added.

ACKNOWLEDGMENTS

The author is only one of many important persons involved in writing a textbook. The third edition of this book would not have been possible without the energy and expertise of several persons. Editor John Weimeister provided me with the resources that I needed, gave me free rein to write the training book I want to write, and was always available to discuss ideas and answer questions. His hospitality at professional meetings is unmatched in publishing. John does business the old-fashioned way—he builds goodwill with authors, which for me has turned into a long friendship. Trina Hauger, John's assistant, did a masterful job of coordinating reviews, helping to choose the cover design, and making sure that completed manuscript made its way to the developmental editors. Marlena Pechan, the project manager, and Karen Dorman, the copy editor, made sure that my writing was readable and interpretable.

I take full responsibility for any errors, omissions, or misstatements of fact in this book. However, regardless of your impression of the book, it would not have been this good had it not been for the reviewers. Special thanks to the manuscript reviewers who provided me with detailed comments that helped to make the final version of the book a better product. These reviewers include

Alton O. Roberts
University of San Francisco
K. Shannon Davis
North Carolina State University

Glenda Barrett
University of Maryland University College
Cathy DuBois
Kent State University

Diane Hartman
Utah Valley State College

Warren Osterndorf
Rensselaer Polytechnic Institute

K. Peter Kuchinke
University of Illinois at Urbana-Champaign

Raymond A. Noe

About the Author

Raymond A. Noe

is the Robert and Anne Hoyt Designated Professor of Management at The Ohio State University. He has taught for more than 18 years at Big Ten universities. Before joining the faculty at Ohio State, he was a professor in the Department of Management at Michigan State University and the Industrial Relations Center of the Carlson School of Management, University of Minnesota. He received his B.S. in psychology from The Ohio State University and his M.A. and Ph.D. in psychology from Michigan State University. Professor Noe conducts research and teaches all levels of students—from undergraduates to executives—in human resource management, managerial skills, quantitative methods, human resource information systems, training and development, and organizational behavior. He has published articles in the *Academy of Management Journal, Academy of Management Review, Journal of Applied Psychology, Journal of Vocational Behavior,* and *Personnel Psychology.* Professor Noe is currently on the editorial boards of several journals, including *Personnel Psychology, Journal of Business and Psychology,* and *Journal of Organizational Behavior.* Besides *Employee Training and Development,* he has co-authored two other textbooks: *Fundamentals of Human Resource Management* and *Human Resource Management: Gaining a Competitive Advantage,* both published with McGraw-Hill/Irwin. Professor Noe has received awards for his teaching and research excellence, including the Herbert G. Heneman Distinguished Teaching Award in 1991, the Ernest J. McCormick Award for Distinguished Early Career Contribution from the Society for Industrial and Organizational Psychology in 1993, and the ASTD Outstanding Research Article of the Year Award for 2001. He is also a fellow of the Society for Industrial and Organizational Psychology. You can see what Professor Noe is doing in his training class by visiting his website at *www.cob.ohio-state.edu.*

Brief Contents

Contents

Chapter 4
Learning: Theories and Program Design   105

Chapter 5
Transfer of Training   145

Chapter 6
Training Evaluation   169

Chapter 7
Traditional Training Methods   201

Chapter 8
E-Learning and Use of Technology in Training   231

Chapter 9
Employee Development   265

Chapter **One**

Introduction to Employee Training and Development

Objectives

After reading this chapter, you should be able to

1. Discuss the forces influencing the workplace and learning, and explain how training can help companies deal with these forces.

2. Discuss various aspects of the training design process.

3. Describe the amount and types of training occurring in U.S. companies.

4. Describe how much money is spent on training in U.S. companies and how the money is used.

5. Discuss the key roles for training professionals.

6. Identify appropriate resources (e.g., journals, websites) for learning about training research and practice.

Forces Affecting the Workplace Make Training a Key Ingredient for Company Success

Customer service, employee retention and growth, doing more with less, quality and productivity—these are some of the issues affecting companies in all industries and sizes and influencing training practices. Four companies—Boston Pizza International, Bowater's Coated and Specialty Paper Division, Americredit, and Home Depot—are examples of how these concerns have affected business and how training has helped these businesses succeed.

Boston Pizza International, based in Vancouver, British Columbia, is the top casual restaurant chain in Canada, with 172 restaurants in Canada and the western United States. Recently, the training and development director noticed a skills gap in the store managers. Most of the managers understand the Boston Pizza concept but they lack the soft skills needed to be successful managers. As a result, Boston Pizza College was started. At Boston Pizza College managers learn and practice skills needed for successful store management, including professional conduct and coaching. Boston Pizza College has paid dividends. Reports from secret shoppers and quality assurance visits have improved since the training began. Also, the restaurant chain has increased retention in an industry in which turnover can approach 300 percent.

Striving to improve quality, Bowater's Coated and Specialty Papers Division in Catawba, South Carolina, trained all employees on continuous improvement techniques. Work teams attended the training together and were given a real-world problem in their area to solve. Skills were taught as they were needed to help employees work on the problem. Each team used the techniques acquired in training to solve their assigned problems, then measured the results of their solutions in dollars. The training teams saved $10 million! In addition, since 1996—the first year training was completed—one production area has increased productivity by 2.5 percent, another by 6 percent, and the amount of poor-quality product has decreased by 55 percent. Americredit, an auto financer with about 5,000 employees, based in Fort Worth, Texas, used training to streamline call handling. Americredit trained a cross-functional team to analyze how systems could be improved on all electronic handoff processes within the company's network of five call centers. After working for six months the team produced an estimated cost savings of $1.5 million.

Home Depot is the world's largest home-improvement retailer, with over 1,500 stores in the United States, Canada, Mexico, and Puerto Rico. Every year about 30,000 Home Depot associates participate in training and development activities designed to help their careers and improve the company's productivity and customer satisfaction. Every associate has a position curriculum they are supposed to complete. The training activities include printed materials distributed to stores, on-site instructions, and e-learning programs. The company is looking for training to better drive sales performance in the stores and to build leaders from within the company. Most of the leadership development is done face-to-face, whereas e-learning, instructors, and printed materials are available learning solutions for in-store training. E-learning is used because it reduces training costs and allows employees to access training anytime. Each store has at least two e-learning computers. Home Depot's vice president of learning has reorganized the learning function to focus on five major areas: needs assessment; cost budgeting and funding; content creation; content delivery; and evaluation. The vice president of learning works closely with the CEO and CFO (chief financial officer) to make sure learning solutions are supporting the company strategy.

Source: Based on T. Sosbe, "Home Depot: Building Continuing Education," *Chief Learning Officer* (March 2003): 56–58; B. Hall, "The Top Training Priorities for 2003," *Training* (February 2003): 38–42; T. Galvin, "The 2003 Training Top 100," *Training* (March 2003):18–38.

INTRODUCTION

Boston Pizza International, Bowater's Coated and Specialty Paper Division, Americredit, and Home Depot illustrate how training can contribute to companies' competitiveness. **Competitiveness** refers to a company's ability to maintain and gain market share in an industry. Although they are different types of businesses, these four companies have training practices that have helped them gain a **competitive advantage** in their markets. That is, the training practices have helped them grow the business and improve customer service by providing employees with the knowledge and skills they need to be successful.

Companies are experiencing great change due to new technologies, rapid development of knowledge, globalization of business, and development of e-commerce. Also, companies have to take steps to attract, retain, and motivate their work forces. Training is not a luxury; it is a necessity if companies are to participate in the global and electronic marketplaces by offering high-quality products and services! Training prepares employees to use new technologies, function in new work systems such as virtual teams, and communicate and cooperate with peers or customers who may be from different cultural backgrounds.

Human resource management refers to the policies, practices, and systems that influence employees' behavior, attitudes, and performance. Human resource practices play a key role in attracting, motivating, rewarding, and retaining employees. Other human resource management practices include recruiting employees, selecting employees, designing work, compensating employees, and developing good labor and employee relations. Chapter 2, "Strategic Training," details the importance placed on training in comparison to other human resource management practices. To be effective, training must play a strategic role in supporting the business.

Human resource management is one of several important functions in most companies. Other functions include accounting and finance, production and operations, research and development, and marketing. Keep in mind that although human resource management practices (such as training) can help companies gain a competitive advantage, the company needs to produce a product or provide a service that customers value. Without financial resources and physical resources (e.g., equipment) needed to produce products or provide services, a company will not survive!

The chapter begins by defining training and discussing how the training function has evolved. Next, the forces that are shaping the workplace and learning are addressed. These forces influence the company's ability to successfully meet stakeholders' needs. **Stakeholders** refers to shareholders, the community, customers, employees, and all of the other parties that have an interest in seeing that the company succeeds. The discussion of the forces (including technology, globalization, attracting and winning talent) highlights the role of training in helping companies gain a competitive advantage.

The second part of the chapter focuses on current trends in the training area. This section also introduces you to the trainer's role in a business and how the training function is organized. This section should help you understand current training practices, the types of jobs that trainers may perform, and the competencies needed to be a successful trainer (or, if you are a manager, to identify a successful trainer). The chapter concludes with an overview of the topics covered in the book.

WHAT IS TRAINING?

Training refers to a planned effort by a company to facilitate employees' learning of job-related competencies. These competencies include knowledge, skills, or behaviors that are critical for successful job performance. The goal of training is for employees to master the knowledge, skill, and behaviors emphasized in training programs and to apply them to their day-to-day activities. Recently it has been acknowledged that to gain a competitive advantage, training has to involve more than just basic skill development.[1] That is, to use training to gain a competitive advantage, training should be viewed broadly as a way to create intellectual capital. Intellectual capital includes basic skills (skills needed to perform one's job), advanced skills (such as how to use technology to share information with other employees), an understanding of the customer or manufacturing system, and self-motivated creativity. Intellectual capital is discussed further in Chapter 2. Keep in mind that traditionally most of the emphasis on training has been at the basic and advanced skill levels. But some estimate that soon up to 85 percent of jobs in the United States and Europe will require extensive use of knowledge. This requires employees to share knowledge and creatively use it to modify a product or serve the customer, as well as to understand the service or product development system.

Many companies have adopted this broader perspective, which is known as high-leverage training. **High-leverage training** is linked to strategic business goals and objectives, uses an instructional design process to ensure that training is effective, and compares or benchmarks the company's training programs against training programs in other companies.[2]

High-leverage training practices also help to create working conditions that encourage continuous learning. **Continuous learning** requires employees to understand the entire work system including the relationships among their jobs, their work units, and the company.[3] Employees are expected to acquire new skills and knowledge, apply them on the job, and share this information with other employees. Managers take an active role in identifying training needs and help to ensure that employees use training in their work. To facilitate the sharing of knowledge, managers may use informational maps that show where knowledge lies within the company (for example, directories that list what individuals do as well as the specialized knowledges they possess) and use technology such as groupware or the Internet that allows employees in various business units to work simultaneously on problems and share information.[4] Chapter 8 discusses how new technology such as the Internet is being used for training.

The emphasis on high-leverage training has been accompanied by a movement to link training to performance improvement.[5] Companies have lost money on training because it is poorly designed, because it is not linked to a performance problem or business strategy, or because its outcomes are not properly evaluated.[6] That is, companies have been investing money into training simply because of beliefs that it is a good thing to do. The perspective that the training function exists to deliver programs to employees without a compelling business reason for doing so is being abandoned. Today, training is being evaluated not on the basis of the number of programs offered and training activity in the company but on how training addresses business needs related to learning, behavior change, and performance improvement. In fact, training is becoming more performance-focused. That is, training is used to improve employee performance, which leads to improved business results. Training is seen as one of several possible solutions to improve performance. Other solutions can include such actions as changing the job or increasing employee motivation through pay and incentives. Today there is a greater emphasis on[7]

- Providing educational opportunities for all employees. These educational opportunities may include training programs, but they also include support for taking courses offered outside the company, self-study, and learning through job rotation.

- An ongoing process of performance improvement that is directly measurable rather than organizing one-time training events.
- The need to demonstrate to executives, managers, and trainees the benefits of training.
- Learning as a lifelong event in which senior management, trainer managers, and employees have ownership.
- Training being used to help attain strategic business objectives, which help companies gain a competitive advantage.

Medtronic is a good example of a company that uses high-leverage training. Medtronic is the world leader in medical technology, providing lifelong solutions for people with chronic heart and neurological diseases. Medtronic has 30,000 employees in more than 120 countries. Medtronic has set a goal of 15 percent annual growth, a goal of doubling the size of the company in five years.[8] To reach this goal, Medtronic believes that people development is important. Medtronic engages employees in learning and development, which links them to the company mission to restore many people to full and productive lives and to make sure that products are available to patients who need them.

Training and development occurs only after business strategies for achieving growth are identified by the company. For example, strong leadership is needed for a growing company. Strategies that the company uses to develop leadership skills include cross-functional, global job rotations as well as mentoring. To keep up with Medtronic's growth, training and development initiatives must be flexible. The training and development staff are continually scanning the company and the broader medical device industry to understand the issues and prepare training solutions to meet them. Because Medtronic is a global company, certain skills are needed by all managers wherever they are in the world. But the various offices have the ability to adapt programs to their locations. In the Medtronic Asia/Pacific location, for example, a developing managers' program placed more emphasis on cultural awareness because the managers were from many different locations and backgrounds. Training also supports new product launches to ensure that customers get a consistent message about the product. For example, Medtronic introduced a new heart therapy with a training event broadcast via satellite to salespeople located throughout the United States.

Measuring the return on investment in research and development, marketing, sales, and human resources is key for demonstrating the value to the business. Each of Medtronic's businesses uses a scorecard to measure success and return on investment. Medtronic is currently developing metrics to measure how training contributes to the company's success.

This discussion is not meant to underestimate the importance of "traditional training" (a focus on acquisition of knowledge, skills, and abilities), but it should alert you that for many companies training is evolving from a focus on skills to an emphasis on learning and creating and sharing knowledge. This evolution of training is discussed in Chapter 2.

DESIGNING EFFECTIVE TRAINING

The **training design process** refers to a systematic approach for developing training programs. Figure 1.1 presents the seven steps in this process. Step 1 is to conduct a needs assessment, which is necessary to identify if training is needed. Step 2 is to ensure that employees have the motivation and basic skills necessary to master training content. Step

FIGURE 1.1 Training design process

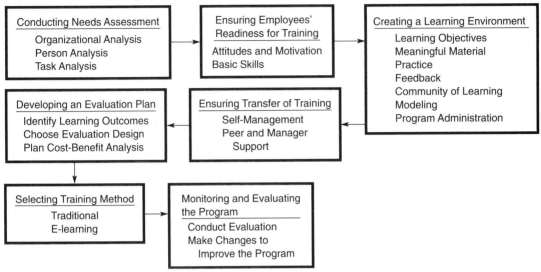

3 is to create a learning environment that has the features necessary for learning to occur. Step 4 is to ensure that trainees apply the training content to their jobs. This step involves having the trainee understand how to manage skill improvement as well as getting co-worker and manager support.

Step 5 is to develop an evaluation plan. Developing an evaluation plan includes identifying what types of outcomes training is expected to influence (for example, learning, behavior, skills), choosing an evaluation design that allows you to determine the influence of training on these outcomes, and planning how to demonstrate how training affects the "bottom line" (that is, using a cost-benefit analysis to determine the monetary benefits resulting from training). Step 6 is to choose the training method based on the learning objectives and learning environment. This step may include a traditional training method of face-to-face interaction with a trainer or e-learning using CD-ROM or Web-based training. Step 7 is to evaluate the program and make changes in it or revisit any of the earlier steps in the process to improve the program so that learning, behavior, change, and the other learning objectives are obtained.

The training design process shown in Figure 1.1 is based on principles of Instructional System Design. **Instructional System Design (ISD)** refers to a process for designing and developing training programs. There is not one universally accepted instructional systems development model. The training design process sometimes is referred to as the ADDIE model because it includes analysis, design, development, implementation, and evaluation.[9] In Figure 1.1, Step 1, conducting needs assessment, and Step 2, ensuring employees' readiness for training, are related to analysis. The next three steps—creating a learning environment, ensuring transfer of training, and developing an evaluation plan—are design issues. Step 6, selecting and using a training method, relates to implementation. Step 7, monitoring and evaluating the program, relates to evaluation. Regardless of the specific ISD approach used, all share the following assumptions:[10]

- Training design is effective only if it helps employees reach instructional or training goals and objectives.
- Measurable learning objectives should be identified before training.
- Evaluation plays an important part in planning and choosing a training method, monitoring the training program, and suggesting changes to the training design process.

Some training professionals argue that the ISD model is flawed for several reasons.[11] First, in organizations the training design process rarely follows the neat, orderly, step-by-step approach of activities shown in Figure 1.1. Second, in trying to standardize their own ISD method used in the training function, some organizations require trainers to provide detailed documents of each activity found in the model. This adds time and cost to developing a training program. Third, the ISD implies an end point: evaluation. However, good instructional design requires an iterative process of design, execution, evaluation, and reconsideration of the needs that the program was designed to meet as well as the learning environment, the transfer of training, and all the other activities in the ISD process. Despite these criticisms, the ISD model can be considered a set of general guidelines that trainers need to follow to ensure effective training.

The training design process should be systematic yet flexible enough to adapt to business needs. Different steps may be completed simultaneously. Keep in mind that designing training unsytematically will reduce the benefits that can be realized. For example, choosing a training method before determining training needs or ensuring employees' readiness for training increases the risk that the method chosen will not be the most effective one for meeting training needs. Also, training may not even be necessary and may result in a waste of time and money! Employees may have the knowledge, skills, or behavior they need but simply not be motivated to use them.

The development of a Web-based training program focusing on teaching managers skills needed to run effective business meetings provides a good example of use of the instructional design process. The first step of the process, needs assessment, involved determining that managers lacked skills for conducting effective meetings and helped to identify the type of meetings that managers were involved in. The needs assessment process involved interviewing managers and observing meetings. The needs assessment process also identified the most appropriate training method.

Because the managers were geographically dispersed and had easy access to computers and because the company wanted a self-directed, self-paced program that the managers could complete during free time in their work schedule, the training designers and company management decided that Web-based training was the appropriate method. Because training was going to be conducted over the Web, the designers had to be sure that managers could access the Web and were familiar with tools for using the Web (e.g., Web browsers). This relates to determining the managers' readiness for training.

The next step was to create a positive learning environment on the Web. Designers made sure that the program objectives were clearly stated to the trainees and provided opportunities within the program for exercises and feedback. For example, trainees were asked to prepare an outline for the steps they would take to conduct an effective meeting. The designers built into the program a feedback system that indicated to the managers which of the steps they outlined were correct and which needed to be changed. The designers also built in assessment tests allowing the trainees to receive feedback through the program and to

TABLE 1.1
Forces Influencing Working and Learning

Globalization
Need for leadership
Increased value placed on knowledge
Attracting and retaining talent
Customer service and quality emphasis
Changing demographics and diversity of the work force
New technology
High-performance models of work systems
Economic changes

skip ahead or return to earlier material based on their scores on the tests. The assessment included a test of meeting skills that the managers completed both prior to and after completing the program. The assessment tests were stored in a data bank that the company could use to evaluate whether trainees' meeting skills improved from pretraining levels.

THE FORCES INFLUENCING WORKING AND LEARNING

Table 1.1 illustrates the forces that are influencing working and learning. Globalization of business, demographic changes, new technologies, and economic changes are several of the forces shown in Table 1.1 that influence all aspects of our lives: how we purchase products and services, how we learn, how we communicate with each other, and what we value in our lives and on the job.[12] These forces are affecting individuals, communities, businesses, and society. To survive, companies must address these forces—with training playing an important role.

Globalization

Every business must be prepared to deal with the global economy. Global business expansion has been made easier by technology. The Internet allows data and information to be instantly accessible and sent around the world. The Internet, e-mail, and video conferencing enable business deals to be completed between companies thousands of miles apart.

Globalization has affected not just businesses with international operations. Companies without international operations may buy or use goods that have been produced overseas, hire employees with diverse backgrounds, or compete with foreign-owned companies operating within the United States.

Many companies are entering international markets by exporting their products overseas, building manufacturing facilities in other countries, entering into alliances with foreign companies, and engaging in e-commerce. Developing nations such as Taiwan, Indonesia, and China may account for over 60 percent of the world economy by 2020.[13] Globalization is not limited to a particular sector of the economy or product market. For example, Procter and Gamble is targeting feminine hygiene products to new markets such as Brazil. The demand for steel in China, India, and Brazil is expected to grow at three times the U.S. rate. Starbucks Coffee recently expanded into Beijing, China.[14] Competition for local managers exceeds the available supply. As a result, companies have to take steps to attract and retain managers. Starbucks researched the motivation and needs of the potential local management work force. The company found that managers were moving from one local Western company to another for several reasons. In the traditional Chinese-owned companies, rules and regulations allow little creativity and autonomy. Also, in many joint U.S.–China ventures, local managers were not trusted. To avoid local management turnover, in its recruiting efforts Starbucks emphasized its casual culture and opportunities for development. Starbucks also spent considerable time in training. New managers were sent to Tacoma, Washington, to learn the corporate culture as well as the secrets of brewing flavorful coffee.

Besides training and developing local employees and managers, many companies are sending U.S. employees and managers to work in international locations. Cross-cultural training is important to prepare employees and their families for overseas assignments. Cross-cultural training prepares employees and their families (1) to understand the culture and norms of the country they are being relocated to and (2) to return to the United States after their assignment.

Cross-cultural training has become even more important since 9/11. Since 9/11 U.S. companies doing business overseas have recognized that many parts of the world have the potential to become dangerous.[15] Before 9/11 many U.S. employees working abroad had lived normal lives without any security concerns. But recent attacks and threats on American interests have shattered that sense of security. Overseas assignments are now considered more risky by many employees. Also, companies with a global work force must manage across boundaries that are more nationalistic. Whereas U.S. citizens have felt united in actions, such as the invasion of Iraq, that they believe are justified as a valid response to hostile intentions, citizens of some countries consider the U.S. military response an act of aggression. Cross-cultural training is discussed in greater detail in Chapter 10.

Globalization also means that employees working in the United States will come from other countries. The United States takes more than 1 million immigrants, some who are illegal. Immigrants provide scientific talent as well as fill low-wage jobs. Immigrants will likely account for an additional million persons in the work force through 2006.[16] The impact of immigration will be especially large in certain areas of the United States, including the states on the Pacific Coast where 70 percent of new entrants to the work force are immigrants.[17] Many of these immigrants will have to be trained to understand the U.S. culture. U.S. employees will need skills to improve their ability to communicate with employees from different cultures. The terrorist attacks of 9/11 have not changed the use of immigrants but have raised security issues, resulting in more deliberate approval of visas (and longer waits for hiring to be approved).

Globalization also means that U.S. companies may move jobs overseas; **offshoring** refers to the process of moving jobs from the United States to other locations in the world. For example, many technical workers are being asked to train their foreign replacements who return to their home countries once the training is completed.[18] The U.S. workers either lose their jobs or are offered other jobs at lower wages. There are two reasons this is occurring. First, U.S. visa program allows companies to transfer workers from overseas offices to the U.S. for seven years. The workers can continue to receive their home country wage, which is usually much less than the wages received by U.S. employees (e.g. Indian workers receive about $10 an hour compared to $60 per hour for U.S. programmers). Second, U.S. colleges are graduating fewer U.S. born engineers, so companies have to look overseas to hire the best employees. The U.S. Congress is considering reducing the number of visas which allow foreign workers to work in the United States because of concerns that the current visa program causes high unemployment among high-tech workers.[19]

The Need for Leadership

The aging of the work force and globalization mean that companies will need to identify, train, and develop employees with managerial talent. Executive, administrative, and managerial occupations will experience the greatest turnover due to death or retirement.[20] This will result in a significant loss of managerial talent.

Many companies do not have employees with the competencies necessary to manage in a global economy.[21] For example, 85 percent of Fortune 500 companies believe that they do not have enough employees with global leadership skills. Among those companies that believe that they have employees with global leadership skills, 60 percent of the firms believe that those employees' skills are not adequate. To successfully manage in a global economy, managers need to be self-aware and be able to build international teams, create global management and marketing practices, and interact and manage employees from diverse cultural backgrounds.

Effective managers are also important because they help retain employees. One of the key reasons that employees leave jobs is because they are uncomfortable with the working environment created by their manager.[22] Effective managers not only perform the basic management functions (planning, organizing, leading, and controlling), but are also good communicators, help employees develop, and work collaboratively with employees (rather than relying on an autocratic leadership style).

Companies need to both identify employees with managerial talent and help potential new managers as well as current managers develop the skills needed to succeed. This includes providing employees with mentors, job experiences, and formal courses to develop their skills. (Employee development and succession planning are discussed in Chapters 9 and 10.) For example, Charles Schwab, the discount stockbroker, uses employee surveys to find out how employees are feeling about work loads, benefits, office culture, and career development.[23] Managers are responsible for identifying any serious problems indicated by the survey. They are expected to meet with their employees and develop plans to solve the problems. Schwab provides managers with coaching and training so that they can develop the skills necessary to be more effective managers. If employees are critical of a manager's interpersonal skills, Schwab may require the manager to take a communications seminar or assign a more senior manager mentor who can model and offer suggestions on effective communications skills.

Increased Value Placed on Knowledge

Today more and more companies are interested in developing intellectual capital as a way to gain an advantage over competitors. As a result, companies are trying to attract, develop, and retain knowledge workers. **Knowledge workers** are employees who contribute to the company not through manual labor, but through what they know about customers or a specialized body of knowledge. Employees cannot simply be ordered to perform tasks; they must share knowledge and collaborate on solutions. Knowledge workers contribute specialized knowledge that their managers may not have, such as information about customers. Managers depend on them to share information. Knowledge workers have many job opportunities. If they choose, they can leave a company and take their knowledge to a competitor. Knowledge workers are in demand because of the growth of jobs requiring them. Service-producing industries will account for much of the job growth to 2010.[24] Health services, business services, social services, and engineering, management, and related services are expected to account for almost one of every two nonfarm wage-and-salary jobs added to the economy.

To completely benefit from employees' knowledge requires a management style that focuses on developing and empowering employees. **Empowering** means giving employees responsibility and authority to make decisions regarding all aspects of product development or customer service.[25] Employees are then held accountable for products and services; in return, they share the rewards and losses of the results. For empowerment to be successful, managers must be trained to link employees to resources within and outside the company (people, websites, etc.), help employees interact with their fellow employees and managers throughout the company, and ensure that employees are updated on important issues and cooperate with each other. Employees must also be trained to understand how to use the Web, e-mail, and other tools for communicating, collecting, and sharing information.

As more companies become knowledge-based, it's important that they promote and capture learning at the employee, team, and company levels. Buckman Laboratories is known for its knowledge management practices.[26] Buckman Laboratories develops and markets specialty chemicals. Buckman's CEO, Robert Buckman, has developed an organizational culture, the technology, and the work processes that encourage the sharing of knowledge. Employees have laptop computers so they can share information anywhere and anytime using the Internet. The company rewards innovation and knowledge creation and exchange by including the sales of new products as part of employees' performance evaluations. Buckman also changed the focus of the company's information systems department, renaming it knowledge transfer department to better match the service it is supposed to provide.

In addition to acquiring and retaining knowledge workers, companies need to be able to adapt to change. **Change** refers to the adoption of a new idea or behavior by a company. Technological advances, changes in the work force or government regulations, globalization, and new competitors are among the many factors that require companies to change. Change is inevitable in companies as products, companies, and entire industries experience shorter life cycles.[27] For example, Samsung Electronics cut one-third of the payroll, replaced half of its senior managers, sold off $1.9 billion in assets, and introduced new products to save itself from bankruptcy. The characteristics of an effective change process are discussed in Chapter 13.

A changing environment means that all employees must embrace a philosophy of learning. A **learning organization** embraces a culture of lifelong learning, enabling all employees to continually acquire and share knowledge. Improvements in product or service quality do not stop when formal training is completed.[28] Employees need to have the financial, time, and content resources (courses, experiences, development opportunities) available to increase their knowledge. Managers take an active role in identifying training needs and helping to ensure that employees use training in their work. Also, employees should be actively encouraged to share knowledge with colleagues and other work groups across the company using e-mail and the Internet.[29] Chapter 5 discusses learning organizations and knowledge management in detail. For a learning organization to be successful requires that teams of employees collaborate to meet customer needs. Managers need to empower employees to share knowledge, identify problems, and make decisions. This allows the company to continuously experiment and improve.

Attracting and Retaining Talent

The economy is expected to add 20 million new jobs; a much larger number of new workers will be needed due to replacement (i.e., job openings due to death, disability, retirement, or leaving the labor force for education or to stay at home).[30] The U.S. population is expected

FIGURE 1.2
Job openings
due to growth
and replacement
needs by major
occupational
group, projected
2000–2010

Source: "Tomorrow's
Jobs" in the 2002–03
*Occupational Outlook
Handbook*, chart 11.
From website http://
stats.bls.gov/oco/oco
2003.htm.

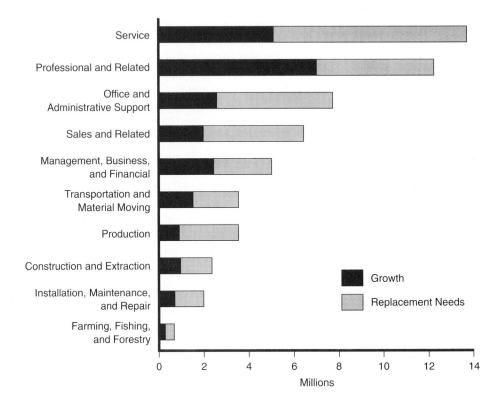

to increase by 24 million over the period from 2000 to 2010. This growth will mean more consumers of goods and services, increasing demand for employees.[31] Figure 1.2 shows expected job openings due to new jobs (growth) and job openings resulting from replacement. Most of the job growth in professional specialties is expected among computer and mathematical occupations; health care practitioners and technical occupations, and education, training, and library occupations. Computer-related positions such as computer engineer, computer support specialist, system analyst, and computer database administrator are projected to be four of the fastest growing jobs in the economy.[32]

As the oldest baby boomers begin to retire in the next several years, the implications for the work force could be enormous.[33] The current tight labor market could be exacerbated, hindering prospects for economic growth and putting a greater burden on those remaining in the work force, perhaps forcing them to work longer hours. Especially in occupations with functions less conducive to technology-driven productivity innovations—many jobs in health services and educational services, for example—service may suffer and needs could go unmet unless older workers can be retained or other sources of workers can be found. Even in occupations in which technological innovations have produced relatively large productivity gains—many of the more complex machining jobs in manufacturing, for example—the learning curves often are steep, meaning that new workers need to enter these occupations soon, so they can become proficient in the necessary skills by the time the baby boomers begin leaving the labor force. As the age of the labor force rises, a greater number of people will leave the labor force due to death, disability, or retirement.

The largest number of job openings will be in occupations requiring a bachelor's degree and on-the-job training. Two-thirds of projected openings require only on-the-job training—but these jobs typically offer low pay and benefits. Seventy percent of the fastest growing occupations require postsecondary education and training. Although companies will need employees with all levels of education and training, those with the most education usually will have more options in the job market and better chances of obtaining higher-paying jobs.

As the occupational structure of the U.S. economy has shifted, skill requirements have changed.[34] The demand for specific skills is being replaced by a need for cognitive skills—mathematical and verbal reasoning ability—and interpersonal skills related to being able to work in teams or to interact with "customers" in a service economy (e.g., patients, students, vendors, suppliers). Cognitive and interpersonal skills are important because in the service-oriented economy employees must take responsibility for the final product or service. Variety and customization require employees who are creative and good problem solvers. Continuous innovation requires the ability to learn. To offer novelty and entertainment value to customers, workers must be creative. Most companies relate these skills with educational attainment, so many firms use a college degree as a standard to screen prospective employees.

Despite the need for high-level skills, many job applicants lack basic skills. According to an American Management Association survey, over 38 percent of job applicants tested for basic skills by companies lacked the necessary reading, writing, and math skills for the jobs they were seeking.[35] Given the tight labor market and numerous job applicants' lack of basic skills, many companies are unable to hire qualified employees. But they are unwilling or unable to leave jobs open. Therefore, they have to hire employees with skill deficiencies and rely on training to correct the deficiencies. A survey of training practices suggests that 34 percent of U.S. companies provide training to employees in basic life and work skills.[36]

Retention is an important part of talent management. Talented employees are looking for growth and a career path. Training and development is a key to attracting and retaining talented employees.[37] A recent survey of changes in the American work force in the context of ongoing and social change identified that a large group of workers are more concerned with opportunities for mentoring and growth than job security and stable employment.[38] Management Recruiters International, an executive search firm based in Cleveland, Ohio, conducted a three-year study of turnover. The researchers found that the number one reason employees left was that the company didn't invest enough in training. At Wellpoint, a California-based health care company, turnover was above industry average and as high as 40 percent in some locations, costing the company millions of dollars annually. Employee attitude survey results suggested that the reason for turnover was lack of training. Training was listed as one of the major influences on employee satisfaction because it increased employees' opportunities for advancement. You will see in Chapter 2 that as companies use training strategically, that is, use it to support business strategy, they find that it also results in retaining talented employees.

Customer Service and Quality Emphasis

Companies' customers judge quality and performance. As a result, customer excellence requires attention to product and service features as well as to interactions with customers. Customer-driven excellence includes understanding what the customer wants and anticipating future needs. Customer-driven excellence includes reducing defects and errors, meeting specifications, and reducing complaints. How the company recovers from defects and errors is also important for retaining and attracting customers.

Due to increased availability of knowledge and competition, consumers are very knowledgeable and expect excellent service. This presents a challenge for employees who interact with customers. The way in which clerks, sales staff, front-desk personnel, and service providers interact with customers influences a company's reputation and financial performance. Employees need product knowledge and service skills, and they need to be clear about the types of decisions they can make when dealing with customers. Customer service as a strategic training and development initiative is discussed in Chapter 2.

To compete in today's economy, whether on a local or global level, companies need to provide a quality product or service. If companies do not adhere to quality standards, their ability to sell their product or service to vendors, suppliers, or customers will be restricted. Some countries even have quality standards that companies must meet to conduct business there. **Total Quality Management (TQM)** is a companywide effort to continuously improve the ways people, machines, and systems accomplish work.[39] Core values of TQM include the following:[40]

- Methods and processes are designed to meet the needs of internal and external customers.
- Every employee in the company receives training in quality.
- Quality is designed into a product or service so that errors are prevented from occurring rather than being detected and corrected.
- The company promotes cooperation with vendors, suppliers, and customers to improve quality and hold down costs.
- Managers measure progress with feedback based on data.

There is no universal definition of quality. The major differences in its various definitions relate to whether customer, product, or manufacturing process is emphasized. For example, quality expert W. Edwards Deming emphasized how well a product or service meets customer needs. Phillip Crosby's approach emphasizes how well the service or manufacturing process meets engineering standards.

The emphasis on quality is seen in the establishment of the **Malcolm Baldrige National Quality Award** and the **ISO 9000:2000** quality standards. The Baldrige award, created by public law, is the highest level of national recognition for quality that a U.S. company can receive. To become eligible for the Baldrige, a company must complete a detailed application that consists of basic information about the firm as well as an in-depth presentation of how it addresses specific criteria related to quality improvement. The categories and point values for the Baldrige award are found in Table 1.2. The award is not given for specific products or services. Three awards may be given annually in each of these categories: manufacturing, service, small business, education, and health care. All applicants for the Baldrige Award undergo a rigorous examination process that takes from 300 to 1,000 hours. Applications are reviewed by an independent board of about 400 examiners who come primarily from the private sector. Each applicant receives a report citing strengths and opportunities for improvement.

Pal's Sudden Service is a 2001 Baldrige Award winner, the first business in the restaurant industry to receive the award.[41] Pal's Sudden Service is a quick-service restaurant chain

TABLE 1.2
Categories and
Point Values
for the
Malcolm
Baldrige
National
Quality Award
Examination

Leadership	**120**
The way senior executives create and sustain corporate citizenship, customer focus, clear values, and expectations and promote quality and performance excellence	
Measurement, Analysis, and Knowledge Management	**90**
The way the company selects, gathers, analyzes, manages, and improves its data, information, and knowledge assets	
Strategic Planning	**85**
The way the company sets strategic direction, how it determines plan requirements, and how plan requirements relate to performance management	
Human Resource Focus	**85**
Company's efforts to develop and utilize the work force and to maintain an environment conducive to full participation, continuous improvement, and personal and organizational growth	
Process Management	**85**
Process design and control, including customer-focused design, product and service delivery, support services, and supply management	
Business Results	**450**
Company's performance and improvement in key business areas (product, service, and supply quality; productivity; and operational effectiveness and related financial indicators)	
Customer and Market Focus	**85**
Company's knowledge of the customer, customer service systems, responsiveness to customer, customer satisfaction	
Total Points	**1,000**

Source: Based on 2003 Baldrige National Quality Program Criteria for Performance Excellence from the website for the National Institute of Standards and Technology, www.quality.nist.gov.

that serves drive-through customers within 60 miles of Kingsport, Tennessee. The restaurant has 465 employees; most are in production and service roles. The restaurants sell hamburgers, hot dogs, chipped ham, chicken, French fries, and breakfast biscuits with ham, sausage, and gravy. The company distinguishes itself from fast-food competitors by offering high-quality food quickly delivered in a cheerful manner and without error. Nothing that Pal's does is done without a good understanding of how it impacts on customer satisfaction. Customer, employee, and supplier feedback is critical to all processes and is gathered both formally and informally. Pal's owners must spend a part of every working day to listening to employees' and customers' views on how the restaurant is performing and ideas for improvement. The company's training and development processes support the business. Managers use a four-step model for staff training: show, do it, evaluate, and perform again. Employees must demonstrate 100 percent competence before they are allowed to work at a work station. Initial training for all employees includes intensive instruction on effective listening skills, health and safety, and organizational culture. Computer-based training, flash cards, and one-on-one coaching is used for training. Cross-training is required of all store-level staff to ensure that they understand all production and service features and quality standards. Pal's believes it has the responsibility to help its employees (who are mainly in their first jobs) to develop knowledge and skills they can use in future jobs. As a result, turnover rates are less than half that of the best competitor, and sales per hour improved by about six dollars per hour since 1998. Customer satisfaction is high, speed of filling orders has improved, and errors are rare.

The ISO 9000:2000 standards were developed by the International Organization for Standardization (ISO) in Geneva, Switzerland.[42] ISO 9000 is the name of a family of standards (ISO 9001, ISO 9004) that include requirements for dealing with issues such as how to establish quality standards and document work processes to help companies understand quality system requirements. ISO 9000:2000 has been adopted as a quality standard in nearly 100 countries including Austria, Switzerland, Norway, Australia, and Japan. The ISO 9000: 2000 standards apply to companies in many different industries—for example, manufacturing, processing, servicing, printing, forestry, electronics, steel, computing, legal services, and financial services. ISO 9001 is the most comprehensive standard because it covers product or service design and development, manufacturing, installation, and customer service. It includes the actual specification for a quality management system. ISO 9004 provides a guide for companies that want to improve.

Why are standards useful? Customers may want to check that the product they ordered from a supplier meets the purpose for which it is required. One of the most efficient ways to do this is when the specifications of the product have been defined in an International Standard. That way, both supplier and customer are on the same wavelength, even if they are based in different countries, because they are both using the same references. Today many products require testing for conformance with specifications or compliance with safety or other regulations before they can be put on many markets. Even simpler products may require supporting technical documentation that includes test data. With so much trade taking place across borders, it may just not be practical for these activities to be carried out by suppliers and customers, but rather by specialized third parties. In addition, national legislation may require such testing to be carried out by independent bodies, particularly when the products concerned have health or environmental implications. One example of an ISO standard is on the back cover of this book and nearly every other book. On the back cover is something called an ISBN number. ISBN stands for International Standard Book Number. Publishers and booksellers are very familiar with ISBN numbers, since they are the method through which books are ordered and bought. Try buying a book on the Internet, and you will soon learn the value of the ISBN number—there is a unique number for the book you want! And it is based on an ISO standard.

In addition to competing for quality awards and seeking ISO certification, many companies are using the Six Sigma process. The **Six Sigma process** refers to a process of measuring, analyzing, improving, and then controlling processes once they have been brought within the narrow Six Sigma quality tolerances or standards. The objective of Six Sigma is to create a total business focus on serving the customer, that is, to deliver what customers really want when they want it. For example, at General Electric introducing the Six Sigma quality initiative meant going from approximately 35,000 defects per million operations—which is average for most companies, including GE—to fewer than 4 defects per million in every element of every process GE businesses perform—from manufacturing a locomotive part to servicing a credit card account to processing a mortgage application to answering a phone.[43] Training is an important component of the process. Six Sigma involves highly trained employees known as Champions, Master Black Belts, Black Belts, and Green Belts who lead and teach teams that are focusing on an ever-growing number of quality projects. The quality projects focus on improving efficiency and reducing errors in products and services. Today GE has over 100,000 employees trained in Six Sigma. Employees are working on more than 6,000 quality projects. Since 1996, when the Six Sigma quality initiative was started, it has produced more than $2 billion in benefits for GE.

Training can help companies meet the quality challenge by teaching employees statistical process control and other quality-related skills that they can use to build quality into a product, rather than fix the product or service after it has been delivered to the customer. Also as a result of the emphasis on quality, employers need to train employees and managers in the interpersonal skills necessary to work together to create high-quality products and services. For example, Nalco Chemical used quality training to increase its presence in the $2.9 billion wastewater management business.[44] Both managers and employees attended Phillip Crosby's quality training program. They were trained in the same basic philosophies of quality so that they could take the same view and speak the same language as their customers. In addition, management closely reviewed how quality training related to specific aspects of each person's job. Managers made certain that employees understood why they were being trained to learn certain things and how training affected their jobs. Quality training is integrated with job training at Nalco. Salespersons learned not only to sell products to customers but also to anticipate customer problems and offer solutions. Nalco Chemical attributes its nearly 50 percent market share to quality training.

Changing Demographics and Diversity of the Work Force

Companies face several challenges as a result of increased diversity in the work force, skill deficiencies, and changes in where work is performed. Population is the single most important factor in determining the size and composition of the labor force, which is composed of people who are either working or looking for work. The U.S. population is expected to increase by 24 million between 2000 and 2010. The work force will be older and more culturally diverse than at any time in the past 40 years. By 2010, the work force is projected to be 69 percent white, 12 percent African American, 13 percent Hispanic, and 6 percent Asian and other ethnic or cultural groups.[45] The Asian and Hispanic labor force increases are due to immigration trends and higher-than-average birth rates. The labor force participation rates of women in nearly all age groups are projected to increase. Not only must companies face the issues of race, gender, ethnicity, and nationality to provide a fair workplace, but they must also develop training programs to help immigrants acquire the technical and customer service skills required in a service economy.

Another factor contributing to diversity is the aging of the labor force. By 2005, the median age of the labor force is expected to be approximately 40, compared to the 1980s' median age of 34.[46] The U.S. Bureau of the Census projects that by 2030, about one-fifth of the total U.S. population will be over 65 years old.[47] The aging population means that companies are likely to employ a growing share of older workers—many of them in their second or third career. Older people want to work, and many say they plan a working retirement. An emerging trend is for qualified older employees to ask to work part-time or for only a few months at a time as a means to transition to retirement. Employees and companies are redefining what it means to be retired to include second careers as well as part-time and temporary work assignments. Another source of work force diversity is greater access to the workplace for people with disabilities.

TABLE 1.3 **How Managing Cultural Diversity Can Provide Competitive Advantage**

1. Cost argument	As organizations become more diverse, the cost of a poor job in integrating workers will increase. Those who handle this well will thus create cost advantages over those who don't.
2. Resource-acquisition argument	Companies develop reputations on favorability as prospective employers for women and ethnic minorities. Those with the best reputations for managing diversity will be the most attractive employers for women and other minority groups. As the labor pool shrinks and changes composition, this edge will become increasingly important.
3. Marketing argument	For multinational organizations, the insight and cultural sensitivity that members with roots in other countries bring to the marketing effort should improve these efforts in important ways. The same rationale applies to marketing to subpopulations within domestic operations.
4. Creativity argument	Diversity of perspectives and less emphasis on conformity to norms of the past (which characterize the modern approach to management of diversity) should improve the level of creativity.
5. Problem-solving argument	Heterogeneity in decisions and problem-solving groups potentially produces better decisions through a wider range of perspectives and more thorough critical analysis of issues.
6. System flexibility argument	An implication of the multicultural model for managing diversity is that the system will become less determinant, less standardized, and therefore more fluid. The increased fluidity should create greater flexibility to react to environmental changes (i.e., reactions should be faster and cost less).

Source: T. H. Cox and S. Blake, "Managing Cultural Diversity: Implications for Organizational Competitiveness," *Academy of Management Executive* 5 (1991): 47.

Because of this diversity, it is unlikely that all employees will hold similar work values. Research suggests that to maximize employees' motivation and commitment to company goals, employees should be given the opportunity to develop their skills, meet their interests, and balance work and nonwork activities.[48] Many companies (e.g., Merck, Marriott, Hewlett-Packard) are trying to attract and keep talented employees through providing training and development opportunities and reimbursing employees for expenses related to obtaining associate, undergraduate, and graduate degrees.[49] For example, Marriott recognizes that most employees don't want to stay in an entry-level job such as housekeeping. So Marriott trains employees to handle a wide variety of positions and rotates them periodically to new jobs. This gives employees opportunities to find the area in which they best like to work. They are encouraged to train for promotion. The goal is to keep employees interested in their work and keep them interested in working for Marriott.

Table 1.3 shows how companies can use this increased diversity to provide a competitive advantage. Training plays a key role in ensuring that employees accept and work more effectively with each other, particularly with minorities and women. To successfully manage a diverse work force, managers and employees must be trained in a new set of skills including

1. Communicating effectively with employees from a wide variety of backgrounds.
2. Coaching, training, and developing employees of different ages, educational backgrounds, ethnicities, physical abilities, and races.

3. Providing performance feedback that is free of values and stereotypes based on gender, ethnicity, or physical handicap.

4. Creating a work environment that allows employees of all backgrounds to be creative and innovative.[50]

As discussed in Chapter 10, many companies have seen managing diversity as a way to reduce costs related to discrimination lawsuits rather than to improve company performance. As Table 1.3 shows, management of diversity contributes to a company's bottom line by its influence on creativity, problem solving, employee retention, and creation of new markets for a company's products and services. Companies that do not manage diversity will find that employees' talents are underutilized and their personal and professional needs are not being met. As a result, they will become dissatisfied and leave, resulting in a poorly performing, less competitive organization. Companies that are known for managing diversity also have an edge in attracting talented employees.

New Technology

Technology has reshaped the way we play (e.g., games on the Internet), communicate (e.g., cell phones), plan our lives (e.g., electronic calendars that include Internet access), and where we work (e.g., small, powerful personal computers allow us to work at home, while we travel, and even while we lie on the beach!). The Internet has created a new business model— **e-commerce,** in which business transactions and relationships can be conducted electronically. The **Internet** is a global collection of computer networks that allow users to exchange data and information. Today more than two-thirds of all Americans age 12 or older have used the Internet; half of these users report they go online every day.[51] Nearly 70 percent access the Internet most often from home, while 17 percent do so from work. A full 86 percent are communicating with others via e-mail, and 50 percent are purchasing products or services.[52] For example, customers can now read the *Wall Street Journal* and many local newspapers online. They can send online greeting cards from Blue Mountain Arts for free. Through the Web you can purchase clothes, flowers, and airline tickets and even have someone pick up groceries for you. Companies can connect with job candidates across the world on *www.monster.com.*

Advances in sophisticated technology along with reduced costs for the technology are changing the delivery of training, making training more realistic and giving employees the opportunity to choose where and when they will work. New technologies allow training to occur at any time and any place. New technologies include the Internet, e-mail, CD-ROMs, DVDs, and satellite or cable television. The Internet and the Web allow employees to send and receive information as well as to locate and gather resources, including software, reports, photos, and videos. The Internet gives employees instant access to experts whom they can communicate with and to newsgroups, which are bulletin boards dedicated to specific areas of interest, where employees can read, post, and respond to messages and articles. Internet sites also have home pages—mailboxes that identify the person or company and contain text, images, sounds, and video. For example, the professional organization for training professionals and those interested in training, the American Society for Training and Development (ASTD), has a website on the Internet. From their website, *www.astd.org,* users can search for and access articles on training topics, review training programs, purchase training materials, and participate in chat rooms on various training topics such as e-learning or evaluation.

Technology has many advantages including reduced travel costs, greater accessibility to training, consistent delivery, the ability to access experts and share learning with others, and the possibility of creating a learning environment with many positive features such as the ability to get feedback, self-pacing, and many practice exercises. While trainer-led classroom instruction remains the most popular way to deliver training, companies report that they plan on delivering a large portion of training through learning technologies such as CD-ROMs and intranets. For example, consider how training at Kinko's, the world's leading supplier of document solutions and business services, with 1,100 locations in nine countries, has changed. Because Kinko's stores are geographically dispersed, the company has had to struggle with costly training programs offered in multiple locations to prepare employees for new products and services. Kinko's recently adopted a blended learning approach including Internet instruction, job aids, virtual classroom training, and mentoring. Cost savings and greater efficiency occurred as a result of the blended approach. The approach has also resulted in increasing staff skills and reducing their time to competence, and in increasing the speed with which new products and services can be brought to market.[53]

Technology is pushing the boundaries of artificial intelligence, speech synthesis, wireless communications, and networked virtual reality.[54] Realistic graphics, dialogue, and sensory cues can now be stored onto tiny, inexpensive computer chips. The advances in technology for toys illustrate potential training applications. For example, The Sims Online is an Internet game that allows players to develop fictional suburban lives. The game has the capacity for over 2,000 players who can directly interact with each other to build bridges and start businesses. The military is already considering similar technology to conduct online team exercises with troops stationed around the world. Virtual sensations (vibrations and other sensory cues) are being incorporated into training applications. For example, in medical training, machines can replicate the feeling of pushing a needle into an artery, using sound and motion to create different situations such as a baby crying or a patient in pain.

Advances in technology, including more powerful computer chips and increasing processing power of handheld computers, have the potential for freeing workers from going to a specific location to work and from traditional work schedules. For example, a recent survey found that 37 percent of employers offer telecommuting on a part-time basis and 23 percent on a full-time basis.[55] Telecommuting has the potential to increase employee productivity, encourage family-friendly work arrangements, and help reduce traffic and air pollution. But at the same time technologies may result in employees being on call twenty-four hours a day, seven days a week. Many companies are taking steps to provide more flexible work schedules to protect employees' free time and to more productively use employees' work time. For example, Hewlett-Packard redesigned its work schedules in response to the loss of talented customer service reps who were forced to answer calls late at night and on weekends. HP allowed employees to volunteer to work at night or on weekends.[56] To protect employees' nonwork time, Ernst and Young allows employees to wait until they return to work or vacation to answer voice mail or e-mail messages.[57]

Technology also allows companies greater use of a contingent work force. **Contingent work force** refers to independent contractors, on-call workers, temporary workers, and contract workers. The Bureau of Labor Statistics estimates that the contingent work force covers about 10 percent of U.S. employees.[58] Use of a contingent work force allows companies to more easily adjust staffing levels based on economic conditions and product and services demand. And when a company downsizes by laying off contingent workers, the damage to the morale of full-time employees is likely to be less severe. Alternative work arrangements also provide employees with flexibility for balancing work and life activities.

A key training issue that alternative work arrangements present is to prepare managers and employees to coordinate their efforts so such work arrangements do not interfere with customer service or product quality. The increased use of contingent employees means that managers need to understand how to motivate employees who may actually be employed by a third party such as a temporary employee service or leasing agency.

High-Performance Models of Work Systems

New technology causes changes in skill requirements and work roles and often results in redesigning work structures (e.g., using work teams).[59] For example, computer-integrated manufacturing uses robots and computers to automate the manufacturing process. The computer allows the production of different products simply by reprogramming the computer. As a result, laborer, material handler, operator/assembler, and maintenance jobs may be merged into one position. Computer-integrated manufacturing requires employees to monitor equipment and troubleshoot problems with sophisticated equipment, share information with other employees, and understand the relationships between all components of the manufacturing process.[60]

Through technology, the information needed to improve customer service and product quality becomes more accessible to employees. This means that employees are expected to take more responsibility for satisfying the customer and determining how they perform their jobs. One of the most popular methods for increasing employee responsibility and control is work teams. **Work teams** involve employees with various skills who interact to assemble a product or provide a service. Work teams may assume many of the activities usually reserved for managers, including selecting new team members, scheduling work, and coordinating activities with customers and other units in the company. To give teams maximum flexibility, cross training of team members occurs. **Cross training** refers to training employees in a wide range of skills so they can fill any of the roles needed to be performed on the team.

Use of new technology and work designs such as work teams needs to be supported by specific human resource management practices. These practices include the following actions:[61]

- Employees choose or select new employees or team members.
- Employees receive formal performance feedback and are involved in the performance improvement process.
- Ongoing training is emphasized and rewarded.
- Rewards and compensation are linked to company performance.
- Equipment and work processes encourage maximum flexibility and interaction between employees.
- Employees participate in planning changes in equipment, layout, and work methods.
- Employees understand how their jobs contribute to the finished product or service.

What role does training play? Employees need job-specific knowledge and basic skills to work with the equipment created with the new technology. Because technology is often used as a means to achieve product diversification and customization, employees must have the ability to listen and communicate with customers. Interpersonal skills, such as negotiation and conflict management, and problem-solving skills are more important than physical strength, coordination, and fine-motor skills—previous job requirements for many manufacturing and service jobs. Although technological advances have made it possible for employees to improve products and services, managers must empower employees to make changes.

Besides changing the way that products are built or services are provided within companies, technology has allowed companies to form partnerships with one or more other companies. **Virtual teams** refer to teams that are separated by time, geographic distance, culture, and/or organizational boundaries and that rely almost exclusively on technology (e-mail, Internet, video conferencing) to interact and complete their projects. Virtual teams can be formed within one company whose facilities are scattered throughout the country or the world. A company may also use virtual teams in partnerships with suppliers or competitors to pull together the necessary talent to complete a project or speed the delivery of a product to the marketplace. For example, the Technology One Alliance was created between BankOne, AT&T Solutions, and IBM Global Services. The success of virtual teams requires a clear mission, good communications skills, trust between members that they will meet deadlines and complete assignments, and understanding of cultural differences (if the teams have global members).

VeriFone, an equipment supplier for credit card verification and automated payments, uses virtual teams in every aspect of its business.[62] Teams of facilities managers work together to determine how to reduce toxins in the office. Marketing and development groups brainstorm new products. Some teams include only VeriFone employees, though others include employees of customers or partners. Virtual teams have distinct training needs. For example, VeriFone makes sure that virtual team members are trained to understand when and how to use communications technology. Guidelines stipulate that for keeping in contact remotely, teams use beepers, cell phones, and voice mail; for disseminating information, they use faxes, e-mail, and application sharing over the network. For brainstorming, discussion, and decision making, teams use e-mail, conference calls, and videoconferencing. VeriFone also emphasizes the psychological problems of virtual communications. Subtleties of meaning are lost and, moreover, misunderstandings and conflict are more common than when teams work face to face. If virtual teams are global, lack of face-to-face contact can worsen cultural differences. Training related to understanding cultural differences in written and verbal communication is important for virtual teams.

Employees must be trained in principles of employee selection, quality, and customer service. They need to understand financial data so they can see the link between their performance and company performance.

Economic Changes

In 2000 the economic picture was positive for the United States.[63] The Dow Jones index hit an all-time record high of 11,722. Unemployment was at under 4 percent nationally. The federal government had a record $236 billion surplus and was considering options for putting the money back into the private sector for investment. There was a shortage of talented employees for all jobs. Employers were importing thousands of workers from overseas to fill shortages in computer science, engineering, systems analysis, and computer programming. From a training perspective, companys' total training expenditures were on the rise (for example, the American Society for Training and Development found that total training expenditures rose from 1.5 percent of payroll in 1996 to 2.0 percent in 2000).

Then came September 11, 2001. . . The loss of lives in the World Trade Center and Pentagon buildings was horrific, and the economic consequences of the attack were devastating. There was billions of dollars lost (e.g., human life, property damage, emergency response, cleanup, personal income, business profits). By September 2001, the Dow had dropped to 8,235, and between September 2001 and 2002 the Federal Reserve Board had cut interest rates 11 times, to their lowest rates in 40 years. The federal government account had a projected deficit of $157 billion for 2002. The events of 9/11 and the dot-com bust were major factors that triggered an economic recession. The unemployment rate increased from less than 4 percent to 5.8 percent in 2002. Between September 2000 and September 2002, manufacturing, retail, hotel, airline, and technology businesses combined to lay off close to 2 million employees.

The events of 9/11 combined with an economic recession put companies into a more uncertain economic period. The implications of this new economic period (which some are calling the "Next Economy") for training are far-reaching. For example, it is likely that training programs and the training function will have increased pressure to relate to the business strategy and show a return on investment. Customer focus needs to be included in all training, even if training addresses a specific skill or problem. New technology combined with economic uncertainty will mean that training will be delivered on an as-needed basis rather than taking employees away from their job sites into a classroom. The aging work force combined with reduced immigration because of security concerns may lead employers to focus more on retraining employees or encouraging older, skilled workers to delay retirement or work part-time. Some suggest that the weak economy and the effects of 9/11 may change the ways employees view work. Employees may not want to travel as much, may spend more time with friends and family, and may be more interested in training and development activities related to personal growth. [64]

SNAPSHOT OF TRAINING PRACTICES

Training can play a key role in helping companies gain a competitive advantage and successfully deal with competitive challenges. Before you can learn how training can be used to help companies meet their business objectives and before you can understand training design, training methods, and other topics covered in the text, you need to become familiar with the amount and type of training that occurs in the United States. Also, you must understand what trainers do. The next sections of this chapter present data regarding training practices (e.g., how much companies spend on training, what type of training is occurring, who is being trained) as well as the skills and competencies needed to be a trainer.

Training Facts and Figures

The snapshot of training practices provided in this section is based on data collected from a number of sources including surveys conducted by *Training* magazine, the American Society for Training and Development (ASTD), and the Bureau of Labor Statistics. [65] Note that these data should be viewed as reasonable estimates of practices rather than exact facts. The generalizability of survey results of training practices to U.S. companies is somewhat limited because of potential biases in the survey methods used. For example, the *Training* survey is based on a random sample of *Training* subscribers. Phone interviews were used to ensure that

TABLE 1.4   **Questions and Answers about Training Practices**

Questions	Answers
What percentage of employers provide some formal training?	70%
How much do employers spend on training?	Between $50 and $60 billion
How much time do employees spend in employer-provided training?	30 hours
Who receives most of the training?	35% of training was received by nonexempt employees.
How do training expenditures as a percentage of payroll vary by company size?	Small companies (under 500 employees) spend less than mid-size or large employers.
Does the amount of money spent vary by industry?	Yes. Technology, finance, insurance, and real estate industries spend the most. Durable and nondurable manufacturing, marketing, and trade industries spend the least.
How much training is being outsourced (provided by outside staff such as consultants and schools)?	Most companies report that they use both in-house and outside suppliers of training for all levels of employees. Outside sources deliver 25% of traditional training programs and 29% of technology-based programs.
Who controls training purchases?	48% of training purchases are controlled by training or HR, 15% by senior management, 13% by the trainee's department, and 5% by the trainee.
How is training delivered	69% is instructor-led in a classroom, 16% is by a computer with no instructor, 10% is instructor-led from a remote location, and 5% reported other delivery methods.

Source: Based on data reported in T. Galvin "Industry Report 2003," *Training* (October 2003): 21–45; H. Frazis, M. Gittleman, M. Horrigan, and M. Joyce, "Results from the 1995 survey of Employer-Provided Training," *Monthly Labor Review* (June 1998):3–13.

the person who was sent the survey was qualified to answer the questions. The response rate was 53 percent (1,650 responses). Also, the most recent survey of employer-provided training conducted by the Bureau of Labor Statistics was done in 1995. While this survey is scientifically accurate, it is not current.

Table 1.4 presents questions and answers about training practices. Seventy percent of employees received formal training. Formal training refers to training that was planned in advance and has a structured format. Of the $5 billion spent on training, 73 percent is for training staff salaries, 7 percent is for custom materials designed and provided by outside suppliers (e.g., consultants or training companies), 11 percent is for seminars and conferences, 6 percent is for off-the-shelf prepackaged training materials (such as software, books, and videos) provided by outside suppliers, and 3 percent is for other training products or services from outside suppliers.

Figure 1.3 shows the percentages of companies providing different types of training. Most companies are offering new employee orientation, leadership training, sexual harassment training, training in product knowledge and equipment operation, safety training, and

FIGURE 1.3   Percentage of companies providing different types of training

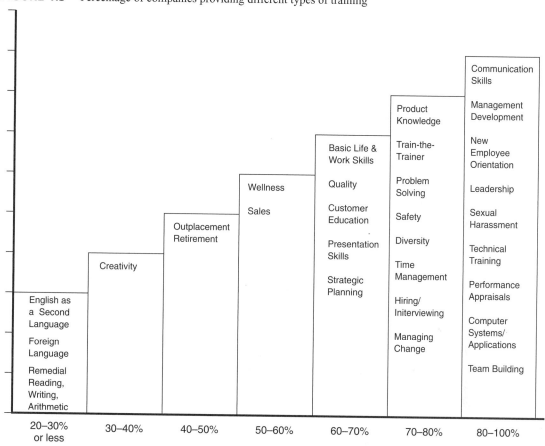

Source: Based on "Industry Report 2002," *Training* (October 2002):51, and T. Gavin, "Industry Report 2003," *Training* (October 2003): 21–45.

training related to problem solving and team building. Fewer companies are offering training in basic life and work skills and language training. Given the changes in the demographics of the work force and the emphasis on quality, it is surprising that only 70 percent of companies are providing diversity and quality training.

The greatest training expenditures are in companies in transportation, communications, and public utilities. This is not surprising given the high level of government regulation and new technologies that have been introduced in these industries. Health or educational services had the lowest level of training expenditures, which may be because employees in these industries receive extensive college, university, and technical school education (e.g., medical education) prior to seeking employment.

Training Investment Leaders

The chapter's opening vignette illustrates how training can be used by companies to gain a competitive advantage. U.S. employers spend approximately $5 billion on formal training per year. Training expenditures as a percentage of payroll are highest in Asia (3.8 percent)

TABLE 1.5
Comparison of Training Investment Leaders and Benchmark Companies

Source: Based on C. Thompson, E. Koon, W. Woodwell Jr., and J. Beauvais, "Training for the Next Economy: An ASTD State of the Industry Report on Trends in Employer-Provided Training in the United States" (Alexandria, VA:ASTD, 2002).

	Benchmark Company	Investment Leader
Percent of eligible employees being trained	78%	91%
Amount of training received per employee	24 hours	57 hours
Amount spent on training		
• Percentage of payroll	2%	4%
• Per employee	$734	$1,647
Average total dollars spent	$3.6m	$11.1m
Percent of training delivered using learning technology	11%	22%
Percent training time in classroom	77%	61%

and lowest in Japan (1.4 percent).[66] By comparison the United States spends 2 percent. Higher spending by companies in the United States is related to use of innovative training practices and high-performance work practices such as teams, employee stock ownership plans, incentive compensation systems (profit sharing), individual development plans, and employee involvement in business decisions. This spending (along with the use of high-performance work practices) has been shown to be related to improved profitability, customer and employee satisfaction, and the ability to retain employees. For example, companies including Pfizer, Century 21, Ritz-Carlton, and Ohio Savings Bank have recognized that training contributes to their competitiveness. They invest 8 to 15 percent of payroll in training. Chapter 2 discusses how training can help companies meet their business goals.

How do the training practices of companies that have recognized training's importance in gaining a competitive advantage differ from other companies? The "2002 ASTD State of the Industry Report" compares the training practices of companies that were part of the ASTD Benchmarking Service with companies that were considered to be Training Investment Leaders.[67] Benchmarking Service companies provided ASTD with a standard set of information on their training practices (e.g., number of hours spent on training); these included 270 companies with an average of 5,000 employees. The Training Investment Leaders represented companies that had made a significant investment in training. This was determined by ranking all companies that participated in the Benchmarking Service on four categories: training investment (expenses for training), total training hours per employee, percentage of employees eligible for training who received it, and percentage of training time delivered through learning technologies (e.g., Web-based training). The 10 percent of the companies with the highest rating across the four categories were identified as Training Investment Leaders; these included 27 companies with an average of 8,000 employees. Table 1.5 compares the Training Investment Leaders with the Benchmark companies. As the table shows, companies that are Investment Leaders train almost all eligible employees, and employees spend about twice as much time training as those in Benchmark firms. Training Investment Leaders made a larger investment in learning technologies and delivered a larger percentage of training using them. CD-ROMs and company intranets were the two most popular learning technologies used to deliver training.

What types of courses were purchased with training dollars? The most money was spent on training related to technical processes and procedures, and the lowest amount of money was spent on basic skills. Training Investment Leaders spent a smaller percentage of expenditures

TABLE 1.6 **Roles of Trainers**

Strategic Adviser	Consults with management on training and development issues that affect business strategy and goals
Systems Design and Developer	Assists management in design and development of systems that affect organizational performance
Organization Change Agent	Advises management on work system design and effective use of human resources
Instructional Designer	Identifies learner needs; develops learning programs; prepares content and learning aids, lesson and program objectives, and delivery technology
Individual Development and Career Counselor	Assists employees in identifying their strengths and weaknesses and development goals
Coach/Performance Consultant	Advises management on ways to improve individual and group performance
Researcher	Evaluates training and development programs to determine their effectiveness; uses these evaluations to make recommendations to managers

Source: Based on P. McLagan, "Great Ideas Revisited," *Training Development* (January 1996): 60–65.

than Benchmarking Service companies on information technology skills and sales and dealer training. They spent a higher percentage on occupational safety.

Roles and Positions of Training Professionals

Trainers can typically hold many jobs, such as instructional designer, technical trainer, or needs analyst (Table 1.7 shows other job titles). Each job has specific roles or functions. For example, one role of the needs analyst is to summarize data collected via interviews, observation, and even surveys to gain an understanding of training needs of a specific job or job family (a grouping of jobs). Special knowledge, skills, or behaviors—also called competencies—are needed to successfully perform each role. For example, the needs analyst must understand basic statistics and research methods to know what type of data to collect and to summarize data to determine training needs.

The most comprehensive study of training professionals has been conducted by the American Society for Training and Development.[68] Table 1.6 shows the different roles of trainers. Note the many roles and responsibilities that trainers can have. Specialists such as instructional designers devote most of their time to analysis, development, or instructional roles. Individual development and career counselors work individually with employees on development plans. In the research role, trainers may evaluate training programs and make recommendations for improving them. Training department managers devote considerable time to the strategic role. Training managers may also still be involved in development or instructional roles, but—because of their administrative and strategic responsibilities—to a smaller extent than specialists. Human resource or personnel managers may also be required to complete many of the training roles, although their primary responsibility is in overseeing the human resources function of the company (e.g., staffing, recruiting, compensation, benefits).

TABLE 1.7
**Median
Salaries for
Training
Professionals**

Source: Based on
J. Vocino, "Annual
Pay and Compensa-
tion," *TD* (January
2003): 44–49.

Top Corporate Organization Development Executive	$149,100
Top Corporate Training Executive	140,000
Management Development Manager	93, 800
Organization Development or Training Manager	92,700
Human Resource Manager	87,600
Training Center Manager	80,800
Training Manager	73,500
Performance Consultant	72,800
Technical Trainer	58,600
Instructional Designer	56,800
Trainer	45,000

Expertise in the roles shown in Table 1.6 continues to be required today. Instructional systems design, adult learning theory, and classroom training are important skills for trainers and training departments. However, traditional narrow jobs in the training department focusing on one set of skills (e.g., instructional designer and technical writer) are changing as new skills are becoming more important. One of these skills is project management, combined with knowledge of new training technologies (e.g., Web-delivered learning, CD-ROM, knowledge management systems), and the ability to manage managers, engineers, scientists, and others who may have more experience or technical saavy than the trainer. For example, at Hewlett-Packard (HP), new learning professionals need to be project managers.[69] They need to know how to create high-impact training solutions that business units in the company want to buy, and they have to do it in short time frames—about six months. Project managers need a solid background in instructional design and knowledge of new technologies that can be used to deliver training.

Hewlett-Packard recently launched "Web Shops," 90-minute Web-delivered sessions that employees can participate in from around the globe. Web Shops include slide shows and presentations by HP experts, followed by online discussions among employees and subject-matter experts. HP also relies heavily on third-party vendors and design contractors for developing training programs. This means that trainers at HP make sure that vendors deliver the promised program on time (i.e., they manage vendors). Although HP continues to put more knowledge on the Web and class time has been reduced, the company realizes that the time in the classroom needs to be well spent. Trainers need to be skilled facilitators who can lead executive dialog discussions, simulations, case studies, and action learning sessions. These training methods are discussed further in Chapters 6 and 7, but for now it is important to know that these are training methods in which the trainee is very actively involved in the learning process. Trainers develop learning content and facilitate hands-on learning experiences. HP trainers are also able to work in global "virtual teams" that include members from different business functions and locations around the world. Personal interaction, reviews of training content, and project coordination occur through e-mail and the Internet.

Table 1.7 shows median salaries for training professionals. Note that very rarely does anyone hold the highest-paying jobs (training manager, personnel manager) without having developed competencies in a number of training roles.

Who Provides Training?

In most companies training and development activities are provided by trainers, managers, in-house consultants, and employee experts. However, as the snapshot of training practices suggests, training and development activities are outsourced. **Outsourcing** means that training and development activities are provided by individuals outside the company. Training providers outside the company include colleges and universities, community and junior colleges, technical and vocational institutions, product suppliers, consultants and consulting firms, unions, trade and professional organizations, and government organizations.

Who Is In Charge of Training?

In small companies training is the responsibility of the founder and all the employees. When organizations grow to 100 employees, typically someone within the company is in charge of human resources as part of their job or their sole responsibility. At this point, training becomes one of the responsibilities of the employee in charge of human resources. In mid to large organizations training can be the responsibility of human resource professionals or can come from a separate function known as human resource development or organizational development. Training is one of several functions that human resource departments and professionals provide. Other functions include staffing (recruitment and selection), compensation, employee relations, health and safety, equal employment opportunities, and human resource planning.

Human resource development refers to the integrated use of training and development, organizational development, and career development to improve individual, group, and organizational effectiveness. Keep in mind that regardless of who is responsible, for training to be successful, employees, managers, training professionals, and top managers all have to take ownership for training! Throughout this book the point is made that although training may be a formal responsibility of someone's job, employees at all levels of the company play a role in the success of training.

As companies grow and/or recognize the important role of training for business success, they form an entire training function (how training functions can be organized is discussed in Chapter 2). The training function may include instructional designers, instructors, technical training, and experts in instructional technology.

The reporting relationship between human resource management and the training function varies across companies.[70] Some organizations include training as part of the human resources function, believing that this provides strategic partnerships with other business functions and consistent company-wide training. For example, at Life Care Centers of America, a Tennessee-based company that operates elder care facilities, training is included in the human resources department because the company believes that training is part of human resources expertise, including the ability to write training curriculum and evaluate learning. Being centrally located in the human resources department makes the best use of resources and helps communicate a common management culture.

Other companies separate training from the human resource function because it allows the training function to be decentralized to better respond to unique needs in different business units. For example, Bank One, a financial services company that has increased in size through merging with other banks, has taken a mixed approach. Following its merger with First Chicago, Bank One had sixty-one independent training units, each with its own training manager. Bank One changed the training function structure to include the strength of a centralized human resource function aligned with a business strategy but at the same time allowed the responsiveness of an independent training unit. The company has a head of education in each of the six business units, along with an educational planning group that includes each head of education and a representative from human resources to establish training policy and make decisions. Bank One centralizes course offerings that are needed across the entire company. But when specific courses related to the business are needed, such as retail banking, the educational unit for the business is responsible for developing the training programs that meet the company's needs. Regardless of the organizational approach used for the training function, it must help meet the training needs of the business.

Preparing to Work in Training

Everyone is a trainer at some point in his or her life! Consider the last time you had to teach some skill to a peer, sibling, spouse, friend, or even your boss. Although some people learn to train by trial and error, the best way is to take courses in training and development or even choose an academic major related to training. For example, training and development courses are usually found in education, business and management, and psychology departments at colleges and universities. Business schools may offer undergraduate and graduate degrees in human resource management with courses in training and development and organizational development. Education departments may have undergraduate and graduate degrees in human resource development. Courses offered with such degrees include instructional design, curriculum development, adult learning, evaluation, and on-the-job training. Psychology departments offer courses in training and development as well. These courses can be part of a degree program in industrial and organizational psychology. If you are fortunate enough to be at a large university, you may have the opportunity to take courses from education, business/management, and the psychology departments that relate to training and development!

To be a successful training professional requires staying up-to-date on current research and training practices. The primary professional organizations for persons interested in training and development include the American Society for Training and Development (ASTD), the Academy of Human Resource Development (AHRD), the Society for Human Resource Management (SHRM), the Society for Industrial and Organizational Psychology (SIOP), the Academy of Management (AOM), and the International Society for Performance Improvement (ISPI). The web addresses for these organizations are listed inside the front cover of this book. Articles about training practices can be found in the following journals: *Training, T&D, Workforce Management, HR Magazine, Academy of Management Executive*, and *Academy of Management Learning and Education*. Training and development research can be found in the following journals: *Human Resource Development Quarterly, Human Resource Development Review, Performance Improvement, Personnel Psychology, Journal of Applied Psychology, Academy of Management Journal,* and *Human Resource Management.*

ORGANIZATION OF THIS BOOK

What is training? Why is it important? What do training professionals do? How much training occurs in U.S. companies? Who is receiving training? How is the training function organized? This chapter answered these questions and offered a broad perspective of training.

Chapter 2 discusses the strategic training and development process. Also, you will see how a company's business strategy influences training practices and the organization of the training department.

The next chapters in the book address specific training issues. Chapters 3 through 8 address different aspects of the instructional system design model, the model used to guide the development of training (see Figure 1.1). Chapter 3 deals with how to determine training needs. Chapter 4 discusses the important issue of learning—specifically, how to create an environment conducive to learning within the training session. Chapter 5 addresses transfer of training, that is, how to ensure that the training environment and the work setting are conducive to the use of knowledge and skills acquired in training. Chapter 6 explains how to evaluate a training program. Chapters 7 and 8 discuss training methods. Chapter 7 looks at traditional training methods such as lecture, behavior modeling simulation, and role play. Chapter 8 examines e-learning and methods that have developed from applications of new technology, for example, Web-based training, virtual reality, and intelligent tutoring systems.

Chapter 9 addresses the important issue of employee development; it discusses four approaches used to develop employee assessments, assignments, relationships, and courses and formal programs. Chapter 10 deals with special topics in training and development including ethics and legal issues, diversity training, cross-cultural training, and the relationship between training and other human resource management practices. Chapters 11 and 12 introduce such career issues as understanding what a career is, the systems companies use to manage careers, and concerns in career management such as plateauing, socialization, downsizing, and outplacement. Chapter 13 discusses how the role of training in organizations may change in the future.

Students should be aware of several important features of the book. Each chapter begins with chapter objectives. These objectives (1) highlight what the student should learn from each chapter and (2) preview the topics. Next comes an opening vignette—an example of a company practice related to the chapter topics. Company examples are liberally used throughout each chapter to help students see how theory and research in training are put into practice. Each chapter ends with key terms, discussion questions, and application assignments. Key terms are related to important concepts emphasized in the chapter. Discussion questions and application assignments can facilitate learning through interacting with other students and actually trying to develop and conduct various training applications. Many application assignments require the use of the World Wide Web, a valuable source of information on training practices.

Key Terms

competitiveness, *2*

competitive advantage, *3*

human resource management, *3*

stakeholders, *3*

training, *3*

high-leverage training, *4*

continuous learning, *4*

training design process, *5*

Instructional Systems Design (ISD), *6*

offshoring, *9*

knowledge workers, *10*

empowering, *11*

change, *11*

learning organizations, *11*

Total Quality Management (TQM), *14*

Malcolm Baldrige National Quality Award, *14*

ISO 9000:2000, *14*

Six Sigma process, *16*

e-commerce, *19*

Internet, *19*

contingent work force, *20*   virtual teams, *22*   human resource
work teams, *21*   outsourcing, *29*   development, *29*
cross training, *21*

Discussion Questions

1. Describe the forces affecting the workplace and learning. How can training help companies deal with these forces?

2. What steps are included in the training design model? What step do you think is most important? Why?

3. How has training contributed to Home Depot?

4. Training professionals continue to debate whether the ISD model is flawed. Some argue that ISD should be treated as a project management approach rather than a step-by-step recipe for building training programs. Others suggest that ISD is too linear and rigid a process, that it is the primary reason training is expensive, and that it takes too long to develop. ISD focuses on inputs; management wants outputs. Businesses want results, not the use of a design technology. Do you believe that ISD is a useful process? Why or why not? Are there certain situations when it is a more (or less) effective way to design training?

5. Which of training professionals' roles do you believe is most difficult to learn? Which is easiest?

6. How might technology influence the importance of training professionals' roles? Can technology reduce the importance of any of the roles? Can it result in additional roles?

7. Describe the training courses that you have taken. How have they helped you? Provide recommendations for improving the courses.

8. How does training differ between companies that are considered Investment Leaders and those that are not?

Application Assignments

1. Go to the American Society for Training and Development (ASTD) home page on the World Wide Web. The address is *www.astd.org.* Investigate the links on the home page. One link is to *Training and Development,* the ASTD journal. Find an article related to training. Summarize the main topic of the article and identify how it relates to course topics or topics covered in this text.

2. Go to *www.quality.nist.gov,* the website for the National Institute of Standards and Technology (NIST). The NIST oversees the Malcolm Baldrige Quality Award. Click on "Criteria for Performance Excellence." Choose either "Business," "Education," or "Healthcare." Download the award criteria. What questions are used to determine a company's education, training, and development focus?

3. For many years General Electric (GE) has been recognized as one of the world's most admired companies. How have training and learning contributed to its success? Visit GE's website at *www.ge.com* and "Click on Careers." Review the links at the top of the page.

4. Conduct a phone or personal interview with a manager. Ask this person to describe the role that training plays in his or her company.

5. Conduct a phone or personal interview with a training manager. Ask this person to discuss how training has changed in the past five years and how he or she believes it will change in the future.

6. *Training* identified the Top 50 Training Organizations (see *Training,* March 2003). The top 10 ranked companies included:

1. Pfizer
2. IBM
3. Sprint
4. Americredit
5. KLA-Tencor
6. Booz Allen Hamilton
7. Ernst and Young LLP
8. Deloitte and Touche LLP
9. Ritz-Carlton Hotel
10. AT&T Business Service

Choose one of these companies to research. Visit the company's website, use a Web search engine, or look for references to the company in publications such as *Training, T&D, Workforce,* or *HR Magazine.* Prepare a report (not to exceed three pages) based on your research (*a*) describing why you believe the company was ranked in the top 10 and (*b*) explaining the relationship between training and the company's competitiveness and business goals and objectives. Your instructor will advise you on whether the report should be submitted electronically or in a paper copy. (Hint: Possible reasons a company might be ranked include the amount of money they devote to training, the level of employee involvement in training, and the type of training used.)

Endnotes

1. J. B. Quinn, P. Anderson, and S. Finkelstein, "Leveraging Intellect," *Academy of Management Executive* 10 (1996): 7–27.

2. A. P. Carnevale, "America and the New Economy," *Training and Development Journal* (November 1990): 31–52; R. Brinkerhoff and A. Apking. High Impact Learning (Cambridge, MA: Perseus Publishing, 2001).

3. J. M. Rosow and R. Zager, *Training the Competitive Edge* (San Francisco: Jossey-Bass, 1988).

4. L. Thornburg, "Accounting for Knowledge," *HR Magazine* (October 1994): 51–56; T. A. Stewart, "Mapping Corporate Brainpower," *Fortune* (October 30, 1995): 209.

5. T. O'Driscoll, "Improving Knowledge Worker Performance," *Performance Improvement* (April 2003): 5–11; F. Wilmouth, C. Prigmore, and M. Bray, "HPT Models: An Overview of the Major Models in the Field," *Performance Improvement* (September 2002): 14–22.

6. B. Pfau and I. Kay, "HR Playing the Training Game and Losing," *HR Magazine* (August 2002): 49–54.

7. D. Zahn, "Training: A Function, Profession, Calling, What?" *Training and Development* (April 2001): 36–41.

8. M. Delahoussaye, K. Ellis, and M. Bolch, "Measuring Corp." (August 2002): 20–35; "Medtronic at a Glance" at Medtronic website, *www.medtronics.com.*

9. M. Molenda, "In Search of the Elusive ADDIE Model," *Performance Improvement* (May/June 2003): 34–36.

10. G. Snelbecker, "Practical Ways for Using Theories and Innovations to Improve Training," in *The ASTD Handbook of Instructional Technology,* ed. G. Piskurich (Burr Ridge, IL: Irwin/McGraw-Hill, 1993): 19.3–19.26.

11. R. Zemke and A. Rosett, "A Hard Look at ISD," *Training* (February 2002): 26–34; Brinkerhoff and Apking, "High Impact Learning."

12. L. Bassi and E. Lewis, eds., *The 1999 ASTD Trends Watch* (Alexandria, VA: American Society for Training and Development, 1999).

13. C. Hill, *Informational Business* (Burr Ridge, IL: Irwin/McGraw-Hill, 1997).

14. J. Lee Young, "Starbucks Expansion into China Is Slated," *The Wall Street Journal,* October 5, 1998, B13C.

15. E. Tahmincioglu, "Opportunities Mingle with Fear Overseas," *The New York Times,* October 24, 2001, G1.

16. M. Cohen, *Labor Shortages as America Approaches the Twenty-First Century* (Ann Arbor: University of Michigan Press, 1995); H. Fullerton, "Another Look at the Labor Force," *Monthly Labor Review* (November 1993): 31–40.

17. "The People Problem," *Inc.* (May 29, 2001): 84–85.

18. R. Konrad, "More U.S. Programmers Training Foreign Replacements," *Columbus Dispatch* (September 1, 2003): D1 & D2.

19. M. Valbrun & S. Thurm, "Foreign Workers Will Soon Get Fewer U.S. Visas," *Wall Street Journal* (October 1, 2003): B1 & B2.

20. A. Dohm, "Gauging the Labor Force Effects of Retiring Babyboomers," *Monthly Labor Review* (July 2000): 17–25.

21. Society for Human Resource Management, *Workplace Visions* 5 (2000): 3–4.

22. K. Dobbs, "Plagued by Turnover? Train Your Managers," *Training* (August 2000): 62–66.

23. Ibid.

24. "BLS Releases 2000–2010 Employment Projections." From U.S. Bureau of Labor Statistics website, *http://stats.bls.gov.*

25. T. J. Atchison, "The Employment Relationship: Untied or Re-Tied," *Academy of Management Executive* 5 (1991): 52–62.

26. "CIO Panel: Knowledge-Sharing Roundtable," Information Week Online, News in Review, April 26, 1999 (from *Information Week* website, *www.informationweek.com*); Buckman Laboratories website, *www.buckman.com.*

27. P. Drucker, *Management Challenges for the 21st Century* (New York: Harper Business, 1999); Howard N. Fullerton Jr., "Labor Force Projections to 2008: Steady Growth and Changing Composition," *Monthly Labor Review* (November 1999): 19–32.

28. D. Senge, "The Learning Organization Made Plain and Simple," *Training and Development Journal* (October 1991): 37–44.

29. L. Thornburg, "Accounting for Knowledge," *HR Magazine* (October 1994): 51–56.

30. C. Bowman, "BLS Projections to 2008: A Summary," *Monthly Labor Review* (November 1999): 3–4.

31. "Tomorrow's Jobs," in the *2002–2003 Occupational Outlook Handbook.* From Bureau of Labor Statistics website, *www.b/s.gov/oco/oco2003.htm.*

32. Ibid.

33. Dohm, "Gauging the Labor Force Effects."

34. A. Carnevale and D. Desrochers, "Training in the Dilbert Economy," *Training and Development* (December 1999): 32–36.

35. M. Van Buren and W. Woodwell Jr., *The 2000 ASTD Trends Report: Staying Ahead of Winds of Change* (Alexandria, VA: American Society for Training and Development, 2000).

36. "Industry Report 2002," *Training* (October 2002): 51.

37. C. Cornell, "Train to Retain," *Human Resource Executive* (June 16, 2003): 34–39.

38. 2002 Spherion Emerging Workforce Study at *www.spherion.com/emergingworkforce.*

39. J. R. Jablonski, *Implementing Total Quality Management: An Overview* (San Diego: Pfeiffer, 1991).

40. R. Hodgetts, F. Luthans, and S. Lee, "New Paradigm Organizations: From Total Quality to Learning World-Class," *Organizational Dynamics* (Winter 1994): 5–19.

41. "Malcolm Baldrige National Quality Award 2001 Award Recipient, Small Business Category, Pal's Sudden Service." From Baldrige Award Recipient Profile at *www.nist.gov,* the website for the National Institute of Standards and Technology.

42. S. L. Jackson, "What You Should Know about ISO 9000," *Training* (May 1992): 48–52; Bureau of Best Practices, *Profile of ISO 9000* (Boston: Allyn and Bacon, 1992); "ISO 9000 International Standards for Quality Assurance," *Design Matters* (July 1995): *http://www.best.com/ISO 9000/att/ISONet.html/.* See *www.iso9000y2k.com,* a website containing ISO 9000:2000 documentation.

43. General Electric 1999 Annual Report. At web address *www.ge.com/annual99.*

44. "Sales and Quality: Marketshare Is Tied to Learning Skills for Both." Total Quality (February 1995): 5.

45. Bureau of Labor Statistics, *"2002–2003 Occupational Outlook Handbook," www.b/s.gov/oco/oco2003.htm.*

46. U.S. Bureau of Labor Statistics, *Employment and Earnings* (Washington DC: U.S. Government Printing Office, January 1990); J. Jarrat and J. Coates, "Employee Development and Job Creation," in *Employees, Careers, and Job Creation,* ed. M. London (San Francisco: Jossey-Bass): 1–25.

47. J. Day, *Population Projections of the United States by Age, Sex, Race, and Hispanic Origin: 1995–2050,* U.S. Bureau of the Census, Current Population Reports, P25–1130 (Washington, D.C.: U.S. Government Printing Office, 1996): 1.

48. D. Hall and J. Richter, "Career Gridlock: Baby Boomers Hit the Wall," *The Executive* 4 (1990): 7–22.

49. K. Dobbs, "Winning the Retention Game," *Training* (September 1999): 50–56.

50. M. Loden and J. B. Rosener, *Workforce America!* (Burr Ridge, IL: Business One Irwin, 1991).

51. "Two Thirds of Americans Online," *CyberAtlas* (May 10, 2000), *http://cyberatlas.internet.com.*

52. Ibid.

53. B. Manville, "Organizing Enterprise-Wide E-learning and Human Capital Management," *Chief Learning Officer* (May 2003): 50–55.

54. A. Weintraub, "High Techs' Future Is in the Toy Chest," *BusinessWeek* (August 26, 2002): 124–26.

55. Society of Human Resource Management, *2002 Benefits Survey* (Alexandria, VA:SHRM Foundation, 2002).

56. C. Johnson, "Don't Forget Your Shift Workers," *HR Magazine* (February 1999): 80-84.

57. J. Cook, "Keeping Work at Work," *Human Resource Executive* (July 2001): 68–71.

58. M. DiNatale, "Characteristics and Preferences for Alternative Work Arrangements, 1999," *Monthly Labor Review* (March 2001): 28–49.

59. P. Choate and P. Linger, *The High-Flex Society* (New York: Knopf, 1986); P. B. Doeringer, *Turbulence in the American Workplace* (New York: Oxford University Press, 1991).

60. K. A. Miller, *Retraining the American Workforce* (Reading, MA: Addison-Wesley, 1989).

61. J. Neal and C. Tromley, "From Incremental Change to Retrofit: Creating High Performance Work Systems," *Academy of Management Executive* 9 (1995): 42–54; M. Huselid, "The Impact of Human Resource Management Practices on Turnover, Productivity, and Corporate Financial Performance," *Academy of Management Journal* 38 (1995): 635–72.

62. W. Pape, "Group Insurance," *Inc. Technology* 2 (1997): 29, 31.

63. C. Thompson, E. Koon, W. Woodwell, Jr., and J. Beauvais, "Training for the Next Economy: An ASTD State of the Industry Report on Trends in Employer-Provided Training in the United States" (Alexandria, VA: ASTD, 2002).

64. "Workplace Visions," *Society for Human Resource Management* 4 (2002).

65. "BLS Reports on the Amount of Employer-Provided Formal Training," press release (July 10, 1996); H. J. Frazis, D. E. Herz, and M. W. Harrigan, "Employer-Provided Training: Results from a New Survey," *Monthly Labor Review* 5 (May 1995): 3–17; C. Thompson, E. Koon, W. Woodwell Jr., and J. Beauvais, "Training for the Next Economy: An ASTD State of the Industry Report on Trends in Employer-Provided Training in the United States" (Alexandria, VA: ASTD, 2002); T. Galvin, "2003 Industry Report," *Training* (October 2003): 21–45.

66. M. Marquardt, S. King, and W. Ershkine, "The 2002 ASTD International Comparisons Report" (Alexandria, VA: American Society for Training and Development 1993).

67. Ibid.

68. W. J. Rothwell, "Selecting and Developing the Professional HRD Staff," in *The ASTD Training and Development Handbook,* 4th ed., ed. R. L. Craig (New York: McGraw-Hill, 1996): 48–76; P. A. McLagan, *The Research Report: Models for HRD Practice* (Alexandria, VA: American Society of Training and Development, 1989); P. McLagan, "Great Ideas Revisited," *Training and Development* (January 1996): 60–65.

69. D. Zielinski, "Training Careers in the 21st Century," *Training* (January 2000): 27–38.

70. J. Schettler, "Should HR Control Training?" *Training* (July 2002): 32–38.

Chapter **Two**

Strategic Training

Objectives

After reading this chapter, you should be able to

1. Discuss how business strategy influences the type and amount of training in a company. *Pg 39*

2. Explain how the role of training is changing. *41*

3. Describe the strategic training and development process. *43*

4. Discuss how a company's staffing and human resource planning strategies influence training. *51*

5. Explain the training needs created by concentration, internal growth, external growth, and disinvestment business strategies. *57*

6. Discuss the advantages and disadvantages of organizing the training function according to the faculty, customer, matrix, and corporate university models. *60 - 63*

7. Discuss the characteristics of the virtual training organization and how it can contribute to the company's business strategy. *65*

Learning Is Business at Nokia

Nokia Corporation, the world leader in mobile communications, has over 50,000 employees and net sales of $30 billion. Nokia consists of two business groups : Nokia Networks and Nokia Mobile Phones. The company also includes the separate Nokia Ventures Organization and the corporate research unit, Nokia Research Center. Nokia's business strategy is to strengthen the company's position as the leading communications and systems provider. Nokia wants to create personalized communication technology that enables people to create their own mobile world. Nokia continues to target and enter segments of the communications market that the company believes will experience faster growth than the industry as a whole. As the demand for wireless access to services increases, Nokia plans to lead the development and commercialization of networks and systems required to make wireless content more accessible and rewarding for customers.

The management approach at Nokia, known as the "Nokia way," consists of the Nokia values, its organizational competencies, and its operations and processes used to maintain operational efficiency. The company has built its current and future strength on the Nokia way. The Nokia way has resulted in a flat, networked company emphasizing speed and flexibility in decision making. Nokia's values include customer satisfaction, respect for the individual, achievement, and continuous learning. Continuous learning provides employees with the opportunity to develop themselves and to stay technologically current. Employees are encouraged to share experiences, take risks, and learn together. Continuous learning goes beyond formal training classes. At Nokia, continuous learning means that employees support each other's growth, developing and improving relationships through the exchange and development of ideas. E-learning is used to provide employees with the freedom to choose the best possible time and place for personal development.

Nokia's top management is committed to continuous learning. For example, the business group presidents are the "owners" of all global management and leadership programs for senior managers. They personally provide input into the development of these programs but they also appoint "godfathers" from their management teams. These godfathers participate actively throughout the program and are also designers of program content. Together with the training and development staff, the godfathers help the learning processes in the programs. Most of the programs involve strategic projects (action learning) that participants are responsible for completing. Top managers invest time in reviewing the projects and have the authority to take action based on the project team recommendations.

The value of continuous learning translates into personal and professional growth opportunities including a commitment to self-development, coaching, learning solutions and training, management training, a vibrant internal job market, and performance management. Employees are encouraged to create their own development plan and use available learning solutions and methods. Coaching with highly skilled colleagues helps employees develop and gives them the opportunity to share ideas and goals with each other. Nokia employees have access to a wide variety of training and development opportunities including learning centers and the Learning Market Place Internet, which has information on all the available learning solutions including e-learning and classroom training. Through the learning centers, Nokia has integrated the learning activities of all the business groups into one place. Nokia believes that by mixing participants from across business groups, knowledge is created because traditions and experiences can be shared between employees. In addition to formal programs offered in classrooms or on the Internet, Nokia emphasizes on-the-job learning through job rotation and through managers giving their employees challenging new job assignments. There is also a wide range of opportunities for managers to improve their management and leadership skills. The emphasis on the internal labor market encourages employees to improve their skills by changing jobs. Nokia's performance management process, known as Investing in People (IIP), involves twice yearly discussions between employees and their managers. The IIP process consists of objective setting, coaching and achievement review, competence analysis, and personal development plan. The entire IIP process is supported electronically. Employees can choose their profile from the company intranet, conduct a self-evaluation, create a personal development plan, and investigate what learning solutions are available at the learning centers.

Nokia emphasizes that learning should result in improved operations and better business results. Therefore, the company uses a combination of measures to evaluate the value of training. Nokia always asks employees for their immediate reactions after they have completed a program. Other measures include attainment of competence and resource strategy in all parts of the company. Top management believes that the largest benefit of the learning is that employees have opportunities to network, creating more knowledge, reinforcing continuous learning, and creating committed employees.

Source: Based on the Nokia Corporation website, *www.nokia.com,* August 22, 2003; L. Masalin, "Nokia Leads Change through Continuous Learning," *Academy of Management Learning and Education,* 2 (2003): 68–72.

INTRODUCTION

As the chapter opening vignette shows, learning is an important part of Nokia's business strategy. Training helps employees at Nokia develop specific skills that enable them to succeed in their current job and develop for the future. Nokia also recognizes that learning involves not just formal training courses but also job experiences and interactions between employees. From Nokia's perspective, training and developing helps the company create a work force that is able to cope with change, meet the increasing demands of the telecommunications industry, and prepare the future leadership of the company. Nokia recognizes that its industry is becoming complex—success will require smart, motivated employees who have the emotional strength to deal with change.

Why is the emphasis on strategic training important? Companies are in business to make money, and every business function is under pressure to show how it contributes to business success or face spending cuts and even outsourcing. To contribute to a company's success, training activities should help the company achieve its business strategy. A **business strategy** is a plan that integrates the company's goals, policies, and actions.[1] The strategy influences how the company uses physical capital (e.g., plants, technology, and equipment), financial capital (e.g., assets and cash reserves), and human capital (employees). The business strategy helps direct the company's activities (production, finance, marketing, human resources) to reach specific goals. The **goals** are what the company hopes to achieve in the medium- and long-term future. Most companies' goals include financial goals, such as to maximize shareholder wealth. But companies have other goals related to employee satisfaction, industry position, and community service.

There is both a direct and indirect link between training and business strategy and goals. Training can help employees develop skills needed to perform their jobs, which directly affects the business. Giving employees opportunities to learn and develop creates a positive work environment, which supports the business strategy by attracting talented employees as well as motivating and retaining current employees.

For example, consider QUALCOMM, which sells Eudora e-mail software and is a leader in developing and delivering innovative digital wireless communications products and services (such as system software and satellite-based systems).[2] QUALCOMM's goal is to produce innovative ideas about communications technology, and to develop and commercialize them. To achieve this goal, QUALCOMM has recognized that it needs bright, creative employees. QUALCOMM has decided to use training and development to help it compete. Employee training and education is critical to nurture the company's entrepreneurial spirit. For example, QUALCOMM now offers more than 250 courses online including technical, computer training/engineering, manufacturing, and management topics. QUALCOMM employs "learning specialists" whose goal is to track the training needs of various business units. QUALCOMM provides an Internet-based self-service tool that allows employees to access their records, analyze their skills, and enroll in training classes. The business units determine what courses employees are required to take. In addition, QUALCOMM offers employees an annual education allowance of $5,200 from which they can pay for additional training. Given the critical role of knowledge in the business, QUAL-COMM has made training an important part of its business strategy to help realize the full potential of its employees and reach business goals.

Business strategy has a major impact on the type and amount of training that occurs and whether resources (money, trainers' time, and program development) should be devoted to training. Also, strategy influences the type, level, and mix of skills needed in the company. Strategy has a particularly strong influence on determining

1. The amount of training devoted to current or future job skills.
2. The extent to which training is customized for the particular needs of an employee or developed based on the needs of a team, unit, or division.
3. Whether training is restricted to specific groups of employees (such as persons identified as having managerial talent) or open to all employees.
4. Whether training is planned and systematically administered, provided only when problems occur, or spontaneously as a reaction to what competitors are doing.
5. The importance placed on training compared to other human resource management practices such as selection and compensation.[3]

This chapter begins with a discussion of how training is evolving. Traditionally, training has been seen as an event or program to develop specific explicit knowledge and skills. But managers and trainers and human resource professionals have begun to recognize the potential contribution to business goals of knowledge that is based on experience and that is impossible to teach in a training program, and they have broadened the role of training to include learning and designing ways to create and share knowledge. The chapter goes on to discuss the process of strategic training and development including identifying the business strategy, choosing strategic training and development initiatives that support the strategy, providing training and development activities that support the strategic initiatives, and identifying and collecting metrics to demonstrate the value of training. The chapter next describes organizational factors that influence how training relates to the business strategy. These include the roles of employees and managers; top management support for training; integration of business units; staffing and human resource planning strategy; degree of unionization; and manager, trainer, and employee involvement in training. The chapter then addresses specific strategic types and their implications for training. The chapter ends with a description of several different ways of organizing the training function, emphasizing that the virtual training organization and corporate university model are gaining in popularity as companies are aligning training activities with business goals.

THE EVOLUTION OF TRAINING'S ROLE

As more companies such as Nokia recognize the importance of continuous learning for meeting business challenges and providing a competitive advantage, the role of training in companies is changing. Figure 2.1 shows the evolution of training's role from a program

FIGURE 2.1
Evolution of
training's role

focus to a broader focus on learning and creating and sharing knowledge.[4] Training will continue to focus on developing programs to teach specific skills; however, to better relate to improving employees' performance and to help meet business needs and challenges (and be considered strategic), training's role has to evolve to include an emphasis on learning and creating and sharing knowledge. **Learning** refers to the acquisition of knowledge by individual employees or groups of employees who are willing to apply that knowledge in their jobs in making decisions and accomplishing tasks for the company.[5] **Knowledge** refers to what individuals or teams of employees know or know how to do (human and social knowledge) as well as company rules, processes, tools, and routines (structured knowledge).[6] Knowledge is either tacit knowledge or explicit knowledge.[7] **Explicit knowledge** refers to knowledge that can be formalized, codified, and communicated. That is, it can be found in manuals, formulas, and specifications. **Tacit knowledge** refers to personal knowledge based on individual experience and is difficult to explain to others. Because tacit knowledge is difficult to communicate, it is passed along to others through direct experience (e.g., interacting with other employees, watching other employees). The types of tacit and explicit knowledge that are important for employees include knowledge about the company, knowledge about customers, and knowledge about the company's business processes.[8] Employees need to understand the company's business, strategy, and financial statements as well as how the company is organized. This gives them some idea of where to go with new ideas, how to seek help with problems, and how to create opportunities for cross-functional businesses. Employees must know who the company's customers are, what they need, and why they choose to do business with the company. Finally, employees must have a general understanding of the major business processes and a more detailed understanding of the business processes they are involved in. Well-designed traditional training courses can successfully help employees learn tacit knowledge. But to learn tacit knowledge requires interpersonal interaction and experiences that are usually not found in training programs.

In traditional approaches to training, training is seen as a series of programs or events that employees attend. After attending the training program, employees are responsible for using what they learned in training on the job, and any support they might receive is based on the whims of their manager. Also, traditional training provides no information that would help employees understand the relationship between the training content and individual performance or development objectives or business goals. This type of training usually fails to improve workplace performance and meet business needs. The role of training as a program or event will continue into the future because employees will always need to be taught specific knowledge and skills. This approach assumes that business conditions are predictable, they can be controlled by the company, and the company can control and predict the knowledge and skills that employees need in the future. These assumptions are true for certain skills such as communication and conflict resolution. However, these training events or programs will need to be more closely tied to performance improvement and business needs to receive support from top management. The training design model presented in Chapter 1 and the different aspects of the model discussed in Chapters 3 though 8 will help you understand how to design training programs that can improve employee performance and meet business needs.

A single training event or program is not likely to give a company a competitive advantage because explicit knowledge is well-known and programs designed to teach it can be easily developed and imitated. However, tacit knowledge developed through experience and shared through interactions between employees is impossible to imitate and can provide companies with a competitive advantage. For example, Blackmer/Dover Resources makes heavy-duty pumps designed to move refined oil and propane gas as well as food products such as chocolate and coconut oil.[9] Blackmer's president believes that it is impossible to document the intelligence of his employees. For example, one employee can tell what's wrong with a malfunctioning pump just by listening to it. Another employee shared knowledge of how to determine whether tiny holes in one type of pump were clogged. The hole is necessary for lubricant to pass through to cool the pump. If the opening isn't wide enough, the pump would pass quality inspection but would burn up when used by the customer. This employee explained that he simply holds the pump up to make sure he sees light passing through the hole.

The emphasis on learning has several implications. First, there is a recognition that to be effective, learning has to be related to helping employees' performance improve and the company achieve its business goals. This connection helps ensure that employees are motivated to learn and that the limited resources (time and money) for learning are focused in areas that will directly help the business succeed. Second, unpredictability in the business environment in which companies operate will continue to be the norm. Because problems cannot be predicted in advance, learning needs to occur on an as-needed basis. Companies need to move beyond the classroom and instead use job experiences and Web-based training to teach employees skills while they focus on business problems. Third, because tacit knowledge is difficult to acquire in training programs, companies need to support informal learning that occurs through mentoring, chat rooms, and job experiences. Fourth, learning has to be supported not only with physical and technical resources but also psychologically. The company work environment needs to support learning, and managers and peers need to encourage learning and help employees find ways to obtain learning on the job. Also, managers need to understand employees' interests and career goals to help them find suitable development activities that will prepare them to be successful in other positions in the company or deal with expansion of their current job. Chapter 5 discusses the characteristics of a learning organization and how to create a work environment that supports training and learning.

Creating and sharing knowledge refers to companies' development of intellectual capital. **Intellectual capital** includes cognitive knowledge (know what), advanced skills (know how), system understanding and creativity (know why), and self-motivated creativity (care why). [10] Traditionally, training has focused on cognitive and advanced skills. But the greatest value for the business may be created by having employees understand the manufacturing or service process and the interrelationships between departments and divisions (system understanding) as well as motivating them to deliver high-quality products and services (care why). To create and share knowledge, companies have to provide the physical space and technology (e-mail, websites) to encourage employee collaboration and knowledge sharing. Ford Motor Company has communities of practice organized around functions.[11] For example, all the painters in every Ford assembly plant around the world belong to the same community. At each plant, one of the painters serves as a "focal point." If a local painter discovers a better way to improve one of the 60 steps involved in painting, the focal person completes a template describing the improvement and its benefits. The template is submitted electronically to a subject matter expert located at Ford headquarters, who reviews the practice and decides whether it is worth sharing with other assembly plants. If so, the practice is approved and sent online to the other assembly plants. Ford has collected $1.3 billion in projected value for the company and realized over $800 million of actual value from its communities of practice.

THE STRATEGIC TRAINING AND DEVELOPMENT PROCESS

Now that you understand how training is evolving in companies and have been introduced to the concept of business strategy and how training can support a business strategy, you are ready to study the process of strategic training and development. Figure 2.2 shows the strategic training and development process with examples of strategic initiatives, training activities, and metrics.

The model shows that the process begins with identifying the business strategy. Next, strategic training and development initiatives that support the strategy are chosen. Translating these strategic training and development initiatives into concrete training and development activities is the next step of the process. The final step of the process involves identifying measures or metrics. These metrics are used to determine if training helped contribute to goals related to the business strategy. The following sections detail each step in the process.

FIGURE 2.2
The strategic training and development process

CONCRETE

Business Strategy	Strategic Training and Development Initiatives	Training and Development Activities	Metrics That Show Value of Training
• Mission • Values • Goals	• Diversify the Learning Portfolio • Improve Customer Service • Accelerate the Pace of Employee Learning • Capture and Share Knowledge	• Use Web-Based Training • Make Development Planning Mandatory • Develop Websites for Knowledge Sharing • Increase Amount of Customer Service Training	• Learning • Performance Improvement • Reduced Customer Complaints • Reduced Turnover • Employee Satisfaction

TABLE 2.1
Decisions a Company Must Make about How to Compete to Reach Its Goals

Source: "Strategy-Decisions about Competition," From R. Noe, J. Hollenbeck, B. Gerhart, and P. Wright, *Human Resource Management: Gaining a Competitive Advantage*, 4th ed. (Burr Ridge, IL: Irwin/McGraw-Hill, 2003): 57.

1. **Where to compete?**
   In what markets (industries, products, etc.) will we compete?
2. **How to compete?**
   On what outcome or differentiating characteristic will we compete? Cost? Quality? Reliability? Delivery? Innovativeness?
3. **With what will we compete?**
   What resources will allow us to beat the competition? How will we acquire, develop, and deploy those resources to compete?

Identify the Company's Business Strategy

Three factors influence the company's business strategy. First, the company's mission, vision, values, and goals help to determine the strategy. These are usually determined by the top management team. The **mission** is the company's reason for existing. It may specify the customers served, why the company exists, what the company does, or the values received by the customer. The **vision** is the picture of the future that the company wants to achieve. **Values** are what the company stands for. Review the chapter opening vignette to see examples of Nokia's business strategy and values. Second, a **SWOT analysis** (strengths, weaknesses, opportunities, threats) involves an analysis of the company's operating environment (e.g., product markets, new technologies) to identify opportunities and threats as well as an internal analysis of the company's strengths and weaknesses including people, technology, and financial resources. The business challenges identified in Chapter 1 may also represent an opportunity (or threat) to the company. Recall that these business challenges include globalization, the need for leadership, increased value of intellectual capital, change, attracting and winning talent, and a focus on customers and quality. Third, the company has to consider its competition. That is, how will the company successfully compete? The decisions that a company has to consider about how to compete are shown in Table 2.1.

Although these decisions are equally important, companies often pay less attention to the "with what will we compete" issue, resulting in failure to reach the goals. The "with what will we compete" decision includes deciding how human, physical, and financial capital will be used. To use human capital to gain a competitive advantage requires linking the company's human resources practices (such as training and development) to the business strategy.

Consider how training contributes to the business strategy at Tires Plus. The mission at Tires Plus's headquarters and 150 stores located in the midwestern United States is to encourage employees to be the same at work as they are in every other area of their lives. Though Tires Plus was once a struggling company, its annual growth rate has exceeded 20 percent over the past five years. It is now a $200 million company—the sixth largest independent tire retailer—and hopes to expand nationally and double in size in the next 10 years. One of the company's most important goals is to ensure that the business strategy promotes employees' growth and loyalty and fairness as economic and social concepts. Tires Plus makes a great effort to differentiate itself from old-fashioned tire shops. Many customers enter the store expecting the same rude staff and dirty service areas they have experienced at other tire shops. But they are pleasantly surprised! Salespeople wear white shirts and ties, and they immediately greet customers. Showrooms are clean and organized. Each store has a customer lounge including television sets, tables, and play areas for children. Fast and friendly service is the norm. Customers are encouraged to walk into the shop to watch the mechanics at work. To reach its business expansion goals will require Tires Plus to expand recruiting efforts and develop its work force while facing a tight labor market. Tires Plus is investing in training to help reach its expansion goals. As one of the company's trainers notes, "The more information and education we can give people, the better equipped they'll be to advance within the company. And if they're moving up, hopefully they'll see opportunities to expand with us."

The company's intensive training and internal promotion programs motivate employees hoping to advance their careers. It's all part of Tires Plus's effort to reduce turnover and improve customer relations. Approximately 1,700 Tires Plus employees spend about 60,000 hours annually in formal training programs offered by Tires Plus University, at a cost of $3 million. The company's training facility includes a 250-seat auditorium, replicas of store showrooms and service shops, a computer lab, media center, and four full-time trainers. New hires receive a week of product, sales, or mechanical training depending on their position. Employees spend hours in classrooms and in simulated tire shops, learning how to create a service environment that encourages customers to do return business and to recommend the company to their friends. Tires Plus career tracks help employees develop into mechanics and store managers—an effort that has helped recruit new employees, retain current employees, and make sure that leadership positions in the company are filled. The company also devotes time and money to giving employees opportunities to advance, which helps retention and recruitment. For example, a tire technician who wants to become a mechanic can take an 11-week course at Tires Plus University, during which the technician learns all the basics of a mechanic's job. After formal training the tire technician works with an on-the-job mentor until he or she is ready to work alone as a mechanic. The course is free and the prospective mechanic gets paid a salary while participating in training. Employees with potential to be managers are given 80 hours of leadership training.

The company's large time and financial investments in training have helped it to meet its strategic goals. Store surveys show a 96 percent customer satisfaction rate. Tires Plus's annual turnover rate is 8 percent—a high rate but it's about 20 percent lower than competitors' rates in the automotive service industry and half of retailers' rates.[12]

Identify Strategic Training and Development Initiatives That Support the Strategy

Strategic training and development initiatives are learning-related actions that a company should take to help it achieve its business strategy.[13] The strategic training and development initiatives vary by company depending on a company's industry, goal, resources, and capabilities. The initiatives are based on the business environment, an understanding of the company's goals and resources, and insight of potential training and development options. They provide the company with a road map to guide specific training and development activities. They also show how the training function will help the company reach its goals (and in doing so, show how the training function will add value).

Table 2.2 shows strategic training and development initiatives and their implications for training practices. *Diversifying the learning portfolio* means that companies may need to provide more learning opportunities than just traditional training programs. These learning opportunities include informal learning that occurs on the job through interactions with peers; new job experiences; personalized learning opportunities using mentors, coaches, and feedback customized to the employee needs; and the use of technology (including Web-based training). Such training is self-paced and available outside a formal classroom environment

TABLE 2.2   **Strategic Training and Development Initiatives and Their Implications**

Strategic Training and Development Initiatives	Implications
Diversify the Learning Portfolio	• Use new technology such as the Internet for training • Facilitate informal learning • Provide more personalized learning opportunities
Expand Who Is Trained	• Train customers, suppliers, and employees • Offer more learning opportunities to nonmanagerial employees
Accelerate the Pace of Employee Learning	• Quickly identify needs and provide a high-quality learning solution • Reduce the time to develop training programs • Facilitate access to learning resources on an as-needed basis
Improve Customer Service	• Ensure that employees have product and service knowledge • Ensure that employees have skills needed to interact with customers • Ensure that employees understand their roles and decision-making authority
Provide Development Opportunities and Communicate to Employees	• Ensure that employees have opportunities to develop • Ensure that employees understand career opportunities and personal growth opportunities • Ensure that training and development addresses employees' needs in current job as well as growth opportunities
Capture and Share Knowledge	• Capture insight and information from knowledgeable employees • Logically organize and store information • Provide methods to make information available (e.g., resource guides, websites)
Align Training and Development with the Company's Strategic Direction	• Identify needed knowledge, skills, abilities, or competencies • Ensure that current training and development programs support the company's strategic needs
Ensure That the Work Environment Supports Learning and Transfer of Training	• Remove constraints to learning, such as lack of time, resources, and equipment • Dedicate physical space to encourage teamwork, collaboration, creativity, and knowledge sharing • Ensure that employees understand the importance of learning • Ensure that managers and peers are supportive of training, development, and learning

Source: Based on S. Tannenbaum, "A Strategic View of Organizational Training and Learning," in *Creating, Implementing and Managing Effective Training and Development*, ed. K. Kraiger (San Francisco: Jossey-Bass, 2002): 10–52.

(these learning opportunities are discussed in Chapters 5, 7, 8, and 9). Consider how Freddie Mac, the mortgage finance company based in Virginia, provides learning when it is needed.[14] A Freddie Mac employee who has a learning need can go to the learning portal on the Web to find solutions. The learning portal includes online courses, books, videos, discussion groups, and articles. Learning consultants are available to help employees use the learning portal, address special needs, and incorporate learning needs into their personal development plan. Accenture Resources Group, a consulting company in New York, uses informal learning as a way to increase communications between executives, managers, and consultants in the field. Each Accenture consultant is assigned to a community of one hundred people that meets four times a year. The community meetings often feature senior executives leading discussions on topics such as leadership and creating shareholder value.

Expand who is trained refers to the recognition that because employees are often the customer's primary point of contact, they need as much if not more training than managers do. Also, to provide better customer service to suppliers, vendors, and consumers, companies need to distribute information about how to use the products and services they offer. Companies are beginning to train suppliers to ensure that the parts that suppliers provide will meet their customers' quality standards. To be successful, companies have to be able to deal with changes in technology, customer needs, and global markets. Training needs have to be quickly identified and effective training provided. That is, companies have to *accelerate the pace of employee learning.* Also, companies are relying on electronic performance support systems (EPSS) that provide employees with immediate access to information, advice, and guidance (EPSS are discussed in more detail in Chapter 5). EPSS can be accessed through personal computers or handheld computers whenever they are needed. Because customers now have access to databases and websites and have a greater awareness of high-quality customer service, they are more knowledgeable, are better prepared, and have higher service expectations than ever before. Employees must be prepared to *provide the best possible customer service.* Employees have to be knowledgeable about the product or service, they need to have customer service skills, and they need to understand the types of decisions they can make (e.g., can they make an exception to the policy of no cash refunds?). *Providing development opportunities* and communicating them to employees is important to ensure that employees believe that they have opportunities to grow and learn new skills. Such opportunities are important for attracting and retaining talented employees. *Creating and sharing knowledge* ensures that important knowledge about customers, products, or processes is not lost if employees leave the company. Also, giving employees access to knowledge that other employees have may quicken response times to customers and improve product and service quality. For example, rather than "reinventing the wheel," service personnel can tap into a database that allows them to search for problems and identify solutions that other service reps have developed. *Aligning training and development* with the company's strategic direction is important to ensure that training contributes to business needs. Companies need to identify what employee capabilities (e.g., knowledge, skills) are needed and whether training programs and services are helping to improve these capabilities. Lastly, *a supportive work environment* is necessary for employees to be motivated to participate in training and learning activities, use what they learn on the job, and share their knowledge with others. Tangible support includes time and money for training and learning as well as work areas that encourage employees to meet and discuss ideas. Psychological support from managers and peers for training and learning is also important. Types of tangible and psychological support for training are discussed in Chapter 5.

Provide Training and Development Activities Linked to Strategic Training and Development Initiatives

After a company chooses its strategic training and development initiatives related to its business strategy, it then identifies specific training and development activities that enable these initiatives to be achieved. These activities include developing initiatives related to use of new technology in training, increasing access to training programs for certain groups of employees, reducing development time, and developing new or expanded course offerings.

TABLE 2.3

Sun Microsystems' Mission Statement

Source: *www.sun.com*, Company Information, Mission Statement, August 22, 2003.

Vision: Everyone and everything connected to the network
Mission: Solve complex network computing problems for governments, enterprises, and service providers
Experience: Two decades on the forefront of network computing
Understanding: The know-how to meet your business challenges
Innovation: A way of computing that connects everyone
Cooperation: Bringing together the best solutions
Commitment: Quality service and support

For example, one of the strategic training and development initiatives for American Express Financial Advisors, located in Minneapolis, Minnesota, is to prepare employees to offer world-class service.[15] Training the company's customer service representatives is especially important because of the breadth of the job requirements. The customer service representatives have to be able to discuss the content of financial products as well as handle transactions of these products over the phone with both customers and financial experts. Also, the representatives work in the securities industry, which is highly regulated, and some are required to have a license to sell securities. American Express's emphasis on training is related not only to the company needs but also to the basic business principle that it costs less to serve customers well and keep them than to try and replace them after they have left. Providing good customer service and maintaining customer loyalty depends on how well customer service representatives work the phones, take orders, offer assistance, and develop relationships with customers.

When new employees report for work in the customer services section of American Express, they begin an eight-week training program designed to help them succeed in building and solidifying the company's client base. First, they split their days into learning about American Express's investment products and practicing how they will work with the company's financial advisers and clients. After employees complete the initial training and begin to work on the phone with actual clients, they still receive at least two weeks of training each year. The ongoing training includes a mix of classroom and Web-based training on subjects such as new financial products or changes in security regulations. Online training modules are used to teach computer skills such as how to use a new software product or how to reduce the number of screens a representative must go through to retrieve a particular piece of information. American Express's training includes active participation by the trainees. Customer service trainees are given time to review material, ask questions, and practice on the computer systems they will be using.

Sun Microsystems, a manufacturer of computer workstations and workstation software based in Santa Clara, California, has made sure its training function and training activities support its business strategy. Sun's mission statement (shown in Table 2.3) discusses how Sun views computers (a vision of computers talking to each other), has established a history of innovation and technology leadership, helps companies in every industry to leverage the power of the Internet, has established relationships with leading suppliers of computing solutions that Sun can rely on to develop integrated solutions, and is committed to high-quality service and technical support. In his letter to stockholders in the 2002 annual report, Scott McNealy, chairman of the board and chief executive officer, states that despite poor economic conditions, intellectual capital and investment in research and development is critical for Sun to stay ahead of its competition and create shareholder value.[16]

TABLE 2.4
SunU's Analysis to Align Training with Business Strategy

Source: Based on P.A. Smith, "Reinventing SunU," *Training and Development* (July 1994): 23–27.

> **Customers**
> Who are our customers and how do we work for them?
>
> **Organization**
> What is the nature of practices required to complete our mission?
>
> **Products and Services**
> How do we ensure that our products and services meet strategic requirements?
>
> **Research and Development**
> How do we stay current in the training and learning fields and use our knowledge in these areas?
>
> **Business Systems**
> What are the processes, products, tools, and procedures required to achieve our goals?
>
> **Continuous Learning**
> How do we recognize that learning at Sun Microsystems is continuous, is conscious, and comes from many sources?
>
> **Results**
> How do we obtain results according to our customers' standards?

A good example of how a training function can contribute to business strategy is evident in the changes made by SunU, the training and development organization of Sun Microsystems.[17] SunU realigned its training philosophy and the types of training it conducted to be more linked to the strategy of Sun. Sun was in a constantly evolving business due to new technologies, products, and product markets. SunU found that its customers wanted training services that could be developed quickly, could train many people, and would not involve classroom training. Because of its importance for the business, Sun was also interested in maintaining and improving the knowledge and competence of its current work force.

Table 2.4 presents the questions that SunU used to determine how to better contribute to the business strategy. Note that the questions SunU asked not only deal with the delivery of training, but also attempt to understand internal customer needs and potential business needs as determined by Sun's business strategy.

As a result of the need to better align the training function with the needs generated by the business strategy, SunU took several steps. First, it developed a new approach to determining the knowledge and skills that the employees needed to meet business goals. SunU identified several basic competencies (such as customer relations). A team of trainers at SunU constantly reviews these competencies and discusses them with key senior managers. For example, in the customer service competency, vice presidents and directors of sales and marketing are interviewed to identify training needs. As a result of this process SunU learns more about the business needs and is able to develop relevant training. To help deliver training quickly to a large number of trainees without relying on the classroom, SunU developed videoconferencing programs that allow training to be delivered simultaneously to several sites without requiring trainees to travel to a central location. To help maintain and improve the knowledge and abilities of its employees, SunU developed a desktop library that enables all employees to access CD-ROMs containing up-to-date information on technologies and products as well as profiles on customers and competitors.

Identify and Collect Metrics to Show Training Success

How does a company determine whether training and development activities actually contribute to the business goals? This determination involves identifying and collecting outcome measures, or metrics. The metrics that are typically used to identify training success or effectiveness include trainees' satisfaction with the training program; whether the trainees' knowledge, skill, ability, or attitudes changed as a result of program participation (cognitive and skill-based outcomes); and whether the program resulted in business-related outcomes for the company.

The business-related outcomes should be directly linked to the business strategy and goals. Examples of business-related outcomes include quicker or higher quality customer service, fewer product defects, higher employee satisfaction, and reduced turnover. Some companies use the balanced scorecard as a process to evaluate all aspects of the business. The **balanced scorecard** is a means of performance measurement that provides managers with a chance to look at the overall company performance or the performance of departments or functions (such as training) from the perspective of internal and external customers, employees, and shareholders.[18] The balanced scorecard considers four different perspectives: customer, internal, innovation and learning, and financial. The emphasis and type of indicators used to measure each of these perspectives is based on the company's business strategy and goals. The four perspectives and examples of metrics used to measure them include:

Customer (time, quality, performance, service, cost).

Internal (processes that influence customer satisfaction).

Innovation and Learning (operating efficiency, employee satisfaction, continuous improvement).

Financial (profitability, growth, shareholder value).

Metrics that might be used to assess training's contribution to the balanced scorecard include employees trained (employees trained divided by total number of employees), training costs (total training cost divided by number of employees trained), and training costs per hour (total training costs divided by total training hours). The process of identifying and collecting metrics is related to training evaluation, the final step in Figure 1.1. Chapter 6 discusses the different types of outcomes in greater detail. Of course, showing that training directly relates to the company "bottom line" (e.g., increased service, sales, product quality) is the most convincing evidence of the value of training!

Best Buy, the consumer electronics retailer based in Richfield, Minnesota, plans to grow the business through expansion.[19] Best Buy plans to open about 60 new stores each year. Training is important to make sure each new store provides the same quality of service and has efficient operations of inventory management and ordering. Best Buy uses Grand Opening University (GOU) to ensure consistency in all new stores. GOU involves several different phases of training prior to a new store opening. Supervisors work with a coach for two weeks in an existing store, learning leadership skills and how to open and operate a new store. Five weeks before the grand opening, one sales manager for each new store attends a five-day course held at Best Buy's corporate campus. The managers learn strategies for successfully training their new supervisors and employees. One day of the course is dedicated to managers' learning about the products they will be training their employees to sell. For example, supervisors who will be working in the digital imaging group are taken to a nature conservatory. The trainer for that group shows them how to take pictures using the functions on the digital cameras they will be selling and brings them back to the corporate campus to print out the pictures. This exercise helps the supervisors understand the strengths and limitations of the digital cameras so they can provide that knowledge to their own employees. What type of metrics does Best Buy use to evaluate whether training is contributing to the business? Best Buy uses turnover and survey data. Reducing turnover is important because if well-trained employees stay, Best Buy provides a consistent, high level of customer service. Otherwise, the company is faced with a constant churn of employees, which means spending more money on training for new employees. One estimate is that Best Buy employee turnover has dropped from between 110 percent and 120 percent to between 70 percent and 80 percent. GOU has also had a positive influence on employee satisfaction. Best Buy surveys employees about how much they like their jobs and the company. At new stores, the survey scores improved at the same time that GOU was started. Best Buy estimates that for every .01 increase in survey scores, the store can realize $100,000 in additional profits. Survey scores have increased .30, which translates into additional profit. Grand Opening University appears to be having a significant impact on Best Buy's bottom line!

ORGANIZATIONAL CHARACTERISTICS THAT INFLUENCE TRAINING

The amount and type of training as well as the organization of the training function in a company is influenced by employee and manager roles; by top management support for training; by the company's degree of integration of business units; by its global presence; by its business conditions; by other human resource management practices, including staffing strategies and human resource planning; by the company's extent of unionization; and by the extent of involvement in training and development by managers, employees, and human resource staff.[20]

Roles of Employees and Managers

The roles that employees and managers have in a company influence the focus of training, development, and learning activity. Traditionally, employees' roles were to perform their jobs according to the managers' directions. Employees were not involved in improving the quality of the products or services. However, with the emphasis on the creation of intellectual capital and the movement toward high-performance work systems using teams, employees today are performing many roles that were reserved for management (e.g., hiring; scheduling work; interacting with customers, vendors, and suppliers).[21] If companies are using teams to manufacture goods and provide services, team members need training in interpersonal problem solving and team skills (e.g., how to resolve conflicts, give feedback). If employees are responsible for the quality of products and services, they need to be trained to use data to make decisions, which involves training in statistical process control techniques. As discussed in Chapter 1, team members may also receive training in skills needed for all positions on the team (cross training), not just for the specific job they are doing. To encourage cross training, companies may adopt skill-based pay systems, which base employees' pay rates on the number of skills they are competent in rather than what skills they are using for their current jobs. Skill-based pay systems are discussed in Chapter 10.

Research suggests that managers in traditional work environments are expected to do the following:[22]

- *Manage individual performance.* Motivate employees to change performance, provide performance feedback, and monitor training activities.
- *Develop employees.* Explain work assignments and provide technical expertise.
- *Plan and allocate resources.* Translate strategic plans into work assignments and establish target dates for projects.
- *Coordinate interdependent groups.* Persuade other units to provide products or resources needed by the work group, and understand the goals and plans of other units.
- *Manage group performance.* Define areas of responsibility, meet with other managers to discuss effects of changes in the work unit on their groups, facilitate change, and implement business strategy.
- *Monitor the business environment.* Develop and maintain relationships with clients and customers, and participate in task forces to identify new business opportunities.
- *Represent one's work unit.* Develop relationships with other managers, communicate the needs of the work group to other units, and provide information on work group status to other groups.

Regardless of their level in the company (e.g., senior management), all managers are expected to serve as spokespersons to other work units, managers, and vendors (i.e., represent the work unit). Of course, the amount of time managers devote to some of these roles is affected by their level. Line managers spend more time managing individual performance and developing employees than midlevel managers or executives do. The most important roles for midlevel managers and executives are planning and allocating resources, coordinating interdependent groups, and managing group performance (especially managing change). Executives also spend time monitoring the business environment by analyzing market trends, developing relationships with clients, and overseeing sales and marketing activities.

The roles and duties of managers in companies that use high-performance work systems (such as teams) are shown in Table 2.5. The managers' duty is to create the conditions necessary to ensure team success. These roles include managing alignment, coordinating activities, facilitating the decision-making process, encouraging continuous learning, and creating and maintaining trust.[23]

To manage successfully in a team environment, managers need to be trained in "people skills," including negotiation, sensitivity, coaching, conflict resolution, and communication skills. A lack of people skills has been shown to be related to managers' failure to advance in their careers.[24]

Top Management Support

The CEO, the top manager in the company, plays a key role in determining the importance of training and learning in the company. The CEO is responsible for[25]

- A clear direction for learning (vision).
- Encouragement, resources, and commitment for strategic learning (sponsor).
- Taking an active role in governing learning, including reviewing goals and objectives and providing insight on how to measure training effectiveness (governor).

TABLE 2.5   **The Roles and Duties of Managers in Companies That Use High-Performance Work Practices**

Roles	Key Duties
Managing Alignment	Clarify team goals and company goals. Help employees manage their objectives. Scan organization environment for useful information for the team.
Coordinating Activities	Ensure that team is meeting internal and external customer needs. Ensure that team meets its quantity and quality objectives. Help team resolve problems with other teams. Ensure uniformity in interpretation of policies and procedures.
Facilitating Decision-Making Process	Facilitate team decision making. Help team use effective decision-making processes (deal with conflict, statistical process control).
Encouraging Continuous Learning	Help team identify training needs. Help team become effective at on-the-job training. Create environment that encourages learning.
Creating and Maintaining Trust	Ensure that each team member is responsible for his or her work load and customers. Treat all team members with respect. Listen and respond honestly to team ideas.

- Developing new learning programs for the company (subject-matter expert).
- Teaching programs or providing resources online (faculty).
- Serving as a role model for learning for the entire company and demonstrating willingness to constantly learn (learner).
- Promoting the company's commitment to learning by advocating it in speeches, annual reports, interviews, and other public relations tools (marketing agent).

For example, John Chambers, CEO of Cisco Systems, declared publicly that learning is a strategic priority for the company. He challenged the training organization at Cisco to develop "best in class" e-learning.[26]

Integration of Business Units

The degree to which a company's units or businesses are integrated affects the kind of training that takes place. In a highly integrated business, employees need to understand other units, services, and products in the company. Training likely includes rotating employees between jobs in different businesses so they can gain an understanding of the whole business.

Global Presence

As noted in Chapter 1, the development of global product and service markets is an important challenge for U.S. companies. For companies with global operations, training is used to prepare employees for temporary or long-term overseas assignments. Also, because employees are geographically dispersed outside the United States, companies need to determine whether training will be conducted and coordinated from a central U.S. facility or will be the responsibility of satellite installations located near overseas facilities.

Business Conditions

When unemployment is low and/or businesses are growing at a high rate and need more employees, companies often find it difficult to attract new employees, find employees with necessary skills, and retain current employees.[27] Companies may find themselves in the position of hiring employees who might not be qualified for the job. Also, in these types of business conditions, companies need to retain talented employees. In the knowledge-based economy (including companies in information technology and pharmaceuticals), product development is dependent on employees' specialized skills. Losing a key employee may cause a project to be delayed or hinder a company's taking on new projects. Training plays a key role in preparing employees to be productive as well as motivating and retaining current employees. Studies of what factors influence employee retention suggest that employees rate working with good colleagues, challenging job assignments, and opportunities for career growth and development as top reasons for staying with a company. Across all industries, from high tech to retailing, companies are increasingly relying on training and development to attract new employees and retain current ones. For example, companies such as Merck (a pharmaceutical company) and Hewlett-Packard (computer technology) are successful in terms of financial returns. They are typically found on lists of great places to work (for example, *Fortune* magazine's list of "Best Companies to Work For"). They are quite successful in attracting and retaining employees. Not only do they provide employees with very competitive pay and benefits, but they also are committed to training and development. Retailers such as Macy's and Nordstroms cannot generate sales unless they have enough skilled employees.[28] For example, Macy's West, headquartered in San Francisco, begins its employee retention strategy by starting with executives. Executives are accountable for retention of the employees who report to them. Managers have been trained to run meetings and conduct performance evaluations (skills that influence employees' perceptions of how they are treated, which ultimately affects whether they remain with Macy's). Macy's has also provided training programs and courses for employees.

For companies in an unstable business environment—one characterized by mergers, acquisitions, or disinvestment of businesses—training may be abandoned, left to the discretion of managers, or become more short term (such as offering training courses only to correct skill deficiencies rather than to prepare staff for new assignments). These programs emphasize the development of skills and characteristics needed (e.g., how to deal with change) regardless of the structure the company takes. Training may not even occur as a result of a planned effort. Employees who remain with a company following a merger, acquisition, or disinvestment usually find that their job now has different responsibilities requiring new skills. For employees in companies experiencing growth—that is, an increased demand for their product and services—there may be many new opportunities for lateral job moves and promotions resulting from the expansion of sales, marketing, and manufacturing operations or from the start-up of new business units. These employees are usually excited about participating in development activities because new positions often offer higher salaries and more challenging tasks.

During periods when companies are trying to revitalize and redirect their business, earnings are often flat. As a result, fewer incentives for participation in training—such as promotions and salary increases—may be available. In many cases, companies downsize their work forces as a way of cutting costs. Training activities under these conditions focus on ensuring that employees are available to fill the positions vacated by retirement or turnover.

Training also involves helping employees avoid skill obsolescence. (Strategies to help employees avoid skill obsolescence are discussed in Chapter 12.)

Other Human Resource Management Practices

Human resource management (HRM) practices consist of the management activities related to investments (time, effort, and money) in staffing (determining how many employees are needed, and recruiting and selecting employees), performance management, training, and compensation and benefits. The type of training and the resources devoted to training are influenced by the strategy adopted for two human resource management practices: staffing and human resource planning.

Staffing Strategy

Staffing strategy refers to the company's decisions regarding where to find employees, how to select them, and the mix of employee skills and statuses (temporary, full-time, etc.). For example, one staffing decision a company has to make is how much to rely on the internal labor market (within the company) or external labor market (outside the company) to fill vacancies. Two aspects of a company's staffing strategy influence training: the criteria used to make promotion and assignment decisions (assignment flow) and the places where the company prefers to obtain the human resources to fill open positions (supply flow).[29]

Companies vary on the extent to which they make promotion and job assignment decisions based on individual performance or on group or business-unit performance. They also vary on the extent to which their staffing needs are met by relying on current employees (internal labor market) or on employees from competitors and recent entrants into the labor market, such as college graduates (external labor market). Figure 2.3 displays the two dimensions of staffing strategy. The interaction between assignment flow and supply flow results in four distinct types of companies: fortresses, baseball teams, clubs, and academies. Each company type places a different emphasis on training activities. For example, some companies (such as medical research companies) emphasize innovation and creativity. These types of companies are labeled baseball teams. Because it may be difficult to train skills related to innovation and creativity, they tend to handle staffing needs by luring employees away from competitors or by hiring graduating students with specialized skills. Figure 2.3 can be used to identify development activities that support a specific staffing strategy. For example, if a company wants to reward individual employee contributions and promote from within (the bottom right quadrant of Figure 2.3), it needs to use lateral, upward, and downward moves within and across functions to support the staffing strategy.

Human Resource Planning

Human resource planning includes the identification, analysis, forecasting, and planning of changes needed in the human resources area to help the company meet changing business conditions.[30] Human resource planning allows the company to anticipate the movement of human resources in the company because of turnover, transfers, retirements, or promotions. Human resource plans can help identify where employees with certain types of skills are needed in the company. Training can be used to prepare employees for increased responsibilities in their current job, promotions, lateral moves, transfers, and downward job opportunities that are predicted by the human resource plan.

FIGURE 2.3

Implications of staffing strategy for training

Source: Adapted from J. A. Sonnenfeld and M. A. Peiperi, "Staffing Policy as a Strategic Response: A Typology of Career Systems," *Academy of Management Review* 13 (1988): 588–600.

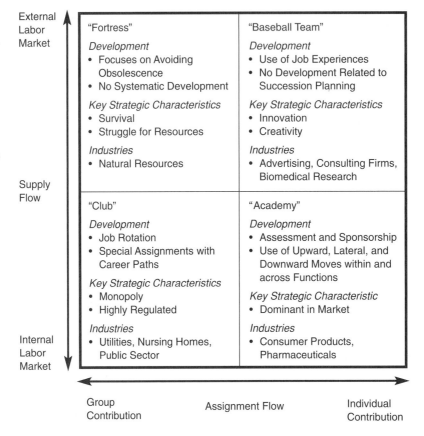

Extent of Unionization

Unions' interest in training has resulted in joint union–management programs designed to help employees prepare for new jobs. When companies begin retraining and productivity-improvement efforts without involving unions, the efforts are likely to fail. The unions may see the programs as just another attempt to make employees work harder without sharing the productivity gains. Joint union–management programs (detailed in Chapter 10) ensure that all parties (unions, management, employees) understand the development goals and are committed to making the changes necessary for the company to make profits and for employees to both keep their jobs and share in any increased profits.

Staff Involvement in Training and Development

How often and how well a company's training program is used is affected by the degree to which managers, employees, and specialized development staff are involved in the process. If managers are not involved in the training process (e.g., determining training needs, being used as trainers), training may be unrelated to business needs. Managers may also not be committed to ensuring that training is effective (e.g., giving trainees feedback on the job). As a result, training's potential impact on helping the company reach its goals may be limited because managers may feel that training is a "necessary evil" forced on them by the training department rather than a means of helping them to accomplish business goals.

If line managers are aware of what development activity can achieve, such as reducing the time it takes to fill open positions, they will be more willing to become involved in it. They will also become more involved in the training process if they are rewarded for participating. At Xerox, performance evaluations are directly related to pay increases.[31] Managers' performance appraisals include their actions to train and develop women and minorities (e.g., moving women and minorities into pivotal jobs that provide them the experience needed to become senior managers).

An emerging trend is that companies expect employees to initiate the training process.[32] Companies with a greater acceptance of a continuous learning philosophy require more development planning. Companies will support training and development activities (such as tuition reimbursement and the offering of courses, seminars, and workshops) but will give employees the responsibility for planning their own development. Training and development planning involve identifying needs, choosing the expected outcome (e.g., behavior change, greater knowledge), identifying the actions that should be taken, deciding how progress toward goal attainment will be measured, and creating a timetable for improvement. To identify strengths and weaknesses and training needs, employees need to analyze what they want to do, what they can do, how others perceive them, and what others expect of them. A need can result from gaps between current capabilities and interests and the type of work or position the employee wants in the future. The needs assessment process is discussed in greater detail in Chapter 3.

TRAINING NEEDS IN DIFFERENT STRATEGIES

Table 2.6 describes four business strategies—concentration, internal growth, external growth, and disinvestment—and highlights the implications of each for training practices.[33] Each strategy differs based on the goal of the business. A **concentration strategy** focuses on increasing market share, reducing costs, or creating and maintaining a market niche for products and services. Southwest Airlines has a concentration strategy. It focuses on providing short-haul, low-fare, high-frequency air transportation. It utilizes one type of aircraft (the Boeing 737), has no reserved seating, and serves no meals. This concentration strategy has enabled Southwest to keep costs low and revenues high. An **internal growth strategy** focuses on new market and product development, innovation, and joint ventures. For example, the merger between two publishing companies, McGraw-Hill and Richard D. Irwin, created one company with strengths in the U.S. and the international college textbook markets. An **external growth strategy** emphasizes acquiring vendors and suppliers or buying businesses that allow the company to expand into new markets. For example, General Electric, a manufacturer of lighting products and jet engines, acquired the National Broadcast Corporation (NBC), a television and communications company. A **disinvestment strategy** emphasizes liquidation and divestiture of businesses. For example, General Mills sold its restaurant businesses.

Preliminary research suggests a link between business strategy and amount and type of training.[34] Table 2.6 shows that training issues vary greatly from one strategy to another. Divesting companies need to train employees in job-search skills and to focus on cross-training remaining employees who may find themselves in jobs with expanding responsibilities. Companies focusing on a market niche (a concentration strategy) need to emphasize

TABLE 2.6 **Implications of Business Strategy for Training**

Strategy	Emphasis	How Achieved	Key Issues	Training Implications
Concentration	• Increased market share • Reduced operating costs • Market niche created or maintained	• Improve product quality • Improve productivity or innovate technical processes • Customize products or services	• Skill currency • Development of existing work force	• Team building • Cross training • Specialized programs • Interpersonal skill training • On-the-job training
Internal Growth	• Market development • Product development • Innovation • Joint ventures	• Market existing products/add distribution channels • Expand global market • Modify existing products • Create new or different products • Expand through joint ownership	• Creation of new jobs and tasks • Innovation	• High-quality communication of product value • Cultural training • Development of organizational culture that values creative thinking and analysis • Technical competence in jobs • Manager training in feedback and communication • Conflict negotiation skills
External Growth (Acquisition)	• Horizontal integration • Vertical integration • Concentric diversification	• Acquire firms operating at same stage in product market chain (new market access) • Acquire business that can supply or buy products • Acquire firms that have nothing in common with acquiring firm	• Integration • Redundancy • Restructuring	• Determination of capabilities of employees in acquired firms • Integration of training systems • Methods and procedures of combined firms • Team building
Disinvestment	• Retrenchment • Turnaround • Divestiture • Liquidation	• Reduce costs • Reduce assets • Generate revenue • Redefine goals • Sell off all assets	• Efficiency	• Motivation, goal setting, time management, stress management, cross training • Leadership training • Interpersonal communications • Outplacement assistance • Job-search skills training

skill currency and development of their existing work force. New companies formed from a merger need to ensure that employees have the skills needed to help the company reach its new strategic goals. For example, Deluxe Corporation is a check printer based in Saint Paul, Minnesota. Factors such as electronic transactions, mergers and acquisitions among financial institutions, and a company reorganization resulted in downsizing and poor employee morale within the company.[35] Fewer than 140 of 400 account managers were still employed with the company. As a result of the downsizing, Deluxe lost many account managers with 5 to 10 years of experience. The account managers who remained had worked at Deluxe less than 3 years or more than 20 years. For these account managers, sales training involved only product training. Deluxe used training to capture and retain not only business but also the hearts and minds of employees.

Account managers developed fundamental sales skills through a combination of online and workshop courses. To build credibility for the training, three high-performing account managers assisted two trainers from Deluxe's training department. Simultaneously with the account managers' training, all employees providing field support for the sales team participated in a one-day training session that emphasized the change from selling product to building relationships with customers. Sales managers and directors participated in a field-coaching program so they could reinforce the account managers' learning. The sales managers now "shadow" the account managers once every business quarter to observe their sales skills and to provide coaching. Another training program focused on strategic time management skills. As a result of the training, customer retention rates have improved to 95 percent, up from 85 percent two years ago.

Companies with an internal growth strategy face the challenge of keeping employees up-to-date on new products and services. For example, Masimo Corporation, located in Orange County, California, develops, licenses, and markets advanced medical signal processing technologies for monitoring patient vital signs.[36] Because employees work with sophisticated technology and because new products are constantly being developed, Masimo is challenged to keep its sales force and distribution partners aware of the latest features, functions, and applications of its monitoring devices. Using an Internet-based corporate university, Masimo has been able to provide programs that enhance revenue by preparing the sales force more quickly to sell new products, and these programs have given the company the ability to bring products to the market faster. Also, the training benefits the clinical staff by increasing brand awareness and product competence among hospital staff and by building a community of users to drive future sales. The Internet-based corporate university is also important because it allows clinical staff who work long hours access to training and because it tracks and documents training as required by government regulations.

Rockwell Collins manufactures cockpit instruments, in-flight entertainment systems, and ground communications tools.[37] Rockwell is trying to reduce operating costs in all areas. The company's new learning strategy involves expanding training courses by 40 percent while saving the company $14 million over three years! How does Rockwell plan to achieve this? The company is moving from training that is primarily classroom based to new instructional delivery methods including Web-based training, computer-based training on CD-ROMs using kiosks and learning labs, and live training delivered by online virtual classrooms. The former reliance on classroom training made it impossible to keep up with the demand for training and the changing training needs. Over half the employees reported that work demands had forced them to cancel their attendance at a training session or to leave a session without completing it. Rockwell created a learning-and-development team to interview and survey employees and determine the costs and savings of using alternative training methods. The team found that the company would save $14 million on labor, travel, and hotel expenses as well as work hours lost to off-site training. Rockwell was able to use the same training budget allocated to classroom training to switch to online and computer-based training. The company purchased a library of information-technology courses, which saved the cost of sending 3,000 employees to classroom courses.

MODELS OF ORGANIZING THE TRAINING DEPARTMENT

This section discusses five models of organizing the training department: faculty model, customer model, matrix model, corporate university model, and virtual model.[38] This review of these structures should help you to understand that the organization of the training department has important consequences for how the training department (and trainers employed in the department) contributes (or fails to contribute) to the business strategy. Keep in mind that—particularly with large, decentralized companies—there may be multiple separate training functions, each organized using a different model. The virtual training organization and the corporate university model are the models that companies are moving to in order to ensure that training is used to help the company achieve its business objectives. These models are also being adopted as companies begin to value intellectual capital and view training as part of a learning system designed to create and share knowledge.

Faculty Model

Training departments organized by the **faculty model** look a lot like the structure of a college. Figure 2.4 shows the faculty model. The training department is headed by a director with a staff of experts who have specialized knowledge of a particular topic or skill area. These experts develop, administer, and update training programs. For example, sales trainers are responsible for sales skills training (cultivating clients, negotiating a sale, closing a sale), and computer experts provide training on topics such as using e-mail and the World Wide Web as well as software design language.

The faculty model has several strengths. First, training staff are clearly experts in the area they train in. Second, the training department's plans are easily determined by staff expertise.

FIGURE 2.4
The faculty model

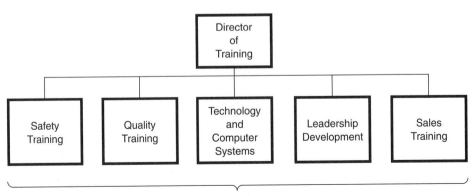

Training Specialty Areas

The content and timing of programs are determined primarily by when they are available and the expertise of the trainers. Organizing by the faculty model also has several disadvantages. Companies that use the faculty model may create a training function that has expertise that does not meet the needs of the organization. Trainers in a faculty model may also be unaware of business problems or unwilling to adapt materials to fit a business need. This can result in demotivated trainees who fail to learn because course content lacks meaning for them—that is, it does not relate to problems or needs of the business. Programs and courses that may be needed may not be offered because trainers are not experts in certain areas. Skill and knowledge emphasized in programs may not match the needs of the company. To overcome these disadvantages of the faculty model, managers need to frequently survey training's customers to ensure that course offerings are meeting their needs. Expert trainers also need to ensure that they adapt course materials so that they are meaningful for participants.

Customer Model

Training departments organized according to the **customer model** are responsible for the training needs of one division or function of the company. For example, trainers might be responsible for programs related to information systems, marketing, or operations. The trainers might also be human resource generalists whose job responsibilities include a broad range of human resource functions such as training, performance management, hiring, and benefits. Figure 2.5 shows the customer model. This model overcomes a major problem of the faculty model. Training programs are developed more in line with the particular needs of a business group rather than on the expertise of the training staff. Selection, training, compensation, and development are all based on a common set of knowledge, skills, abilities, or competencies. That is, training is integrated with other human resource responsibilities. Trainers in this model are expected to be aware of business needs and to update courses and content to reflect them. If needs change such that training is no longer available from a source inside the company, the trainers may use outside experts (e.g., consultants). Materials provided by a training staff organized by this model are likely to be meaningful to trainees.

There are several disadvantages to this model. First, trainers have to spend considerable time learning the business function before they can be useful trainers. Second, a large number of programs covering similar topics may be developed by customers. These programs may also vary greatly in effectiveness. It may be difficult for the training director to oversee

FIGURE 2.5
The customer model

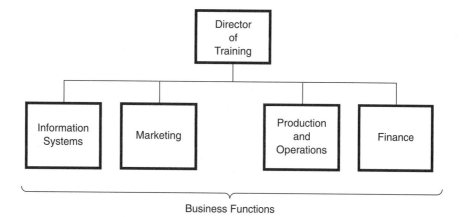

Business Functions

FIGURE 2.6

The matrix model

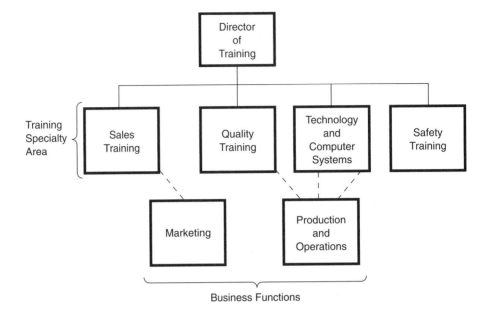

each function to ensure that (1) a common instructional design process is used or (2) the company's quality philosophy is consistently emphasized in each program. For example, quality training may be developed separately for marketing and for operations employees. This type of structure is likely to be unattractive to trainers who consider presentation and teaching to be their primary job function. In the customer model, trainers are likely to be employees from the functional area (e.g., manufacturing engineers) who have great functional expertise but lack training in instructional design and learning theory. As a result, courses may be meaningful but poor from a design perspective (e.g., have inadequate feedback and practice opportunities).

For example, Transamerica Life Companies have identified skills that are needed companywide.[39] These skills include communications, accountability, initiative, and collaboration. They also identified technical knowledge that is only needed in certain business units of the company. These skills and knowledge will be used to make hiring, promotion, and compensation decisions. All employee training and development activity will focus on the skills.

Matrix Model

The **matrix model** involves trainers reporting to both a manager in the training department and a manager in a particular function. Figure 2.6 shows the matrix model. The trainer has the responsibility of being both a training expert and a functional expert. For example, as Figure 2.6 shows, sales trainers report to both the director of training and the marketing manager. One advantage of the matrix model is that it helps ensure that training is linked to needs of the business. Another advantage is that the trainer gains expertise in understanding a specific business function. Because the trainer is also responsible to the training director, it is likely that the trainer will stay professionally current (e.g., up-to-date on new training delivery mechanisms such as the Internet). A major disadvantage of the matrix model is that trainers likely will have more time demands and conflicts because they report to two managers: a functional manager and a training director.

FIGURE 2.7
The corporate university model

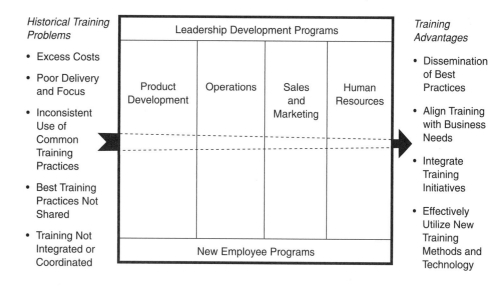

Historical Training Problems

- Excess Costs
- Poor Delivery and Focus
- Inconsistent Use of Common Training Practices
- Best Training Practices Not Shared
- Training Not Integrated or Coordinated

Leadership Development Programs

Product Development	Operations	Sales and Marketing	Human Resources

New Employee Programs

Training Advantages

- Dissemination of Best Practices
- Align Training with Business Needs
- Integrate Training Initiatives
- Effectively Utilize New Training Methods and Technology

Corporate University Model (Corporate Training Universities)

An emerging model for organizing training is the corporate university model in Figure 2.7. The **corporate university model** differs from the other models in that the client group includes not only employees and managers but also stakeholders outside the company including community colleges, universities, high schools, and grade schools. Training functions organized by the university model tend to offer a wider range of programs and courses than functions organized by the other models. Important culture and values also tend to be emphasized more often in the training curriculum of corporate universities than the other models. The university model centralizes training to make sure that "best training practices" that may be used in one unit of the company are disseminated across the company. Also, the corporate university enables the company to control costs by developing consistent training practices and policies.

Both large and small companies have started their own universities to train new employees and to retain and update the skills and knowledge of current employees. Companies are finding that the benefits of corporate universities include improved recruitment, increased revenues, reduced turnover, better employee advancement, and a deeper pool of employee talent.[40] For example, CoreTech Consulting Group in King of Prussia, Pennsylvania, found that compensaton was less of an issue with its employees than growth opportunities and career development. CoreTech started CoreTech University, which offers short training courses to help employees improve their technical and interpersonal skills. While the company spends approximately $4,500 per employee each year on training, it helps certify employees in different areas of information technology (e.g., a Microsoft certified systems engineer), which is tied directly to the company's mission and goals. CoreTech even used the in-house courses offered by the university to create a separate for-profit training company that offers courses to the public. It has generated $325,000 in revenues through courses offered primarily to chief information officers and information technology managers.

At Unitel, a call-center company in Virginia, average monthly turnover has dropped from 12 percent to 6 percent since Unitel University was started a few years ago. The company is staffed primarily by low-wage employees. Giving employees the opportunity to take courses such as computer training and customer service has improved retention and satisfaction. After 90 days at Unitel, new employees can become "freshmen" at the university and can take additional courses. If they "pass," they receive a raise of up to 8 percent of their pay. Every 90 days, employees can take more in-depth courses in telephone sales, customer service, and computer skills. They receive additional raises of 8 percent for successfully completing each level. Although the program is not mandatory, employees realize that training is the quickest path to increased pay and responsibility.

I-Cube, a Massachusetts information technology consulting services company, found that its corporate university improved the available employee talent pool. One program, called I-Attitude, allowed the company to hire employees who lacked experience and gave them the technical skills they needed to serve clients. Rather than competing for scarce talented employees who have both experience and education (and who demand high levels of compensation for their services), the university allowed I-Cube to attract and hire college graduates who were well educated but lacked experience.

The Center for Performance Excellence developed by Booz Allen Hamilton, a management consulting firm, is a good example of the university model.[41] The consultants work in a rapidly changing business environment so they have to be kept current on the knowledge they need. The Center for Performance Excellence provides both virtual learning and face-to-face learning opportunities. Face-to-face learning opportunities include classroom training, seminars, workshops, conferences, partnerships with universities and training providers, counseling, and coaching. The center includes full-time and part-time instructors and university faculty. In 2002 the center conducted 23,000 days of training. The center's Virtual Campus provides access to a training center, university center, external training, leadership center, resource library, and information about new learning opportunities. Not only can employees enroll in more than 600 online courses on a variety of topics (e.g., stress management, technology), but they can also search for courses that are related to their training needs or they can research other development opportunities.

Creating a corporate university from scratch involves several steps.[42] First, senior managers and business managers need to form a governing body that develops a vision for the university. (In other words, what are the university's policies, systems, and procedures? What are the key functional areas for which training courses will be developed?) Second, a vision needs to be developed. The vision statement links to the business strategy. At Ranstad North American, an Atlanta-based company, Ranstad University's mission statement includes mention of continuous learning opportunities and performance management tools aligned to the business strategy.[43] Three managing directors who report directly to the CEO sit on Ramstad's executive advisory boards, which ensures that the university is directly linked to business strategy by way of certification, training, and an annual review process. Third, the company has to decide how to fund the university. The university can be funded by charging fees to business units and/or by monies allocated directly from the corporate budget. Fourth, the degree to which all training will be centralized needs to be determined. Many universities centralize the development of a learning philosophy, core curriculum design, and policies and procedures related to registration, administration, measurement, marketing, and distance learning. Local and regional on-site delivery and specialized business-unit curriculum are developed by business units. Fifth, it is important to identify the needs of university "customers" including employees, managers, suppliers, and external customers. Sixth, products and services need to be developed. The Bank of Montreal uses a service team that includes a client- relationship manager, a subject-matter expert, and a learning manager. The client-relationship manager works with the business units to identify their needs. The subject-matter expert identifies the skill requirements for meeting those needs. The learning manager recommends the best mix of learning, including classroom training as well as training based on, say, the Web or CD-ROM. The seventh step is to choose learning partners including suppliers, consultants, colleges, and companies specializing in education. Eighth, the company needs to develop a strategy for using technology to train more employees, more frequently, and more cost-effectively than instructor-led training. Ninth, learning that occurs as a result of a corporate university should be linked to performance improvement. This involves identifying how performance improvement will be measured (tests, sales data, etc.). For example, Sprint's corporate university, the University of Excellence, has developed the Standard Training Equivalent (STE) unit, an evaluation tool for its customers who are internal business units.[44] The STE unit is equal to one hour of the traditional instructor-led classroom time that would be required to deliver a course to a group of employees at a central location. An STE unit consisting of a one-hour course over the company intranet is worth much more than the same amount of time spent in the classroom. The STE program helps the University of Excellence demonstrate its value to Sprint's business units, who fund the university. Finally, the value of the corporate university needs to be communicated to potential "customers." Questions about the types of programs offered, how learning will occur, and how employees will enroll need to be addressed.

Virtual Model (Virtual Training Organizations)

Many organizations such as Corning and Apple Computer are organizing their training function so that they can respond to client needs quickly and provide high-quality services.[45] **Virtual training organizations** operate according to three principles. First, employees (not the company) have primary responsibility for learning. Second, the most effective learning takes place on the job, not in the classroom. Third, for training to translate into improved job performance, the manager–employee relationship (not employee–trainer relationship) is critical. That is, for employees to use training content on the job, they are responsible for learning course content and understanding how content may be applied to their work. Managers are responsible for (1) holding employees accountable to use training on the job and (2) removing obstacles that may interfere with their doing so.

A virtual training organization (VTO) is characterized by five competencies: strategic direction, product design, structural versatility, product delivery, and accountability for result. Strategic direction includes a clearly described goal and direction to the department as well as a customer focus that includes customizing training to meet customer needs and continuously improving programs. A virtual training organization views not only trainees as customers, but also managers who make decisions to send employees to training and senior-level managers who allocate money for training. Table 2.7 contrasts a virtual training organization with a traditional training department. Compared to a traditional training department, a virtual training organization is customer focused. It takes more responsibility for learning and evaluating training effectiveness, provides customized training solutions based on customer needs, and determines when and how to deliver training based on customer needs. The most noticeable difference between a VTO and a traditional training department is its structure. The traditional training organization tends to operate with a fixed staff of trainers and administrators who perform very specific functions such as

TABLE 2.7 Comparison between a Virtual Training Organization and a Traditional Training Department

A Traditional Training Department	A Virtual Training Organization
Strategic Direction Leaves objectives unstated or vague Assumes that class participants are its only customers Limits offerings to predetermined courses Continues to supply products that are no longer useful Organizes its offerings by courses Tries to mandate training	Broadly disseminates a clearly articulated mission Recognizes that its customer base is segmented Provides customized solutions to its clients' needs Understands product life cycles Organizes its offerings by competencies Competes for internal customers
Product Design Uses rigid and cumbersome design methodologies Views suppliers as warehouses of materials	Uses benchmarking and other innovative design strategies to develop products quickly Involves suppliers strategically
Structural Versatility Employs trainers who serve primarily as facilitators and classroom instructors Operates with a fixed number of staff Relies solely on training staff to determine the department's offerings	Employs professionals who serve as product managers and internal consultants Leverages resources from many areas Involves line managers in determining direction and content
Product Delivery Distributes a list of courses Offers courses on a fixed schedule at fixed locations	Offers a menu of learning options Delivers training at the work site
Accountability for Results Believes that the corporation manages employee development Ends its involvement with participants when courses end Considers the instructor the key player in supporting learning Relies on course critiques as its primary source of feedback Vaguely describes training outcomes	Believes individual employees must take responsibility for their personal growth Provides follow-up on the job to ensure that learning takes place Considers the manager the key player in supporting learning Evaluates the strategic effects of training and its bottom-line results Guarantees that training will improve performance

Source: S. S. McIntosh, "Envisioning Virtual Training Organization," *Training and Development* (May 1995): 47.

instructional design. In traditional training departments developers and instructors often take a "silo" approach, focusing only on their particular responsibilities.[46] This approach can hinder the development of successful training programs. In VTO all persons who are involved in the training process communicate and share resources. Trainers—who are responsible for developing training materials, delivering instruction, and supporting trainees—work together to ensure that learning occurs. For example, access to project managers and subject-matter experts can be provided by developers to instructors who usually do not have contact with these groups. The number of trainers in VTOs varies according to the demand for products and services. The trainers not only have specialized competencies (e.g., instructional design) but can also serve as internal consultants and provide a wide range of services (e.g., needs assessment, content improvement, customization of programs, results measurement).

Dell Computer is an example of a company that has a virtual training organization.[47] Dell's training organization includes three parts: corporate training, regional (HR) training, and regional (non-HR) training run by the senior management team. The corporate group includes

- Corporate and Regional Operations, which is concerned with global education, planning, financial management and reporting, and process and infrastructures.
- Dell Learning Services, which provides instructional design and consulting.
- Dell Learning Technology Services, which disseminates new learning technologies.
- Education Services, a centralized support function that handles administrative services, vendor management, registration, and facilities.
- The New Product Training Group, which provides training materials for sales and technology support for all of the company's products.
- The Program Management Office, which develops strategies and global curricula to support strategic initiatives.

The corporate group reports to human resources as do business-based training groups that may be functional (finance), geographic (Brazil), or in a business segment (small business). Decisions about where to locate the training groups are based on business needs. Dell believes in the principle of the learner being in charge of learning. As a result, more than half of all training occurs outside of a classroom (primarily on the Internet). Dell's technology-based training allows learners to control not only what they learn but also when learning starts and stops or is interrupted. Dell requires employees to create development plans that are supported by their managers. Self-assessments help employees determine the gaps between their current abilities and the training curriculum so they can customize their training and development plans. Dell links training statistics to business goals. Studies on sales, new hires, new products, and software training were conducted, and the company found that training programs reduced the time it took new hires to be productive, increased sales revenue and sales margins, reduced employee turnover and classroom hours, and generated new business. Dell also tracks all training activity (including classes taken, enrollments, and total hours by region and business), type of training (e.g., management executive, sales), online training, and employees' evaluations of training programs.

Because many companies are recognizing training's critical role in meeting competitive challenges, there is an increasing trend for the training function, regardless of company size, to be organized as a virtual training organization and also for companies to develop a separate corporate university. For example, Gates Bar-B-Q, a restaurant chain in Kansas City, Missouri, has created Rib Tech, the College of Barbecue Knowledge.[48] Although the company has only 300 employees, the owner has invested in training because it has helped him solve a major problem facing businesses with multiple locations: maintaining consistent quality. The college offers seven basic courses in such topics as sandwich cutting. All employees must attend classes to maintain their current position, and training attendance is considered in determining promotions. Advanced classes include how to cook ribs (covering such topics as the right combination of hickory and oak in a barbecue pit) and the best way to season meat. The College of Barbecue Knowledge is responsible for the consistency in food, service, and staff appearance found across the chain of restaurants. Because of this consistency, the chain is a Kansas City landmark, lines often form outside the restaurant, it ships barbecue sauce nationwide, and it operates its own catering service.

MARKETING THE TRAINING FUNCTION

Despite the increased recognition of the importance of training and learning on achieving business goals, many managers and employees may not recognize the value of training. Internal marketing involves making employees and managers excited about training and learning. Internal marketing is especially important for trainers who act as internal consultants to business units. For internal consultants to survive, they must generate fees for their services. Some if not all of their operating expenses comes from fees paid for their services. Here are some successful internal marketing tactics:[49]

- Involve the target audience in developing the training or learning effort.
- Demonstrate how a training and development program can be used to solve specific business needs.
- Showcase an example of how training has been used within the company to solve specific business needs.
- Identify a "champion" (e.g., top-level manager) who actively supports training.
- Listen and act on feedback received from clients, managers, and employees.
- Advertise on e-mail, on company websites, in employee break areas.
- Designate someone in the training function as an account representative who interacts between the training designer or team and the business unit that is the customer.

Summary

For training to help a company gain a competitive advantage, it must help the company reach business goals and objectives. This chapter emphasized how changes in work roles, organizational factors, and the role of training influence the amount and type of training as well as the organization of the training functions. The process of strategic training and development was discussed. The chapter explained how different strategies (concentration, internal growth, external growth, and disinvestment) influence the goals of the business and create different training needs. The chapter concluded with a discussion of different models of the training function and how to market training. As training is expected to make a greater contribution to achievement of business strategies and goals, the virtual training organization and corporate university models will become more prevalent.

Key Terms

business strategy, *39*
goals, *39*
learning, *41*
knowledge, *41*
explicit knowledge, *41*
tacit knowledge, *41*
intellectual capital, *42*
mission, *44*
vision, *44*
values, *44*

SWOT analysis, *44*
strategic training and
development initiatives, *45*
balanced scorecard, *50*
human resource
management (HRM)
practices, *55*
staffing strategy, *55*
human resource planning, *55*
concentration strategy, *57*

internal growth strategy, *57*
external growth strategy, *57*
disinvestment strategy, *57*
faculty model, *60*
customer model, *61*
matrix model, *62*
corporate university
model, *63*
virtual training
organizations, *65*

Discussion Questions

1. How would you expect the training activities of a company that is dominant in its product market to differ from those of a company that emphasizes research and development?

2. What do you think is the most important organizational characteristic that influences training? Why?

3. Which model or combination of models is best for organizing the training function? Why?

4. Chesebrough-Pond's, a producer of health and beauty aids, decided several years ago to expand its product lines by repackaging Vaseline Petroleum Jelly in pocket-size squeeze tubes called Vaseline Lip Therapy. The company decided to place a strategic emphasis on developing markets for this product. The company knew from market research studies that its petroleum jelly customers were already using the product in its original container to prevent chapped lips. Company managers reasoned that their market could be expanded significantly if the product were repackaged to fit conveniently in consumers' pockets and purses. Identify the business strategy. What training needs result from this strategy? What are the training implications of this decision for (1) manufacturing and (2) the sales force?

5. Which strategic training and development initiatives do you think all companies should support in today's economic climate? Why?

6. Are any of the strategic training and development initiatives more important for small business? Explain.

7. Evaluate Dell Computer's training organization using the five competencies of a virtual training organization. Would you consider Dell's training organization to be a virtual training organization?

8. Compare and contrast the corporate university model with the faculty model. How are they similar? How do they differ?

9. What is intellectual capital? How is intellectual capital influencing the changing role of training from skill and knowledge acquisition to creating and sharing knowledge?

10. How could SWOT analysis be used to align training activities with business strategies and goals?

11. What are the training implications of the increased use of teams to manufacture products or provide services?

12. How would you design a corporate university? Explain each step you would take.

Application Assignments

1. Go to *www.pfizer.com,* the website for Pfizer, a company that researches, develops, manufactures, and markets leading prescription medicines for humans and animals. Identify Pfizer's mission statement, vision, and values. Go to the Careers section of the website. Click on Working for Pfizer. Review the links on this page. Describe how leader behavior and education support Pfizer's vision and values.

2. Find a company's annual report by using the World Wide Web or visiting a library. Using the annual report, do the following:

   a. Identify the company's mission, values, and goals.

b. Find any information provided in the report regarding the company's training practices and how they relate to the goals and strategies. Be prepared to give a brief presentation to the class on your research.

3. Go to *www.qualcomm.com,* the website for QUALCOMM. What is the company's mission? How does the company use training and development to help reach its business goals? Be specific.

4. *www.milliken.com* is the website for Milliken and Company, which produces high-quality textiles and chemical products. Click on Industry Leadership and then Education. What is the mission of Milliken University? What learning resources are used? What courses and curricula are offered? How does the university relate to the company's business strategy, mission, and goals?

5. *www.corpu.com* is the website for Corporate University Exchange, a corporate education and research and consulting firm that is expert on corporate universities. What kind of information about corporate universities is available on this site? Why is it useful?

Endnotes

1. J. Meister, "The CEO-Driven Learning Culture," *Training and Development* (June 2000): 52–70.

2. S. Greengard, "Keyboard Courses at Work or Home," *Workforce* (March 2000): 88–92; QUALCOMM website *www.qualcomm.com.*

3. R. S. Schuler and S. F. Jackson, "Linking Competitive Strategies with Human Resource Management Practices," *Academy of Management Executive* 1 (1987): 207–19.

4. T. T. Baldwin, C. Danielson, and W. Wiggenhorn, "The Evolution of Learning Strategies in Organizations: From Employee Development to Business Redefinition," *Academy of Management Executive* 11 (1997): 47–58; J. J. Martocchio and T. T. Baldwin, "The Evolution of Strategic Organizational Training," in *Research in Personnel and Human Resource Management* 15, ed. G. R. Ferris (Greenwich, CT: JAI Press, 1997): 1–46; R. Brinkerhoff and A. Apking, *High Impact Learning* (Cambridge, MA: Perseus, 2001).

5. D. Miller, "A Preliminary Typology of Organizational Learning: Synthesizing the Literature," *Strategic Management Journal* 22 (1996): 484–505; S. Jackson, M. Hitt, and A. DeNisi (eds.), *Managing Knowledge for Sustained Competitive Advantage* (San Francisco:Jossey-Bass, 2003).

6. D. Delong and L. Fahey, "Diagnosing Cultural Barriers to Knowledge Management," *Academy of Management Executive* 14 (2000): 113–127; A. Rossett, "Knowledge Management Meets Analysis," *Training and Development* (May 1999): 71–78.

7. I. Nonaka and H. Takeuchi, *The Knowledge Creating Company* (New York: Oxford University Press, 1995).

8. D. Tobin, *The Knowledge-Enabled Organization* (New York: AMACOM, 1998).

9. T. Aeppel, "On Factory Floors, Top Workers Hide Secrets to Success," *Wall Street Journal* (July 1, 2002): A1, A10.

10. J. B. Quinn, P. Andersen, and S. Finkelstein, "Leveraging Intellect," *Academy of Management Executive* 10 (1996): 7–39.

11. K. Ellis, "Share Best Practices Globally," *Training* (July 2001): 32–38.

12. K. Dobbs, "Tires Plus Takes the Training High Road," *Training* (April 2000):57–63.

13. S. Tannenbaum, "A Strategic View of Organizational Training and Learning," ed. Kraiger, K. *Creating, Implementing, and Managing Effective Training and Development* (San Francisco: Jossey-Bass, 2002): 10–52.

14. K. Ellis, "Top Training Strategies," *Training* (July/August 2003): 30–36.

15. F. Jossi, "Lesson Plans," *HR Magazine* (February 2003): 72–76.

16. *www.sun.com,* 2002 Annual Report, Letter from the Chairman.

17. P. A. Smith, "Reinventing SunU," *Training and Development* (July 1994): 23–27.

18. R. Kaplan and D. Norton, "The Balanced Scorecard—Measures That Drive Performance," *Harvard Business Review* (January–February 1992): 71–79. R. Kaplan and D. Norton, "Putting the Balanced Scorecard to Work," *Harvard Business Review* (September–October 1993): 134–147.

19. "Grand Opening University," *Training* (July/August 2003):16.

20. R. J. Campbell, "HR Development Strategies," in *Developing Human Resources,* ed. K. N. Wexley (Washington, DC: BNA Books, 1991): 5-1–5-34; J. K. Berry, "Linking Management Development to Business Strategy," *Training and Development Journal* (August 1990): 20–22.

21. D. F. Van Eynde, "High Impact Team Building Made Easy," *HR Horizons* (Spring 1992): 37–41; J. R. Hackman, ed., *Groups That Work and Those That Don't: Creating Conditions for Effective Teamwork* (San Francisco: Jossey-Bass, 1990); D.McCann and C. Margerison, "Managing High-Performance Teams," *Training and Development Journal* (November 1989): 53–60.

22. A. I. Kraut, P. R. Pedigo, D. D. McKenna, and M. D. Dunnette, "The Role of the Manager: What's Really Important in Different Managerial Jobs," *Academy of Management Executive* 4 (1988): 36–48; F. Luthans, "Successful versus Effective Real Managers," *Academy of Management Executive* 2 (1988): 127–132; H. Mintzberg, *The Nature of Managerial Work* (New York: Harper and Row, 1973); S. W. Floyd and B. Wooldridge, "Dinosaurs or Dynamos? Recognizing Middle Management's Strategic Role," *Academy of Management Executive* 8 (1994): 47–57.

23. B. Gerber, "From Manager into Coach," *Training* (February 1992): 25–31; C. Carr, "Managing Self-Managed Workers," *Training and Development Journal* (September 1991): 37–42.

24. P. Kizilos, "Fixing Fatal Flaws," *Training* (September 1991): 66–70; F. S. Hall, "Dysfunctional Managers: The Next Human Resource Challenge," *Organizational Dynamics* (August 1991): 48–57.

25. J. Meister, "The CEO-Driven Learning Culture."

26. P. Galagan, "Mission E-Possible: The Cisco E-Learning Story," *Training and Development* (February 2001): 46–55.

27. K. Dobbs, "Winning the Retention Game," *Training* (September 1999): 50–56.

28. N. Breuer, "Shelf Life," *Workforce* (August 2000): 28–32.

29. J. A. Sonnenfeld and M. A. Peiperl, "Staffing Policy as a Strategic Response: A Typology of Career Systems," *Academy of Management Review* 13 (1988): 588–600.

30. V. R. Ceriello and C. Freeman, *Human Resource Management Systems: Strategies, Tactics, and Techniques* (Lexington, MA: Lexington Books, 1991).

31. V. Sessa, "Managing Diversity at the Xerox Corporation: Balanced Workforce Goals and Caucus Groups," in *Diversity in the Workplace: Human Resource Initiatives,* ed. S. E. Jackson and Associates (New York: Guilford Press, 1992): 37–64.

32. D. T. Jaffe and C. D. Scott, "Career Development for Empowerment in a Changing Work World," in *New Directions in Career Planning and the Workplace,* ed. J. M. Kummerow (Palo Alto, CA: Consulting Psychologist Press, 1991): 33–60; L. Summers, "A Logical Approach to Development Planning," *Training and Development* 48 (1994): 22–31; D. B. Peterson and M. D. Hicks, *Development First* (Minneapolis, MN: Personnel Decisions, 1995).

33. A. P. Carnevale, L. J. Gainer, and J. Villet, *Training in America* (San Francisco: Jossey-Bass, 1990); L. J. Gainer, "Making the Competitive Connection: Strategic Management and Training," *Training and Development* (September 1989): s1–s30.

34. S. Raghuram and R. D. Arvey, "Business Strategy Links with Staffing and Training Practices," *Human Resource Planning* 17 (1994): 55–73.

35. K. Ellis, "Smarter, Faster, Better," *Training* (April 2003): 27–31.

36. B. Manville, "Organizing Enterprise-Wide E-Learning and Human Capital Management," *Chief Learning Officer* (May 2003): 50–55.

37. S. Fister, "Reinventing Training at Rockwell Collins," *Training* (April 2000): 65–70.

38. M. London, *Managing the Training Enterprise* (San Francisco: Jossey-Bass, 1994); D. Laird, *Approaches to Training and Development,* 2d ed. (Boston: Addison-Wesley, 1985).

39. S. Caudron, "Integrate HR and Training," *Workforce* (May 1998): 89–91.

40. D. Fenn, "Corporate Universities for Small Companies," *Inc* (February 1999): 95–96.

41. G. Johnson, "Nine Tactics to Take Your Corporate University from Good to Great," *Training* (July/August 2003): 38–42.

42. J. Meister, "Ten Steps to Creating a Corporate University," *Training and Development* (November 1998): 38–43.

43. Johnson, "Nine Tactics."

44. Ibid.

45. S. S. McIntosh, "Envisioning Virtual Training Organization," *Training and Development* (May 1995): 46–49.

46. B. Mosher, "How 'Siloed' Is Your Training Organization?" *Chief Learning Officer* (July 2003): 13.

47. J. Meister, "The CEO-Driven Learning Culture."

48. K. S. Breaux, "In Ribs 101, Star Pupils Win Promotions," *Wall Street Journal* (September 10, 1996): B1–B2.

49. W. Webb, "Who Moved My Training?" *Training* (January 2003): 22–26.

Chapter **Three**

Needs Assessment

Objectives

After reading this chapter, you should be able to

1. Discuss the role of organization analysis, person analysis, and task analysis in needs assessment.
2. Identify different methods used in needs assessment and identify the advantages and disadvantages of each method.
3. Discuss the concerns of upper-level and midlevel managers and trainers in needs assessment.
4. Explain how person characteristics, input, output, consequences, and feedback influence performance and learning.
5. Create conditions to ensure that employees are receptive to training.
6. Discuss the steps involved in conducting a task analysis.
7. Analyze task analysis data to determine the tasks in which people need to be trained.
8. Explain competency models and the process used to develop them.

Determining Training Needs at Union Pacific Railroad

Union Pacific Railroad is the largest railroad in North America, operating in the western two-thirds of the United States. The railroad serves 23 states, linking every major West Coast and Gulf Coast port, and provides service to the east through its four major gateways in Chicago, St. Louis, Memphis, and New Orleans. Additionally, Union Pacific operates key north/south corridors and connects with the Canadian and Mexican rail systems, and it is the only railroad to serve all six gateways to Mexico. The railroad transports a large number of products including chemicals, coal, food and food products, forest products, grain and grain products, metals and minerals, and automobiles and parts. For 2003, Union Pacific ranked first among railroads in *Fortune* magazine's published list of "America's Most Admired Companies."

But Union Pacific Railroad was not always one of America's most admired companies. The timeliness and accuracy of shipments to customers was less than 70 percent. Union Pacific installed computers and satellites on the railroad engines, giving conductors better ability to communicate and locate railcars that needed to be delivered. A consultant was hired to provide training for the new system. To better understand the training that conductors needed in order to use the computers and satellites to increase the accuracy of deliveries, the consultant conducted a needs analysis. During meetings with conductors, the consultant found out that the conductors disliked management and did not understand the business aspects of a successful railroad. The consultant informed Union Pacific that given the conductors' frustration with management and lack of business knowledge, training would be a waste of time. Although the consultant could train the conductors to use the computers and satellites, the consultant believed that the conductors would be unwilling to learn and would be unmotivated to use the system effectively. The top management of Union Pacific agreed with the consultant's recommendations and asked the consultant to conduct a more in-depth analysis of the reasons for the conductors' feelings. What the consultant found was a lack of trust and poor communication between the conductors and management. To address these issues, the consultant produced a country music video that was distributed to all of Union Pacific's employees. One of the singers in the video was dressed as a conductor and sang about the conductors' frustrations. Another singer was dressed as a manager and sang from the manager's point of view. The music video helped improve employee morale and eliminate distrust between management and the conductors. The music video made it possible for Union Pacific to develop training courses that improved the company's delivery accuracy (which is now about 90 percent).

The needs assessment helped identify a larger organizational issue that needed to be addressed before skills training could be successful. Both the conductors and management had to understand each other's roles and how those roles affected the company's ability to deliver to customers.

Source: D. Goldwasser, "First Things First." *Training* (January 2001): 88.

INTRODUCTION

As discussed in Chapter 1, effective training practices involve the use of a training design process. The design process begins with a needs assessment. Subsequent steps in the process include ensuring that employees have the motivation and basic skills necessary to learn, creating a positive learning environment, making sure that trainees use learned skills on the job, choosing the training method, and evaluating whether training achieved the desired outcomes. As the Union Pacific Railroad example highlights, before you choose a training method, it is important to determine what type of training is necessary and whether trainees are willing to learn. **Needs assessment** refers to the process used to determine whether training is necessary.

Needs assessment typically involves organizational analysis, person analysis, and task analysis.[1] An organizational analysis considers the context in which training will occur. That is, **organizational analysis** involves determining the appropriateness of training, given the company's business strategy, its resources available for training, and support by managers and peers for training activities. You are already familiar with one aspect of organizational analysis. Chapter 2 discussed the role of the company's business strategy in determining the frequency and type of training.

Person analysis helps to identify who needs training. **Person analysis** involves (1) determining whether performance deficiencies result from a lack of knowledge, skill, or ability (a training issue) or from a motivational or work-design problem, (2) identifying who needs training, and (3) determining employees' readiness for training. **Task analysis** identifies the important tasks and knowledge, skill, and behaviors that need to be emphasized in training for employees to complete their tasks.

WHY IS NEEDS ASSESSMENT NECESSARY?

Needs assessment is the first step in the instructional design process, and if it is not properly conducted any one or more of the following situations could occur:

- Training may be incorrectly used as a solution to a performance problem (when the solution should deal with employee motivation, job design, or a better communication of performance expectations).
- Training programs may have the wrong content, objectives, or methods.
- Trainees may be sent to training programs for which they do not have the basic skills, prerequisite skills, or confidence needed to learn.
- Training will not deliver the expected learning, behavior change, or financial results that the company expects.
- Money will be spent on training programs that are unnecessary because they are unrelated to the company's business strategy.

Figure 3.1 shows the three types of analysis involved in needs assessment and the causes and outcomes resulting from needs assessment. There are many different "pressure points" that suggest that training is necessary. These pressure points include performance problems, new technology, internal or external customer requests for training, job redesign, new legislation, changes in customer preferences, new products, or employees' lack of basic skills. Note that these pressure points do not guarantee that training is the correct solution. As was shown in the chapter opening vignette, a needs assessment conducted at Union Pacific Railroad found that there were organizational issues (lack of understanding of business operations, distrust between the conductors and management) that needed to be dealt with before training occurred. Otherwise, conductors' unwillingness and lack of motivation to use training would have reduced its contribution to helping Union Pacific increase delivery accuracy. Also consider, for example, a delivery truck driver whose job is to deliver anesthetic gases to medical facilities. The driver mistakenly hooks up the supply line of a mild anesthetic to the supply line of a hospital's oxygen system, contaminating the hospital's oxygen supply. Why did the driver make this mistake, which is clearly a performance problem? The driver may have made this mistake because of a lack of knowledge about the appropriate line hookup for the anesthetic, because of anger over a requested salary increase that the

FIGURE 3.1   Causes and outcomes of needs assessment

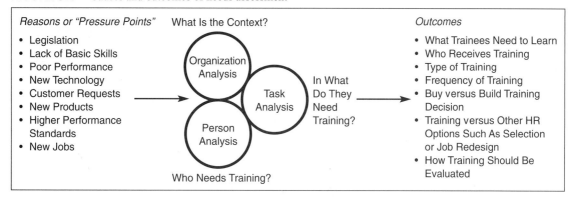

driver's manager recently denied, or because of mislabeled valves for connecting the gas supply. Only the lack of knowledge can be addressed by training. The other pressure points require addressing issues related to the consequence of good performance (pay system) or the design of the work environment.

What outcomes result from a needs assessment? Needs assessment provides important input into most of the remaining steps in the training design. As shown in Figure 3.1, the needs assessment process results in information related to who needs training and what trainees need to learn, including the tasks in which they need to be trained plus knowledge, skill, behavior, or other job requirements. Needs assessment helps to determine whether the company will purchase training from a vendor or consultant or else develop training using internal resources. Determining exactly what trainees need to learn is critical for the next step in the instructional design process: identifying learning outcomes and objectives. Chapter 4 explores identifying learning outcomes and learning objectives and creating a training environment so that learning occurs. Needs assessment also provides information regarding the outcomes that should be collected to evaluate training effectiveness. Training evaluation is discussed in Chapter 6.

WHO SHOULD PARTICIPATE IN NEEDS ASSESSMENT?

Since the goal of needs assessment is to determine whether a training need exists, who it exists for, and what tasks need to be trained, it is important to include managers, trainers, and employees in the needs assessment process. Traditionally, only trainers were concerned with the needs assessment process. But, as Chapter 2 showed, as training increasingly becomes used to help the company achieve its strategic goals, both upper- and top-level managers are involved in the needs assessment process.

Table 3.1 shows the questions that upper-level managers, mid-level managers, and trainers are interested in answering for organization analysis, person analysis, and task analysis. Upper-level managers include directors, chief executive officers (CEOs), and vice presidents. Upper-level managers view the needs assessment process from the broader company perspective. They do not focus on specific jobs. Upper-level managers are involved in the needs assessment process to identify the role of training in relation to other human resource practices in the company (e.g., selection, compensation). That is, upper-level managers help to determine if training is related to the company's business strategy—and, if so, what type of training. Upper-level managers are also involved in identifying what business functions or units need training (person analysis) and in determining if the company has the knowledge, skills, and abilities in the work force that are necessary to meet its strategy and be competitive in the marketplace. Mid-level managers are more concerned with how training may affect the attainment of financial goals for the units they supervise. As a result, for midlevel managers organizational analysis focuses on identifying (1) how much of their budgets they want to devote to training, (2) the types of employees who should receive training (e.g., engineers, or core employees who are directly involved in producing goods or providing services), and (3) for what jobs training can make a difference in terms of improving products or customer service.

As discussed in Chapter 2, trainers (including training managers and instructional designers) need to consider if training is aligned with the business strategy. However, trainers are primarily interested in needs assessment to provide them with information that they need to

TABLE 3.1   Key Concerns of Upper-Level and Mid-Level Managers and Trainers in Needs Assessment

	Upper-Level Managers	*Mid-Level Managers*	*Trainers*
Organizational Analysis	Is training important to achieve our business objectives? How does training support our business strategy?	Do I want to spend money on training? How much?	Do I have the budget to buy training services? Will managers support training?
Person Analysis	What functions or business units need training?	Who should be trained? Managers? Professionals? Core employees?	How will I identify which employees need training?
Task Analysis	Does the company have the people with the knowledge, skills, and ability needed to compete in the marketplace?	For what jobs can training make the biggest difference in product quality or customer service?	What tasks should be trained? What knowledge, skills, ability, or other characteristics are necessary?

administer, develop, and support training programs. This includes determining if training should be purchased or developed in-house, identifying the tasks that need to be trained, and determining top-level and mid-level managers' interest and support for training.

Upper-level managers are usually involved to determine if training meets the company's strategy and then to provide appropriate financial resources. Upper-level managers are not usually involved in identifying which employees need training; the tasks for which training is needed; and the knowledge, skills, abilities, and other characteristics needed to complete those tasks. This is the role of subject-matter experts (SMEs). **Subject-matter experts (SMEs)** are employees, academics, managers, technical experts, trainers, and even customers or suppliers who are knowledgeable in regard to (1) training issues including tasks to be performed; (2) knowledge, skills, and abilities required for successful task performance; (3) necessary equipment; and (4) conditions under which the tasks have to be performed. A key issue with SMEs is making sure they are knowledgeable about the content that training must cover as well as realistic enough to be able to prioritize what content is critical to cover in the time allotted for the subject in the training curriculum. SMEs must also have information that is relevant to the company's business and have an understanding of the company language, tools, and products. There is no rule regarding how many types of employees should be represented in the group conducting the needs assessment. Still, it is important to get a sample of job incumbents involved in the process because they tend to be most knowledgeable about the job and can be a great hindrance to the training process if they do not feel they have had input into the needs assessment. **Job incumbents** are employees who are currently performing the job.

For example, Netg, an Illinois company that develops courseware for training information technology skills, uses academics or trainers who are familiar with course content.[2] To develop the courseware, Netg's development team includes a project manager; one or more SMEs; a curriculum planner who determines what the course will cover; an instructional designer who makes sure the course development covers all aspects of the instructional system design model; and writers, programmers, and graphic artists to build the simulations included in the course. The SME leads a group training session to determine what the subject matter is for the course, the different elements the course needs to cover, and the goals for the course. The instructional designer meets with the SMEs to review the learning objectives. To keep the SMEs on track, Netg asks them to consider not only the value of the information that is being communicated to the trainee but also what trainees need to know at the end of the course.

METHODS USED IN NEEDS ASSESSMENT

Several methods are used to conduct needs assessment, including observing employees performing the job, reading technical manuals and other documentation, interviewing SMEs, conducting focus groups with SMEs, and asking SMEs to complete questionnaires designed to identify tasks and knowledge, skills, abilities, and other characteristics required for a job. Table 3.2 presents advantages and disadvantages of each method. Texas Instruments was trying to determine how to train engineering experts to become trainers for new engineers.[3] All of the engineers had technical expertise. The problem was that their level of instructional expertise varied. Some had no experience teaching, whereas others taught courses at local colleges. When new engineers became inexperienced instructors, both the trainees and the instructors were frustrated. In assessing the engineers' training needs, training and development specialists used all five methods shown in Table 3.2. They collected information that was useful for organization and task analysis. Training course listings and mission statements were used to identify the engineering department mission, and current and previous course offerings were used to develop engineers. Competency studies and project checklists were used to identify relevant tasks. Classroom observation of new and experienced instructors was used to identify strengths and weaknesses of instructors' presentations (person analysis). Both instructors and noninstructors were interviewed to validate the information gathered though the written documentation and surveys. Boeing uses a process borrowed from the field of artificial intelligence. Experts are observed and interviewed to identify their thinking processes for solving problems, dealing with uncertainty, and minimizing risks. The expert practices that are uncovered are then included in the training curriculum.[4]

For newly created jobs, trainers often do not have job incumbents to rely on for this information. Rather, technical diagrams, simulations, and equipment designers can provide information regarding the training requirements, tasks, and conditions under which the job is performed.

Because no one method is superior to the others, multiple methods are usually used. The methods vary in the type of information as well as the level of detail of the information. Questionnaires have the advantage of being able to collect information from a large number of persons. Also, questionnaires allow many employees to participate in the needs assessment process. However, when using questionnaires it is difficult to collect detailed information regarding training needs. Face-to-face and telephone interviews are time consuming. However, more detailed information regarding training needs can be collected. **Focus groups** are a type of SME interview that involves a face-to-face meeting with groups of SMEs in which the questions that are asked relate to specific training needs. It is important to verify the results of interviews and observations because what employees and managers say they do and what they really do may differ. For example, the author was involved

TABLE 3.2   **Advantages and Disadvantages of Needs Assessment Techniques**

Technique	Advantages	Disadvantages
Observation	• Generates data relevant to work environment • Minimizes interruption of work	• Needs skilled observer • Employees' behavior may be affected by being observed
Questionnaires	• Inexpensive • Can collect data from a large number of persons • Data easily summarized	• Requires time • Possible low return rates, inappropriate responses • Lacks detail • Only provides information directly related to questions asked
Interviews	• Good at uncovering details of training needs as well as causes and solutions of problems • Can explore unanticipated issues that come up • Questions can be modified	• Time consuming • Difficult to analyze • Needs skilled interviewer • Can be threatening to SMEs • Difficult to schedule • SMEs only provide information they think you want to hear
Focus groups	• Useful with complex or controversial issues that one person may be unable or unwilling to explore • Questions can be modified to explore unanticipated issues	• Time-consuming to organize • Group members only provide information they think you want to hear • Group members may be reluctant to participate if status or position differences exist among members
Documentation (Technical Manuals, Records)	• Good source of information on procedure • Objective • Good source of task information for new jobs and jobs in the process of being created	• You may be unable to understand technical language • Materials may be obsolete

Source: Based on S. V. Steadham, "Learning to Select a Needs Assessment Strategy," *Training and Development Journal* (January 1980): 56–61; R. J. Mirabile, "Everything You Wanted to Know about Competency Modeling," *Training and Development* (August 1997): 74; K. Gupta, *A Practical Guide to Needs Assessment* (San Francisco: Jossey-Bass, 1999); Needs Assessment Decision Aid from http://mine1.marc.gatech.edu/mm_Tools/NADA.html.

in a needs assessment project for the educational services division of a financial services company. The company wanted to determine the training needs of 3,000 employees including managers, nonmanagers, and regional trainers in the needs assessment process. The company had five regional sites geographically dispersed across the United States (e.g., Midwest region, West region).

One of the potential training needs identified by the corporate training staff was that employees were unable to use new technologies such as the Internet to access training programs. Questionnaires administered to all 3,000 employees to help determine their training needs included questions related to skills in using new technology. Because there were too many skills and tasks related to the use of technology to include all of them on the questionnaire (e.g., how to use the personal computer operating system, Web browsers, CD-ROM, spreadsheets), several general questions were included—for instance, "To what extent do you believe you need training to use new technologies that the company is implementing at your workplace?" Phone interviews were conducted with a small sample of the employees to gather more detailed information regarding specific skill needs.

With the increasing emphasis on Total Quality Management, many companies are often also using information about other companies' training practices (a process known as **benchmarking**) to help determine the appropriate type, level, and frequency of training.[5] For example, Chevron, Federal Express, GTE, Xerox, and several other companies are members of the American Society for Training and Development (ASTD) benchmarking forum. A common survey instrument is completed by each company. The survey includes questions on training costs, staff size, administration, design, program development, and delivery. The information is summarized and shared with the participating companies.

THE NEEDS ASSESSMENT PROCESS

This section examines the three elements of needs assessment: organizational analysis, person analysis, and task analysis. Figure 3.2 illustrates the needs assessment process. In practice, organizational analysis, person analysis, and task analysis are not conducted in any order. Whether time and money is devoted to training is contingent on the results of organizational, person, and task analyses. While any one analysis can indicate the need for training,

FIGURE 3.2
The needs
assessment
process

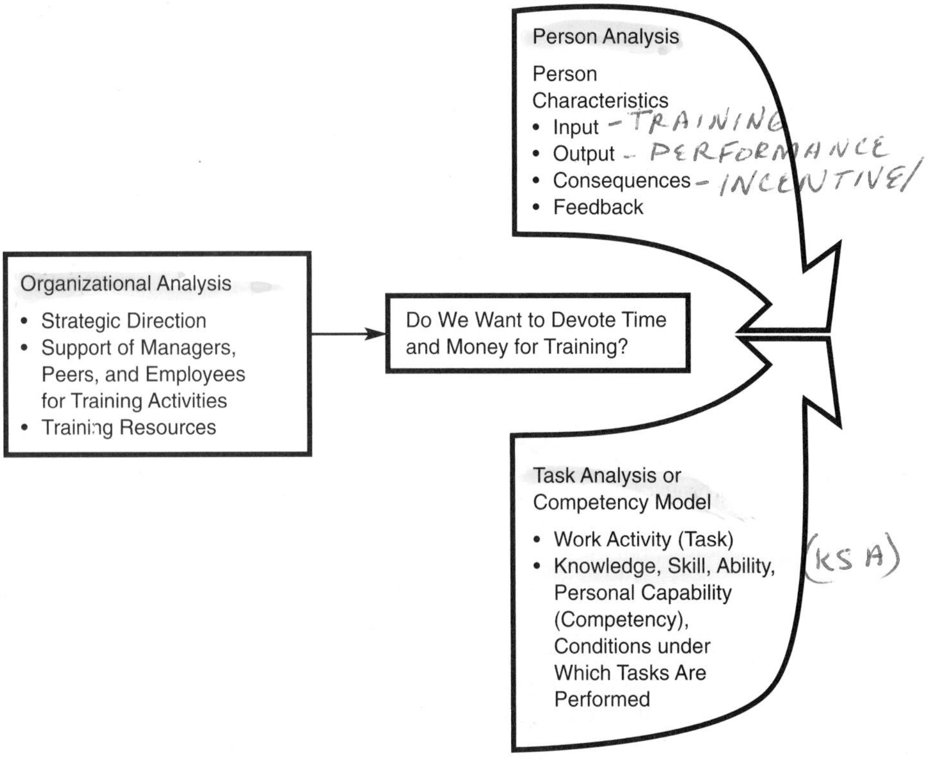

TABLE 3.3
Questions to Ask in an Organizational Analysis

Source: Based on S. Tannenbaum, "A Strategic View of Organizational Training and Learning," in *Creating, Implementing, and Managing Effective Training and Development*, ed. K. Kraiger (San Francisco: Jossey-Bass, 2002): 10–52.

How might the training content affect our employees' relationship with our customers?

What might suppliers, customers, or partners need to know about the training program?

How does this program align with the strategic needs of the business?

Should organizational resources be devoted to this program?

What do we need from managers and peers for this training to succeed?

What features of the work environment might interfere with training (e.g., lack of equipment, no time to use new skills)?

Do we have experts who can help us develop the program content and ensure that we understand the needs of the business as we develop the program?

Will employees perceive the training program as an opportunity? reward? punishment? waste of time?

companies need to consider the information from all three types of analysis before the decision is made to devote time and money for training. Because organizational analysis is concerned with identifying whether training fits with the company's strategic objectives and whether the company has the budget, time, and expertise for training (the context for training), it is usually conducted first. Person analysis and task analysis are often conducted at the same time because it is difficult to determine whether performance deficiencies are a training problem without understanding the tasks and the work environment. An initial organizational analysis may suggest that a company does not want to spend financial resources on training. However, if person analysis reveals that a large number of employees lack a skill in an important area that is related to the company's business objectives (such as customer service), upper-level managers may decide to reallocate financial resources for training.

Organizational Analysis

Organizational analysis involves identifying whether training supports the company's strategic direction; whether managers, peers, and employees support training activity; and what training resources are available. Table 3.3 provides questions that trainers should answer in an organizational analysis. Some combination of documentation, interviews, or focus groups of managers and individuals in the training function should be used to answer these questions.

Company's Strategic Direction

How the company's business strategy influences training was discussed in Chapter 2. The strategic role of training influences the frequency and type of training and how the training function is organized in the company. In companies in which training is expected to contribute to the achievement of business strategies and goals, the amount of money allocated to training and the frequency of training will likely be higher than in companies in which training is done haphazardly or with no strategic intent in mind. For example, companies that believe learning contributes to their competitive advantage or that have adopted high-performance work systems (e.g., teams) are likely to have greater training budgets and conduct more training. The business strategy also influences the type of training. For example, as noted in Chapter 2, companies that have adopted a disinvestment strategy are more likely to focus on outplacement assistance and job search skills training than are companies with other strategic initiatives. Last, the greater the strategic role of training, the more likely the company will organize the training function using the virtual training organization or corporate university models. Both of these models emphasize that training is used to help solve business problems.

Support of Managers, Peers, and Employees for Training Activities

A number of studies have found that peer and manager support for training is critical along with employee enthusiasm and motivation to attend training. The key factors for success are a positive attitude among peers, managers, and employees about participation in training activities; managers' and peers' willingness to provide information to trainees about how they can more effectively use knowledge, skill, or behaviors learned in training on the job; and opportunities for trainees to use training content in their jobs.[6] If peers' and managers' attitudes and behaviors are not supportive, employees are not likely to apply training content to their jobs.

Training Resources

It is necessary to identify whether the company has the budget, time, and expertise for training. For example, if the company is installing computer-based manufacturing equipment in one of its plants, it has three possible strategies for dealing with the need to have computer-literate employees. First, the company can decide that given its staff expertise and budget, it can use internal consultants to train all affected employees. Second, the company may decide that it is more cost-effective to identify employees who are computer-literate by using tests and work samples. Employees who fail the test or perform below standards on the work sample can be reassigned to other jobs. Choosing this strategy suggests that the company has decided to devote resources to selection and placement rather than training. Third, because it lacks time or expertise, the company may decide to purchase training from a consultant.

One way to identify training resources is for companies that have similar operations or departments located across the country or the world to share practices.[7] For example, Pfizer Pharmaceuticals created a "virtual learning team" to promote the sharing of "best practices" in technical training among its U.S. manufacturing sites. Training managers from New York, Brooklyn, New Jersey, Missouri, Nebraska, Indiana, Puerto Rico, and Belgium serve on the team. The team members meet face-to-face once every business quarter and also have a regular conference call every six weeks. The objectives of the team are to (1) provide a centralized focus to Pfizer's training strategies, (2) enable training managers to mentor peers and exchange training practices, and (3) establish training standards for each of the manufacturing sites. The team has made some valuable contributions, including the development of a new operator training standard, a 10-step method for teaching and evaluating the skills of employees who make drug products or operate machinery. The team based the standard on an existing practice at one of the manufacturing sites. Another accomplishment was that the Brooklyn and Puerto Rico team representatives found that they had similar work areas in their plants, so they decided to each create one module of a new training plan and transfer each module to the other location.

If a company decides to purchase a training program from a consultant or vendor rather than build the program in-house, it is important to choose a high-quality provider. Training providers may include individual consultants, consulting firms, or academic institutions. Many companies identify vendors and consultants who can provide training services by

TABLE 3.4
**Questions
to Ask
Vendors and
Consultants**

Source: Based on
R. Zemke and J. Arm-
strong, "Evaluating
Multimedia Develop-
ers," *Training* (Novem-
ber 1996): 33–38.

How much and what type of experience does your company have in designing and delivering training?

What are the qualifications and experiences of your staff?

Can you provide demonstrations or examples of training programs you have developed?

Would you provide references of clients for whom you worked?

What evidence do you have that your programs work?

using requests for proposals.[8] A **request for proposal (RFP)** is a document that outlines for potential vendors and consultants the type of service the company is seeking, the type and number of references needed, the number of employees who need to be trained, funding for the project, the follow-up process used to determine level of satisfaction and service, expected date of completion of the project, and the date when proposals must be received by the company. The RFP may be mailed to potential consultants and vendors or posted on the company's website. The RFP is valuable because it provides a standard set of criteria against which all consultants will be evaluated. The RFP also helps eliminate the need to evaluate outside vendors that cannot provide the needed services.

Usually the RFP helps to identify several vendors who meet the criteria. The next step is to choose the preferred provider. Table 3.4 provides examples of questions to ask vendors. Managers and trainers should check the vendor's reputation by contacting prior clients and professional organizations (such as the American Society for Training and Development). The consultant's experience should be evaluated. (For example, in what industry has the vendor worked?) Managers should carefully consider the services, materials, and fees outlined in the consulting contract. For example, it is not uncommon for training materials, manuals, and handouts to remain the property of the consultant. If the company wishes to use these materials for training at a later date, it would have to pay additional fees to the consultant.

When using a consultant or other outside vendor to provide training services, it is also important to consider the extent to which the training program will be customized based on the company's needs or whether the consultant is going to provide training services based on a generic framework that it applies to many different organizations. For example, Towers Perrin, a well-known, successful New York consulting firm, told several clients that it would study their companies in detail and provide a customized diversity training program to fit their needs. However, six companies (including Nissan USA, Thompson Consumer Electronics, and Harris Bank) were given the same 18 recommendations (e.g., separate the concept of affirmative action from that of managing diversity)![9]

How long should it take a vendor or consultant to develop a training program? The answer is "It depends."[10] Some consultants estimate that development time ranges from 10 to 20 hours for each hour of instruction. Highly technical content requiring more frequent meetings with SMEs can add an additional 50 percent more time. For training programs using new technology (such as a CD-ROM) development time can range from 300 to 1,000 hours per hour of program time depending on how much animation, graphics, video, and audio are included; how much new content needs to be developed; the number of practice exercises and type of feedback to be provided to trainees; and the amount of "branches" to different instructional sequences. Chapter 8 details the use of new technologies in training.

FIGURE 3.3

Process for analyzing the factors that influence employee performance and learning

Source: G. Rummler, "In Search of the Holy Performance Grail," *Training and Development* (April 1996): 26–31.

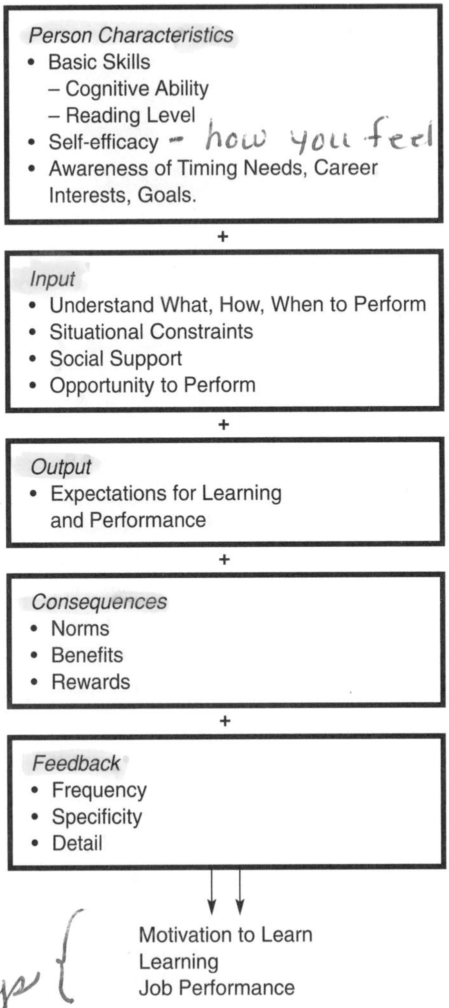

Person Characteristics
- Basic Skills
  - Cognitive Ability
  - Reading Level
- Self-efficacy — *how you feel about yourself*
- Awareness of Timing Needs, Career Interests, Goals.

+

Input
- Understand What, How, When to Perform
- Situational Constraints
- Social Support
- Opportunity to Perform

+

Output
- Expectations for Learning and Performance

+

Consequences
- Norms
- Benefits
- Rewards

+

Feedback
- Frequency
- Specificity
- Detail

Keys {

Motivation to Learn
Learning
Job Performance

Person Analysis

Person analysis helps to identify employees who need training, that is, whether current performance or expected performance indicates a need for training. The need for training may result from the pressure points in Figure 3.1, including performance problems, changes in the job, or use of new technology.

A major pressure point for training is poor or substandard performance. Poor performance is indicated by customer complaints, low performance ratings, or on-the-job incidents such as accidents and unsafe behavior. Another potential indicator of the need for training is if the job changes such that current levels of performance need to be improved or employees must be able to complete new tasks.

Figure 3.3 shows a process for analyzing the factors that influence performance and learning. This process involves determining employees' readiness for training. **Readiness for training** refers to whether (1) employees have the personal characteristics (ability, attitudes, beliefs, and motivation) necessary to learn program content and apply it on the job and (2) the work environment will facilitate learning and not interfere with performance. This process includes evaluating person characteristics, input, output, consequences, and feedback.[11] **Person characteristics** refer to the employees' knowledge, skill, ability, and attitudes. **Input** relates to the instructions that tell employees what, how, and when to perform. Input also refers to the resources that the employees are given to help them perform. These resources may include equipment, time, or budget. **Output** refers to the job's performance standards. **Consequences** refer to the type of incentives that employees receive for performing well. **Feedback** refers to the information that employees receive while they are performing.

Interviews or questionnaires can be used to measure person characteristics, input, output, consequences, and feedback. For example, a package delivery company believed that lead drivers were valuable for providing on-the-job training for new employees.[12] The company employed 110 lead drivers. The lead driver job involved driving, delivery, and bookkeeping duties. The lead drivers benefited from training because coaching and training made their jobs more interesting. The company benefited because on-the-job training was relatively inexpensive and effective. Lead drivers often quickly spotted and corrected performance problems with new trainees. Lead drivers knew the technical aspects of the delivery job quite well. Although many of the lead drivers were good trainers and coaches, the company believed they needed to learn how to coach and train the new drivers. The company used interviews to identify what type of coaching and training skills the lead drivers needed. Interviews were conducted with 14 lead drivers, six supervisors, and two regional vice presidents. The interview for the lead drivers consisted of questions such as

- What types of situations call for coaching on your part?
- What keeps you from being a good coach on the job?
- How do you encourage or motivate other lead drivers? Do you use incentives or rewards? Do you try other things (compliments, personal attention)?
- What common types of performance problems do new hires have?
- What were the biggest problems you encountered as a new coach and trainer? What mistakes did you make? What lessons have you learned over time?
- Tell me about a successful coaching experience and an unsuccessful coaching experience.

Recurring trends in the interview data were noted and categorized. For example, interview questions on obstacles to coaching related to three themes: lack of time to coach, the physical environment (no privacy), and reluctance to coach peers. These three topics were covered in the coaching course.

Person characteristics, input, output, consequences, and feedback also influence motivation to learn. **Motivation to learn** is trainees' desire to learn the content of training programs.[13] Consider how your motivation to learn may be influenced by personal characteristics and the environment. You may have no problem understanding and comprehending the contents of this textbook. But your learning may be inhibited because of your attitude toward the course. That is, perhaps you don't believe the course will be important for your career. Maybe you're taking the course only because it fits your schedule or is required in your degree program. Learning may also be inhibited by the environment. For example, maybe you want to learn, but your study environment prevents you from doing so. Every time you are prepared to read and review your notes and the textbook, your roommates could be having a party. Even if you don't join them, the music may be so loud that you can't concentrate!

Marriott International, the hotel and restaurant chain, found that personal characteristics were having a significant influence on the success rate of the company's welfare-to-work program.[14] This program involved training welfare recipients for jobs in the company's hotels and restaurants. (These types of programs are discussed in greater detail in Chapter 9.) Many trainees were unable to complete the training program because of poor attendance resulting from unreliable child care, drug problems, or abusive husbands or boyfriends. As a result, Marriott has instituted tight standards for selecting welfare recipients into the training program. These standards include requiring trainees to have child care, transportation, and housing arrangements. Also, Marriott plans to add an additional drug test during training. Currently, trainees are tested for drugs only at the beginning of training.

A number of research studies have shown that motivation to learn is related to knowledge gained, behavior change, or skill acquisition resulting from training.[15] Besides considering the factors of person characteristics, input, output, consequences, and feedback in determining whether training is the best solution to a performance problem, managers should also consider these factors prior to sending employees to a training program. These factors relate to the employees' motivation to learn. The following sections describe each of these factors and its relationship to performance and learning.

Person Characteristics

Basic skills refer to skills that are necessary for employees to successfully perform on the job and learn the content of training programs. Basic skills include cognitive ability and reading and writing skills. For example, one assumption that your professor is making in this course is that you have the necessary reading level to comprehend this textbook and the other course materials such as overhead transparencies, videos, or readings. If you lacked the necessary reading level, you likely would not learn much about training in this course. As Chapter 1 mentioned, recent forecasts of skill levels of the U.S. work force indicate that managers will likely have to work with employees who lack basic skills. A literacy audit can be used to determine employees' basic skill levels. Table 3.5 shows the activities involved in conducting a literacy audit.

Cognitive Ability Research shows that cognitive ability influences learning and job performance. **Cognitive ability** includes three dimensions: verbal comprehension, quantitative ability, and reasoning ability.[16] Verbal comprehension refers to the person's capacity to understand and use written and spoken language. Quantitative ability refers to how fast and accurately a person can solve math problems. Reasoning ability refers to the person's capacity to invent solutions to problems. Research shows that cognitive ability is related to successful performance in all jobs.[17] The importance of cognitive ability for job success increases as the job becomes more complex.

For example, a supermarket cashier needs low to moderate levels of all three dimensions of cognitive ability to successfully perform that job. An emergency room physician needs higher levels of verbal comprehension, quantitative ability, and reasoning ability than the cashier. The supermarket cashier needs to understand basic math operations (addition, subtraction, etc.) to give customers the correct amount of change. The cashier also needs to invent solutions to problems. (For example, how does the cashier deal with items that are not priced that the customer wants to purchase?) The cashier also needs to be able to understand

TABLE 3.5
Steps in Performing a Literacy Audit

Source: U.S. Department of Education, U.S. Department of Labor, *The Bottom Line: Basic Skills in the Workplace* (Washington, DC: 1988): 14–15.

Step 1: Observe employees to determine the basic skills they need to be successful in their job. Note the materials the employee uses on the job, the tasks performed, and the reading, writing, and computations completed by the employee.

Step 2: Collect all materials that are written and read on the job and identify computations that must be performed to determine the necessary level of basic skill proficiency. Materials include bills, memos, and forms such as inventory lists and requisition sheets.

Step 3: Interview employees to determine the basic skills they believe are needed to do the job. Consider the basic skill requirements of the job yourself.

Step 4: Determine whether employees have the basic skills needed to successfully perform the job. Combine the information gathered by observing and interviewing employees and evaluating materials they use on their job. Write a description of each job in terms of reading, writing, and computation skills needed to perform successfully.

Step 5: Develop or buy tests that ask questions relating specifically to the employees' job. Ask employees to complete the tests.

Step 6: Compare test results with the description of the basic skills required for the job (from step 5). If the level of employees' reading, writing, and computation skills does not match the basic skills required by the job, then a basic skills problem exists.

and communicate with customers (verbal comprehension). The physician also needs quantitative ability, but at a higher level. For example, when dealing with an infant experiencing seizures in an emergency situation, the physician needs to be able to calculate the correct dosage of medicine (based on an adult dosage) to stop the seizures after considering the child's weight. The physician has to be able to quickly diagnose the situation and determine what actions (blood tests, X-rays, respiratory therapy) are necessary. The physician also needs to communicate clearly to the patient's parents the treatment and recovery process.

Cognitive ability influences job performance and ability to learn in training programs. If trainees lack the cognitive ability level necessary to perform job tasks, they will not perform well. Also, trainees' level of cognitive ability can influence how well they can learn in training programs.[18] Trainees with low levels of cognitive ability are more likely to fail to complete training or (at the end of training) receive lower grades on tests to measure how much they have learned.

To identify employees without the cognitive ability to succeed on the job or in training programs, companies use paper-and-pencil cognitive ability tests. Determining a job's cognitive ability requirement is part of the task analysis process discussed later in this chapter.

Reading Ability   Lack of the appropriate reading level can impede performance and learning in training programs. Material used in training should be evaluated to ensure that its reading level does not exceed that required by the job. **Readability** refers to the difficulty level of written materials.[19] A readability assessment usually involves analysis of sentence length and word difficulty.

If trainees' reading level does not match the level needed for the training materials, four options are available. First, determine whether it is feasible to lower the reading level of training materials or use video or on-the-job training, which involves learning by watching and practicing rather than by reading. Second, employees without the necessary reading level could be identified through reading tests and reassigned to other positions more congruent with their skill levels. Third, again using reading tests, identify employees who lack the necessary reading skills and provide them with remedial training. Fourth, determine whether the job can be redesigned to accommodate employees' reading levels. The fourth option is certainly the most costly and least practical. Therefore, alternative training methods need to be considered, or managers can elect a nontraining option. Nontraining options include selecting employees for jobs and training opportunities on the basis of reading, computation, writing, and other basic skill requirements.

Many companies are finding that employees lack the basic skills needed to successfully complete training programs. For example, a training program for 1,800 hourly employees at Georgia-Pacific (a paper manufacturer) was ineffective.[20] Employees reported that they understood training content but once they left training and returned to their jobs, they couldn't successfully perform maintenance tasks. In trying to determine the cause of the failed training, employees' basic skills were tested. Tests revealed that many employees had difficulty reading and writing. As a result, they were unable to understand the materials used in training. This translated into reduced learning and poor job performance.

To help ensure that employees have the necessary basic skills needed to succeed in training, Georgia-Pacific developed a basic skills assessment and training program. The first step involved assessment (or measurement) of employees' basic skills. A test of reading and math skills was given to employees. People who scored at or above a ninth grade reading level were eligible to attend training programs. Those with literacy levels below ninth grade were counseled to attend basic skills training. Because Georgia-Pacific's primary concern was how to convince employees to attend training, the company had to establish trust with the employees. In general, employees who lack basic skills are embarrassed to admit they have difficulty and are afraid that their lack of literacy will cost them their jobs. To alleviate these fears, employees received confidential counseling about their test results, they were not required to start basic skills training immediately after the assessment, and the company did not put information regarding test results (pass or fail) in employees' personnel files.

A local community college supplied the basic skills training. Classes were set up close to Georgia-Pacific's plants so employees could attend classes before or after their work shifts. There was no charge for the classes. Now the work force has the necessary basic skills. To ensure that new employees do not lack basic skills, Georgia-Pacific has changed its hiring qualifications. The company does not accept applications from anyone who hasn't completed a specific 18-month schedule of courses at the community college.

Another approach to improving basic skills is incorporating basic skills instruction into training programs. An example is the electronics technician training program developed by the Ford Foundation.[21] Before the start of the program, students are given information about electronic technician jobs. Students are told they will learn how to think about operating, maintaining, and repairing electrical equipment that they are familiar with such as flashlights, curling irons, and lamps. These appliances were selected because they are useful for introducing basic electronic concepts and procedures.

Trainees are given a book that covers the basic literacy skills needed to read training and job-related material in electronics. The book's exercises and worksheets help the trainee master "reading-to-do" and "reading-to-learn" skills that have been identified as required in the majority of jobs.[22] Reading-to-do involves searching for and reading information in manuals, books, or charts (e.g., looking up information such as repair specifications in a technical manual or scanning tables and graphs to locate information). Reading-to-learn involves reading information to apply it in the future, such as reading instructions on how to use a piece of equipment (e.g., paraphrasing and summarizing information).

Besides learning reading skills related to electronics, trainees study how electronics is used in flashlights and table lamps. The textbook introduces students to math concepts and their applications, including scientific notation needed to understand waves that appear on an oscilloscope. This training program has prepared competent electronic technicians for entry-level positions.

Self-Efficacy **Self-efficacy** is employees' belief that they can successfully perform their job or learn the content of the training program. The job environment can be threatening to many employees who may not have been successful performers in the past. For example, as you will see in Chapter 10, people who are hired through a welfare-to-work program—a program designed to help find jobs for welfare recipients—may lack self-efficacy. The training environment can also be threatening to people who have not received training or formal education for some length of time, lack education, or are not experienced in the training program's subject matter. For example, training employees to use equipment for computer-based manufacturing may represent a potential threat, especially if they are intimidated by new technology and do not have the confidence in their ability to master the skills needed to use a computer. Research has demonstrated that self-efficacy is related to performance in training programs.[23] Employees' self-efficacy level can be increased by

1. Letting employees know that the purpose of training is to try to improve performance rather than to identify areas in which employees are incompetent.
2. Providing as much information as possible about the training program and purpose of training prior to the actual training.
3. Showing employees the training success of their peers who are now in similar jobs.
4. Providing employees with feedback that learning is under their control and they have the ability and the responsibility to overcome any learning difficulties they experience in the program.

Awareness of Training Needs, Career Interests, and Goals To be motivated to learn in training programs, employees must be aware of their skill strengths and weaknesses and of the link between the training program and improvement of their weaknesses.[24] Managers should make sure that employees understand why they are asked to attend training programs, and they should communicate the link between training and improvement of skill weaknesses or knowledge deficiencies. This can be accomplished by sharing performance feedback with employees, holding career development discussions, or having employees complete a self-evaluation of their skill strengths and weaknesses as well as career interests and goals.

If possible, employees need to be given a choice of what programs to attend and must understand how actual training assignments are made to maximize motivation to learn. Several recent studies have suggested that giving trainees a choice regarding which programs to attend and then honoring those choices maximizes motivation to learn. Giving employees choices but not necessarily honoring them can undermine motivation to learn.[25]

Input

Employees' perceptions of two characteristics of the work environment—situational constraints and social support—are determinants of performance and motivation to learn. **Situational constraints** include lack of proper tools and equipment, materials and supplies, budgetary support, and time. **Social support** refers to managers' and peers' willingness to provide feedback and reinforcement.[26] If employees have the knowledge, skills, attitudes, and behavior needed to perform but do not have the proper tools and equipment needed, their performance will be inadequate.

To ensure that the work environment enhances trainees' motivation to learn, managers should take the following steps:

1. Provide materials, time, job-related information, and other work aids necessary for employees to use new skills or behavior before participating in training programs.
2. Speak positively about the company's training programs to employees.
3. Let employees know they are doing a good job when they are using training content in their work.
4. Encourage work-group members to involve each other in trying to use new skills on the job by soliciting feedback and sharing training experiences and situations in which training content was helpful.
5. Provide employees with time and opportunities to practice and apply new skills or behaviors to their work.

Output

Poor or substandard performance can occur on the job because employees do not know at what level they are expected to perform. For example, they may not be aware of quality standards related to speed or degree of personalization of service that is expected. Employees may have the knowledge, skill, and attitudes necessary to perform, but fail to perform because they are not aware of the performance standards. Lack of awareness of the performance standards is a communications problem, but it is not a problem that training can "fix."

Understanding the need to perform is important for learning. Trainees need to understand what specifically they are expected to learn in the training program. To ensure that trainees master training content at the appropriate level, trainees in training programs also need to understand the level of proficiency that is expected of them. For example, for tasks, level of proficiency relates to how well employees are to perform a task. For knowledge, level of proficiency may relate to a score on a written test. The standards or level of performance is part of the learning objectives (discussed in Chapter 4).

Consequences

If employees do not believe that rewards or incentives for performance are adequate, they will be unlikely to meet performance standards even if they have the necessary knowledge, behavior, skill, or attitudes. Also, work-group norms may encourage employees not to meet performance standards. **Norms** refer to accepted standards of behavior for work-group members. For example, during labor contract negotiations baggage handlers for Northwest Airlines worked slowly loading and unloading baggage from airplanes. As a result, many passenger departures and arrivals were delayed. The baggage handlers had the knowledge, skills, and behaviors necessary to unload the planes, but they worked slowly because they were trying to send a message to management that the airlines could not perform effectively if their contract demands were not met.

Consequences also affect learning in training programs. Employees' motivation to learn can be enhanced by communicating to them the potential job-related, personal, and career benefits they may receive as a result of attending training and learning the content of the training program. These benefits may include learning a more efficient way to perform a process or procedure, establishing contacts with other employees in the company (also known as networking), or increasing their opportunity to pursue other jobs in the company. It is important that the communication from the manager about potential benefits be realistic. Unmet expectations about training programs can hinder motivation to learn.[27]

Feedback

Performance problems can result when employees do not receive feedback regarding the extent to which they are meeting performance standards. Training may not be the best solution to this type of problem if employees know what they are supposed to do (output), but do not understand how close their performance is to the standard. Employees need to be given specific, detailed feedback of effective and ineffective performance. For employees to perform to standard, feedback needs to be given to employees frequently, not just during a yearly performance evaluation.

In Chapter 4 the role of feedback in learning is discussed in detail. Keep in mind that feedback is critical for shaping trainees' behaviors and skills.

Determining Whether Training Is the Best Solution

To determine whether training is needed to solve a performance problem, managers need to analyze characteristics of the performer, input, output, consequences, and feedback. How might this be done?[28] Managers should assess the following:

1. Is the performance problem important? Does it have the potential to cost the company a significant amount of money from lost productivity or customers?
2. Do the employees know how to perform effectively? Perhaps they received little or no previous training or the training was ineffective. (This problem is a characteristic of the person.)
3. Can the employees demonstrate the correct knowledge or behavior? Perhaps employees were trained but they infrequently or never used the training content (knowledge, skills, etc.) on the job. (This is an input problem.)
4. Were performance expectations clear (input)? Were there any obstacles to performance such as faulty tools or equipment?
5. Were positive consequences offered for good performance? Was poor performance not rewarded? For example, if employees are dissatisfied with their compensation, their peers or a union may encourage them to slow down their pace of work. (This involves consequences.)
6. Did employees receive timely, relevant, accurate, constructive, and specific feedback about their performance (a feedback issue)?
7. Were other solutions—such as job redesign or transferring employees to other jobs—too expensive or unrealistic?

If employees lack the knowledge and skill to perform and the other factors are satisfactory, training is needed. If employees have the knowledge and skill to perform but input, output, consequences, or feedback is inadequate, training may not be the best solution. For example, if poor performance results from faulty equipment, training cannot solve this problem but repairing the equipment will! If poor performance results from lack of feedback, then employees may not need training, but their managers may need training on how to give performance feedback!

Task Analysis

Task analysis results in a description of work activities, including tasks performed by the employee and the knowledge, skills, and abilities required to complete the tasks. A **job** is a specific position requiring the completion of certain tasks. (The job exemplified in Figure 3.4 is that of an electrical maintenance worker.) A **task** is the employee's work activity in a specific job. Figure 3.4 shows several tasks for the electrical maintenance worker job. These tasks include replacing light bulbs, electrical outlets, and light switches. To complete tasks, employees must have specific levels of knowledge, skill, ability, and other considerations (KSAOs). **Knowledge** includes facts or procedures (e.g., the chemical properties of gold). **Skill** indicates competency in performing a task (e.g., negotiation skill, a skill in getting another person to agree to take a certain course of action). **Ability** includes the physical and mental capacities to perform a task (e.g., spatial ability, the ability to see the relationship between objects in physical space). **Other** refers to the conditions under which tasks are performed. These conditions include identifying the equipment and environment that the employee works in (e.g., the need to wear an oxygen mask, work in extremely hot conditions), time constraints for a task (e.g., deadlines), safety considerations, or performance standards.

Task analysis should be undertaken only after the organizational analysis has determined that the company wants to devote time and money for training. Why? Task analysis is a time-consuming, tedious process that involves a large time commitment to gather and summarize data from many different persons in the company including managers, job incumbents, and trainers.

FIGURE 3.4

Sample items from task analysis questionnaires for the electrical maintenance job

Source: E. F. Holton III and C. Bailey, "Top to Bottom Curriculum Redesign," *Training & Development* (March 1995): 40–44

Job: Electrical Maintenance Worker

Task Performance Ratings

Task #s	Task Description	Frequency of Performance	Importance	Difficulty
199-264	Replace a light bulb	0 1 2 3 4 5	0 1 2 3 4 5	0 1 2 3 4 5
199-265	Replace an electrical outlet	0 1 2 3 4 5	0 1 2 3 4 5	0 1 2 3 4 5
199-266	Install a light fixture	0 1 2 3 4 5	0 1 2 3 4 5	0 1 2 3 4 5
199-267	Replace a light switch	0 1 2 3 4 5	0 1 2 3 4 5	0 1 2 3 4 5
199-268	Install a new circuit breaker	0 1 2 3 4 5	0 1 2 3 4 5	0 1 2 3 4 5

Frequency of Performance	Importance	Difficulty
0=never	1=negligible	1=easiest
5=often	5=extremely high	5=most difficult

Steps in a Task Analysis

A task analysis involves four steps:[29]

1. Select the job(s) to be analyzed.

2. Develop a preliminary list of tasks performed on the job by (1) interviewing and observing expert employees and their managers and (2) talking with others who have performed a task analysis.

3. Validate or confirm the preliminary list of tasks. This involves having a group of subject matter experts (job incumbents, managers, etc.) answer in a meeting or on a written survey several questions regarding the tasks. The types of questions that may be asked include the following: How frequently is the task performed? How much time is spent performing each task? How important or critical is the task for successful performance of the job? How difficult is the task to learn? Is performance of the task expected of entry-level employees?

Table 3.6 presents a sample task analysis questionnaire. This information is used to determine which tasks will be focused on in the training program. The person or committee conducting the needs assessment must decide the level of ratings across dimensions that will determine that a task should be included in the training program. Tasks that are important, frequently performed, and of moderate-to-high level of difficulty should be trained for. Tasks that are not important and infrequently performed will not be trained for. It is difficult for managers and trainers to decide if tasks that are important, are performed infrequently, and require minimal difficulty should be included in training. Managers and trainers must determine whether or not important tasks—regardless of how frequently they are performed or their level of difficulty—will be included in training.

4. Once the tasks are identified, it is important to identify the knowledge, skills, or abilities necessary to successfully perform each task. This information can be collected through interviews and questionnaires. Recall this chapter's discussion of how ability influences learning. Information concerning basic skill and cognitive ability requirements is critical for determining if certain levels of knowledge, skills, and abilities will be prerequisites for entrance to the training program (or job) or if supplementary training in underlying skills is needed. For training purposes, information concerning how difficult it is to learn the knowledge, skill, or ability is important—as is whether the knowledge, skill, or ability is expected to be acquired by the employee before taking the job.[30]

Table 3.7 summarizes key points to remember regarding task analysis.

Example of a Task Analysis

Each of the four steps of a task analysis can be seen in this example from a utility company. Trainers were given the job of developing a training system in six months.[31] The purpose of the program was to identify tasks and knowledge, skills, abilities, and other considerations that would serve as the basis for training program objectives and lesson plans.

The first phase of the project involved identifying potential tasks for each job in the utility's electrical maintenance area. Procedures, equipment lists, and information provided by subject matter experts (SMEs) were used to generate the tasks. SMEs included managers, instructors, and senior technicians. The tasks were incorporated into a questionnaire administered to all technicians in the electrician maintenance department. The questionnaire included 550 tasks. Figure 3.4 shows sample items from the questionnaire for the electrical maintenance job. Technicians were asked to rate each task on importance, difficulty, and frequency of performance. The rating scale for frequency included zero. A zero rating indicated

TABLE 3.6 **Sample Task Statement Questionnaire**

Name   Date

Position

Please rate each of the task statements according to three factors: the *importance* of the task for effective performance, how *frequently* the task is performed, and the degree of *difficulty* required to become effective in the task. Use the following scales in making your ratings.

Importance

4 = Task is critical for effective performance.

3 = Task is important but not critical
for effective performance.

2 = Task is of some importance for
effective performance.

1 = Task is of no importance for
effective performance.

0 = Task is not performed.

Frequency

4 = Task is performed once a day.

3 = Task is performed once a week.

2 = Task is performed once every few months.

1 = Task is performed once or twice a year.

0 = Task is not performed.

Difficulty

4 = Effective performance of the task requires extensive prior experience and/or training
(12–18 months or longer).

3 = Effective performance of the task requires minimal prior experience and training
(6–12 months).

2 = Effective performance of the task requires a brief period of prior training and experience
(1–6 months).

1 = Effective performance of the task does not require specific prior training and/or experience.

0 = This task is not performed.

Task	Importance	Frequency	Difficulty
1. Ensuring maintenance on equipment, tools, and safety controls			
2. Monitoring employee performance			
3. Scheduling employees			
4. Using statistical software on the computer			
5. Monitoring changes made in processes using statistical methods			

that the technician rating the task had never performed the task. Technicians who rated a task zero were asked not to evaluate the task's difficulty and importance.

Customized software was used to analyze the ratings collected via the questionnaire. The primary requirement used to determine whether a task required training was its importance rating. A task rated "very important" was identified as one requiring training regardless of its frequency or difficulty. If a task was rated moderately important but difficult, it also was designated for training. Tasks rated unimportant, not difficult, or done infrequently were not designated for training.

The list of tasks designated for training was reviewed by the SMEs to determine if it accurately described job tasks. The result was a list of 487 tasks. For each of the 487 tasks,

TABLE 3.7
Key Points to Remember When Conducting a Task Analysis

Source: Adapted from A. P. Carnevale, L. J. Gainer, and A.S. Meltzer, *Workplace Basics Training Manual* (San Francisco: Jossey-Bass, 1990).

A task analysis should identify both what employees are actually doing and what they should be doing on the job.

Task analysis begins by breaking the job into duties and tasks.

Use more than two methods for collecting task information to increase the validity of the analysis.

For task analysis to be useful, information needs to be collected from subject matter experts (SMEs). SMEs include job incumbents, managers, and employees familiar with the job.

In deciding how to evaluate tasks, the focus should be on tasks necessary to accomplish the company's goals and objectives. These may not be the tasks that are the most difficult or take the most time.

two SMEs identified the necessary knowledge, skills, abilities, and other factors required for performance. This included information on working conditions, cues that initiate the task's start and end, performance standards, safety considerations, and necessary tools and equipment. All data were reviewed by plant technicians and members of the training department. More than 14,000 knowledge, skill, ability, and other considerations were grouped into common areas and assigned an identification code. These groups were then combined into clusters. The clusters represented qualification areas. That is, the task clusters related to linked tasks that the employees must be certified in to perform the job. The clusters were used to identify training lesson plans and course objectives. Trainers also reviewed the clusters to identify prerequisite skills for each cluster.

COMPETENCY MODELS

In today's global and competitive business environment, many companies are finding that it is difficult to determine whether employees have the capabilities needed for success. The necessary capabilities may vary from one business unit to another and even across roles within a business unit. As a result, many companies have started to use competency models to help them identify the knowledge, skills, and personal characteristics (attitudes, personality) needed for successful performance in a job. Competency models are also useful for ensuring that training and development systems are contributing to the development of such knowledge, skills, and personal characteristics.

Traditionally, needs assessment has involved identifying knowledge, skills, abilities, and tasks. However, a current trend in training is for needs assessment to focus on competencies. A **competency** refers to areas of personal capability that enable employees to successfully perform their jobs by achieving outcomes or accomplishing tasks.[32] A competency can be knowledge, skills, attitudes, values, or personal characteristics. A **competency model** identifies the competencies necessary for each job as well as the knowledge, skills, behavior, and personality characteristics underlying each competency.[33] Table 3.8 shows a competency model for a systems engineer. The left side of the table lists technical competencies within the technical cluster (systems architecture, data migration, documentation). The right side shows behaviors that might be used to determine a systems engineer's level of proficiency for each competency.

TABLE 3.8   Example of Competencies and a Competency Model

Technical Cluster	Proficiency Ratings
Systems Architecture Ability to design complex software applications, establish protocols, and create prototypes.	**0**—Is not able to perform basic tasks. **1**—Understands basic principles; can perform tasks with assistance or direction. **2**—Performs routine tasks with reliable results; works with minimal supervision. **3**—Performs complex and multiple tasks; can coach or teach others. **4**—Considered an expert in this task; can describe, teach, and lead others.
Data Migration Ability to establish the necessary platform requirements to efficiently and completely coordinate data transfer.	**0**—Is not able to perform basic tasks. **1**—Understands basic principles; can perform tasks with assistance or direction. **2**—Performs routine tasks with reliable results; works with minimal supervision. **3**—Performs complex and multiple tasks; can coach or teach others. **4**—Considered an expert in this task; can describe, teach, and lead others.
Documentation Ability to prepare comprehensive and complete documentation including specifications, flow diagrams, process control, and budgets.	**0**—Is not able to perform basic tasks. **1**—Understands basic principles; can perform tasks with assistance or direction. **2**—Performs routine tasks with reliable results; works with minimal supervision. **3**—Performs complex and multiple tasks; can coach or teach others. **4**—Considered an expert in this task; can describe, teach, and lead others.

Source: R. J. Mirabile, "Everything You Wanted to Know about Competency Modeling," *Training and Development* (August 1997): 73–77.

One way to understand competency models is to compare them to job analysis. As you may recall from other classes or experiences, **job analysis** refers to the process of developing a description of the job (tasks, duties, and responsibilities) and the specifications (knowledge, skills, and abilities) that an employee must have to perform it. How does job analysis compare to competency models? Job analysis is more work- and task-focused (what is accomplished), whereas competency modeling is worker-focused (how objectives are met or how work is accomplished). Focusing on "how" versus "what" provides valuable information for training and development. A recent study asked competency modeling experts (consultants, HR practitioners, academics, industrial psychologists) to compare and contrast competency modeling to job analysis.[34] The study found several differences between job analysis and competency models. Competency models are more likely to link competencies and the company's business goals. Competency models provide descriptions of competencies that are common for an entire occupational group, level of jobs, or an entire organization. Job analysis describes what is different across jobs, occupational groups, or organization levels. Finally, job analysis generates specific knowledge, skill, and abilities for particular jobs. It is used to generate specific requirements to be used for employee selection. The competencies generated by competency modeling are more general and believed to have greater application to a wider variety of purposes including selection, training, employee development, and performance management.

Another way to think about competency models is by considering performance management.[35] Unfortunately, many performance management systems suffer from a lack of agreement on what outcomes should be used to evaluate performance. Manager–employee discussions about performance deficiencies tend to lack specificity. By identifying the areas of personal capability that enable employees to successfully perform their jobs, competency models ensure an evaluation of both what gets done and how it gets done. Performance feedback can be directed toward specific concrete examples of behavior; and knowledge, skills, ability, and other characteristics that are necessary for success are clearly described.

How are competencies identified and competency models developed? First, the job or position to be analyzed needs to be identified. Second, any changes in the business strategy need to be identified. The implications of business strategy for training were discussed in Chapter 2. Changes in the business strategy might cause new competencies to be needed or old competencies to be altered. Third, effective and ineffective performers need to be identified. Fourth, the competencies responsible for effective and ineffective performance need to be identified. There are several approaches for identifying competencies. These include analyzing one or several "star" performers, surveying persons who are familiar with the job (subject-matter experts), and developing competencies based on benchmark data of good performers in other companies.[36] Fifth, the model needs to be validated. That is, a determination must be made as to whether the competencies included in the model truly are related to effective performance. In Table 3.8's example of the technical competencies for the system engineer, it is important to verify that (1) the three competencies shown are needed to be successful in the job and (2) the level of proficiency of the competency is appropriate.

Competency models are useful for training and development in several ways[37]:

- They identify behaviors needed for effective job performance. These models ensure that feedback given to employees as part of a development program (such as 360-degree feedback) relate specifically to individual and organizational success.
- They provide a tool for determining what skills are needed to meet today's needs as well as the company's future skill needs. They can be used to evaluate the relationship between the company's current training programs and present needs. That is, they help align training and development activities with the company's business goals. They can be used to evaluate how well the offerings relate to anticipated future skill needs.
- They help to determine what skills are needed at different career points.
- They provide a framework for ongoing coaching and feedback to develop employees for current and future roles. By comparing their current personal competencies to those required for a job, employees can identify competencies that need development and choose actions to develop those competencies. These actions may include courses, job experiences, and other types of development. (Development methods are detailed in Chapter 9.)
- They create a "road map" for identifying and developing employees who may be candidates for managerial positions (succession planning).

For example, consider the use of competency models at Cross Country TravCorps, a staffing company that provides short-term employment for nurses, operating room technologists, therapists, and allied health professionals at facilities across the nation.[38] Departmental training managers and the training department developed a job-specific competency checklist that identifies skills and job tasks that new employees need to learn to be effective. The checklist is used for on-the-job training. Sprint Corporation, the global communications company, identifies competencies that are used for performance management and development. The seven Sprint Dimensions include leadership, communications, management, personal effectiveness, professional knowledge/global awareness, customer focus, and team approach. The dimensions are used to help employees to improve. Based on the Sprint Dimensions, managers identify suitable development experiences for employees.

SCOPE OF NEEDS ASSESSMENT

Up to this point, the chapter has discussed the various aspects of needs assessment including organizational, person, and task analyses. This involves interviews, observations, and potentially even surveying employees. You might be saying to yourself, This sounds good, but it appears to be a very elaborate process that takes time. What happens if I don't have time to conduct a thorough needs assessment? Should I abandon the process?

Time constraints can limit the length and detail obtained from a needs assessment. However, even if managers demand a training course right now, needs assessment should still be conducted. There are several ways to reduce the time for needs assessment without sacrificing the quality of the process.[39] First, the scope of needs assessment depends on the size of the potential "pressure point." If the pressure point seems to be local and has a potentially small impact on the business, then the information-gathering part of needs assessment could consist of only a few interviews with managers or job incumbents. If the pressure point will have a large impact on the business, then more information gathering should be conducted. If, after interviewing subject-matter experts and job incumbents, you can tell that you are not learning anything new about the job, then interviewing could be stopped. Second, you should consider using already available data collected for other purposes. For example, error data, sales data, customer complaints, and exit interviews might provide valuable clues as to the source of performance problems. The Web may be a useful source for quickly conducting interviews with subject-matter experts in different locations. Finally, if you are attuned to the business problems, technological developments, and other issues facing the organization, you will be able to anticipate training needs. For example, if the company is opening sales offices in an international location and introducing new technology in the manufacturing plants, cross-cultural training and training designed to help employees use the new technology undoubtedly will be needed. Be prepared by understanding the business!

Needs Assessment in Practice

The manufacturing operations of the Owens-Corning Insulation Business were interested in increasing the productivity, product quality, and safety performance of the business. This was consistent with the company-wide strategy of trying to increase shareholder value, ensure individual dignity, and deliver customer service. To help meet the strategic goals, plant-based specialists in human resources, training, organization development, and project management created a group to direct training activities. The first priority of this group was to establish supervisor training. At that time there was no formal training for manufacturing supervisors. Therefore, the group worked on developing such a program. Interviews with plant human resource managers and trainers suggested that creation of a generic training program would not be effective. As a result, the group developed a survey that was administered to employees in all of the plants. The survey asked specific questions about the supervisors' skill needs—for example, "The supervisor actively listens to individuals or teams to check for understanding" and "The supervisor meets all deadlines on projects, action items, and special requests." The data collected from the survey indicated that supervisors' greatest skill deficiencies included two-way communications, active listening skills, setting performance expectations, providing feedback, handling conflict, and time management. Each plant supervisor training program was designed based on these needs, taking into account the uniqueness of the facility and its culture.

This example illustrates several things. First, training was viewed as critical for helping the company meet its strategic objectives. As a result, resources and time were allocated for needs assessment and training. Second, the person analysis consisted of a survey of supervisor skills. This information was used to identify overall skill deficiencies across the plants. Training programs were developed to improve the skill deficiencies identified using methods that were congruent with the plant environment and culture. For example, one plant used a three-day skills workshop, a one-day quarterly leadership skills conference (which updates and refreshes supervisors' skills), and an informal once-per-month leadership discussion.

Summary

The first step in a successful training effort is to determine that a training need exists through a process known as needs assessment. Needs assessment involves three steps: organizational analysis, person analysis, and task analysis. Various methods—including observation, interviews, and surveys or questionnaires—are used to conduct a needs assessment. Each has advantages and disadvantages. Organizational analysis involves determining (1) the extent to which training is congruent with the company's business strategy and resources and (2) if peers and managers are likely to provide the support needed for trainees to use training content in the work setting.

Person analysis focuses on identifying whether there is evidence that training is the solution, who needs training, and whether employees have the prerequisite skills, attitudes, and beliefs needed to ensure they master the content of training programs. Because performance problems are one of the major reasons companies consider training employees, it is important to consider how personal characteristics, input, output, consequences, and feedback relate to performance and learning. This means that managers and trainers need to be concerned about employees' basic skill levels, attitudes, and the work environment in determining if performance problems can be solved using training.

Training is likely the best solution to a performance problem if employees don't know how to perform. If employees have not received feedback about their performance, if they lack the equipment needed to perform the job, if the consequences for good performance are negative, or if they are unaware of an expected standard for performance, then training is not likely to be the best solution.

To maximize employees' motivation to learn in training programs, managers and trainers need to understand these factors prior to sending employees to training. For example, lack of basic skills or reading skills can inhibit both job performance and learning.

A task analysis involves identifying the task and knowledge, skills, and abilities that will be trained for. Competency modeling is a new approach to needs assessment that focuses on identifying personal capabilities including knowledge, skills, attitudes, values, and personal characteristics.

Key Terms

needs assessment, *74*
organizational analysis, *74*
person analysis, *74*
task analysis, *74*
subject-matter experts
(SMEs), *77*
job incumbent, *77*
focus groups, *78*
benchmarking, *80*
request for proposal
(RFP), *83*
readiness for training, *84*

person characteristics, *85*
input, *85*
output, *85*
consequences, *85*
feedback, *85*
motivation to learn, *85*
basic skills, *86*
cognitive ability, *86*
readability, *87*
self-efficacy, *89*
situational constraints, *90*
social support, *90*

norms, *90*
job, *92*
task, *92*
knowledge, *92*
skill, *92*
ability, *92*
other, *92*
competency, *95*
competency model, *95*
job analysis, *96*

Discussion Questions

1. Which of the factors that influence performance and learning do you think is most important? Which is least important?
2. If you had to conduct a needs assessment for a new job at a new plant, describe the method you would use.
3. Needs assessment involves organization, person, and task analysis. Which one of these analyses do you believe is most important? Which is least important? Why?
4. Why should upper-level managers be included in the needs assessment process?
5. Explain how you would determine if employees had the reading level necessary to succeed in a training program.
6. What conditions would suggest that a company should buy a training program from an outside vendor? Which would suggest that the firm should develop the program itself?
7. Assume you have to prepare older employees with little computer experience to attend a training course on how to use the World Wide Web. How will you ensure that they have high levels of readiness for training? How will you determine their readiness for training?
8. Review the accompanying sample tasks and task ratings for the electronic technician's job. What tasks do you believe should be emphasized in the training program? Why?

Task	Importance	Frequency	Learning Difficulty
1. Replaces components	1	2	1
2. Repairs equipment	2	5	5
3. Interprets instrument readings	1	4	5
4. Uses small tools	2	5	1

Explanation of ratings:
Frequency: 1 = very infrequently to 5 = very frequently.
Importance: 1 = very important to 5 = very unimportant.
Learning difficulty: 1 = easy to 5 = very difficult.

9. Discuss the types of evidence that you would look for in order to determine whether a needs analysis has been improperly conducted.

10. How is competency modeling similar to traditional needs assessment? How does it differ?

Application Assignments

1. Develop a competency model for a job held by a friend, spouse, or roommate (someone other than yourself). Use the process discussed in this chapter to develop your model. Note the most difficult part of developing the model. How could the model be used?

2. The Department of Social Services represents a large portion of your county's budget and total number of employees. The job of eligibility technician is responsible for all client contact, policy interpretation, and financial decisions related to several forms of public aid (e.g., food stamps, aid to families with dependent children). Eligibility technicians must read a large number of memos and announcements of new and revised policies and procedures. Eligibility technicians were complaining they had difficulty reading and responding to this correspondence. The county decided to send the employees to a speed reading program costing $250 per person. The county has 200 eligibility technicians.

   Preliminary evaluation of the speed reading program was that trainees liked it. Two months after the training was conducted, the technicians told their managers that they were not using the speed reading course in their jobs, but were using it in leisure reading at home. When their managers asked why they weren't using it on the job, the typical response was "I never read those memos and policy announcements anyway."

   A. Evaluate the needs assessment process used to determine that speed reading was necessary. What was good about it? Where was it faulty?

   B. How would you have conducted the needs assessment? Be realistic.

3. Consider the interview questions for the lead drivers that are shown on page 85. Write questions that could be used to interview the six lead driver supervisors and the two regional vice presidents. How do these questions differ from those for the lead drivers? How are they similar?

4. Several companies are known for linking their values and human resource practices in ways that have led to business success as well as employee satisfaction. These companies include Southwest Airlines (*www.iflyswa.com*), Cisco Systems (*www.cisco.com*), SAS Institute (*www.sas.com*), the Mens Wearhouse (*www.menswearhouse.com*), and

Intel (www.intel.com). Choose one of these companies' websites and perform an organizational needs analysis. Read about the company's values and vision; look for statements about the importance of training and personal development. Is training important in the company? Why or why not? Provide supporting evidence from the website.

Endnotes

1. I. L. Goldstein, E. P. Braverman, and H. Goldstein, "Needs Assessment," in *Developing Human Resources,* ed. K. N. Wexley (Washington, DC: Bureau of National Affairs, 1991): 5–35 to 5–75.

2. L. Simpson, "In Search of Subject Matter Excellence," *Training* (January 2003): 44–47.

3. J. Wircenski, R. Sullivan, and P. Moore, "Assessing Training Needs at Texas Instruments," *Training and Development* (April 1989).

4. L. Overmyer-Day and G. Benson, "Training Success Stories," *Training and Development* (June 1996): 24–29.

5. L. E. Day, "Benchmarking Training," *Training and Development* (November 1995): 27–30.

6. J. Rouiller and I. Goldstein, "The Relationship between Organizational Transfer Climate and Positive Transfer of Training," *Human Resource Development Quarterly* 1993 (4): 377–90; R. Noe and J. Colquitt, "Planning for Training Impact," in *Creating, Implementing, and Managing Effective Training and Development,* ed. K. Kraiger (San Francisco: Jossey-Bass, 2002): 53–79.

7. D. Zielinski, "Have You Shared a Bright Idea Today?" *Training* (July 2000): 65–68.

8. B. Gerber, "How to Buy Training Programs," *Training* (June 1989): 59–68.

9. D. A. Blackmon, "Consultants' Advice on Diversity Was Anything but Diverse," *Wall Street Journal* (March 11, 1997): A1, A16.

10. R. Zemke and J. Armstrong, "How Long Does It Take? (The Sequel)," *Training* (May 1997): 69–79.

11. G. Rummler, "In Search of the Holy Performance Grail," *Training and Development* (April 1996): 26–31; D. G. Langdon, "Selecting Interventions," *Performance Improvement* 36 (1997): 11–15.

12. K. Gupta, *A Practical Guide to Needs Assessment* (San Francisco: Jossey-Bass/Pfeiffer, 1999).

13. R. A. Noe, "Trainee Attributes and Attitudes: Neglected Influences on Training Effectiveness," *Academy of Management Review* 11 (1986): 736–49.

14. D. Milibank, "Marriott Tightens Job Program Screening," *Wall Street Journal* (July 15, 1997): A1, A12.

15. T. T. Baldwin, R. T. Magjuka, and B. T. Loher, "The Perils of Participation: Effects of Choice on Trainee Motivation and Learning," *Personnel Psychology* 44 (1991): 51–66; S. I. Tannenbaum, J. E. Mathieu, E. Salas, and J. A. Cannon-Bowers, "Meeting Trainees' Expectations: The Influence of Training Fulfillment on the Development of Commitment, Self-Efficacy, and Motivation," *Journal of Applied Psychology* 76 (1991): 759–69.

16. J. Nunally, *Psychometric Theory* (New York: McGraw-Hill, 1978).

17. L. Gottsfredson, "The g Factor in Employment," *Journal of Vocational Behavior* 19 (1986): 293–96.

18. M. J. Ree and J. A. Earles, "Predicting Training Success: Not Much More Than g," *Personnel Psychology* 44 (1991): 321–32.

19. D. R. Torrence and J. A. Torrence, "Training in the Face of Illiteracy," *Training and Development Journal* (August 1987): 44–49.

20. M. Davis, "Getting Workers Back to the Basics," *Training and Development* (October 1997): 14–15.

21. J. M. Rosow and R. Zager, *Training: The Competitive Edge* (San Francisco: Jossey-Bass, 1988), Chapter 7 ("Designing Training Programs to Train Functional Illiterates for New Technology").

22. A. P. Carnevale, L. J. Gainer, and A. S. Meltzer, *Workplace Basics Training Manual, 1990* (San Francisco: Jossey-Bass, 1990).

23. M. E. Gist, C. Schwoerer, and B. Rosen, "Effects of Alternative Training Methods on Self-Efficacy and Performance in Computer Software Training," *Journal of Applied Psychology* 74 (1990): 884–91; J. Martocchio and J. Dulebohn, "Performance Feedback Effects in Training: The Role of Perceived Controllability," *Personnel Psychology* 47 (1994): 357–73; J. Martocchio, "Ability Conceptions and Learning," *Journal of Applied Psychology* 79 (1994): 819–25.

24. R. A. Noe and N. Schmitt, "The Influence of Trainee Attitudes on Training Effectiveness: Test of a Model," *Personnel Psychology* 39 (1986): 497–523.

25. M. A. Quinones, "Pretraining Context Effects: Training Assignments as Feedback," *Journal of Applied Psychology* 80 (1995): 226–38; Baldwin, Magjuka, and Loher, "The Perils of Participation."

26. L. H. Peters, E. J. O'Connor, and J. R. Eulberg, "Situational Constraints: Sources, Consequences, and Future Considerations," in *Research in Personnel and Human Resource Management,* ed. K. M. Rowland and G. R. Ferris (Greenwich, CT: JAI Press, 1985), 3: 79–114; E. J. O'Connor, L. H. Peters, A. Pooyan, J. Weekley, B. Frank, and B. Erenkranz, "Situational Constraints Effects on Performance, Affective Reactions, and Turnover: A Field Replication and Extension," *Journal of Applied Psychology* 69 (1984): 663–72; D. J. Cohen, "What Motivates Trainees?" *Training and Development Journal* (November 1990): 91–93; J. S. Russell, J. R. Terborg, and M. L. Power, "Organizational Performance and Organizational Level Training and Support," *Personnel Psychology* 38 (1985): 849–63.

27. W. D. Hicks and R. J. Klimoski, "Entry into Training Programs and Its Effects on Training Outcomes: A Field Experiment," *Academy of Management Journal* 30 (1987): 542–52.

28. R. F. Mager and P. Pipe, *Analyzing Performance Problems: Or You Really Oughta Wanna,* 2d ed. (Belmont, CA: Pittman Learning, 1984); Carnevale, Gainer, and Meltzer, *Workplace Basics Training Manual;* Rummler, "In Search of the Holy Performance Grail"; C. Reinhart, "How to Leap over Barriers to Performance," *Training Development* (January 2000): 46–49.

29. C. E. Schneier, J. P. Guthrie and J. D. Olian, "A Practical Approach to Conducting and Using Training Needs Assessment," *Public Personnel Management* (Summer 1988): 191–205.

30. I. Goldstein, "Training in Organizations," in *Handbook of Industrial/Organizational Psychology,* 2d ed., ed. M. D. Dunnette and L. M. Hough (Palo Alto, CA: Consulting Psychologists Press, 1991), 2: 507–619.

31. E. F. Holton III and C. Bailey, "Top-to-Bottom Curriculum Redesign," *Training and Development* (March 1995): 40–44.

32. A. Reynolds, *The Trainer's Dictionary: HRD Terms, Abbreviations, and Acronyms* (HRD Press, 1993).

33. M. Dalton, "Are Competency Models a Waste?" *Training and Development* (October 1997): 46–49.

34. J. S. Shippmann, R. A. Ash, M. Battista, L. Carr, L. D. Eyde, B. Hesketh, J. Kehoe, K. Pearlman and J. I. Sanchez, "The Practice of Competency Modeling," *Personnel Psychology* 53 (2000): 703–40.

35. A. Lucia and R. Lepsinger, *The Art and Science of Competency Models* (San Francisco: Jossey-Bass, 1999).

36. J. Kochanski, "Competency-Based Management," *Training and Development* (October 1997): 41–44.

37. A. D. Lucia and R. Lepsinger, *The Art and Science of Competency Models* (San Francisco: Jossey-Bass, 1999).

38. J. Barbarian, "The Best-Laid Plans," *Training* (March 2003): 30–31.

39. K. Gupta, *A Practical Guide to Needs Assessment* (San Francisco: Jossey-Bass, 1999); and R. Zemke, "How to Do a Needs Assessment When You Don't Have the Time," *Training* (March 1998): 38–44.

Chapter **Four**

Learning: Theories and Program Design

Objectives

After reading this chapter, you should be able to

1. Discuss the five types of learner outcomes.

2. Explain the implications of learning theory for instructional design.

3. Incorporate adult learning theory into the design of a training program.

4. Describe how learners receive, process, store, retrieve, and act upon information.

5. Discuss the internal conditions (within the learner) and external conditions (learning environment) necessary for the trainee to learn each type of capability.

6. Be able to choose and prepare a training site.

7. Explain the four components of program design: course parameters, objectives, lesson overview, and detailed lesson plan.

A Positive Learning Environment Energizes Training

At Exelon Energy Delivery, based in Chicago, Illinois, training incorporates many of the features of a positive learning environment that ensure that training is successful. Exelon is the parent company of ComEd and PECO, energy distribution companies that bring electrical power to homes and industry. Creating a meaningful training environment and practice is an important part of training regardless of the type of job employees are performing. For example, for customer service training Exelon developed a human practice lab. Before starting to work in customer service, employees handle simulated telephone calls in a environment that is an exact replica of the customer service center. Employees are required to demonstrate customer service skills and are tested to make sure they have learned the training content. Another important part of helping trainees learn is ensuring that they have the prerequisite skills to complete the program. Exelon's Aerial Line School is a program designed to train employees in all aspects of an electrician's job, from climbing poles to maintaining electrical systems. Because of the physical strength requirement of the training and the job itself, the company developed a strength and conditioning program for newly hired employees. For two to three months before starting Aerial Line School, employees work with a personal trainer at the company's expense. As a result, new employees have been better able to handle the rigors of aerial training, and program dropout rates fell more than two-thirds, to 10 percent.

In addition to having job-related training that is based on principles of effective learning environments, Exelon also gives employees the opportunity to choose learning and development opportunities that meet their personal needs. All employees are encouraged to take advantage of learning opportunities that will prepare them for their careers. The company reimburses 100 percent of the tuition costs for employees taking degree-related courses. Every management employee completes an individual development plan that includes career aspirations and short-term goals.

Source: Based on J. Schettler, "Exelon Energy Delivery," *Training* (March 2003): 64.

INTRODUCTION

Training at Exelon Energy Delivery is designed to teach employees to successfully perform their jobs. Depending on the job, successful performance may be providing quality customer service or it may be climbing a pole to make repairs. These are examples of learning outcomes. Exelon's programs highlight a couple of conditions necessary for learning to occur: (1) opportunities for trainees to practice and (2) meaningful content. Also, Exelon demonstrates successful program design by identifying any prerequisites for completing the program (e.g., physical strength).

As the Exelon training illustrates, for learning to occur it is important to identify *what* is to be learned—that is, to identify learning outcomes. As a student you are probably most familiar with one type of learning outcome: intellectual skills. However, training programs often focus on other outcomes such as motor skills (e.g., climbing) and attitudes. Understanding learning outcomes is crucial because they influence the characteristics of the training environment that are necessary for learning to occur. These characteristics include using materials in training that are meaningful to the trainees, providing opportunities to practice, and receiving feedback. For example, if trainees are to master motor skills such as climbing a pole, they must have opportunities to practice climbing and receive feedback about their climbing skills.

Also, the design of the training program is important for learning to occur. This includes creating the program schedule, providing a physically comfortable training environment, and arranging the seating in the training environment to facilitate interaction among trainees and between trainer and trainees.

This chapter begins by defining learning and acquainting you with the different learning outcomes. Next is a discussion of various theories of learning and their implications for creating a learning environment designed to help the trainee learn the desired outcomes. The last section of the chapter looks at practical issues in training program design, including selecting and preparing a training site and developing lesson plans.

WHAT IS LEARNING? WHAT IS LEARNED?

Learning is a relatively permanent change in human capabilities that is not a result of growth processes.[1] These capabilities are related to specific learning outcomes, as Table 4.1 shows.

Verbal information includes names or labels, facts, and bodies of knowledge. Verbal information includes specialized knowledge that employees need in their jobs. For example, a manager must know the names of different types of equipment as well as the body of knowledge related to Total Quality Management.

Intellectual skills include concepts and rules. These concepts and rules are critical to solve problems, serve customers, and create products. For example, a manager must know the steps in the performance appraisal process (e.g., gather data, summarize data, prepare for appraisal interview with employee) in order to conduct an employee appraisal.

Motor skills include coordination of physical movements. For example, a telephone repair person must have the coordination and dexterity necessary to climb ladders and telephone poles.

Attitudes are a combination of beliefs and feelings that predispose a person to behave a certain way. Attitudes include a cognitive component (beliefs), an affective component (feeling), and an intentional component (the way a person intends to behave in regard to the subject of the attitude). Important work-related attitudes include job satisfaction, commitment to the organization, and job involvement. Suppose you say that an employee has a "positive attitude" toward her work. This means the person likes her job (the affective component). She may like her job because it is challenging and provides an opportunity to meet people (the cognitive component). Because she likes her job, she intends to stay with the company and do her best at work (the intentional component). Training programs may be used to develop or change attitudes because attitudes have been shown to be related to physical and mental withdrawal from work, turnover, and behaviors that impact the well-being of the company (e.g., helping new employees).

TABLE 4.1   **Learning Outcomes**

Type of Learning Outcome	Description of Capability	Example
Verbal Information	State, tell, or describe previously stored information	State three reasons for following company safety procedures
Intellectual Skills	Apply generalizable concepts and rules to solve problems and generate novel products	Design and code a computer program that meets customer requirements
Motor Skills	Execute a physical action with precision and timing	Shoot a gun and consistently hit a small moving target
Attitudes	Choose a personal course of action	Choose to respond to all incoming mail within 24 hours
Cognitive Strategies	Manage one's own thinking and learning processes	Selectively use three different strategies to diagnose engine malfunctions

Source: R. Gagne and K. Medsker, *The Conditions of Learning* (New York: Harcourt-Brace, 1996).

Cognitive strategies regulate the processes of learning. They relate to the learner's decision regarding what information to attend to (i.e., pay attention to), how to remember, and how to solve problems. For example, a physicist recalls the colors of the light spectrum through remembering the name "Roy G. Biv" (red, orange, yellow, green, blue, indigo, violet).

As this chapter points out, each learning outcome requires a different set of conditions for learning to occur. Before this chapter investigates the learning process in detail, it looks at the theories that help to explain how people learn.

LEARNING THEORIES

Several theories relate to how people learn. Each theory relates to different aspects of the learning process. Many of the theories also relate to trainees' motivation to learn, which was discussed in Chapter 3.

Reinforcement Theory

Reinforcement theory emphasizes that people are motivated to perform or avoid certain behaviors because of past outcomes that have resulted from those behaviors.[2] There are several processes in reinforcement theory. Positive reinforcement is a pleasurable outcome resulting from a behavior. Negative reinforcement is the removal of an unpleasant outcome. The process of withdrawing positive or negative reinforcers to eliminate a behavior is known as extinction. Punishment is presenting an unpleasant outcome after a behavior, leading to a decrease in that behavior.

From a training perspective, reinforcement theory suggests that for learners to acquire knowledge, change behavior, or modify skills, the trainer needs to identify what outcomes the learner finds most positive (and negative). Trainers then need to link these outcomes to learners acquiring knowledge, skills, or changing behaviors. As was mentioned in Chapter 3, learners can obtain several types of benefits from participating in training programs. The benefits may include learning an easier or more interesting way to perform their job (job-related), meeting other employees who can serve as resources when problems occur (personal), or increasing opportunities to consider new positions in the company (career-related). According to reinforcement theory, trainers can withhold or provide these benefits to learners who master program content. The effectiveness of learning depends on the pattern or schedule for providing these reinforcers or benefits. Schedules of reinforcement are shown in Table 4.2.

Behavior modification is a training method that is primarily based on reinforcement theory. For example, a training program in a bakery focused on eliminating unsafe behaviors such as climbing over conveyor belts (rather than walking around them) and sticking hands into equipment to dislodge jammed materials without turning off the equipment.[3] Employees were shown slides depicting safe and unsafe work behaviors. After viewing the slides, employees were shown a graph of the number of times safe behaviors were observed during past weeks. Employees were encouraged to increase the number of safe behaviors they demonstrated on the job. They were given several reasons for doing so: for their own protection, to decrease costs for the company, and to help their plant get out of last place in the safety rankings of the company's plants. Immediately after the training, safety reminders were posted in employees' work areas. Also, after training, data about the number of safe

TABLE 4.2   **Schedules of Reinforcement**

Type of Schedule	Description	Effectiveness
Ratio Schedules		
Fixed-Ratio Schedule	Reinforcement whenever target behavior has taken place a given number of times	Rapid learning; frequent instances of target behavior; rapid extinction
Continuous Reinforcement	Reinforcement after each occurrence of target behavior	Same direction of behavior as with fixed-ratio schedules but more extreme
Variable-Ratio Schedule	Reinforcement after several occurrences of target behavior: number of occurrences before reinforcement may differ each time	Target behavior less susceptible to extinction than with fixed-ratio schedules
Interval Schedules		
Fixed-Interval Schedule	Reinforcement at a given time interval after performance of target behavior	Lower performance of target behavior than with ratio schedules; lower effectiveness if time interval is long
Variable-Interval Schedule	Reinforcement occurring periodically after performance of target behavior; time intervals may differ each time	Target behavior less susceptible to extinction than with fixed-interval schedules; lower performance of target behavior than with ratio schedules

Source: P. Wright and R. A. Noe, *Management of Organizations* (Burr Ridge, IL: Irwin/McGraw-Hill, 1996).

behaviors performed by employees continued to be collected and displayed on the graph in the work area. Employees' supervisors were also instructed to recognize the workers whenever they saw them perform a safe work behavior. In this example, the data of safe behavior posted in the work areas and supervisors' recognition of safe work behavior represent positive reinforcers.

Social Learning Theory

Social learning theory emphasizes that people learn by observing other persons (models) whom they believe are credible and knowledgeable.[4] Social learning theory also recognizes that behavior that is reinforced or rewarded tends to be repeated. The models' behavior or skill that is rewarded is adopted by the observer. According to social learning theory, learning new skills or behaviors comes from (1) directly experiencing the consequences of using that behavior or skill, or (2) the process of observing others and seeing the consequences of their behavior.[5]

According to social learning theory, learning also is influenced by a person's self-efficacy. **Self-efficacy** is a person's judgment about whether he or she can successfully learn knowledge and skills. Chapter 3 emphasizes self-efficacy as an important factor to consider in the person analysis phase of needs assessment. Why? Self-efficacy is one determinant of readiness to learn. A trainee with high self-efficacy will put forth effort to learn in a training program and is most likely to persist in learning even if an environment is not conducive to learning (e.g., noisy training room). In contrast, a person with low self-efficacy will have self-doubts about mastering the content of a training program and is more likely to withdraw psychologically and/or physically (daydream or fail to attend the program).

FIGURE 4.1 Processes of social learning theory

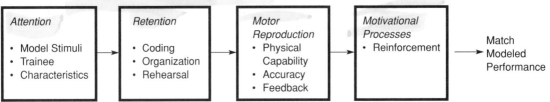

Source: Based on A. Bandura, *Social Foundations of Thoughts and Actions* (Englewood Cliffs, NJ: Prentice-Hall, 1986).

These persons believe that they are unable to learn, and regardless of their effort level, they will be unable to learn.

A person's self-efficacy can be increased using several methods: verbal persuasion, logical verification, observation of others (modeling), and past accomplishments.[6] **Verbal persuasion** means offering words of encouragement to convince others they can learn. **Logical verification** involves perceiving a relationship between a new task and a task already mastered. Trainers and managers can remind employees when they encounter learning difficulties that they have been successful at learning similar things. **Modeling** involves having employees who already have mastered the learning outcomes demonstrate them for trainees. As a result, employees are likely to be motivated by the confidence and success of their successful peers. **Past accomplishments** refers to allowing employees to build a history of successful accomplishments. Managers can place employees in situations where they are likely to succeed and provide training so that employees know what to do and how to do it.

Social learning theory suggests that four processes are involved in learning: attention, retention, motor reproduction, and motivational processes (see Figure 4.1).

Attention suggests that persons cannot learn by observation unless they are aware of the important aspects of a model's performance. Attention is influenced by characteristics of the model and the learner. Learners must be aware of the skills or behavior they are supposed to observe. The model must be clearly identified and credible. The learner must have the physical capability (sensory capability) to observe the model. Also, a learner who has successfully learned other skills or behavior by observing the model is more likely to attend to the model.

Learners must remember the behaviors or skills that they observe. This is the role of *retention*. Learners have to code the observed behavior and skills in memory in an organized manner so they can recall them for the appropriate situation. Behaviors or skills can be coded as visual images (symbols) or verbal statements.

Motor reproduction involves trying out the observed behaviors to see if they result in the same reinforcement that the model received. The ability to reproduce the behaviors or skills depends on the extent to which the learner can recall the skills or behavior. The learner must also have the physical capability to perform the behavior or exhibit the skill. For example, a firefighter can learn the behaviors necessary to carry a person away from a dangerous situation, but may be unable to demonstrate the behavior because he lacks upper body strength. Note that performance of behavior is usually not perfect on the first attempt. Learners must have the opportunity to practice and receive feedback to modify their behavior to be similar to the model's behavior.

Learners are more likely to adopt a modeled behavior if it results in positive outcomes. Social learning theory emphasizes that behaviors that are reinforced (a *motivational process*) will be repeated in the future. For example, a major source of conflict and stress for managers often relates to the performance appraisal interview. A manager may, through observing successful managers, learn behaviors that allow employees to be more participative in a performance appraisal interview (e.g., give employees the opportunity to voice their concerns). If the manager uses this behavior in the performance appraisal interview and the behavior is rewarded by employees (e.g., they make comments such as "I really felt the feedback meeting was the best we have ever had") or the new behavior leads to reduced conflicts with employees (e.g., negative reinforcement), the manager will more likely use this behavior in subsequent appraisal interviews.

As you will see in the discussion of training methods in Chapters 7 and 8, social learning theory is the primary basis for behavior modeling training and has influenced the development of multimedia training programs. For example, in the training program called "Getting Your Ideas Across," trainees are first presented with the five key behaviors for getting their ideas across: (1) state the point and purpose of the message, (2) present points to aid understanding, (3) check the audience for reactions and understanding, (4) handle reactions from the audience to what was presented, and (5) summarize the main point. The trainer provides a rationale for each key behavior. Next, trainees view a video of a business meeting in which a manager is having difficulty getting subordinates to accept his ideas regarding how to manage an impending office move. The manager, who is the model, is ineffective in getting his ideas across to his subordinates. As a result, the video shows that the subordinates are dissatisfied with the manager and his ideas. The video is turned off and the trainer leads the trainees in a discussion of what the manager did wrong in trying to get his ideas across. Trainees again view the video. But this time the manager, in the same situation, is shown using the key behaviors. As a result, subordinates react quite positively to their boss (the model). Following this video segment, the trainer leads a discussion of how the model used the key behaviors to successfully get his ideas across.

After observing the model and discussing the key behaviors, each trainee is paired with another trainee for practice. Each group is given a situation and message to communicate. The trainees take turns trying to get their ideas across to each other using the key behaviors. Each trainee is expected to provide feedback regarding the partner's use of the key behaviors. The trainer also observes and provides feedback to each group. Before leaving training, the trainees are given a pocket-size card with the key behaviors, which they take back with them to the job. Also, they complete a planning guide in which they describe a situation where they want to use the key behaviors and how they plan to use them.

Goal Theories

Goal Setting Theory

Goal setting theory assumes that behavior results from a person's conscious goals and intentions.[7] Goals influence behavior by directing energy and attention, sustaining effort over time, and motivating the person to develop strategies for goal attainment.[8] Research suggests that specific challenging goals result in better performance than vague, unchallenging goals.[9] Goals have been shown to lead to high performance only if people are committed to the goal. Employees are less likely to be committed to a goal if they believe it is too difficult.

An example of how goal setting theory influences training methods is seen in a program designed to improve pizza deliverers' driving practices.[10] The majority of pizza deliverers are young (age 18 to 24), inexperienced drivers, who are compensated based on the number of pizzas they can deliver. This created a situation where deliverers are rewarded for fast but unsafe driving practices—for example, not wearing a safety belt, failing to use turn signals, and not coming to complete stops at intersections. These unsafe practices have resulted in a high driving accident rate.

Prior to goal setting, pizza deliverers were observed by their managers leaving the store and then returning from deliveries. The managers observed the number of complete stops at intersections over a one-week period. In the training session, managers and trainers presented the deliverers with a series of questions for discussion. Here are examples: In what situations should you come to a complete stop? What are the reasons for coming to a complete stop? What are the reasons for not coming to a complete stop?

After the discussion, pizza deliverers were asked to agree on the need to come to a complete stop at intersections. Following the deliverers' agreement, the managers shared the data they collected regarding the number of complete stops at intersections they had observed the previous week. (Complete stops were made 55 percent of the time.) The trainer asked the pizza deliverers to set a goal for complete stopping over the next month. They decided on a goal of 75 percent complete stops.

After the goal setting session, managers at each store continued observing their drivers' intersection stops. The following month in the work area, a poster showed the percentages of complete stops for every four-day period. The current percentage of total complete stops was also displayed.

Goal setting theory also is used in training program design. Goal setting theory suggests that learning can be facilitated by providing trainees with specific challenging goals and objectives. Specifically, the influence of goal setting theory can be seen in the development of training lesson plans. As explained later in the chapter, these lesson plans begin with specific goals providing information regarding the expected action that the learner will demonstrate, conditions under which learning will occur, and the level of performance that will be judged acceptable.

Goal Orientation

Goal orientation refers to the goals held by a trainee in a learning situation. Goal orientation can include a mastery orientation or a performance orientation. **Mastery orientation** relates to trying to increase ability or competence in a task. People with a mastery orientation believe that training success is defined as showing improvement and making progress, prefer trainers who are more interested in how trainees are learning than in how they are performing, and view errors and mistakes as part of the learning process. **Performance orientation** refers to a focus of learners on task performance and how they compare to others. Persons with a performance orientation define success as high performance relative to others, value high ability more than learning, and find that errors and mistakes cause anxiety and want to avoid them.

Goal orientation is believed to affect the amount of effort a trainee will expend in learning (motivation to learn). Learners with a high mastery orientation will direct greater attention to the task and learn for the sake of learning in comparison to learners with a performance orientation. Learners with a performance orientation will direct more attention to performing well and less effort to learning. Research has shown that trainees with a learning orientation exert greater effort to learn and use more complex learning strategies than trainees with a performance orientation.[11]

Need Theories

Need theories help to explain the value that a person places on certain outcomes. A **need** is a deficiency that a person is experiencing at any point in time. A need motivates a person to behave in a manner to satisfy the deficiency. Maslow's and Alderfer's need theories focused on physiological needs, relatedness needs (needs to interact with other persons), and growth needs (self-esteem, self-actualization).[12] Both Maslow and Alderfer believed that persons start by trying to satisfy needs at the lowest level, then progress up the hierarchy as lower-level needs are satisfied. That is, if physiological needs are not met, a person's behavior will focus first on satisfying these needs before relatedness or growth needs receive attention. The major difference between Alderfer's and Maslow's hierarchies of needs is that Alderfer allows the possibility that if higher-level needs are not satisfied, employees will refocus on lower-level needs.

McClelland's need theory focused primarily on needs for achievement, affiliation, and power.[13] According to McClelland, these needs can be learned. Need for achievement relates to a concern for attaining and maintaining self-set standards of excellence. Need for affiliation involves concern for building and maintaining relationships with other people and for being accepted by others. The need for power is a concern for obtaining responsibility, influence, and reputation.

Need theories suggest that to motivate learning, trainers should identify trainees' needs and communicate how training program content relates to fulfilling these needs. Also, if certain basic needs of trainees (e.g., physiological and safety needs) are not met, they are unlikely to be motivated to learn. For example, consider a word processing training class for secretaries in a downsizing company. It is doubtful that even the best designed training class will result in learning if employees believe their job security is threatened (unmet need for security) by the company's downsizing strategy. Also, it is unlikely the secretaries will be motivated to learn if they believe that word processing skills emphasized in the program cannot help them keep their current employment or increase their chances that they can find another job inside or outside the company.

Another implication of need theory relates to providing employees with a choice of training programs to attend. As Chapter 3 mentioned, giving employees a choice of which training course to attend can increase their motivation to learn. This occurs because trainees are able to choose programs that best match their needs.

Expectancy Theory

Expectancy theory suggests that a person's behavior is based on three factors: expectancy, instrumentality, and valence.[14] Beliefs about the link between trying to perform a behavior and actually performing well are called **expectancies.** Expectancy is similar to self-efficacy. In expectancy theory, a belief that performing a given behavior (e.g., attending a training program) is associated with a particular outcome (e.g., being able to better perform your job) is called **instrumentality. Valence** is the value that a person places on an outcome (e.g., how important it is to perform better on the job).

FIGURE 4.2 Expectancy theory of motivation

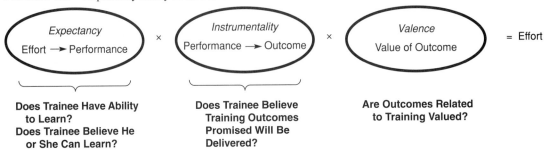

According to expectancy theory, various choices of behavior are evaluated according to their expectancy, instrumentality, and valence. Figure 4.2 shows how behavior is determined based on finding the mathematical product of expectancy, instrumentality, and valence. People choose the behavior with the highest value.

From a training perspective, expectancy theory suggests that learning is most likely to occur when employees believe they can learn the content of the program (expectancy); learning is linked to outcomes such as better job performance, a salary increase; or peer recognition (instrumentality); and employees value these outcomes.

Adult Learning Theory

Adult learning theory was developed out of a need for a specific theory of how adults learn. Most educational theories as well as formal educational institutions were developed exclusively to educate children and youth. Pedagogy, the art and science of teaching children, dominated educational theory. Pedagogy gives the instructor major responsibility for making decisions about learning content, method, and evaluation. Students are generally seen as (1) being passive recipients of directions and content and (2) bringing few experiences that may serve as resources to the learning environment.[15]

Educational psychologists, recognizing the limitations of formal education theories, developed **andragogy,** the theory of adult learning. Malcolm Knowles is most frequently associated with adult learning theory. This model is based on several assumptions:[16]

1. Adults have the need to know why they are learning something.
2. Adults have a need to be self-directed.
3. Adults bring more work-related experiences into the learning situation.
4. Adults enter into a learning experience with a problem-centered approach to learning.
5. Adults are motivated to learn by both extrinsic and intrinsic motivators.

Adult learning theory is especially important to consider in developing training programs because the audience for many such programs tends to be adults, most of whom have not spent a majority of their time in a formal education setting. Table 4.3 shows implications of adult learning theory for learning. For example, many adults are intimidated by math and finance.[17] In a day-long seminar to teach basic accounting principles, the course designers considered the trainees' readiness. They created a program filled with fun and music, in which participants start their own lemonade stand. This reduced trainees' anxiety, which

TABLE 4.3
Implications of Adult Learning Theory for Training

Source: Based on M. Knowles, *The Adult Learner,* 4th ed. (Houston, TX: Gulf Publishing, 1990).

Design Issue	Implications
Self-Concept	Mutual planning and collaboration in instruction
Experience	Use learner experience as basis for examples and applications
Readiness	Develop instruction based on the learner's interests and competencies
Time Perspective	Immediate application of content
Orientation to Learning	Problem-centered instead of subject-centered

could have inhibited their learning. Many adults believe that they learn through experience. As a result, trainers need to provide opportunities for trainees to experience something new and discuss it or review training materials based on their experiences.

Note that a common theme in these applications is mutuality. That is, the learner and the trainer are both involved in creating the learning experience and making sure that learning occurs.

Information Processing Theory

Compared to other learning theories, information processing theories give more emphasis to the internal processes that occur when training content is learned and retained. Figure 4.3 shows a model of information processing. Information processing theories propose that information or messages taken in by the learner undergo several transformations in the human brain.[18] Information processing begins when a message or stimuli (which could be sound, smell, touch, or pictures) from the environment is received by receptors (ears, nose, skin, eyes). The message is registered in the senses and stored in short-term memory. The message is then transformed or coded for storage in long-term memory. A search process occurs in memory during which time a response to the message or stimulus is organized. The response generated relates to one of the five learning outcomes: verbal information, cognitive skills, motor skills, intellectual skills, or attitudes. The final link in the model is feedback from the environment. This feedback provides the learner with an evaluation of the response given. This information can come from another person or the learner's own observation of the results of his or her action. A positive evaluation of the response provides reinforcement that the behavior is desirable to be stored in long-term memory for use in similar situations.

FIGURE 4.3
A model of human information processing

Source: Adapted from R. Gagne, "Learning Processes and Instruction, *Training Research Journal* 1 (1995/96):17–28.

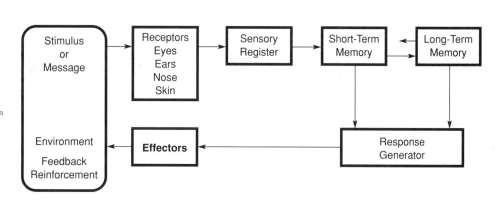

Besides emphasizing the internal processes needed to capture, store, retrieve, and respond to messages, the information processing model highlights how external events influence learning. These events include[19]

1. Changes in the intensity or frequency of the stimulus that affect attention.
2. Informing the learner of the objectives to establish an expectation.
3. Enhancing perceptual features of the material (stimulus), drawing the attention of the learner to certain features.
4. Verbal instructions, pictures, diagrams, and maps suggesting ways to code the training content so that it can be stored in memory.
5. Meaningful learning context (examples, problems) creating cues that facilitate coding.
6. Demonstration or verbal instructions helping to organize the learner's response as well as facilitating the selection of the correct response.

THE LEARNING PROCESS

Now that you have reviewed learning theories, you are ready to address three questions: What are the physical and mental processes involved in learning? How does learning occur? Do trainees have different learning styles?

Mental and Physical Processes

Figure 4.4 shows the learning processes. These processes include expectancy, perception, working storage, semantic encoding, long-term storage, retrieval, generalizing, and gratification.[20] **Expectancy** refers to the mental state that the learner brings to the instructional process. This includes factors such as readiness for training (motivation to learn, basic skills) as well as an understanding of the purpose of the instruction and the likely benefits that may result from learning and using the learned capabilities on the job. **Perception** refers to the ability to organize the message from the environment so that it can be processed and acted upon. Both working storage and semantic encoding relate to short-term memory. In **working storage,** rehearsal and repetition of information occur, allowing material to be coded for memory.

Working storage is limited by the amount of material that can be processed at any one time. Research suggests that not more than five messages can be prepared for storage at any one time. **Semantic encoding** refers to the actual coding process of incoming messages.

Different learning strategies influence how training content is coded. Learning strategies include rehearsal, organizing, and elaboration.[21] **Rehearsal,** the simplest learning strategy, focuses on learning through repetition (memorization). **Organizing** requires the learner to find similarities and themes in the training material. **Elaboration** requires the trainee to relate the training material to other more familiar knowledge, skills, or behaviors. Trainees use a combination of these strategies to learn. The "best" strategy depends on the learning outcome. For knowledge outcomes, rehearsal and organization are most appropriate. For skill application, elaboration is necessary. After messages have been attended to, rehearsed, and coded, they are ready for storage in long-term memory.

FIGURE 4.4   The relationship between learning processes, instructional events, and forms of instruction

Processes of Learning	External Instructional Events	Forms of Instruction
1. Expectancy	1. Informing the learner of the lesson objective	1a. Demonstrate the expected performance. 1b. Indicate the kind of verbal question to be answered.
2. Perception	2. Presenting stimuli with distinctive features	2a. Emphasize the features of the subject to be perceived. 2b. Use formatting and figures in text to emphasize features.
3. Working Storage	3. Limiting the amount to be learned	3a. Chunk lengthier material. 3b. Provide a visual image of material to be learned. 3c. Provide practice and overlearning to aid the attainment of automaticity.
4. Semantic Encoding	4. Providing learning guidance	4a. Provide verbal cues to proper combining sequence. 4b. Provide verbal links to a larger meaningful context. 4c. Use diagrams and models to show relationships among concepts.
5. Long-Term Storage	5. Elaborating the amount to be learned	5a. Vary the context and setting for presentation and recall of material. 5b. Relate newly learned material to previously learned information. 5c. Provide a variety of contexts and situations during practice.
6. Retrieval	6. Providing cues that are used in recall	6a. Suggest cues that elicit the recall of material. 6b. Use familiar sounds or rhymes as cues.
7. Generalizing	7. Enhancing retention and learning transfer	7a. Design the learning situation to share elements with the situation of use. 7b. Provide verbal links to additional complexes of information.
8. Gratifying	8. Providing feedback about performance correctness	8a. Provide feedback on degree of accuracy and timing of performance. 8b. Confirm whether original expectancies were met.

Source: R. Gagne, "Learning Processes and Instruction," *Training Research Journal* 1 (1995/96): 17–28.

To use learned material (e.g., cognitive skills, verbal information), it must be retrieved. **Retrieval** involves identifying learned material in long-term memory and using it to influence performance. An important part of the learning process is not only being able to reproduce exactly what was learned but also being able to adapt the learning to use in similar but not identical situations. This is known as **generalizing.** Finally, **gratifying** refers to the feedback that the learner receives as a result of using learning content. Feedback is necessary to allow the learner to adapt responses to be more appropriate. Feedback also provides information about the incentives or reinforcers that may result from performance.

The Learning Cycle

Learning can be considered a dynamic cycle that involves four stages: concrete experience, reflective observation, abstract conceptualization, and active experimentation.[22] First, a trainee encounters a concrete experience (e.g., a work problem). This is followed by thinking and reflective observation about the problem, which leads to generation of ideas of how to solve the problem (abstract conceptualization) and finally to implementation of the ideas directly to the problem (active experimentation). Implementing the ideas provides feedback as to their effectiveness, so the learner can see the results of their action and start the learning process over again. Trainees continually develop concepts, translate them into ideas, implement them, and adapt them as a result of their personal observations about their experiences.

Researchers have developed questionnaires to measure trainees' weak and strong points in the learning cycle. Some people have a tendency to over- or underemphasize one stage of the learning cycle or to avoid certain stages. The key to effective learning is to be competent in each of the four stages. Four fundamental learning styles are believed to exist. These learning styles combine elements of each of the four stages of the learning cycle. Table 4.4 shows the characteristics and dominant learning stage of these styles, called Divergers, Assimilators, Convergers, and Accommodators.[23] Although the questionnaires have been widely used as part of training programs, few studies have investigated the reliability and validity of the learning styles.

Trainers who are aware of trainees' learning styles can try to customize instruction to match their preferences. If a group of trainees tend to be hands-on learners, trying to teach mechanics of a technical application online by having them read it will not result in learning. They need applications and the ability to get feedback from an instructor. (Effective online learning is discussed in Chapter 8.)

For example, AmeriCredit, an auto finance company located in Fort Worth, Texas, is trying to modify training to better match employees' learning styles.[24] The company has created a database to identify and track each employee's learning style. Also, employees' learning styles are being considered in course design. In a new e-learning class, employees who prefer learning by action will receive information in bullet points and complete activities that help them learn. Employees who prefer thought and reasoning will receive more conceptual material during the course and be involved in fewer experiences. The company plans to compare the new e-learning class that takes into account learning styles with one that does not to determine whether the adaptation to learning styles makes a difference in trainee satisfaction and learning.

Age Influences on Learning

There is biological evidence that certain mental capacities decrease from age 20 to age 70.[25] Short-term memory and the speed at which people process information decline as we age. However, with age comes experience, which can compensate for the loss of memory and mental quickness. Although mental quickness and memory losses diminish at a steady pace, at older ages the memory loss is much greater because mental resources are more depleted than at earlier ages. Some trainers believe that there are four generations of employees with distinct attitudes toward work and preferred ways to learn. Those generations have been called millenniums (or nexters), Gen Xers, baby boomers, and traditionalists.

But note that members of the same generation are no more alike than members of the same gender or race. Each generation may be characterized by certain characteristics that

TABLE 4.4   **Learning Styles**

Learning Style Type	Dominant Learning Abilities	Learning Characteristics
Diverger	• Concrete experience • Reflective observation	• Is good at generating ideas, seeing a situation from multiple perspectives, and being aware of meaning and value • Tends to be interested in people, culture, and the arts
Assimilator	• Abstract conceptualization • Reflective observation	• Is good at inductive reasoning, creating theoretical models, and combining disparate observations into an integrated explanation • Tends to be less concerned with people than ideas and abstract concepts
Converger	• Abstract conceptualization • Active experimentation	• Is good at decisiveness, practical application of ideas, and hypothetical deductive reasoning • Prefers dealing with technical tasks rather than interpersonal issues
Accommodator	• Concrete experience • Active experimentation	• Is good at implementing decisions, carrying out plans, and getting involved in new experiences • Tends to be at ease with people but may be seen as impatient or pushy

Source: Based on D. Kolb Learning Style Inventory version 3 (Boston, MA: Hay/McBer Training Resources Group, 1999).

can influence learning. Also note that there has been no research that follows different generations of employees over their life spans to identify differences. Trainers should consider generational differences in designing learning environments but keep in mind that definite conclusions regarding generational differences cannot be made.

The terms **millenniums** and **nexters** refer to people born after 1980. They are optimistic, willing to work and learn, and technology-literate; they appreciate diversity. The term **Gen Xers** refers to people born from 1961 to 1980. Gen Xers need feedback and flexibility; they dislike close supervision. They have experienced change all their lives (in terms of parents, homes, and cities). Gen Xers value a balance between work and nonwork. **Baby boomers** are people born between 1945 and 1960. They are competitive, hard working, and concerned that all employees be fairly treated. **Traditionalists** are people born between 1920 and 1944. They are patriotic and loyal, and they have a great deal of knowledge of the history of organizations and work life. Each generation may have specific preferences for the arrangement of the learning environment, type of instruction, and learning activities.[26] (Chapter 11 discusses implications of generational differences for career management.)

Traditionalists prefer a traditional training room with a stable, orderly learning environment. They do not like to be put on the spot in front of other trainees. They value direct presentation of information and training materials organized logically. They like trainers to ask them to share their experiences or anecdotes. But they also look to the trainer to provide expertise.

Baby boomers respond well to interactive training activities—they like group activities. They like well-organized training materials with an overview of the information and an easy way to access more detailed information. Compared to the other groups, they are especially motivated to learn if they believe training content will benefit them personally. Baby boomers need to work on translating the knowledge they have into skills.

Gen Xers prefer a self-directed learning environment. They respond best to training methods that allow them to work at their own pace: videos, CD-ROMs, and Web-based training. Gen Xers are highly motivated learners who view training as a way to increase their employability. They like to learn by doing, through experimentation and feedback. They respond best to training materials that provide visual stimulation with relatively few words.

Nexters prefer a learning environment that includes teamwork and technology. They like to learn by both working alone and helping others. They are motivated to learn skills and acquire knowledge that will help make their working lives less stressful and increase their employability. They place a high value on money so linking training to monetary incentives may facilitate learning. Nexters (like Gen Xers) prefer entertaining training activities. Training needs to be interactive and to utilize music, art, and games.

The potential for generational differences to affect learning suggests that trainers need to be aware of trainees' ages before the session so they can try to create a learning environment and develop materials that meet their preferences. Most training groups probably have a mix of generations. Employees can learn much from cross-generation interaction if it is managed well. Trainees of all age groups need to feel that participation in the session through questioning, providing answers, and discussing issues is valued and rewarded. If a group of trainees includes all generations, it must take a blended approach—use examples that include people from different generations and use different training approaches (experts, audience involvement, group work, self-directed learning activities).

Implications of the Learning Process for Instruction

Instruction refers to the characteristics of the environment in which learning is to occur.[27] The right side of Figure 4.4 shows the forms of instruction that support the learning process. These forms of instruction can also be considered features of a positive learning environment or good instruction. Subsequent sections discuss the features of good instruction.

Employees Need to Know Why They Should Learn

Employees learn best when they understand the objective of the training program. The **objective** refers to the purpose and expected outcome of training activities. There may be objectives for each training session as well as overall objectives for the program. Training objectives based on the training needs analysis help employees understand why they need training. Objectives are also useful for identifying the types of training outcomes that should be measured to evaluate a training program's effectiveness.

A training objective has three components:[28]

1. A statement of what the employee is expected to do (performance or outcome).

2. A statement of the quality or level of performance that is acceptable (criterion).

3. A statement of the conditions under which the trainee is expected to perform the desired outcome (conditions).

The objective should not describe performance that cannot be observed, such as "understand" or "know." Table 4.5 shows verbs that can be used for cognitive, affective, and psychomotor (physical abilities and skills) outcomes.

TABLE 4.5   **Examples of Performance or Outcomes for Objectives**

Domain	Performance
Knowledge (recall of information)	Arrange, define, label, list, recall, repeat
Comprehension (interpret in own words)	Classify, discuss, explain, review, translate
Application (apply to new situation)	Apply, choose, demonstrate, illustrate, prepare
Analysis (break down into parts and show relationships)	Analyze, categorize, compare, diagram, test
Synthesis (bring together to form a whole)	Arrange, collect, assemble, propose, set up
Evaluation (judgments based on criteria)	Appraise, attack, argue, choose, compare
Receiving (pay attention)	Listen to, perceive, be alert to
Responding (minimal participation)	Reply, answer, approve, obey
Valuing (preferences)	Attain, assume, support, participate
Organization (development of values)	Judge, decide, identify with, select
Characterization (total philosophy of life)	Believe, practice, carry out
Reflexes (involuntary movement)	Stiffen, extend, flex
Fundamental Movements (simple movements)	Crawl, walk, run, reach
Perception (response to stimuli)	Turn, bend, balance, crawl
Physical Abilities (psychomotor movements)	Move heavy objects, make quick motions
Skilled Movements (advanced learned movements)	Play an instrument, use a hand tool

Source: Based on H. Sredl and W. Rothwell, "Setting Instructional Objectives," Chapter 16 in *The ASTD Reference Guide to Professional Training Roles and Competencies, Vol. II* (New York: Random House, 1987); and Robert Mager, *Preparing Instructional Objectives,* 3rd ed. (Atlanta, GA: Center for Effective Performance, 1997).

For example, a training objective for a customer-service training program for retail salespeople might be "After training, the employee will be able to express concern [performance] to all irate customers by a brief (fewer than 10 words) apology, only after the customer has stopped talking [criteria] and no matter how upset the customer is [conditions]."

Good training objectives provide a clear idea of what the trainees are expected to do at the end of training. Good training should include standards of satisfactory performance that can be measured or evaluated (e.g., speed, quality, products, reactions). The program needs to spell out any resources (equipment, tools) that the trainees need in order to perform the action or behavior specified in the objective. Good training objectives also describe the conditions under which performance of the objective is expected to occur. These conditions can relate to the physical work setting (e.g., at night), mental stresses (e.g., an angry customer), or equipment failure (e.g., malfunctioning landing gear on an airplane).

Employees Need Meaningful Training Content

Employees are most likely to learn when the training is linked to their current job experiences and tasks—that is, when it is meaningful to them.[29] To enhance the meaningfulness of training content, the message should be presented using concepts, terms, and examples familiar to trainees. Also, the training context should mirror the work environment. The **training context** refers to the physical, intellectual, and emotional environment in which training occurs. For example, in a retail salesperson customer-service program, the meaningfulness of the material will be increased by using scenarios of unhappy customers actually encountered by salespersons in stores. Recent research indicates that learning can be enhanced not just by linking training to current job experiences but also by providing trainees with the opportunity to choose their practice strategy and other characteristics of the learning environment.[30]

Employees Need Opportunities to Practice

Practice refers to the physical or mental rehearsal of a task, knowledge, or skill to achieve proficiency in performing the task or skill or demonstrating the knowledge. Practice involves having the employee demonstrate the learned capability (e.g., cognitive strategy, verbal information) emphasized in the training objectives under conditions and performance standards specified by the objectives. For practice to be effective, it needs to actively involve the trainee, include overlearning (repeated practice), take the appropriate amount of time, and include the appropriate unit of learning (amount of material). Practice also needs to be relevant to the training objectives. Some examples of ways to practice include case studies, simulations, role plays, games, and oral and written questions.

Pre-practice Conditions   There are several things that trainers can do within the training course prior to practice to enhance trainees' motivation to learn and facilitate retention of training content. Before practice, trainers can[31]

1. Provide information about the process or strategy that will result in the greatest learning. For example, let trainees in a customer service class know about the types of calls they will receive (irate customer, request for information on a product, challenge of a bill), how to recognize such calls, and how to complete the calls.

2. Encourage trainees to develop a strategy **(metacognition)** to reflect on their own learning process. (Why am I choosing this type of action? Do I understand the relationship between this material and my job? What is the next step in the task?) Metacognition helps trainees monitor learning and decide what content needs more energy and attention.

3. Provide **advance organizers**—outlines, texts, diagrams, and graphs that help trainees organize the information that will be presented and practiced.

4. Help trainees set challenging mastery or learning goals.

5. Create realistic expectations for the trainees by communicating what will occur in training.

6. When training employees in teams, communicate performance expectations and clarify roles and responsibilities of team members.

Practice Involves Experience   Learning will not occur if employees practice only by talking about what they are expected to do. For example, using the objective for the customer service course previously discussed, practice would involve having trainees participate in role playing with unhappy customers (customers upset with poor service, poor merchandise, or exchange policies). Trainees need to continue to practice even if they have been able to perform the objective several times **(overlearning).** Overlearning helps the trainee become more comfortable using new knowledge and skills and increases the length of time the trainee will retain the knowledge, skill, or behavior.

Massed versus Spaced Practice   The frequency of practice has been shown to influence learning, depending on the type of task being trained.[32] **Massed practice** conditions are those in which individuals practice a task continuously without rest. In **spaced practice** conditions, individuals are given rest intervals within the practice session. Spaced practice is superior to massed practice. However, the effectiveness of massed versus spaced practice varies by the characteristics of the task. Task characteristics include overall task complexity, mental requirements, and physical requirements. **Overall task complexity** refers to the degree to which a task requires a number of distinct behaviors, the number of choices

TABLE 4.6 Mental, Overall, and Physical Requirements for Tasks

Mental Requirements	Overall Complexity	Physical Requirements	Tasks
Low	Low	High	Rotary pursuit, typing, ball toss, ladder climb, peg reversal, bilateral transfer, crank turning
High	Average	Low	Free recall task, video games, foreign language, slide bar task, voice recognition, classroom lecture, sound localization, word processing, stoop task, verbal discrimination, maze learning, connecting numbers, upside down alphabet printing, distance learning, Web training
Low	High	High	Gymnastic skills, balancing task
High	High	High	Air traffic controller simulation, milk pasteurization simulation, airplane control simulation, hand movement memorization, puzzle box task, music memorization and performance

Source: J. Donovan and D. Radosevich, "A Meta-analytic Review of the Distribution of Practice Effect: Now You See It, Now You Don't," *Journal of Applied Psychology* 84 (1999):795–805.

involved in performing the task, and the degree of uncertainty in performing the task. **Mental requirements** refer to the degree to which the task requires the subject to use or demonstrate mental skills or cognitive skills or abilities to perform the task. **Physical requirements** refer to the degree to which the task requires the person to use or demonstrate physical skills and abilities to perform and complete the task. Table 4.6 shows how tasks can differ.

For more complex tasks (including those that are representative of training settings such as Web-based instruction, lecture, and distance learning), relatively long rest periods appear to be beneficial for task learning.

After practice, trainees need specific feedback to enhance learning. This includes feedback from the task or job itself, trainers, managers, and peers.

Whole versus Part Practice A final issue related to practice is how much of the training should be practiced at one time. One option is that all tasks or objectives should be practiced at the same time **(whole practice).** Another option is that an objective or task should be practiced individually as soon as each is introduced in the training program **(part practice).** It is probably best to employ both whole and part practice in a training session. Trainees should have the opportunity to practice individual skills or behaviors. If the skills or behaviors introduced in training are related to one another, the trainee should demonstrate all of them in a practice session after they are practiced individually.

For example, one objective of the customer service training for retail salespeople is learning how to deal with an unhappy customer. Salespeople are likely to have to learn three key behaviors: (1) greeting disgruntled customers, (2) understanding their complaints, and then (3) identifying and taking appropriate action. Practice sessions should be held for each of the three behaviors (part practice). Then another practice session should be held so that trainees can practice all three skills together (whole practice). If trainees were only given the opportunity to practice the behaviors individually, it is unlikely that they would be able to deal with an unhappy customer.

Effective Practice Conditions For practice to be relevant to the training objectives, several conditions must be met.[33] Practice must involve the actions emphasized in the training objectives, be completed under the conditions specified in the training objectives, help trainees perform to meet the criteria or standard that was set, provide some means to evaluate the extent to which trainees' performance meets the standards, and allow trainees to correct their mistakes.

Practice must be related to the training objectives. The trainer should identify what trainees will be doing when practicing the objectives (performance), the criteria for attainment of the objective, and the conditions under which they may perform. These conditions should be present in the practice session. Next, the trainer needs to consider the adequacy of the trainees' performance. That is, how will trainees know whether their performance meets performance standards? Will they see a model of desired performance? Will they be provided with a checklist or description of desired performance? Can the trainees decide if their performance meets standards, or will the trainer or a piece of equipment compare their performance with standards?

The trainer must also decide—if trainees' performance does not meet standards—whether trainees understand what is wrong and how to fix it. That is, trainers need to consider if trainees can diagnose their performance and take corrective action or if they will need help from the trainer or a fellow trainee.

Employees Need to Commit Training Content to Memory

Memory works by processing stimuli we perceive through our senses into short-term memory. If the information is determined to be "important," it moves to long-term memory where new interconnections are made between neurons or electrical connections in the brain. There are several things that trainers can do to help employees store knowledge, skills, behavior, and other training in long-term memory.[34] One way is to make trainees aware of how they are creating, processing, and accessing memory. It is important for trainees to understand how they learn. A discussion of learning styles (discussed earlier) can be a useful way to determine the ways that trainees prefer to learn.

To create long-term memory it is important to be explicit on content and elaborate on details. There are several ways to create long-term memory. One approach trainers use is to create a concept map to show relationships among ideas. Another is to use multiple forms of review including writing, drawings, and role plays to access memory through multiple methods. Teaching key words, a procedure, or a sequence, or providing a visual image gives trainees another way to retrieve information. Reminding trainees of knowledge, behavior, and skills that they already know that are relevant to the current training content creates a link to long-term memory that provides a framework for recalling the new training content. External retrieval cues can also be useful. Consider a time when you misplaced your keys or wallet. In trying to remember, we often review all of the information we can recall that was close in time to the event or preceded the loss. We often go to the place where we were when we last saw the item because the environment can provide cues that aid in recall.

Research suggests that no more than four or five items can be attended to at one time. If a lengthy process or procedure is to be taught, instruction needs to be delivered in relatively small chunks or short sessions in order to not exceed memory limits.[35] Long-term memory is also enhanced by going beyond one-trial learning. That is, often once trainees correctly demonstrate a behavior or skill or correctly recall knowledge, it is assumed that they have learned it. However, that is often not the case. Making trainees review and practice over multiple days (overlearning) can help retain information in long-term memory. Overlearning also helps to automize a task.

Automatization refers to making performance of a task, recall of knowledge, or demonstration of a skill so automatic that it requires little thought or attention. Automatization also helps to reduce memory demands. The more automatization occurs, the more memory is freed up to concentrate on other learning and thinking. The more active a trainee is in rehearsal and practice, the greater the amount of information retained in long-term memory and the less memory decay occurs over time.

Employees Need Feedback

Feedback is information about how well people are meeting the training objectives. To be effective, feedback should focus on specific behaviors and be provided as soon as possible after the trainees' behavior.[36] Also, positive trainee behavior should be verbally praised or reinforced. Videotape is a powerful tool for giving feedback. Trainers should view the videotape with trainees, provide specific information about how behaviors need to be modified, and praise trainee behaviors that meet objectives. Feedback can also come from tests and quizzes, on-the-job observation, performance data, a mentor or coach, written communications, or interpersonal interactions.

Employees Learn through Observation, Experience, and Interacting with Others

As mentioned earlier in the chapter, one way employees learn is through observing and imitating the actions of models. For the model to be effective, the desired behaviors or skills need to be clearly specified and the model should have characteristics (e.g., age or position) similar to the target audience.[37] After observing the model, trainees should have the opportunity to reproduce the skills or behavior shown by the model in practice sessions. According to adult learning theory, employees also learn best if they learn by doing.[38] This involves giving employees hands-on experiences or putting them with more experienced employees and providing them with the tools and materials needed to manage their knowledge gaps. Learning also occurs through interacting with other trainees in small groups during the training session as well as back at work. By working in small groups, trainees can obtain diverse perspectives on problems and issues, perspectives they would never hear if they learned alone.

Communities of practice refer to groups of employees who work together, learn from each other, and develop a common understanding of how to get work accomplished.[39] The idea of communities of practice suggests that learning occurs on the job as a result of social interaction.

Communities of practice also take the form of discussion boards, list servers, or other forms of computer-mediated communication in which employees communicate electronically. In doing so, each employee's knowledge can be accessed in a relatively quick manner. It is as if employees are having a conversation with a group of experts. Every company has naturally occurring communities of practice that arise as a result of relationships employees develop to accomplish work and as a result of the design of the work environment. For example, at Siemens Power Transmission in Wendell, North Carolina, managers were wondering how to stop employees from gathering in the employee cafeteria for informal discussions.[40]

But that was before the managers discovered that the informal discussions actually encouraged learning. In the discussions, employees were developing problem-solving strategies, sharing product and procedural information, and providing career counseling to each other. Now Siemens is placing pads of paper and overhead projectors in the lunchroom as aids for informal meetings. Managers who were previously focused on keeping workers on the job are now encouraging employees by providing essential tools and information and giving employees the freedom to meet.

Websites can also be developed on company intranets to create communities of practice in virtual organizations. For example, a consulting firm developed a website called Management University for about 500 managers of a software development group in six locations in the United States and United Kingdom.[41] Management University consists of three sections: Resource Center, Management Forum, and Executive Perspective. The Resource Center has a virtual library that consists of a prescreened selection of books, articles, videos, and CD-ROMs on management topics. It includes links to other significant management websites. The Resource Center also offers a "manager's toolkit," which consists of searchable cases, topics, and issues. The main topics for this organization include coaching, performance management, consulting and influencing, leadership, team building, innovation, and professional development. The Management Forum is a message board for managers to post questions on difficult management situations and get answers from others who have dealt with similar problems. Managers can search the message board and browse postings by topic. The forum includes success stories (for example, how coaching skills were used for positive results) and management trends for discussion. The Executive Perspective allows senior executives to communicate with their managers.

Despite the benefits of improved communication, a drawback to these communities is that participation is often voluntary, so some employees may not share their knowledge unless the organizational culture supports participation. That is, employees may be reluctant to participate without an incentive or may be fearful that if they share their knowledge with others, they will give away their personal advantage in salary and promotion decisions.[42] (The role of organizational culture in learning is discussed in Chapter 5.) Another potential drawback is information overload. Employees may receive so much information that they fail to process it. This may cause them to withdraw from the community of practice.

Employees Need the Training Program to Be Properly Coordinated and Arranged

Training coordination is one of several aspects of training administration. **Training administration** refers to coordinating activities before, during, and after the program.[43] Training administration involves

1. Communicating courses and programs to employees.
2. Enrolling employees in courses and programs.
3. Preparing and processing any pretraining materials such as readings or tests.
4. Preparing materials that will be used in instruction (e.g., copies of overheads, cases).
5. Arranging for the training facility and room.
6. Testing equipment that will be used in instruction.
7. Having backup equipment (e.g., paper copy of slides, an extra overhead projector bulb) should equipment fail.

8. Providing support during instruction.
9. Distributing evaluation materials (e.g., tests, reaction measures, surveys).
10. Facilitating communications between trainer and trainees during and after training (e.g., coordinating exchange of e-mail addresses).
11. Recording course completion in the trainees' training records or personnel files.

Good coordination ensures that trainees are not distracted by events (such as an uncomfortable room or poorly organized materials) that could interfere with learning. Activities before the program include communicating to trainees the purpose of the program, the place it will be held, the name of a person to contact if they have questions, and any preprogram work they are supposed to complete. Books, speakers, handouts, and videotapes need to be prepared. Any necessary arrangements to secure rooms and equipment (such as VCRs) should be made. The physical arrangement of the training room should complement the training technique. For example, it would be difficult for a team-building session to be effective if the seats could not be moved for group activities. If visual aids will be used, all trainees should be able to see them. Make sure that the room is physically comfortable with adequate lighting and ventilation. Trainees should be informed of starting and finishing times, break times, and location of bathrooms. Minimize distractions such as phone messages. If trainees will be asked to evaluate the program or take tests to determine what they have learned, allot time for this activity at the end of the program. Following the program, any credits or recording of the names of trainees who completed the program should be done. Handouts and other training materials should be stored or returned to the consultant. The end of the program is also a good time to consider how the program could be improved if it will be offered again. Practical issues in selecting and preparing a training site and designing a program are discussed later in the chapter.

An interesting example that illustrates many of the features of good instruction that have just been explained can be found in the training programs of the Culinary Institute of America (CIA), located in the rolling hills of the Hudson River Valley, a 90-minute drive from New York City. The CIA, the world's finest training facility for chefs, has approximately 2,000 full-time students in its degree programs. CIA graduates are chefs in some of the best restaurants in the world and in prestigious private dining rooms (such as the White House), and they direct food service operations for large hotel chains such as the Marriott, Hyatt, Radisson, and Hilton. Besides offering degree programs, the CIA also hosts more than 6,000 trainees from a wide variety of companies that have food service operations.

Whether an instructor is teaching meat-cutting or sautéing techniques, the programs' learning environments are basically the same. A lecture is followed by demonstration and several hours of guided hands-on practice. The trainee then receives feedback from the instructor. The trainer moves from a show-and-tell approach to become a coach over the course of the training session. Videos are produced for every class that a student will take. They can be viewed from residence halls or can be seen at the video learning center where students can review the tapes at their own pace; the students control what they see.

CIA programs deal not only with cognitive learning but also with physical and emotional learning. In addition to cooking and baking courses, students are required to study psychology, Total Quality Management, languages, marketing, communications, restaurant management, and team supervision. Physical fitness and stress management are required parts of the curriculum. Why? Running a commercial kitchen involves long hours and high levels of stress—it is very physically demanding. Thanks to the learning environment created at CIA, the institute is recognized as the world leader in gastronomic training as it provides a foundation of basic knowledge for chefs from around the world.[44]

INSTRUCTIONAL EMPHASIS FOR LEARNING OUTCOMES

The discussion of the implications of the learning process for instruction provided general principles regarding how to facilitate learning. However, you should understand the relationship between these general principles and the learning process. Different internal and external conditions are necessary for learning each outcome. **Internal conditions** refer to processes within the learner that must be present for learning to occur. These processes include how information is registered, stored in memory, and recalled. **External conditions** refer to processes in the learning environment that facilitate learning. These conditions include the physical learning environment as well as opportunities to practice and to receive feedback and reinforcement. The external conditions should directly influence the design or form of instruction. Table 4.7 shows what is needed during instruction at each step of the learning process. For example, during the process of committing training content to memory, verbal cues, verbal links to a meaningful context, and diagrams and models are necessary. If training content is not coded (or is incorrectly coded), learning will be inhibited.

TABLE 4.7   **Internal and External Conditions Necessary for Learning Outcomes**

Learning Outcome	Internal Conditions	External Conditions
Verbal Information Labels, facts, and propositions	Previously learned knowledge and verbal information Strategies for coding information into memory	Repeated practice Meaningful chunks Advance organizers Recall cues
Intellectual Skills Knowing how		Link between new and previously learned knowledge
Cognitive Strategies Process of thinking and learning	Recall of prerequisites, similar tasks, and strategies	Verbal description of strategy Strategy demonstration Practice with feedback Variety of tasks that provide opportunity to apply strategy
Attitudes Choice of personal action	Mastery of prerequisites Identification with model Cognitive dissonance	Demonstration by a model Positive learning environment Strong message from credible source Reinforcement
Motor Skills Muscular actions	Recall of part skills Coordination program	Practice Demonstration Gradual decrease of external feedback

Source: Based on R. M. Gagne and K. L. Medsker, *The Conditions of Learning* (Fort Worth, TX: Harcourt-Brace College Publishers, 1996).

CONSIDERATIONS IN DESIGNING EFFECTIVE TRAINING PROGRAMS

This chapter has discussed implications of learning theory for instruction. The importance of objectives, meaningful material, properly coordinated and arranged training, and opportunities for practice and feedback has been emphasized. How do trainers ensure that these conditions are present in training programs? The last section of the chapter discusses the practical steps in designing effective training programs, courses, and lessons. This includes selecting and preparing the training site and program design.

Selecting and Preparing the Training Site

The **training site** refers to the room where training will be conducted. A good training site offers the following features:[45]

1. It is comfortable and accessible.
2. It is quiet, private, and free from interruptions.
3. It has sufficient space for trainees to move easily around in, offers enough room for trainees to have adequate work space, and has good visibility for trainees to see each other, the trainer, and any visual displays or examples that will be used in training (e.g., videos, product samples, charts, slides).

Details to Be Considered in the Training Room

Table 4.8 presents characteristics of the meeting room that a trainer, program designer, or manager should use to evaluate a training site. Keep in mind that many times trainers do not have the luxury of choosing the "perfect" training site. Rather, they use their evaluation of the training site to familiarize themselves with the site's strengths and weaknesses in order to adjust the training program and/or physical arrangements of the site (e.g., rearrange the trainer's position so it is closer to electrical outlets needed to run a VCR).

Because of technology's impact on the delivery of training programs, many training sites include instructor- and trainee-controlled equipment. For example, at Microsoft's customer briefing center in Chicago, Illinois, 16 different computer platforms, ranging from laptops to mainframe systems, are available to use for training. Two seminar rooms include videoconferencing technology, which allows training sessions to be transmitted from Microsoft's corporate headquarters in Redmond, Washington, to Chicago. The Chicago site can link up to any of 25 Microsoft locations or a combination of 11 sites at once. Presenters have access to a VCR, CD player, cassette decks, and document camera. The seminar rooms have touchscreen systems controlling both the audiovisual equipment and the room environment.[46]

Although the use of technology in training is discussed in more detail in Chapter 8, it is important to note that laptop computers create a desktop training environment that is replacing trainers as the primary way to present training content. For example, at Ernst and Young, an accounting and consulting firm, laptops are used by employees in tax, finance, consulting, and auditing training courses to view visuals, work on case-study exercises, ask questions, and access other information stored on the company's intranet.[47] The laptop connects employees to Web-based training designed to help them gain prerequisites for training sessions as well as provide follow-up information after they attend training. Instead of

TABLE 4.8
Details to Consider When Evaluating a Training Room

Source: Based on C. L. Finkel, "Meeting Facilities," in *The ASTD Training and Development Handbook*, 3d ed., ed. R. L. Craig (New York: McGraw-Hill, 1996): 978–89.

Noise. Check for noise from heating and air conditioning systems, from adjacent rooms and corridors, and from outside the building.

Colors. Pastel hues such as oranges, greens, blues, and yellows are warm colors. Variations of white are cold and sterile. Blacks and brown shades will close in psychologically and become fatiguing.

Room structure. Use rooms that are somewhat square in shape. Long, narrow rooms make it difficult for trainees to see, hear, and identify with the discussion.

Lighting. Main source of lighting should be fluorescent lights. Incandescent lighting should be spread throughout the room and used with dimmers when projection is required.

Wall and floor covering. Carpeting should be placed in the meeting area. Solid colors are preferable because they are not distracting. Only meeting-related materials should be on the meeting room walls.

Meeting room chairs. Chairs should have wheels, swivels, and backs that provide support for the lower lumbar region.

Glare. Check and eliminate glare from metal surfaces, TV monitors, and mirrors.

Ceiling. Ten-foot-high ceilings are preferable.

Electrical outlets. Outlets should be available every six feet around the room. A telephone jack should be next to the outlets. Outlets for the trainer should be available.

Acoustics. Check the bounce or absorption of sound from the walls, ceiling, floor, and furniture. Try voice checks with three or four different people, monitoring voice clarity and level.

playing a major role as presenters of content, trainers are devoting their time to coaching, providing feedback, and monitoring progress of trainees. Trainers can "see" how trainees are working and provide individualized feedback and coaching. Trainers can use the computer to ask questions about what trainees are finding difficult in a particular training session. These responses can be shared with other trainees or used to guide the trainer to hold special "help" sessions or provide supplemental learning modules. The desktop training environment can handle different sizes of training groups even if they are in assorted geographical areas.

Seating Arrangements   Seating arrangements at the training site should be based on an understanding of the desired type of trainee interaction and trainee–trainer interaction.[48] Figure 4.5 shows several types of seating arrangements.

Fan-type seating is conducive to allowing trainees to see from any point in the room. Trainees can easily switch from listening to a presentation to practicing in groups, and trainees can communicate easily with everyone in the room. Fan-type seating is effective for training that includes trainees working in groups and teams to analyze problems and synthesize information.

If the training primarily involves knowledge acquisition, with lecture and audiovisual presentation being the primary training method used, traditional classroom-type seating is appropriate. Traditional classroom instruction allows for trainee interaction with the trainer, but makes it difficult for trainees to work in teams (particularly if the seats are not movable to other locations in the room).

FIGURE 4.5
Examples
of seating
arrangements

Source: Based on F. H.
Margolis and C. R.
Bell, *Managing the
Learning Process*
(Minneapolis, MN:
Lakewood
Publications, 1984).

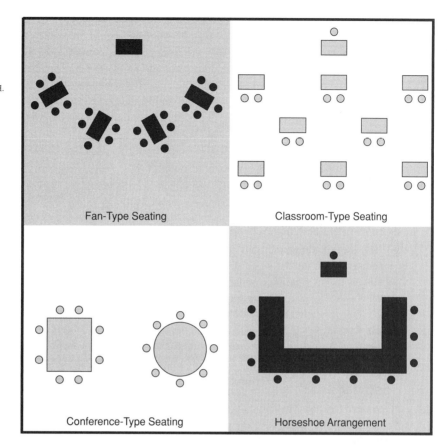

If training emphasizes total-group discussion with limited presentation and no small-group interaction, a conference-type arrangement may be most effective. If the training requires both presentation and total-group instruction, the horseshoe arrangement will be useful.

Selecting Trainers

Selecting professional trainers or consultants is one obvious possibility for companies. Trainers, whether from inside or outside the company, should have expertise in the topic and experience in training.[49] Train-the-trainer programs are necessary for managers, employees, and "experts" who may have content knowledge but need to improve presentation and communications skills, gain an understanding of the key components of the learning process (e.g., feedback, practice), or learn to develop lesson plans. This may involve having employees and managers earn a certificate that verifies they have the skills needed to be effective trainers. To increase their chances of success in their first courses, new trainers should be observed and should receive coaching and feedback from more experienced trainers. When companies use in-house experts for training, it is important to emphasize that these experts convey training content in as concrete a manner as possible (e.g., use examples), especially if the audience is unfamiliar with the content. Experts may have a tendency to use more abstract and advanced concepts that may confuse trainees.[50]

Using managers and employees as trainers may help increase the perceived meaningfulness of the training content. Because they understand the company's business, employee and manager trainers tend to make the training content more directly applicable to the trainees' work. Also, use of managers and employees can help increase their support for learning and reduce the company's dependency on expensive outside consultants. Serving as trainers can be rewarding for employees and managers if they are recognized by the company or if the training experience is linked to their personal development plans.

How Trainers Can Make the Training Site and Instruction Conducive to Learning

As a trainer, you can take several steps to make the room and instruction conducive to learning.[51]

Creating a Learning Setting

Think about the type of room you require for learning to occur. Do the trainees need to be able to concentrate and write? Do they need to be able to see detailed visuals? Do they need breakout rooms, that is, rooms where they can leave the main training setting to work on problems and discuss issues in their teams? Choose a room large enough to meet your purpose, not just to accommodate a certain number of trainees. Avoid putting 25 people in a room that can seat 250. A small number of trainees in a large room makes it impersonal and leaves people feeling insignificant. Consider the room design well in advance of the session and work with the training site coordinator to design a setting that meets your learning needs.

Preparation

You need to know your content very well. Use mental and physical rehearsals to help build confidence and to evaluate the pace and timing of material. Observe master trainers to get new ideas. Design the training from the audience's perspective—ask "So what?" about everything you plan to do. If you are using computers, CD-ROMs, the Internet, distance learning, or other technologies, make sure you know how to work the equipment and have backup materials in case the technology fails. Make sure your visuals are available in at least two formats (e.g., Powerpoint slides and overheads). Arrive at the training room at least 15 minutes early to make sure the room is set up correctly, materials are available, and technology is functioning. Greet the trainees as they enter the room.

Classroom Management

Monitor the room for extra chairs, overflowing trash cans, and piles of materials left over from previous training sessions. A messy, disorganized, uninviting training room creates learning distractions. Give trainees frequent breaks so they can leave the room and return ready to learn.

Engaging Trainees

You as a trainer carry the responsibility for the trainees' learning experience. You need to communicate the topics that will be covered, the learning approach that will be used, and the expectations for trainees. You need to be dramatic to draw attention to important points. Research suggests that trainees have the best recall of training content when the trainer is enthusiastic and avoids vocal distractions (e.g., use of "er" and "um").[52]

How you should engage trainees is based on both the size of the room and the number of trainees. The larger the room, the more your gestures and movements must be exaggerated to get the audience's attention. To create intimacy with the training group, you must move close to them. Standing in the front of the room is a way to establish authority. One of the best ways to gain trainees' attention is to facilitate discussion from different places in the room. Strive to lead the instruction but focus on the trainees. Help trainees develop their own answers, apply tools and techniques, and use reference materials to reach solutions that are effective in training and on the job. Use questions that lead trainees to answers or points you want to make. Continually strive for interaction with trainees—trainees may have more "real-life" experiences, exposure to, or applications related to training topics than you do. Create a training environment where trainees can learn from each other. Listen to trainees, summarize learning points, and provide feedback.

Managing Group Dynamics

To ensure an even distribution of knowledge or expertise in groups, ask trainees to indicate whether they consider themselves novices, experienced, or experts on a topic. Arrange the groups so that they contain a mix of novices, experienced, and expert trainees. Group dynamics can be changed by changing learners' positions in the room. Pay attention to group dynamics by wandering through the room and noticing which groups are frustrated or stalled, who is withdrawn, and who is dominating the group. Your role is to make sure that everyone in a group has an opportunity to contribute. Seating arrangements such as rectangular tables often give trainees authority based on where they are seated. For example, the end of a rectangular table is the position of authority. Putting a quiet person in the "power seat" creates an opportunity for that person to assume a leadership role within the group.

Program Design

For learning to occur, training programs require meaningful material, clear objectives, and opportunities for practice and feedback. However, even if a training program contains all of these conditions, it still may not result in learning for several reasons. Proper equipment and materials may not be available during the session, trainers may be rushed to present content and fail to allow adequate time for practice, or the actual activities that occur in the training session may not relate to the learning objectives. **Program design** refers to the organization and coordination of the training program. A training program may include one or several courses. Each course may contain one or more lessons. Program design includes considering the purpose of the program as well as designing specific lessons within the program. Effective program design includes course parameters, objectives, a lesson plan overview, and a detailed lesson plan.[53]

Keep in mind that although the responsibility for designing the training program may belong to the instructional designer, human resource professional, or manager, the "clients" of the program should also be involved in program design. As already discussed in Chapter 3, managers and employees should be involved in the needs assessment process. In addition, their role may include reviewing prototypes of the program, providing example and program content, and participating in the program as instructors. [54]

The explanation of each feature of effective program design is accompanied by an example based on a training program developed to increase managers' effectiveness in conducting performance appraisal feedback interviews. Performance appraisal feedback sessions

TABLE 4.9
Course
Parameters

Course title: Conducting an Effective Performance Feedback Session

Target audience: Managers

Purpose: To prepare managers to conduct effective performance feedback sessions with their direct reports

Goals: Managers will be able to conduct a performance feedback session using the problem-solving approach

Total time: 1 day

Number of participants per session: 20–25

Locations: Various

Prerequisites: None

Instructor: Caroline O'Connell

are meetings between managers and subordinates during which the strengths and weaknesses of an employee's performance are discussed. Improvement goals are usually agreed upon. Based on a needs assessment, one company discovered that managers were uncomfortable conducting performance appraisal feedback sessions. In this company, managers often were very authoritarian in the sessions. That is, they tended to tell employees what aspects of their job performance needed to be improved rather than allowing the employees to participate in the session or working with them to identify and solve performance problems.

Course Parameters

The **course parameters** refer to general information about the training program including the course title, description of the audience, statement of purpose, goals of the course, location, time, prerequisites, and name of the trainer. The course parameters are based on the information obtained from the needs assessment discussed in Chapter 3.

Table 4.9 presents the course parameters for the performance appraisal feedback course. The course was designed for managers. The purpose of the course was to prepare managers to conduct effective performance appraisal feedback sessions with their subordinates.

Objectives

Earlier in this chapter was a discussion about characteristics of good objectives. Within a training program, there are usually different types of objectives. **Program objectives** are broad summary statements of the purpose of the program. **Course objectives,** or **lesson objectives,** relate to goals of the course or the lesson. These objectives are more specific than the program objectives in terms of the expected behaviors, the content, the conditions, and the standards.

For the performance appraisal feedback training program, objectives included "Describe the eight steps in the problem-solving approach without error" and "Demonstrate the eight steps in the problem-solving approach in a role play exercise without error." The eight steps were: Explain the purpose of the meeting; ask the employee to describe what he has done that deserves recognition; ask the employee to describe what he should stop doing, start doing, or do differently; ask the employee for areas in which you can provide assistance; give

TABLE 4.10   Sample of a Detailed Lesson Plan

Course title: Conducting an Effective Performance Feedback Session

Lesson title: Using the problem-solving style in the feedback interview

Lesson length: Full day

Learning objectives:
1. Describe the eight key behaviors used in the problem-solving style of giving appraisal feedback without error
2. Demonstrate the eight key behaviors in an appraisal feedback role play without error

Target audience: Managers

Prerequisites:

Trainee: None
Instructor: Familiarity with the tell-and-sell, tell-and-listen, and problem-solving approaches used in performance appraisal feedback interviews

Room arrangement: Fan-type

Materials and equipment needed: VCR, overhead projector, pens, transparencies, VCR tape titled "Performance Appraisal Interviews," role play exercises

Evaluation and assignments: Role-play; read article titled "Conducting Effective Appraisal Interviews"

Comment: Article needs to be distributed two weeks prior to session

Lesson Outline	Instructor Activity	Trainee Activity	Time
Introduction	Presentation	Listening	8–8:50 A.M.
View videos of three styles		Watching	8:50–10 A.M.
Break			10–10:20 A.M.
Discussion of strengths and weaknesses of each style	Facilitator	Participation	10:20–11:30 A.M.
Lunch			11:30 A.M.–1 P.M.
Presentation of eight key behaviors of problem-solving style	Presentation	Listening	1–2 P.M.
Role plays	Watch exercise	Practice using key behaviors	2–3 P.M.
Wrap-up	Answer questions	Questions	3–3:15 P.M.

him your opinion of his performance; ask for and listen to the employee's concerns about your evaluation; agree on steps to be taken by each of you; and agree to a follow-up date.[55]

The Detailed Lesson Plan

Lesson plans can be designed for programs lasting a day, a week, or several hours. If training takes place over several days, a separate lesson plan is prepared for each day.

The **detailed lesson plan** translates the content and sequence of training activities into a guide that is used by the trainer to help deliver the training. That is, lesson plans include the sequence of activities that will be conducted in the training session and identify the administrative details. Table 4.10 shows a lesson plan. The lesson plan provides a table of

TABLE 4.11   **Features of an Effective Lesson Plan**

Feature	
Learning Objectives or Outcomes	What is the lesson designed to accomplish? What is the standard for successful learning?
Target Audience	Who is in the lesson? What are the characteristics of the audience?
Prerequisites (trainees and instructor)	What will trainees need to be able to do before they can benefit from the course? Who is qualified to be in the program? Who is qualified to be an instructor?
Time	How much time is devoted to each part of the lesson?
Lesson Outline	What topics will be covered? In what sequence?
Activity	What will trainees' and instructor's role be during each topic covered?
Support Materials	What materials and/or equipment is needed for delivery of instruction or to facilitate instruction?
Physical Environment	Is a certain size or arrangement of room necessary?
Preparation	Do the trainees have homework that needs to be completed before the lesson? What does the instructor need to do?
Lesson Topic	What topic is the lesson going to cover?
Evaluation	How will learning be evaluated (e.g., tests, role plays)?
Transfer and Retention	What will be done to ensure that training content is used on the job?

Source: Based on R. Vaughn, *The Professional Trainer* (Eudid, OH: Williams Custom Publishing, 2000); R. F. Mager, *Making Instruction Work* 2nd ed. (Atlanta, GA: Center for Effective Performance, 1997); L. Nadler and Z. Nadler, *Designing Training Programs* (2nd ed.), (Houston, TX: Gulf Publishing, 1992); Big Dog's Human Resource Development page: http://www.nwlink.com/~donclarkd/hrd.html.

contents for the training activity. This helps to ensure that training activities are consistent regardless of the trainer. Lesson plans also help to ensure that both the trainee and trainer are aware of the course and program objectives. Most training departments have written lesson plans that are stored in notebooks or in electronic databases. Because lesson plans are documented, they can be shared with trainees and customers of the training department (i.e., managers who pay for training services) to provide them with detailed information of program activities and objectives.

Table 4.11 shows the features of an effective lesson plan. The lesson plan includes the course title, learning objective, topics to be covered, target audience, time of session, instructor activity (what the instructor will do during the session), learner activity (e.g., listen, practice, ask questions), and any prerequisites.[56]

In developing the lesson outline, trainers need to consider the proper sequencing of topics. Trainers must answer questions such as "What knowledge and skills need to be learned first?" "In what order should the knowledge, skills, and behavior be taught?" "What order will make sense to the trainees?" It is also important to consider the target audience. Any information about their training and experience, their motivation for taking the course, their interests, learning styles, and background (e.g., education, work experience) will be useful for choosing meaningful examples, determining program content, deciding on support materials, and building the credibility of the training. Information about the target audience should be available from the person analysis of the needs assessment (see Chapter 3). Additional information can be collected by talking to the "clients" (e.g., managers) who requested the training program and to past program participants, if available. Support materials include any equipment needed for delivery of instruction, such as computers; DVD, CD, or video players; or overhead projectors. Trainers should arrange for the purchase of any whiteboards, flip charts, or markers that may be used in instruction. Any exercises needed for trainees' practice or preparation, such as readings, role play exercises, assessments, or pretests, need to be ordered or reproduced (after copyright permission is obtained). In considering instructor and trainee activity, the focus should be on ensuring that the lesson has as many features of a positive learning process as possible, including communication of objectives, feedback, opportunities for practice, opportunities for trainees to share experiences and ask questions, and modeling or demonstration. Transfer and retention strategies might include chat rooms, follow-up meetings with the manager, and action planning. Transfer and retention strategies are discussed in Chapter 5.

Because the lesson objective involves having trainees successfully demonstrate the key behaviors, meeting this objective requires that trainees both understand the key behaviors and practice using them. The example shows that the instructor is involved in presenting key behaviors to the trainees, facilitating discussion, and overseeing role play exercises. The trainees in the session are involved in both passive learning (listening) and active learning (discussion, role play exercises).

The prerequisites include (1) arrangement of the training site, equipment, and materials needed; (2) instructor preparation; and (3) trainee prerequisites. In the example, the trainer needs a VCR to show a video of performance appraisal feedback styles. The trainer also needs an overhead projector to record points made by the trainees during the planned discussion of the strengths and weaknesses of the appraisal styles presented on the video. The room needs to be fan-shaped so trainees can see the trainer and each other. Also, the fan arrangement is good for role play exercises that involve trainees working in groups of two or three.

Trainee prerequisites refer to any preparation, basic skills, or knowledge that the trainee needs prior to participating in the program. Trainee prerequisites may include basic math and reading skills, completion of prior training sessions, or successful completion of tests or certificate or degree programs. Instructor prerequisites indicate what the instructor needs to do to prepare for the session (e.g., rent equipment, review previous day's training session) and any educational qualifications the instructor needs. Lesson plans also may cover how the lesson will be evaluated and any assignments that the trainees need to complete. In the example, trainees are required to read an article on effective performance appraisal feedback interviews. The instructor needs to be familiar with the eight key behaviors for conducting problem-solving appraisal feedback interviews.

Lesson Plan Overview

The **lesson plan overview** matches major activities of the training program and specific times or time intervals.[57] Table 4.12 provides an example of a lesson plan overview for the performance appraisal feedback training.

Completing a lesson plan overview helps the trainer determine the amount of time that needs to be allocated for each topic covered in the program. The lesson plan overview is

TABLE 4.12
Sample Lesson
Overview

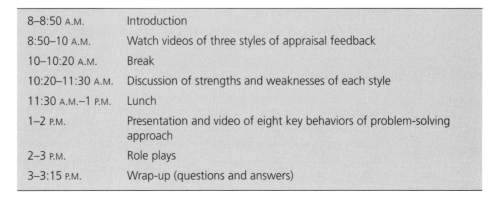

8–8:50 A.M.	Introduction
8:50–10 A.M.	Watch videos of three styles of appraisal feedback
10–10:20 A.M.	Break
10:20–11:30 A.M.	Discussion of strengths and weaknesses of each style
11:30 A.M.–1 P.M.	Lunch
1–2 P.M.	Presentation and video of eight key behaviors of problem-solving approach
2–3 P.M.	Role plays
3–3:15 P.M.	Wrap-up (questions and answers)

also useful in determining when trainers are needed during a program; time demands on trainees; program breaks for snacks, lunch, and dinner; and opportunities for practice and feedback. For the performance appraisal feedback, the lesson plan shows that approximately half of the training time is devoted to active learning by the trainees (discussion, role plays, question-and-answer session).

The experience of Health Partners, which administers Medicaid and Medicare coverage for patients in the Philadelphia, Pennsylvania, area, illustrates the importance of lesson planning and program design.[58] The company installed a major upgrade to its data processing system, but the program was unfamiliar to most employees. To conduct the training, Health Partners identified employees who were familiar with the program and asked them to be part-time instructors. Instead of providing day-long classes that would likely be boring and overwhelming, the company's training staff broke the training into a series of 45-minute sessions that employees could easily fit into their work schedules. The curriculum was organized by department rather than by tasks, and staff from other departments were invited to attend the program so they could understand how the entire company used the system. Portions of the training time were devoted to discussing with employees the stress of change in the workplace and the benefits of the new system. The management teams also met periodically with the instructors to keep them up-to-date on the types of problems that employees faced in working with the new system so those issues could be incorporated into the training.

Summary

Learning must occur for training to be effective. This chapter began by defining learning and identifying the capabilities that can be learned: verbal information, intellectual skills, motor skills, attitudes, and cognitive strategies. To understand how these capabilities can be learned, the chapter discussed several theories of learning: reinforcement theory, social learning theory, goal setting theory, need theories, expectancy theory, adult learning theory, and information processing theory. Next, the chapter investigated the learning process and the implications of how people learn. The learning process emphasized that internal processes (expectancy, storage, and retrieval) as well as external processes (gratifying) influence learning. The potential influence of learning styles and age differences in learning was examined. The chapter then discussed the relationship between the implications of the learning process and design of instruction. Important design elements include providing learners with an understanding of why they should learn, meaningful content, practice opportunities, feedback, a model, a coordinated program, and a good physical learning environment.

The chapter concluded by discussing how to select and prepare a training site and by discussing effective program design. Effective program design includes developing course parameters, objectives, a lesson plan overview, and a detailed lesson plan.

Key Terms

learning, *107*
verbal information, *107*
intellectual skills, *107*
motor skills, *107*
attitudes, *107*
cognitive strategies, *108*
reinforcement theory, *108*
social learning theory, *109*
self-efficacy, *109*
verbal persuasion, *110*
logical verification, *110*
modeling, *110*
past accomplishments, *110*
goal setting theory, *111*
goal orientation, *112*
mastery orientation, *112*
performance
orientation, *112*
need, *113*
expectancies, *113*
instrumentality, *113*
valence, *113*
andragogy, *114*

expectancy, *116*
perception, *116*
working storage, *116*
semantic encoding, *116*
rehearsal, *116*
organizing, *116*
elaboration, *116*
retrieval, *117*
generalizing, *117*
gratifying, *117*
millennium (nexter), *119*
Gen Xers, *119*
baby boomers, *119*
traditionalists, *119*
instruction, *120*
objective, *120*
training context, *121*
practice, *122*
metacognition, *122*
advance organizer, *122*
overlearning, *122*
massed practice, *122*
spaced practice, *122*

overall task
complexity, *122*
mental requirement, *123*
physical requirement, *123*
whole practice, *123*
part practice, *123*
automatization, *125*
feedback, *125*
communities of
practice, *125*
training administration, *126*
internal conditions, *128*
external conditions, *128*
training site, *129*
program design, *133*
course parameters, *134*
program objectives, *134*
course objectives (lesson
objectives), *134*
detailed lesson plan, *135*
lesson plan overview, *137*

Discussion Questions

1. Compare and contrast any two of the following learning theories: expectancy theory, social learning theory, reinforcement theory, information processing theory.
2. What learning condition do you think is most necessary for learning to occur? Which is least critical? Why?
3. What value would it be to know that you were going to be training a class of persons between the ages of 20 and 35? Would it influence the approach you would take? How?
4. Consider the ages of persons in the class mentioned in the previous question. What suggestions would you make to the instructor or trainer as to how to better teach the course, given the generations represented in the class?
5. How do instructional objectives help learning to occur?
6. Assume you are training an employee to diagnose and repair a loose wire in an electrical socket. After demonstrating the procedure to follow, you let the trainee show you how

to do it. The trainee correctly demonstrates the process and repairs the connection on the first attempt! Has learning occurred? Justify your answer.

7. Your boss says, "Why do I need to tell you what type of learning capability I'm interested in? I just want a training program to teach employees how to give good customer service!" Explain to the boss how "good customer service" can be translated into different learning outcomes.

8. How does practice aid in the learning process?

9. What learning conditions are necessary for short- and long-term retention of training content to occur?

10. Under what circumstances might a traditional seating arrangement be superior to a fan-type seating arrangement?

11. Detailed lesson plans have important information for trainers. List the different types of information found in a detailed lesson plan. Also, indicate the importance of each type of information for learning.

Application Assignments

1. Using any source possible (magazines, journals, personal conversation with a trainer), find a description of a training program. Consider the learning process and the implications of the learning process for instruction discussed in the chapter. Evaluate the degree to which the program facilitates learning. Provide suggestions for improving the program.

2. You are the training director of a hotel chain, Noe Suites. Each Noe Suites hotel has 100 to 150 rooms, a small indoor pool, and a restaurant. Hotels are strategically located near exit ramps of major highways in college towns such as East Lansing, Michigan, and Columbus, Ohio. You received the following e-mail message from the vice president of operations:

To: You, Training Director

From: Vice President of Operations, Noe Suites

As you are probably aware, one of the most important aspects of quality service is known as "recovery"—that is, the employee's ability to respond effectively to customer complaints. There are three possible outcomes to a customer complaint: The customer complains and is satisfied by the response, the customer complains and is dissatisfied with the response, and the customer does not complain but remains dissatisfied. Many dissatisfied customers do not complain because they want to avoid confrontation, there is no convenient way to complain, or they do not believe that complaining will do much good.

I have decided that to improve our level of customer service, we need to train our hotel staff in the "recovery" aspect of customer service. My decision is based on the results of recent focus groups we held with customers. One theme that emerged from these focus groups was that we had some weaknesses in the recovery area. For example, last month in one of the restaurants, a waiter dropped the last available piece of blueberry pie on a customer as he was serving her. The waiter did not know how to correct the problem other than offer an apology.

I have decided to hire two well-known consultants in the service industry to discuss recovery as well as to provide an overview of different aspects of quality customer service. These consultants have worked in service industries as well as manufacturing industries.

I have scheduled the consultants to deliver a presentation in three training sessions. Each session will last three hours. There will be one session for each shift of employees (day, afternoon, and midnight shifts).

The sessions will consist of a presentation and question-and-answer session. The presentation will last one and a half hours and the question-and-answer session approximately 45 minutes. There will be a half-hour break.

My expectations are that following this training, the service staff will be able to successfully recover from service problems.

Because you are an expert on training, I want your feedback on the training session. Specifically, I am interested in your opinion regarding whether our employees will learn about service recovery from attending this program. Will they be able to recover from service problems in their interactions with customers? What recommendations do you have for improving the program?

3. Identify what is wrong with each of the following training objectives. Then rewrite it.
   a. To be aware of the safety rules for operating the ribbon-cutting machine in three minutes.
   b. Given a personal computer, a table, and a chair, enter the data into a Microsoft Excel spreadsheet.
   c. Use the World Wide Web to learn about training practices.
   d. Given a street address in the city of Dublin, Ohio, be able to drive the ambulance from the station to the address in less than 10 minutes.

4. Go to *www.nwlink.com/~donclark/hrd/sat.html,* Big Dog's ISD (Instructional System Design page). This website is an excellent resource that describes all aspects of the instructional system design model. Scroll down the page. Under Appendix, click on Learning Style Inventory. Complete the Learning Style Inventory. What are the implications of your learning style for how you best learn? What type of learning environment is best suited for your style? Be as specific as possible.

5. Go to *www.cne.gmu.edu/modules/dau/stat,* the website for an interactive tutorial that provides a refresher on probability and statistics. Click on Index. Choose a topic (such as Data Analysis). Review the module for the topic. What does the module include that can help make the learning process effective? Why?

Endnotes

1. R. M. Gagne and K. L. Medsker, *The Conditions of Learning* (Fort Worth, TX: Harcourt-Brace, 1996).

2. B. F. Skinner, *Science and Human Behavior* (New York: Macmillan).

3. J. Komaki, K. D. Barwick, and L. R. Scott, "A Behavioral Approach to Occupational Safety: Pinpointing and Reinforcing Safe Performance in a Food Manufacturing Plant," *Journal of Applied Psychology* 63 (1978): 434–45.

4. A. Bandura, *Social Foundations of Thought and Action* (Englewood Cliffs, NJ: Prentice-Hall, 1986); A. Bandura, "Self-Efficacy Mechanisms in Human Behavior," *American Psychologist* 37 (1982): 122–47.

5. Bandura, *Social Foundations of Thought and Action.*

6. M. E. Gist and T. R. Mitchell, "Self-Efficacy: A Theoretical Analysis of Its Determinants and Malleability," *Academy of Management Review* 17 (1992): 183–221.

7. E. A. Locke and G. D. Latham, *A Theory of Goal Setting and Task Performance* (Englewood Cliffs, NJ: Prentice Hall, 1990).

8. Ibid.

9. E. A. Locke, K. N. Shaw, L. M. Saari, and G. P. Latham, "Goal Setting and Task Performance," *Psychological Bulletin* 90 (1981): 125–52.

10. T. D. Ludwig and E. S. Geller, "Assigned versus Participative Goal Setting and Response Generalization: Managing Injury Control among Professional Pizza Drivers," *Journal of Applied Psychology* 82 (1997): 253–61.

11. S. Fisher and J. Ford, "Differential Effects of Learner Effort and Goal Orientation on Two Learning Outcomes," *Personnel Psychology* 51 (1998): 397–420.

12. A. H. Maslow, "A Theory of Human Motivation," *Psychological Reports* 50 (1943): 370–96; C. P. Alderfer, "An Empirical Test of a New Theory of Human Needs," *Organizational Behavior and Human Performance* 4 (1969): 142–75.

13. D. McClelland, "Managing Motivation to Expand Human Freedom," *American Psychologist* 33 (1978): 201–10.

14. V. H. Vroom, *Work and Motivation* (New York: John Wiley, 1964).

15. M. S. Knowles, "Adult Learning," in *The ASTD Training and Development Handbook,* ed. R. L. Craig (New York: McGraw-Hill): 253–65.

16. M. Knowles, *The Adult Learner,* 4th ed. (Houston: Gulf Publishing, 1990).

17. S. Caudron, "Learners Speak Out," *Training and Development* (April 2000): 52–57.

18. Gagne and Medsker, *The Conditions of Learning;* W. C. Howell and N. J. Cooke, "Training the Human Information Processor: A Review of Cognitive Models," in *Training and Development in Organizations,* ed. I. L. Goldstein and Associates (San Francisco: Jossey-Bass, 1991): 121–82.

19. R. M. Gagne, "Learning Processes and Instruction," *Training Research Journal* 1 (1995/96): 17–28.

20. Ibid.

21. "Cognitive Strategies," Chapter 6 in Gagne and Medsker, *The Conditions of Learning;* M. Gist, "Training Design and Pedagogy: Implications for Skill Acquisition, Maintenance, and Generalization," in *Training for a Rapidly Changing Workplace,* ed. R. Quinches and A. Ehrenstein (Washington, DC: American Psychological Association, 1997): 201–22.

22. D. Kolb, "Management and the Learning Process," *California Management Review* 18 (1996): 21–31.

23. See D. Kolb, I. Rubin, J. McIntyre, *Organizational Psychology: An Experimental Approach,* 3rd ed. (Englewood Cliffs, NJ: Prentice Hall, 1984):27–54; M. Delahoussaye, "The Perfect Learner: An Expert Debate on Learning Styles," *Training* (March 2002): 28–36.

24. H. Dolezalek, "AmeriCredit," *Training* (March 2003): 46–47.

25. R. Boyd, "Steady Drop in Brain's Prowess Starts in 20s," *Columbus Dispatch* (November 17, 2000): A5.

26. R. Zemke, C. Raines, and B. Filipczak, "Generation Gaps in the Classroom," *Training* (November 2000): 48–54; J. Salopek, "The Young and the Rest of Us," *Training and Development* (February 2000): 26–30.

27. Gagne, "Learning Processes and Instruction."

28. B. Mager, *Preparing Instructional Objectives,* 5th ed. (Belmont, CA: Lake Publishing, 1997); B. J. Smith and B. L. Delahaye, *How to Be an Effective Trainer,* 2d ed. (New York: John Wiley and Sons, 1987).

29. K. A. Smith-Jentsch, F. G. Jentsch, S. C. Payne, and E. Salas, "Can Pre-training Experiences Explain Individual Differences in Learning?" *Journal of Applied Psychology* 81 (1996): 110–16; Caudron, "Learners Speak Out."

30. J. K. Ford, D. A. Weissbein, S. M. Guly, and E. Salas, "Relationship of Goal Orientation, Metacognitive Activity, and Practice Strategies with Learning Outcomes and Transfer," *Journal of Applied Psychology,* 83 (1998): 218–33; A. Schmidt and J. Ford, "Learning within a Learner Control Training Environment: The Interactive Effect of Goal Orientation and Metacognitive Instruction on Learning Outcomes," *Personnel Psychology* 56 (2003): 405–30.

31. J. Cannon-Bowers, L. Rhodenizer, E. Salas, and C. Bowers, "A Framework for Understanding Pre-practice Conditions and Their Impact on Learning," *Personnel Psychology* 51 (1998): 291–320.

32. J. Donovan and D. Radosevich, "A Meta-analytic Review of the Distribution of Practice Effect: Now You See It, Now You Don't," *Journal of Applied Psychology* 84 (1999): 795–805.

33. R. M. Mager, *Making Instruction Work* (Belmont, CA: David Lake, 1988).

34. R. Weiss, "Memory and Learning," *Training and Development* (October 2000): 46–50; R. Zemke, "Toward a Science of Training," *Training* (July 1999): 32–36.

35. J. C. Naylor and G. D. Briggs, "The Effects of Tasks Complexity and Task Organization on the Relative Efficiency of Part and Whole Training Methods," *Journal of Experimental Psychology* 65 (1963): 217–24.

36. Gagne and Medsker, *The Conditions of Learning.*

37. P. J. Decker and B. R. Nathan, *Behavior Modeling Training: Principles and Applications* (New York: Praeger, 1985).

38. Caudron, "Learners Speak Out."

39. D. Stamps, "Communities of Practice," *Training* (February 1997): 35–42.

40. D. Goldwasser, "Me, a Trainer," *Training* (April 2001): 61–66.

41. A. Newman and M. Smith, "How to Create a Virtual Learning Community," *Training and Development* 53, no. 7 (1999): 44–48.

42. R. Williams and J. Cothrel, "Four Smart Ways to Run On-Line Communities," *Sloan Management Review* (Summer, 2000): 81–91.

43. Smith and Delahaye, *How to Be an Effective Trainer;* M. Van Wart, N. J. Cayer, and S. Cook, *Handbook of Training and Development for the Public Sector* (San Francisco: Jossey-Bass, 1993).

44. R. Zemke, "Cooking Up World-Class Training," *Training* 34 (1997): 52–58.

45. Smith and Delahaye, *How to Be an Effective Trainer;* Van Wart, Cayer, and Cook, *Handbook of Training and Development for the Public Sector.*

46. "Top Training Facilities," *Training* (March 1995): special section.

47. Harrison Conference Centers, "Outlook 2000," *Training* (February 2000): S1–S21.

48. L. Nadler and Z. Nadler, *Designing Training Programs,* 2d ed. (Houston: Gulf Publishing Company, 1994); T. W. Goad, "Building Presentations: A Top-Down Approach," in *Effective Training Delivery* (Minneapolis: Lakewood Publishing, 1989): 21–24; F. H. Margolis and C. R. Bell, *Managing the Learning Process* (Minneapolis: Lakewood, 1984).

49. M. Welber, "Save by Growing Your Own Trainers," *Workforce* (September 2002): 44–48.

50. P. Hinds, M. Patterson, and J. Pfeffer, "Bothered by Abstraction: The Effects of Expertise on Knowledge Transfer and Subsequent Novice Performance," *Journal of Applied Psychology* 86: (2001) 1232–43.

51. D. Booher, "Make the Room Work for You," *Training and Development,* S5–S7; D. Abernathy, "Presentation Tips from the Pros," *Training and Development* (October 1999): 19–25.

52. A. Towler and R. Dipboye, "Effects of Trainer Expressiveness, Organizations, and Trainee Goal Orientation on Training Outcomes," *Journal of Applied Psychology* 86 (2001): 664–73.

53. Van Wart, Cayer, and Cook, *Handbook of Training and Development for the Public Sector.*

54. P. Kirschner, C. Carr, and P. Sloep, "How Expert Designers Design," *Performance Improvement Quarterly* 15 (2002): 86–104.

55. G. P. Latham and K. N. Wexley, *Increasing Productivity through Performance Appraisal,* 2d ed. (Reading, MA: Addison-Wesley, 1994).

56. Van Wart, Cayer, and Cook, *Handbook of Training and Development for the Public Sector.*

57. Ibid.

58. P. Kiger, "Health Partners Delivers Training That Works," *Workforce* (November 2002): 60–64.

Chapter **Five**

Transfer of Training

Objectives

After reading this chapter, you should be able to

1. Diagnose and solve a transfer of training problem.
2. Create a work environment that will facilitate transfer of training.
3. Explain to a manager how to ensure that transfer of training occurs.
4. Discuss the implications of identical elements, stimulus generalization, and cognitive theories for transfer of training.
5. Develop a self-management module for a training program.
6. Discuss the technologies that can be used to support transfer of training.
7. Discuss the key features of the learning organization.
8. Provide recommendations of how to manage knowledge.

Training Makes the Grade at KLA-Tencor

At KLA-Tencor, a supplier of process control solutions for the semiconductor industry and based in San Diego, California, employees average 200 hours of training per year. The training budget is $41.8 million per year, and the company has a ratio of one training professional for every 49 employees. Employee training is part of business at KLA-Tencor, a company that values training and development, invests in training and development, and ties it to the business strategy. For example, the company was recently ranked fifth in *Training* magazine's Top 100. Because of the high level of investment in training, KLA-Tencor is taking several steps with employees and mangers to ensure that training is taken seriously and is used on the job.

One of the company's concerns was that too many employees were viewing training as a vacation from their job. To deal with this concern, KLA-Tencor has incorporated a pass/fail policy into its training curriculum. If an employee fails any section within a training course, management action is immediately taken. The employee is removed from the course, and a performance improvement plan is developed that requires the employee to retake the course. The pass/fail policy has resulted in improved employee competency levels, a reduction in marginally performing employees, and savings of $1.4 million. But the most important result was that the policy has changed employees' view of training. Instead of quickly leaving when a training session has ended, trainees are staying late and forming study groups to complete homework and assignments. The class tardiness rate has dropped from 20 percent to zero. The pass/fail policy has also boosted the morale of the technical instructors because they can see that students are actually learning and are interested in the courses.

Managers pay attention to the development of their staff because part of their incentive plan is based on training and development. The three components of the incentive plan include fiscal, productivity, and strategic goals. Training and development is considered a strategic goal. Typically, 10 percent to 30 percent of a manager's bonus pay is based on development. For some managers, as much as 75 percent of their bonus pay can be based on staff development as measured by employee training and certification levels. The percentage varies depending on how critical the training is for business operations. The incentive plans also help the employees receive bonuses which are tied to productivity goals. Only employees who maintain training and certification levels can be eligible for productivity bonuses. For some jobs, such as service engineer, bonuses can range from 10 percent to 15 percent. This incentive plan makes training the responsibility not only of the managers but also of each employee.

Source: Based on K. Ellis, "Developing for Dollars," *Training* (May 2003): 34–39; G. Johnson, "KLA-Tencor," *Training* (March 2003): 48–49.

INTRODUCTION

KLA-Tencor helps ensure that training supports the company's business strategy by creating conditions under which learning will occur and by increasing the likelihood that training content will be used on the job. By using the pass/fail grading system and by linking manager and employee pay bonuses to training, the company shapes perceptions that training is important and learning is valuable. As you will see in this chapter, trainee motivation to learn as well as manager support for training are key issues for ensuring learning and the application of training to the job.

Recall the instructional system design model presented in Chapter 1. After a company conducts a needs assessment, ensures that employees are ready for training, and creates a learning environment, its next step is to ensure that what is learned in training is applied on the job. **Transfer of training** refers to trainees effectively and continually applying what they learned in training (knowledge, skills, behaviors, cognitive strategies) to their jobs.[1] As KLA-Tencor illustrates, the work environment plays an important role in ensuring that transfer of training occurs. Transfer of training is also influenced by trainee characteristics and training design.

Figure 5.1 presents a model of the transfer process. As the model shows, transfer of training includes both the generalization of training to the job and the maintenance of learned material. **Generalization** refers to a trainee's ability to apply learned capabilities (verbal knowledge, motor skills, etc.) to on-the-job work problems and situations that are similar but not completely identical to those problems and situations encountered in the learning environment. **Maintenance** refers to the process of continuing to use newly acquired capabilities over time.

FIGURE 5.1

A model of the transfer process

Source: Adapted from T. T. Baldwin and J. K. Ford, "Transfer of Training: A Review and Directions for Future Research," *Personnel Psychology* 41 (1988): 63–103.

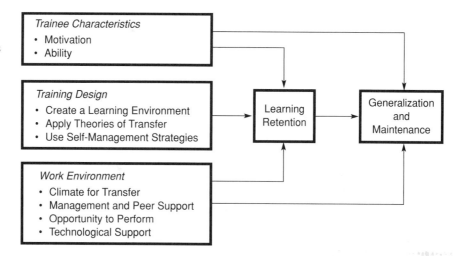

For generalization and maintenance to occur, capabilities must be learned and retained. Training design, trainee characteristics, and the work environment influence learning, retention, maintenance, and generalization. **Training design** refers to the characteristics of the learning environment. Chapter 4 covered important features of the learning environment—including meaningful material, opportunities to practice, feedback, learning objectives, and program organization—and physical features of the training site. Another factor that influences learning and retention is **trainee characteristics.** Trainee characteristics include ability and motivation that affect learning. The influence of trainee characteristics on learning was discussed in Chapters 3 and 4. If trainees lack the basic skills needed to master learned capabilities (e.g., cognitive ability, reading skills), are not motivated to learn, and do not believe that they can master the learned capabilities (low self-efficacy), it is doubtful the learning and transfer of training will occur. The third factor that influences the learning, retention, and transfer is the work environment. The **work environment** includes factors on the job that influence transfer of training including managers' support, peer support, technology support, the climate for transfer, and the opportunity to use newly acquired capabilities on the job.

This chapter will focus on identifying additional factors besides the learning environment and trainee characteristics already discussed that influence transfer of training. This chapter includes a detailed discussion of transfer of training theories and how the work environment influences transfer of training.

The chapter organization is based on the model shown in Figure 5.1. The model shows that three factors influence learning and transfer of training. These three factors are trainee characteristics, training design, and the work environment. Although transfer of training sounds like something that is considered *after* training occurs, it is important to emphasize that it should be planned for *before* training. Recall from Chapter 3 that assessment of trainee characteristics and the work environment is part of needs assessment. Transfer of training does occur after training occurs. However, the conditions that facilitate transfer need to be provided before training actually occurs. For example, to motivate trainees to attend a training program, communications about the program need to emphasize the benefit of training. Design of the learning process needs to include desirable features such as objectives, meaningful material, and opportunities to practice and receive feedback (recall the learning process from Chapter 4). Managers' and peers' attitudes toward training can influence the level of motivation to learn that trainees bring to a program.

The chapter begins with a discussion of training design issues related to transfer of training. This discussion includes (1) application of theories of transfer of training to training design and (2) an emphasis on self-management as part of the training program. Next, the chapter addresses how the work environment influences the transfer of training process. Trainees', managers', and trainers' roles in ensuring that transfer of training occurs are emphasized. Through discussions of learning organizations and knowledge management, you will gain a perspective on how the work climate can influence transfer of training. The chapter also points out that transfer of training can be enhanced by holding trainees accountable for using information learned in training and sharing that information with their colleagues. The chapter concludes with a discussion of learning organizations—a multifaceted approach for encouraging learning and transfer of training.

TRAINING DESIGN

Training design refers to factors built into the training program to increase the chances that transfer of training will occur. Chapter 4 discussed the important factors needed for learning to occur (objective, practice, feedback, meaningful material, etc.). For transfer of training to occur, managers need to apply transfer of training theories and principles of self-management.

Applications of Transfer of Training Theory

Three theories of transfer of training have implications for training design (the learning environment): the theory of identical elements, the stimulus generalization approach, and cognitive theory.[2] Table 5.1 shows each theory's primary emphasis and the conditions under which it is most appropriate to consider.

TABLE 5.1
Transfer of Training Theories

Theory	Emphasis	Appropriate Conditions	Type of Transfer
Identical Elements	Training environment is identical to work environment.	Work environment features are predictable and stable. *Example:* training to use equipment.	Near
Stimulus Generalization	General principles are applicable to many different work situations.	Work environment is unpredictable and highly variable. *Example:* training in interpersonal skills.	Far
Cognitive Theory	Meaningful material and coding schemes enhance storage and recall of training content.	All types of training and environments.	Near and far

Theory of Identical Elements

The **theory of identical elements** proposes that transfer of training occurs when what is being learned in the training session is identical to what the trainee has to perform on the job.[3] Transfer will be maximized to the degree that the tasks, materials, equipment, and other characteristics of the learning environment are similar to those encountered in the work environment.

The use of identical elements theory is shown in the hostage training simulation used by the Baltimore Police Department. The Baltimore Police Department needed to teach police sergeants the skills to handle hostage-barricade situations in which lives are at stake—skills such as negotiating with a troubled husband holding his wife and/or children hostage. The first hour of a hostage situation is critical. The sergeant must quickly organize resources to achieve a successful end to the situation with minimal or no injuries. A simulation was chosen because it provides a model of reality, a mock-up of a real situation without the danger. Multiple scenarios can be incorporated into the simulation, allowing the sergeants to practice the exact skills they will need when faced with a hostage crisis.

The simulation begins by having the trainees briefed on the hostage situation. Then they are directed to take charge of resolving the incident in the presence of an instructor who has personally been involved in similar real-life incidents. Each trainee supervises one difficult and one easy scenario. The simulation is designed to emphasize the importance of clear thinking and decision making in a situation in which time is critical. It is essential that the trainees take actions according to a set of priorities. These priorities place the greatest value on minimizing the risks to the hostages and isolating suspects before communicating with them. The simulation scenarios include elements of many actual hostage incidents such as forced entry, taking persons against their will, the presence of a weapon, and threats. As trainees work in the simulation, their actions are evaluated by the instructor. The instructor provides feedback to the trainees in writing after they complete the simulation or the instructor can correct mistakes as they happen.

The training simulation mirrors exactly the circumstances of actual hostage situations that police officers encounter. Also, a checklist of activities and behaviors that the sergeants are provided with in training is the exact checklist used in hostage situations that occur on the street. Evidence of generalization is provided by police sergeants who have successfully dealt with a bank-hostage situation by using the skills emphasized in the simulation. The Baltimore Police Department is also concerned with maintenance. At the conclusion of the simulation, officers may be able to demonstrate how to successfully free hostages. However, the incidence of hostage situations is fairly low compared to other tasks that police officers perform (e.g., issuing traffic citations, investigating burglaries). As a result, the police department is concerned that officers may forget what they learned in training and therefore have difficulties in hostage situations. To ensure that officers have opportunities to practice these infrequently used but important skills, the training department will occasionally schedule mock hostage situations.[4]

Another application of the theory of identical elements is found in the use of simulators for training airline pilots. Pilots are trained in a simulator that looks exactly like the cockpit of a commercial aircraft. All aspects of the cockpit in the simulator (e.g., gauges, dials, lights) are the same as in a real aircraft. In psychological terms, the learning environment has complete fidelity with the work environment. **Fidelity** refers to the extent to which the training environment is similar to the work environment. If skills in flying, taking off, landing, and dealing with emergency situations are learned in the simulator, they will be transferred to the work setting (commercial aircraft).

The identical elements approach has also been used to develop instruments designed to measure the similarity of jobs.[5] Job similarity can be used as one measure of the extent to which training in the knowledge and skills required for one job prepares an employee to perform a different job.

The theory of identical elements has been applied to many training programs, particularly those that deal with the use of equipment or that involve specific procedures that must be learned. Identical elements theory is particularly relevant to make sure that near transfer occurs. **Near transfer** refers to trainees' ability to apply learned capabilities exactly to the work situation. Programs that emphasize near transfer should include the following training designs:[6]

- The program should teach specific concepts and procedures.
- Trainees should be given an explanation as to any differences between training tasks and work tasks.
- Trainees should be encouraged to focus only on important differences between training tasks and work tasks (e.g., speed of completion) rather than unimportant differences (e.g., equipment with the same features but a different model).
- Behaviors or skills that trainees learn in the program should contribute to effective performance.

For example, in police officer training, new hires (cadets) practice shooting targets. During practice sessions, cadets fire a round of shells, empty the cartridges into their hands, and dispose of the empty cartridges into the nearest garbage can. This process is repeated several times. After graduation from the police academy, one new officer was involved in a shooting. He fired his gun, emptied the cartridges into his hand, and proceeded to look for a garbage can for the empty cartridges. As a result, he was seen by the gunman, shot, and killed!

Identical elements theory does not encourage transfer where the learning environment and the training environment are not necessarily identical. This situation arises particularly in interpersonal skills training. For example, a person's behavior in a conflict situation is not easily predictable. Therefore, trainees must learn general principles of conflict resolution that they can apply to a wide variety of situations as the circumstances dictate (e.g., an irate customer versus a customer who lacks product knowledge).

Stimulus Generalization Approach

The **stimulus generalization approach** suggests that the way to understand the transfer of training issue is to construct training so that the most important features or general principles are emphasized. It is also important to identify the range of work situations in which these general principles can be applied. The stimulus generalization approach emphasizes far transfer. **Far transfer** refers to the trainee's ability to apply learned capabilities to the work environment, even though the work environment (equipment, problems, tasks) is not identical to that of the training session. Programs that emphasize far transfer should include the following training designs:[7]

- The program should teach general concepts and broad principles.
- Trainees should be made aware of examples from their experiences that are similar to those emphasized in training so that connections can be made among strategies that have been effective in different situations.

- The program should emphasize that the general principles might be applied to a greater set of contexts than those that are presented in the training setting.

The stimulus generalization approach can be seen in the design of managerial skill training programs, known as behavior modeling training, which are based on social learning theory. Recall from the discussion of social learning theory in Chapter 4 that modeling, practice, feedback, and reinforcement play key roles in learning. One step in developing behavior modeling programs is to identify key behaviors that are needed to be successful in a situation. **Key behaviors** refer to a set of behaviors that can be used successfully in a wide variety of situations. The model demonstrates these key behaviors on a video, and trainees have opportunities to practice the behaviors. In behavior modeling training, the key behaviors are believed to be applicable to a wide variety of situations. In fact, the practice sessions in behavior modeling training require the trainee to use the behaviors in a variety of situations that are not identical.

Cognitive Theory of Transfer

The cognitive theory of transfer is based on the information processing model of learning discussed in Chapter 4. Recall that the storage and retrieval of information are key aspects of this model of learning. According to the **cognitive theory of transfer,** the likelihood of transfer depends on the trainees' ability to retrieve learned capabilities. This theory suggests that the likelihood of transfer is enhanced by providing trainees with meaningful material that enhances the chances that they will link what they encounter in the work environment to the learned capability. Also important is providing the trainee with cognitive strategies for coding learned capabilities in memory so that they are easily retrievable. (These strategies were discussed in Chapter 4.)

The influence of cognitive theory is seen in training design by encouraging trainees, as part of the program, to consider potential applications of the training content to their jobs. Many training programs include having trainees identify a work problem or situation and discuss the potential application of training content. Application assignments increase the likelihood that trainees will recall the training content and apply it to the work setting when they encounter the appropriate cues (problems, situations) in the environment. **Application assignments** are work problems or situations in which trainees are asked to apply training content to solve them. The use of application assignments in training helps the trainee understand the link between the learned capability and real-world application, which makes it easier to recall the capability when needed.

Self-Management Strategies

Self-management refers to a person's attempt to control certain aspects of decision making and behavior. Training programs should prepare employees to self-manage their use of new skills and behaviors on the job. Self-management involves

1. Determining the degree of support and negative consequences in the work setting for using newly acquired capabilities.
2. Setting goals for using learned capabilities.
3. Applying learned capabilities to the job.
4. Monitoring use of learned capabilities on the job.
5. Engaging in self-reinforcement.[8]

TABLE 5.2   Examples of Obstacles in the Work Environment That Inhibit Transfer

Obstacle	Description of Influence
Work Conditions Time pressures Inadequate equipment Few opportunities to use skills Inadequate budget	Trainee has difficulty using new knowledge, skills, or behavior.
Lack of Peer Support Discourage use of new knowledge and skills on the job Are unwilling to provide feedback See training as waste of time	Peers do not support use of new knowledge, skills, or behavior.
Lack of Management Support Do not accept ideas or suggestions that are learned in training. Do not discuss training opportunities Oppose use of skills learned in training Communicate that training is a waste of time Are unwilling to provide reinforcement, feedback, and encouragement needed for trainees to use training content	Managers do not reinforce training or provide opportunities to use new knowledge, skills, or behavior

Source: Based on R. D. Marx, "Self-Managed Skill Retention," *Training and Development Journal* (January 1986): 54–57.

Research suggests that trainees exposed to self-management strategies exhibit higher levels of transfer of behavior and skills than do trainees who are not provided with self-management strategies.[9]

Self-management is important because the trainee is likely to encounter several obstacles in the work environment that inhibit transfer of training. Table 5.2 shows these obstacles. They include (1) lack of support from peers and managers and (2) factors related to the work itself (e.g., time pressure). Given the restructuring, downsizing, and cost cutting occurring in many companies, these obstacles are often a reality for trainees.

For example, new technologies allow employees to gain access to resources and product demonstrations using the World Wide Web or personal computers equipped with CD-ROM drives. But while employees are being trained to use these resources with state-of-the-art technology, they often become frustrated because comparable technology is not available to them at their work site. Employees' computers may lack sufficient memory or links to the World Wide Web for them to use what they have learned.

These obstacles inhibit transfer because they cause lapses. **Lapses** refer to the trainee using previously learned, less effective capabilities instead of trying to apply the capability emphasized in the training program. Lapses into old behavior and skill patterns are common. Trainees should try to avoid a consistent pattern of slipping back or using old, ineffective learned capabilities (e.g., knowledge, skills, behaviors, strategies). Also, trainees should understand that lapses are common and be prepared to cope with them. Trainees who are unprepared for lapses may give up trying to use new capabilities—especially trainees with low self-efficacy and self-confidence.

TABLE 5.3 **Sample Content of Self-Management Module**

1. Discuss lapses. • Note evidence of inadequacy • Provide direction for improvement	**5. Identify when lapses are likely.** • Situations • Actions to deal with lapses
2. Identify skills targeted for transfer.	**6. Discuss resources to ensure transfer of skills.** • Manager • Trainer • Other trainees
3. Identify personal or environment factors contributing to lapse. • Low self-efficacy • Time pressure • Lack of manager or peer support	
4. Discuss coping skills and strategies. • Time management • Setting priorities • Self-monitoring • Self-rewards • Creating a personal support network	

Source: Adapted from R. D. Marx, "Relapse Prevention for Managerial Training: A Model for Maintenance of Behavior Change," *Academy of Management Review* 7 (1982): 433–41; R. D. Marx, "Improving Management Development through Relapse Prevention Strategies," *Journal of Management Development* 5 (1986): 27–40; M. L. Broad and J. W. Newstrom, *Transfer of Training* (Reading, MA: Addison-Wesley, 1992).

One way to prepare trainees to deal with these obstacles is to provide instruction in self-management techniques at the end of the training program. Table 5.3 shows an example of self-management instruction. The module begins with a discussion of lapses emphasizing that lapses are not evidence of personal inadequacy; rather, they result from habits of usage of knowledge and skill that have developed over time. Lapses provide information necessary for improvement. They help identify the circumstances that will have the most negative influence on transfer of training. Next, a specific behavior, skill, or strategy is targeted for transfer. Then, obstacles that inhibit transfer of training are identified; these can include both work environment characteristics and personal characteristics (such as low self-efficacy). Trainees are then provided with an overview of coping skills or strategies that they can use to deal with these obstacles. These skills and strategies include time management, creating a personal support network (persons to talk with about how to transfer skills to the work setting), and self-monitoring to identify successes in transferring skills to the job. Next, to deal with lapses trainees are instructed to be aware of where the situations are most likely to occur. The final part of the module deals with the use of resources to aid transfer of training. These resources may include communications with the trainer or fellow trainees via e-mail as well as discussions with their boss.

For example, a manager may have attended a training program designed to increase her leadership skills. After a discussion of lapses, the manager identifies a target skill, say, participative decision making—that is, discussing problems and potential solutions with subordinates before making decisions that will affect the work group. Next, the manager identifies factors that may contribute to a lapse. One factor may be the manager's lack of confidence in being able to deal with subordinates who disagree with her view. Potential coping strategies that the manager identifies may include (1) scheduling time on the calendar to meet with subordinates (time management), (2) communicating to the boss the transfer goal and asking for help (create a support group), and (3) taking an assertiveness training course. In what situation may the manager be especially likely to experience a lapse? The manager identifies that she may be most likely to lapse back into an autocratic style when faced with a short time frame for making a decision (time pressure being an obstacle). The manager recognizes that it may be inappropriate to try to gain consensus for a decision when time constraints are severe and subordinates lack expertise. In the last step of the module, the manager suggests that she will (1) meet with her mentor to review her progress, (2) talk with other managers about how they effectively use participative decision making, and (3) resolve to communicate with other managers who attended the training session with her. The manager also commits to monitoring her use of participative decision making, noting successes and failures in a diary.

WORK ENVIRONMENT CHARACTERISTICS THAT INFLUENCE TRANSFER OF TRAINING

As Figure 5.1 showed, several work environment characteristics influence transfer of training, including the climate for transfer, managerial and peer support, opportunity to perform, and technological support.

Climate for Transfer

Climate for transfer refers to trainees' perceptions about a wide variety of characteristics of the work environment that facilitate or inhibit use of trained skills or behavior. These characteristics include manager and peer support, opportunity to use skills, and the consequences for using learned capabilities.[10] Table 5.4 shows characteristics of a positive climate for transfer of training. Research has shown that transfer of training climate is significantly related to positive changes in managers' administrative and interpersonal behaviors following training. To ensure transfer of training for its customer service representatives, Welch Allyn, a medical equipment manufacturer in New York, sends out e-mail reminders with skills update information, posts information that employees display in their cubicles, and monitors calls to check on employees' progress. [11]

Consider how Patagonia's work environment supports transfer of training. Patagonia, a subsidiary of Lost Arrow Corporation, sells outdoor sports clothing and equipment through specialty retailers, a catalog, and stores in North America, Australia, Europe, and Japan. Patagonia is known for having a culture that emphasizes quality products and environmental awareness, and gives employees the opportunity to grow and develop. This culture has attracted employees who have casual tastes, a motivation and passion to learn, and an active lifestyle.

All of Patagonia's human resource management practices, including training and development, support the company's mission. For example, the company hires "dirtbags"—passionate outdoor people who are customers. Patagonia believes that it is easier to teach these people business than to turn a businessperson into someone with a passion for the outdoor.

Because Patagonia believes it is a stable-growth company, it hires primarily from within its current work force. Employee education is emphasized as much as product research and promotion. Patagonia provides employees with a minimum of 45 hours of training per year. New employee orientation is handled by employees, not trainers or human resource professionals.

TABLE 5.4 **Characteristics of a Positive Climate for Transfer of Training**

Characteristic	Example
Supervisors and co-workers encourage and set goals for trainees to use new skills and behaviors acquired in training.	Newly trained managers discuss how to apply their training on the job with their supervisors and other managers.
Task cues: Characteristics of a trainee's job prompt or remind him or her to use new skills and behaviors acquired in training.	The job of a newly trained manager is designed in such a way as to allow him or her to use the skills taught in training.
Feedback consequences: Supervisors support the application of new skills and behaviors acquired in training.	Supervisors notice newly trained managers who use their training.
Lack of punishment: Trainees are not openly discouraged from using new skills and behaviors acquired in training.	When newly trained managers fail to use their training, they are not reprimanded.
Extrinsic reinforcement consequences: Trainees receive extrinsic rewards for using new skills and behaviors acquired in training.	Newly trained managers who successfully use their training will receive a salary increase.
Intrinsic reinforcement consequences: Trainees receive intrinsic rewards for using new skills and behaviors acquired in training.	Supervisors and other managers appreciate newly trained managers who perform their job as taught in training.

Source: Adapted from J. B. Tracey, S. I. Tannenbaum, and M. J. Kavanagh, "Applying Trained Skills on the Job: The Importance of the Work Environment," *Journal of Applied Psychology* 80 (1995): 235–52.

Patagonia offers a wide range of classes that are designed to keep employees learning but are not necessarily related to their current jobs. These courses include introduction to French culture, business and communications, Japanese style, and beginning sewing. Patagonia also has an internship program that allows employees to take time off work. The Patagonia Internship Program offers eligible employees or groups the opportunity to take a paid leave of up to two months to work full- or part-time for a nonprofit group of their choice. Employees continue to earn their regular paycheck and benefits while lending their talents and energy to a worthy cause and while learning more about issues that are important to them. For example, one employee spent seven weeks on the Coromandel Peninsula of New Zealand's north island working with the Mist Preservation Society to protect the biodiversity of subtropical forests. Cross training is expected at Patagonia. If an employee leaves to go on vacation or pursue an internship opportunity, the temporary opening is filled with another employee who is interested in the vacated job. The temporary employee has the opportunity to grow and learn.

What are the benefits to Patagonia of having a culture that gives employees the opportunities to pursue their outdoor passion, to balance work and nonwork, to make shoes an optional part of their dress code, and to grow and learn; of having a culture that allows employees to pursue sports and environmental interests during work time; of having a culture that uses business to help implement solutions to protect and preserve the natural environment? Few employees leave voluntarily, and the company has no problem attracting new ones. The company has been successful at making the best clothing and equipment for outdoor sports. It has received awards from many professional publications and organizations

FIGURE 5.2

Levels of management support for training

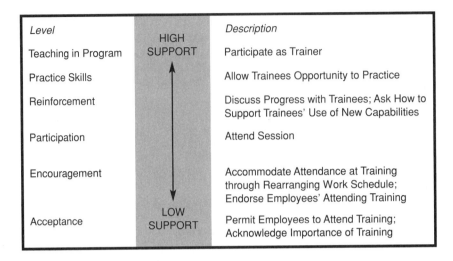

Level		Description
Teaching in Program	HIGH SUPPORT	Participate as Trainer
Practice Skills		Allow Trainees Opportunity to Practice
Reinforcement		Discuss Progress with Trainees; Ask How to Support Trainees' Use of New Capabilities
Participation		Attend Session
Encouragement		Accommodate Attendance at Training through Rearranging Work Schedule; Endorse Employees' Attending Training
Acceptance	LOW SUPPORT	Permit Employees to Attend Training; Acknowledge Importance of Training

for its proactive approach to contributing to employees' worklife and the environment. The company also is a financial success. In 2002 Lost Arrow Corporation, including Patagonia, grossed $220 million in sales.[12]

Manager Support

Manager support refers to the degree to which trainees' managers (1) emphasize the importance of attending training programs and (2) stress the application of training content to the job. For example, trainers at the California Housing Partnership train project managers of rental housing on how to schedule complex tasks. Unfortunately, many trainees do not implement the scheduling system because when they return to their community agencies, their managers are not convinced that the scheduling system is worthwhile to use.[13]

Managers can provide different levels of support for training activities, as illustrated in Figure 5.2.[14] The greater the level of support, the more likely that transfer of training will occur. Managers should be actively involved in the design and delivery of training programs. The basic level of support that a manager can provide is acceptance, allowing trainees to attend training. The greatest level of support is to participate in training as an instructor (teaching in the program). Managers who serve as instructors are more likely to provide many of the lower-level support functions, such as reinforcing use of newly learned capabilities, discussing progress with trainees, and providing opportunities to practice. To maximize transfer of training, trainers need to achieve the highest level of support possible. Managers can also facilitate transfer through reinforcement (use of action plans). An **action plan** is a written document that includes the steps that the trainee and manager will take to ensure that training transfers to the job (see Figure 5.3). The action plan includes (1) a goal identifying what training content will be used and how it will be used (project, problem), (2) strategies for reaching the goal (including what the trainee will do differently, resources needed, and type of support from managers and peers), (3) strategies for getting feedback, and (4) expected outcome. The action plan also provides a progress check schedule of specific dates and times when the manager and trainee agree to meet to discuss the progress being made in using learned capabilities on the job. The action planning process

FIGURE 5.3
Sample action
plan

Training Topic _____

Goal *Include training content (knowledge, skill, behavior, competency, etc.) and application (project, problem, etc.)*

Strategies for reaching goal
Modifying behavior (What I will do differently?)

_____
_____
_____
_____

Resources needed (equipment, financial)

_____
_____
_____

Support from peers and manager (Be as specific as possible.)

_____
_____
_____
_____

Strategies for receiving feedback about my progress *(Include meetings with peers and managers, self-monitoring of progress, customer reactions, etc.)*

_____
_____
_____
_____

Expected outcome *(When I reach the goal, what will be different? Who will notice the difference? What will they notice?)*

What will be different?

_____
_____

Who will notice?

_____
_____

What will they notice?

_____
_____
_____

Progress Date Checks _____   _____   _____

should start by identifying the goal and the strategies for reaching the goal. Once those are determined, strategies for obtaining feedback and identifying what goal accomplishment will look like are completed.

Table 5.5 presents a checklist that can be used to determine the level of manager support for training. The more statements that managers agree with, the greater their level of support for the training program. There are several ways to gain managers' support for training.[15]

TABLE 5.5
Checklist for Determining Level of Manager Support for Training

Source: A. Rossett, "That Was a Great Class, But . . . ," *Training and Development* (July 1997): 21.

	Agree	Disagree
I have a good sense of what the class is about.		
I know how the training matches what I need employees to do.		
There are tangible ways that the training will help employees.		
There are tangible ways that the training will help our unit.		
I can see why the organization is interested in providing the training.		
In performance appraisals, I can evaluate employees on what they learn in the class.		
I know enough about the training to support employees when they return to work.		
We have the tools and technologies that will be discussed in the class.		
I'm glad employees are attending the class.		
I've discussed the topic and the class with the employees who will participate.		
They know that I care about what will be taught in the class.		

First, managers need to be briefed on the purpose of the program and its relationship to business objectives and the business strategy. Managers should be given the schedule of topics and a checklist of what they should do after the training to ensure that transfer occurs. Second, trainees should be encouraged to bring to the training session work problems and situations they face on the job. These can be used as practice exercises or input into action plans. Trainees should jointly identify the problems and situations with their manager. Third, information regarding the benefits of the course collected from past participants should be shared with managers. Fourth, trainers can assign trainees to complete action plans with their managers. Fifth, if possible, use managers as trainers. That is, train the managers first, and then give them responsibility to train their subordinates.

At a minimum, special sessions should be scheduled with managers to explain the purpose of the training and set expectations that they will encourage attendance at the training session, provide practice opportunities, reinforce use of training, and follow up with trainees to determine the progress in using newly acquired capabilities.

Men's Wearhouse exhibits strong management support by having few employees dedicated exclusively to training. Company executives are able to influence training by not providing a training budget; senior managers are expected to spend on training as necessary. A series of manager meetings, each geared toward a different level of manager, provide the information and motivation required to facilitate employee development. At Johnson and Johnson, managers learn online about how to support training and development. Using a Web-based resource, managers can assess employees' skills, develop learning plans, and confidentially ask for feedback. Because the site is used by a consortium of companies (including AT&T and Metropolitan Life Insurance), managers have access to the development lessons learned in other companies.[16]

Peer Support

Transfer of training can also be enhanced by a support network among the trainees.[17] A **support network** is a group of two or more trainees who agree to meet and discuss their progress in using learned capabilities on the job. This could involve face-to-face meetings or communications via e-mail. Trainees could share successful experiences in using training content on the job. They can also discuss how they obtained resources needed to use training content or how they coped with a work environment that interfered with use of training content.

Trainers might also use a newsletter to show how trainees are dealing with transfer of training issues. Distributed to all trainees, the newsletter might feature interviews with trainees who were successful in using new skills. Trainers may also provide trainees with a mentor—a more experienced employee who previously attended the same training program. The mentor may be a peer. The mentor can provide advice and support related to transfer of training issues (e.g., how to find opportunities to use the learned capabilities).

Opportunity to Use Learned Capabilities

Opportunity to use learned capabilities (**opportunity to perform**) refers to the extent to which the trainee is provided with or actively seeks experience with newly learned knowledge, skill, and behaviors from the training program. Opportunity to perform is influenced by both the work environment and trainee motivation. One way trainees have the opportunity to use learned capabilities is through assigned work experiences (e.g., problems, tasks) that require their use. The trainees' manager usually plays a key role in determining work assignments. Opportunity to perform is also influenced by the degree to which trainees take personal responsibility to actively seek out assignments that allow them to use newly acquired capabilities.

Opportunity to perform includes breadth, activity level, and task type.[18] *Breadth* includes the number of trained tasks performed on the job. *Activity level* is the number of times or the frequency with which trained tasks are performed on the job. *Task type* refers to the difficulty or criticality of the trained tasks that are actually performed on the job. Trainees who are given opportunities to use training content on the job are more likely to maintain learned capabilities than trainees given few opportunities.[19]

Opportunity to perform can be measured by asking former trainees to indicate (1) whether they perform a task, (2) how many times they perform the task, and (3) the extent to which they perform difficult and challenging tasks. Individuals who report low levels of opportunity to perform may be prime candidates for "refresher courses" (courses designed to let trainees practice and review training content). Refresher courses are necessary because these persons have likely experienced a decay in learned capabilities since they haven't had opportunities to perform. Low levels of opportunity to perform may also indicate that the work environment is interfering with using new skills. For example, the manager may not support training activities or give the employee the opportunity to perform tasks using skills emphasized in training. Finally, low levels of opportunity to perform may indicate that training content is not important for the employee's job.

Technological Support

Electronic performance support systems (EPSSs) are computer applications that can provide, as requested, skills training, information access, and expert advice.[20] An EPSS may be used to enhance transfer of training by providing trainees with an electronic information source that they can refer to on an as-needed basis while they attempt to apply learned capabilities on the job. EPSS use in training is discussed in detail in Chapter 8.

Cagle's, an Atlanta-based poultry processor, uses EPSS for employees who maintain the chicken-processing machines.[21] Because the machines that measure and cut chickens are constantly increasing in sophistication, it is impossible to continually train technicians so that they know the equipment's details. However, technicians are trained on the basic procedures they need to know to maintain these types of machines. When the machines encounter a problem, the technicians rely on what they have learned in training as well as the EPSS system, which provides more detailed instructions about the repairs. The EPSS system also tells technicians the availability of parts and where in inventory to find replacement parts. The EPSS system consists of a postage-stamp–size computer monitor attached to a visor that magnifies the screen. The monitor is attached to a three-pound computer about half the size of a portable CD player. Attached to the visor is a microphone that the technician uses to give verbal commands to the computer. The EPSS helps employees diagnose and fix the machines very quickly. This speed is important, given that the plant processes more than 100,000 chickens a day and chicken is a perishable food product!

Trainers can also monitor trainees' use of EPSS, which provides the trainer with valuable information about the transfer of training problems that trainees are encountering. These problems might relate to the training design (e.g., lack of understanding of process or procedure) or work environment (e.g., trainees not having or being able to find resources or equipment needed to complete an assignment).

ORGANIZATIONAL ENVIRONMENTS THAT ENCOURAGE TRANSFER

To ensure that trainees have the opportunity to perform, that managers and peers support training activities, that trainees motivated to learn, and that the work environment is favorable for learning, many companies are attempting to become learning organizations and are concerned with knowledge management.

The Learning Organization

A **learning organization** is a company that has an enhanced capacity to learn, adapt, and change.[22] Training processes are carefully scrutinized and aligned with company goals. In a learning organization, training is seen as one part of a system designed to create intellectual capital. Recall from Chapter 2 that intellectual capital includes not only teaching employees basic capabilities needed to perform their current jobs, but also stimulating creativity and innovation plus motivating employees to acquire and apply knowledge.

The essential features of a learning organization appear in Table 5.6. Note that the learning organization emphasizes that learning occurs not only at the individual–employee level (as we traditionally think of learning), but also at the group and organizational levels. The learning organization emphasizes knowledge management.

To become a successful learning organization, companies may be required not only to place a greater emphasis on training but also to change human resource management systems to support learning. Skandia Sweden is the world's tenth largest life insurance company; it operates in more than 20 countries.[23] Skandia has many of the features of a learning organization. It supports training and development, which is linked to the company's business goals. As part

TABLE 5.6
Key Features of a Learning Organization

Source: Adapted from M. A. Gephart, V. J. Marsick, M. E. Van Buren, and M. S. Spiro, "Learning Organizations Come Alive," *Training and Development* 50 (1996): 34–45.

Feature	Description
Continuous Learning	Employees share learning with each other and use job as a basis for applying and creating knowledge.
Knowledge Generation and Sharing	Systems are developed for creating, capturing, and sharing knowledge.
Critical Systematic Thinking	Employees are encouraged to think in new ways, see relationships and feedback loops, and test assumptions.
Learning Culture	Learning is rewarded, promoted, and supported by managers and company objectives.
Encouragement of Flexibility and Experimentation	Employees are free to take risks, innovate, explore new ideas, try new processes, and develop new products and services.
Valuing of Employees	System and environment focus on ensuring the development and well-being of every employee.

of Skandia's continuous learning efforts, the company developed a corporate university, provided tuition reimbursement, and encouraged employees to take advantage of learning opportunities. But despite the encouragement Skandia noticed an increase in turnover. Interviews revealed that employees were burned out from the pressure to both work and learn. Employees were having difficulties meeting their personal obligations at home because they were busy developing new competencies at work. Skandia came up with a solution to support both learning and work. The company created a new benefit: a competency savings account in which, like a 401(k) account, Skandia matches the employee contribution. Employees can take time off to learn while still receiving a full salary, and the company uses the funds in the competency account to hire a temporary employee to fill the position. Skandia matches, at a rate of 3 to 1, the contributions by employees with minimum education, employees with 15 or more years experience, or employees who are more than 45 years old. The company views these employees as being at risk because their knowledge or skill is inadequate for current and future business. Skandia also created a website where employees can develop and manage their own growth plans.

Knowledge and Knowledge Management

Recall from Chapter 2 that knowledge refers to what individuals or teams of employees know or know how to do (human and social knowledge) as well as a company's rules, processes, tools, and routines (structured knowledge). Knowledge is either tacit knowledge or explicit knowledge. Tacit knowledge is personal knowledge based on individual experience and influenced by perceptions and values. The communication of tacit knowledge requires personal communications through discussion and demonstrations. Explicit knowledge refers to manuals, formulas, and specifications that are described in formal language. Explicit knowledge can either be managed by placing it in a knowledge database or be managed by a knowledge management system.

There are four modes of knowledge sharing: socialization, externalization, combination, and internalization. These are shown in Figure 5.4. **Socialization** involves sharing tacit

FIGURE 5.4

Four modes of knowledge sharing

Source: I. Nonaka and H. Takeuchi, *The Knowledge Creating Company* (New York: Oxford University Press, 1995).

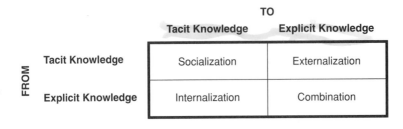

knowledge by sharing experiences. Knowledge is shared and learning occurs through observation, imitation, and practice. **Externalization** involves translating tacit knowledge into explicit knowledge. This takes the form of metaphors, models, concepts, and equations. **Combination** involves systematizing explicit concepts into a knowledge system by analyzing, categorizing, and using information in a new way. Formal courses and seminars convert knowledge in this way. **Internalization** refers to converting explicit knowledge to tacit knowledge. Training methods such as simulations, action learning, and on-the-job experiences are used to create tacit knowledge from explicit knowledge.

Knowledge management refers to the process of enhancing company performance by designing and implementing tools, processes, systems, structures, and cultures to improve the creation, sharing, and use of knowledge.[24] Knowledge management can help companies get products to market quicker, better serve customers, develop innovative products and services, and attract new employees and retain current ones by giving people the opportunity to learn and develop.

How might knowledge management occur? There are several ways to create and share knowledge:[25]

1. Use technology and software such as LOTUS Notes and e-mail, or create a company intranet that allows people to store information and share it with others.
2. Publish directories that list what employees do, how they can be contacted, and the type of knowledge they have.
3. Develop informational maps that identify where specific knowledge is stored in the company.
4. Create chief information officer and chief learning officer positions for cataloging and facilitating the exchange of information in the company.
5. Require employees to give presentations to other employees about what they have learned from training programs they have attended.
6. Allow employees to take time off from work to acquire knowledge, study problems, attend training, and use technology.
7. Create an online library of learning resources such as journals, technical manuals, training opportunities, and seminars.
8. Design office space to facilitate interaction between employees.

For example, KLA-Tencor employees have access to the company's best practices, proposals, experiences, references, marketing information, and other intellectual capital. Ernst and Young has information on employees' skills and competencies to help assemble project teams.[26] Xerox has created a database of "communities of interests," employees throughout the organization who have a common interest in a technology, product, service, or process who may not be working formally together but communicate informally to share and build knowledge for themselves and the company. Dow Chemical's database of patents, trademarks, and copyrights also includes vital business processes and practices. This helps employees avoid spending time, effort, and money on practices or processes that have already been completed in another part of the company.

BP Exploration, the division of BP that explores for and produces oil and gas, organized its regional operating centers into 42 autonomous business assets.[27] BP wanted these units to have the freedom to develop the processes and solutions appropriate to their specific problems. Best practices and innovations could be "shared" in other places in the company. As a result, BP launched a project designed to develop effective ways for team members to collaborate across different locations. The program ("The Virtual Teamwork Program") recognized that knowledge is important and that the company needed to develop appropriate ways to share it. The program's goal was to build a network of people and to allow knowledgeable people to talk to each other. The hardware and software used for the program included desktop videoconferencing equipment, multimedia e-mail, shared chalkboards, document scanners, groupware, and a Web browser. This equipment was chosen because the emphasis was on capturing the richness of communications and duplicating actual human interactions as much as possible. BP has instituted "virtual coffee breaks," where up to 20 people at up to eight separate locations discuss current work problems and ideas that have developed. BP hopes that these conversations will pay off in two ways. First, employees will have a better idea of what is happening in other places in the company. Second, participants discovering a connection between projects or suggestions might help solve a difficult problem.

For knowledge management to be effective, the training department and information technology department must collaborate.[28] Training can help develop the culture as well as the content and learning strategies. Information technology develops the systems for accessing, sharing, and storing knowledge and delivering training. For example, the Royal Bank of Canada intranet serves as the central depository for information about initiatives completed, planned, or under way in the company. It also contains templates and other "tools" for training project managers. A separate website features "lessons learned"—summaries posted by employees who have attended conferences and courses. Technologists developed the infrastructure and trainers recommended what features should be included. Raytheon's Project Library system allows a user to search the library for specific projects (e.g., cycle time reduction), then narrow the search to projects specific to a function (e.g., engineering) and even limit the search to a certain geographic area.[29] Descriptions of project leaders and their phone numbers are included with the project information. The project website now contains over 2,000 projects and is accessed by over 5,000 employees.

Some companies, including Xerox, IBM, and Plante and Moran, have created leadership positions to foster continuous learning and knowledge management.[30] By creating a position that is considered to be part of the company's top management team, a signal is sent to all employees that learning is valued and knowledge management is seen as related to business strategy and critical for the company's success. **Chief learning, or knowledge, officers (CLOs)** are leaders of a company's knowledge management efforts. The CLO's job is to develop, implement, and link a knowledge/learning culture with the company's technology infrastructure including databases and intranet. CLOs locate knowledge and find ways to create, capture, and distribute it. The CLO has to ensure that trainers, information technologists, and business units support and contribute to the development of knowledge management practices. The CLO also is responsible for ensuring that knowledge management is translated into visible benefits to the business. For example, the head of knowledge management at Aventis, a pharmaceutical company, is involved with figuring out how much information the company should share with its partners in joint ventures. Joint ventures in the industry are growing as companies look to share the costs of developing new drugs. At Whirlpool, an appliance company, knowledge management led to the development of "innovation mentors" around the world who encouraged employees to try out new ideas.[31]

An important issue in knowledge management is whether employees are willing to share knowledge with others. Employees may believe that sharing knowledge makes them susceptible to downsizing, takes away their power, or forces them into taking on more work.[32] Sharing information needs to be encouraged by the company culture and reward system. Viant, a consulting company specializing in building e-businesses, is a learning organization that successfully manages knowledge.[33] Viant consultants work and create in a community of shared learning, mutual respect, and energetic collaboration, where inspiration happens and innovation results. All new employees begin their careers at the home office in Boston learning about the company. They learn team skills and Viant's consulting strategy and tools; they are exposed to the company culture and meet its upper-level management team. Viant's open-office arrangement encourages interactions between work teams by setting up snack areas that intersect where teams are working. The company's nonhierarchical structure promotes the free flow of ideas, and it values expertise over job titles. Viant's leadership team includes rotating "fellows" nominated by peers. Performance reviews emphasize growth in employees' skill levels, while knowledge sharing is rewarded with stock options. Viant rewards employees for how they contribute to the company and the culture, including how they share knowledge, master new skills, take ownership, and mentor and teach. At Viant, before every project, consultants complete a brief document that describes what knowledge they need, what knowledge from other projects can be used, what they will need to create, and what lessons they hope to learn that they can share with other consultants. The documents end up in Viant's internal website. Every six weeks, the company's internal knowledge management group prepares and posts online a summary of what has been learned. To further stimulate knowledge management Viant has created the role of "project catalyst" for its consultants. Project catalysts are assigned to multiple projects. Their job is to challenge and question the teams, to push them to think of innovative solutions and insightful approaches and ideas for business problems.

How does knowledge management translate into Viant's business practices? Viant's team helped BlueTape build and launch a digital entertainment business. BlueTape's first offering is sputnik7, an online interactive music video channel for Web- and music-savvy trendspotters. The technologists on the sputnik7.com team pushed current technology to its limits, delivering inline, synchronized streaming media through a Web browser. They weren't stopped by not knowing if something could be done; they questioned processes and technology and experimented.

Because knowledge management can potentially improve a company's competitive position, companies that are managing knowledge use several measures to evaluate the effectiveness of their knowledge management practices. Evaluation is discussed in greater detail in Chapter 6.) These measures include the ability to attract and retain key employees, employee commitment to the company, new product introductions, customer satisfaction, repeat relationships with customers, and percentage of employees involved in designing and developing new products and services.[34]

Summary	Learning is an important aspect of any training program. But equally important is encouraging trainees to use learned capabilities on the job (transfer of training). This chapter discussed how trainee characteristics, trainee design features, and the work environment influence transfer of training. From a design standpoint, the chapter emphasized that it is important to consider identical elements, stimulus generalization, and cognitive theories related to transfer of training in program design. Trainees may need self-management skills to cope with a work environment that is not always conducive to transfer of training. The climate for transfer, manager and peer support, technology support, and opportunity to perform are features of the work environment that influence transfer of training. Transfer of training is an important issue to companies that consider themselves to be learning organizations. Recognizing the value of human, social, and structural knowledge, many companies are attempting to become learning organizations and to manage knowledge in order to develop better products and improve customer service.

Key Terms

transfer of training, *146*
generalization, *146*
maintenance, *146*
training design, *147*
trainee characteristics, *147*
work environment, *147*
theory of identical
elements, *149*
fidelity, *149*
near transfer, *150*
stimulus generalization
approach, *150*
far transfer, *150*

key behavior, *151*
cognitive theory of
transfer, *151*
application
assignments, *151*
self-management, *151*
lapses, *152*
climate for transfer, *154*
manager support, *156*
action plan, *156*
support network, *159*
opportunity to
perform, *159*

electronic performance
support system
(EPSS), *159*
learning organization, *160*
socialization, *161*
externalization, *162*
combination, *162*
internalization, *162*
knowledge
management, *162*
chief learning, or
knowledge, officer
(CLO), *163*

Discussion Questions

1. Consider three time periods (pretraining, during training, and after training) and three parties involved in transfer of training (manager, trainer, trainee). Construct a matrix showing what each party can do to facilitate transfer of training at each time period.
2. Distinguish between the following: (1) maintenance and generalization and (2) learning and transfer.
3. What could be done to increase the likelihood of transfer of training if the work environment conditions are unfavorable and cannot be changed?
4. Discuss how trainees can support each other so that transfer of training occurs.
5. What is the most important feature of the learning organization? Which is least important? Why?
6. What technologies might be useful for ensuring transfer of training? Briefly describe each technology and how it could be used.
7. How might you motivate managers to play a more active role in ensuring transfer of training?

8. Is training transfer an important issue in the companies where you have worked? How is transfer evaluated in those companies?

9. Discuss the major emphases of identical elements, stimulus generalization, and cognitive theories of transfer.

10. What is knowledge? Why is knowledge important? How can companies manage knowledge?

Application Assignments

1. Develop a questionnaire to measure the degree to which the work environment supports transfer of training. Include the questions and the rating scales you would use. Use the checklist in Table 5.5 as an example.

2. Design an action planning sheet that a manager and employee could use to facilitate transfer of training. Justify each category included in the action plan.

3. Develop specific recommendations that the instructor could use to make this class a learning organization.

4. This assignment relates to Application Assignment 2 in Chapter 4. You received the following e-mail from the vice president of operations:
   Thanks for your recommendations regarding how to make the "Improving Service Quality Program" a success. To improve hotel staff ability to respond effectively to customer complaints (that is, "recovery") we have incorporated many of your ideas into the program, including

   a. Having trainees bring an example of a customer problem to class.

   b. Giving trainees the opportunity to practice dealing with irate customers.

   c. Providing trainees with feedback during role plays.

   d. Having trainers identify and communicate objectives of the program to trainees.

   e. Having trainers communicate to the trainees specific key behaviors related to customer service.

   I am now concerned about how to make sure our training investments pay off. That is, I am really interested in the effective, continuous application of the skills and knowledge gained in training to employees' jobs.
   What recommendations do you have?

5. Go to *www.buckman.com,* the website for Buckman Laboratories. Buckman Laboratories works with industries worldwide, providing advanced chemical treatment technologies and extensive technical service to help solve complex industrial problems. Its expertise spans a broad range of specialty chemicals including microbiocides, scale inhibitors, corrosion inhibitors, polymers, dispersants, and defoamers. Buckman has been recognized as a leader in knowledge management practices. Click on Customer Value. Next, click on Knowledge Nurture. How does Buckman Laboratories manage knowledge? How has knowledge management contributed to the business?

6. Go to *www.boozallenhamilton.com,* the website for Booz Allen Hamilton, a consulting firm. Click on Careers. Review the links in this section of the website. Find out information about the company's training programs. Does the company have a work environment that supports training? Explain.

Endnotes

1. M. L. Broad and J. W. Newstrom, *Transfer of Training* (Reading, MA: Addison-Wesley, 1992).

2. J. M. Royer, "Theories of the Transfer of Learning," *Educational Psychologist* 14 (1979): 53–69.

3. E. L. Thorndike and R. S. Woodworth, "The Influence of Improvement of One Mental Function upon the Efficiency of Other Functions," *Psychological Review* 8 (1901): 247–61.

4. J. F. Reintzell, "When Training Saves Lives," *Training and Development* 51 (1997): 41–42.

5. J. A. Sparrow, "The Measurement of Job Profile Similarity for the Prediction of Transfer of Learning," *Journal of Occupational Psychology* 62 (1989): 337–41.

6. M. Machin, "Planning, Managing, and Optimizing Transfer of Training," in *Creating, Implementing, and Managing Effective Training and Development,* ed. K. Kraiger (San Francisco: Jossey-Bass, 2002): 263–301; J. Kim and C. Lee, "Implications of Near and Far Transfer of Training on Structured On-the-Job Training," *Advances in Developing Human Resources* (November 2001): 442–51.

7. Ibid.

8. C. A. Frayne and J. M. Geringer, "Self-Management Training for Joint Venture General Managers," *Human Resource Planning* 15 (1993): 69–85; L. Burke and T. Baldwin, "Workforce Training Transfer: A Study of the Effect of Relapse Prevention Training and Transfer Climate," *Human Resource Management* (Fall 1999): 227–42; C. Frayne and J. Geringer, "Self-Management Training for Improving Job Performance: A Filed Experiment Involving Salespeople," *Journal of Applied Psychology* (2000): 361–72.

9. A. Tziner, R. R. Haccoun, and A. Kadish, "Personal and Situational Characteristics Influencing the Effectiveness of Transfer of Training Strategies," *Journal of Occupational Psychology* 64 (1991): 167–77; R. A. Noe, J. A. Sears, and A. M. Fullenkamp, "Release Training: Does It Influence Trainees' Post-Training Behavior and Cognitive Strategies?" *Journal of Business and Psychology* 4 (1990): 317–28; M. E. Gist, C. K. Stevens, and A. G. Bavetta, "Effects of Self-Efficacy and Post-Training Intervention on the Acquisition and Maintenance of Complete Interpersonal Skills," *Personal Psychology* 44 (1991): 837–61.

10. J. B. Tracey, S. I. Tannenbaum, and M. J. Kavanaugh, "Applying Trained Skills on the Job: The Importance of the Work Environment," *Journal of Applied Psychology* 80 (1995): 239–52; P. E. Tesluk, J. L. Farr, J. E. Mathieu, and R. J. Vance, "Generalization of Employee Involvement Training to the Job Setting: Individual and Situational Effects," *Personnel Psychology* 48 (1995): 607–32; J. K. Ford, M. A. Quinones, D. J. Sego, and J. S. Sorra, "Factors Affecting the Opportunity to Perform Trained Tasks on the Job," *Personnel Psychology* 45 (1992): 511–27.

11. F. Jossi, "Lesson Plans," *HR Magazine* (February 2003): 72–76.

12. J. Laabs, "Mixing Business with Passion," *Workforce* (March 2000): 80–87, information about company culture and training from Patagonia website, *www.patagonia.com.*

13. A. Rossett, "That Was a Great Class, But . . . ," *Training and Development* (July 1997): 19–24.

14. J. M. Cusimano, "Managers as Facilitators," *Training and Development* 50 (1996): 31–33.

15. S. B. Parry, "Ten Ways to Get Management Buy-In," *Training and Development* (September 1997): 21–22; Broad and Newstrom, *Transfer of Training.*

16. D. Goldwasser, "Me, a Trainer," *Training* (April 2001): 61–66.

17. C. M. Petrini, ed., "Bringing It Back to Work," *Training and Development Journal* (December 1990): 15–21.

18. Ford, Quinones, Sego, and Sorra, "Factors Affecting the Opportunity to Perform Trained Tasks on the Job."

19. Ibid.; M. A. Quinones, J. K. Ford, D. J. Sego, and E. M. Smith, "The Effects of Individual and Transfer Environment Characteristics on the Opportunity to Perform Trained Tasks," *Training Research Journal* 1 (1995/96): 29–48.

20. G. Stevens and E. Stevens, "The Truth about EPSS," *Training and Development* 50 (1996): 59–61.

21. "In Your Face EPSs," *Training* (April 1996): 101–2.

22. M. A. Gephart, V. J. Marsick, M. E. Van Buren, and M. S. Spiro, "Learning Organizations Come Alive," *Training and Development* 50 (1996): 35–45; C. M. Solomon, "HR Facilitates the Learning Organization Concept," *Personnel Journal* (November 1994): 56–66; T. A. Stewart, "Getting Real about Brainpower," *Fortune* (November 27, 1995): 201–3; L. Thornburg, "Accounting for Knowledge," *HR Magazine* (October 1994): 51–56.

23. S. Hawkins, "The Competence Marketplace," *TD* (December 2002): 60–62.

24. D. DeLong and L. Fahey, "Diagnosing Cultural Barriers to Knowledge Management," *Academy of Management Executive* 14 (2000): 113–127; A. Rossett, "Knowledge Management Meets Analysis," *Training & Development* (May 1999): 63–68; M. Van Buren, "A Yardstick for Knowledge Management," *Training and Development* (May 1999): 71–78.

25. Gephart, Marsick, Van Buren, and Spiro, "Learning Organizations Come Alive."

26. D. Tobin, *The Knowledge-Enabled Organization* (New York: AMACOM. 1998).

27. T. Davenport and L. Prusak, *Working Knowledge* (Boston, MA: Harvard Business School Press, 1998).

28. J. Gordon, "Intellectual Capital and You," *Training* (September 1999): 30–38; D. Zielinski, "Have You Shared a Bright Idea Today?" *Training* (July 2000): 65–68.

29. K. Ellis, "Share Best Practices Globally," *Training* (July 2001): 32–38.

30. D. Bonner, "Enter the Chief Knowledge Officer," *Training and Development* (February 2000): 36–40.

31. D. Pringle, "Learning Gurus Adapt to Escape Corporate Axes," *The Wall Street Journal,* January 7, 2003: B1, B4.

32. T. Aeppel, "On Factory Floor, Top Workers Hide Secrets to Success," *The Wall Street Journal,* July 1, 2002: A1, A10; D. Lepak and S. Snell, "Managing Human Resource Architecture for Knowledge-Based Competition," in *Managing Knowledge for Sustained Competitive Advantage,* ed. S. Jackson, M. Hitt, and A. Denisi (San Francisco: Jossey-Bass, 2003): 127–54.

33. T. Stewart, "The House That Knowledge Built," *Fortune* (October 2, 2000): 278–80; Viant's website, *www.viant.com.*

34. M. Van Buren, "A Yardstick for Knowledge Management."

Chapter **Six**

Training Evaluation

Objectives

After reading this chapter, you should be able to

1. Explain why evaluation is important.
2. Identify and choose outcomes to evaluate a training program.
3. Discuss the process used to plan and implement a good training evaluation.
4. Discuss the strengths and weaknesses of different evaluation designs.
5. Choose the appropriate evaluation design based on the characteristics of the company and the importance and purpose of the training.
6. Conduct a cost-benefit analysis for a training program.

Training Is Flying High at Northwest Airlines

The Northwest Airlines technical operations training department includes 72 instructors who are responsible for training thousands of aircraft technicians and over 10,000 outside vendors who work on maintaining the Northwest aircraft fleet. Each of the training instructors works with one type of aircraft, such as the Airbus 320. Most of the department's training is instructor-led in a classroom, but other instruction programs use a simulator or take place in an actual airplane.

By tracking department training data, which allowed for training evaluation, the technical operations department was able to demonstrate its worth by showing how its services contribute to the airline's business. For example, the technical operations department reduced the cost of training an individual technician by 16 percent; increased customer satisfaction through training; increased training productivity; made the case for upper management to provide financial resources for training; and improved post-course evaluations, knowledge, and performance gains.

To achieve these results, the technical operations training department developed the Training Quality Index (TQI). The TQI is a computer application that collects data about training department performance, productivity, budget, and courses and allows for detailed analysis of the data. TQI tracks all department training data into five categories: effectiveness, quantity, perceptions, financial impact, and operational impact.

The quality of training is included under the effectiveness category. For example, knowledge gain relates to the difference in trainees' pretraining and posttraining knowledge measured by exams. The system can provide performance reports that relate to budgets and the cost of training per student per day and other costs of training. The measures that are collected are also linked to department goals, to department strategy, and ultimately, to Northwest Airline's overall strategy. Questions that were often asked before TQI was developed but couldn't easily be answered—such as how can the cost of training be justified, what is the operational impact of training, and what amount of training have technicians received—can now be answered through the TQI system. Training demand can be compared against passenger loads and the number of flying routes to determine the right number of trainers in the right locations to support business needs. These adjustments increase customer satisfaction and result in positive views of the training operations.

Source: J. Schettler, "Homegrown Solution," *Training* (November 2002): 76–79.

INTRODUCTION

As the opening vignette illustrates, Northwest Airlines wanted to show that the time, money, and effort devoted to training technicians actually made a difference. That is, the company was interested in assessing the effectiveness of the training program. **Training effectiveness** refers to the benefits that the company and the trainees receive from training. Benefits for trainees may include learning new skills or behavior. Benefits for the company may include increased sales and more satisfied customers. A training evaluation includes measuring specific outcomes or criteria to determine the benefits of the program. **Training outcomes or criteria** refer to measures that the trainer and the company use to evaluate training programs. To determine the effectiveness of the program, Northwest Airlines had to conduct an evaluation. **Training evaluation** refers to the process of collecting the outcomes needed to determine if training is effective. For Northwest Airlines, outcomes included trainees' satisfaction with the program and knowledge gained. Northwest Airlines also collected information that it used to highlight the financial benefits of training courses and the training department. Northwest Airlines also had to be confident that its information-gathering process was providing it with accurate conclusions about the effectiveness of its training programs. The **evaluation design** refers to the collection of information—including what, when, how, and from whom—that will be used to determine the effectiveness of the training program. Northwest Airlines used pretraining and posttraining measures of knowledge that were easily accessible from a database.

Recall the Instructional Systems Design model shown in Figure 1.1 and the topics covered in Chapters 2 through 5. The information from the needs assessment, the characteristics of the learning environment, and the steps taken to ensure transfer of training should all be used to develop an evaluation plan. In order to identify appropriate training outcomes, a company needs to look at its business strategy, at its organizational analysis (Why are we conducting training? How is it related to the business?), at its person analysis (Who needs training?), at its task analysis (What is the training content?), at the learning objectives of the training, and at its plan for training transfer.

This chapter will help you understand why and how to evaluate training programs. The chapter begins by discussing the types of outcomes used in training program evaluation. The next section of the chapter discusses issues related to choosing an evaluation design. An overview of the types of designs is presented. The practical factors that influence the type of design chosen for an evaluation are discussed. The chapter concludes by reviewing the process involved in conducting an evaluation.

REASONS FOR EVALUATING TRAINING

Companies are investing millions of dollars in training programs to help gain a competitive advantage: One estimate is that companies' direct spending on education and training was 2 percent of payroll in 2001. Regardless of industry or size, companies make substantial investment in training programs. For example, small companies (1–499 employees) who are members of ASTD's benchmarking service spend $1,027 in training per employee compared to $660 for large companies (2,000 or more employees).[1] Companies invest in training because learning creates knowledge, which differentiates between those companies and employees who are successful and those who are not. Because companies have made large dollar investments in training and education and view training as a strategy to be successful, they expect the outcomes or benefits related to training to be measurable.

For example, consider LensCrafters. LensCrafters brings the eye doctor, a wide selection of frames and lenses, and the lens-making laboratory together in one location. LensCrafters has convenient locations and hours of operations, and it has the ability to make eyewear on-site. Emphasizing customer service, the company offers a one-stop location and promises to make eyewear in one hour. Dave Palm, a training professional at LensCrafters, received a call from a concerned regional manager.[2] He called to tell Palm that although executives knew LensCrafters employees had to be well trained to design eyewear and that employees were satisfied with the training, they wanted to know whether the money they were investing in training was providing any return. Training evaluation provides a way to understand the investments that training produces and provides information needed to improve training.[3] If the company receives an inadequate return on its investment in training, the company will likely reduce its investment in training or look for training providers outside the company who can provide training experiences that improve performance, productivity, customer satisfaction, or whatever other outcomes the company is interested in achieving. Training evaluation provides the data needed to demonstrate that training does provide benefits to the company.

Training evaluation involves both formative and summative evaluation.[4] **Formative evaluation** refers to evaluation conducted to improve the training process. That is, formative evaluation helps to ensure that (1) the training program is well organized and runs smoothly and (2) trainees learn and are satisfied with the program. Formative evaluation provides information about how to make the program better; it usually involves collecting qualitative data about the program. Qualitative data includes opinions, beliefs, and feelings about the program. This information is collected through questionnaires or interviews with potential trainees and/or managers who are purchasing or paying for trainees to attend the program. Employees and managers, either individually or in groups, participate in the program before it is made available to the rest of the company. They are asked to evaluate the training materials' clarity and ease of use. Trainers measure the time requirements of the program. As a result of the formative evaluation, training content may be changed to be more accurate, easier to understand, or more appealing. The training method can be adjusted to improve learning (e.g., provide trainees with more opportunities to practice or give feedback).

Pilot testing refers to the process of previewing the training program with potential trainees and managers or with other customers (persons who are paying for the development of the program). Pilot testing can be used as a "dress rehearsal" to show the program to managers, trainees, and customers. It should also be used for formative evaluation. For example, a group of potential trainees and their managers may be asked to preview or pilot test a Web-based training program. As they complete the program, trainees and managers may be asked to provide their opinions as to whether graphics, videos, or music used in the program contributed to (or interfered with) learning. They may also be asked how easy it was to move through the program and complete the exercises, and they may be asked to evaluate the quality of feedback the training program provided after they completed the exercises. The information gained from this preview would be used by program developers to improve the program before it is made available to all employees.

Summative evaluation refers to evaluation conducted to determine the extent to which trainees have changed as a result of participating in the training program. That is, have trainees acquired knowledge, skills, attitudes, behavior, or other outcomes identified in the training objectives? Summative evaluation may also include measuring the monetary benefits (also known as return on investment) that the company receives from the program. Summative evaluation usually involves collecting quantitative (numerical) data through tests, ratings of behavior, or objective measures of performance such as volume of sales, accidents, or patents.

From the discussion of summative and formative evaluation, it is probably apparent to you why a training program should be evaluated:

1. To identify the program's strengths and weaknesses. This includes determining if the program is meeting the learning objectives, if the quality of the learning environment is satisfactory, and if transfer of training to the job is occurring.

2. To assess whether the content, organization, and administration of the program—including the schedule, accommodations, trainers, and materials—contribute to learning and the use of training content on the job.

3. To identify which trainees benefit most or least from the program.

4. To assist the marketing programs through the collection of information from participants about whether they would recommend the program to others, why they attended the program, and their level of satisfaction with the program.

5. To determine the financial benefits and costs of the program.

6. To compare the costs and benefits of training versus nontraining investments (such as work redesign or a better employee selection system).

7. To compare the costs and benefits of different training programs to choose the best program.

OVERVIEW OF THE EVALUATION PROCESS

Before you look at each aspect of training evaluation in detail, you need to understand the evaluation process, which is summarized in Figure 6.1. The previous discussion of formative and summative evaluation suggests that training evaluation involves scrutinizing the

FIGURE 6.1

The evaluation process

Source: Based on D. A. Grove and C. Ostroff, "Program Evaluation," in *Developing Human Resources*, ed. K. N. Wexley (Washington, DC: Bureau of National Affairs, 1991): 5-185 to 5-220.

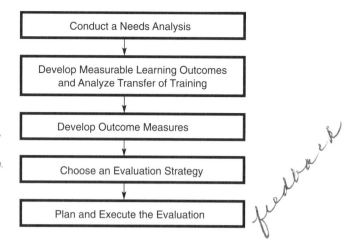

program both before and after the program is completed. Figure 6.1 emphasizes that training evaluation be considered by managers and trainers before training has actually occurred. As was suggested earlier in this chapter, information gained from the training design process shown in Figure 1.1 is valuable for training evaluation.

The evaluation process should begin with determining training needs (as discussed in Chapter 3). Needs assessment helps identify what knowledge, skills, behavior, or other learned capabilities are needed. Once the learned capabilities are identified, the next step in the process is to identify specific, measurable training objectives to guide the program. The characteristics of good objectives are discussed in Chapter 4. The more specific and measurable these objectives are, the easier it is to identify relevant outcomes for the evaluation. Analysis of the work environment to determine transfer of training (discussed in Chapter 5) is also useful for determining how training content will be used on the job. Based on the learning objectives and analysis of transfer of training, outcome measures are designed to assess the extent to which learning and transfer have occurred. Once the outcomes are identified, the next step is to determine an evaluation strategy. Factors such as expertise, how quickly the information is needed, change potential, and the organizational culture should be considered in choosing a design. Planning and executing the evaluation involves previewing the program (formative evaluation) as well as collecting training outcomes according to the evaluation design. The results of the evaluation are used to modify, market, or gain additional support for the program. Next is an examination of each aspect of the evaluation process, starting with the development of outcome measures.

OUTCOMES USED IN THE EVALUATION OF TRAINING PROGRAMS

To evaluate a training program, it is necessary to identify how you will determine if the program is effective. As mentioned earlier in the chapter, this involves identifying training outcomes or criteria.

Table 6.1 shows D. L. Kirkpatrick's four-level framework for categorizing training outcomes.[5] Both level 1 and level 2 criteria (reactions and learning) are collected before trainees return to their job. Level 3 and level 4 criteria (behavior and results) measure the

TABLE 6.1
Kirkpatrick's
Four-Level
Framework of
Evaluation
Criteria

Source: Based on
D. L. Kirkpatrick,
"Evaluation" in *The
ASTD Training and
Development
Handbook* (2nd ed.),
R. L. Craig (ed.)
(New York: McGraw-
Hill, 1996): 294–312.

Level	Criteria	Focus
4	Results	Business results achieved by trainees
3	Behavior	Improvement of behavior on the job
2	Learning	Acquisition of knowledge, skills, attitudes, behavior
1	Reactions	Trainee satisfaction

degree to which trainees are using training content on the job. That is, level 3 and level 4 criteria are used to determine transfer of training.

The hierarchical nature of Kirkpatrick's framework suggests that higher level outcomes should not be measured unless positive changes occur in lower level outcomes. For example, if trainees do not like a course, no learning will occur. Also, the framework implies that changes at a higher level (e.g., results) are more beneficial than changes at a lower level (e.g., learning). However, the framework has been criticized for a number of reasons. First, research has not found that each level is caused by the level that precedes it in the framework, nor does evidence suggest that the levels differ in importance.[6] Second, the approach does not take into account the purpose of the evaluation. The outcomes used for evaluation should relate to the training needs, the program learning objectives, and the strategic reasons for training. Third, use of the approach suggests that outcomes can and should be collected in an orderly manner, that is, measures of reaction followed by measures of learning, behavior, and results. Realistically, learning measures need to be collected at approximately the same time as reaction measures, near the end of the training program, in order to determine whether learning has occurred.

As a result of these criticisms, both training practitioners and academic researchers have argued that more comprehensive models of training criteria are needed, that is, that additional training outcomes are useful for evaluating training programs. These outcomes include attitudes, motivation, and return on investment. Accordingly, training outcomes have been classified into five categories: cognitive outcomes, skill-based outcomes, affective outcomes, results, and return on investment.[7] Table 6.2 shows examples of these outcomes and how they are measured.

Cognitive Outcomes

Cognitive outcomes are used to determine the degree to which trainees are familiar with principles, facts, techniques, procedures, or processes emphasized in the training program. Cognitive outcomes—which include the level 2 (learning) criteria from Kirkpatrick's framework—measure what knowledge trainees learned in the program. Typically, paper-and-pencil tests are used to assess cognitive outcomes. Table 6.3 provides an example of items from a pencil-and-paper test used to measure trainees' knowledge of decision-making skills. These items help to measure whether a trainee knows how to make a decision (the process he or she would use). They do not help to determine if the trainee will actually use decision-making skills on the job.

Skill-Based Outcomes

Skill-based outcomes are used to assess the level of technical or motor skills and behaviors. Skill-based outcomes include acquisition or learning of skills (skill learning) and use of skills on the job (skill transfer). The extent to which trainees have learned skills can be

TABLE 6.2 **Outcomes Used in Evaluating Training Programs**

Outcome	Example	How Measured	What Is Measured
Cognitive Outcomes	• Safety rules • Electrical principles • Steps in appraisal interview	• Pencil-and-paper tests • Work sample	• Acquisition of knowledge
Skill-Based Outcomes	• Jigsaw use • Listening skills • Coaching skills • Airplane landings	• Observation • Work sample • Ratings	• Behavior • Skills
Affective Outcomes	• Satisfaction with training • Beliefs regarding other cultures	• Interviews • Focus groups • Attitude surveys	• Motivation • Reaction to program • Attitudes
Results	• Absenteeism • Accidents • Patents	• Observation • Data from information system or performance records	• Company payoff
Return on Investment	• Dollars	• Identification and comparison of costs and benefits of the program	• Economic value of training

TABLE 6.3
Sample Test Items Used to Measure Learning

Source: Based on A. P. Carnevale, L. J. Gainer, and A. S. Meltzer, *Workplace Basics Training Manual* (San Francisco: Jossey-Bass, 1990): 8.12.

For each question, check all that apply.

1. If my boss returned a piece of work to me and asked me to make changes on it, I would:

___ Prove to my boss that the work didn't need to be changed.
___ Do what the boss said, but show where changes are needed.
___ Make the changes without talking to my boss.
___ Request a transfer from the department.

2. If I were setting up a new process in my office, I would:

___ Do it on my own without asking for help.
___ Ask my boss for suggestions.
___ Ask the people who work for me for suggestions.
___ Discuss it with friends outside the company.

evaluated by observing their performance in work samples such as simulators. Skill transfer is usually determined by observation. For example, a resident medical student may perform surgery while the surgeon carefully observes, giving advice and assistance as needed. Peers and managers may also be asked to rate trainees' behavior or skills based on their observations. Table 6.4 shows a sample rating form. This form was used as part of an evaluation of a training program developed to improve school principals' management skills. Skill-based outcomes relate to Kirkpatrick's level 2 (learning) and level 3 (behavior).

TABLE 6.4   Sample Rating Form Used to Measure Behavior

Rating task: Consider your opportunities over the past three months to observe and interact with the principal/assistant principal you are rating. Read the definition and behaviors associated with the skill. Then complete your ratings using the following scale:

Always	Usually	Sometimes	Seldom	Never
1	2	3	4	5

I. *Sensitivity:* Ability to perceive the needs, concerns, and personal problems of others; tact in dealing with persons from different backgrounds; skill in resolving conflict; ability to deal effectively with people concerning emotional needs; knowing what information to communicate to whom.

To what extent in the past three months has the principal or assistant principal:

___ 1. Elicited perceptions, feelings, and concerns of others?
___ 2. Expressed verbal and nonverbal recognition of the feelings, needs, and concerns of others?
___ 3. Taken actions that anticipated the emotional effects of specific behaviors?
___ 4. Accurately reflected the point of view of others by restating it, applying it, or encouraging feedback?
___ 5. Communicated all information to others that they needed to perform their job?
___ 6. Diverted unnecessary conflict with others in problem situations?

II. *Decisiveness:* Ability to recognize when a decision is required and act quickly. (Disregard the quality of the decision.)

To what extent in the past three months has this individual:

___ 7. Recognized when a decision was required by determining the results if the decision was made or not made?
___ 8. Determined whether a short- or long-term solution was most appropriate to various situations encountered in the school?
___ 9. Considered decision alternatives?
___ 10. Made a timely decision based on available data?
___ 11. Stuck to decisions once they were made, resisting pressures from others?

Affective Outcomes

Affective outcomes include attitudes and motivation. One type of affective outcome is trainees' reactions toward the training program. **Reaction outcomes** refer to trainees' perceptions of the program including the facilities, trainers, and content. (Reaction outcomes are often referred to as a measure of "creature comfort.") This information is typically collected at the program's conclusion. Reactions are useful for identifying what trainees thought was successful or inhibited learning.

Reaction outcomes are typically collected via a questionnaire completed by trainees. A reaction measure should include questions related to the trainee's satisfaction with the instructor, training materials, and training administration (ease of registration, accuracy of course description) as well as the clarity of course objectives and usefulness of the training content.[8] Table 6.5 shows a reaction measure that contains questions about these areas. Keep in mind that while reactions provide useful information, they usually only weakly relate to learning or transfer of training.

An **instructor evaluation** measures a trainer's or instructor's success. An accurate instructor evaluation needs to include the complete range of factors that make a trainer successful.[9]

TABLE 6.5 **Sample Reaction Measure**

Read each statement below. Indicate the extent to which you agree or disagree with each statement using the scale below.

Strongly Disagree	Disagree	Neither	Agree	Strongly Agree
1	2	3	4	5

1. I had the knowledge and skills needed to learn in this course.
2. The facilities and equipment made it easy to learn.
3. The course met all of the stated objectives.
4. I clearly understood the course objectives.
5. The way the course was delivered was an effective way to learn.
6. The materials I received during the course were useful.
7. The course content was logically organized.
8. There was enough time to learn the course content.
9. I felt that the instructor wanted us to learn.
10. I was comfortable asking the instructor questions.
11. The instructor was prepared.
12. The instructor was knowledgeable about the course content.
13. I learned a lot from this course.
14. What I learned in this course is useful for my job.
15. The information I received about the course was accurate.
16. Overall, I was satisfied with the instructor.
17. Overall, I was satisfied with the course.

Most instructor evaluations include items related to the trainer's preparation, delivery, ability to lead a discussion, organization of the training materials and content, use of visual aids, presentation style, ability and willingness to answer questions, and ability to stimulate trainees' interest in the course. These items come from trainer's manuals, trainer certification programs, and observation of successful trainers.

Other affective outcomes that might be collected in an evaluation include tolerance for diversity, motivation to learn, safety attitudes, and customer service orientation. Affective outcomes can be measured using surveys. The specific attitude of interest depends on the program objectives. For example, attitudes toward equal employment opportunity laws might be an appropriate outcome to use to evaluate a diversity training program.

Results

Results are used to determine the training program's payoff for the company. Examples of results outcomes include increased production and reduced costs related to employee turnover, accidents, and equipment downtime as well as improvements in product quality or customer service.[10] For example, Kroger, the supermarket chain, hires more than 100,000 new employees each year who need to be trained.[11] Kroger collected productivity data for an evaluation comparing cashiers who received computer-based training to those who were trained in the classroom and on the job. The measures of productivity included rate of scanning grocery items, recognition of produce that had to be identified and weighed at the checkout, and the amount of time that store offices spent helping the cashiers deal with more complex transactions such as food stamps and checks.

Return on Investment

Return on investment (ROI) refers to comparing the training's monetary benefits with the cost of the training. Training costs can be direct and indirect.[12] **Direct costs** include salaries and benefits for all employees involved in training, including trainees, instructors, consultants, and employees who design the program; program material and supplies; equipment or classroom rentals or purchases; and travel costs. **Indirect costs** are not related directly to the design, development, or delivery of the training program. They include general office supplies, facilities, equipment, and related expenses; travel and expenses not directly billed to one program; training department management and staff salaries not related to any one program; and administrative and staff support salaries. **Benefits** are the value that the company gains from the training program.

The last section in this chapter includes a detailed example of how to determine the costs, benefits, and return on investment from a training program.

DETERMINING WHETHER OUTCOMES ARE GOOD

An important issue in choosing outcomes is to determine whether they are good. That is, are these outcomes the best ones to measure to determine if the training program is effective? Good training outcomes need to be relevant, reliable, discriminative, and practical.[13]

Relevance

Criteria relevance refers to the extent to which training outcomes are related to the learned capabilities emphasized in the training program. The learned capabilities required to succeed in the training program should be the same as those required to be successful on the job. The outcomes collected in training should be as similar as possible to what trainees learned in the program. That is, the outcomes need to be valid measures of learning. One way to ensure the relevancy of the outcomes is to choose outcomes based on the learning objectives for the program. Recall from Chapter 4 that the learning objectives show the expected action, conditions under which the trainee is to perform, and the level or standard of performance.

Figure 6.2 shows two ways that training outcomes may lack relevance. **Criterion contamination** refers to the extent that training outcomes measure inappropriate capabilities or are affected by extraneous conditions. For example, if managers' evaluations of job performance are used as a training outcome, trainees may receive higher ratings of job performance simply because the managers know they attended the training program, believe the program is valuable, and therefore give high ratings to ensure that the training looks like it positively affects performance. Criteria may also be contaminated if the conditions under which the outcomes are measured vary from the learning environment. That is, trainees may be asked to perform their learned capabilities using equipment, time constraints, or physical working conditions that are not similar to those in the learning environment.

For example, trainees may be asked to demonstrate spreadsheet skills using a newer version of spreadsheet software than they used in the training program. This demonstration likely will result in no changes in their spreadsheet skills from pretraining levels. In this case, poor-quality training is not the cause for the lack of change in their spreadsheet skills. Trainees may have learned the necessary spreadsheet skills, but the environment for the

FIGURE 6.2
Criterion
deficiency,
relevance, and
contamination

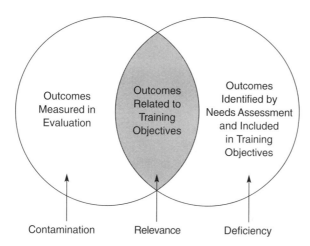

evaluation differs substantially from the learning environment, so no change in their skill levels is observed.

Criteria may also be deficient. **Criterion deficiency** refers to the failure to measure training outcomes that were emphasized in the training objectives. For example, the objectives of a spreadsheet skills training program emphasize that trainees both understand the commands available on the spreadsheet (e.g., compute) and use the spreadsheet to calculate statistics using a data set. An evaluation design that uses only learning outcomes such as a test of knowledge of the purpose of keystrokes is deficient, because the evaluation does not measure outcomes that were included in the training objectives (e.g., use spreadsheet to compute the mean and standard deviation of a set of data).

Reliability

Reliability refers to the degree to which outcomes can be measured consistently over time. For example, a trainer gives restaurant employees a written test measuring knowledge of safety standards to evaluate a safety training program they attended. The test is given before (pretraining) and after (posttraining) employees attend the program. A reliable test includes items for which the meaning or interpretation does not change over time. A reliable test allows the trainer to have confidence that any improvements in posttraining test scores from pretraining levels result from learning that occurred in the training program, not from test characteristics (e.g., items are more understandable the second time) or the test environment (e.g., trainees performed better on the posttraining test because the classroom was more comfortable and quieter).

Discrimination

Discrimination refers to the degree to which trainees' performances on the outcome actually reflect true differences in performance. For example, a paper-and-pencil test that measures electricians' knowledge of electrical principles must detect true differences in trainees' knowledge of electrical principles. That is, the test should discriminate on the basis of trainees' knowledge of electrical principles. (People who score high on the test have better understanding of principles of electricity than those who score low.)

FIGURE 6.3

Training evaluation practices

Source: Based on C. Thompson, E. Koon, W. Woodwell Jr. and J. Beauvais, "Training for the Next Economy: An ASTD State of the Industry Report on Trends in Employer-Provided Training in the United States" (Washington, DC: American Society for Training and Development, 2002), p.33.

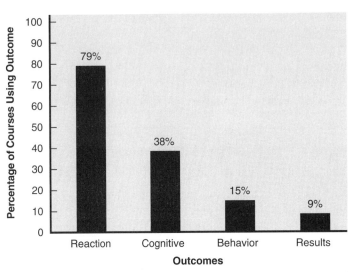

Note: Respondents were companies that participated in ASTD Benchmarking Service or Benchmarking Forum, or that were identified as Training Investment Leaders.

Practicality

Practicality refers to the ease with which the outcomes measures can be collected. One reason that companies give for not including learning, performance, and behavior outcomes in their evaluation of training programs is that collecting them is too burdensome. (It takes too much time and energy, which detracts from the business.) For example, in evaluating a sales training program, it may be impractical to ask customers to rate the salesperson's behavior because this would place too much of a time commitment on the customer (and probably damage future sales relationships).

EVALUATION PRACTICES

Figure 6.3 shows outcomes used in training evaluation practices. Surveys of companies' evaluation practices indicate that reactions (an affective outcome) and cognitive outcomes are the most frequently used outcomes in training evaluation.[14] Keep in mind that while most companies are conducting training evaluations, some surveys indicate that 20 percent of all companies are not!

It is important to recognize the limitations of using only reaction and cognitive outcomes. Consider the previous discussions of learning (Chapter 4) and transfer of training (Chapter 5). Remember that for training to be successful, learning *and* transfer of training must occur. Figure 6.4 shows the multiple objectives of training programs and their implication for choosing evaluation outcomes. Training programs usually have objectives related to both learning and transfer. That is, they want trainees to acquire knowledge and cognitive skill and also to demonstrate the use of the knowledge or strategy in their on-the-job behavior. As a result, to ensure an adequate training evaluation, companies must collect outcome measures related to both learning and transfer.

FIGURE 6.4

Training program objectives and their implications for evaluation

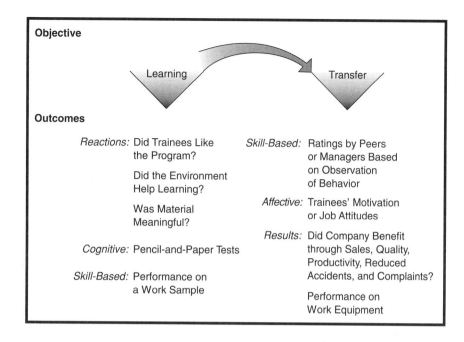

Note that outcome measures are independent of each other. That is, it is tempting to assume that satisfied trainees learn more and will apply their knowledge and skill to the job, resulting in behavior change and positive results for the company. However, research indicates that the relationships among reaction, cognitive, behavior, and results outcomes are small.[15]

Which training outcomes measure is best? The answer depends on the training objectives. For example, if the instructional objectives identified business-related outcomes such as increased customer service or product quality, then results outcomes should be included in the evaluation. As Figure 6.4 shows, both reaction and cognitive outcomes may affect learning. Reaction outcomes provide information regarding the extent to which the trainer, facilities, or learning environment may have hindered learning. Cognitive outcomes directly measure the extent to which trainees have mastered training content. Reaction and cognitive outcomes do not help determine the extent to which trainees actually use the training content in their jobs. To the extent possible, evaluation should include skill-based, affective, or results outcomes to determine the extent to which transfer of training has occurred—that is, training has influenced a change in behavior, skill, or attitude or has directly influenced objective measures related to company effectiveness (e.g., sales).

Positive transfer of training is demonstrated when learning occurs and positive changes in skill-based, affective, or results outcomes are also observed. No transfer of training is demonstrated if learning occurs but no changes are observed in skill-based, affective, or learning outcomes. Negative transfer is evident when learning occurs but skills, affective outcomes, or results are less than at pretraining levels. Results of evaluation studies that find no transfer or negative transfer suggest that the trainer and the manager need to investigate whether a good learning environment (e.g., opportunities for feedback and practice) was provided in the training program, trainees were motivated and able to learn, and the needs assessment correctly identified training needs.

EVALUATION DESIGNS

The design of the training evaluation determines the confidence that can be placed in the results, that is, how sure a company can be that training is responsible for changes in evaluation outcomes or that training failed to influence the outcomes. No evaluation design can ensure that the results of the evaluation are completely due to training. What the evaluator strives for is to use the most rigorous design possible (given the circumstances under which the evaluation occurs) to rule out alternative explanations for the results of the evaluation.

This discussion of evaluation designs begins by identifying these "alternative explanations" that the evaluator should attempt to control for. Next, various evaluation designs are compared. Finally, this section discusses practical circumstances that the trainer needs to consider in selecting an evaluation design.

Threats to Validity: Alternative Explanations for Evaluation Results

Table 6.6 presents threats to validity of an evaluation. **Threats to validity** refer to factors that will lead an evaluator to question either (1) the believability of the study results or (2) the extent to which the evaluation results are generalizable to other groups of trainees and situations.[16] The believability of study results refers to **internal validity.** The internal threats to validity relate to characteristics of the company (history), the outcome measures (instrumentation, testing), and the persons in the evaluation study (maturation, regression toward the mean, mortality, initial group differences). These characteristics can cause the evaluation study to reach the wrong conclusions about training effectiveness. An evaluation study needs internal validity to provide confidence that the results of the evaluation (particularly if they are positive) are due to the training program and not to another factor. For example, consider a group of managers who have attended a communication skills training program. At the same time that they attend the program, it is announced that the company will be restructured. After the program, the managers may become better communicators simply because they are scared that otherwise they will lose their jobs. Perhaps no learning actually occurred in the training program!

Trainers are also interested in the generalizability of the study results to other groups and situations (i.e., they are interested in the **external validity** of the study). As shown in Table 6.6, threats to external validity relate to how study participants react to being included in the study and the effects of multiple types of training. Because evaluation usually does not involve all employees who have completed a program (or who may take training in the future), trainers want to be able to say that the training program will be effective in the future with similar groups.

Methods to Control for Threats to Validity

Because trainers often want to use evaluation study results as a basis for changing training programs or demonstrating that training does work (as a means to gain additional funding for training from those who control the training budget), it is important to minimize the threats to validity. There are three ways to minimize threats to validity: the use of pretest and posttest in evaluation designs, comparison groups, and random assignment.

TABLE 6.6 **Threats to Validity**

Threats to Internal Validity	Description
Company	
History	Event occurs, producing changes in training outcomes.
Persons	
Maturation	Changes in training outcomes result from trainee's physical growth or emotional state.
Mortality	Study participants drop out of study, e.g., leave company.
Initial Group Differences	Training group differs from comparison group on individual differences that influence outcomes (knowledge, skills, ability, behavior).
Outcome Measures	
Testing	Trainees are sensitized to perform well on posttest measures.
Instrumentation	Trainee interpretation of outcomes changes over course of evaluation.
Regression toward the Mean	High- and low-scoring trainees move toward middle or average on posttraining measure.
Threats to External Validity	**Description**
Reaction to Pretest	Use of test before training causes trainee to pay attention to material on test.
Reaction to Evaluation	Being evaluated causes trainee to try harder in training program.
Interaction of Selection and Training	Characteristics of trainee influence program effectiveness.
Interaction of Methods	Results of trainees who received different methods can be generalized only to trainees who receive same training in the same order.

Source: Based on T. D. Cook, D. T. Campbell, and L. Peracchio, "Quasi-Experimentation," in *Handbook of Industrial and Organizational Psychology,* 2d ed., Vol. 1, eds. M. D. Dunnette and L. M. Hough (Palo Alto, CA: Consulting Psychologists Press, 1990): 491–576.

Pretests and Posttests   One way to improve the internal validity of the study results is to first establish a baseline or **pretraining measure** of the outcome. Another measure of the outcomes can be taken after training. This is referred to as a **posttraining measure.** A comparison of the posttraining and pretraining measures can indicate the degree to which trainees have changed as a result of training.

Use of Comparison Groups   Internal validity can be improved by using a control or comparison group. A **comparison group** refers to a group of employees who participate in the evaluation study but do not attend the training program. The comparison employees have personal characteristics (e.g., gender, education, age, tenure, skill level) as similar to the trainees as possible. Use of a comparison group in training evaluation helps to rule out the possibility that changes found in the outcome measures are due to factors other than training. The **Hawthorne effect** refers to employees in an evaluation study performing at a high level simply because of the attention they are receiving. Use of a comparison group helps to show that any effects observed are due specifically to the training rather than to the attention the trainees are receiving. Use of a comparison group helps to control for the effects of history, testing, instrumentation, and maturation because both the comparison group and training group are treated similarly, receive the same measures, and have the same amount of time to develop.

For example, consider an evaluation of a safety training program. Safe behaviors are measured before and after safety training for both trainees and a comparison group. If the level of safe behavior improves for the training group from pretraining levels but remains relatively the same for the comparison group at both pretraining and posttraining, the reasonable conclusion is that the training (not some other factor, such as the attention given to both the trainees and comparison group by asking them to participate in the study) was responsible for the observed differences in safe behaviors.

Random Assignment   **Random assignment** refers to assigning employees to the training or comparison group on the basis of chance. That is, employees are assigned to the training program without consideration of individual differences (ability, motivation) or prior experiences. Random assignment helps to ensure that trainees are similar in individual differences such as age, gender, ability, and motivation. Because it is often impossible to identify and measure all of the individual characteristics that might influence the outcome measures, random assignment ensures that these characteristics are equally distributed in the comparison group and the training group. Random assignment helps to reduce the effects of employees dropping out of the study (mortality) and differences between the training group and comparison group in ability, knowledge, skill, or other personal characteristics.

Keep in mind that random assignment is often impractical. Companies want to train employees who need training. Also, companies may be unwilling to provide a comparison group. One solution to this problem is to identify the factors in which the training and comparison groups differ and control for these factors in the analysis of the data (a statistical procedure known as analysis of covariance). Another method is to determine trainees' characteristics after they are assigned and ensure that the comparison group includes employees with similar characteristics.

Types of Evaluation Designs

A number of different designs can be used to evaluate training programs.[17] Table 6.7 compares each design on the basis of who is involved (trainees, comparison group), when measures are collected (pretraining, posttraining), the costs, the time it takes to conduct the evaluation, and the strength of the design for ruling out alternative explanations for the results. As shown in Table 6.7, research designs vary based on whether they include pretraining and posttraining measurement of outcomes and a comparison group. In general, designs that use pretraining and posttraining measures of outcomes and include a comparison group reduce the risk that alternative factors (other than the training itself) are responsible for the results of the evaluation. This increases the trainer's confidence in using the results to make decisions. Of course, the trade-off is that evaluations using these designs are more costly and take more time to conduct than do evaluations not using pretraining and posttraining measures or comparison groups.

Posttest Only

The **posttest-only** design refers to an evaluation design in which only posttraining outcomes are collected. This design can be strengthened by adding a comparison group (which helps to rule out alternative explanations for changes). The posttest-only design is appropriate when trainees (and the comparison group, if one is used) can be expected to have similar levels of knowledge, behavior, or results outcomes (e.g., same number of sales, equal awareness of how to close a sale) prior to training.

TABLE 6.7   *Comparison of Evaluation Designs*

Design	Groups	Measures				
		Pretraining	Posttraining	Cost	Time	Strength
Posttest Only	Trainees	No	Yes	Low	Low	Low
Pretest/Posttest	Trainees	Yes	Yes	Low	Low	Med.
Posttest Only with Comparison Group	Trainees and Comparison	No	Yes	Med.	Med.	Med.
Pretest/Posttest with Comparison Group	Trainees and Comparison	Yes	Yes	Med.	Med.	High
Time Series	Trainees	Yes	Yes, several	Med.	Med.	Med.
Time Series with Comparison Group and Reversal	Trainees and Comparison	Yes	Yes, several	High	Med.	High
Solomon Four-Group	Trainees A	Yes	Yes	High	High	High
	Trainees B	No	Yes			
	Comparison A	Yes	Yes			
	Comparison B	No	Yes			

For example, pharmacy technicians wait on customers, take refill information over the phone from doctors, and provide customers with information regarding generic drugs in place of brand-name drugs when the two are identical (generic drugs cost the customer less money).[18] At Walgreen Company, a training course for new technicians was developed to replace the on-the-job training technicians had received from the pharmacists who hired them. The new training course involved 20 hours of classroom training and 20 hours of supervision on the job. Because the company has several thousand stores, large amounts of money and time were being invested in the training. As a result, the company decided to evaluate the program.

The evaluation consisted of comparing technicians who had completed the program with some who had not. Surveys about new employees' performance were sent to the pharmacists who supervised the technicians. Some questions related to speed of entering patient and drug data into the store computer and how often the technician offered customers generic drug substitutes. The results of the comparison showed that formally trained technicians were more efficient and wasted less of the pharmacist's time than technicians who received traditional on-the-job training. Sales in pharmacies with formally trained technicians exceeded sales in pharmacies with on-the-job-trained technicians by an average of $9,500 each year.

Pretest/Posttest

The **pretest/posttest** refers to an evaluation design in which both pretraining and posttraining outcomes measures are collected. There is no comparison group. The lack of a comparison group makes it difficult to rule out the effects of business conditions or other factors as explanations for changes. This design is often used by companies that want to evaluate a training program but are uncomfortable with excluding certain employees or that only intend to train a small group of employees.

TABLE 6.8

Example of a Pretest/Posttest Comparison Group Design

Source: Based on S. J. Simon and J. M. Werner, "Computer Training through Behavior Modeling, Self-Paced and Instructional Approaches: A Field Experiment," *Journal of Applied Psychology* 81 (1996): 648–59.

	Pretraining	Training	Posttraining Time 1	Posttraining Time 2
Lecture	Yes	Yes	Yes	Yes
Self-Paced	Yes	Yes	Yes	Yes
Behavior Modeling	Yes	Yes	Yes	Yes
No Training (Comparison)	Yes	No	Yes	Yes

Pretest/Posttest with Comparison Group

The **pretest/posttest with comparison group** refers to an evaluation design that includes trainees and a comparison group. Pretraining and posttraining outcome measures are collected from both groups. If improvement is greater for the training group than the comparison group, this finding provides evidence that training is responsible for the change. This type of design controls for most of the threats to validity.

Table 6.8 presents an example of a pretest/posttest comparison group design. This evaluation involved determining the relationship between three conditions or treatments and learning, satisfaction, and use of computer skills.[19] The three conditions or treatments (types of computer training) were behavior modeling, self-paced studying, and lecturing. A comparison group was also included in the study. Behavior modeling involved watching a video showing a model performing key behavior necessary to complete a task. In this case the task was procedures on the computer. (Behavior modeling is discussed in detail in Chapter 7.)

Forty trainees were included in each condition. Measures of learning included a test consisting of 11 items designed to measure information that trainees needed to know to operate the computer system (e.g., "Does formatting destroy all data on the disk?"). Also, trainees' comprehension of computer procedures (procedural comprehension) was measured by presenting trainees with scenarios on the computer screens and asking them what would appear next on the screen. Use of computer skills (skill-based learning outcome) was measured by asking trainees to complete six computer tasks (e.g., changing directories). Satisfaction with the program (reaction) was measured by six items (e.g., "I would recommend this program to others").

As shown in Table 6.8, measures of learning and skills were collected from the trainees prior to attending the program (pretraining). Measures of learning and skills were also collected immediately after training (posttraining time 1) and four weeks after training (posttraining time 2). The satisfaction measure was collected immediately following training.

The posttraining time 2 measures collected in this study help to determine the occurrence of training transfer and retention of the information and skills. That is, immediately following training, trainees may have appeared to learn and acquire skills related to computer training. Collection of the posttraining measures four weeks after training provides information about trainees' level of retention of the skills and knowledge.

Statistical procedures known as analysis of variance and analysis of covariance were used to test for differences between pretraining measures and posttraining measures for each condition. Also, differences between each of the training conditions and the comparison group were analyzed. These procedures test to determine if differences between the groups are large enough to conclude with a high degree of confidence that the differences were caused by training rather than by chance fluctuations in trainees' scores on the measures.

TABLE 6.9
**Example of a
Time Series
Design**

Source: J. Komaki,
K. D. Badwick, and
L. R. Scott, "A
Behavioral Approach
to Occupational
Safety: Pinpointing
Safe Performance in a
Food Manufacturing
Plant," *Journal of
Applied Psychology* 63
(1978). Copyright
1978 by the American
Psychological Associa-
tion. Adapted by
permission.

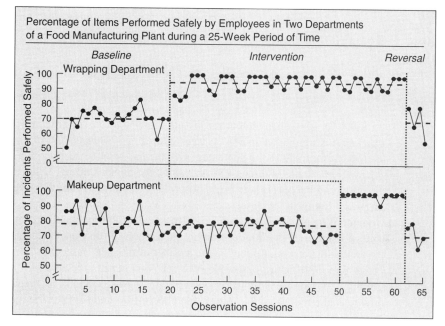

Percentage of Items Performed Safely by Employees in Two Departments of a Food Manufacturing Plant during a 25-Week Period of Time

Time Series

Time series refers to an evaluation design in which training outcomes are collected at periodic intervals both before and after training. (In the other evaluation designs discussed here, training outcomes are collected only once after and maybe once before training.) The strength of this design can be improved by using **reversal,** which refers to a time period in which participants no longer receive the training intervention. A comparison group can also be used with a time series design. One advantage of the time series design is that it allows an analysis of the stability of training outcomes over time. Another advantage is that using both the reversal and comparison group helps to rule out alternative explanations for the evaluation results. The time series design is frequently used to evaluate training programs that focus on improving readily observable outcomes (such as accident rates, productivity, and absenteeism) that vary over time.

Table 6.9 shows a time series design that was used to evaluate how much a training program improved the number of safe work behaviors in a food manufacturing plant.[20] This plant was experiencing an accident rate similar to that of the mining industry, the most dangerous area of work. Employees were engaging in unsafe behaviors such as putting their hands into conveyors to unjam them (resulting in crushed limbs).

To improve safety, a training program was developed to teach employees safe behavior, provide them with incentives for safe behaviors, and encourage them to monitor their own behavior.

To evaluate the program, the design included a comparison group (the Makeup Department) and a trained group (the Wrapping Department). The Makeup Department is responsible for measuring and mixing ingredients, preparing the dough, placing the dough in the oven and removing it when it is cooked, and packaging the finished product. The Wrapping Department is responsible for bagging, sealing, and labeling the packaging and stacking it

TABLE 6.10

Example of a Solomon Four-Group Design

Source: Based on R. D. Bretz and R. E. Thompsett, "Comparing Traditional and Integrative Learning Methods in Organizational Training Programs," *Journal of Applied Psychology* 77 (1992): 941–51.

	Pretest	Training	Posttest
Group 1	Yes	IL-based	Yes
Group 2	Yes	Traditional	Yes
Group 3	No	IL-based	Yes
Group 4	No	Traditional	Yes

on skids for shipping. Outcomes included observations of safe work behaviors. These observations were taken over a 25-week period.

The baseline shows the percentage of safe acts prior to introduction of the safety training program. Training directed at increasing the number of safe behaviors was introduced after approximately five weeks (20 observation sessions) in the Wrapping Department and 10 weeks (50 observation sessions) in the Makeup Department. Training was withdrawn from the Wrapping and Makeup Departments after approximately 62 observation sessions. The withdrawal of training resulted in a reduction of the work incidents performed safely (to pretraining levels). As shown, the number of safe acts observed varied across the observation period for both groups. However, the number of safe behaviors increased after the training program was conducted for the trained group (Wrapping Department). The level of safe acts remained stable across the observation period. (See the intervention period.) When the Makeup Department received training (at 10 weeks, or after 50 observations) a similar increase in the percentage of safe behaviors was observed.

Solomon Four-Group

The **Solomon four-group** design combines the pretest/posttest comparison group and the posttest-only control group design. In the Solomon four-group design, a training group and a comparison group are measured on the outcomes both before and after training. Another training group and control group are measured only after training. This design controls for most threats to internal and external validity.

An application of the Solomon four-group design is shown in Table 6.10. This design was used to compare the effects of training based on integrative learning (IL) with traditional (lecture-based) training of manufacturing resource planning. Manufacturing resource planning is a method for effectively planning, coordinating, and integrating the use of all resources of a manufacturing company.[21] The IL-based training differed from the traditional training in several ways. IL-based training sessions began with a series of activities intended to create a relaxed, positive environment for learning. The students were asked what manufacturing resource planning meant to them, and attempts were made to reaffirm their beliefs and unite the trainees around a common understanding of manufacturing resource planning. Students presented training material and participated in group discussions, games, stories, and poetry related to the manufacturing processes.

Because the company was interested in the effects of IL related to traditional training, groups who received traditional training were used as the comparison group (rather than groups who received no training).

A test of manufacturing resource planning (knowledge test) and a reaction measure were used as outcomes. The study found that participants in the IL-based learning groups learned slightly less than participants in the traditional training groups. IL-group participants had much more positive reactions than those in the traditional training program.

TABLE 6.11
Factors That Influence the Type of Evaluation Design

Source: Based on S. I. Tannenbaum and S. B. Woods, "Determining a Strategy for Evaluating Training: Operating within Organizational Constraints," *Human Resource Planning* 15 (1992): 63–81.

Factor	How Factor Influences Type of Evaluation Design
Change Potential	Can program be modified?
Importance	Does ineffective training affect customer service, product development, or relationships among employees?
Scale	How many trainees are involved?
Purpose of Training	Is training conducted for learning, results, or both?
Organization Culture	Is demonstrating results part of company norms and expectations?
Expertise	Can a complex study be analyzed?
Cost	Is evaluation too expensive?
Time Frame	When do we need the information?

Considerations in Choosing an Evaluation Design

There is no one appropriate evaluation design. An evaluation design should be chosen based on an evaluation of the factors shown in Table 6.11. There are several reasons why no evaluation or a less rigorous evaluation design may be more appropriate than a more rigorous design that includes a comparison group, random assignment, pretraining and posttraining measures. First, managers and trainers may be unwilling to devote the time and effort necessary to collect training outcomes. Second, managers or trainers may lack the expertise to conduct an evaluation study. Third, a company may view training as an investment from which it expects to receive little or no return. You should consider a more rigorous evaluation design (pretest/posttest with comparison group) if any of the following conditions are true:[22]

1. The evaluation results can be used to change the program.
2. The training program is ongoing and has the potential to affect many employees (and customers).
3. The training program involves multiple classes and a large number of trainees.
4. Cost justification for training is based on numerical indicators. (Here the company has a strong orientation toward evaluation.)
5. You or others have the expertise (or the budget to purchase expertise from outside the company) to design and evaluate the data collected from an evaluation study.
6. The cost of the training creates a need to show that it works.
7. There is sufficient time for conducting an evaluation. Here, information regarding training effectiveness is not needed immediately.
8. There is interest in measuring change (in knowledge, behavior, skill, etc.) from pretraining levels or in comparing two or more different programs.

For example, if you are interested in determining how much employees' communications skills have changed as a result of a training program, a pretest/ posttest comparison group design is necessary. Trainees should be randomly assigned to training and no-training conditions. These evaluation design features give you a high degree of confidence that any communication skill change is the result of participation in the training program.[23] This type of evaluation design is also necessary if you are asked to compare the effectiveness of two training programs.

Evaluation designs without pretest or comparison groups are most appropriate in situations where you are interested in identifying if a specific level of performance has been achieved. (For example, are employees who participated in training able to adequately communicate their ideas?) In this situation, you are not interested in determining how much change has occurred. Rather, you are interested in whether the trainees achieved a certain proficiency level.

One company's evaluation strategy for a training course delivered to the company's tax professionals shows how company norms regarding evaluation and the purpose of training influence the type of evaluation design chosen.[24] This accounting firm views training as an effective method for developing human resources. Training is expected to provide a good return on investment. The company used a combination of affective, cognitive, behavior, and results criteria to evaluate a five-week course designed to prepare tax professionals to understand state and local tax law. The course involved two weeks of self-study and three weeks of classroom work. A pretest/posttest comparison design was used. Before they took the course, trainees were tested to determine their knowledge of state and local tax laws, and they completed a survey designed to assess their self-confidence in preparing accurate tax returns. The evaluators also identified the trainees' (accountants') billable hours related to calculating state and local tax returns and the revenue generated by the activity. After the course, evaluators again identified billable hours and surveyed trainees' self-confidence. The results of the evaluation indicated that the accountants were spending more time doing state and local tax work than before training. Also, the trained accountants produced more revenue doing state and local tax work than accountants who had not yet received the training (comparison group). There was also a significant improvement in the accountants' confidence following training, and they were more willing to promote their expertise in state and local tax preparation. Finally, after 15 months, the revenue gained by the company more than offset the cost of training. On average, the increase in revenue for the trained tax accountants was more than 10 percent.

DETERMINING RETURN ON INVESTMENT

Return on investment (ROI) is an important training outcome. This section discusses how to calculate ROI through a cost-benefit analysis. **Cost-benefit analysis** in this situation is the process of determining the economic benefits of a training program using accounting methods that look at training costs and benefits. Training cost information is important for several reasons:[25]

1. To understand total expenditures for training, including direct and indirect costs.
2. To compare the costs of alternative training programs.
3. To evaluate the proportion of money spent on training development, administration, and evaluation as well as to compare monies spent on training for different groups of employees (exempt versus nonexempt, for example).
4. To control costs.

Recall Dave Palm's dilemma at LensCrafters that was discussed earlier in the chapter. Palm needed to show that training provided a return on investment. He decided to partner with the operations people to identify how to link training to measurable outcomes such as profitability, quality, and sales. After conversations with the operations employees, he decided to link training to waste from mistakes in quality and remakes, store performance and sales, and customer satisfaction. He chose two geographic regions for the evaluation study. He compared the results from these two regions with results from one that had not yet received the training. Palm found that all stores in the two regions that received training reduced waste, increased sales, and improved customer satisfaction. As a result, LensCrafters allotted its training department more financial resources—$10 million a year for training program development and administration—than did any other optical retail competitor. Because the training department demonstrated that it does contribute to business operations, it also received money to develop a multimedia-based training system.

The process of determining ROI begins with an understanding of the objectives of the training program.[26] Plans are developed for collecting data related to measuring these objectives. The next step is to isolate, if possible, the effects of training from other factors that might influence the data. Last, the data are converted to a monetary value and ROI is calculated. Choosing evaluation outcomes and designing an evaluation that helps isolate the effects of training were explained earlier in the chapter. The remainder of this chapter discusses how to determine costs and benefits and provides examples of cost-benefit analysis and ROI calculations.

Determining Costs

One method for comparing costs of alternative training programs is the resource requirements model.[27] The resource requirements model compares equipment, facilities, personnel, and materials costs across different stages of the training process (needs assessment, development, training design, implementation, and evaluation). Use of the resource requirements model can help determine overall differences in costs among training programs. Also, costs incurred at different stages of the training process can be compared across programs.

Accounting can also be used to calculate costs.[28] Seven categories related to the cost sources are calculated. These costs include those related to program development or purchase, instructional materials for trainers and trainees, equipment and hardware, facilities, travel and lodging, and salary of trainer and support staff as well as the cost of lost productivity while trainees attend the program (or cost of temporary employees who replace the trainees while they are at training). This method also identifies when the costs are incurred. One-time costs include those related to needs assessment and program development. Costs per offering relate to training site rental fees, trainer salaries, and other costs that are realized every time the program is offered. Costs per trainee include meals, materials, and lost productivity or expenses incurred to replace the trainees while they attend training.

Determining Benefits

To identify the potential benefits of training, the company must review the original reasons that the training was conducted. For example, training may have been conducted to reduce production costs or overtime costs or to increase the amount of repeat business. A number of methods may be helpful in identifying the benefits of training:

1. Technical, academic, and practitioner literature summarizes the benefits that have been shown to relate to a specific training program.
2. Pilot training programs assess the benefits from a small group of trainees before a company commits more resources.

3. Observance of successful job performers helps a company determine what successful job performers do differently than unsuccessful job performers.[29]
4. Trainees and their managers provide estimates of training benefits.

For example, a training and development consultant at Apple Computer was concerned with the quality and consistency of the training program used in assembly operations.[30] She wanted to show that training was not only effective but also resulted in financial benefits. To do this, the consultant chose an evaluation design that involved two separately trained groups—each consisting of 27 employees—and two untrained groups (comparison groups). The consultant collected a pretraining history of what was happening on the production line in each outcome she was measuring (productivity, quality, and labor efficiency). She determined the effectiveness of training by comparing performance between the comparison and training groups for two months after training. The consultant was able to show that the untrained comparison group had 2,000 more minutes of downtime than the trained group did. This finding meant that the trained employees built and shipped more products to customers—showing definitively that training was contributing to Apple's business objectives.

To conduct a cost-benefit analysis, the consultant had each employee in the training group estimate the effect of behavior change on a specific business measure (e.g., breaking down tasks will improve productivity or efficiency). The trainees assigned a confidence percentage to the estimates. To get a cost-benefit estimate for each group of trainees, the consultant multiplied the monthly cost-benefit by the confidence level and divided by the number of trainees. For example, one group of 20 trainees estimated a total overall monthly cost benefit of $336,000 related to business improvements and showed an average 70 percent confidence level with that estimate. Seventy percent multiplied by $336,000 gave a cost-benefit of $235,200. This number was divided by 20 ($235,200/20 trainees) to give an average estimated cost benefit for the 20 trainees ($11,760). To calculate return on investment, follow these steps:[31]

1. Identify outcomes (e.g., quality, accidents).
2. Place a value on the outcomes.
3. Determine the change in performance after eliminating other potential influences on training results.
4. Obtain an annual amount of benefits (operational results) from training by comparing results after training to results before training (in dollars).
5. Determine the training costs (direct costs + indirect costs + development costs + overhead costs + compensation for trainees).
6. Calculate the total savings by subtracting the training costs from benefits (operational results).
7. Calculate the ROI by dividing benefits (operational results) by costs. The ROI gives an estimate of the dollar return expected from each dollar invested in training.

Example of a Cost-Benefit Analysis

A cost-benefit analysis is best explained by an example.[32] A wood plant produced panels that contractors used as building materials. The plant employed 300 workers, 48 supervisors, 7 shift superintendents, and a plant manager. The business had three problems. First, 2 percent of the wood panels produced each day were rejected because of poor quality. Second, the production area was experiencing poor housekeeping, such as improperly stacked

TABLE 6.12
Determining Costs for a Cost-Benefit Analysis

Direct Costs	
Instructor	$ 0
In-house instructor (12 days @ $125 per day)	1,500
Fringe benefits (25% of salary)	375
Travel expenses	0
Materials ($60 × 56 trainees)	3,360
Classroom space and audiovisual equipment (12 days @ $50 per day)	600
Refreshments ($4 per day × 3 days × 56 trainees)	672
Total direct costs	6,507
Indirect Costs	
Training management	0
Clerical and administrative salaries	750
Fringe benefits (25% of salary)	187
Postage, shipping, and telephone	0
Pre- and posttraining learning materials ($4 × 56 trainees)	224
Total indirect costs	1,161
Development Costs	
Fee for program purchase	3,600
Instructor training	
Registration fee	1,400
Travel and lodging	975
Salary	625
Benefits (25% of salary)	156
Total development costs	6,756
Overhead Costs	
General organizational support, top management time (10% of direct, indirect, and development costs)	1,443
Total overhead costs	1,443
Compensation for Trainees	
Trainees' salaries and benefits (based on time away from job)	16,969
Total training costs	32,836
Cost per trainee	587

finished panels that would fall on employees. Third, the number of preventable accidents was higher than the industry average. To correct these problems, the supervisors, shift superintendents, and plant manager attended training in (1) performance management and interpersonal skills related to quality problems and poor work habits of employees and (2) rewarding employees for performance improvement. Training was conducted in a hotel close to the plant. The training program was a purchased videotape, and the instructor for the program was a consultant. Table 6.12 shows each type of cost and how it was determined.

The benefits of the training were identified by considering the objectives of the training program and the type of outcomes the program was to influence. These outcomes included the quality of panels, housekeeping, and accident rate. Table 6.13 shows how the benefits of the program were calculated.

TABLE 6.13 Determining Benefits for a Cost-Benefit Analysis

Operational Results Area	How Measured	Results before Training	Results after Training	Differences (+ or –)	Expressed in Dollars
Quality of panels	Percentage rejected	2 percent rejected— 1,440 panels per day	1.5 percent rejected— 1,080 panels per day	.5 percent— 360 panels	$720 per day, $172,800 per year
Housekeeping	Visual inspection using 20-item checklist	10 defects (average)	2 defects (average)	8 defects	Not measurable in $
Preventable accidents	Number of accidents	24 per year	16 per year	8 per year	$48,000 per year
	Direct cost of accidents	$144,000 per year	$96,000 per year	$48,000 per year	

$$ROI = \frac{Return}{Investment} = \frac{Operational\ results}{Training\ costs} = \frac{\$220,800}{\$32,836} = 6.7$$

Total savings: $187,964

Source: Adapted from D. G. Robinson and J. Robinson, "Training for Impact," *Training and Development Journal* (August 1989): 30–42.

Once the costs and benefits of the program are determined, ROI is calculated by dividing return or benefits by costs. In our example, ROI was 6.7. That is, every dollar invested in the program returned approximately seven dollars in benefits. How do you determine if the ROI is acceptable? One way is for managers and trainers to agree on what level of ROI is acceptable. Another method is to use the ROI that other companies obtain from similar types of training. Table 6.14 provides examples of ROI obtained from several types of training programs.

Other Methods for Cost-Benefit Analysis

Other, more sophisticated, methods are available for determining the dollar value of training. For example, **utility analysis** is a cost-benefit analysis method that involves assessing the dollar value of training based on estimates of the difference in job performance between trained and untrained employees, the number of individuals trained, the length of time a training program is expected to influence performance, and the variability in job performance in the untrained group of employees.[33] Utility analysis requires the use of a pretest/posttest design with a comparison group to obtain an estimate of the difference in job performance for trained versus untrained employees. Other types of economic analyses evaluate training as it benefits the firm or the government using direct and indirect training costs, government incentives paid for training, wage increases received by trainees as a result of completion of training, tax rates, and discount rates.[34]

Practical Considerations in Determining Return on Investment

ROI analysis may not be appropriate for all training programs. Training programs best suited for ROI analysis have clearly identified outcomes, are not a one-time events, are highly visible in the company, are strategically focused, and have effects that can be isolated.[35] In the

TABLE 6.14
Example of
Return on
Investment

Source: Based on
J. J. Philips, "ROI:
The Search for Best
Practices," *Training
and Development*
(February 1996): 45.

Industry	Training Program	ROI
Bottling company	Workshops on managers' roles	15:1
Large commercial bank	Sales training	21:1
Electric and gas utility	Behavior modification	5:1
Oil company	Customer service	4.8:1
Health maintenance organization	Team training	13.7:1

examples of ROI analysis in this chapter, the outcomes were very measurable. That is, it was easy to see changes in quality, to count accident rates, and to observe housekeeping behavior. For training programs that focus on soft outcomes (e.g., attitudes, interpersonal skills), it may be more difficult to estimate the value.

Showing the link between training and market share gain or other higher level strategic business outcomes can be very problematic. These outcomes can be influenced by too many other factors not directly related to training (or even under the control of the business), such as competitors' performance and economic upswings and downturns. Business units may not be collecting the data needed to identify the ROI of training programs on individual performance. Also, the measurement of training can often be very expensive. Verizon Communications employs 240,000 employees. The company estimates that it spends approximately $5,000 for an ROI study. Given the large number of training programs the company offers, it is too expensive to conduct an ROI for each program.

Companies are finding that, despite these difficulties, the demand for measuring ROI is still high. As a result, companies are using creative ways to measure the costs and benefits of training.[36] For example, to calculate ROI for a training program designed to cut absenteeism, trainees and their supervisors were asked to estimate the cost of an absence. The values were averaged to obtain an estimate. Cisco Systems tracks how often its partners return to its website for additional instruction. A. T. Kearney, a management consulting firm, tracks the success of its training by how much business is generated from past clients. Rather than relying on ROI, Verizon Communications uses training ROE, or return on expectations. Prior to training, the senior managers who are financially accountable for the training program are asked to identify their expectations regarding what the training program should accomplish as well as a cost estimate of the current issue or problem. After training, the senior managers are asked whether their expectations were met, and they are encouraged to attach a monetary value to those met expectations. The ROE is used as an estimate in an ROI analysis. Verizon Communications continues to conduct ROI analysis for training programs and courses in which objective numbers are available (e.g., sales training) and in which the influence of training can be better isolated (evaluation designs that have comparison groups and that collect pretraining and posttraining outcomes).

Summary

Evaluation provides information used to determine training effectiveness. Evaluation involves identifying the appropriate outcomes to measure. The outcomes used in evaluating training programs include trainees' satisfaction with the training program, learning of knowledge or skills, use of knowledge and skills on the job, and results such as sales, productivity, or accident prevention. Evaluation may also involve comparing the costs of training to the benefits received (return on investment). Outcomes used in training evaluation help to determine the degree to which the program resulted in both learning and transfer of training. Evaluation also involves choosing the appropriate design to maximize the confidence that can be placed in the results. The design is based on a careful analysis of how to minimize threats to internal and external validity as well as the purpose, expertise, and other company and training characteristics. The types of designs used for evaluation vary on the basis of whether they include pretraining and posttraining measures of outcomes and a training and a comparison group. The chapter concludes by noting that a good evaluation requires thinking about the evaluation in advance of conducting the training program. Information from the needs assessment and specific and measurable learning objectives can help identify measurable outcomes that should be included in the evaluation design.

Key Terms

training effectiveness, *170*
training outcomes (criteria), *170*
training evaluation, *170*
evaluation design, *170*
formative evaluation, *171*
pilot testing, *172*
summative evaluation, *172*
cognitive outcomes, *174*
skill-based outcomes, *174*
affective outcomes, *176*
reaction outcomes, *176*
instructor evaluation, *176*
results, *177*

return on investment (ROI), *178*
direct costs, *178*
indirect costs, *178*
benefits, *178*
criteria relevance, *178*
criterion contamination, *178*
criterion deficiency, *179*
reliability, *179*
discrimination, *179*
practicality, *180*
threats to validity, *182*
internal validity, *182*
external validity, *182*

pretraining measure, *183*
posttraining measure, *183*
comparison group, *183*
Hawthorne effect, *183*
random assignment, *184*
posttest-only, *184*
pretest/posttest, *185*
pretest/posttest with comparison group, *186*
time series, *187*
reversal, *187*
Solomon four-group, *188*
cost-benefit analysis, *190*
utility analysis, *194*

Discussion Questions

1. What can be done to motivate companies to evaluate training programs?
2. What do threats to validity have to do with training evaluation? Identify internal and external threats to validity. Are internal and external threats similar? Explain.
3. What are the strengths and weaknesses of each of the following designs: posttest-only, pretest/posttest comparison group, pretest/posttest only?
4. What are results outcomes? Why do you think that most organizations don't use results outcomes for evaluating their training programs?
5. This chapter discussed several factors that influence the choice of evaluation design. Which of these factors would have the greatest influence on your choice of an evaluation design? Which would have the smallest influence? Explain your choices.
6. How might you estimate the benefits from a training program designed to teach employees how to use the World Wide Web to monitor stock prices?

7. A group of managers ($N = 25$) participated in the problem-solving module of a leadership development program two weeks ago. The module consisted of two days in which the group focused on the correct process to use in problem solving. Each manager supervises 15 to 20 employees. The company is willing to change the program, and there is an increasing emphasis in the company to show that training expenses are justifiable. You are asked to evaluate this program. Your boss would like the results of the evaluation no later than six weeks from now. Discuss the outcomes you would collect and the design you would use. How might your answer change if the managers have not yet attended the program?

8. What practical considerations need to be taken into account when calculating a training program's ROI?

Application Assignments

1. Consider this course as a training program. In teams of up to five students, identify (a) the types of outcomes you would recommend to use in evaluating this course and (b) the evaluation design you would use. Justify your choice of a design based on minimizing threats to validity and practical considerations.

2. Domino's Pizza was interested in determining whether a new employee could learn how to make a pizza using a computer-based training method (CD-ROM). The CD-ROM application addresses the proper procedure for "massaging" a dough ball and stretching it to fit a 12-inch pizza pan. Domino's quality standards emphasize the roundness of the pizza, an even border, and uniform thickness of the dough. Traditionally, on-the-job training is used to teach new employees how to stretch pizza dough to fit the pizza pan.

   a. What outcomes or criteria should Domino's Pizza measure to determine if CD-ROM training is an effective method for teaching new employees how to stretch pizza dough to fit a 12-inch pan? Who would be involved in the evaluation?

   b. Describe the evaluation design you would recommend that Domino's Pizza use to determine if CD-ROM training is more effective than on-the-job training.

3. Ask your instructor for a copy of the evaluation form, survey, or rating sheet that is used by your college, university, or business to evaluate the course or program in which you are using this text. As you look over the evaluation, answer the following questions:

   a. What are the strengths and weaknesses of the evaluation form?

   b. What changes would you suggest to improve the evaluation form (e.g., different questions, additional questions)?

   c. How should the evaluation be used to actually improve the instruction that you receive?

4. Sears designed a training program to improve tool and hardware sales. The two-hour program involved distance learning and was broadcast from the Sears training facility to 50 salespersons at 10 store locations in the United States. The salespersons are paid $15 per hour. The program involved training salespeople in how to set up merchandise displays so they attract buyers' attention. Sales of tools and merchandise at the 10 stores included in the program averaged $5,000 per week before the program and $6,500 per week after the program. Program costs included:

Instructor	$10,000
Distance learning (satellite space rental)	5,000
Materials ($100 per trainee @ 50 trainees)	5,000
Trainees' salaries and benefits	
(50 trainees with wages of $15 per hour in a 2-hour training program)	1,500

What is the return on investment (ROI) from this program?

5. Cablevision developed an e-learning course that trained salespersons how to increase the number of cable television subscribers, thereby increasing revenue. The company wants to know if salespersons will increase upselling of cable television services (e.g., premium channels) and will try to sell other products (e.g., e-mail and Web access). The company also wants to know the ROI of this training program.

   a. What training outcomes should the company collect? From whom should the outcomes be collected?

   b. What evaluation design would you recommend? Defend your recommendation.

   c. Show how Cablevision can conduct an ROI analysis. Describe the information they should collect and how it should be collected.

Endnotes

1. C. Thompson, E. Koon, W. Woodwell, Jr., and J. Beauvais, *Training for the Next Economy: An ASTD State of the Industry Report on Trends in Employer-Provided Training in the United States* (Washington, DC: ASTD, 2002).

2. A. Purcell, " 20/20 ROI," *Training and Development* (July 2000): 28–33.

3. Ibid.

4. M. Van Wart, N. J. Cayer, and S. Cook, *Handbook of Training and Development for the Public Sector* (San Francisco: Jossey-Bass, 1993).

5. D. L. Kirkpatrick, "Evaluation," in *The ASTD Training and Development Handbook,* 2d ed., ed. R. L. Craig (New York: McGraw-Hill, 1996): 294–312.

6. K. Kraiger, J. K. Ford, and E. Salas, "Application of Cognitive, Skill-Based, and Affective Theories of Learning Outcomes to New Methods of Training Evaluation," *Journal of Applied Psychology* 78 (1993): 311–28; J. J. Phillips, "ROI: The Search for Best Practices," *Training and Development* (February 1996): 42–47; G. M. Alliger, S. I. Tannenbaum, W. Bennet, Jr., H. Traver, and A. Shortland, "A Meta-analysis of the Relations among Training Criteria," *Personnel Psychology* 50 (1997): 341–55; K. Kraiger, "Decision-Based Evaluation," in *Creating, Implementing, and Managing Effective Training and Development,* ed. K. Kraiger (San Francisco: Jossey-Bass, 2002): 331–75; G. Alliger and E. Janek , "Kirkpatrick's Levels of Training Criteria: Thirty Years Later," *Personnel Psychology* 42 (1989): 331–42.

7. Kraiger, Ford, and Salas, "Application of Cognitive, Skill-Based, and Affective Theories"; J. J. Phillips, "ROI: The Search for Best Practices"; D. L. Kirkpatrick, "Evaluation of Training," in *Training and Development Handbook,* 2d ed., ed. R. L. Craig (New York: McGraw-Hill, 1976): 18-1 to 18-27.

8. R. Morgan and W. Casper, "Examining the Factor Structure of Participant Reactions to Training: A Multidimensional Approach," *Human Resource Development Quarterly* 11 (2000): 301–17.

9. G. Hopkins, "How to Design an Instructor Evaluation," *Training and Development* (March 2000): 51–53.

10. J. J. Phillips, "Was It the Training?" *Training and Development* (March 1996): 28–32.

11. T. Murphy and S. Zandvakili, "Data- and Metrics-Driven Approach to Human Resource Practices: Using Customers, Employees, and Financial Metrics," *Human Resource Management* 39: (Spring 2000) 93–105.

12. Phillips, "ROI: The Search for Best Practices."

13. D. A. Grove and C. Ostroff, "Program Evaluation," in *Developing Human Resources,* ed. K. N. Wexley (Washington, DC: Bureau of National Affairs, 1991): 5-185 to 5-220.

14. H. J. Frazis, D. E. Herz, and M. W. Horrigan, "Employer-Provided Training: Results from a New Survey," *Monthly Labor Review* 118 (1995): 3–17.

15. G. M. Alliger and E. A. Janak, "Kirkpatrick's Levels of Training Criteria: Thirty Years Later," *Personnel Psychology* (Summer 1989): 331–42.

16. T. D. Cook, D. T. Campbell, and L. Peracchio, "Quasi Experimentation," in *Handbook of Industrial and Organizational Psychology,* 2d ed., Vol. 1, eds. M. D. Dunnette and L. M. Hough (Palo Alto, CA: Consulting Psychologists Press, 1990): 491–576.

17. Ibid.; J. J. Phillips, *Handbook of Training Evaluation and Measurement Methods,* 2d ed. (Houston, TX: Gulf Publishing, 1991).

18. B. Gerber, "Does Your Training Make a Difference? Prove It!" *Training* (March 1995): 27–34.

19. S. J. Simon and J. M. Werner, "Computer Training through Behavior Modeling, Self-Paced, and Instructional Approaches: A Field Experiment," *Journal of Applied Psychology* 81 (1996): 648–59.

20. J. Komaki, K. D. Bardwick, and L. R. Scott, "A Behavioral Approach to Occupational Safety: Pinpointing and Reinforcing Safe Performance in a Food Manufacturing Plant," *Journal of Applied Psychology* 63 (1978): 434–45.

21. R. D. Bretz and R. E. Thompsett, "Comparing Traditional and Integrative Learning Methods in Organizational Training Programs," *Journal of Applied Psychology* 77 (1992): 941–51.

22. S. I. Tannenbaum and S. B. Woods, "Determining a Strategy for Evaluating Training: Operating within Organizational Constraints," *Human Resource Planning* 15 (1992): 63–81; R. D. Arvey, S. E. Maxwell, and E. Salas, "The Relative Power of Training Evaluation Designs under Different Cost Configurations," *Journal of Applied Psychology* 77 (1992): 155–60.

23. P. R. Sackett and E. J. Mullen, "Beyond Formal Experimental Design: Toward an Expanded View of the Training Evaluation Process," *Personnel Psychology* 46 (1993): 613–27.

24. Gerber, "Does Your Training Make a Difference? Prove It!"

25. A. P. Carnevale and E. R. Schulz, "Return on Investment: Accounting for Training," *Training and Development Journal* (July 1990): S1–S32.

26. J. Phillips and P. Phillips, "Using Action Plans to Measure ROI," *Performance Improvement* 42 (2003): 22–31.

27. Carnevale and Schulz, "Return on Investment: Accounting for Training"; G. Kearsley, *Costs, Benefits, and Productivity in Training Systems* (Boston: Addison-Wesley, 1982).

28. S. D. Parry, "Measuring Training's ROI," *Training and Development* (May 1996): 72–77.

29. D. G. Robinson and J. Robinson, "Training for Impact," *Training and Development Journal* (August 1989): 30–42. J. J. Phillips, "How Much Is the Training Worth?" *Training and Development* (April 1996): 20–24.

30. A. Purcell, "20/20 ROI."

31. J. Phillips, *Handbook of Training Evaluation and Measurement Methods,* 2nd ed. (Houston: Gulf Publishing, 1991); J. Phillips. "ROI: The Search for the Best Practices," *Training and Development* (February 1996): 42–47.

32. Robinson and Robinson, "Training for Impact."

33. J. E. Matheiu and R. L. Leonard, "Applying Utility Analysis to a Training Program in Supervisory Skills: A Time-Based Approach," *Academy of Management Journal* 30 (1987): 316–35; F. L. Schmidt, J. E. Hunter, and K. Pearlman, "Assessing the Economic Impact of Personnel Programs on Work-Force Productivity," *Personnel Psychology* 35 (1982): 333–47; J. W. Boudreau, "Economic Considerations in Estimating the Utility of Human Resource Productivity Programs," *Personnel Psychology* 36 (1983): 551–76.

34. U. E. Gattiker, "Firm and Taxpayer Returns from Training of Semiskilled Employees," *Academy of Management Journal* 38 (1995): 1151–73.

35. B. Worthen, "Measuring the ROI of Training," *CIO* (February 15, 2001): 128–36.

36. D. Abernathy, "Thinking Outside the Evaluation Box," *Training and Development* (February 1999): 19–23; E. Krell, "Calculating Success," *Training* (December 2002): 47–52; D. Goldwater, "Beyond ROI," *Training* (January 2001): 82–90.

Chapter **Seven**

Traditional Training Methods

Objectives

After reading this chapter, you should be able to

1. Discuss the strengths and weaknesses of presentational, hands-on, and group building training methods.
2. Provide recommendations for effective on-the-job training.
3. Develop a case study.
4. Develop a self-directed learning module.
5. Discuss the key components of behavior modeling training.
6. Explain the conditions necessary for adventure learning to be effective.
7. Discuss what team training should focus on to improve team performance.

Training Gets Products to Market

Kimberly-Clark, the Dallas, Texas, consumer products company, is used to marketing and selling new products. But after unsuccessful training efforts to familiarize employees with the process of using PowerPoint presentations and meetings to launch new products, senior managers wanted a new training approach. The charge was to make sure that 15,000 employees understood the process without a lot of money being spent and without much development time, and the training had to be distributed to employees very quickly.

The director of organizational effectiveness at Kimberly-Clark used training methods that included simulations, games, and videos. All 15,000 employees attended four-hour sessions in which they watched a video about Kimberly-Clark's supply chain (known as Go To Market). Small teams of employees discussed the company's key customers and other supply-chain issues presented on a map. Team members were given roles in a fictitious company that was bringing a product to market and that encountered the problems of supply-chain management. At the end of the role play, the employees discovered that a competitor had beaten them to the market. Exposure to the problems of supply-chain management served as the basis for a second map that led employees through a discussion of the future of Kimberly-Clark's supply chain. Teams earned points for finding information on the map, and the winning team received inexpensive prizes. After completing the second map, the employees watched a video from the CEO and product sector presidents and heard presentations from line managers. The three levels of management each gave more specific information about the meaning of Go To Market and how employees could contribute to it.

Employee reactions to the program were overwhelmingly positive. Employees felt that for the first time they understood how Kimberly-Clark's supply chain worked. As a result of the training program, employees suggested ways to eliminate waste and redundancies in the supply chain. These suggestions resulted in $275 million in cost savings.

Source: Based on H. Dolezalek, "Pretending to Learn," *Training* (July/August 2003): 20–26.

INTRODUCTION

Kimberly-Clark uses a combination of training methods to ensure that employees understand how to get products to market and how to recognize their own role in making the process efficient and effective. Many companies face similar conditions when choosing a training method. The method has to be developed or purchased within a budget, has to be quickly developed, and must be distributed to all employees. The challenge is to purchase or develop a training program that meets these conditions and is effective, that is, that trainees like the program, that learning occurs, and that employees put the learning into practice at work.

Figure 7.1 provides an overview of the frequency of use of instructional methods. The figure shows that traditional training methods, those that do not involve technology to deliver lessons, are more frequently used than is training that involves technology to deliver programs. For example, instructor-led classrooms, videos, workbooks and manuals, and role plays are used more frequently than virtual reality, computer-based games and simulations, and virtual classrooms with instructor. Note that there is one important exception: Technology-based programs involving CD-ROM/DVD/diskettes and Internet/intranet are frequently used by over 40 percent of the companies surveyed.

Regardless of whether the training method is traditional or technology based, for training to be effective it needs to be based on the training design model shown in Figure 1.1. Needs assessment, a positive learning environment, and transfer of training are critical for training program effectiveness. Recall the discussions of needs assessment, learning, and transfer of training in Chapters 3, 4, and 5.

Chapters 7 and 8 present various training methods. Chapter 7 focuses on traditional training methods, methods that do not require new technology (e.g., Internet) for delivery. However, most methods discussed in this chapter can be delivered using CD-ROM or the Internet. For example, a classroom lecture can occur face-to-face with trainees (traditional training) or can be delivered through a virtual classroom in which the instructor is not in the same room as the trainees. Also, instruction can be real-time (synchronous) or time-delayed (asynchronous). Through technology, a lecture can be attended live although the trainees are not in the same classroom as the trainer, or the lecture can be videotaped or burned onto a CD-ROM or DVD. The lecture can be viewed by the trainees at their convenience on a personal computer that gives them access to the appropriate medium for viewing the lecture (e.g., CD-ROM, player, DVD player, or Internet connection). Chapter 8 discusses technology-based training methods, including Web-based training, e-learning, and virtual reality. The increased

FIGURE 7.1 Overview of use of instructional methods

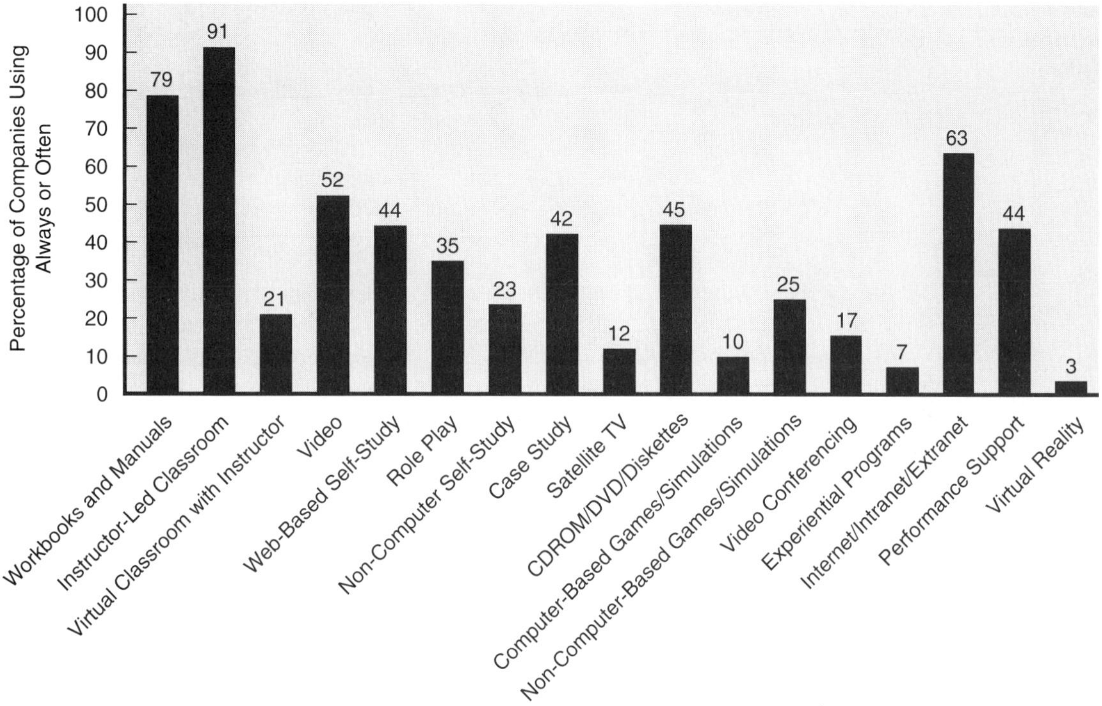

Source: Based on T. Galvin "Industry Report 2003," *Training* (October 2003): 30, 31.

use of technology-based training for delivery of instruction is occurring because of the potential increases in learning effectiveness as well as the reductions in training costs.

The traditional training methods discussed in this chapter are organized into three broad categories: presentation methods, hands-on methods, and group building methods.[1] The following sections provide a description of each method, a discussion of its advantages and disadvantages, and tips for the trainer who is designing or choosing the method. The chapter concludes by comparing methods based on several characteristics including the learning outcomes influenced; the extent to which the method facilitates learning; and transfer, cost, and effectiveness.

PRESENTATION METHODS

Presentation methods are methods in which trainees are passive recipients of information. This information may include facts, processes, and problem-solving methods. Presentation methods include lectures and audiovisual techniques.

Lecture

A **lecture** involves trainers communicating through spoken words what they want the trainees to learn. The communication of learned capabilities is primarily one-way—from

TABLE 7.1
Variations of the Lecture Method

Method	Description
Standard Lecture	Trainer talks while trainees listen and absorb information.
Team Teaching	Two or more trainers present different topics or alternative views of the same topic.
Guest Speakers	Speaker visits the session for a predetermined time period. Primary instruction is conducted by the guest or speaker.
Panels	Two or more speakers present information and ask questions.
Student Presentations	Groups of trainees present topics to the class.

the trainer to the audience. As Figure 7.1 shows, lecture remains a popular training method despite new technologies such as interactive video and computer-assisted instruction.

A lecture is one of the least expensive, least time-consuming ways to present a large amount of information efficiently in an organized manner.[2] The lecture format is also useful because it is easily employed with large groups of trainees. Besides being the primary means to communicate large amounts of information, lectures are also used to support other training methods such as behavior modeling and technology-based techniques. For example, a lecture may be used to communicate information regarding the purpose of the training program, conceptual models, or key behaviors to trainees prior to their receiving training that is more interactive and customized to their specific needs.

Table 7.1 describes several variations of the standard lecture method. All have advantages and disadvantages.[3] Team teaching brings more expertise and alternative perspectives to the training session. Team teaching does require more time on the part of trainers to not only prepare their particular session but also coordinate with other trainers, especially when there is a great deal of integration between topics. Panels are good for showing trainees different viewpoints in a debate. A potential disadvantage of a panel is that trainees who are relatively naive about a topic may have difficulty understanding the important points. Guest speakers can motivate learning by bringing to the trainees relevant examples and applications. For guest speakers to be effective, trainers need to set expectations with speakers regarding how their presentation should relate to the course content. Student presentations may increase the material's meaningfulness and trainees' attentiveness, but it can inhibit learning if the trainees do not have presentation skills.

The lecture method has several disadvantages. Lectures tend to lack participant involvement, feedback, and meaningful connection to the work environment—all of which inhibit learning and transfer of training. Lectures appeal to few of the trainees' senses because trainees focus primarily on hearing information. Lectures also make it difficult for the trainer to judge quickly and efficiently the learners' level of understanding. To overcome these problems, the lecture is often supplemented with question-and-answer periods, discussion, or case studies. These techniques allow the trainer to build into the lecture more active participation, job-related examples, and exercises, which facilitate learning and transfer of training.

Audiovisual Techniques

Audiovisual instruction includes overheads, slides, and video. As Figure 7.1 shows, video is one of the most popular instructional methods.[4] It has been used for improving communications skills, interviewing skills, and customer-service skills and for illustrating how procedures (e.g., welding) should be followed. Video is, however, rarely used alone. It is usually used in conjunction with lectures to show trainees real-life experiences and examples. Here is how one company is using video in its training program.

At 5:30 A.M. the Morse Bros. drivers prepare to deliver the first of many loads of concrete. In the concrete business, a perishable product needs to be delivered on a timely basis to construction sites. Morse Bros., located in Tangent, Oregon, is one of only a few ready-mix firms in the Northwest that provide regular training for their drivers. Drivers play a key role in determining the success of the business. Morse Bros. has been able to reduce costs and raise customer satisfaction by providing drivers with product training and by instructing drivers to avoid rollovers and excessive idling at construction sites.

What method does Morse Bros. use to train its drivers? The company produces training videos that are presented by mentor-drivers. The mentor-driver's job is to select the weekly video, schedule viewing sessions, keep attendance records, and guide a wrap-up discussion following each video. The mentor-drivers are trained to call attention to key learning points covered in the video and relate the topic to issues the drivers deal with on the job. Because training sessions are scheduled early in the morning at the beginning of the drivers' shift, time is limited. Videos seldom run more than 10 minutes. For example, one called *Another Pair of Eyes* trains drivers to observe test procedures used by testing agencies at job sites. Samples are tested several times a month. A sample that fails can leave the company liable for demolition and removal of the concrete structure. Morse Bros. provides training on test procedures because samples often fail a test due to contamination (e.g., dirt) that gets into the test cylinder. Another video emphasizes cold-weather precautions: Drain all tanks and hoses at the end of the day, park the drum in neutral. At each training session, drivers are asked to answer several questions related to the content of the program. At the end of a session, drivers and the mentor-driver discuss anything that might be interfering with the quality of the product or timeliness of delivery. Mentor-drivers then share this information with company managers.[5]

Video is also a major component of behavior modeling and, naturally, interactive video instruction. The use of video in training has a number of advantages. First, trainers can review, slow down, or speed up the lesson, which gives them flexibility in customizing the session depending on trainees' expertise. Second, trainees can be exposed to equipment, problems, and events that cannot be easily demonstrated, such as equipment malfunctions, angry customers, or emergencies. Third, trainees are provided with consistent instruction. Program content is not affected by the interests and goals of a particular trainer. Fourth, videotaping trainees allows them to see and hear their own performance without the interpretation of the trainer. As a result, trainees cannot attribute poor performance to the bias of external evaluators such as the trainer or peers.

Most problems in video result from the creative approach used.[6] These problems include too much content for the trainee to learn, poor dialogue between the actors (which hinders the credibility and clarity of the message), overuse of humor or music, and drama that makes it confusing for the trainee to understand the important learning points emphasized in the video.

HANDS-ON METHODS

Hands-on methods are training methods that require the trainee to be actively involved in learning. These methods include on-the-job training, simulations, case studies, business games, role plays, and behavior modeling. These methods are ideal for developing specific skills, understanding how skills and behaviors can be transferred to the job, experiencing all aspects of completing a task, or dealing with interpersonal issues that arise on the job.

On-the-Job Training (OJT)

Companies spend between $90 billion and $180 billion annually on informal on-the-job training compared with $30 billion on formal off-the-job training.[7] **On-the-job training (OJT)** refers to new or inexperienced employees learning through observing peers or managers performing the job and trying to imitate their behavior. OJT can be useful for training newly hired employees, upgrading experienced employees' skills when new technology is introduced, cross-training employees within a department or work unit, and orienting transferred or promoted employees to their new jobs.

OJT takes various forms, including apprenticeships and self-directed learning programs. (Both are discussed later in this section.) OJT is an attractive training method because, compared to other methods, it needs less investment in time or money for materials, trainer's salary, or instructional design. Managers or peers who are job knowledge experts are used as instructors. As a result, it may be tempting to let them conduct the training as they believe it should be done.

There are several disadvantages to this unstructured approach to OJT.[8] Managers and peers may not use the same process to complete a task. They may pass on bad habits as well as useful skills. Also, they may not understand that demonstration, practice, and feedback are important conditions for effective on-the-job training. Unstructured OJT can result in poorly trained employees, employees who use ineffective or dangerous methods to produce a product or provide a service, and products or services that vary in quality.

OJT must be structured to be effective. Table 7.2 shows the principles of structured OJT. Because OJT involves learning by observing others, successful OJT is based on the principles emphasized by social learning theory. These include the use of a credible trainer, a manager or peer who models the behavior or skill, communication of specific key behaviors, practice, feedback, and reinforcement. For example, at Rochester Gas and Electric in Rochester, New York, radiation and chemistry instructors teach experienced employees how to conduct OJT.[9] While teaching these employees how to demonstrate software to new employees, the trainer may ask the employees to watch other OJT instructors as they train new recruits so they can learn new teaching techniques. Regardless of the specific type, effective OJT programs include

1. A policy statement that describes the purpose of OJT and emphasizes the company's support for it.
2. A clear specification of who is accountable for conducting OJT. If managers conduct OJT, this is mentioned in their job descriptions and is part of their performance evaluations.
3. A thorough review of OJT practices (program content, types of jobs, length of program, cost savings) at other companies in similar industries.
4. Training of managers and peers in the principles of structured OJT (see Table 7.2).
5. Availability of lesson plans, checklists, procedure manuals, training manuals, learning contracts, and progress report forms for use by employees who conduct OJT.
6. Evaluation of employees' levels of basic skills (reading, computation, writing) before OJT.[10]

TABLE 7.2   **Principles of On-the-Job Training**

Preparing for Instruction
1. Break down the job into important steps.
2. Prepare the necessary equipment, materials, and supplies.
3. Decide how much time you will devote to OJT and when you expect the employees to be competent in skill areas.

Actual Instruction
1. Tell the trainees the objective of the task and ask them to watch you demonstrate it.
2. Show the trainees how to do it without saying anything.

3. Explain the key points or behaviors. (Write out the key points for the trainees, if possible.)
4. Show the trainees how to do it again.
5. Have the trainees do one or more single parts of the task and praise them for correct reproduction (optional).
6. Have the trainees do the entire task and praise them for correct reproduction.
7. If mistakes are made, have the trainees practice until accurate reproduction is achieved.
8. Praise the trainees for their success in learning the task.

Source: Based on W. J. Rothwell and H. C. Kazanas, "Planned OJT Is Productive OJT," *Training and Development Journal* (October 1990): 53–55; P. J. Decker and B. R. Nathan, *Behavior Modeling Training* (New York: Praeger Scientific, 1985).

For example, the OJT program utilized by Borden's North American Pasta Division has many of these characteristics.[11] Not all managers and peers are used as trainers. Borden's invests in trainer selection, training, and rewards to ensure OJT's effectiveness. Employees and managers interested in being instructors are required to apply for the position. Those chosen as instructors are required to complete a demanding train-the-trainer course that involves classroom training as well as time on the manufacturing floor to learn how to operate machinery such as pasta machines and to correctly teach other employees to use the equipment. Borden's also builds accountability into the OJT program. Trainees are responsible for completing a checklist that requires them to verify that the trainer helped them learn the skills needed to operate the equipment and used effective instructional techniques.

Self-Directed Learning

Self-directed learning has employees take responsibility for all aspects of learning—when it is conducted and who will be involved.[12] Trainees master predetermined training content at their own pace without an instructor. Trainers may serve as facilitators. That is, trainers are available to evaluate learning or answer questions for the trainee. The trainer does not control or disseminate instruction. The learning process is controlled by the trainee.

For example, at Corning Glass, new engineering graduates participate in an OJT program called SMART (Self-Managed, Awareness, Responsibility, and Technical competence).[13] Each employee is responsible for seeking the answers to a set of questions (e.g., "Under what conditions would a statistician be involved in the design of engineering experiments?") by visiting plants and research facilities and meeting with technical engineering experts and managers. After employees complete the questions, they are evaluated by a committee of peers who have already completed the SMART program. Evaluations have shown that the program cuts employees' start-up time in their new jobs from six weeks to three. The program is effective for a number of reasons. It encourages new employees' active involvement in learning and allows flexibility in finding time for training. A peer-review evaluation component motivates employees to complete the questions correctly. And, as a result of participating in the program, employees make contacts throughout the company and gain a better understanding of the technical and personal resources available within the company.

Self-directed learning has several advantages and disadvantages.[14] It allows trainees to learn at their own pace and receive feedback about the learning performance. For the company, self-directed learning requires fewer trainers, reduces costs associated with travel and meeting rooms, and makes multiple-site training more realistic. Self-directed learning provides consistent training content that captures the knowledge of experts. Self-directed learning also makes it easier for shift employees to gain access to training materials. For example, Four Seasons hotels faced the challenge of opening a new hotel in Bali, Indonesia.[15] It needed to teach English skills to 580 employees, none of whom spoke English or understood Western cuisine or customs. Four Seasons created a self-directed learning center that enabled employees to teach themselves English. The center emphasizes communications, not simply learning to speak English. As a result of this emphasis, the center features video recorders, training modules, books, and magazines. Monetary incentives were provided for employees to move from the lowest to the highest level of English skills. Besides English, the center also teaches Japanese (the language of 20 percent of the hotel visitors) and provides training for foreign managers in Bahasa Indonesian, the native language of Indonesia.

A major disadvantage of self-directed learning is that trainees must be willing and comfortable learning on their own. That is, trainees must be motivated to learn. From the company perspective, self-directed learning results in higher development costs, and development time is longer than with other types of training programs.

Several steps are necessary to develop effective self-directed learning:[16]

1. Conduct a job analysis to identify the tasks that must be covered.
2. Write trainee-centered learning objectives directly related to the tasks. Because the objectives take the place of the instructor, they must indicate what information is important, what actions the trainee should take, and what the trainee should master.
3. Develop the content for the learning package. This involves developing scripts (for video) or text screens (for computer-based training). The content should be based on the trainee-centered learning objectives. Another consideration in developing the content is the media (e.g., paper, video, computer, website) that will be used to communicate the content.
4. Break the content into smaller pieces ("chunks"). The chunks should always begin with the objectives that will be covered and include a method for trainees to evaluate their learning. Practice exercises should also appear in each chunk.
5. Develop an evaluation package that includes evaluation of the trainee and evaluation of the self-directed learning package. Trainee evaluation should be based on the objectives (a process known as criterion referencing). That is, questions should be developed that are written directly from the objectives and can be answered directly from the materials. Evaluation of the self-directed learning package should involve determining ease of use, how up-to-date the material is, whether the package is being used as intended, and whether trainees are mastering the objectives.

Self-directed learning is likely to become more common in the future as companies seek to train staff flexibly, take advantage of technology, and encourage employees to be proactive in their learning rather than driven by the employer.

TABLE 7.3
Example of a Machinist Apprenticeship

Source: A. H. Howard III, "Apprenticeship," in *The ASTD Training and Development Handbook*, 4th ed., ed. R. L. Craig (New York: McGraw-Hill, 1996): 808.

Hours	Weeks	Unit
240	6.0	Bench work
360	9.0	Drill press
240	6.0	Heat treat
200	5.0	Elementary layout
680	17.0	Turret lathe (conventional and numerical control)
800	20.0	Engine lathe
320	8.0	Tool grind
640	16.0	Advanced layout
960	24.0	Milling machine
280	7.0	Profile milling
160	4.0	Surface grinding
240	6.0	External grinding
280	7.0	Internal grinding
200	5.0	Thread grinding
520	13.0	Horizontal boring mills
240	6.0	Jig bore/jig grinder
160	4.0	Vertical boring
600	15.0	Numerical control milling
240	6.0	Computer numerical control
640	16.0	Related training
8,000	200.0	TOTAL

***Probationary:* The following hours are included in the totals above, but must be completed in the first 1,000 hours of apprenticeship:**

Hours	Weeks	Unit
80	2.0	Drill press (probation)
280	7.0	Lathe work (probation)
360	9.0	Milling machine (probation)
40	1.0	Elementary layout (probation)
80	2.0	Related training (probation)
840	21.0	TOTAL

Apprenticeship

Apprenticeship is a work-study training method with both on-the-job and classroom training.[17] To qualify as a registered apprenticeship program under state or federal guidelines, at least 144 hours of classroom instruction and 2,000 hours, or one year, of on-the-job experience are required.[18] Apprenticeships can be sponsored by individual companies or by groups of companies cooperating with a union. The majority of apprenticeship programs are in the skilled trades such as plumbing, carpentry, electrical work, and bricklaying.

Table 7.3 shows an example of an apprenticeship program for a machinist. The hours and weeks that must be devoted to completing specific skill units are clearly defined. OJT involves assisting a certified tradesperson (a journeyman) at the work site. The on-the-job training portion of the apprenticeship follows the guidelines for effective on-the-job training.[19] Modeling, practice, feedback, and evaluation are involved. First, the employer verifies that the trainee has the required knowledge of the operation or process. Next, the trainer (who is usually a more experienced, licensed employee) demonstrates each step of the process, emphasizing safety issues and key steps. The senior employee provides the apprentice with the opportunity to perform the process until all are satisfied that the apprentice can perform it properly and safely.

A major advantage of apprenticeship programs is that learners can earn pay while they learn. This is important because programs can last several years. Learners' wages usually increase automatically as their skills improve. Also, apprenticeships are usually effective learning experiences because they involve learning why and how a task is performed in classroom instruction provided by local trade schools, high schools, or community colleges. Apprenticeships also usually result in full-time employment for trainees when the program is completed. Will-Burt Corporation of Orrville, Ohio, started an apprenticeship program two years ago.[20] The program offers coursework for two career paths: machinist and brake press set-up operator. Each requires classroom study plus 160 hours of on-the-job training. Employees who want to become journeymen will take additional training off-site after completing their apprentice training. Classes are taught on-site through a partnership with Wayne College, University of Akron, and are free to employees. Many new employees work through the preapprenticeship program, while others take advantage of refreshing their skills in a single class or two. About 40 people signed up for geometric and tolerancing class as a refresher.

One disadvantage of many apprenticeship programs is limited access for minorities and women.[21] Another disadvantage is that there is no guarantee that jobs will be available when the program is completed. Finally, apprenticeship programs prepare trainees who are well trained in one craft or occupation. Due to the changing nature of jobs (thanks to new technology and use of cross-functional teams), many employers may be reluctant to employ workers from apprenticeship programs. Employers may believe that because apprentices are narrowly trained in one occupation or with one company, program graduates may have only company-specific skills and may be unable to acquire new skills or adapt their skills to changes in the workplace.

Apprenticeship programs are a more important part of training in countries such as Germany and Denmark than in the United States.[22] For example, the German apprenticeship experience is similar to that in the United States in that it combines classroom-based and on-the-job training. But the apprenticeship system is more linked with the education and training systems in Germany. The German apprenticeship system has been highlighted as a model for providing young people with the skills and credentials needed for an occupation. The system relies on the belief that students who do not attend college should be encouraged to learn an occupation. Two-thirds of secondary school graduates participate in apprenticeship programs. The German system identifies more than 300 occupations, each with its own set of standards and curriculum. Government, business, labor, and education are all involved at all stages of the process of managing and implementing apprenticeships.

The German apprenticeship model has recently had its problems.[23] German businesses such as Siemens and Daimler Benz have been experiencing high wage and welfare costs, so they are creating most new jobs outside the country. These firms want flexible workers who will upgrade their skills rather than employees from the apprenticeship program who are well trained in just one trade or occupation. As a result, the availability of apprenticeships for trainees has declined.

Simulations

A **simulation** is a training method that represents a real-life situation, with trainees' decisions resulting in outcomes that mirror what would happen if they were on the job. Simulations, which allow trainees to see the impact of their decisions in an artificial, risk-free environment, are used to teach production and process skills as well as management and interpersonal skills. As you will see in Chapter 8, new technology has helped the development of virtual reality, a type of simulation that even more closely mimics the work environment.

Simulators replicate the physical equipment that employees use on the job. For example, Time Warner cable installers learn how to correctly install cable and high-speed Internet connections by crawling into two-story houses that have been built inside the company's training center.[24] Trainees drill through the walls and crawl around inside these houses, learning how to work with different types of homes. New call center employees at American Express learn in a simulated environment that replicates a real call center.[25] Trainees go to a lab that contains cubicles identical to those in the call center. All materials (binders, reference materials, supplies) are exactly the same as they would be in the call center. The simulator uses a replica of the call center database and includes a role play that uses speech recognition software to simulate live calls. After the call center trainees learn transactions, they answer simulated calls that require them to practice the transactions. The simulator gives them feedback about errors they made during the calls and shows them the correct action. The simulator also tracks the trainees' performance and alerts the instructors if a trainee is falling behind. The simulator prepares call center employees in 32 days, an improvement over the previous 12-week program of classroom and on-the-job training. Turnover among call center employees is 50 percent lower since employees began training in the simulated environment. American Express believes that the reduction in turnover is because the training environment better prepares new employees to deal with the noise and pace of a real call center.

Simulations are also used to develop managerial skills. Looking Glass© is a simulation designed to develop both teamwork and individual management skills.[26] In this program, participants are assigned different roles in a glass company. On the basis of memos and correspondence, each participant interacts with other members of the management team over the course of six hours. The simulation records and evaluates participants' behavior and interactions in solving the problems described in correspondence. At the conclusion of the simulation, participants are given feedback regarding their performance.

A key aspect of simulators is the degree to which they are similar to the equipment and situation that the trainee will encounter on the job. Recall the discussion of near transfer in Chapter 5. Simulators need to have identical elements to those found in the work environment. The simulator needs to respond exactly like the equipment would under the conditions and response given by the trainee. For this reason simulators are expensive to develop and need constant updating as new information about the work environment is obtained. For example, American Airlines Flight 965 crashed into the mountains near Cali, Colombia, after one of the pilots entered the wrong code into a navigational computer.[27] The crew set the onboard computer to direct the plane to a radio beacon called "Romeo" instead of "Rozo." As the plane turned into the mountains, the pilots became confused and failed to revert back to basic radio navigation. An investigation of the accident suggested that the pilots may have been fooled by a discrepancy between standard navigation charts and the

TABLE 7.4
Process for Case Development

Source: Based on J. Alden and J. K. Kirkhorn, "Case Studies," in *The ASTD Training and Development Handbook*, 4th ed., ed. R. L. Craig (New York: McGraw-Hill, 1996): 497–516.

1. Identify a story.
2. Gather information.
3. Prepare a story outline.
4. Decide on administrative issues.
5. Prepare case materials.

navigation computer. Charts used by airlines list a radio beacon designation "R" as "Rozo," but the computer does not recognize "R" as "Rozo." It recognizes "R" as "Romeo." As a result of this tragic accident, pilot training in simulators will place greater emphasis on dealing with navigational errors.

Case Studies

A **case study** is a description about how employees or an organization dealt with a difficult situation. Trainees are required to analyze and critique the actions taken, indicating the appropriate actions and suggesting what might have been done differently.[28] A major assumption of the case study approach is that employees are most likely to recall and use knowledge and skills if they learn through a process of discovery.[29] Cases may be especially appropriate for developing higher order intellectual skills such as analysis, synthesis, and evaluation. These skills are often required by managers, physicians, and other professional employees. Cases also help trainees develop the willingness to take risks given uncertain outcomes, based on their analysis of the situation. To use cases effectively, the learning environment must give trainees the opportunity to prepare and discuss their case analyses. Also, face-to-face or electronic communication among trainees must be arranged. Because trainee involvement is critical for the effectiveness of the case method, learners must be willing and able to analyze the case and then communicate and defend their positions.

Table 7.4 presents the process used for case development. The first step in the process is to identify a problem or situation. It is important to consider whether the story is related to the instructional objectives, will provoke a discussion, forces decision making, can be told in a reasonable time period, and is generalizable to the situations that trainees may face. Information on the problem or situation must also be readily accessible. The next step is to research documents, interview participants, and obtain data that provide the details of the case. The third step is to outline the story and link the details and exhibits to relevant points in the story. Fourth, the media used to present the case should be determined. Also, at this point in case development, the trainer should consider how the case exercise will be conducted. This may involve determining if trainees will work individually or in teams, and how the students will report results of their analysis. Finally, the actual case materials need to be prepared. This includes assembling exhibits (figures, tables, articles, job descriptions, etc.), writing the story, preparing questions to guide trainees' analysis, and writing an interesting, attention-getting case opening that attracts trainees' attention and provides a quick orientation to the case.

There are a number of available sources for preexisting cases. A major advantage of preexisting cases is that they are already developed. A disadvantage is that the case may not actually relate to the work situation or problem that the trainee will encounter. It is especially important to review preexisting cases to determine how meaningful they will be to the trainee. Preexisting cases on a wide variety of problems in business management (e.g., human resource management, operations, marketing, advertising) are available from Harvard Business School, The Darden Business School at the University of Virginia, Ivey Business School at the University of Western Ontario, and various other sources.

One organization that has effectively used case studies is the Central Intelligence Agency (CIA).[30] The cases are historically accurate and use actual data. For example, "The Libyan Attack" is used in management courses to teach leadership qualities. "The Stamp Case" is used to teach new employees about the agency's ethics structure. The CIA uses approximately 100 cases. One-third are focused on management; the rest focus on operations training, counterintelligence, and analysis. The cases are used in the training curriculum where the objectives include teaching students to analyze and resolve complex, ambiguous situations. The CIA found that for the cases used in training programs to be credible and meaningful to trainees, the material had to be as authentic as possible and stimulate students to make decisions similar to those they must make in their work environment. As a result, to ensure case accuracy, the CIA uses retired officers to research and write cases. The CIA has even developed a case writing workshop to prepare instructors to use the case method.

Business Games

Business games require trainees to gather information, analyze it, and make decisions. Business games are primarily used for management skill development. Games stimulate learning because participants are actively involved and because games mimic the competitive nature of business. The types of decisions that participants make in games include all aspects of management practice: labor relations (agreement in contract negotiations), marketing (the price to charge for a new product), and finance (financing the purchase of new technology).

Many companies are using board games to teach employees finance because employee pay is based on the financial performance of the business function employees work in.[31] In pay-for-performance plans, companies must ensure that employees understand basic financial concepts such as how to read balance sheets and income statements. Employees also need to understand how their actions and decisions affect profits. Most of the board games are similar to Monopoly.® Trainees guide their companies through a series of decisions challenged by various obstacles such as a rival introducing a competing product or a strike by plant workers. Trainees have to track key financial measures over two years.

Harley-Davidson, the motorcycle company, uses a business game to help prospective dealers understand how dealerships make money.[32] The game involves 15 to 35 people working in teams. The game consists of five simulated rounds, each round challenging a team to manage a Harley dealership in competition with other teams. Between rounds of the game, lectures and case studies reinforce key concepts. The facilitators change the business situation in each round of the game. The facilitators can increase or decrease interest rates, add new products, cause employee turnover, or even set up a bad event such as a fire at the business. The game helps dealers develop skills needed for business success. Participants must work well as a team, listen to each other, and think strategically.

Documentation of learning from games is anecdotal.[33] Games may give team members a quick start at developing a framework for information and help develop cohesive groups. For some groups (such as senior executives), games may be more meaningful training activities (because the game is realistic) than presentation techniques such as classroom instruction.

Role Plays

Role plays have trainees act out characters assigned to them.[34] Information regarding the situation (e.g., work or interpersonal problem) is provided to the trainees. Role plays differ from simulations on the basis of response choices available to the trainees and the level of detail of the situation given to trainees. Role plays may provide limited information regarding the situation, whereas the information provided for simulation is usually quite detailed. A simulation focuses on physical responses (e.g., pull a lever, move a dial). Role plays focus on interpersonal responses (e.g., asking for more information, resolving conflict). In a simulation, the outcome of the trainees' response depends on a fairly well-defined model of reality. (If a trainee in a flight simulator decreases the angle of the flaps, that influences the direction of the aircraft.) In a role play, outcomes depend on the emotional (and subjective) reactions of the other trainees.

For role plays to be effective, trainers need to engage in several activities before, during, and after the role play. Before the role play, it is critical to explain the purpose of the activity to the trainees. This increases the chances that they will find the activity meaningful and be motivated to learn. Second, the trainer needs to clearly explain the role play, the characters' roles, and the time allotted for the activity. A short video may also be valuable for quickly showing trainees how the role play works. During the activity, the trainer needs to monitor the time, degree of intensity, and focus of the group's attention. (Is the group playing the roles or discussing other things unrelated to the exercise?) The more meaningful the exercise is to the participants, the less trouble the trainer should have with focus and intensity. At the conclusion of the role play, debriefing is critical. Debriefing helps trainees understand the experience and discuss their insights with each other. Trainees should also be able to discuss their feelings, what happened in the exercise, what they learned, and how the experience, their actions, and resulting outcomes relate to incidents in the workplace.

Behavior Modeling

Behavior modeling presents trainees with a model who demonstrates key behaviors to replicate and provides trainees with the opportunity to practice the key behaviors. Behavior modeling is based on the principles of social learning theory (discussed in Chapter 4), which emphasize that learning occurs by (1) observing behaviors demonstrated by a model and (2) vicarious reinforcement. **Vicarious reinforcement** occurs when a trainee sees a model being reinforced for using certain behaviors.

Behavior modeling is more appropriate for teaching skills and behaviors than factual information. Research suggests that behavior modeling is one of the most effective techniques for teaching interpersonal and computer skills.[35]

Table 7.5 presents the activities in a behavior modeling training session. These activities include an introduction, skill preparation and development, and application planning.[36] Each training session, which typically lasts four hours, focuses on one interpersonal skill such as coaching or communicating ideas. Each session includes a presentation of the rationale behind the key behaviors, a videotape of a model performing the key behaviors, practice opportunities using role playing, evaluation of a model's performance in the videotape, and a planning session devoted to understanding how the key behaviors can be used on the job. In the practice sessions, trainees are provided with feedback regarding how closely their behavior matches the key behaviors demonstrated by the model. The role playing and modeled performance are based on actual incidents in the employment setting in which the trainee needs to demonstrate success.

TABLE 7.5
Activities in a Behavior Modeling Training Program

Introduction	**(45 mins.)**
• Present key behaviors using video.	
• Give rationale for skill module.	
• Trainees discuss experiences in using skill.	
Skill Preparation and Development	**(2 hrs., 30 mins.)**
• View model.	
• Participate in role plays and practice.	
• Receive oral and video feedback on performance of key behaviors.	
Application Planning	**(1 hr.)**
• Set improvement goals.	
• Identify situations to use key behaviors.	
• Identify on-the-job applications of the key behaviors.	

Well-prepared behavior modeling training programs identify the key behaviors, create the modeling display, provide opportunities for practice, and facilitate transfer of training.[37] The first step in developing behavior modeling training programs is to determine (1) the tasks that are not being adequately performed due to lack of skill or behavior and (2) the key behaviors that are required to perform the task. A **key behavior** is one of a set of behaviors that are necessary to complete a task. In behavior modeling, key behaviors are typically performed in a specific order for the task to be completed. Key behaviors are identified through a study of the skills and behavior necessary to complete the task and the skills or behaviors used by employees who are effective in completing the task.

Table 7.6 presents key behaviors for a behavior modeling training program on problem analysis. The table specifies behaviors that the trainee needs to engage in to be effective in problem analysis skills. Note that the key behaviors do not specify the exact behaviors needed at every step of solving a problem. Rather, the key behaviors in this skill module specify more general behaviors that are appropriate across a wide range of situations. If a task involves a clearly defined series of specific steps that must be accomplished in a specific order, then the key behaviors that are provided are usually more specific and explained in greater detail. For example, in teaching tennis players how to serve, a detailed sequence of activities must be followed to be effective (e.g., align feet on service line, take the racquet back over the head, toss the ball, bring the racquet over the head, pronate the wrist, and strike the ball). In teaching interpersonal skills, because there is more than one way to complete the task, more general key behaviors should be developed. This helps to promote far transfer (discussed in Chapter 5). That is, trainees are prepared to use the key behaviors in a variety of situations.

Another important consideration in developing behavior modeling programs is the modeling display. The **modeling display** provides the key behaviors that the trainees will practice to develop the same set of behaviors. Videotape is the predominant method used to present modeling displays, although computerized modeling displays are also being used. (New technology is discussed in Chapter 8.) Effective modeling displays have six characteristics:[38]

1. The display clearly presents the key behaviors. Music and characteristics of the situation shown in the display do not interfere with the trainee seeing and understanding the key behaviors.

TABLE 7.6
Example of Key Behaviors in Problem Analysis

Get all relevant information by
  Rephrasing the question or problem to see if new issues emerge.
  Listing the key problem issues.
  Considering other possible sources of information.
Identify possible causes.
If necessary, obtain additional information.
Evaluate the information to ensure that all essential criteria are met.
Restate the problem considering new information.
Determine what criteria indicate that the problem or issue is resolved.

2. The model is credible to the trainees.

3. An overview of the key behaviors is presented.

4. Each key behavior is repeated. The trainee is shown the relationship between the behavior of the model and each key behavior.

5. A review of the key behaviors is included.

6. The display presents models engaging in both positive use of key behaviors and negative use (ineffective models not using the key behaviors).

Providing opportunities for practice involves (1) having trainees cognitively rehearse and think about the key behaviors and (2) placing trainees in situations (such as role plays) where they have to use the key behaviors. Trainees may interact with one other person in the role play or in groups of three or more where each trainee can practice the key behaviors. The most effective practice session allows trainees to practice the behaviors multiple times, in a small group of trainees where anxiety or evaluation apprehension is reduced, with other trainees who understand the company and the job.

Practice sessions should include a method for providing trainees with feedback. This feedback should provide reinforcement to the trainee for behaviors performed correctly as well as information needed to improve behaviors. For example, if role plays are used, trainees can receive feedback from the other participants who serve as observers when not playing the role. Practice sessions may also be videotaped and played back to the trainees. The use of video objectively captures the trainees' behavior and provides useful, detailed feedback. Having the trainees view the video shows them specifically how they need to improve their behaviors and identifies behaviors they are successfully replicating.

Behavior modeling helps to ensure that transfer of training occurs by using application planning. **Application planning** prepares trainees to use the key behaviors on the job (i.e., enhances transfer of training). Application planning involves having each participant prepare a written document identifying specific situations where they should use the key behaviors. Some training programs actually have trainees complete a "contract" outlining the key behaviors they agree to use on the job. The trainer may follow up with the trainees to see if they are performing according to the contract. Application planning may also involve preparing trainees to deal with situational factors that may inhibit their use of the key behaviors (similar to relapse prevention discussed in Chapter 5). As part of the application planning process, a trainee may be paired with another participant, with the stated expectation that they should periodically communicate with each other to discuss successes and failures of the use of key behaviors.

GROUP BUILDING METHODS

Group building methods are training methods designed to improve team or group effectiveness. Training is directed at improving the trainees' skills as well as team effectiveness. In group building methods, trainees share ideas and experiences, build group identity, understand the dynamics of interpersonal relationships, and get to know their own strengths and weaknesses and those of their co-workers. Group techniques focus on helping teams increase their skills for effective teamwork. A number of training techniques are available to improve work group or team performance, to establish a new team, or to improve interactions among different teams. All involve examination of feelings, perceptions, and beliefs about the functioning of the team; discussion; and development of plans to apply what was learned in training to the team's performance in the work setting. Group building methods include adventure learning, team training, and action learning.

Group building methods often involve experiential learning. **Experiential learning** training programs involve four stages: (1) gain conceptual knowledge and theory; (2) take part in a behavioral simulation; (3) analyze the activity; (4) and connect the theory and activity with on-the-job or real-life situations.[39]

For experiential training programs to be successful, several guidelines should be followed. The program needs to tie in to a specific business problem. The trainees need to be moved outside their personal comfort zones but within limits so as not to reduce trainee motivation or ability to understand the purpose of the program. Multiple learning modes should be used, including audio, visual, and kinesthetic. When preparing activities for an experiential training program, trainers should ask trainees for input on the program goals. Clear expectations about the purpose, expected outcomes, and trainees' role in the program are important. Finally, the training program needs to be evaluated. Training programs that include experiential learning should be linked to changes in employee attitudes, behaviors, and other business results. If training programs that involve experiential learning do not follow these guidelines, they may be questioned. For example, the U.S. Postal Inspector resigned after criticisms surfaced about postal team training activities. Current and former postal employees complained to several senators about training activities that included having employees wrap each other in toilet paper and dress as cats and hold signs that spelled "teamwork."[40]

California-based Quantum Corporation developed a project to overhaul the company's online infrastructure across global operations.[41] The project included a diverse group of team members from the information technology, engineering, marketing, and graphic design departments. The team consisted of very talented employees who were not used to working with each other. Many of the team members were geographically dispersed, which increased the difficulties in working together. Quantum hired an actors' group to lead the team through a series of improvisational activities designed to get the team members to share personal stories. Using music, props, lighting, and costumes, the actors interpreted the stories told by team members. The actors portrayed team members who, for example, expressed isolation and frustration. Other times, team members would play the parts. The sessions allowed each team member to ask questions of the actors or each other. The team came away from the activity with more empathy and understanding for each other. Development of the personal relationships created positive interpersonal bonds that helped the team meet deadlines and complete projects.

Adventure Learning

Adventure learning focuses on the development of teamwork and leadership skills through structured outdoor activities.[42] Adventure learning is also known as *wilderness training* and *outdoor training*. Adventure learning appears to be best suited for developing skills related to group effectiveness such as self-awareness, problem solving, conflict management, and risk taking. Adventure learning may involve strenuous, challenging physical activities such as dogsledding or mountain climbing. Adventure learning can also use structured individual and group outdoor activities such as wall climbing, rope courses, trust falls, ladder climbing, and traveling from one tower to another using a device attached to a wire that connects the two towers.

For example, "The Beam" requires team members to get over a six-foot-high beam placed between two trees using only help from the team. Trainees can help by shouting advice and encouragement.[43] Rope-based activities may be held 3 to 4 feet or 25 to 30 feet above the ground. The high-ropes course is an individual-based exercise whose purpose is to help the trainee overcome fear. The low-ropes course requires the entire team of trainees to complete the course successfully. The purpose is to develop team identity, cohesiveness, and communication skills.

In one adventure learning program, a Chili's restaurant manager was required to scale a three-story-high wall.[44] About two-thirds of the way from the top of the wall, the manager became very tired. She successfully reached the top of the wall using the advice and encouragement shouted from team members on the ground below. When asked to consider what she learned from the experience, she reported that the exercise made her realize that reaching personal success depends on other people. At her restaurant, everyone has to work together to make the customers happy.

For adventure learning programs to be successful, exercises should relate to the types of skills that participants are expected to develop. Also, after the exercises a skilled facilitator should lead a discussion about what happened in the exercise, what was learned, how events in the exercise relate to the job situation, and how to set goals and apply what was learned on the job.[45] Trust falls require each trainee to stand on a platform five to six feet above the ground and fall backward into the arms of fellow group members. If trainees are reluctant to fall, this suggests they don't trust the team members. After completing the trust fall, the facilitator may question trainees to identify sources of their anxiety and to relate this anxiety to specific workplace incidents (e.g., a project delegated to a peer was not completed on time, resulting in distrust of the peer).

The physical demands of adventure learning and the requirement that trainees often touch each other in the exercises may increase a company's risk for negligence claims due to personal injury, intentional infliction of emotional distress, and invasion of privacy. Also, the Americans with Disabilities Act raises questions about requiring disabled employees to participate in physically demanding training experiences.[46]

Given the physically demanding nature of adventure learning, it is important to consider when to use it instead of another training method. Adventure learning allows trainees to interact interpersonally in a situation not governed by formal business rules. This type of environment may be important for employees to mold themselves into a cohesive work team. Also, adventure learning exercises allow trainees to share a strong emotional experience. Significant emotional experiences can help trainees break difficult behavior patterns

FIGURE 7.2
Components of team performance

Source: Based on E. Salas and J. A. Cannon-Bowers, "Strategies for Team Training," in *Training for 21st Century Technology: Applications of Psychological Research*, eds. M. A. Quinones and A. Dutta (Washington, DC: American Psychological Association, 1997): 249–81.

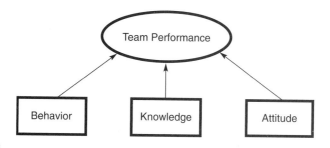

and open up trainees to change their behaviors. One of the most important characteristics of adventure learning is that the exercises can serve as metaphors for organizational behavior. That is, trainees will behave in the same way in the exercises that they would when working as a team (e.g., developing a product launch plan). As a result, by analyzing behaviors that occur during the exercise, trainees gain insight into ineffective behaviors.

Does adventure learning work? Rigorous evaluations of its impact on productivity or performance have not been conducted. However, former participants often report that they gained a greater understanding of themselves and how they interact with co-workers.[47] One key to an adventure learning program's success may be the insistence that whole work groups participate together so that group dynamics that inhibit effectiveness can emerge and be discussed.

Team Training

Team training coordinates the performance of individuals who work together to achieve a common goal. Figure 7.2 shows the three components of team performance: knowledge, attitudes, and behavior.[48] The behavioral requirement means that team members must perform actions that allow them to communicate, coordinate, adapt, and complete complex tasks to accomplish their objective. The knowledge component requires team members to have mental models or memory structures that allow them to function effectively in unanticipated or new situations. Team members' beliefs about the task and feelings toward each other relate to the attitude component. Team morale, cohesion, and identity are related to team performance. For example, in the military as well as the private sector (e.g., nuclear power plants, commercial airlines), much work is performed by crews, groups, or teams. Successful performance depends on coordination of individual activities to make decisions, on team performance, and on readiness to deal with potentially dangerous situations (e.g., an overheating nuclear reactor). Research suggests that teams that are effectively trained develop procedures to identify and resolve errors, coordinate information gathering, and reinforce each other.[49]

Figure 7.3 illustrates the four main elements of the structure of team training (tools, methods, strategies, and team training objectives). Several tools help to define and organize the delivery of team training.[50] These tools also provide the environment (e.g., feedback) needed for learning to occur. These tools work in combination with different training methods to help create instructional strategies. These strategies are a combination of methods, tools, and content required to perform effectively.

The strategies include cross training, coordination training, and team leader training. **Cross training** has team members understand and practice each other's skills so that

FIGURE 7.3

Main elements of the structure of team training

Source: Based on E. Salas and J. A. Cannon-Bowers, "Strategies for Team Training," in *Training for 21st Century Technology: Applications of Psychological Research*, eds. M. A. Quinones and A. Dutta (Washington, DC: American Psychological Association, 1997): 270.

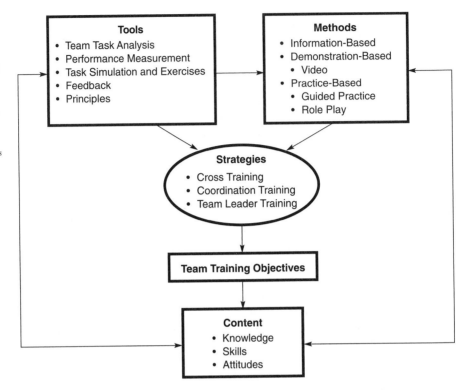

members are prepared to step in and take the place of a member who may temporarily or permanently leave the team. Research suggests that most work teams would benefit from providing members with at least enough understanding of teammates' roles to discuss trade-offs of various strategies and behaviors that affect team performance.[51] **Coordination training** instructs the team in how to share information and decision-making responsibilities to maximize team performance. Coordination training is especially important for commercial aviation or surgical teams who are in charge of monitoring different aspects of equipment and the environment but who must share information to make the most effective decisions regarding patient care or aircraft safety and performance. **Team leader training** refers to training that the team manager or facilitator receives. This may involve training the manager on how to resolve conflict within the team or helping the team coordinate activities or other team skills.

Employees obviously need technical skills that can help the team accomplish its task. But team members also need skills in communication, adaptability, conflict resolution, and other teamwork issues.[52] Team training usually involves multiple methods. For example, a lecture or video may be used to disseminate knowledge regarding communication skills to trainees. Role plays or simulations may be used to give trainees the opportunity to put into practice the communication skills emphasized in the lecture. Regardless of the method chosen, opportunities for practice and feedback need to be included. Boeing utilized team training to improve the effectiveness of teams used to design the Boeing 777.[53] At Boeing, 250 teams with 8 to 15 members each worked on the design of the aircraft. Team members included engineers with different specialties (e.g., design engineers, production engineers), reliability specialists, quality experts, and marketing professionals. This type of team is known as a concurrent engineering team because employees from all the business functions needed to design the aircraft work together at the same time. This system contrasts with the traditional linear method of building an aircraft in which each business function works with the product and then passes it along to another function. One advantage of concurrent engineering teams is that design and marketing problems can be addressed earlier in the assembly process (at lower costs) because engineers and marketing employees are working together. For concurrent engineering teams to be successful, team members must understand how the process or product they are working on fits with the finished product. Because each 777 aircraft contains millions of parts, it is important that they fly together!

Boeing's team training approach began with an extensive orientation for team members. The orientation emphasized how team members were supposed to work together. Following orientation, the teams were given their work assignments. Trainers helped the teams work through issues and problems on an as-needed basis. That is, trainers were available to help the teams if the teams requested help. Trainers provided training in communication skills, conflict resolution, and leadership.

Action Learning

Action learning gives teams or work groups an actual problem, has them work on solving it and committing to an action plan, and then holds them accountable for carrying out the plan.[54] Several types of problems are used in action learning, including how to change the business, better utilize technology, remove barriers between the customer and company, and develop global leaders. Typically, action learning involves between 6 and 30 employees. It may also include customers and vendors. There are several variations in the composition of the group. One variation is that the group includes a single customer for the problem being dealt with. Sometimes the groups include cross-functional representatives who all have a stake in the problem. Or the group may involve employees from multiple functions who all focus on their own functional problems, each contributing to solving the problems identified. Employees are asked to develop novel ideas and solutions in a short period of time. The teams usually need to gather data for problem solving by visiting customers, employees, academics, and/or industry leaders. Once the teams have gathered data and developed their recommendations they are required to present them to top-level executives.

ATC, a public transportation services management company in Illinois, used action learning to help boost profitability by reducing operating costs.[55] Employees were divided into Action Workout Teams to identify ways of reducing costs and to brainstorm effective solutions. The process assumed that employees closest to where the work gets done have the best ideas about how to solve problems. Teams of five to seven employees met once a week for a couple of hours for 45 to 60 days. For example, a team working on parts inventory might have had a parts clerk, a couple of people from maintenance, a supervisor, and an operations employee. These teams studied problems and issues such as overtime, preventive maintenance, absenteeism, parts inventory, and inefficient safety inspection procedures. The teams brainstormed ideas, prioritized them according to their highest potential, developed action plans, installed them, tested them, and measured the outcomes. The solutions that the teams generated resulted in more than $1.8 million in savings for the company.

Six Sigma and black belt training programs involve principles of action learning. Six Sigma provides employees with measurement and statistical tools to help reduce defects and to cut costs.[56] Six Sigma is a quality standard with a goal of only 3.4 defects per million processes. Six Sigma was born at Motorola. It has saved the company an estimated $15 billion since the early 1990s. There are several levels of Six Sigma training, resulting in employees becoming certified as green belts, champions, or black belts.[57] To become black belts, trainees must participate in workshops and written assignments coached by expert instructors. The training involves four 4-day sessions over about 16 weeks. Between training sessions, candidates apply what they learn to assigned projects and then use them in the next training session. Trainees are also required to complete not only oral and written exams but also two or more projects that have a significant impact on the company's bottom line. After completing black belt training, employees are able to develop, coach, and lead Six Sigma teams; mentor and advise management on determining Six Sigma projects; and provide Six Sigma tools and statistical methods to team members. After black belts lead several project teams, they can take additional training and be certified as master black belts. Master black belts can teach other black belts and help senior managers integrate Six Sigma into the company's business goals.

McKesson Corporation trained 15 to 20 black belts and reassigned them to their original business units as their team's Six Sigma representatives.[58] When the two-year commitment ends, the black belts return to the business at higher positions, helping to spread the approach throughout the organization and ensuring that key leaders are committed to the Six Sigma philosophy. In most divisions of the company, Six Sigma training is mandated for senior vice presidents, who attend training that introduces Six Sigma and details how to identify a potential Six Sigma project. Across the company, every manager and director is expected to attend basic training. The Six Sigma effort has shown benefits every year since the program started in 1999.

Although action learning has not been formally evaluated, the process appears to maximize learning and transfer of training because it involves real-time problems that employees are facing. Also, action learning can be useful for identifying dysfunctional team dynamics that can get in the way of effective problem solving.

CHOOSING A TRAINING METHOD

As a trainer or manager, you will likely be asked to choose a training method. Given the large number of training methods available to you, this task may seem difficult. One way to choose a training method is to compare methods. Table 7.7 evaluates each training method discussed in this chapter on a number of characteristics. The types of learning outcomes related to each method are identified. Also, for each method, a high, medium, or low rating is provided for each characteristic of the learning environment, for transfer of training, for cost, and for effectiveness.

How might you use this table to choose a training method? The first step in choosing a method is to identify the type of learning outcome that you want training to influence. As discussed in Chapter 4, these outcomes include verbal information, intellectual skills, cognitive strategies, attitudes, and motor skills. Training methods may influence one or several learning outcomes. Once you have identified a learning method, the next step is to consider the extent to which the method facilitates learning and transfer of training, the costs related to development and use of the method, and its effectiveness.

TABLE 7.7 Comparison of Training Methods

	Presentation		OJT	Self-Directed Learning	Hands-on						Group Building		
	Lecture	Video			Appren-ticeship	Simulation	Case Study	Business Games	Role Play	Behavior Modeling	Adventure Learning	Team Training	Action Learning
Learning Outcome													
Verbal information	Yes	Yes	Yes	Yes	Yes	No	Yes	Yes	No	No	No	No	No
Intellectual skills	Yes	No	No	Yes	Yes	Yes	Yes	Yes	No	No	No	Yes	No
Cognitive strategies	Yes	No	Yes	Yes	No	Yes	Yes	Yes	Yes	Yes	Yes	Yes	Yes
Attitudes	Yes	Yes	No	No	No	No	No	No	Yes	No	Yes	Yes	Yes
Motor skills	No	Yes	Yes	No	Yes	Yes	No	No	No	Yes	No	No	No
Learning Environment													
Clear objective	Medium	Low	High	High	High	High	Medium	High	Medium	High	Medium	High	High
Practice	Low	Low	High	High	High	High	Medium	Medium	Medium	High	Medium	High	Medium
Meaningfulness	Medium	Medium	High	Medium	High	High	Medium	Medium	Medium	Medium	Low	High	High
Feedback	Low	Low	High	Medium	High	High	Medium	High	Medium	High	Medium	Medium	High
Observe and interact with others	Low	Medium	High	Medium	High	High	High	High	High	High	High	High	High
Transfer of Training	Low	Low	High	Medium	High	High	Medium	Medium	Medium	High	Low	High	High
Cost													
Development	Medium	Medium	Medium	High	High	High	Medium	High	Medium	Medium	Medium	Medium	Low
Administrative	Low	Low	Low	Medium	High	Low	Low	Medium	Medium	Medium	Medium	Medium	Medium
Effectiveness	High for verbal information	Medium	High for structured OJT	Medium	High	High	Medium	Medium	Medium	High	Low	Medium	High

As Chapter 4 said, for learning to occur, trainees must understand the objectives of the training program, training content should be meaningful, and trainees should have the opportunity to practice and receive feedback. Also, a powerful way to learn is through observing and interacting with others. As you may recall from Chapter 5, transfer of training refers to the extent to which training will be used on the job. In general, the closer the training content and environment prepare trainees for use of learning outcomes on the job, the greater the likelihood that transfer will occur. As discussed in Chapter 6, two types of costs are important: development costs and administrative costs. Development costs relate to design of the training program, including costs to buy or create the program. Administrative costs are incurred each time the training method is used. These include costs related to consultants, instructors, materials, and trainers. The effectiveness rating is based on both academic research and practitioner recommendations.

Several trends in Table 7.7 are worth noting. First, there is considerable overlap between learning outcomes across the training methods. Group building methods are unique because they focus on individual as well as team learning (e.g., improving group processes). If you are interested in improving the effectiveness of groups or teams, you should choose one of the group building methods (e.g., action learning, team training, action learning). Second, comparing the presentation methods to the hands-on methods illustrates that most hands-on methods provide a better learning environment and transfer of training than do the presentation methods. The presentation methods are also less effective than the hands-on methods. If you are not limited by the amount of money that can be used for development or administration, choose a hands-on method over a presentation method. The training budget for developing training methods can influence the method chosen. If you have a limited budget for developing new training methods, use structured on-the-job training—a relatively inexpensive yet effective hands-on method. If you have a larger budget, you might want to consider hands-on methods that facilitate transfer of training, such as simulators. Keep in mind that many of the methods discussed in this chapter can be adapted for use in online learning, e-learning, or distance learning. These training methods are discussed in Chapter 8.

Summary

This chapter discussed presentation, hands-on, and group building training methods. Presentation methods (such as lecture) are effective for efficiently communicating information (knowledge) to a large number of trainees. Presentation methods need to be supplemented with opportunities for the trainees to practice, discuss, and receive feedback to facilitate learning. Hands-on methods get the trainee directly involved in learning. Hands-on methods are ideal for developing skills and behaviors. Hands-on methods include on-the-job training, simulations, self-directed learning, business games, case studies, role plays, and behavior modeling. These methods can be expensive to develop but incorporate the conditions needed for learning and transfer of training to occur. Group building methods such as team training, action learning, and adventure learning focus on helping teams increase the skills needed for effective teamwork (e.g., self-awareness, conflict resolution, coordination) and help to build team cohesion and identity. Group building techniques may include the use of presentation methods as well as exercises during which team members interact and communicate with each other. Team training has a long history of success in preparing flight crews and surgical teams, but its effectiveness for developing management teams has not been clearly established.

Key Terms

presentation methods, *203*
lecture, *203*
audiovisual instruction, *204*
hands-on methods, *205*
on-the-job training
(OJT), *206*
self-directed learning, *207*
apprenticeship, *209*
simulation, *211*

case study, *212*
business games, *213*
role plays, *214*
behavior modeling, *214*
vicarious
reinforcement, *214*
key behavior, *215*
modeling display, *215*
application planning, *216*

group building
methods, *217*
Experiential learning, *217*
adventure learning, *218*
team training, *219*
cross training, *219*
coordination training, *220*
team leader training, *220*
action learning, *221*

Discussion Questions

1. What are the strengths and weaknesses of the lecture, the case study, and behavior modeling?

2. If you had to choose between adventure learning and action learning for developing an effective team, which would you choose? Defend your choice.

3. Discuss the process of behavior modeling training.

4. How can the characteristics of the trainee affect self-directed learning?

5. What are the components of effective team performance? How might training strengthen these components?

6. Table 7.7 compares training methods on a number of characteristics. Explain why simulation and behavior modeling receive high ratings for transfer of training.

7. What are some reasons why on-the-job training can be ineffective? What can be done to ensure its effectiveness?

Application Assignments

1. Choose a job you are familiar with. Develop a self-directed learning module for a skill that is important for that job.

2. Click on *www.sabrehq.com,* the website for Sabre Corporate Development. Click on Best Selling Team Building Concepts. Choose one of the activities and events found on this page, and review it. Discuss what you would do to ensure that the team building event you selected is successful.

3. Divide into teams of two students. One student should be designated as a "trainer," the other as a "trainee." The trainee should briefly leave the room while the trainers read the instructions for folding a paper cup (see p. 226). After the trainers have read the instructions, the trainees should return to the room. The trainers should then train the trainees in how to fold a paper cup (about 15 minutes). When the instructor calls time, the trainers should note the steps they followed to conduct the training. The trainees should record their evaluations of the strengths and weaknesses of the training session (5–10 minutes). If time allows, switch roles.

   Be prepared to discuss the training process and your reactions as a trainer or trainee. Also, be prepared to discuss the extent to which the training followed the steps for effective on-the-job training.

SUPPLEMENT TO APPLICATION ASSIGNMENT 3
Steps and Key Points in Folding a Paper Cup

Steps in the Operation	Key Points
Step: A logical segment of the operation in which something is done to advance the work.	Key point: Any directions or bits of information that help to perform the step correctly, safely, and easily.
Place 8½" x 11" sheet of paper in front of you on flat surface.	1. Be sure surface is flat—free of interfering objects.
Fold lower left corner up.	2a. Line up the right edges. b. Make a sharp crease.
Turn paper over.	3a. Pick up lower right corner with right hand and place it at the top. b. Folded flap should not be underneath.
Fold excess lower edge up.	4a. Line up right edges. b. Fold should line up with bottom edge. c. Make sharp crease.
Fold lower left corner flush with edge "A."	5a. Keep edges "B" and "C" parallel. b. Hold bottom edge in the center with finger while making fold.
Fold upper corner to point "D."	6a. Hold cup firmly with left hand. b. Bring upper corner down with right hand.
Separate lower right corner and fold back.	7a. Hold cup with left hand. b. Fold back with right hand. c. Make sharp creases.
Turn cup over and fold remaining flap back.	8. Make sharp creases.
Check cup to be sure it will hold water.	9. Open cup and look inside.

Source: From P. Decker and B. Nathan, *Behavior Modeling Training* (New York: Praeger Scientific, 1985).

4. Review one of the following websites, which feature simulations: *www.income-outcome.com, www.celemi.com,* or *www.riskybusiness.com.*

   Describe the situation that the simulation is designed to represent. What elements in the simulation replicate the work environment? How could the simulation be improved to ensure that learning and transfer of training occur?

Endnotes

1. D. McMurrer, M. Van Buren, W. Woodrell, Jr., "The 2000 ASTD State of the Industry Report" (Alexandra, VA: American Society for Training and Development, 2000); Industry Report 2000, *Training* (October 2000) 57–66; A. P. Carnevale, L. J. Gainer, and A. S. Meltzer, *Workplace Basics Training Manual* (San Francisco: Jossey-Bass, 1990).

2. M. Van Wart, N. J. Cayer, and S. Cook, *Handbook of Training and Development for the Public Sector* (San Francisco: Jossey-Bass, 1993); R. S. House, "Classroom Instruction," in *The ASTD Training and Development Handbook,* 4th ed., ed. R. L. Craig (New York: McGraw-Hill, 1996): 437–52.

3. Van Wart, Cayer, and Cook, *Handbook of Training and Development for the Public Sector.*

4. C. Lee, "Who Gets Trained in What?"

5. T. Skylar, "When Training Collides with a 35-Ton Truck," *Training* (March 1996): 32–38.

6. R. B. Cohn, "How to Choose a Video Producer," *Training* (July 1996): 58–61.

7. A. P. Carnevale, "The Learning Enterprise," *Training and Development Journal* (February 1989): 26–37.

8. B. Filipczak, "Who Owns Your OJT?" *Training* (December 1996): 44–49.

9. Ibid.

10. W. J. Rothwell and H. C. Kazanas, "Planned OJT is Productive OJT," *Training and Development Journal* (October 1996): 53–56.

11. Filipczak, "Who Owns Your OJT?"

12. G. M. Piskurich, *Self-Directed Learning* (San Francisco: Jossey-Bass, 1993).

13. D. B. Youst and L. Lipsett, "New Job Immersion without Drowning," *Training and Development Journal* (February 1989): 73–75.

14. G. M. Piskurich, "Self-Directed Learning," in *The ASTD Training and Development Handbook:* 453–72; G. M. Piskurich, "Developing Self-Directed Learning," *Training and Development* (March 1994): 31–36.

15. C. M. Solomon, "When Training Doesn't Translate," *Workforce* (March 1997): 40–44.

16. P. Warr and D. Bunce, "Trainee Characteristics and the Outcomes of Open Learning," *Personnel Psychology* 48 (1995): 347–75; T. G. Hatcher, "The Ins and Outs of Self-Directed Learning," *Training and Development* (February 1997): 35–39.

17. R. W. Glover, *Apprenticeship Lessons from Abroad* (Columbus, OH: National Center for Research in Vocational Education, 1986).

18. Commerce Clearing House, *Orientation-Training* (Chicago: Personnel Practices Communications, Commerce Clearing House, 1981): 501–5.

19. A. H. Howard III, "Apprenticeships," in *The ASTD Training and Development Handbook:* 803–13.

20. K. Ellis, "More Than an Assembly Line," *Training* (January 2002): 33.

21. *Eldredge* v. *Carpenters JATC* (1981), 27 Fair Employment Practices (Bureau of National Affairs) 479.

22. M. McCain, "Apprenticeship Lessons from Europe," *Training and Development* (November 1994): 38–41.

23. K. L. Miller and K. N. Anhalt, "Without Training, I Can't Start My Real Life," *Business Week* (September 16, 1996): 60.

24. M. Pramik, "Installers Learn on Practice Dwellings," *Columbus Dispatch,* February 7, 2003: F1.

25. H. Dolezalek, "Pretending to Learn," *Training* (July/August 2003): 20–26.

26. M. W. McCall Jr. and M. M. Lombardo, "Using Simulation for Leadership and Management Research," *Management Science* 28 (1982): 533–49.

27. S. McCartney, "Colombia Says Pilot Error Was Cause of '95 Crash of American Airlines Plane," *The Wall Street Journal,* September 30, 1996: B5.

28. J. Alden and J. Kirkhorn, "Case Studies," in *The ASTD Training and Development Handbook:* 497–516.

29. H. Kelly, "Case Method Training: What It Is and How It Works," in *Effective Training Delivery,* ed. D. Zielinski (Minneapolis: Lakewood Books, 1989): 95–96.

30. T. W. Shreeve, "On the Case at the CIA," *Training and Development* (March 1997): 53–54.

31. E. Krell, "Learning to Love the P&L," *Training* (September 1999): 66–72.

32. "Business War Games," *Training* (December 2002): 18.

33. M. Hequet, "Games That Teach," *Training* (July 1995): 53–58.

34. S. Thiagarajan, "Instructional Games, Simulations, and Role Plays," in *The ASTD Training and Development Handbook:* 517–33.

35. S. J. Simon and J. M. Werner, "Computer Training through Behavior Modeling, Self-Paced, and Instructional Approaches: A Field Experiment," *Journal of Applied Psychology* 81 (1996): 648–59.

36. W. C. Byham and A. Pescuric, "Behavior Modeling at the Teachable Moment," *Training* (December 1996): 51–56.

37. P. Decker and B. Nathan, *Behavior Modeling Training* (New York: Praeger Scientific, 1985).

38. Ibid.; T. T. Baldwin, "Effects of Alternative Modeling Strategies on Outcomes of Interpersonal-Skills Training," *Journal of Applied Psychology* 77 (1992): 147–54.

39. D. Brown and D. Harvey, *An Experiential Approach to Organizational Development* (Englewood Cliffs, NJ: Prentice-Hall, 2000); J. Schettler, "Learning by Doing," *Training* (April 2002): 38–43.

40. S. Lueck, "Postal Service's Top Inspector Should Be Fired, Senators Say," *The Wall Street Journal,* May 2, 2003: A2.

41. J. Schettler, "Learning by Doing."

42. R. J. Wagner, T. T. Baldwin, and C. C. Rowland, "Outdoor Training: Revolution or Fad?" *Training and Development Journal* (March 1991): 51–57; C. J. Cantoni, "Learning the Ropes of Teamwork," *The Wall Street Journal,* October 2, 1995: A14.

43. C. Steinfeld, "Challenge Courses Can Build Strong Teams," *Training and Development* (April 1997): 12–13.

44. Ibid.

45. G. M. Tarullo, "Making Outdoor Experiential Training Work," *Training* (August 1992): 47–52.

46. C. Clements, R. J. Wagner, and C. C. Roland, "The Ins and Outs of Experiential Training," *Training and Development* (February 1995): 52–56.

47. G. M. McEvoy, "Organizational Change and Outdoor Management Education," *Human Resource Management* 36 (1997): 235–50.

48. E. Salas and J. A. Cannon-Bowers, "Strategies for Team Training," in *Training for 21st Century Technology: Applications for Psychological Research,* eds. M. A. Quinones and A. Dutta (Washington, DC: American Psychological Association, 1997).

49. R. L. Oser, A. McCallum, E. Salas, and B. B. Morgan, Jr., "Toward a Definition of Teamwork: An Analysis of Critical Team Behaviors," Technical Report 89-004 (Orlando, FL: Naval Training Research Center, 1989).

50. E. Salas and J. A. Cannon-Bowers, "Strategies for Team Training."

51. M. Marks, M. Sabella, C. Burke, and S. Zaccaro, "The Impact of Cross-Training on Team Effectiveness," *Journal of Applied Psychology* 87 (2002): 3–13.

52. E. Salas, C. Burke, and J. Cannon-Bowers, "What We Know about Designing and Delivering Team Training: Tips and Guidelines," *Creating, Implementing, and Managing Effective Training and Development,* ed. K. Kraiger (San Francisco: Jossey-Bass, 2002): 234–62.

53. B. Filipczak, "Concurrent Engineering," *Training* (August 1996): 54–59.

54. D. Dotlich and J. Noel, *Active Learning: How the World's Top Companies Are Recreating Their Leaders and Themselves* (San Francisco: Jossey-Bass, 1998).

55. "A Team Effort," *Training* (September 2002): 18.

56. H. Lancaster, "This Kind of Black Belt Can Help You Score Some Points at Work," *The Wall Street Journal,* September 14, 1999: B1; S. Gale, "Building Frameworks for Six Sigma Success," *Workforce* (May 2003: 64–66.

57. J. DeFeo, "An ROI Story," *Training and Development* (July 2000): 25–27.

58. S. Gale, "Six Sigma is a Way of Life," *Workforce* (May 2003): 67–68.

Chapter **Eight**

E-Learning and Use of Technology in Training

Objectives

After reading this chapter, you should be able to

1. Explain how new technologies are influencing training.
2. Discuss potential advantages and disadvantages of multimedia training.
3. Evaluate a Web-based training site.
4. Explain how learning and transfer of training are enhanced by new training technologies.
5. Explain the strengths and limitations of e-learning.
6. Describe to a manager the different types of distance learning.
7. Recommend what should be included in an electronic performance support system.
8. Compare and contrast the strengths and weaknesses of traditional training methods with those of training methods based on new technology.
9. Identify and explain the benefits of new technologies that can be used to improve the efficiency of training administration.

Technology Makes Training an Easy Sale at Cisco Systems

Cisco Systems of San Jose, California, is a leading company that develops networking for the Internet. Cisco Systems grew from nothing in 1986 to a peak of 46,000 employees worldwide. However, Cisco fell on hard times during the 2001 economic downturn as the company's value fell by $430 billion and the company had to lay off more than 4,000 employees. Despite the downturn, Cisco did not cut back on its commitment to employee learning. CEO John Chambers believed that e-learning was an important force for helping Cisco recover from its economic woes, for creating strong ties with information technology, and for demonstrating real business results. It doesn't hurt that the more e-learning that companies use, the more demand there will be for the video, voice, and data network products that Cisco provides! Cisco believes that the future of the Internet is the convergence of voice, video, and data (telephone, television, computer) networks into one common network.

Through a partnership with the company's Internet Learning Solutions Group, the Information Technology Unit, and Chambers, the Cisco Media Network was developed. This collaboration was necessary to ensure a match between the company's tools and technology infrastructure, its business purpose, and effective learning principles. The Cisco Media Network is a large, private broadcasting network linked via satellite to a worldwide grid of servers. The network serves about 1,000 users. The content comes from business units, technology groups, and product marketing groups. The network broadcasts include the company's annual meeting, video briefings by executives, and learning portals for employees and customers. The Media Network allows Cisco to broadcast high-quality material over the intranet. Sound and images are production quality.

The Media Network has been useful for developing e-learning for Cisco's account managers, who are the company's frontline sales force. To determine the account managers' needs, Cisco carried out a needs assessment that included interviews with them. The needs assessment helped identify what they needed to learn and the time they had available for learning. A common concern raised by the account managers was that learning content was not delivered to them in a way that fit their work patterns or learning styles. Because account managers spend a lot of time traveling, they wanted to get on the Internet, find what they needed, and get out again. They preferred not to sit in front of a personal computer for a long e-learning course.

As a result, the Account Manager Learning Environment (AMLE) was created. The AMLE is a development tool and performance support system based on four business objectives: increase sales, increase time-to-revenue, increase speed that account managers become competent in a topic, and reduce travel and costs. The goal in developing AMLE was to create a learning environment that would motivate the account managers to use it. The AMLE consists of a suite of learning tools, each with its own characteristics. The learning tools include small chunks of information to meet the managers' "get in and get out" needs, short skill-building sessions to help develop account managers' competencies, and a scenario-based, sales call simulator that provides real-world practice. The virtual sales calls are designed to make the account managers field difficult questions. The questions are provided by a realistic audio feed, and once a response is selected, feedback is immediate and specific about what the account manager could have done better.

Account managers can choose remote access or can download lessons to their hard drive. They are offered two ways to access lessons while traveling. First, a talk show can be accessed remotely, saved to a laptop, or downloaded to an MP3 player. The talk show discusses key issues of account management and the sales process. Second, a magazine is available to give account managers fast facts and advice.

Source: Based on M. Delahoussaye and R. Zemke, "Ten Things We Know For Sure about On-Line Learning," *Training* (September 2001): 48–59; P. Galagan, "Delta Force," *T&D* (July 2002): 21–28.

INTRODUCTION

As the chapter opening vignette illustrates, technology is having a major impact on the delivery of training programs. Cisco Systems is using new technology for training because of the learning and accessibility advantages that new technology offers over traditional classroom training. The use of technology for learning requires collaboration among the areas of training, information technology, and top management. For technology in training to be effective, it needs to be designed with good learning principles (recall the discussion in Chapter 4), to match the capabilities of the company's technology infrastructure, and to have top management support. Again, needs assessment, design, transfer, and evaluation (training design) are critical components of the effective use of training technology! Although technologies such as MP3 players, digital video discs (DVDs), and wireless handheld computers provide exciting capabilities and possibilities, it is critical that companies use training technologies that support the business and learner needs. Cisco Systems is not alone in its efforts to use new training technologies. Technology is changing learning and training in corporate settings as well as in grade schools, high schools, colleges, and universities.

For example, students at several dental schools are being asked to purchase a DVD containing the entire dental curriculum including textbooks, manuals, and lecture slides.[1] Students are required to buy a laptop computer with a DVD player. The DVD contains 2.2 million pages of text and images from books and manuals plus 300,000 other images including diagrams, figures, microscopic images, charts, photographs, and illustrations. Each DVD also has 20 hours of video that demonstrates various dental techniques. Each DVD weighs less than one-third of an ounce but replaces at least 300 pounds of textbooks and other materials! The DVD makes it easy for students to search for information and allows students to skip sections, learn new material, and review material as they feel appropriate. The DVD helps students learn by appealing to multiple senses. A student can search for a term such as *maxilla* (the word for jaw), read the definition, and see a video of various types of jaws.

Using videoconferencing equipment, students at New Albany High School in New Albany, Ohio, are taking a college Spanish course without leaving their school.[2] Other students in Ohio schools are taking virtual field trips, reading homework assignments posted on the Internet, and watching live open-heart surgery.

Several surveys of company training practices suggest that although face-to-face classroom instruction is used by almost all companies, new technologies are gaining in popularity. Table 8.1 provides a snapshot of the use of technology in training. The use of training technologies is expected to increase dramatically in the next decade as technology improves, as the cost of technology decreases, as companies recognize the potential cost savings of

TABLE 8.1
Use of New Technology in Training

Source: Based on T. Gavin, "Industry Report," *Training* (October 2003): 21–45; M. Hequet, "The State of the E-Learning Market," *Training* (September 2003): 24–29.

- 24 percent of companies have a separate technology-based training budget.
- 18 percent of companies have full-time trainers who are paid from the information technology department's budget.
- The most frequently used technology in training is the Internet/intranet/extranet (54 percent of companies).
- 60 percent of training that is delivered by the computer and that is not instructor-led is done through self-paced Web courses, and 32 percent uses CD-ROM/DVD/diskettes.
- 34 percent of online learning follows the classroom learning model that connects trainees with an instructor or other students.
- 80 percent of companies who use e-learning are creating the content of these programs internally.
- Of those companies who use e-learning, 56 percent offer it to all employees, 45 percent offer it to select groups of employees, and 26 percent offer it to customers.

training via desktop and personal computers (PCs), and as the need for customized training increases while the economy moves from a one-size-fits-all approach to mass customization in the delivery of goods and services.[3] As you will see later in this chapter, new training technologies are unlikely to totally replace face-to-face instruction. Rather, face-to-face instruction will be combined with new training technologies (a combination known as blended training) to maximize learning.

This chapter begins by discussing new technologies' influence on training delivery, support, and administration. How technology has changed the learning environment is addressed. Next, the chapter explores emerging multimedia training techniques (computer-based training, CD-ROM, interactive video, the Internet). E-learning, a comprehensive training strategy that involves several multimedia training techniques (Internet, CD-ROM), is discussed. E-learning emphasizes learning through interaction with training content, sharing with other trainees, and using Internet resources. More sophisticated technologies that are just beginning to be marketed commercially for training delivery (expert systems, virtual reality, intelligent tutoring systems) are introduced. The use of expert systems and groupware exemplifies how technology supports training through its role as a storage place for intellectual capital (information and learned capabilities), which facilitates access to information and communication of knowledge among employees. The chapter also shows how technology such as interactive voice responses and imaging is used in training administration. The last section of the chapter compares the various training methods that are based on new technology, employing the characteristics used to evaluate the traditional training methods discussed in Chapter 7. As you will see, several training methods discussed in this chapter can replace or substitute for traditional training methods under certain conditions.

TECHNOLOGY'S INFLUENCE ON TRAINING AND LEARNING

Chapters 1 and 2 discussed the role that training and development should play in helping companies to execute their business strategy and deal with forces influencing the workplace. For training to help a company gain a competitive advantage, it needs to support business goals and to be delivered as needed to geographically dispersed employees who may be working at home or in another country. Training costs (such as travel costs) should be minimized and maximum benefits gained, including learning and transfer of training. For learning and transfer to occur (i.e., for the benefits of training to be realized), the training environment must include learning principles such as practice, feedback, meaningful material, and the ability to learn by interacting with others.

New technologies have made it possible to reduce the costs associated with delivering training to employees, to increase the effectiveness of the learning environment, and to help training contribute to business goals. New training technologies include multimedia, distance learning, expert systems, electronic support systems, and training software applications. These new technologies have influenced the delivery of training, training administration, and training support. Technology has made several benefits possible:[4]

- Employees can gain control over when and where they receive training.
- Employees can access knowledge and expert systems on an as-needed basis.

- Employees can choose the type of media (print, sound, video) they want to use in a training program.
- Course enrollment, testing, and training records can be handled electronically, reducing the paperwork and time needed for administrative activities.
- Employees' accomplishments during training can be monitored.
- Traditional training methods such as classroom instruction and behavior modeling can be delivered to trainees rather than requiring them to come to a central training location.

Technology allows digital collaboration to occur. **Digital collaboration** is the use of technology to enhance and extend employees' abilities to work together regardless of their geographic proximity.[5] Digital collaboration includes electronic messaging systems, electronic meeting systems, online communities of learning organized by subject where employees can access interactive discussion areas and share training content and Web links, and document-handling systems with collaboration technologies that allow interpersonal interaction. For example, at *www.buzzsaw.com,* contractors, suppliers, and engineers can buy and sell products and services as well as exchange blueprints, designs, and other data to cut building time. Digital collaboration requires a computer, but collaborative applications for handheld devices and personal digital assistants are becoming available that will allow employees to collaborate anytime or anywhere. Digital collaboration can be synchronous or asynchronous.[6] In **synchronous communication,** trainers, experts, and learners interact with each other live and in real time in the same way they would in face-to-face classroom instruction. Technologies such as video teleconferencing and live online courses (virtual classrooms) make synchronous communications possible. **Asynchronous communication** refers to non–real-time interactions. That is, persons are not online and cannot communicate with each other without a time delay, but learners can still access information resources when they desire them. E-mail, self-paced courses on the Web or on CD-ROM, discussion groups, and virtual libraries allow asynchronous communications.

The Shoney's and Captain D's restaurant chains have more than 350 restaurants in more than 20 states.[7] Over 8,000 employees each year must be trained on the basics of the operational parts of the business, including how to make french fries, hush puppies, and coleslaw. Also, each year 600 new managers must be trained in business issues and back-office operations of the restaurants. The biggest challenge that Shoney's faced was how to consistently train geographically dispersed employees. Shoney's solution was to implement OneTouch, a live integrated video and two-way voice and data application that combines synchronous video, voice, and data and live Web pages so that team members can interact with trainers. OneTouch can be delivered to desktop PCs as well as to warehouses and repair bays. Desktop systems can be positioned in any appropriate locations in the restaurant. Individuals or group of employees can gather around the PC for training. The training modules include such topics as orientation, kitchen, and dining room. Each module is interactive. Topics are introduced and are followed up by quizzes to ensure that learning occurs. For example, the coleslaw program shows trainees what the coleslaw ingredients are and where they can be found in the restaurant. The coleslaw program includes a video that trainees can watch and practice with. After they practice, they have to complete a quiz, and their manager has to verify that they completed the topic before they move on to the next program. The training is consistent and is easy to update so as to ensure it is current. The program

FIGURE 8.1 Types of learning environments

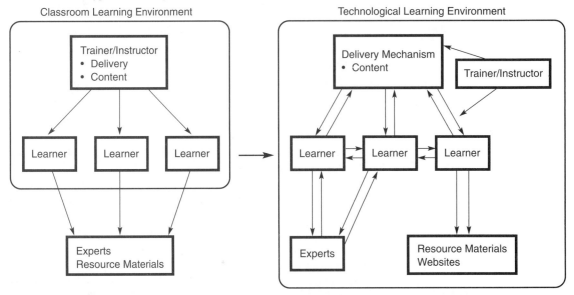

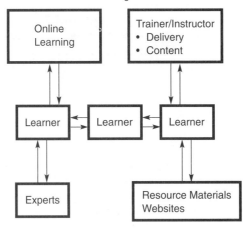

also allows kitchen and counter staff to learn each other's skills, which gives Shoney's flexibility in its staffing (e.g., counter employees who know how to cook).

The Internet is primarily responsible for creating our revolution in learning. Internet technology has permitted the development of electronic networks that integrate voice, video, and data connections among learners, instructors, and experts. Figure 8.1 shows three different types of learning environments. Learning used to be a very linear process. That is, instructors presented information to the learners; practice and applications then occurred after instruction was completed (see the classroom learning environment in Figure 8.1). Traditionally, the learning environment included only the instructor or trainer and the learners.

The trainer was responsible for delivering content, answering questions, and testing learning. Trainees played a passive role in learning. Communication on course content was one-way: from the instructor to the learner. Experts and resource materials were separate from the learning environment. Contact with resource materials and experts beyond the instructor and course materials assigned for the course required learners to go outside the formal learning environment. Also, learners had to wait to access resource materials and experts until instruction was completed. Interaction between learners occurred primarily outside the training room and tended to be limited to those who worked in the same geographic area.

Technology has allowed learning to become a more dynamic process. As shown on the right side of Figure 8.1, the learning environment has expanded to include greater interaction between learners and the training content as well as between learners and the instructor. The trainer helps design the instruction, but the instruction is primarily delivered to the learners online using the Internet. The instructor becomes more of a coach and resource person to answer students' questions and is less involved in delivery of training content. Learning occurs not only through interaction with the instructor or trainer but also through communicating with other learners, working on virtual team projects, exchanging ideas, interacting with experts (engineers, managers, etc.), and discovering ideas and applications using hyperlinks that take the learner to other websites. Experts and resource materials are part of the learning environment. While learners interact with the training content through exercises, applications, and simulations, they can discuss what they are learning with other learners or access experts or resource materials available on the Internet. Training delivery and administration (e.g., tracking learner progress) is all done by the computer. In the blended learning environment, shown at the bottom of Figure 8.1, trainees have access to a blended training curriculum that consists of both online and classroom instruction. Collaboration occurs between learners, between learners and instructors, and between learners and experts.

MULTIMEDIA TRAINING

Multimedia training combines audiovisual training methods with computer-based training.[8] These programs integrate text, graphics, animation, audio, and video. Because multimedia training is computer-based, the trainee can interact with the content. Interactive video, Internet, or intranets may be used to deliver training.

How prevalent is multimedia training? Most companies use it. Multimedia-based training is used most frequently to train employees in software and basic computer skills (42 percent of the managers mentioned these skills); training in management skills and technical training is also occurring (25 percent).[9] Almost all companies that use multimedia training deliver it using CD-ROM, with approximately one-third using the World Wide Web. The high use of CD-ROMs relates to how multimedia training is delivered.

Table 8.2 shows the major advantages and disadvantages of multimedia training. Multimedia training motivates trainees to learn, provides immediate feedback and guidance (through online help), tests employees' level of mastery, and allows employees to learn at their own pace.[10] A major disadvantage of multimedia training is the cost. Initial development costs for a computerized version of training can range from $25,000 to $250,000 depending on the complexity of material and media used.[11] These costs can be recovered over time by savings gained from reductions in travel costs and instruction costs if the content does

TABLE 8.2
Advantages and Disadvantages of Multimedia Training

Source: Based on S.V. Bainbridge, "The Implications of Technology-Assisted Training," *IHRIM-Link* (December 1996/January 1997): 62–68; M. Hequet, "How Does Multimedia Change Training?" *Training* (February 1997): A20–A22.

Advantages	Disadvantages
Is self-paced	Is expensive to develop
Is interactive	Is ineffective for certain training content
Has consistency of content	May lead to trainee anxiety with using technology
Has consistency of delivery	Is difficult to quickly update
Offers unlimited geographic accessibility	Can be a lack of agreement on effectiveness
Provides immediate feedback	
Has a built-in guidance system	
Appeals to multiple senses	
Can test and certify mastery	
Provides privacy	

not require frequent updating.[12] Multimedia training may also be difficult to use for training interpersonal skills, especially where the learner needs to recognize and/or practice subtle behavioral cues or cognitive processes.

Medtronic is a 12,000-employee company based in Minneapolis, Minnesota, that specializes in developing and selling medical technology. Multimedia was first used at Medtronic purely for marketing purposes. Salespeople would use a laptop personal computer equipped with a CD player to show physicians the benefits and correct usage of heart valves. When the interactive program was introduced at a national sales meeting, demand for the CD exceeded supply.

Medtronic is exploring the use of multimedia for training as well as marketing. Currently, Medtronic extensively uses classroom-based training for salespeople. Although the product CDs are being used as a learning tool by staff preparing for sales presentations, the CDs are only one step the company is taking toward the goal of enhancing learning. The current manager of sales training is pushing for expanded use of multimedia training because it can cut salespeople's time in the classroom. The manager believes that multimedia training will increase the consistency and efficiency of training and provide salespeople with feedback regarding which dimensions of the product they "know." The current CD-based product programs work best for experienced salespeople who already are familiar with the product. New salespeople need feedback and help screens, available from multimedia applications. New salespeople need to be able to interact with the product at their own pace, so that they are comfortable explaining and demonstrating all aspects of the product to physicians. Salespeople's time is also in great demand. Multimedia provides accessibility to training wherever and whenever salespeople can access their laptop computer. Multimedia can also help the entire sales force learn about new products as quickly as possible.[13]

Note that few conclusions can be made regarding the effectiveness of multimedia training compared to traditional training methods.[14] For example, a division of PepsiCo used a multimedia training program for meal packers at fast-food restaurants. Employees' reactions to the program were positive. However, the multimedia delivery method was discontinued because less costly methods including use of technical manuals and job aids (laminated cards at workstations) resulted in the same level of learning and behavior as the more expensive multimedia program.

COMPUTER-BASED TRAINING

Computer-based training (CBT) is an interactive training experience in which the computer provides the learning stimulus, the trainee must respond, and the computer analyzes the responses and provides feedback to the trainee.[15] CBT includes interactive video, CD-ROM, and other systems when they are computer-driven. The most common CBT programs consist of software on a floppy disk that runs on a personal computer. CBT, one of the first new technologies to be used in training, has become more sophisticated with the development of laser discs, DVDs, and CD-ROMs and with increasing use of the Internet. These technologies allow greater use of video and audio than do technologies that rely solely on the computer.

For example, to teach managers how to complete performance reviews, Vidicon Enterprises, which operates convenience stores in Washington, purchased software called "Performance Now!"[16] Managers learned how to write better performance reviews and to improve their management skills. The program works by asking managers to identify which of several job dimensions they want to evaluate. For the dimension "job quality," the manager is asked to rate the employee in various categories such as "Strives to Achieve Goals." The program automatically summarizes the ratings into a paragraph that the manager can edit. The program teaches the managers effective language to use in performance evaluations. If the manager writes something inappropriate (e.g., "the employee is too young for the position"), a box appears on the screen with a warning not to equate age with experience. Also, use of the categories underlying each job dimension has broadened managers' views of employee performance.

Computer-based training can also involve simulations. For example, during training needs assessment, Bayer Pharmaceuticals discovered that its technical experts needed new skills to manage large projects.[17] These skills related to keeping project managers focused on the task, managing competing priorities, managing large cross-functional teams, and supervising employees who did not report to them. These skills are important to reduce the time needed to bring research discoveries to the marketplace. To train in these skills, Bayer used a computer-based simulation that requires teams of trainees to manage a large-scale project. The management decisions they make impact their odds of being successful. A computer calculates each team's probability of succeeding. The simulation includes obstacles that can negatively impact a project such as unmotivated employees, absenteeism, and projects being completed late. The simulation also includes online work that trainees complete prior to training. The prework provides trainees with an overview of the steps involved in project management. All trainees complete a self-assessment of their team-related behavior (e.g., conflict resolution). The assessments are used for discussing leader/team-member relationships. After completing the simulation, trainees can access a program website that includes a newsletter and tips for project management. Employees who have completed the simulation are demonstrating increased confidence in their ability to manage a project and to handle changing priorities, and they are addressing team issues more quickly.

CD-ROM, DVD, Laser Disc

A personal computer enables animation, video clips, and graphics to be integrated into a training session. Also, the user can interact with the training material through using a joystick or touch-screen monitor. **CD-ROMs** and **DVDs** utilize a laser to read text, graphics, audio, and video off an aluminum disc. A **laser disc** uses a laser to provide high-quality video and sound. A laser disc can be used alone (as a source of video) or as part of a computer-based instruction delivery system.

For example, at Pilgrim Nuclear Power Plant in Plymouth, Massachusetts, a newly hired security guard learns the layout of the facility by using a computer, television, monitor, joystick, and video disc.[18] The new hire can tour the trash-compactor facility, examine the components on a panel of electrical controls, ride elevators, and listen to colleagues discuss machinery, equipment, and high-radiation areas that the new hire should be aware of. With more than 77,000 photos on the laser disc, the new security guard can travel at normal walking speed, look upward or downward, quickly change location, and store images for future reference!

Moody's Risk Management Services uses a CD-ROM course to train bank loan agents.[19] The CD-ROM includes a number of case studies that require the trainee to research commercial loan applications and make recommendations. The trainee can access virtual resources including a fax machine, a telephone, background articles, colleagues' advice, and interviews with the loan applicant. After making the loan recommendation, the trainee receives feedback about the accuracy of the recommendation and the process used to make the recommendation.

Interactive Video

Interactive video combines the advantages of video and computer-based instruction. Instruction is provided one-on-one to trainees via a monitor connected to a keyboard. Trainees use the keyboard or touch the monitor to interact with the program. Interactive video is used to teach technical procedures and interpersonal skills. The training program may be stored on a videodisc or CD.

Apple Computer's and Federal Express's experiences with CD-ROMs provide good examples of how a CD-ROM not only can provide greater accessibility to consistent training but can also facilitate learning. Apple Computer's managers wanted access to training, but their busy schedules made it difficult for them to leave their jobs to attend training sessions.[20] As a result of this need for an alternative to classroom instruction, Apple connected CD-ROM drives to all of its computers. CD-ROM training programs were created for the managers. One CD-ROM–based program covered basics of employment law, offering both narrated text and video. The CD-ROM also allowed the manager to access reference materials included on the CD, such as a list of legal interview questions and demonstrations of violations of law (e.g., sexual harassment).

Federal Express's 25-disc interactive video curriculum includes courses related to customer etiquette, defensive driving, and delivery procedures.[21] As Federal Express discovered, interactive video has many advantages. First, training is individualized. Employees control what aspects of the training program they view. They can skip ahead where they feel competent, or they can review topics. Second, employees receive immediate feedback concerning their performance. Third, training is accessible on a 24-hour basis regardless of employees' work schedules. From the employer's standpoint, the high cost of developing interactive video programs and purchasing the equipment was offset by the reduction in instructor costs and travel costs related to a central training location. At Federal Express, interactive video has made it possible to train 35,000 customer-contact employees in 650 locations nationwide, saving the company millions of dollars. Without interactive video, Federal Express could not deliver consistent high-quality training.

The Internet, Web-Based Training, and E-Learning

The **Internet** is a widely used tool for communications, a method for sending and receiving communications quickly and inexpensively, and a way to locate and gather resources, such as software and reports.[22] According to a recent survey, more than 66 percent of Americans age 12 or older use the Internet, and half of these users report that they go online daily.[23] To gain access to the Internet, you need a personal computer with a direct connection via an existing network or a modem to dial into the Internet. Educational institutions, government agencies, and commercial service providers such as Microsoft and America Online provide access to the Internet.

Employees can communicate with managers nearby or across the globe, can leave messages or documents, and can gain access to "rooms" designated for conversation on certain topics (the Americans with Disabilities Act, for example). Various newsgroups, bulletin boards, and discussion groups are dedicated to areas of interest. There you can read, post, and respond to messages and articles. Internet sites can have home pages—mailboxes that identify the person or company and contain text, images, sounds, or even moving pictures.

The **World Wide Web (WWW)** is a user-friendly service on the Internet.[24] The Web provides browser software (e.g., Microsoft Internet Explorer, Netscape) that enables you to explore the Web. Besides browser software, you also need a search engine (e.g., Yahoo, Google) to find information on topics of your choice.

Every home page on the Web has a uniform resource locator (URL), or Web address. For example, the Web address for the Cisco Systems website is *http://www.cisco.com.*

The Internet is a valuable source of information on a wide range of topics. The inside of the front cover of this book provides Internet and website addresses related to training topics. For example, one manager at Hydro Quebec, a large Canadian utility, used the Internet to research topics related to TQM and business process reengineering. When the company wanted information on diversity and women's issues, the manager logged onto a Cornell University website and quickly downloaded two dozen reports on the topic. When the company needed to develop a satisfaction survey, the manager used the Internet to identify similar-sized companies that had conducted comprehensive surveys. Within one day, 30 human resources professionals, including managers at Federal Express and United Parcel Service, responded. The Hydro Quebec manager has also networked with human resources managers at Motorola, IBM, and other companies.[25]

Internet-based training refers to training that is delivered on public or private computer networks and displayed by a Web browser.[26] **Intranet-based training** refers to training that uses the company's own computer network. The training programs are accessible only to the company's employees, not to the general public. Both Internet-based and intranet-based training is stored in a computer and accessed using a computer network. The two types of training use similar technologies. The major difference is that access to the intranet is restricted to a company's employees. For example, Amdahl Corporation (a mainframe computer manufacturer) has set up an intranet.[27] Employees use Netscape to browse the Web along with a company-developed Web browser. Every department at Amdahl has its own Web home page. The home page describes what services the department provides. Many employees also have their own personal home pages. The training department home page includes a list of courses offered by the training department. The manufacturing department gives employees access to technical manuals via the intranet.

FIGURE 8.2 Levels of technology-based training

Communications	Online Referencing	Testing Assessment	Delivery of Computer-based Training & Multimedia (synchronous or asynchronous)	Blended Learning	Electronic Performance Support Systems
1	2	3	4	5	6

Source: Based on K. Kruse, "Five Levels of Internet-Based Training," *Training and Development* (February 1997): 60–61; R. Clark and C. Lyons, "Using Web-Based Training Wisely," *Training* (July 1999): 51–56; J. Coné and D. Robinson, "The Power of E-Performance," *T&D* (August 2001): 32–41.

Web-based training and e-learning support virtual reality, animation, interactions, communications between trainees, and real-time audio and video. As Figure 8.2 shows, there are six levels of technology-based training. The difference between the highest and lowest levels is that at the higher levels learning is more job-related and helps meet a business need. The simplest level facilitates communications between trainers and trainees. More complex uses of technology involve actual delivery of training. Trainees are very actively involved in learning. Sound, automation, and video are used in Web-based training. In addition, trainees are linked to other resources on the Web. They are also required to share information with other trainees and to deposit knowledge and their insights from the training (such as potential applications of the training content) in a database that is accessible to other company employees. At the highest level—electronic performance support systems—employees receive training while they perform their jobs.

E-learning or **online learning** refers to instruction and delivery of training by computer online through the Internet or the Web.[28] E-learning includes Web-based training, distance learning, and virtual classrooms; it may involve a CD-ROM. E-learning can include task-based support, simulation-based training, distance learning, and learning portals. There are three important characteristics of e-learning. First, e-learning involves electronic networks that enable information and instruction to be delivered, shared, and updated instantly. Second, e-learning is delivered to the trainee using computers with Internet technology. Third, it focuses on learning solutions that go beyond traditional training by including the delivery of information and tools that improve performance.

Figure 8.3 shows the features of e-learning. These features include collaboration and sharing, links to resources, learner control, delivery, and administration. As Figure 8.3 shows, not only does e-learning provide the trainee with content, but it also can give learners the ability to control what they learn, the speed at which they progress through the program, how much they practice, and even when they learn. In addition, e-learning allows learners to collaborate or interact with other trainees and experts and provides links to other learning resources such as reference materials, company websites, and other training programs. Text, video, graphics, and sound can be used to present course content. E-learning may also include various aspects of training administration such as course enrollment, testing and evaluating trainees, and monitoring of trainees' learning progress.

These features of e-learning give it advantages over other training methods. The advantages of e-learning are shown in Table 8.3. E-learning initiatives are designed to contribute to a company's strategic business objectives.[29] E-learning supports company initiatives such

FIGURE 8.3 Characteristics of e-learning

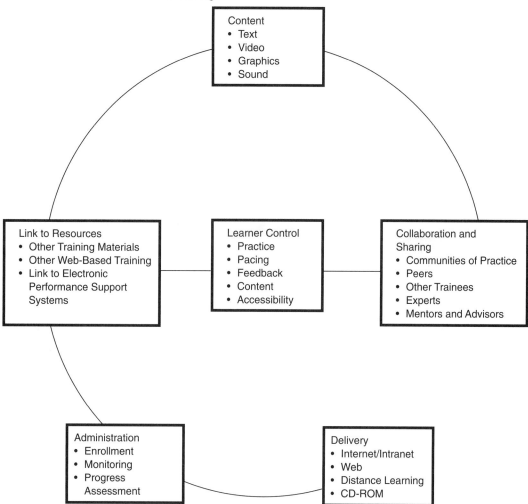

as expanding the number of customers, initiating new ways to carry out business such as e-business, and speeding the development of new products or services. E-learning may involve a larger audience than do traditional training programs that focus on employees. E-learning may involve partners, suppliers, vendors, and potential customers. For example, Lucent Technologies, which designs and delivers communications network technologies, has devoted significant resources to ensure that customers and business partners have access to e-learning.[30] Training affects customer satisfaction with Lucent's products and solutions. It also influences employees' ability to sell to and service customers. Product training courses that deal with installing, repairing, and operating Lucent equipment are available to customers on the company's website. Users can take the courses, register and pay for the classes, and track their progress. Lucent also provides training to its business partners, who

TABLE 8.3
Advantages of E-Learning

Source: Based on D. Hartley, "All Aboard the E-Learning Train," *Training and Development* (July 2000): 37–42; V. Beer, *The Web Learning Field Book: Using the World Wide Web to Build Workplace Learning Environments* (San Francisco: Jossey-Bass, 2000).

It supports the company's business strategy and objectives.
It is accessible at any time and any place.
The audience can include employees and managers as well as vendors, customers, and clients.
Training can be delivered to geographically dispersed employees.
Training can be delivered faster and to more employees in a shorter period of time.
Updating is easy.
Practice, feedback, objectives, assessment, and other positive features of a learning environment can be built into the program. Learning is enhanced through use of multiple media (sound, text, video, graphics) and trainee interaction.
Paperwork related to training management (enrollment, assessment, etc.) can be eliminated.
It can link learners to other content, experts, and peers.

are required to be certified in Lucent's products before they can receive special discounts. As Lucent increases its electronically delivered courses, the company is also trying to increase the percentage of learners who take courses online. Today, about half of the users attend classroom-based training.

E-learning can reduce training time and allow companies to train more employees in a shorter period of time than with traditional training methods, thus reducing training costs. Learning is enhanced through e-learning because learners are more engaged through the use of video, graphics, sound, and text, which appeal to multiple senses of the learner. Also, e-learning requires learners to actively practice, ask questions, and interact with other learners and experts.

E-learning offers training to geographically dispersed employees at their own locations, reducing travel costs associated with bringing trainees to a central location. Aetna US Health Care is using e-learning over the company intranet to teach employees how to enroll a customer and settle a medical claim.[31] Aetna has found that training time per employee has been reduced from one to three weeks from an average of six weeks for traditional classroom training. This has cut training costs and enhanced the company's ability to meet customer needs. BellSouth Cellular Corporation in Atlanta, has been able to train employees quicker with online learning than with classroom approaches without a decrease in effectiveness.[32] New supervisors traditionally enrolled in a basic supervisory skills class after 11 months on the job. The new supervisors are now able to take the online training just three weeks into their jobs. At USA Group, a student loan company, online ethics training class time was reduced from four hours in the classroom to two hours. The audience for the classroom course, taught by a company vice president, was limited to 25 employees. Now all 2,880 employees have access to the course. Some companies have training requirements that all employees have to complete for the company to meet quality or legal requirements. Online learning allows more employees to gain access to these types of programs in a quicker time period than if face-to-face instruction is used. E-learning allows Circuit City, the consumer electronics retailer, to track every employee's course performance and match it with his or her sales performance.[33] Product lines are tied to specific certificate tracks. To sell those products, employees must first complete the learning for that track and pass the certification exam. The more training employees take, the more products they can sell. At Continental Airlines, e-learning modules

TABLE 8.4
**Factors
Limiting
the Use of
E-Learning**

Source: Based on
M. Hequet, "The
State of the
E-Learning Market,"
Training (September
2003): 24–29.

Cost
Lack of motivation among employees to learn online
Lack of management buy-in
Lack of employee intranet access
Lack of proof concerning return on investment
Lack of high-quality content

have been especially helpful for bringing staff up to speed on new security regulations.[34] "It's hard to have someone away from their job for a whole day," says Jennifer Boubel, senior manager of airport services training for Continental Airlines. "This way, they can spend 30 minutes here and 45 minutes there to complete the modules."

E-learning is also easy to update, thanks to user-friendly authoring languaging such as HTML. Changes can be made on the server that stores the e-learning program. Employees worldwide can access the updated program. The administrative features of e-learning make training management a more efficient, paperless process. For example, CCH Inc. developed Shared Learning, an online administration module that allows companies to monitor employees' completion of e-learning. It tracks how many times employees complete the same class and how much time employees spend per class, and it bookmarks the point at which trainees leave an online class so they can enter the program at the place they left it when they again begin training.[35]

Table 8.4 lists factors that have limited companies' use of e-learning. Approximately one-third of the companies participating in a survey reported that significant factors in not using e-learning were that it cost too much, that employees were not motivated to learn online, and that management had not bought into the idea of e-learning.[36] Twenty-five percent of the companies reported that their use of e-learning was limited because employees lacked intranet access and because the company lacked evidence showing e-learning's return on investment. The following sections discuss some ways to overcome these problems.

Developing Effective Online Learning

Table 8.5 provides tips for developing effective online learning.[37] Needs assessment, design and method, and evaluation are three central issues that need to be addressed for effective online learning, including Web-based training and e-learning.

The information technology department needs to be involved in the design of any Web-based program to ensure that the technology capabilities of the company network are understood and to guarantee that trainees can get access to the browsers and connections they need to participate in e-learning and utilize all of the tools (e.g., e-mail, chat rooms, hyperlinks) that may accompany it. Online tutorials may be needed to acquaint trainees with the capabilities of the e-learning system and how to navigate through the Web. Recall from Chapter 3 that a needs assessment determines the company's resources for training and the tasks to be trained for, and it analyzes the employees who may need training. The needs assessment process for Web-based training or any other type of online learning should include a technology assessment (as part of the organizational analysis) and an assessment of the skills that users need for online training (person analysis). Needs assessment also includes getting management to support online learning.

TABLE 8.5 **Tips for Developing Effective Online Learning**

Needs Assessment	Identify the connection between online learning and the business's needs.
	Get management to buy in.
	Make sure employees have access to technology.
	Consult with information technology experts about system requirements.
	Identify specific training needs (knowledge, skills, competencies, behaviors).
Design/Method	Incorporate learning principles (practice; feedback; meaningful material; an appeal to active learner involvement; an appeal to multiple senses).
	Keep learning modules short.
	Design the course for the available bandwidth or increase the bandwidth.
	Avoid using plug-ins.
	Allow trainees the opportunity to collaborate.
	Consider blended instruction.
	Use games and simulations, which are attractive to learners.
	Structure materials properly.
Evaluation	Make trainees and managers accountable for course completion and learning.
	Conduct a formative evaluation (pilot test) before large-scale use of online learning.

Source: Based on K. Dobbs, "What the Online World Needs Now: Quality," *Training* (September 2000): 84–94; K. Kiser, "10 Things We Know So Far about Online Training," *Training* (November 1999): 66–70; P. Galagan, "Getting Started with E-Learning." *Training and Development* (May 2000): 62–64; D. Zielinski, "Can You Keep Learners Online?" *Training* (March 2000): 65–75; A. Rossett and J. Barnett, "Designing under the Influence," *Training* (December 1996): 39–42.; V. Beer, *The Web Learning Field Book: Using the World Wide Web to Build Workplace Learning Environments* (San Francisco Jossey-Bass, 2000); E. Zimmerman "Better Training Is Just a Click Away." *Workforce* (January 2001): 36–42; R. Clark and R. Mayer, *E-Learning and the Science of Instruction* (San Francisco: John Wiley, 2003).

Grant Thornton, a global accounting, tax, and business advisory firm, created Grant Thornton University (GTU), one place for all of its employees' training needs.[38] Through GTU, employees can register for any course, whether its classroom-based or online, and have access to more than 1,000 hours of self-paced live Webcasts and virtual classroom courses. To ensure that GTU was successful, the company investigated its business learning needs and the best delivery method for each topic (a needs assessment). Learning paths are broken down by competencies and skill requirements and are related to job performance. For example, if employees receive performance feedback suggesting that they need to improve their teamwork skills, managers can identify an appropriate course by position and required competencies. A combination of self-paced lessons and live virtual classroom is the optimal instructional method. The self-paced lessons deliver content, and the live training is used for question-and-answer sessions and case studies. Live training also provides trainees with the opportunity to interact with peers and course experts. To obtain support for GTU, the company's chief learning officer invited managers to participate in a virtual kickoff from their desktop personal computers. The kickoff covered the strategic goals of the initiative, showed managers how the technology worked, and let them sample various content.

PSS/World Medical based in Jacksonville, Florida, is a holding company for three different businesses, including a supplier of imaging supplies and medical equipment for hospitals and nursing homes.[39] The business has 4,500 employees, with half working in the field as truck drivers and warehouse employees. The company wanted to use e-learning to deliver training but was faced with the issue of employee access. Ninety percent of the computers at the company's distribution centers could not run the e-learning program. PSS/World

Medical decided to install a kiosk with printer and headphones in every warehouse. Any field worker can access training on important topics ranging from blood-borne pathogens to department of transportation regulations.

When designing Web training, keep in mind the principles of learning that were discussed in Chapter 4. Remember that just putting text online isn't necessarily an effective way to learn. **Repurposing** refers to directly translating an instructor-led face-to-face training program to an online format. Online learning that involves merely repurposing an ineffective training program will still result in ineffective training. Unfortunately, in their haste to develop online learning, many companies are repurposing bad training. The best e-learning uses the advantages of the Internet in combination with the principles of a good learning environment. Effective online learning takes advantage of the Web's dynamic nature and ability to use many positive learning features including linking to other training sites and content through the use of hyperlinks, providing learner control, and allowing the trainee to collaborate with other learners. Effective online learning uses video, sound, text, and graphics to hold learners' attention. Effective online learning provides trainees with meaningful content, relevant examples, and the ability to apply content to work problems and issues. Also, trainees have opportunities to practice and receive feedback through use of problems, exercises, assignments, and tests.

To ensure that materials are not confusing or overwhelming to the learner, online learning content needs to be properly arranged.[40] Materials in online learning need to be organized in small, meaningful modules of information. Each module should relate to one idea or concept. The modules should be connected in a way that encourages the learner to be actively involved in learning. Objectives, videos, practice exercises, links to material that elaborates on the module content, and tests should be accessible within each module. The modules should be linked in an arrangement that makes sense, such as by importance or by the order in which content has to be learned (prerequisites). Trainees can choose to skip over material that they are familiar with or that they are competent in, based on a test of the content, or they can return to modules they need more practice in.

One of the Web's major potential advantages is that it gives learners control. **Learner control** refers to the ability for trainees to actively learn though self-pacing, exercises, exploring links to other material, and conversations with other trainees and experts. That is, online learning allows activities typically led by the instructor (presentation, visuals, slides) or trainees (discussion, questions) as well as group interaction (discussion of application of training content) to be incorporated into training without trainees or the instructor having to be physically present in a training room. Simply providing learner control does not ensure that trainees will use all the features provided by online learning (e.g., practice exercises).[41] Companies must communicate the importance and meaningfulness of the training content for employees' jobs and must hold employees accountable for completing the training.

Online learning blurs the distinction between training and work. Expectations that trainees will be motivated and able to complete Web-based training during breaks in their normal workday or on their personal time are unrealistic.[42] Managers need to give employees time in their schedules, and employees need to schedule "training time" to complete training and avoid interruptions that can interfere with learning. Some companies are moving away from their initial expectation that online learning can be completed at the employee's desktop without time away from the job; instead they are setting up learning labs for online learning to occur without the distractions of the workplace. "Chunking," or using one- to two-hour training modules, helps trainees learn and retain more than they might in a standard full-day or half-day training class. Training can also be more easily integrated into the typical workday. Trainees can devote one to two hours to a learning session from their office and then return to their work responsibilities. Using formative evaluation of prototypes of Web training can be helpful in identifying the appropriate length and time of modules (formative evaluations were discussed in Chapter 6). End users (managers, potential trainees) should be involved in a formative evaluation to ensure that music, graphics, icons, animation, video, and other features facilitate rather than interfere with learning. Also, end users need to test the content, the navigator, or the site map to guarantee that they can easily move through the learning module and access resources and links to other websites as needed.

Technology limitations and preferences also need to be taken into account. Web-based training must be designed for the bandwidth that is available. **Bandwidth** refers to the number of bytes and bits (information) that can travel between computers per second. Graphics, photos, animation, and video in courses can be slow to download and can "crash" the system. Online learning courses should be designed for the available bandwidth on the company's system. Bandwidth can be increased by upgrading access speed on the users' computers, buying and installing faster servers and switches (computer hardware) on the company's network, or encouraging trainees to access the Web when demand is not high.[43] Soon bandwidth may not be an issue because computer servers will be able to transfer more data faster, personal computers will have greater processing speed, and cables and wireless communications systems that carry data will have greater capacity. Online learning should also try to build in interactivity without requiring the use of plug-ins. **Plug-ins** refer to additional software that needs to be loaded on the computer to listen to sound or watch video. Plug-ins can be expensive because they may require the company to pay licensing fees. Plug-ins also can affect how the computer processes tasks. If trainees experience repeated technology problems (such as slow download times, network downtimes, or plug-in difficulties), they are likely to lose patience and be reluctant to participate in online learning.

Chapter 4 emphasized that learning often occurs as a result of interaction or sharing between employees. Employees learn by informal, unstructured contact with experts and peers. Collaboration can involve an exchange among two or more trainees or among the trainer or other experts. Some of the more common ways that trainees can collaborate in online learning are shown in Table 8.6. Berlitz International's worldwide learning system uses communication technology to enhance and reinforce employee learning.[44] When language instructors take a course, they have to access an electronic bulletin board in order to answer three posted questions and give three new ones. Berlitz uses its communications technology to enhance communications, encourage information sharing, and create a sense of online community. Berlitz employees share ideas in online live chats, threaded discussions, or electronic bulletin boards, giving e-learners the opportunity to meet classmates online to discuss assignments, ask instructors questions, or participate in virtual roundtables. Employees can share ideas and experiences—important ways to learn from others.

Hyperlinks are links that allow a trainee to access other websites that include printed materials as well as communications links to experts, trainers, and other learners. Owens-Corning's learning resource home page has hyperlinks to all available forms of training information including CD-ROM, Web-based, and trainer-led programs. The site supports online course registration and allows tests to be sent to trainees, scored, and used to register trainees in appropriate courses.[45]

TABLE 8.6
Common Ways of Collaboration in Online Learning

Source: Based on R. Clark and R. Mayer, *E-Learning and the Science of Instruction* (San Francisco: John Wiley, 2003); J. Cone and D. Robinson, "The Power of E-Performance," *T&D* (August 2001): 32–41.

Chat Rooms	Trainees communicate at the same time by text or audio. Chat rooms may be moderated by a facilitator.
Message Boards	Trainees communicate at different times by typing comments that remain on the board for others to read and respond to.
Threaded Discussion	Trainees communicate via a message board in which related comments appear together. A discussion occurs over time.
Online Conferencing	Trainees are online with a moderator. They can hear comments, send messages, display visuals, vote, or work together on a project.
E-mail	Trainees communicate at different times. Communications are received and managed at each trainee's mail site.
List-Servs	In these group e-mails, trainees comment on a topic, and comments are sent to everyone on the mailing list.

Research suggests that the reason why some employees fail to complete online learning and prefer instructor-led face-to-face instruction over online learning is that they want to be able to learn and network with their peers.[46] Effective online learning connects trainees and facilitates interaction and sharing through the use of chat rooms, e-mail, electronic bulletin boards, and discussion groups. Other methods for learner interaction and sharing include having trainees participate in collaborative online projects and receive tutoring, coaching, and mentoring by experts. Online learning also should provide a link between the trainees and the "instructor," who can answer questions, provide additional learning resources, and stimulate discussion between trainees on topics such as potential applications of the training content and common learning problems.

Given the work demands that employees face, trainees need incentives to complete online learning. Some companies present cash awards and merchandise to employees who pass online competency tests that show they have completed and learned online course content. Other companies use certification programs to ensure that online courses are completed. For example, at Symbol Technologies, a manufacturer of handheld bar-code scanners and computers, sales trainees must complete online courses to be certified as salespersons.[47] If they don't complete the training, they can't continue into other training programs needed to be a successful salesperson. Aventis Pharma AG, a pharmaceutical company, has simply eliminated other training options such as classroom learning. If employees want training, their only option is online learning.

Blended Learning

Because of the limitations of online learning related to technology (e.g., insufficient bandwith, lack of high-speed Web connections), because of trainee preference for face-to-face contact with instructors and other learners, and because of employees' inability to find unscheduled time during their workday to devote to learning from their desktops, many companies are moving to a hybrid, or blended, learning approach. **Blended learning** combines online learning, face-to-face instruction, and other methods for distributing learning content and instruction. CAN, a Chicago-based company with employees across the United States and Canada, developed a blended learning approach.[48] Live seminars kick off a class and conclude it. But in between are online case studies, question-and-answer sessions, and simulations. Trainees work in teams of 10 people. They communicate with each other through chat rooms, threaded discussions, and virtual meetings. For example, employees might be assigned to come up with 10 questions. The instructor answers the questions, and the trainees discuss them. Trainees may be asked to put ideas into practice, using message rooms to provide updates and ask questions. Coaches or mentors may guide the trainees to additional reference materials. To be certified that they have completed training, trainees must complete an accountability plan. The plan summarizes actions that the trainees will take to prove to their managers that they have achieved proficiency.

Belgacom SA, the leading supplier of global telecommunications solutions in Belgium, created the Learning and Development Academy (LDA) to identify, analyze, develop, and implement training solutions.[49] The company's learning philosophy is that training and continuing education responsibilities are shared by the company, employees, and managers. The LDA uses e-learning to cut travel costs and time for training; to create anywhere, anytime learning; to deliver a consistent training message; and to shorten course development and distribution time. LDA uses a blended approach with e-learning. For example, trainees attend a half-day information session and are given three months to complete coursework at work, at home, or at one of the company's open learning centers. During the first month of study, trainees interact with a coach, who discusses their progress and provides advice. The LDA uses a number of ways to present training content, including videoconferencing, desktop video coaching, virtual lectures, Web-based training, and CD-ROMs.

Learning Portals

Learning portals are websites or online learning centers that provide, via e-commerce transactions, access to training courses, services, and online learning communities from many sources.[50] Learning portals provide not only one-stop shopping for a variety of training programs from different vendors but also access to online classes. Learning portals may also offer services to track employees' enrollment and progress in training programs. They were initially set up with the idea that an individual purchaser (an employee or other "customer") could purchase training using a credit card. The characteristics of learning portals vary.[51] Some allow users to pay, register, and attend courses online; others offer access only to classroom training programs at colleges or universities. In addition to instruction, some sites provide mentors who can tutor students as well as discussion groups where students can communicate with each other. W. R. Grace, a specialty chemicals company, uses its online learning center to support employee development, to link learning to performance and talent management, and to improve communications.[52] The learning center is organized around a set of core competencies that define the knowledge, skills, and abilities all employees are expected to achieve. A search option is provided so that employees can explore and access resources relevant to a specific topic. The learning center includes training sessions, recommended readings, a rental library (providing videotapes and CD-ROMs for self-paced learning), and a strategy guide (providing quick ideas and learning assignments to develop a competency). Every six weeks the learning center sends an electronic newsletter to every employee's personal computer. The newsletter keeps employees up to date on the latest learning center offerings, reports on how employees are effectively using the learning center, and encourages employees to use the center. Ford Motor Company has developed the Ford Learning Network (FLN), which includes 48,000 twenty-minute pieces of information using different media.[53] The FLN has more than 400,000 titles, including 1,500 online courses, 800 classroom courses, 1,900 e-books, and numerous internal resources from websites, journals, and industry periodicals. The learning can occur when the employee needs it or as a refresher that can be accessed at the employee's convenience. Ford is adding an automated survey tool that tracks the value of training received to see how training is being used and applied on the job. Ford also hopes that the network can make it possible for novices to gain access to expert employee information. For example, the knowledge and skills of experts in braking systems can be made available throughout the company. Ford's goal is to capture the intellectual property of in-house experts via video and other media and to make that information searchable on the FLN.

Virtual Reality

Virtual reality is a computer-based technology that provides trainees with a three-dimensional learning experience. Using specialized equipment or viewing the virtual model on the computer screen, trainees move through the simulated environment and interact with its components.[54] Technology is used to stimulate multiple senses of the trainee.[55] Devices relay information from the environment to the senses. For example, audio interfaces, gloves that provide a sense of touch, treadmills, or motion platforms are used to create a realistic, artificial environment. Devices also communicate information about the trainee's movements to a computer. These devices allow the trainee to experience **presence** (the perception of actually being in a particular environment). Presence is influenced by the amount of sensory information available to the trainee, control over sensors in the environment, and the trainees' ability to modify the environment.

For example, Motorola uses virtual reality in its advanced manufacturing courses for employees learning to run the Pager Robotic Assembly facility. Employees are fitted with a head-mount display that allows them to view the virtual world, which includes the actual lab space, robots, tools, and assembly operation. Trainees hear and see the actual sounds and sights as if they were using the real equipment. Also, the equipment responds to the employees' actions (e.g., turning on a switch or dial).

One advantage of virtual reality is that it allows trainees to practice dangerous tasks without putting themselves or others in danger. Research suggests that virtual reality training is likely to have the greatest impact on complex tasks or tasks that involve extensive use of visual cues.[56] The virtual reality environment can be virtually identical to the actual work environment. Another potential advantage relates to the cognitive processing required by the learner. The use of such a realistic environment in training may make more memory available for learning. Memory that was previously used to convert one- or two-dimensional training scenarios into three-dimensional space can now be used for processing information.

Obstacles to developing effective virtual reality training include poor equipment that results in a reduced sense of presence (e.g., poor tactile feedback and inappropriate time lags between sensing and responding to trainees' actions). Poor presence may result in the trainee experiencing vomiting, dizziness, and headaches (simulator sickness) because senses are distorted.

INTELLIGENT TUTORING SYSTEMS

Intelligent tutoring systems (ITS) are instructional systems that use artificial intelligence.[57] There are three types of ITS: tutoring, coaching, and empowering environments. Tutoring is a structured attempt to increase trainee understanding of a content domain.

Coaching provides trainees with the flexibility to practice skills in artificial environments. Empowering refers to the student's ability to freely explore the content of the training program. The five components of ITS are shown in Figure 8.4. The ITS has information about the content domain as well as expectations about the trainee's level of knowledge.

ITS can be distinguished from other new training technologies in several ways:[58]

- ITS has the ability to match instruction to individual student needs.
- ITS can communicate and respond to the student.
- ITS can model the trainee's learning process.
- ITS can decide, on the basis of a trainee's previous performance, what information to provide.
- ITS can make decisions about the trainee's level of understanding.
- ITS can complete a self-assessment resulting in a modification of its teaching process.

ITS has been used by NASA in astronaut training.[59] For example, the Remote Maneuvering System ITS was used to teach astronauts how to use the robotic arm on the space shuttle. Astronauts had to learn to complete tasks and procedures related to grappling a payload. The ITS generated processes that were matched to individual astronauts. Feedback was matched to their pattern of success and failure in learning the tasks. The system recorded performance data for each astronaut, made decisions regarding the student's level of understanding, and used those decisions to provide appropriate feedback.

FIGURE 8.4

Components of intelligent tutoring systems

Source: Based on D. Steele-Johnson and B. G. Hyde, "Advanced Technologies in Training: Intelligent Tutoring Systems and Virtual Reality," in *Training for a Rapidly Changing Workplace*, eds. M. A. Quinones and A. Ehrenstein (Washington, DC: American Psychological Association, 1997): 225–48.

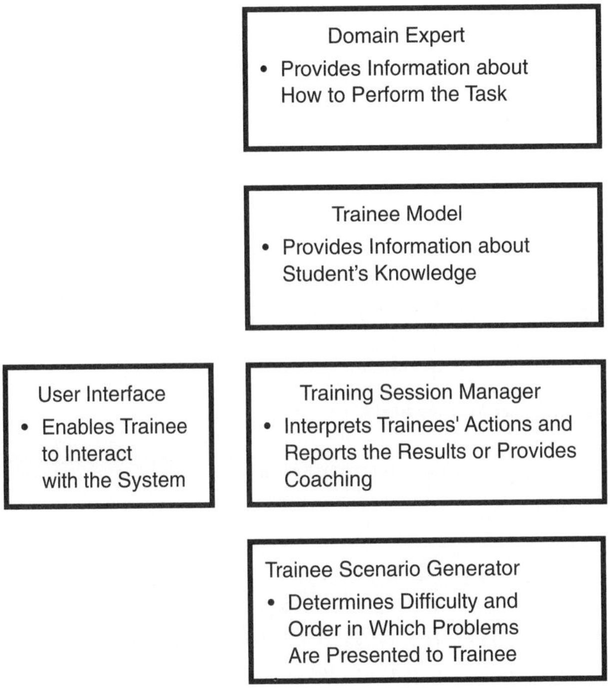

Domain Expert
- Provides Information about How to Perform the Task

Trainee Model
- Provides Information about Student's Knowledge

User Interface
- Enables Trainee to Interact with the System

Training Session Manager
- Interprets Trainees' Actions and Reports the Results or Provides Coaching

Trainee Scenario Generator
- Determines Difficulty and Order in Which Problems Are Presented to Trainee

DISTANCE LEARNING

Distance learning is used by geographically dispersed companies to provide information about new products, policies, or procedures as well as skills training and expert lectures to field locations.[60] Distance learning features two-way communications between people. Distance learning currently involves two types of technology.[61] First, it includes teleconferencing. **Teleconferencing** refers to synchronous exchange of audio, video, and/or text between two or more individuals or groups at two or more locations. Trainees attend training programs in training facilities in which they can communicate with trainers (who are at another location) and other trainees using the telephone or personal computer. A second type of distance learning also includes individualized, personal-computer–based training.[62] Employees participate in training anywhere they have access to a personal computer. This type of distance learning may involve multimedia training methods such as Web-based training. Course material and assignments can be distributed using the company's intranet, video, or CD-ROM. Trainers and trainees interact using e-mail, bulletin boards, and conferencing systems.

Teleconferencing usually includes a telephone link so that trainees viewing the presentation can call in questions and comments to the trainer. Also, satellite networks allow companies to link up with industry-specific and educational courses for which employees receive college credit and job certification. IBM, Digital Equipment, and Eastman Kodak are among the many firms that subscribe to the National Technological University, which broadcasts courses throughout the United States that technical employees need to obtain advanced degrees in engineering.[63]

An advantage of distance learning is that the company can save on travel costs. It also allows employees in geographically dispersed sites to receive training from experts who would not otherwise be available to visit each location. FileNeT Corporation, was concerned with how their sales force was going to keep up with new software and software updates.[64] FileNeT tried self-paced online learning but discovered that salespeople did not like to read a lot of material about new products on the Web. Enrollment in online courses dwindled, and salespeople flooded the company's training department with requests for one-on-one assistance. To solve the training problem, the company decided to use webcasting. **Webcasting** involves classroom instructions that are provided online through live broadcasts. Webcasting helped spread the sales force training throughout the year rather than cramming it into twice-a-year sales meetings. Webcasting also helped ensure that the salespeople all received the same information. The salespeople liked the webcasts because of the timely information that helped them have conversations with customers. The live sessions were also popular because participants could ask questions. Webcasting has not replaced face-to-face training at FileNeT; classroom training is still about 80 percent of training, but that percentage has decreased by 10 percent. Webcasting has also resulted in savings of $500,000 annually (one of the twice-yearly sales meetings was canceled).

The major disadvantage of distance learning is the potential for lack of interaction between the trainer and the audience. A high degree of interaction between trainees and the trainer is a positive learning feature that is missing from distance learning programs that merely use technology to broadcast a lecture to geographically dispersed employees. All that is done in this case is repurposing a traditional lecture (with its limitations for learning and

TABLE 8.7
Conditions When Training Support Technologies Are Most Needed

- Performance of task is infrequent.
- The task is lengthy, difficult, and information intensive.
- The consequences of error are damaging.
- Performance relies on knowledge, procedures, or approaches that frequently change.
- There is high employee turnover.
- Little time is available for training, or resources for training are few.
- Employees are expected to take full responsibility for learning and performing tasks.

Source: Based on A. Rossett, "Job Aids and Electronic Performance Support Systems," in *The ASTD Training and Development Handbook*, 4th ed., ed. R. L. Craig (New York: McGraw-Hill, 1996): 554–77.

transfer of training) for a new training technology! That's why establishing a communications link between employees and the trainer is important. Also, on-site instructors or facilitators should be available to answer questions and moderate question-and-answer sessions.

TECHNOLOGIES FOR TRAINING SUPPORT

New technologies such as expert systems, groupware, and electronic support systems are being used to support training efforts. Training support means that these technologies are helping to capture training content so that it is available to employees who may not have attended training. Training support also means that these technologies provide information and decision rules to employees on an as-needed basis (i.e., they are job aids). Employees can access these technologies in the work environment.

Table 8.7 shows when training support technologies are most needed. Many conditions shown in the table relate to characteristics of the task or the environment that can inhibit transfer of training. For example, employees may work some distance away from their manager, the manager may be difficult to contact, or employees may need special expertise that the manager lacks. These situations make it difficult for employees to find answers to problems that arise on the job. Training support technologies can help to ensure that transfer of training occurs by helping employees generalize training content to the work environment and by providing employees with new information (not covered in training).

Expert Systems

Expert systems refer to technology (usually software) that organizes and applies the knowledge of human experts to specific problems.[65] Expert systems have three elements:

1. A knowledge base that contains facts, figures, and rules about a specific subject.
2. A decision-making capability that, imitating an expert's reasoning ability, draws conclusions from those facts and figures to solve problems and answer questions.
3. A user interface that gathers and gives information to the person using the system.

Expert systems are used as a support tool that employees refer to when they have problems or decisions they feel exceed their current knowledge and skills. For example, a large international food processor uses an expert system called Performer, which is designed to provide training and support to its plant operators. One problem the company was facing was determining why potato chips were being scorched in the fryer operation. A operator solved the problem using Performer. He selected the "troubleshooting" menu, then "product texture/ flavor," then "off oil flavor." The program listed probable causes, beginning with high oxidation during frying. The operator chose that cause, and the system recommended adjusting the cooking line's oil flush, providing detailed steps for that procedure. Following those steps resolved the problem.[66]

Although expert systems are discussed as a technology that supports training, expert systems can also be used as a delivery mechanism. Expert systems can be used to train employees in the decision rules of the experts.

Expert systems can deliver both high quality and lower costs. By using the decision processes of experts, the system enables many people to arrive at decisions that reflect experts' knowledge. An expert system helps avoid the errors that can result from fatigue and decision biases. The efficiencies of an expert system can be realized if it can be operated by fewer or less skilled (and likely less costly) employees than the company would otherwise require.

Groupware

Groupware (electronic meeting software) is a special type of software application that enables multiple users to track, share, and organize information and to work on the same document simultaneously.[67] A groupware system combines such elements as e-mail, document management, and an electronic bulletin board. A popular brand of groupware is Lotus Notes.

Companies have been using groupware to improve business processes such as sales and account management and to improve meeting effectiveness as well as to identify and share knowledge in the organization. (See Chapter 5's discussion of creating a learning organization.) Monsanto uses Lotus Notes to link salespeople, account managers, and competitor-intelligence analysts.[68] The database contains updated news on competitors and customers, information from public news sources, salespersons' reports, an in-house directory of experts, and attendees' notes from conventions and conferences.

As noted earlier in the chapter, many companies are creating their own intranets. Intranets are cheaper and simpler to use than groupware programs but pose potential security problems because of the difficulty of keeping persons out of the network.[69]

Electronic Performance Support Systems

An **electronic performance support system (EPSS)** is an electronic infrastructure that captures, stores, and distributes individual and corporate knowledge assets throughout an organization to enable individuals to achieve required levels of performance in the fastest possible time and with a minimum of support from other people.[70] An EPSS includes all the software needed to support the work of individuals (not just one or two specific software applications). It integrates knowledge assets into the interface of the software tools rather than separating them as add-on components. For example, company policy information may be presented in a dialog box message rather than in a separate online document. The typical EPSS includes

- An "assistant" to automate tasks and lighten the work load.
- A "librarian" to provide task-specific information.
- A "teacher" to guide the user through the process step by step.
- An "advisor" to provide expert advice.

Chapter 5 discussed EPSS as a means to help training transfer. EPSS can also be used as a substitute for training. Microsoft's Office software has "wizards," a help function that recognizes the task that the user is starting to perform (e.g., writing a letter) and offers information related to that task. First Union Commercial Bank wanted to decrease the time needed for new users to become proficient with software that processed commercial loans.[71] The company trained over 3,000 employees using computer-based instruction followed by classroom training in which the employees had opportunities to use the software. An EPSS was developed to run at the same time as the loan processing software. The EPSS included job-based assistance at several levels. If users wanted to understand the function of a software window, to perform a task, to use a document, or to understand how the software supported the loan process, information was provided at their request.

To use EPSS as a substitute for training, trainers must determine whether problems and tasks require employees to actually acquire knowledge, skill, or ability (learned capability) and whether periodic assistance through an EPSS is sufficient.

TECHNOLOGIES FOR TRAINING ADMINISTRATION

New technology is making training administration more efficient and effective. Training administration includes record keeping, employee enrollment in courses, and testing and certification. Interactive voice technology, imaging, and software applications have made it easier to track training information. They also provide easy access to training information for trainers to use in decision making.

Interactive Voice Technology

Interactive voice technology uses a conventional personal computer to create an automated phone response system. This technology is especially useful for benefits administration. For example, at Hannaford Brothers—a supermarket chain spread through the northeastern United States—the human resources department installed an interactive voice response system that allows employees to get information on their retirement accounts, stock purchases, and benefit plans by using the push buttons on their phones.[72] Employees can also directly enroll in training programs and speak to a human resources representative if they have questions. As a result of the technology, the company was able to reduce its human resources staff and more quickly serve employees' benefit needs.

Imaging

Imaging refers to scanning documents, storing them electronically, and retrieving them.[73] Imaging is particularly useful because paper files take a large volume of space and are difficult to access. Training records can be scanned and stored in a database for access at a later date. Some software applications allow the user to scan documents based on key words such as *job history, education,* and *experience.* This is a valuable feature when answering managers' and other customers' questions regarding employees' training and skills. For example, inquiries such as "I need an engineer to take an expatriate assignment in France. Do we have any engineers who speak French?" can be easily and quickly answered by scanning training databases. Imaging can also help a training department better serve its customers by reducing the time needed to locate a file or service a phone inquiry from an

FIGURE 8.5
Example of
an employee
training progress
report

Source:
www.trainersoft.com.,
"Trainersoft Manager
Demo," January 29,
2001.

Progress Report for: Joe Trainee

Course Name	ID	Completed	Length	Score	Manager
Customer Service Level 1	CUST1	01/12/2000	60:00	98%	dcutter@rd.com
Customer Service Level 2	CUST2	02/03/2000	60:00	No	ldelkin@rd.com
Delivering Value—The RD Way	VALU1	02/08/2000	20:00	No	dcutter@rd.com
Employee Orientation 1	ORIEN1	02/18/2000	30:00	No	ldelkin@rd.com
Employee Orientation—Benefits	ORIEN2	03/07/2000	20:00	No	acarter@rd.com
Managing Conflict	CONF1	03/19/2000	20:00	97%	ldelkin@rd.com

employee, by providing the ability for employee training records to be shared simultaneously, by eliminating the need to refile, and by reducing the physical space needed to store training records.

Training Software Applications

Training software applications have primarily been used to track information related to training administration (e.g., course enrollments, tuition reimbursement summaries, and training costs), employee skills, and employees' training activities. Important database elements for training administration include training courses completed, certified skills, and educational experience. Georgia Power uses a database system that tracks internal training classes, available classroom space, instructor availability, costs, and the salaries of training class members.[74] Figure 8.5 illustrates a screen showing an employee's training activity. Some applications provide cost information that can be used by managers to determine which departments are exceeding their training budgets. This information can be used to reallocate training dollars during the next budget period. Other databases give access to summaries of journal articles, legal cases, and books to help professional employees such as engineers and lawyers keep up to date.[75]

Software applications can be useful for decision making. Managers can use skills inventories to ensure that they get the maximum benefit out of their training budget. Using skill inventories, managers can determine which employees need training and can suggest training programs to them that are appropriate for their job and skill levels. Skill inventories are also useful for identifying employees who are qualified for promotions and transfers. Finally, they can also be useful for helping managers to quickly build employee teams with the necessary skills to respond to customer needs, product changes, international assignments, or work problems.

CHOOSING NEW TECHNOLOGY TRAINING METHODS

Table 8.8 compares training methods that use new technology on the same characteristics used to compare traditional training programs in Chapter 7. Several trends are apparent in this table. First, these methods require considerable investment in development. Development costs are related to purchasing hardware and software as well as developing programs and transferring programs to new media (e.g., CD-ROM). However, although development costs are high, costs for administering the program are low. Advantages of these methods include (1) cost savings due to training being accessible to employees at their home or office and (2) reduced costs

TABLE 8.8 **Comparison of Training Methods Using New Technology**

	Computer-Based Training	CD-ROM	Internet	Intranet	E-Learning	Distance Learning	Intelligent Tutoring	Virtual Reality
Learning Outcome								
Verbal information	Yes	Yes	Yes	Yes	Yes	Yes	Yes	Yes
Intellectual skills	Yes	Yes	Yes	Yes	Yes	Yes	Yes	Yes
Cognitive strategies	Yes	Yes	Yes	Yes	Yes	Yes	Yes	Yes
Attitudes	No	Yes	No	No	Yes	No	No	No
Motor skills	No	No	No	No	No	No	Yes	Yes
Learning Environment								
Clear objective	Medium	High	High	High	High	Medium	High	High
Practice	Medium	High	Medium	Medium	High	Low	High	High
Meaningfulness	Medium	High	High	High	High	Medium	High	High
Feedback	Medium	High	Medium	Medium	High	Low	High	High
Observation and interaction with others	Low	High	Medium	Medium	High	Low	Low	Low
Transfer of Training	Medium	High	Medium	Medium	High	Low	High	High
Cost								
Development	High	High	High	High	High	Medium	High	High
Administrative	Low	Low	Low	Low	Low	Low	Low	Low
Effectiveness	Medium	High	?	?	?	Medium	?	High

associated with employees traveling to a central training location (e.g., airfare, food, lodging). Moreover, with the exception of distance learning, most of the important characteristics needed for learning to occur (practice, feedback, etc.) are built into these methods. Note that limited studies of the effectiveness of several methods (Web-based training, intelligent tutoring) are available because companies are just starting to use these technologies for training. However, their effectiveness is likely to be high if characteristics of a positive learning environment and learner control, sharing, and linking are built into these methods.

You might assume that Web-based training and e-learning are superior to other methods, but this is not necessarily the case. A comparison between Web-based training and the CD-ROM highlights that both methods have distinct advantages (and disadvantages). Two advantages that the CD-ROM has over Web-based training are the CD's greater ability for interaction between the learner and the material in the training program, and its greater use of audio and video. Web-based training, in turn, has several advantages over the CD-ROM. Its major advantage is that Web-based programs offer collaboration and sharing (connecting trainees to other trainees, experts, and chat rooms) and links to resources available on the Web. Second, Web-based training allows the learner to be given assignments requiring open-ended responses (e.g., write a report on a customer's needs) rather than only yes/no or multiple-choice responses. In Web-based training, the instructor can read the assignment and provide detailed feedback. CD-ROMs can only score close-ended questions with true/false, yes/no, or multiple-choice answers. Finally, Web-based training is easier to update and change than a CD-ROM is. If a company's e-learning program has complex simulations requiring a high degree of interaction with the trainee, the company will likely provide the trainee with a CD-ROM for the simulation and will rely on the Web for linking to resources, collaboration and sharing, and testing trainees.

How do new technology training methods relate to traditional training methods discussed in Chapter 7? Virtual reality and intelligent tutoring systems are best suited for teaching complex processes related to operating machinery, tools, and equipment. These methods are an extension of simulations. CD-ROMs, the Internet, the intranet, and e-learning are best suited for teaching facts, figures, cognitive strategies (e.g., how to hold an effective meeting), and interpersonal skills (e.g., closing a sale). These methods are technological extensions of traditional training methods such as behavior modeling, on-the-job training, and apprenticeship. Although traditional training methods can be effective, managers and trainers should consider using new technology training methods under certain conditions:

1. Sufficient budget has been provided to develop and use new technology.
2. Trainees are geographically dispersed and travel costs related to training are high.
3. Trainees are comfortable using technology including the Web, personal computers, and CD-ROMs.
4. The increased use of new technology is part of the company's business strategy. New technology is being used or implemented in manufacturing of products or service processes.
5. Employees have a difficult time attending scheduled training programs.
6. Current training methods allow limited time for practice, feedback, and assessment.

Summary   This chapter provided an overview of new technologies' use in training delivery, support, and administration. Many new technologies have features that help to ensure learning and transfer of training (e.g., multimedia training methods such as CD-ROM and e-learning). These technologies appeal to multiple senses and allow employees to pace themselves, receive feedback and reinforcement, and find information from experts on an as-needed basis. New technologies also enable employees to participate in training from home or work on a 24-hour basis. Employees control not only the presentation of training content but also when and where they participate in training! New technologies such as virtual reality also can create a more realistic training environment, which can make the material more meaningful and increase the probability that training will transfer to the job. Expert systems and electronic support systems are tools that employees can access on an as-needed basis to obtain knowledge and information. Groupware and intranets help to capture the knowledge that employees gain from training and facilitate their sharing of information. Interactive voice technologies, imaging, and software applications especially designed for training make it easier to store and record training information such as course enrollments and employee training records. This technology also makes it easier to retrieve training-related information for managerial decision making.

The chapter concludes by showing that most new technology training methods can be superior to traditional methods because a positive learning environment can be built into the method. But development costs of new technology training methods are high. Considerations include monies for development, geographic dispersion of employees, employees' difficulty in attending training, and whether new technologies are part of the company's business strategy.

Key Terms

digital collaboration, *235*

synchronous communication, *235*

asynchronous communication, *235*

multimedia training, *237*

computer-based training (CBT), *239*

CD-ROM, *239*

DVD (digital video disc), *239*

laser disc, *239*

interactive video, *240*

Internet, *241*

World Wide Web (WWW), *241*

Internet-based training, *241*

intranet-based training, *241*

e-learning, *242*

online learning, *242*

repurposing, *247*

learner control, *247*

bandwidth, *248*

plug-in, *248*

hyperlink, *248*

blended learning, *249*

learning portal, *250*

virtual reality, *251*

presence, *251*

intelligent tutoring systems (ITS), *251*

distance learning, *253*

teleconferencing, *253*

webcasting, *253*

expert systems, *254*

groupware (electronic meeting software), *255*

electronic performance support system (EPSS), *255*

interactive voice technology, *256*

imaging, *256*

Discussion Questions

1. Explain how technology has changed the learning environment.
2. What are some advantages and disadvantages of multimedia training?
3. What are the differences between expert systems and electronic performance tools?
4. Are training support technologies always needed? Justify your answer.
5. Discuss how new technologies make it easier to learn. How do they facilitate transfer of training?
6. Is all Internet training the same? Explain.
7. What are some potential problems with using virtual reality technology for training?
8. How can interactive voice technology and imaging help with training administration?
9. Explain learner control, sharing, and linking. How do they contribute to the effectiveness of e-learning?
10. What is repurposing? How does it affect use of new technologies in training?
11. Distance learning can be used to deliver a lecture to geographically dispersed trainees. How might distance learning be designed and used to avoid some of the learning and transfer of training problems of the traditional lecture method?
12. Why would a company use a combination of face-to-face instruction and Web-based training?

Application Assignments

1. Using only the Web, further investigate any new technology discussed in this chapter. Utilizing any browser on the Web (e.g., Google), conduct a search for information about the technology you have chosen. Find information describing the technology, hints for developing or purchasing the technology, and examples of companies marketing and/or using the technology. Include Web addresses in your summary.

2. The Interactive Patient is a realistic interactive computer simulation of a patient's visit to a physician's office. The Interactive Patient is a Web-based training program used to train medical students at Marshall University and to provide continuous education credits to practicing physicians. Visit and review the Interactive Patient at *http://nt.media.hku. hk/InteractivePatient/medicus.htm* or go to *www.nyerrn.com/simulators.htm,* a website of patients with emergency situations. Choose one of the patient simulators.

   a. What are the program's strengths and weaknesses?

   b. How would you improve the program?

3. Go to *www.cisco.com,* the website for Cisco Systems. Click on Business Industries and Solutions. Click on E-Learning. On the drop-down menu, click on Presentations. Review one of the presentations provided. For the presentation you choose to review, list and discuss the features of the programs shown that (a) enhance learning and (b) motivate employees to complete the training.

4. Go to *www.knowledgeplanet.com.* KnowledgePlanet is a leading global Internet e-learning software provider. Review the information available on the website. What e-learning solutions does KnowledgePlanet provide to its customers? Do you believe that these solutions are effective? Why?

5. Go to *www.golearn.com,* the website for the Government Online Learning Center, a resource that supports development of the federal work force through simplified and one-stop access to high quality e-training products and services. What learning resources are provided at this center? How do they support the development of the work force?

6. Go to *www.vrgroup.com,* the website for VRGroup Consulting, a technology consulting company. Click on Consulting, then click on Virtual Reality. Review one of the virtual reality simulations. What are the advantages of the simulation you reviewed? What are the potential weaknesses?

7. Go to *www.capellauniversity.edu,* the website for Capella University—a university that offers online courses. Enter the website. Click on How E-Learning at Capella Works. View the course demo. What are the strengths and weaknesses of the online course (based on the demo)? What will be most effective for helping students learn?

Endnotes

1. L. Guernsey, "Bookbag of the Future," *The New York Times,* March 2, 2000: D1, D7.

2. M. Pramik, "Learning Crosses the Line," *The Columbus Dispatch,* November 6, 2000: F1.

3. M. Van Buren and W. Woodwell, Jr., *The 2000 ASTD Trends Report: Staying Ahead of the Winds of Change* (Alexandria, VA: American Society for Training and Development, 2000).

4. S. E. O'Connell, "New Technologies Bring New Tools, New Rules," *HR Magazine* (December 1995): 43–48; S. E. O'Connell, "The Virtual Workplace Moves at Warp Speed," *HR Magazine* (March 1996): 51–57.

5. J. Salopek, "Digital Collaboration," *Training and Development* (June 2000): 39–43.

6. A. Chute, P. Sayers, and R. Gardner, "Network Learning Environments," *New Directions for Teaching and Learning* 71 (1997): 75–83.

7. E. Hollis, " Shoney's: Workforce Development on the Side," *Chief Learning Officer* (March 2003): 32–34.

8. J. J. Howell and L. O. Silvey, "Interactive Multimedia Systems," in *The ASTD Training and Development Handbook,* 4th ed., ed. R. L. Craig (New York: McGraw-Hill, 1996): 534–53.

9. "Multimedia Training in the Fortune 1000," *Training* (September 1996): 53–60.

10. R. Zemke and J. Armstrong, "Evaluating Multimedia," *Training* (August 1996): 48–52.

11. K. Murphy, "Pitfalls vs. Promise in Multimedia Training," May 6, 1996 (from *The New York Times* website, *www.nytimes.com*).

12. Howell and Silvey, "Interactive Multimedia Systems."

13. W. Webb, "High-Tech in the Heartland," *Training* (May 1997): 51–56.

14. Murphy, "Pitfalls vs. Promise in Multimedia Training."

15. W. Hannum, *The Application of Emerging Training Technologies* (Alexandria, VA: American Society for Training and Development, 1990).

16. A. Field, "Class Act," *Inc.* (January 1997): 55–57.

17. "Project Leadership," *Human Resource Executive* (2000): A16.

18. S. Greengard, "How Technology Is Advancing HR," *Personnel Journal* (September 1993): 80–90.

19. R. Clark and C. Lyons, "Using Web-Based Training Wisely," *Training* (July 1999): 51–56.

20. L. Keegan and S. Rose, "The Good News about Desktop Learning," *Training and Development* (June 1997): 24–27.

21. F. Filipowski, "How Federal Express Makes Your Package Its Most Important," *Personnel Journal* (February 1992): 40–46.

22. S. Greengard, "Catch the Wave as HR Goes Online," *Personnel Journal* (July 1995): 54–68; M. I. Finney, "It's All in the Knowing How," *HR Magazine* (July 1995): 36–43; "A Survey of the Internet" (special section), *The Economist* (July 1, 1995): 3–18; A. Doran, "The Internet: The New Tool for the HR Professional," *The Review* (August/September 1995): 32–35.

23. "Two-Thirds of Americans On-Line," *CyberAtlas,* May 10, 2000 (from Cyber Atlas website, *cyberatlas.internet.com*).

24. S. Greengard, "Leverage the Power of the Internet," *Workforce* (March 1997): 76–85.

25. S. Greengard, "Catch the Wave as HR Goes Online."

26. "What Is Web-Based Training?" (from *www.clark.net/pub/nractive/fl.html*).

27. B. Filipczak, "An Internet of Your Very Own," in *Using Technology-Delivered Training,* ed. D. Zielinski (Minneapolis, MN: Lakewood, 1997): 127–28.

28. M. Rosenberg, *E-Learning: Strategies for Delivering Knowledge in the Digital Age* (New York: McGraw-Hill, 2001).

29. P. Galagan, "The E-Learning Revolution," *Training and Development* (December 2000): 24–30; D. Khirallah, "A New Way to Learn," *Information Week Online,* May 22,

2000; G. Wang, R. Von Der Linn, D. Facar-szocki, O. Griffin, and E. Sceiford, "Measuring the Business Impact of E-Learning—An Empirical Study," *Performance Improvement Quarterly* 16 (2003): 17–30.

30. M. Gold, "E-Learning, the Lucent Way," *T&D* (July 2003): 46–50.

31. D. Khirallah, "A New Way to Learn."

32. D. Schaaf, "The View from the Middle," *Training* (September 1999): OL 4–OL12.

33. S. Gale, "Making E-Learning More Than 'Pixie Dust,'" *Workforce* (March 2003): 58–62.

34. H. Baldwin, *Q Magazine* (May/June 2003) at *cisco.com/en/us/strategy/index.html* ("The Travel Industry's Journey Forward").

35. Shared learning demo, January 24, 2001 (from CCH website, *hr.cch.com*).

36. M. Hequet, "The State of the E-Learning Market," *Training* (September 2003): 24–29.

37. K. Kiser, "10 Things We Know So Far about Online Training," *Training* (November 1999): 66–70; R. Wells, "Back to the (Internet) Classroom," *Training* (March 1999): 50–54.

38. S. Gale, "Making E-Learning More Than 'Pixie dust.'"

39. "Going Online," *Human Resource Executive* (2003): A6.

40. K. Brown and J. Ford, "Using Computer Technology in Training: Building an Infrastructure for Active Learning," *Creating, Implementing, and Managing Effective Training and Development,* ed. K. Kraiger (San Francisco: Jossey-Bass, 2002): 192–233.

41. K. Brown, "Using Computers to Deliver Training: Which Employees Learn and Why?" *Personnel Psychology* (2001): 271–96.

42. D. Zielinski, "The Lie of Online Learning," *Training* (February 2000): 38–40; D.Zielinski, "Can You Keep Learners On-line?" *Training* (March 2000): 65–75.

43. D. Schaaf, "Bandwidth Basics," *Training* (September 1999): OL23–OL37.

44. C. Osberg, "How to Keep E-Learners Online," *T&D* (October 2002): 45–46.

45. C. Pollack and R. Masters, "Using Internet Technologies to Enhance Training," *Performance Improvement* (February 1997): 28–31.

46. Zielinski, "Can You Keep Learners On-Line?"

47. Ibid.

48. P. Collins, D. Dorbolo, and L. Vandresse, "E-Learning @ Belgacom," *T&D* (August 2002): 54–56.

49. G. Yohe, "The E-Collaborators," *Human Resource Executive* (August 2002): 41–44.

50. J. Armstrong, "The Biggest, Baddest Learning Portals," *Training* (June 2000): 61–63.

51. Ibid.; B. Hall, "One-Stop Shopping: Learning Portals Proliferate," 1999–2000 (from website *www.internetconnect.net/bhall/portals/portals.html*).

52. K. Boxer and B. Johnson, "How to Build an Online Learning Center," *T&D* (August 2002): 36–42.

53. T. Sosbe, "Ed Sketch: Ford's Drive toward Quality Education," *Chief Learning Officer* (May 2003): 36–39.

54. N. Adams, "Lessons from the Virtual World," *Training* (June 1995): 45–48.

55. D. Steele-Johnson and B. G. Hyde, "Advanced Technologies in Training: Intelligence Tutoring Systems and Virtual Reality," in *Training for a Rapidly Changing Workplace,*

eds. M. A. Quinones and A. Ehrenstein (Washington, DC: American Psychological Association, 1997): 225–48.

56. Ibid.

57. Ibid.

58. R. J. Seidel, O. C. Park, and R. S. Perez, "Expertise of ICAI: Developmental Requirements," *Computers in Human Behavior* 4 (1988): 235–56.

59. Steele-Johnson and Hyde, "Advanced Technologies in Training: Intelligent Tutoring Systems and Virtual Reality."

60. "Putting the Distance into Distance Learning," *Training* (October 1995): 111–18.

61. D. Picard, "The Future Is Distance Training," *Training* (November 1996): s3–s10.

62. A. F. Maydas, "On-Line Networks Build the Savings into Employee Education," *HR Magazine* (October 1997): 31–35.

63. J. M. Rosow and R. Zager, *Training: The Competitive Edge* (San Francisco: Jossey-Bass, 1988).

64. S. Alexander, "Reducing the Learning Burden," *Training* (September 2002): 32–34.

65. Hannum, *The Application of Emerging Training Technologies.*

66. P. A. Galagan, "Think Performance: A Conversation with Gloria Gery," *Training and Development* (March 1994): 47–51.

67. J. Clark and R. Koonce, "Meetings Go High-Tech," *Training and Development* (November 1995): 32–38; A. M. Townsend, M. E. Whitman, and A. R. Hendrickson, "Computer Support Adds Power to Group Processes," *HR Magazine* (September 1995): 87–91.

68. T. A. Stewart, "Getting Real about Brainpower," *Fortune* (November 27, 1995): 201–3.

69. B. Ziegler, "Internet Software Poses Big Threat to Notes, IBM's Stake in Lotus," *The Wall Street Journal,* November 7, 1995: A1, A8.

70. S. Caudron, "Your Learning Technology Primer," *Personnel Journal* (June 1996): 120–36; A. Marquardt and G. Kearsley, *Technology-Based Learning* (Boca Raton, FL: St. Lucie Press, 1999).

71. "A VisionCor Case Study, Electronic Performance Support" (from *www.visioncor .com*).

72. S. Greengard, "How Technology Is Advancing HR."

73. A. L. Lederer, "Emerging Technology and the Buy-Wait Dilemma: Sorting Fact from Fantasy," *The Review* (June/July 1993): 16–19.

74. S. E. Forrer and Z. B. Leibowitz, *Using Computers in Human Resources* (San Francisco: Jossey-Bass, 1991); V. R. Ceriello and C. Freeman, *Human Resource Management Systems* (Lexington, MA: Lexington Books, 1991).

75. L. Granick, A. Y. Dessaint, and G. R. VandenBos, "How Information Systems Can Help Build Professional Competence," in *Maintaining Professional Competence,* eds. S. L. Willis and S. S. Dubin (San Francisco: Jossey-Bass, 1990): 278–305.

Chapter **Nine**

Employee Development

Objectives

After reading this chapter, you should be able to

1. Discuss current trends in using formal education for development.
2. Relate how assessment of personality type, work behaviors, and job performance can be used for employee development.
3. Describe the benefits that protégés and mentors receive from a mentoring relationship.
4. Explain the characteristics of successful mentoring programs.
5. Tell how job experiences can be used for skill development.
6. Explain how to train managers to coach employees.
7. Explain the key features of an effective development strategy and how e-learning incorporates them.
8. Describe the steps in the development planning process.
9. Discuss the employee's and company's responsibilities in the development planning process.

Employees in Motion at PPG Industries

PPG Industries, based in Pittsburgh, Pennsylvania, manufactures coatings for transportation and other industries. PPG is a decentralized company with 16 different businesses. Although the businesses differ in many aspects, they share a need: to develop employees to fill the role of general manager, an important position within PPG. General management positions help employees build competencies needed for top leadership positions with PPG. Recently, senior executives of PPG have taken an aggressive approach to developing the company's future leaders by moving employees to new positions. For example, a sales position is now occupied by a human resource manager. A new plant manager was previously an experienced salesperson. What's the reason for putting employees in motion, that is, moving them to new positions? PPG anticipates a significant need for leaders because of retirements and turnover. Replacements for these leaders are not available from the positions that are traditionally used to staff leadership positions.

To build leadership talent, PPG requires each business to complete an annual ranking of all managers in order to identify those with potential for moving into leadership positions based on the company's competency model. Participants in the development program, known as Aggressive Career Management (ACM), are typically managers who are ranked in the top 10 percent. However, any employee who meets the standards can be nominated by his or her business unit. The standards include having a personal goal of moving into senior leadership or a general manager position, five years of experience as a professional, and a record of demonstrating potential. Executive management committees identify who will be invited to join ACM. Not all nominees accept the invitation to join ACM. Some employees decline the invitation because they don't want to relocate. ACM is a very exclusive group—in a company with over 30,000 employees, only 40 people are in the program.

Development plans include training, job moves, and mentors. Also, each ACM participant is paired with a senior executive who is responsible for monitoring the participant's career. Participation in the ACM program is not widely publicized in PPG to protect the careers of individuals who may decide to leave the program. PPG has also been concerned about the turnover of high-potential employees who were not included in ACM.

Source: K. Ellis, "Making Waves," *Training* (June 2003): 16–21.

INTRODUCTION

As the PPG Industries example illustrates, management development is a key component of employee development efforts. Traditionally, development has focused on management-level employees, while line employees received training designed to improve a specific set of skills needed for their current job. However, with the greater use of work teams and employees' increased involvement in all aspects of business, development is becoming more important for all employees. **Development** refers to formal education, job experiences, relationships, and assessments of personality and abilities that help employees perform effectively in their current or future job and company.[1] Because development is future oriented, it involves learning that is not necessarily related to the employee's current job. Table 9.1 shows the differences between training and development. It is important to note that although training and development are similar, there are important differences between them. Traditionally, training is focused on helping improve employees' performance in their current jobs. Development helps prepare them for other positions in the company and increases their ability to move into jobs that may not yet exist.[2] Development also helps employees prepare for changes in their current job that may result from new technology, work designs, customers, or product markets. Because training often focuses on improving employees' performances in their current jobs, attendance at training programs is required. Development may be mandatory for employees who have been identified to have managerial potential. However, most employees must take the initiative to become involved in development. Although development is sometimes enhanced through planned development programs (as the PPG Industries example shows), it often results from work experiences. Chapter 2 emphasized the strategic role of training. Note that as training continues to become more strategic (more related to business goals), the distinction between training and

TABLE 9.1
Comparison
between
Training and
Development

	Training	Development
Focus	Current	Future
Use of work experiences	Low	High
Goal	Preparation for current job	Preparation for changes
Participation	Required	Voluntary

development will blur. Both training and development will be required and will focus on current and future personal and company needs.

Why is employee development important? Employee development is a necessary component of a company's efforts to improve quality, to retain key employees, to meet the challenges of global competition and social change, and to incorporate technological advances and changes in work design. Increased globalization of product markets compels companies to help their employees understand cultures and customs that affect business practices. For high-involvement companies and work teams to be successful, their employees need strong interpersonal skills. Employees must also be able to perform roles traditionally reserved for managers. Legislation (such as the Civil Rights Act of 1991), labor market forces, and a company's social responsibility dictate that employers provide women and minorities with access to development activities that will prepare them for managerial positions. Companies must help employees overcome stereotypes and attitudes that inhibit the innovative contributions that can come from a work force made up of employees with diverse ethnic, racial, and cultural backgrounds.

As noted in Chapter 1, employees' commitment and retention are directly related to how they are treated by their managers. Managers need to be able to identify high-potential employees, make sure that their talents are used, and reassure them of their value before they become dissatisfied and leave the company. Managers also must be able to listen. While new employees need strong direction and a boss who can make quick decisions, they expect to be able to challenge a manager's thinking and be treated with respect and dignity. Because of their skills, many employees are in high demand and can easily leave for a competitor. Development activities can help companies reduce turnover in two ways: (1) by showing employees that the company is investing in the employees' skill development, and (2) by developing managers who can create a positive work environment that makes employees want to come to work and contribute to the company goals. One of the major reasons that good employees leave companies is poor relationships with their managers. Companies need to retain their talented employees or risk losing their competitive advantage. Development activities can help companies with employee retention by developing managers' skills. Sprint PCS used 360-degree feedback as a way to help develop people skills in its managers of customer contact centers.[3] That is, the company wanted its managers to develop skills in communication, creating trust, coaching, and other interpersonal actions that would help the company retain good employees. Managers who scored high on the 360-degree assessment were also ranked by their employees as high in providing career development help and support (key reasons employees stayed with Sprint). The 360-degree assessment was linked to a development plan, and each interpersonal skill could be developed through online training. Sprint set a goal to reduce turnover to 48 percent. Every Sprint location that completed the 360-degree assessment met the goal!

This chapter discusses approaches that companies use to develop employees as well as the development process itself. The chapter begins by exploring development approaches including formal education, assessment, job experiences, and interpersonal relationships. The chapter emphasizes the types of skills, knowledge, and behaviors that are strengthened by each development method. Developmental approaches are one part of the development planning process. Before one or multiple developmental approaches are used, the employee and the company must have an idea of the employee's development needs and the purpose of development. Identifying needs and purpose of development is part of the development planning process. The chapter provides an overview of the development planning process, including a discussion of the roles of the employee and the company. The chapter concludes with a discussion of employee development strategies, including the use of e-learning.

APPROACHES TO EMPLOYEE DEVELOPMENT

Four approaches are used to develop employees: formal education, assessment, job experiences, and interpersonal relationships.[4] Many companies use a combination of these approaches. Cardinal Health, the largest provider of health care products and services in the world, is headquartered in Dublin, Ohio.[5] The company has 50,000 employees in 22 countries. Cardinal Health has 10 leadership core competencies: customer orientation, personal leadership, business acumen, team player, innovation/risk taker, results orientation, integrity, strategic thinker, interpersonal skills, and maturity. Development activities are designed to assess the strengths and weaknesses of managers (or potential managers) in these core competencies. Training programs, job experiences, and mentoring programs are designed to improve individuals' competencies and the leadership capabilities of the company.

Regardless of the approach used to ensure that development programs are effective, the programs should be developed through the same process used for training design: needs assessment, creating a positive development environment, ensuring employees' readiness for development, identifying the objectives for development, choosing a combination of development activities that will help achieve the objectives, ensuring that the work environment supports development activities and the use of skills and experiences acquired, and program evaluation. To determine the development needs of an individual, department, or company, an analysis of strengths and weaknesses needs to be completed so that appropriate development activities can be chosen. Many companies have identified key competencies for successful managers. Recall from the discussion in Chapter 3 that competencies are areas of personal capability that enable employees to successfully perform their jobs. Competencies can include knowledge, skills, abilities, or personal characteristics.

Two companies that first determined the need for development and then used assessment to determine appropriate development activities were Schwan and General Physics. Schwan, a Minnesota-based frozen food delivery service, created its own corporate university.[6] As part of the process, the company had to determine what kind of managers it wanted and how they were supposed to perform. Schwan identified 15 important competencies, including "managing vision and purpose," and "developing direct reports." After the competencies were identified, the company used 360-degree feedback to measure managers' competency strengths and weaknesses and created development activities related to strengthening the competencies (e.g., coaches, training programs, job experiences).

General Physics (GP), a training and work force development company, believed that the company's managers needed development.[7] GP assessed its current leaders before determining what type of development activity was appropriate and what skills needed to be developed. GP used 360-degree feedback to evaluate managers' competencies in managing change, leadership, motivation, managing conflict, performance, and empowerment. GP also developed an organizational climate survey that was completed by other employees in the company. The climate survey measured the same competencies that the 360-degree assessment did. Based on the results of the 360-degree assessment and the climate survey, GP determined that all of the competencies needed development. GP management also decided that a nontraditional approach was needed to get managers to change, so it adopted a "boot camp" philosophy. The official announcement of the new program was made at a business meeting attended by GP directors and other top-level managers. One of the members of the management team in charge of development initiatives described the program while dressed in battle fatigues. Many in the audience applauded the program, signifying important support from top management. The two-day intensive leadership development program included physically challenging teamwork exercises, motivational speakers, classroom training, and action learning in which teams of program participants worked on issues affecting corporate human performance and briefed senior management on how to deal with them. To reinforce the importance of the program, participants remained at the camp away from business activities and ate all meals together. All participants were issued uniforms. Did the program result in improved leadership competencies? In a follow-up climate survey that was completed six months after the program, employees indicated an improvement in the managers: there was a 17 percent to 25 percent improvement in all of the competencies.

Keep in mind that although the large majority of development activity is targeted at managers, all levels of employees may be involved in one or more development activity. For example, clerks in a grocery store usually receive performance appraisal feedback (a development activity related to assessment). As a result of the appraisal process, they are asked to complete an individual development plan outlining (1) how they plan to change their weaknesses and (2) their future plans (including positions or locations desired and education or experience needed). Specific issues related to developing managers (succession planning, dealing with dysfunctional managers, creating more opportunities for women and minorities to become managers) are discussed in Chapter 10.

Formal Education

Formal education programs include off-site and on-site programs designed specifically for the company's employees, short courses offered by consultants or universities, executive MBA programs, and university programs in which participants actually live at the university while taking classes. These programs may involve lectures by business experts or professors, business games and simulations, adventure learning, and meetings with customers. For example, Harvard University offers several different programs for executives, high-potential upper-level managers, and general managers (e.g., an advanced management program). Harvard also offers programs on managerial issues such as negotiations and programs for specific audiences (e.g., Senior Executive Program for South Africa). Many companies (e.g., Motorola, IBM, GE, Metropolitan Financial, Dow) have training and development centers or corporate universities that offer one- or two-day seminars, week-long programs, and their own degree programs. For example, General Electric's Management Development Institute

FIGURE 9.1 Examples of development programs at General Electric

Program	Description	Target Audience	Courses
Executive Development Sequence	Courses emphasize strategic thinking, leadership, cross-functional integration, competing globally, customer satisfaction	Senior professionals and executives identified as high-potential	Manager Development Course Global Business Management Course Executive Development Course
Core Leadership Program	Courses develop functional expertise, business excellence, management of change	Managers	Corporate Entry Leadership Conference Professional Development Course New Manager Development Course Experienced Manager Course
Professional Development Program	Courses emphasize preparation for specific career path	New employees	Audit Staff Course Financial Management Program Human Resources Program Technical Leadership Program

Source: Based on World Wide Web site *http://www.ge.com/ibcrucl8.htm.*

in Crotonville, New York, offers courses in manufacturing and sales, marketing, and advanced management training.[8] Tuition ranges from $800 for a half-week conference to $14,000 for a four-week executive development course. Tuition is paid for by the employee's business unit. The types of development programs used at GE and their target audiences are shown in Figure 9.1. Here are descriptions of several courses to help you understand the techniques used to facilitate development:

- *Corporate entry leadership conferences.* New hires learn about global competition and GE's values and are asked to examine their personal values. Three years after attending this program, the employees return for a program on total business competitiveness. They are given real projects to work on and have to agree to make changes in their business units.

- *New manager development course.* New managers learn how to manage at GE. The program has special emphasis on teaching people skills to be used in hiring, appraising, and building work teams.

- *Senior functional program.* Senior functional managers attend programs on leadership development in their specific functional areas (e.g., marketing, finance). Managers work on real business problems as part of the program.

- *Executive programs.* Executive programs include adventure learning and projects. In one program, the head of a business unit presents an unresolved business problem that teams of managers must solve. The managers interview customers and competitors and collect background information on which they base their recommendations.

TABLE 9.2 **Examples of Institutions Providing Executive Education**

Provider (Location)	2000–01 Revenue (millions)	No. of Executive Nondegree Programs	No. of Executives Attending Programs	Range of Costs for Programs	Top Corporate Clients
Harvard (Boston)	$91.0	47	4,051	$2,450–$47,000	NA
University of Pennsylvania Wharton School (Philadelphia)	43.0	43	3,946	4,750–49,000	Merrill Lynch Verizon Merck
University of Michigan (Ann Arbor)	28.6	50	4,175	2,400–25,000	AT&T Ford Motor Company Pfizer
Center for Creative Leadership (Greensboro, North Carolina)	49.0	13	8,679	2,900–8,900	General Motors SAP America Maytag Corporation
INSEAD (Fontainbleau, France)	47.7	41	2,932	4,410–22,660	IBM Credit Suisse Dow Chemical

Source: Based on "Exec-Ed Rankings and Profiles," *Business Week Online*, October 15, 2001, *www.businessweek.com*; M. Schneider and B. Hindo, "A Mid-Career Boost," *Business Week Online*, October 15, 2001, *www.businessweek.com*.

- *Officer workshops.* In these workshops, the CEO and the company officers meet to try to solve company wide issues.

These descriptions emphasize that most formal programs actively involve the employees in learning. Separate programs are usually offered for supervisors, middle managers, and executives. Special programs for particular jobs (such as engineer) are also available. (One course at Honeywell is called "Personal Computers in Manufacturing Operations.") Companies may also include personal development courses as part of their education programs. American Medical Systems, a division of Pfizer, offers courses in stress management and preretirement planning.

Leadership, entrepreneurship, and e-business are the most important topics in executive education programs. Programs directed at developing executives' understanding of global business issues and management of change are other important parts of executive development.[9]

Table 9.2 shows examples of institutions that provide executive education. There are several important trends in executive education. Increasingly, many companies and universities are using distance learning (which was discussed in Chapter 8) to reach executive audiences.[10] For example, Duke University's Fuqua School of Business is offering an electronic executive MBA program in both Frankfurt, Germany, and Durham, North Carolina.[11] The program consists of eight terms, each with one week on campus and six weeks of online work. Using their personal computers, students "attend" CD-ROM video lectures. They can download study aids and additional videos and audio programs. Students discuss lectures and work on team projects using computer bulletin boards, e-mail, and live chat rooms. They use the Internet to research specific companies and class topics. Besides the electronic learning environment, students spend time in traditional face-to-face instruction for several weeks at their home. They also travel to attend courses held either in Germany or on the U.S. campus.

Another trend in executive education is for companies and the education provider (business school or other educational institution) to work together to create short, custom courses with content designed specifically to meet the needs of the audience. For example, in the Global Leadership Program run by Columbia University's business school, executives work on real problems they face in their jobs. A manager for window maker Pella Corporation left the program with a plan for international sales![12]

The final important trend in executive education is to supplement formal courses from consultants or university faculty with other types of training and development activities. Avon Products has used action learning (discussed in Chapter 7) for management development. Its "Passport Program" is targeted at employees the company thinks can become general managers.[13] To learn Avon's global strategy, they meet for each session in a different country. The program brings a team of employees together for six-week periods spread over 18 months. Participants are provided with a general background of a functional area by university faculty and consultants. Then teams work with senior executives on a country project such as how to penetrate a new market. The team projects are presented to Avon's top managers.

Managers who attend the Center for Creative Leadership development program in Greensboro, North Carolina, take psychological tests, receive feedback from managers, peers, and direct reports; participate in group building activities (like adventure learning, discussed in Chapter 7); receive counseling; set improvement goals; and write development plans.[14]

Enrollment in executive education programs is susceptible to economic trends and world events such as the 9/11 terrorist attacks. If company training budgets are reduced, the money spent on travel and executive training declines. However, responding to world events and economic changes often requires new knowledge and ways of thinking. For example, Wharton School at the University of Pennsylvania offered a five-day program for executives called "Competing in a Changed World."[15]

Most companies consider the primary purpose of education programs to be providing the employee with job-specific skills.[16] Unfortunately, little research has been done on the effectiveness of formal education programs. In a study of Harvard University's Advanced Management Program, participants reported that they had acquired valuable knowledge from the program (e.g., how globalization affects a company's structure). They said the program broadened their perspective on issues facing their company, increased their self-confidence, and helped them learn new ways of thinking and looking at problems.[17]

Assessment

Assessment involves collecting information and providing feedback to employees about their behavior, communication style, or skills.[18] The employees as well as their peers, managers, and customers may be asked to provide information. Assessment is most frequently used to identify employees with managerial potential and to measure current managers' strengths and weaknesses. Assessment is also used to identify managers with the potential to move into higher-level executive positions, and it can be used with work teams to identify individual team members' strengths and weaknesses as well as the decision processes or communication styles that inhibit the team's productivity.

Companies vary in the methods and sources of information they use in developmental assessment. Many companies provide employees with performance appraisal information.

Companies with sophisticated development systems use psychological tests to measure employees' skills, personality types, and communication styles. Self, peer, and manager's ratings of employees' interpersonal styles and behaviors may also be collected. The following sections look at several popular assessment tools.

Myers-Briggs Type Indicator

The **Myers-Briggs Type Indicator® (MBTI)** is the most popular psychological test for employee development. As many as 2 million people take the MBTI in the United States each year. The test consists of more than 100 questions about how the person feels or prefers to behave in different situations (e.g., "Are you usually a good 'mixer' or rather quiet and reserved?"). The MBTI is based on the work of psychologist Carl Jung, who believed that differences in individuals' behavior resulted from people's preferences in decision making, interpersonal communication, and information gathering.

The MBTI identifies individuals' preferences for energy (introversion versus extroversion), information gathering (sensing versus intuition), decision making (thinking versus feeling), and lifestyle (judging versus perceiving).[19] The energy dimension determines where individuals gain interpersonal strength and vitality. Extroverts (E) gain energy through interpersonal relationships. Introverts (I) gain energy by focusing on personal thoughts and feelings. The information-gathering preference relates to the actions individuals take when making decisions. Individuals with a Sensing (S) preference tend to gather facts and details. Intuitives (I) tend to focus less on facts and more on possibilities and relationships between ideas. Differences in decision-making styles are based on the amount of consideration the person gives to others' feelings in making a decision. Individuals with a Thinking (T) preference tend to be very objective in making decisions. Individuals with a Feeling (F) preference tend to evaluate the impact of potential decisions on others and be more subjective in making a decision. The lifestyle preference reflects an individual's tendency to be flexible and adaptable. Individuals with a Judging (J) preference focus on goals, establish deadlines, and prefer to be conclusive. Individuals with a Perceiving (P) preference tend to enjoy surprises, like to change decisions, and dislike deadlines.

Sixteen unique personality types result from the combination of the four MBTI preferences (see Table 9.3). Each of us has developed strengths and weaknesses as a result of our preferences. For example, individuals who are Introverted, Sensing, Thinking, and Judging (known as ISTJs) tend to be serious, quiet, practical, orderly, and logical. They can organize tasks, be decisive, and follow through on plans and goals. ISTJs have several weaknesses because they have not used the opposite preferences of Extroversion, Intuition, Feeling, and Perceiving. Potential weaknesses for ISTJs include problems dealing with unexpected opportunities, appearing too task-oriented or impersonal to colleagues, and being overly quick to make decisions. Visit the website *www.keirsey.com* for more information on the personality types.

The MBTI is used for understanding such things as communication, motivation, teamwork, work styles, and leadership. For example, it can be used by salespeople or executives who want to become more effective at interpersonal communication by learning things about their own personality styles and the way they are perceived by others. The MBTI can help a company develop teams by matching team members with assignments that allow them to capitalize on their preferences and by helping employees understand how the different preferences of team members can lead to useful problem solving.[20] For example,

TABLE 9.3 **Personality Types Used in the Myers-Briggs Type Indicator Assessment**

	Sensing Types (S)		Intuitive Types (N)	
	Thinking (T)	Feeling (F)	Feeling (F)	Thinking (T)
Introverts (I) Judging (J)	**ISTJ** Quiet, serious, earn success by thoroughness and dependability. Practical, matter-of-fact, realistic, and responsible. Decide logically what should be done and work toward it steadily, regardless of distractions. Take pleasure in making everything orderly and organized— their work, their home, their life. Value traditions and loyalty.	**ISFJ** Quiet, friendly, responsible, and conscientious. Committed and steady in meeting their obligations. Thorough, painstaking, and accurate. Loyal, considerate, notice and remember specifics about people who are important to them, concerned with how others feel. Strive to create an orderly and harmonious environment at work and at home.	**INFJ** Seek meaning and connection in ideas, relationships, and material possessions. Want to understand what motivates people and are insightful about others. Conscientious and committed to their firm values. Develop a clear vision about how best to serve the common good. Organized and decisive in implementing their vision.	**INTJ** Have original minds and great drive for implementing their ideas and achieving their goals. Quickly see patterns in external events and develop long-range explanatory perspectives. When committed, organize a job and carry it through. Skeptical and independent, have high standards of competence and performance—for themselves and others.
Perceiving (P)	**ISTP** Tolerant and flexible, quiet observers until a problem appears, then act quickly to find workable solutions. Analyze what makes things work and readily get through large amounts of data to isolate the core of practical problems, interested in cause and effect, organize facts using logical principles, value efficiency.	**ISFP** Quiet, friendly, sensitive, and kind. Enjoy the present moment, what's going on around them. Like to have their own space and to work within their own time frame. Loyal and committed to their values and to people who are important to them. Dislike disagreements and conflicts, do not force their opinions or values on others.	**INFP** Idealistic, loyal to their values and to people who are important to them. Want an external life that is congruent with their values. Curious, quick to see possibilities, can be catalysts for implementing ideas. Seek to understand people and to help them fulfill their potential. Adaptable, flexible, and accepting unless a value is threatened.	**INTP** Seek to develop logical explanations for everything that interests them. Theoretical and abstract, interested more in ideas than in social interaction. Quiet, contained, flexible and adaptable. Have unusual ability to focus in depth to solve problems in their area of interest. Skeptical, sometimes critical, always analytical.

employees with an Intuitive preference can be assigned brainstorming tasks. Employees with a Sensing preference can be given the responsibility of evaluating ideas.

Research on the validity, reliability, and effectiveness of the MBTI is inconclusive.[21] People who take the MBTI find it a positive experience and say it helps them change their behavior. MBTI scores appear to be related to one's occupation. Analysis of managers' MBTI scores in the United States, England, Latin America, and Japan suggests that a large majority of all managers have certain personality types (ISTJ, INTJ, ESTJ, or ENTJ). However, MBTI scores are not necessarily stable or reliable over time. Studies administering the MBTI at two different times found that as few as 24 percent of those who took the test were classified as the same type the second time.

The MBTI is a valuable tool for understanding communication styles and the ways people prefer to interact with others. Because it does not measure how well employees perform their preferred functions, it should not be used to appraise performance or evaluate employees' promotion potential. Furthermore, MBTI types should not be viewed as unchangeable personality patterns.

TABLE 9.3 *(concluded)*

	Sensing Types (S)		Intuitive Types (N)	
	Thinking (T)	Feeling (F)	Feeling (F)	Thinking (T)
Extroverts (E) Perceiving (P)	**ESTP** Flexible and tolerant, they take a pragmatic approach focused on immediate results. Theories and conceptual explanations bore them—they want to act energetically to solve the problem. Focus on the here-and-now, spontaneous, enjoy each moment that they can be active with others. Enjoy material comforts and style. Learn best through doing.	**ESFP** Outgoing, friendly, and accepting. Exuberant lovers of life, people, and material comforts. Enjoy working with others to make things happen. Bring common sense and a realistic approach to their work, and make work fun. Flexible and spontaneous, adapt readily to new people and environments. Learn best by trying a new skill with other people.	**ENFP** Warmly enthusiastic and imaginative. See life as full of possibilities. Make connections between events and information very quickly, and confidently proceed based on the patterns they see. Want a lot of affirmation from others, and readily give appreciation and support. Spontaneous and flexible, often rely on their ability to improvise and their verbal fluency.	**ENTP** Quick, ingenious, stimulating, alert, and outspoken. Resourceful in solving new and challenging problems. Adept at generating conceptual possibilities and then analyzing them strategically. Good at reading other people. Bored by routine, will seldom do the same thing the same way, apt to turn to one new interest after another.
Judging (J)	**ESTJ** Practical, realistic, matter-of-fact. Decisive, quickly move to implement decisions. Organize projects and people to get things done, focus on getting results in the most efficient way possible. Take care of routine details. Have a clear set of logical standards, systematically follow them and want others to also. Forceful in implementing their plans.	**ESFJ** Warmhearted, conscientious, and cooperative. Want harmony in their environment, work with determination to establish it. Like to work with others to complete tasks accurately and on time. Loyal, follow through even in small matters. Notice what others need in their day-by-day lives and try to provide it. Want to be appreciated for who they are and for what they contribute.	**ENFJ** Warm, empathetic, responsive, and responsible. Highly attuned to the emotions, needs, and motivations of others. Find potential in everyone, want to help others fulfill their potential. May act as catalysts for individual and group growth. Loyal, responsive to praise and criticism. Sociable, facilitate others in a group, and provide inspiring leadership.	**ENTJ** Frank, decisive, assume leadership readily. Quickly see illogical and inefficient procedures and policies, develop and implement comprehensive systems to solve organizational problems. Enjoy long-term planning and goal setting. Usually well informed, well read, enjoy expanding their knowledge and passing it on to others. Forceful in presenting their ideas.

Assessment Center

The **assessment center** is a process in which multiple raters or evaluators (also known as assessors) evaluate employees' performance on a number of exercises.[22] An assessment center is usually held at an off-site location such as a conference center. From 6 to 12 employees usually participate at one time. Assessment centers are primarily used to identify if employees have the personality characteristics, administrative skills, and interpersonal skills needed for managerial jobs. They are also increasingly being used to identify if employees have the necessary skills to work in teams.

The types of exercises used in assessment centers include leaderless group discussions, interviews, in-baskets, and role plays.[23] In a **leaderless group discussion,** a team of five to seven employees must work together to solve an assigned problem within a certain time period. The problem may involve buying and selling supplies, nominating a subordinate for an award, or assembling a product. An **in-basket** is a simulation of the administrative tasks of the manager's job. The exercise includes a variety of documents that may appear in the in-basket on a manager's desk. The participant is asked to read the materials and decide how to respond to them. Responses might include delegating tasks, scheduling meetings, writing replies, or completely ignoring the memo!

In **role plays,** participants take the part or role of a manager or other employee. For example, an assessment center participant may be asked to take the role of a manager who has to give a negative performance review to a subordinate. The participant is provided with information regarding the subordinate's performance. The participant is asked to prepare for and actually hold a 45-minute meeting with the subordinate to discuss the performance problems. The role of the subordinate is played by a manager or other member of the assessment center design team or the company. The assessment center might also include testing. Interest and aptitude tests may be used to evaluate employees' vocabulary, general mental ability, and reasoning skills. Personality tests may be used to determine if employees can get along with others, their tolerance for ambiguity, and other traits related to success as a manager.

The exercises in the assessment center are designed to measure employees' administrative and interpersonal skills. Skills that are typically measured include leadership, oral communication, written communication, judgment, organizational ability, and stress tolerance. Table 9.4 shows an example of the skills measured by the assessment center. Each exercise allows participating employees to demonstrate several skills. For example, the exercise requiring scheduling to meet production demands evaluates employees' administrative and problem-solving abilities. The leaderless group discussion measures interpersonal skills such as sensitivity toward others, stress tolerance, and oral communications skills.

Managers are usually used as assessors. The managers are trained to look for behaviors related to the skills that will be assessed. Typically, each assessor is assigned to observe and record one or two employees' behaviors in each exercise. The assessors review their notes and rate the employee's level of skills. (For example, 5 equals a high level of leadership skills, 1 equals a low level of leadership skills.) After all employees have completed the exercises, the assessors meet to discuss their observations of each employee. They compare their ratings and try to agree on each employee's rating for each skill.

Research suggests that assessment center ratings are related to performance, salary level, and career advancement.[24] Assessment centers may also be useful for development purposes because employees who participate in the process receive feedback regarding their attitudes, skill strengths, and weaknesses.[25] For example, Steelcase, the office furniture manufacturer based in Grand Rapids, Michigan, uses assessment centers for first-level managers.[26] The assessment center exercises include in-basket, interview simulation, and a timed scheduling exercise requiring participants to fill positions created by absences. Managers are also required to confront an employee on a performance issue, getting the employee to commit to improve. Because the exercises relate closely to what managers are required to do at work, feedback given to managers based on their performance in the assessment center can target specific skills or competencies that they need to be successful managers.

TABLE 9.4 **Examples of Skills Measured by Assessment Center Exercises**

	Exercises				
Skills	**In-Basket**	**Scheduling Exercise**	**Leaderless Group Discussion**	**Personality Test**	**Role Play**
Leadership (Dominance, coaching, influence, resourcefulness)	X		X	X	X
Problem solving (Judgment)	X	X	X		X
Interpersonal (Sensitivity, conflict resolution, cooperation, oral communication)			X	X	X
Administrative (Organizing, planning, written communications)	X	X	X		
Personal (Stress tolerance, confidence)			X	X	X

Note: An "X" indicates that the skill is measured by the exercise.

Benchmarks

Benchmarks© is an instrument designed to measure important factors in being a successful manager. Items measured by Benchmarks are based on research that examines the lessons executives learn at critical events in their careers.[27] Items that are measured included dealing with subordinates, acquiring resources, and creating a productive work climate. Table 9.5 shows the 16 skills and perspectives believed to be important in becoming a successful manager. These skills and perspectives have been shown to relate to performance evaluations, bosses' ratings of promotability, and actual promotions received.[28] To get a complete picture of managers' skills, the managers' supervisors, their peers, and the managers themselves all complete the instrument. A summary report presenting the self-ratings and ratings by others is provided to the manager along with information about how the ratings compare with those of other managers. Also available is a development guide with examples of experiences that enhance each of the skills and how successful managers use the skills.

Performance Appraisals and 360-Degree Feedback Systems

Performance appraisal is the process of measuring employees' performance. There are several different approaches for measuring performance, including ranking employees, rating their work behaviors, rating the extent to which employees have desirable traits believed to be necessary for job success (e.g., leadership), and directly measuring the results of work performance (e.g., productivity).

These approaches can be useful for employee development under certain conditions.[29] The appraisal system must give employees specific information about their performance problems and ways they can improve their performance. Appraisals should provide a clear understanding of the differences between current performance and expected performance,

TABLE 9.5 **Skills Related to Managerial Success**

Resourcefulness	Can think strategically, engage in flexible problem-solving behavior, and work effectively with higher management.
Doing Whatever It Takes	Has perseverance and focus in the face of obstacles.
Being a Quick Study	Quickly masters new technical and business knowledge.
Building and Mending Relationships	Knows how to build and maintain working relationships with co-workers and external parties.
Leading Subordinates	Delegates to subordinates effectively, broadens their opportunities, and acts with fairness toward them.
Compassion and Sensitivity	Shows genuine interest in others and sensitivity to subordinates' needs.
Straightforwardness and Composure	Is honorable and steadfast.
Setting a Developmental Climate	Provides a challenging climate to encourage subordinates' development.
Confronting Problem Subordinates	Acts decisively and fairly when dealing with problem subordinates.
Team Orientation	Accomplishes tasks through managing others.
Balance between Personal Life and Work	Balances work priorities with personal life so that neither is neglected.
Decisiveness	Prefers quick and approximate actions to slow and precise ones in many management situations.
Self-Awareness	Has an accurate picture of strengths and weaknesses and is willing to improve.
Hiring Talented Staff	Hires talented people for his or her team.
Putting People at Ease	Displays warmth and a good sense of humor.
Acting with Flexibility	Can behave in ways that are often seen as opposites.

Source: Adapted from C. D. McCauley, M. M. Lombardo, and C. J. Usher, "Diagnosing Management Development Needs: An Instrument Based on How Managers Develop," *Journal of Management* 15 (1989): 389–403.

identify the causes of the performance discrepancy, and develop action plans to improve performance. Managers must be trained in providing performance feedback and must frequently give employees performance feedback. Managers also need to monitor employees' progress in carrying out the action plan.

A recent trend in the use of performance appraisals for management development is the upward feedback and 360-degree feedback process. Dow Chemical, Hallmark, The Limited stores, Raychem, and AT&T, for example, use this type of appraisal process. In **upward feedback,** the appraisal process involves collecting subordinates' evaluations of managers' behaviors or skills. The **360-degree feedback** process (see Figure 9.2) is a special case of the upward feedback process. In 360-degree feedback systems, employees' behaviors or skills are evaluated not only by subordinates, but also by peers, customers, their boss, and themselves. The raters complete a questionnaire that rates the person on a number of different dimensions. Table 9.6 provides an example of the types of competencies that are rated in a 360-degree feedback questionnaire. This example evaluates the management competency of decision making. Each of the five items relates to a specific aspect of decision making (e.g., takes accountability for results of individual and team decisions). Typically, raters are asked to assess the manager's strength in a particular item or whether development is needed. Raters may also be asked to identify how frequently they observe a competency or skill (e.g., always, sometimes, seldom, never).

FIGURE 9.2
360-degree
feedback system

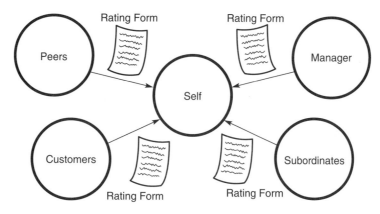

TABLE 9.6
Sample
Competency
and Items from
a 360-Degree
Feedback
Instrument

Decision Making
Identifies the key decisions that have the greatest impact on business goals. Understands and integrates conflicting or contradictory information. Balances business sense with data and logic to make effective decisions. Takes accountability for results of individual and team decisions. Makes appropriate trade-offs between complete analysis and speed when making decisions.

The results of a 360-degree feedback system show managers how they are seen on each item. The results reveal how self-evaluations differ from evaluations from the other raters. Typically, managers are asked to review their results, seek clarification from the raters, and participate in development planning designed to set specific development goals based on the strengths and weaknesses identified.[30] For example, U S West used 360-degree feedback as part of a manager development program.[31] The 360-degree feedback results showed one manager that she had a tendency to avoid confrontation. With this information, she focused her training and development activity on role plays and discussions that would help her become more comfortable with confrontation. She left the program with an individualized list of training and development activities linked directly to the skill she needed to improve.

Table 9.7 shows the types of activities involved in development planning using the 360-degree feedback process.[32] The first step for the manager being rated is to gain an understanding of skill strengths and weaknesses. This includes comparing self-ratings to other ratings (i.e., manager, peers, customers, subordinates) to identify areas of agreement and disagreement. A manager may overrate herself (rate herself too high) in comparison to the other raters. This means that the manager believes she has greater skill than the other raters believe. The manager may also underrate herself (rate herself too low) in comparison to the other raters. This suggests that the manager may lack confidence in her skills. The second step is for the manager to identify a skill or behavior to develop. Third the manager needs to identify how she will determine her progress toward meeting her development goal. The final step in the process is to provide the manager with strategies for reaching her goal. This includes three components. First, the manager needs to identify specific actions she can take to reach

TABLE 9.7
Development-
Planning
Activities from
360-Degree
Feedback

1. **Understand strengths and weaknesses.**
   Review ratings for strengths and weaknesses.
   Identify skills or behaviors where self and others' (managers', peers', customers') ratings agree and disagree.
2. **Identify a development goal.**
   Choose a skill or behavior to develop.
   Set a clear, specific goal with a specified outcome.
3. **Identify a process for recognizing goal accomplishment.**
4. **Identify strategies for reaching the development goal.**
   Establish strategies such as reading, job experiences, courses, and relationships.
   Establish strategies for receiving feedback on progress.
   Establish strategies for receiving reinforcement for new skill or behavior.

her goal (e.g., job experiences, courses). Next, the manager needs to identify whom she will ask to provide feedback about her progress. Third, the manager needs to consider how she will find reinforcement for her progress. Recall from Chapter 5's discussion of transfer of training that it is often difficult to receive reinforcement for using trained skills in the workplace. Similarly, the manager needs to consider self-reinforcement for development progress. This reinforcement could involve buying herself a gift or rewarding herself with a night out on the town.

Benefits of 360-degree feedback include collecting multiple perspectives of managers' performance, allowing employees to compare their own personal evaluation with the views of others, and formalizing communications between employees and their internal and external customers. For example, Robert Allen, a high-level AT&T executive, now more freely airs his opinions in executive committee meetings based on the feedback he received from his subordinates as part of a 360-degree feedback system. Several studies have shown that performance improvement and behavior change occur as a result of participation in upward feedback and 360-degree feedback systems.[33] The most change occurs in individuals who receive lower ratings from others than they gave themselves (overraters).

Potential limitations of 360-degree feedback systems include the time demands placed on the raters to complete the evaluation, managers seeking to identify and punish raters who provided negative information, the need to have a facilitator to help interpret results, and companies' failure to provide ways that managers can act on the feedback they receive (e.g., development planning, meeting with raters, taking courses).

In developing (or hiring a consultant to develop) a 360-degree feedback system, several factors are necessary for the system to be effective. The system must provide reliable or consistent ratings; feedback must be job-related (valid); the system must be easy to use, understandable, and relevant; and the system must lead to managerial development. Important issues to consider include[34]

- Who will the raters be?
- How will you maintain confidentiality of the raters?
- What behaviors and skills are job-related?
- How will you ensure full participation and complete responses from every employee who is asked to be a rater?

- What will the feedback report include?
- How will you ensure that managers receive and act on the feedback?

Both Capital One and World Bank have developed effective 360-degree feedback systems.[35] Capitol One, a consumer credit company, has included a number of features in its 360-degree feedback system to minimize the chance that the ratings will be used as ways to get back at an employee or turned into popularity contests. The 360-degree assessments are based on the company's competency model, so raters are asked for specific feedback on a competency area. Rather than a lengthy form that places a large burden on raters to assess many different competencies, Capital One's assessment asks the raters to concentrate on three or four strengths or development opportunities. It also seeks comments rather than limiting raters to merely circling numbers corresponding to how much of each competency the employee has demonstrated. These comments often provide specific information about what aspect of a competency needs to be developed or identifies work situations in which a competency needs to be improved. This comment system helps tailor development activities to fit competency development. To increase the chances that the assessment will result in change, the feedback from the 360-degree assessment is linked to development plans, and the company offers coaching and training to help employees strengthen their competencies. Employees are encouraged to share feedback with their co-workers. This creates a work environment based on honest and open feedback that helps employees personally grow. The World Bank's 360-degree feedback system offers anonymity to raters, but employees who are being assessed are responsible for nominating those who provide feedback. Similar to Capital One's approach, the World Bank system encourages written commentary along with ratings. Although the bank leaves it up to each employee to make use of the 360-degree feedback, it does link development opportunities directly to the items included in the assessment. The bank also helps facilitate the feedback of the assessment information, either in person or through video conferencing.

New technology has allowed 360-degree questionnaires to be delivered electronically to the raters via their personal computers. This increases the number of completed questionnaires, makes it easier to process the information, and speeds delivery of feedback reports to managers.

Regardless of the assessment method used, the information must be shared with the employee for development to occur. Along with the assessment information, the employee needs suggestions for correcting skill weaknesses and using skills already learned.[36] These suggestions might be to participate in training courses or develop skills through new job experiences. Based on the assessment information and available development opportunities, employees should develop an action plan to guide their self-improvement efforts.

Job Experiences

Most employee development occurs through job experiences.[37] **Job experiences** refer to relationships, problems, demands, tasks, or other features that employees face in their jobs. A major assumption of using job experiences for employee development is that development is most likely to occur when there is a mismatch between the employee's skills and past experiences and the skills required for the job. To be successful in their jobs, employees must stretch their skills—that is, they must be forced to learn new skills, apply their skills and knowledge in a new way, and master new experiences.[38] At Dave and Busters, which runs several large-volume restaurant-entertainment complexes across the United States, the company uses job experiences to strengthen employees' management competencies.[39] Employees are placed in departments where they have to deal with real-life issues such as working with the kitchen staff or dealing with difficult customers.

Most of what is known about development through job experiences comes from a series of studies conducted by the Center for Creative Leadership in Greensboro, North Carolina.[40] Executives were asked to identify key events in their careers that made a difference in their managerial styles and the lessons they learned from these experiences. The key events included those involving the job assignment (e.g., fixing a failing operation), interpersonal relationships (e.g., getting along with supervisors), and making transitions (e.g., handling situations in which the executive did not have the necessary education or work background). Job demands and what employees can learn from them are shown in Table 9.8. One concern in the use of demanding job experiences for employee development is whether they are viewed as positive or negative stressors. Job experiences that are seen as positive stressors challenge employees to stimulate learning. Job challenges viewed as negative stressors create high levels of harmful stress for employees who are exposed to them. Recent research suggests that all job demands, with the exception of obstacles, are related to learning.[41] Managers reported that obstacles and job demands related to creating change were more likely to lead to negative stress than were other job demands. This suggests that companies should carefully weigh the potential negative consequences before placing employees in development assignments involving obstacles or creation of change.

Although research on development through job experiences has focused on executives and managers, line employees can also learn from job experiences. As was noted earlier, for a work team to be successful, its members now need the kinds of skills that only managers were once thought to need (e.g., dealing directly with customers, analyzing data to determine product quality, resolving conflict among team members). Besides the development that occurs when a team is formed, employees can further develop their skills by switching work roles within the team.

Figure 9.3 shows the various ways that job experiences can be used for employee development. These include enlarging the current job, job rotation, transfers, promotions, downward moves, and temporary assignments with other organizations.

Enlarging the Current Job

Job enlargement refers to adding challenges or new responsibilities to an employee's current job. This could include special project assignments, switching roles within a work team, or researching new ways to serve clients and customers. For example, an engineering employee may be asked to join a task force charged with developing new career paths for technical employees. Through this project work, the engineer may be asked to take leadership for certain aspects of career path development (such as reviewing the company's career development process). As a result, the engineer has the opportunity not only to learn about the company's career development system but also to use leadership and organizational skills to help the task force reach its goals.

Some companies are allowing their employees to redesign their jobs. Deloitte Consulting was concerned with losing valuable senior consultants. These consultants have important knowledge about the company and its clients, so losing them would cripple the company's

TABLE 9.8 Job Demands and the Lessons Employees Learn from Them

Making Transitions	*Unfamiliar responsibilities:* The manager must handle responsibilities that are new, very different, or much broader than previous ones.
	Proving yourself: The manager has added pressure to show others she can handle the job.
Creating Change	*Developing new directions:* The manager is responsible for starting something new in the organization, making strategic changes in the business, carrying out a reorganization, or responding to rapid changes in the business environment.
	Inherited problems: The manager has to fix problems created by his predecessor or take over problem employees.
	Reduction decisions: Decisions about shutting down operations or staff reductions have to be made.
	Problems with employees: Employees lack adequate experience, are incompetent, or are resistant.
Having High Level of Responsibility	*High stakes:* Clear deadlines, pressure from senior managers, high visibility, and responsibility for key decisions make success or failure in this job clearly evident.
	Managing business diversity: The scope of the job is large with responsibilities for multiple functions, groups, products, customers, or markets.
	Job overload: The sheer size of the job requires a large investment of time and energy.
	Handling external pressure: External factors that affect the business (e.g., negotiating with unions or government agencies; working in a foreign culture; coping with serious community problems) must be dealt with.
Being Involved in Nonauthority Relationships	*Influencing without authority:* Getting the job done requires influencing peers, higher management, external parties, or other key people over whom the manager has no direct authority.
Facing Obstacles	*Adverse business conditions:* The business unit or product line faces financial problems or difficult economic conditions.
	Lack of top management support: Senior management is reluctant to provide direction, support, or resources for current work or new projects.
	Lack of personal support: The manager is excluded from key networks and gets little support and encouragement from others.
	Difficult boss: The manager's opinions or management styles differ from those of the boss, or the boss has major shortcomings.

Source: C. D. McCauley, L. J. Eastman, and J. Ohlott, "Linking Management Selection and Development through Stretch Assignments," *Human Resource Management* 84 (1995): 93–115. Copyright © 1995 John Wiley and Sons, Inc. Reprinted by permission of John Wiley and Sons, Inc.

expansion plans. As a result, Deloitte allows long-tenured and experienced consultants to customize their jobs so they are less stressful but more challenging.[42] For example, some senior consultants may decide on a work schedule that involves less travel and fewer deadlines, and more focus on internal consulting and mentoring. Not only does this plan help retain senior consultants, but it also shows less senior consultants that the company will treat them reasonably if they stay with Deloitte Consulting, which has a positive effect on retention of the younger generation of consultants.

FIGURE 9.3

How job experiences are used for employee development

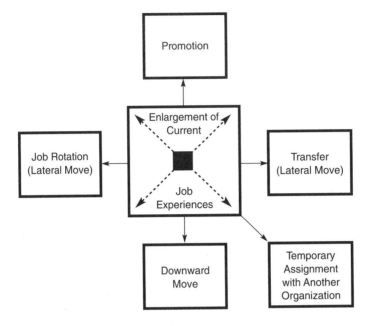

Job Rotation

Job rotation involves providing employees with a series of job assignments in various functional areas of the company or movement among jobs in a single functional area or department. Arrow Electronics allows employees to take a 10-week sabbatical after seven years with the company.[43] While an employee is taking the sabbatical, the company uses the job vacancy as a job rotation for a different employee. Assignments to open positions are based on an employee's development needs. Employees who rotate to new positions are required to document their experiences and learning, especially emphasizing how the position helped them better understand the business. W. W. Grainger, a distributor of business maintenance products in Lake Forest, Illinois, regularly moves employees across functions—for example, from marketing to information technology, from field-office work to corporate-office work, from regional sales offices to distribution centers—to help employees think strategically about different parts of the business.[44] Each employee has a customized development plan, and employees are assigned new positions based on the skills they need. The length of time in each position varies, depending on the skills and experience the employees need. Some employees return to their original jobs, while others may move to another department.

Job rotation helps employees gain an overall appreciation of the company's goals, increases their understanding of different company functions, develops a network of contacts, and improves their problem-solving and decision-making skills.[45] Job rotation has also been shown to be related to skill acquisition, salary growth, and promotion rates. There are several potential problems with job rotation from both the employee's and the work unit's points of view. The rotation may create a short-term perspective on problems and solutions in the employees being rotated and their peers. Employees' satisfaction and motivation may be adversely affected because they find it difficult to develop functional specialties and because

TABLE 9.9
Characteristics of Effective Job Rotation Systems

Source: Based on L. Cheraskin and M. Campion, "Study Clarifies Job Rotation Benefits," *Personnel Journal* (November 1996): 31–38.

1. Job rotation is used to develop skills as well as give employees experience needed for managerial positions.
2. Employees understand specific skills that will be developed by rotation.
3. Job rotation is used for all levels and types of employees.
4. Job rotation is linked with the career management process so employees know the development needs addressed by each job assignment.
5. Benefits of rotation are maximized and costs are minimized through timing the rotations to reduce work load costs and help employees understand the job rotation's role in their development plans.
6. All employees have equal opportunities for job rotation assignments regardless of their demographic group.

they don't spend enough time in one position to receive a challenging assignment. Productivity losses and work load increases may be experienced by both the department gaining a rotating employee and the department losing the employee due to training demands and loss of a resource.

Table 9.9 shows characteristics of effective job rotation systems. Effective job rotation systems are linked to the company's training, development, and career management systems. Also, job rotation is used for all types of employees, not just those with managerial potential.

Transfers, Promotions, and Downward Moves

Upward, lateral, and downward mobility is available for development purposes in most companies.[46] In a **transfer,** an employee is given a different job assignment in a different area of the company. Transfers do not necessarily involve increased job responsibilities or compensation. They are likely lateral moves (a move to a job with similar responsibilities). **Promotions** are advancements into positions with greater challenges, more responsibility, and more authority than in the previous job. Promotions usually include pay increases.

Transfers may involve relocation within the United States or to another country, which can be stressful for a number of reasons. The employee's work role changes. If the employee has a family, they have to join a new community. Employed spouses may have to find new employment. Transfers disrupt employees' daily lives, interpersonal relationships, and work habits.[47] Employees have to find new housing as well as new shopping, health care, and leisure facilities, and they may be many miles from the emotional support of friends and family. They have to learn a new set of work norms and procedures as well as develop interpersonal relationships with their new managers and peers, and they are expected to be as productive in their new jobs as they were in their old jobs even though they may know very little about the products, services, processes, or employees for whom they are responsible.

Because transfers can be anxiety provoking, many companies have difficulty getting employees to accept them. Research has identified the employee characteristics associated with a willingness to accept transfers:[48] high career ambitions, a belief that one's future with the company is promising, and a belief that accepting a transfer is necessary for success in the company. Employees who are not married and not active in the community are most willing to accept transfers. Among married employees, the spouse's willingness to move is the most important influence on whether an employee will accept a transfer.

A **downward move** occurs when an employee is given a reduced level of responsibility and authority.[49] This may involve a move to another position at the same level but with less authority and responsibility (lateral demotion), a temporary cross-functional move, or a demotion because of poor performance. Temporary cross-functional moves to lower-level positions, which give employees experience working in different functional areas, are most frequently used for employee development. For example, engineers who want to move into management often take lower-level positions (e.g., shift supervisor) to develop their management skills.

Because of the psychological and tangible rewards of promotions (e.g., an increased feeling of self-worth, high salary, and higher status in the company), employees are more willing to accept promotions than they are to accept lateral or downward moves. Promotions are most readily available when a company is profitable and growing. When a company is restructuring and/or experiencing stable or declining profits, promotion opportunities may be limited, especially if a large number of employees are interested in promotions and if the company tends to rely on the external labor market to staff higher-level positions.[50]

Unfortunately, many employees have difficulty associating transfers and downward moves with development. They see them as punishments rather than as opportunities to develop skills that will help them achieve long-term success with the company. Many employees decide to leave a company rather than accept a transfer. Companies need to successfully manage transfers not only because of the costs of replacing employees but because of the costs directly associated with managing them. For example, GTE spends approximately $60 million a year on home purchases and other relocation costs such as temporary housing and relocation allowances.[51] One challenge companies face is learning how to use transfers and downward moves as development opportunities—convincing employees that accepting these opportunities will result in long-term benefits for them.

To ensure that employees accept transfers, promotions, and downward moves as development opportunities, companies can provide[52]

- Information about the content, challenges, and potential benefits of the new job and location.
- Involvement in the transfer decision by sending the employees to preview the new locations and giving them information about the community and other employment opportunities.
- Clear performance objectives and early feedback about their job performance.
- A host at the new location who will help them adjust to the new community and workplace.
- Information about how the job opportunity will affect their income, taxes, mortgage payments, and other expenses.
- Reimbursement and assistance in selling, purchasing, and/or renting a place to live.
- An orientation program for the new location and job.
- A guarantee that the new job experiences will support employees' career plans.
- Assistance for dependent family members, including helping to identify schools as well as child and elder care options.
- Help for spouses in identifying and marketing their skills and finding employment.

Externships allow employees to take full-time, temporary operational roles at another company. Mercer Management, a consulting firm, uses its externship program to develop employees who have an interest in gaining experience in a specific industry.[53] Mercer Management promises to re-employ the externs after their assignments end. For example, one employee who has been a consultant for Mercer for five years is now vice president of Internet services for Binney and Smith, the maker of Crayola crayons. A year ago he was working on an Internet consulting project for Binney and Smith, but he wanted to actually implement his recommendations rather than just provide them to the client and move on to another project. As a result he started working at Binney and Smith. He remains on Mercer Management's payroll, though his salary comes from Binney and Smith. Mercer believes that employees who participate in the externship program will remain committed to the company because they have had the opportunity to learn and grow professionally and have not had to disrupt their personal and professional lives with a job search. Although externships provide employees with new employment options and although some employees will leave, Mercer believes that the program is not only a good development strategy but also helps in recruitment. The externship program signals to potential employees that Mercer is creative and flexible with its employees.

Temporary Assignment with Other Organizations

Employee exchange is another example of temporary assignments. Two companies can agree to exchange employees. First Chicago National Bank and Kodak participated in an employee exchange program so that the two companies could better understand each other's business and how to improve the services provided.[54] For example, an employee from First Chicago helped the business imaging division of Kodak identify applications for compact disc technology. The Kodak employee helped First Chicago understand areas within the bank that could benefit from imaging technology.

Interpersonal Relationships

Employees can also develop skills and increase their knowledge about the company and its customers by interacting with a more experienced organizational member. Mentoring and coaching are two types of interpersonal relationships used to develop employees.

Mentoring

A **mentor** is an experienced, productive senior employee who helps develop a less experienced employee (the protégé). Most mentoring relationships develop informally as a result of interests or values shared by mentor and protégé. Research suggests that employees with certain personality characteristics (e.g., high needs for power and achievement, emotional stability, ability to adapt their behavior based on the situation) are more likely to seek a mentor and be an attractive protégé for a mentor.[55]

Mentoring relationships can also develop as part of a planned company effort to bring together successful senior employees with less experienced employees (a formal mentoring programs).

KLA-Tencor, a supplier of process control solutions for the semiconductor industry, uses mentoring to improve senior managers' skills.[56] The senior managers receive mentoring from company board members as well as retired company executives. The senior managers are expected to increase their functional expertise, identify specific performance goals and developmental activities to address job-related weaknesses, and increase their understanding of the company's culture, vision, and political structure. KLA-Tencor also has an online

TABLE 9.10
Characteristics of Successful Formal Mentoring Programs

1. Mentor and protégé participation is voluntary. Relationship can be ended at any time without fear of punishment.
2. Mentor–protégé matching process does not limit the ability of informal relationships to develop. For example, a mentor pool can be established to allow protégés to choose from a variety of qualified mentors.
3. Mentors are chosen on the basis of their past record in developing employees, willingness to serve as a mentor, and evidence of positive coaching, communication, and listening skills.
4. The purpose of the program is clearly understood. Projects and activities that the mentor and protégé are expected to complete are specified.
5. The length of the program is specified. Mentor and protégé are encouraged to pursue the relationship beyond the formal time period.
6. A minimum level of contact between the mentor and protégé is specified.
7. Protégés are encouraged to contact one another to discuss problems and share successes.
8. The mentor program is evaluated. Interviews with mentors and protégés are used to obtain immediate feedback regarding specific areas of dissatisfaction. Surveys are used to gather more detailed information regarding benefits received from participating in the program.
9. Employee development is rewarded, which signals managers that mentoring and other development activities are worth their time and effort.

mentoring program for managers identified as having high potential for upper-level positions. The program includes an automated relationship pairing function and a 360-degree assessment that is used in the mentoring relationship to improve skill weaknesses.

Developing Successful Mentoring Programs Although many mentoring relationships develop informally, one major advantage of formalized mentoring programs is that they ensure access to mentors for all employees, regardless of gender or race. An additional advantage is that participants in the mentoring relationship tend to know what is expected of them.[57] One limitation of formal mentoring programs is that mentors may not be able to provide counseling and coaching in a relationship that has been artificially created.[58]

Table 9.10 presents characteristics of a successful formal mentoring program. A key to successful mentoring programs is that the mentor and protégé actually interact with each other. Face-to-face contact can be difficult, but with e-mail and videoconferencing, virtual mentoring is possible.

Cardinal Health's mentoring program is designed to expose mentors and protégés to the company's different business units (e.g., pharmaceutical formulation, manufacturing, packaging, and distribution) for the purpose of developing managers who have a broad understanding of the Cardinal Health businesses. This cross-unit perspective is especially important because Cardinal Health has grown to be a global business through acquisitions. To ensure that mentors and protégés interact, Cardinal Health's program includes four formal sessions in which mentors and protégés meet at a business location. Both mentors and protégés are expected to make a specific time commitment to the program each month.

Mentors should be chosen based on interpersonal and technical skills. They also need to be trained. For example, New York Hospital–Cornell Medical Center developed a mentoring program for housekeeping employees. Each mentor has 5 to 10 protégés who meet on a quarterly basis. To qualify as mentors, employees must receive outstanding performance evaluations, demonstrate strong interpersonal skills, and be able to perform basic cleaning tasks and essential duties of all housekeeping positions including safety procedures (such as handling infectious waste). Mentors undergo a two-day training program that emphasizes communication skills. They are taught how to convey information about the job and give directions effectively without criticizing employees.[59]

Fannie Mae provides financial products and services that make it possible for families to purchase homes. At Fannie Mae, the company's mentoring program is designed to encourage the advancement of high-potential employees, especially women and minorities.[60] To ensure that the mentor and protégé are compatible, a pairing committee conducts detailed screening and matching based on the mentor's and protégé's interests and expectations (e.g., What skills, experiences, and knowledge would you like your mentor to possess?). Fannie Mae provides guidelines to both mentors and protégés that identify what is expected of the relationship. Orientation sessions help the mentor and protégé become acquainted with each other. Both mentor and protégé sign a confidentiality agreement to build trust between the parties. To help ensure the success of the mentoring program, Fannie Mae uses surveys to conduct formal and informal evaluations that help the company understand the strengths and weaknesses of the program.

Benefits of Mentoring Relationships Both mentors and protégés can benefit from a mentoring relationship. Research suggests that mentors provide career and psychosocial support to their protégés. **Career support** includes coaching, protection, sponsorship, and providing challenging assignments, exposure, and visibility. **Psychosocial support** includes serving as a friend and a role model, providing positive regard and acceptance, and providing an outlet for the protégé to talk about anxieties and fears. Additional benefits for protégés include still development, higher rates of promotion, larger salaries, and greater organizational influence.[61]

Mentoring relationships provide opportunities for mentors to develop their interpersonal skills and increase their feelings of self-esteem and worth to the organization. Adobe Systems, located in San Jose, California, provides digital imaging, design, and document technology for consumers and businesses (you may have read a document using Adobe's PDF file format). For example, Melissa Dyrdahl, a manager at Adobe Systems, and Bruce Chizen, a senior vice president at Adobe, have multiple mentors that they benefit from.[62] Chizen considers the founders of Adobe as mentors. The founders have taught him how to preserve the company's culture by hiring people smarter than he is. The founders' technical creativity has inspired him to offer new ideas to engineers at the company. He knows that the founders care about him personally but are honest in their opinions. Dyrdahl considers one of the Abode board members a mentor. She asked the mentor for career advice and exposure to new ideas without changing jobs. Her mentor encouraged her to pursue a seat on a public company board of directors, especially a company needing her marketing skills. Another of Dyrdahl's mentors, who works for a marketing agency, has encouraged her to advance her career by highlighting her accomplishments to others.

For individuals in management positions as well as technical fields such as engineering and health services, the protégé may help them gain knowledge about important new scientific developments in their field and therefore prevent them from becoming technically obsolete. For example, General Electric recently launched an initiative in e-business. However, many veteran managers faced the challenge of trying to understand how to effectively use the Internet. John Welch, then CEO of General Electric, created a mentoring program for his top 600 managers in which younger employees who were experienced with the Internet served as mentors for the top managers.[63] Welch generated interest in the program by getting his own mentor, who was approximately half his age and had much less business experience than he does. However, she was a Web expert who ran the company's website! The purpose of the program was to help managers to become familiar with competitors' websites, to experience the difficulty of ordering products online, and to understand what the best websites are doing well. Welch started the program believing that e-business knowledge is generally inversely related to age and position in the company hierarchy— younger employees at the lower levels of the organization are more Web-savvy. GE managers meet with their younger mentors for Web lessons, where they critique websites, discuss assigned articles and books about e-commerce, and ask questions. The sessions benefited both the mentor and the protégé. The protégés learned about the Web, and the mentoring sessions made the younger employees feel more comfortable talking to their bosses while learning about the skills that a manager needs to run a large business operation (e.g., ability to communicate with different people).

Purposes of Mentoring Programs   One estimate is that about 20 percent of companies have a formal mentoring program.[64] The purpose of these programs varies. Mentor programs are used to socialize new employees and to increase the likelihood of skill transfer from training to the work setting. Mentor programs may also be developed specifically for women and minorities to enable them to gain the experience and skills needed for managerial positions. Mentoring programs can also be used to develop managers for top-level management positions or to help them acquire specific skills. Consider the New York Hospital–Cornell Medical Center mentoring program just discussed. The program is designed to help new employees more quickly learn housekeeping duties and understand the culture of the hospital. One benefit of the program is that new employees' performance deficiencies are more quickly corrected. Although formal mentoring of new employees lasts only two weeks, mentors are available to provide support many months later.

Steve Croft and Janet Graham have met at least once a month for the past two years to share problems, information, and advice at E. I. du Pont de Nemours and Company corporate headquarters.[65] He is a planning manager in the company's research division. She is an administrative assistant in the toxicology lab where Steve Croft used to work. Croft and Graham are part of the DuPont Company's eight-year-old mentoring program. Mentees choose from a list of volunteer mentors (managers and executives) whose skills and experience they want to learn about. Croft, the mentor, has provided Graham, the mentee, with answers to her questions about corporate programs and has given her the opportunity to meet scientists and managers in the company. Graham has also learned more about other departments' roles in the company and about budgetary priorities. Croft has also benefited from the relationship. He has learned how management decisions affect employees. For example, when the toxicology lab was forced to begin to charge departments for its services (rather than being supported from the company's general fund), Croft learned about employees' reactions and anxieties from Graham.

Group mentoring programs have been initiated by some companies that lack potential mentors or a formal reward system supporting mentoring or that believe that the quality of mentorships developed in a formal program is poorer than informal mentoring relationships. In **group mentoring programs,** a successful senior employee is paired with four to six less experienced protégés. One potential advantage of the mentoring group is that protégés can learn from each other as well as from a more experienced senior employee. The leader helps protégés understand the organization, guides them in analyzing their experiences, and helps them clarify career directions. Each member of the group may have specific assignments to complete, or the group may work together on an issue.[66]

Coaching Relationships

A **coach** is a peer or manager who works with employees to motivate them, help them develop skills, and provide reinforcement and feedback. There are three roles that a coach can play.[67] Part of coaching may be one-on-one with an employee, providing feedback based on psychological tests, 360-degree assessment, or interviews with bosses, peers, and subordinates. A second role is to help employees learn for themselves by putting them in touch with experts who can help them with their concerns and by teaching them how to obtain feedback from others. Third, the coach may provide the employee with resources such as mentors, courses, or job experiences that the employee may not otherwise have access to. For example, at National Semiconductor, managers participate in a 360-degree feedback program. Each manager selects another manager as a coach. They both attend a coaching workshop that focuses on skills such as active listening. The workshop presents a coaching process that includes creating a contract outlining members' roles and expectations, discussing 360-degree feedback, and identifying specific improvement goals and a plan for achieving them. After each pair works alone for six to eight months, they evaluate their progress.

The best coaches are empathetic, tough, practical, interested in helping others do better, and self-confident. Coaches need to be able to suggest effective improvement actions and must respect employee confidentiality. If assessment instruments are part of the coaching process, the coach must be familiar with them.

Some companies are using coaching specifically to groom future chief executive officers.[68] Several companies (including Toys 'R' Us and Coca-Cola) unfortunately discovered the development needs of newly appointed CEOs too late. The new CEOs had been successful in their previous jobs, but were quickly forced out of their new positions. An executive director with a telecommunications and outsourcing company was known for his tough management style.[69] He tended to fire poorly performing employees in a brusque and unfeeling manner. Employees who did satisfactory work were treated coldly; they received infrequent praise and were publicly criticized for mistakes. Eventually, this manager's style kept him from moving into higher management levels. Based on complaints that he was a "toxic manager," the company hired a coach to work with him. The coach put him through a series of psychological tests and asked for assessment from former bosses, peers, and subordinates. Based on the assessments and tests, the manager learned that he saw people as instruments to get things done but he didn't concern himself with their feelings. The coach helped the manager make a list of desired behaviors and gave him homework in which he focused on one person a week, emphasizing the positive things the person did. After coaching and feedback, the manager has learned to concentrate on fixing problems, not criticizing the person who made the mistake.

Training programs that develop coaching skills need to focus on four issues related to managers' reluctance to provide coaching.[70] First, managers may be reluctant to discuss performance issues even with a competent employee because they want to avoid confrontation—especially if the manager is less of an expert than the employee. Second, managers may be better able to identify performance problems than to help employees solve them.

Third, managers may feel that the employee might interpret coaching as criticism. Fourth, as companies downsize and operate with fewer employees, managers may feel that there is not enough time for coaching. For example, a middle manager at PG&E, an energy company, was hurting her relationships with her associates, and her career, by her brash personality.[71] PG&E hired a coach to work with her. The coach videotaped her as she role-played an actual clash that she had had with another manager over a new information system. During the confrontation (and the role play), she was aloof, abrasive, cold, and condescending. The coach helped her see the limitations of her approach. She apologized to the colleague and listened to the colleague's ideas. Coaching helped this manager learn how to maintain her composure and focus on what is being said rather than on the person.

THE DEVELOPMENT PLANNING PROCESS

The **development planning process** involves identifying development needs, choosing a development goal, identifying the actions that need to be taken by the employee and the company to achieve the goal, determining how progress toward goal attainment will be measured, investing time and energy to achieve the goal, and establishing a timetable for development.[72] Table 9.11 shows the development planning process, identifying responsibilities of employees and the company. An emerging trend in development is that the employee must initiate the development planning process.[73] Note that the development approach is dependent on the needs and developmental goal. To identify development needs, employees must consider what they want to do, what they are interested in doing, what they can do, and what others expect of them. A development need can result from gaps between current capabilities and/or interests and the type of work or position that the employee wants in the future.

TABLE 9.11 **Responsibilities in the Development Planning Process**

Development Planning Process	Employee Responsibility	Company Responsibility
Opportunity	How do I need to improve?	Company provides assessment information to identify strengths, weaknesses, interests, and values.
Motivation	Am I willing to invest the time and energy to develop?	Company assists in identifying personal and company reasons for change. Manager discusses steps for dealing with barriers and challenges to development.
Goal Identification	What do I want to develop?	Company provides development planning guide. Manager has developmental discussion with employee.
Criteria	How will I know I am making progress?	Manager provides feedback on criteria.
Actions	What will I do to reach my development goal?	Company provides assessment, courses, job experiences, and relationships.
Accountability	What is my timetable? How can I ask others for feedback on progress toward my goal?	Manager follows up on progress toward development goal and helps employee set a realistic timetable for goal achievement.

The company responsibility is primarily taken by the employee's manager. The role of the manager in development planning is to provide coaching, communicate information about development opportunities (e.g., job experiences, courses), help eliminate barriers to development, and refer the employee to other people (human resources) and resources (assessment tools). Managers must also help employees set realistic development goals and measure their progress in attaining them.

How might the development planning process work? Take the example of Robert Brown, a program manager in an information systems department. He needs to increase his knowledge of available project management software. His performance appraisal indicated that only 60 percent of the projects he is working on are being approved due to incomplete information. (Assessment identified his development need.) As a result, Robert and his manager agree that his development goal is to increase his knowledge of available project management software. This software can increase his effectiveness in project management. To boost his knowledge of such software, Robert will read articles (formal education), meet with software vendors, and contact vendors' customers for their evaluations of the project management software they have used (job experiences). His manager will provide the names of customers to contact. Robert and his manager set six months as the target date for completing these activities.

COMPANY STRATEGIES FOR PROVIDING DEVELOPMENT

There are several company strategies for providing development. One strategy is to provide development only for top-level executives, senior managers, and employees identified as having high potential. Lower-level managers who play a critical role in motivating and retaining employees are neglected. Another strategy is to require all employees to devote a specific number of hours or spend a certain amount of money on development. While this approach guarantees that employees will partake in development, it tends to emphasize formal courses as the only viable development method. This is counter to adult learning theory (see Chapter 4), which emphasizes that adults want to interact in the learning process and are more motivated to learn when they get to choose the learning topics and the delivery method (e.g., classroom, mentoring, job experiences).

The most effective development strategies involve individualization, learner control, and ongoing support.[74] Individualization makes sure that development efforts are directed at the employee's weaknesses. Personality and interest inventories as well as 360-degree feedback provide information about an employee's interests, values, strengths, and weaknesses. Instead of requiring employees to attend courses or workshops, companies should offer a menu of development options. These might include courses offered in the classroom or on the Web, mentoring, discussion groups, support networks, and job experiences.

Nationwide Financial, a 5,000-employee life insurance company based in Columbus, Ohio, found that their management development program contained four kinds of prospective managers.[75] The first category, reluctant leaders, have all the necessary skills to be successful managers but lack confidence. Arrogant leaders, the second category, believe they have all the leadership skills they need. The problem is that they lack empathy and humility. Unknown leaders have the right skills but their talents are unknown to top managers in the company. Workaholics, the final category, have been rewarded for spending long hours at work, but they lack the perspective and personality to successfully manage others. Nationwide Financial tries to tailor development to the needs of the four types of prospective leaders. The company's development activities include coaching, mentoring, job experiences, training classes, and feedback sessions. For example, one reluctant leader's development focused on 360-degree feedback to show her that she already had strong managerial skills. The prospective manager was asked to work on hypothetical managerial problems with a coach and mentor. As she became more expert at thinking through managerial decisions, she gained confidence and learned to trust her own thinking, business knowledge, and decision-making ability.

Booz Allen Hamilton, a strategy and technology consulting company headquartered in McLean, Virginia, uses a program they call the Development Framework to help managers and employees choose the right combination of development activities to strengthen competencies.[76] The Development Framework consists of four sections:

1. *Development roles:* Managers, mentors, development staff, and other roles in the development process.
2. *Performance expectations:* A description of competencies, performance results, and major job experiences required to succeed at each level of the company.
3. *Development needs:* Needs that frequently occur at each career level, those that vary by individual, and the derailers that can stall career progress and negatively affect performance. Ways to prevent or deal with derailers are provided.
4. *Development road map:* Descriptions of development activities that should occur at each career level and that support development needs and prevent derailers. These activities include job experiences, training and education, coaching and mentoring, and self-directed experiences.

Employees can access the Development Framework online via the company's virtual campus and website. Managers can use the tool to discuss development needs in their departments. The framework includes the competencies for each staff level and for each employee, which allows employees to view their personal development needs online. By identifying the competencies that employees want to strengthen, the framework provides a list of activities employees can use to develop those competencies. Employees can use Development Framework to take charge of their own careers. The framework helps employees answer questions such as "I'm at this level and this person is above me; how can I get there?"

The framework was provided by Booz Allen Hamilton to help employees better understand how to develop themselves. Booz Allen views development as a shared responsibility between employees and the company. The framework helps employees realize that development can occur through activities other than training classes. The framework makes a strong business case for employee development by aligning development to the business strategy and to different levels of the company; the program provides a process for simultaneously building the company's intellectual capital and helping employees build successful careers. The framework also provides a map for preparing potential leaders, which is important because the company is growing 20 percent per year.

E-Learning and Employee Development

With the development of e-learning, many companies are moving development activities online. For example, IBM's "Basic Blue for Managers" program replaces a widely successful New Manager School.[77] The yearlong program includes a combination of online self-study, simulations, competency assessment, coaching, and classroom experience. The program helps managers understand their responsibilities in managing performance, employee relations, diversity, and multicultural issues. It moves the learning of all basic management skills to the Web, using classroom experiences for more complex management issues. It also gives managers and their bosses greater responsibility for development, while the company provides support in the form of unlimited access to development activities and support networks. The learning model includes four levels:

1. *Management Quick Views:* Management Quick Views provide practical information on more than 40 common management topics related to business, leadership/management competencies, productivity, and HR issues.
2. *Interactive Learning Modules and Simulations:* These interactive simulations emphasize people and task management. Employees learn by viewing videos; interacting with models and problem employees; making decisions on how to deal with the problem, issue, or request; and getting feedback on their decision. Case studies are also available for review.
3. *Collaborative Learning:* The learner can connect via the company intranet with tutors, team members, customers, or other learners to discuss problems, issues, and approaches and to share learnings.
4. *Learning Labs:* These five-day in-class workshops build on the learnings acquired during the previous phases of e-learning. The workshops emphasize peer learning and the development of a learning community. Through challenging activities and assignments, managers gain increased self-awareness of themselves, their work teams, and IBM.

Management Quick Views, Interactive Learning Modules and Simulations, and Collaborative Learning are delivered by technology. Learning Labs is a face-to-face classroom experience. The Basic Blue for Managers program recognizes the role of the boss as coach, supporter, and role model. The boss is involved in the program through coaching and feedback, on-the-job learning experiences, assessment of the manager's development needs and progress, and assistance in completing individual development plans.

IBM believes that utilization of e-learning and the classroom environment enables managers to participate in self-directed learning, try out skills in a "safe" environment, gain access to communities of learning, and use just-in-time learning. The advantages of e-learning are complemented by the strengths of an interactive classroom experience and support from the manager's boss to create the best development program possible. Evaluations of the program have been positive. Participants report satisfaction with program content and delivery. Nearly all the participants have achieved mastery in the 15 subject areas included in the program. Program alumni report that business value related to leadership skill improvement averages $450,000 per employee.

Summary

This chapter emphasized that there are several development methods: formal education, assessment, job experiences, and interpersonal relationships. Most companies use one or more of these approaches to develop employees. Formal education involves enrolling employees in courses or seminars offered by the company or educational institutions. Assessment involves measuring the employees' performance, behavior, skills, and/or personality characteristics. Job experiences include job enlargement, rotating to a new job, promotions, downward moves, temporary assignments, and transfers. A more experienced senior employee (a mentor) can help employees understand the company and gain exposure and visibility to key persons in the organization. Part of a manager's job responsibility may be to coach employees. Regardless of the development approach used, employees need a development plan to identify the type of development needed, development goals, the best approach for development, and a means to determine whether development goals have been reached. For development plans to be effective, the employee, the company, and managers all have responsibilities that need to be completed. An effective development strategy involves individualization, learner control, and support. Development programs based on e-learning can provide these features.

Key Terms

development, *266*
formal education
programs, *269*
assessment, *272*
Myers-Briggs Type
Indicator® (MBTI), *273*
assessment center, *275*
leaderless group
discussion, *276*
in-basket, *276*

role plays, *276*
Benchmarks©, *277*
performance appraisal, *277*
upward feedback, *278*
360-degree feedback, *278*
job experiences, *281*
job enlargement, *282*
job rotation, *284*
transfer, *285*
promotions, *285*

downward move, *286*
externship, *286*
mentor, *287*
career support, *289*
psychosocial support, *289*
group mentoring
programs, *290*
coach, *291*
development planning
process, *292*

Discussion Questions

1. How could assessment be used to create a productive work team?
2. How can competencies be used in employee development?
3. List and explain the characteristics of effective 360-degree feedback systems.
4. Why do companies develop formal mentoring programs? What are the potential benefits for the mentor and for the protégé?
5. Your boss is interested in hiring a consultant to help identify potential managers from current employees of a fast-food restaurant. The manager's job is to help wait on customers and prepare food during busy times, oversee all aspects of restaurant operations (including scheduling, maintenance, on-the-job training, and food purchase), and motivate employees to provide high-quality service. The manager is also responsible for resolving disputes between employees. The position involves working under stress and coordinating several activities at one time. Your boss asks you to outline the type of assessment program you believe would best identify employees who could be successful managers. What will you tell your boss?
6. Many employees are unwilling to relocate geographically because they like their current community and because spouses and children prefer not to move. As a result, it is difficult to develop employees through job experiences that require relocation (e.g., transfer to a new location). How could an employee's current job be changed to develop that employee's leadership skills?
7. What is coaching? Is there only one type of coaching? Explain.

8. Discuss reasons why many managers are reluctant to coach their employees.

9. Discuss the characteristics of the most effective company development strategies. Which characteristic do you believe is most important? Why?

Application Assignments

1. Your manager wants you to develop a one-page form for development planning. Develop the form. Provide a rationale for each category you include on the form.

2. Read the article "Baby Boomers Seek New Ways to Escape Career Claustrophobia in the *Wall Street Journal,* June 24, 2003: B1. It describes the challenges of motivating managers who have limited opportunities for advancement. Write a two-page memo outlining your recommendations for developing managers who are stuck in their jobs or feel underutilized.

3. Go to General Electric's website at *www.gecareers.com.* Click on Leadership Programs. Review the entry-level leadership and experienced leadership programs. Overall, what type of development activities are included in these programs? Choose one program and describe it (development activities, length, participants). Compare the development activities used in the entry-level and experienced leadership programs. How are they similar? How are they different? Why might they differ?

4. Go to *www.keirsey.com.* Complete the Keirsey Temperament Sorter or the Keirsey Character Sorter. These are examples of assessment instruments that can be used for development. What did you learn about yourself? How could the instrument you completed be useful for management development? What might be some disadvantages of using this instrument?

Endnotes

1. M. London, *Managing the Training Enterprise* (San Francisco: Jossey-Bass, 1989); C. McCauley and S. Heslett, "Individual Development in the Workplace," in *Handbook of Industrial, Work, and Organizational Psychology*, vol. 1, ed. N. Anderson, D. Ones, H. Sinangil, and C. Viswesvaran (London: Sage Publications, 2001): 313–35.

2. R. W. Pace, P. C. Smith, and G. E. Mills, *Human Resource Development* (Englewood Cliffs, NJ: Prentice-Hall, 1991); W. Fitzgerald, "Training versus Development," *Training and Development Journal* (May 1992): 81–84; R. A. Noe, S. L. Wilk, E. J. Mullen, and J. E. Wanek, "Employee Development: Issues in Construct Definition and Investigation of Antecedents," in *Improving Training Effectiveness in Work Organizations,* ed. J. K. Ford (Mahwah, NJ: Lawrence Erlbaum, 1997): 153–89.

3. C. Taylor, "Focus on Talent," *T&D* (December 2002): 26–31.

4. R. J. Campbell, "HR Development Strategies," in *Developing Human Resources,* ed. K. N. Wexley (Washington, DC: BNA Books. 1991): 5–1 to 5–34; M. A. Sheppeck and C. A. Rhodes, "Management Development: Revised Thinking in Light of New Events of Strategic Importance," *Human Resource Planning* 11 (1988): 159–72; B. Keys and J. Wolf, "Management Education: Current Issues and Emerging Trends," *Journal of Management* 14 (1988): 205–29; L. M. Saari, T. R. Johnson, S. D. McLaughlin, and D. Zimmerle, "A Survey of Management Training and Education Practices in U.S. Companies," *Personnel Psychology* 41 (1988): 731–44.

5. Cardinal Health a Tradition of Performance (Dublin, Ohio: Cardinal Health, 2003), brochure.

6. C. Cornell, "Fail Safe," *Human Resource Executive* (June 2, 2003): 33–36.

7. J. Ronan, "A Boot to the System," *T&D* (March 2003): 38–45.

8. T. A. Stewart, "GE Keeps Those Ideas Coming," *Fortune* (August 12, 1991): 41–49; N. M. Tichy, "GE's Crotonville: A Staging Ground for a Corporate Revolution," *The Executive* 3 (1989): 99–106.

9. J. Bolt, *Executive Development* (New York: Harper Business, 1989); H. S. Jonas, R. E. Fry, and S. Srivasta, "The Office of the CEO: Understanding the Executive Experience," *Academy of Management Executive* 4 (1990): 36–48; J. Noel and R. Charam, "GE Brings Global Thinking to Light," *Training and Development Journal* (July 1992): 29–33; B. O'Reilly, "How Execs Learn Now," *Fortune* (April 5, 1993); M. A. Hitt, B. B. Tyler, C. Hardee, and D. Park, "Understanding Strategic Intent in the Global Marketplace," *Academy of Management Executive* 9 (1995): 12–19.

10. J. A. Byrne, "Virtual Business Schools," *Business Week* (October 23, 1995): 64–68.

11. J. Reingold, "How B-Schools Are Making It Easier to Juggle Work, Classes, and Family," *Business Week On-line,* October 18, 1999, *www.businessweek.com.*

12. J. Reingold, "Corporate America Goes to School," *Business Week* (October 20, 1997): 66–72.

13. Ibid.

14. L. Bongiorno, "How'm I Doing," *Business Week* (October 23, 1995): 72, 74.

15. M. Schneider and B. Hindo, "A Midcareer Boost," *Business Week Online,* October 15, 2001, *www.businessweek.com.*

16. T. A. Stewart, "GE Keeps Those Ideas Coming," *Fortune* (August 12, 1991): 41–49.

17. G. P. Hollenbeck, "What Did You Learn in School? Studies of a University Executive Program," *Human Resource Planning* 14 (1991): 247–60.

18. A. Howard and D. W. Bray, *Managerial Lives in Transition: Advancing Age and Changing Times* (New York: Guilford, 1988); Bolt, *Executive Development;* J. R. Hinrichs and G. P. Hollenbeck, "Leadership Development," in K. N. Wexley (ed), *Developing Human Resources,* 5–221 to 5–237.

19. S. K. Hirsch, *MBTI Team Member's Guide* (Palo Alto, CA: Consulting Psychologists Press, 1992); A.L. Hammer, *Introduction to Type and Careers* (Palo Alto, CA: Consulting Psychologists Press, 1993).

20. A. Thorne and H. Gough, *Portraits of Type* (Palo Alto, CA: Consulting Psychologists Press, 1991).

21. D. Druckman and R. A. Bjork, *In the Mind's Eye: Enhancing Human Performance* (Washington, DC: National Academy Press, 1991); M. H. McCaulley, "The Myers-Briggs Type Indicator and Leadership," in *Measures of Leadership,* eds. K. E. Clark and M. B. Clark (West Orange, NJ: Leadership Library of America, 1990): 381–418.

22. G. C. Thornton III and W. C. Byham, *Assessment Centers and Managerial Performance* (New York: Academic Press, 1982); L. F. Schoenfeldt and J. A. Steger, "Identification and Development of Management Talent," in *Research in Personnel and Human Resource Management,* vol. 7, eds. K. N. Rowland and G. Ferris (Greenwich, CT: JAI Press, 1989): 151–81.

23. Thornton and Byham, *Assessment Centers and Managerial Performance.*

24. B. B. Gaugler, D. B. Rosenthal, G. C. Thornton, III, and C. Bentson, "Meta-analysis of Assessment Center Validity," *Journal of Applied Psychology* 72 (1987): 493–511; D. W. Bray, R. J. Campbell, and D. L. Grant, *Formative Years in Business: A Long-Term AT&T Study of Managerial Lives* (New York: Wiley, 1974).

25. R. G. Jones and M. D. Whitmore, "Evaluating Developmental Assessment Centers as Interventions," *Personnel Psychology* 48 (1995): 377–88.

26. J. Schettler, "Building Bench Strength," *Training* (June 2002): 55–58.

27. C. D. McCauley and M. M. Lombardo, "Benchmarks: An Instrument for Diagnosing Managerial Strengths and Weaknesses," in Clark and Clark, *Measures of Leadership,* 535–45.

28. C. D. McCauley, M. M. Lombardo, and C. J. Usher, "Diagnosing Management Development Needs: An Instrument Based on How Managers Develop," *Journal of Management* 15 (1989): 389–403.

29. S. B. Silverman, "Individual Development through Performance Appraisal," in K. N. Wexley (ed), *Developing Human Resources,* 5–120 to 5–151.

30. J. S. Lublin, "Turning the Tables: Underlings Evaluate Bosses," *The Wall Street Journal,* October 4, 1994: B1, B14; B. O'Reilly, "360 Feedback Can Change Your Life," *Fortune* (October 17, 1994): 93–100; J. F. Milliman, R. A. Zawacki, C. Norman, L. Powell, and J. Kirksey, "Companies Evaluate Employees from All Perspectives," *Personnel Journal* (November 1994): 99–103.

31. S. Caudron, "Building Better Bosses," *Workforce* (May 2000): 33–39.

32. Center for Creative Leadership, *Skillscope for Managers: Development Planning Guide* (Greensboro, NC: Center for Creative Leadership, 1992); G. Yukl and R. Lepsinger, "360 Feedback," *Training* (December 1995): 45–50.

33. L. Atwater, P. Roush, and A. Fischthal, "The Influence of Upward Feedback on Self- and Follower Ratings of Leadership," *Personnel Psychology* 48 (1995): 35–59; J. F. Hazucha, S. A. Hezlett, and R. J. Schneider, "The Impact of 360-Degree Feedback on Management Skill Development," *Human Resource Management* 32 (1993): 325–51; J. W. Smither, M. London, N. Vasilopoulos, R. R. Reilly, R. E. Millsap, and N. Salvemini, "An Examination of the Effects of an Upward Feedback Program Over Time," *Personnel Psychology* 48 (1995): 1–34; J. Johnson and K. Ferstl, "The Effects of Interrater and Self-Other Agreement on Performance Improvement following Feedback," *Personnel Psychology* 2 (1999): 271–303.

34. D. Bracken, "Straight Talk about Multirater Feedback," *Training and Development* (September 1994): 44–51; K. Nowack, J. Hartley, and W. Bradley, "How to Evaluate Your 360 Feedback Efforts," *Training and Development* (April 1999): 48–52.

35. A. Freedman, "The Evolution of 360s," *Human Resource Executive* (December 2002): 47–51.

36. C. Seifert, G. Yukl, and R. McDonald, "Effects of Multisource Feedback and a Feedback Facilitator on the Influence Behavior of Managers toward Subordinates," *Journal of Applied Psychology* 88 (2003): 561–69.

37. M. W. McCall, Jr., M. M. Lombardo, and A. M. Morrison, *Lessons of Experience* (Lexington, MA: Lexington Books, 1988).

38. R. S. Snell, "Congenial Ways of Learning: So Near Yet So Far," *Journal of Management Development* 9 (1990): 17–23.

39. C. Cornell, "Fail Safe."

40. McCall, Lombardo, and Morrison, *Lessons of Experience;* M. W. McCall, "Developing Executives through Work Experiences," *Human Resource Planning* 11 (1988): 1–11; M. N. Ruderman, P. J. Ohlott, and C. D. McCauley, "Assessing Opportunities for Leadership Development," in Clark and Clark, *Measures of Leadership,* 547–62; C. D. McCauley, L. J. Estman, and P. J. Ohlott, "Linking Management Selection and Development through Stretch Assignments," *Human Resource Management* 34 (1995): 93–115.

41. C. D. McCauley, M. N. Ruderman, P. J. Ohlott, and J. E. Morrow, "Assessing the Developmental Components of Managerial Jobs," *Journal of Applied Psychology* 79 (1994): 544–60.

42. B. Gerber, "Who Will Replace Those Vanishing Executives?" *Training* (July 2000): 49–53.

43. T. Galvin, "Best Practice: Job Rotation, Arrow Electronics," *Training* (March 2003): 59.

44. M. Solomon, "Trading Places," *ComputerWorld*, November 5, 2002, *www.computerworld.com/careertopics/careers/labor/story/0,10801,75527,00.html.*

45. M. London, *Developing Managers* (San Francisco: Jossey-Bass, 1985); M. A. Campion, L. Cheraskin, and M. J. Stevens, "Career-Related Antecedents and Outcomes of Job Rotation," *Academy of Management Journal* 37 (1994): 1518–42; M. London, *Managing the Training Enterprise* (San Francisco: Jossey-Bass, 1989).

46. D. C. Feldman, *Managing Careers in Organizations* (Glenview, IL: Scott-Foresman, 1988).

47. J. M. Brett, L. K. Stroh, and A. H. Reilly, "Job Transfer," in *International Review of Industrial and Organizational Psychology: 1992,* eds. C. L. Cooper and I. T. Robinson (Chichester, England: John Wiley and Sons, 1992); D. C. Feldman and J. M. Brett, "Coping with New Jobs: A Comparative Study of New Hires and Job Changers," *Academy of Management Journal* 26 (1983): 258–72.

48. R. A. Noe, B. D. Steffy, and A. E. Barber, "An Investigation of the Factors Influencing Employees' Willingness to Accept Mobility Opportunities," *Personnel Psychology* 41 (1988): 559–80; S. Gould and L. E. Penley, "A Study of the Correlates of Willingness to Relocate," *Academy of Management Journal* 28 (1984): 472–78; J. Landau and T. H. Hammer, "Clerical Employees' Perceptions of Intraorganizational Career Opportunities," *Academy of Management Journal* 29 (1986): 385–405; R. P. Duncan and C. C. Perruci, "Dual Occupation Families and Migration," *American Sociological Review* 41 (1976): 252–61; J. M. Brett and A. H. Reilly, "On the Road Again: Predicting the Job Transfer Decision," *Journal of Applied Psychology* 73 (1988): 614–20.

49. D. T. Hall and L. A. Isabella, "Downward Moves and Career Development," *Organizational Dynamics* 14 (1985): 5–23.

50. H. D. Dewirst, "Career Patterns: Mobility, Specialization, and Related Career Issues," in *Contemporary Career Development Issues,* eds. R. F. Morrison and J. Adams (Hillsdale, NJ: Lawrence Erlbaum, 1991): 73–108.

51. N. C. Tompkins, "GTE Managers on the Move," *Personnel Journal* (August 1992): 86–91.

52. J. M. Brett, "Job Transfer and Well-Being," *Journal of Applied Psychology* 67 (1992): 450–63; F. J. Minor, L. A. Slade, and R. A. Myers, "Career Transitions in Changing Times," in Morrison and Adams, *Contemporary Career Development Issues,* 109–20; C. C. Pinder and K. G. Schroeder, "Time to Proficiency Following Job Transfers," *Academy of Management Journal* 30 (1987): 336–53; G. Flynn, "Heck No—We Won't Go!" *Personnel Journal* (March 1996): 37–43.

53. R. E. Silverman, "Mercer Tries to Keep Employees through Its 'Externship' Program," *The Wall Street Journal,* November 7, 2000: B18.

54. D. Gunsch, "Customer Service Focus Prompts Employee Exchange," *Personnel Journal* (October 1992): 32–38.

55. D. B. Turban and T. W. Dougherty, "Role of Protégé Personality in Receipt of Mentoring and Career Success," *Academy of Management Journal* 37 (1994): 688–702; E. A. Fagenson, "Mentoring: Who Needs It? A Comparison of Protégés' and Nonprotégés' Needs for Power, Achievement, Affiliation, and Autonomy," *Journal of Vocational Behavior* 41 (1992): 48–60.

56. T. Galvin, "Best Practices: Mentoring, KLA-Tencor Corp," *Training* (March 2003): 58.

57. A. H. Geiger, "Measures for Mentors," *Training and Development Journal* (February 1992): 65–67; K. Dunham, "Mentors May Not Help," *The Wall Street Journal* (September 23, 2003): B8.

58. K. E. Kram, *Mentoring at Work: Developmental Relationships in Organizational Life* (Glenview, IL: Scott-Foresman, 1985); L. L. Phillips-Jones, "Establishing a Formalized Mentoring Program," *Training and Development Journal* 2 (1983): 38–42; K. Kram, "Phases of the Mentoring Relationship," *Academy of Management Journal* 26 (1983): 608–25; G. T. Chao, P. M. Walz, and P. D. Gardner, "Formal and Informal Mentorships: A Comparison of Mentoring Functions and Contrasts with Nonmentored Counterparts," *Personnel Psychology* 45 (1992): 619–36; B. Ragins, J. Cotton, and J. Miller, "Marginal Mentoring: The Effects of Type of Mentor, Quality of Relationship, and the Program Design on Work and Career Attitudes," *Academy of Management Journal* 43 (2000): 1177–94.

59. C. M. Solomon, "Hotel Breathes Life into Hospital's Customer Service," *Personnel Journal* (October 1995): 120.

60. A. Poe, "Establishing Positive Mentoring Relationships," *HR Magazine* (February 2002): 62–69.

61. G. F. Dreher and R. A. Ash, "A Comparative Study of Mentoring among Men and Women in Managerial, Professional, and Technical Positions," *Journal of Applied Psychology* 75 (1990): 539–46; J. L. Wilbur, "Does Mentoring Breed Success?" *Training and Development Journal* 41 (1987): 38–41; R. A. Noe, "Mentoring Relationships for Employee Development," in *Applying Psychology in Business: The Handbook for Managers and Human Resource Professionals,* eds. J. W. Jones, B. D. Steffy, and D. W. Bray (Lexington, MA: Lexington Books, 1991): 475–82; M. M. Fagh and K. Ayers, Jr., "Police Mentors," *FBI Law Enforcement Bulletin* (January 1985): 8–13; Kram, "Phases of the Mentoring Relationship"; R. A. Noe, "An Investigation of the Determinants of Successful Assigned Mentoring Relationships," *Personnel Psychology* 41 (1988): 457–79; B. J. Tepper, "Upward Maintenance Tactics in Supervisory Mentoring and Nonmentoring Relationships," *Academy of Management Journal* 38 (1995): 1191–205; B. R. Ragins and

T. A. Scandura, "Gender Differences in Expected Outcomes of Mentoring Relationships," *Academy of Management Journal* 37 (1994): 957–71; M. Lankau and T. Scandura, "An Investigation of Personal Learning in Mentoring Relationships: Content, Antecedents, and Consequences," *Academy of Management Journal* 45 (2002): 779–90.

62. J. Lublin, "Even Top Executives Could Use Mentors to Benefit Careers," *The Wall Street Journal,* July 1, 2003: B1.

63. M. Murray, "GE Mentoring Program Turns Underlings into Teachers of the Web," *The Wall Street Journal,* February 15, 2000: B1, B16.

64. C. Douglas and C. McCauley, "Formal Development Relationships: A Survey of Organizational Practices," *Human Resource Development Quarterly* 10 (1999): 203–21.

65. F. Jossi, "Mentoring in Changing Times," *Training* (August 1997): 50–54.

66. B. Kaye and B. Jackson, "Mentoring: A Group Guide," *Training and Development* (April 1995): 23–27.

67. D. B. Peterson and M. D. Hicks, *Leader as Coach* (Minneapolis, MN: Personnel Decisions, 1996); L. Thach and T. Heinselman, "Executive Coaching Defined," *Training and Development* (March 1999): 200–4; D. Cole, "Even Executives Can Use Help from the Sidelines," *The New York Times,* November 5, 2002, *www.nytimes.com/2002/10/29/ business/businessspecial/29COLE.html.*

68. J. S. Lublin, "Building a Better CEO," *The Wall Street Journal,* April 14, 2000: B1, B4; J. W. Smither and S. Reilly, "Coaching in Organizations: A Social Psychological Perspective," In *How People Evaluate Others in Organizations,* ed. M. London (Mahwah, NJ: Erlbaum, 2001).

69. H. Lancaster, "Given a Second Chance, a Boss Learns to Favor Carrots over Sticks," *The Wall Street Journal,* November 30, 1999: B1.

70. R. Zemke, "The Corporate Coach," *Training* (December 1996): 24–28.

71. J. Lublin, "Did I Just Say That?! How You Can Recover from Foot-in-Mouth," *The Wall Street Journal,* June 18, 2002: B1.

72. L. Summers, "A Logical Approach to Development Planning," *Training and Development* 48 (1994): 22–31; D. B. Peterson and M. D. Hicks, *Development First* (Minneapolis, MN: Personnel Decisions, 1995); D. Peterson, "Management Development," In *Creating, Implementing, and Managing Effective Training and Development,* ed. K. Kraiger (San Francisco: Jossey-Bass, 2002): 160–91.

73. D. T. Jaffe and C. D. Scott, "Career Development for Empowerment in a Changing Work World," in *New Directions in Career Planning and the Workplace,* ed. J. M. Kummerow (Palo Alto, CA: Consulting Psychologists Press, 1991): 33–60.

74. S. Caudron, "Building Better Bosses," *Workforce* (May 2000): 33–39.

75. N. Griffin, "Personalize Your Management Development," *Harvard Business Review* (March 2003): 113–19.

76. G. Johnson, "The Development Framework," *Training* (February 2003):32–36.

77. N. Lewis and P. Orton, "The Five Attributes of Innovative E-Learning," *Training and Development* (June 2000): 47–51; K. Mantyla, *Blending E-Learning* (Alexandria, VA: ASTD, 2001).

Chapter **Ten**

Special Issues in Training and Employee Development

Objectives

After reading this chapter, you should be able to

1. Discuss the potential legal issues that relate to training.

2. Develop a program for effectively managing diversity.

3. Design a program for preparing employees for cross-cultural assignments.

4. Discuss the implications of a skill-based pay plan for training.

5. Discuss what a trainer needs to do to ensure that school-to-work and hard-core–unemployed training programs are effective.

6. Describe the necessary steps in a program for helping dysfunctional managers.

Capitalizing on Local Talent

Nonprofit groups or employment brokers serve as liaisons between employers and potential employees by developing training programs for low-income workers. The relationship is beneficial for both the employee and the companies. Employees receive wage-paying jobs, and companies throughout a region of the country and within a specific industry get the employees they need. Most of the companies are located in urban areas and help a wide range of people by raising living and working standards. For example, Jane Addams Resource Corporation (JARC) in Chicago was started as an industry-specific training organization in 1985 by local government and area businesses when the metal working and stamping industry needed skilled workers. Chicago-based S&C Electric, a provider of equipment and services for the electric utility industry, partnered with JARC because it could no longer find skilled workers. S&C Electric and JARC worked together to help the company's 1,700 employees improve their machinery skills. Classes were also offered in math and English as a Second Language. Regence BlueShield, part of the Regence Group, which provides health plans in Idaho, Washington, Utah, and Oregon, teamed up with the Seattle Jobs Initiative (SJI) to create a curriculum that would train potential interns for customer service positions at Regence.

SJI tailors its training to the company culture and requires that individuals show up for a 40-hour workweek and dress professionally. Trainees also are evaluated three times during training, similar to what they would encounter in a performance evaluation on the job.

Training partnerships to prepare economically disadvantaged workers benefit both the company and the employees. California-based Tucker Technology, which provides telecommunications installation and maintenance to large companies, was able to build 15 percent of its work force from community-based organizations throughout the country. The company believes that it receives many benefits from hiring through community centers, including a trained work force without the training costs and a highly committed work force with a low turnover rate. Participants of industry-specific training programs were surveyed before they entered the training program and after they completed the program, and the results suggest that the program also offers many benefits for the employees. Most employees improved their position in the labor market, and 66 percent remained employed two years after the survey was conducted. Seventy-eight percent had access to health insurance, paid vacation, sick leave, and a pension plan. Most employees felt that their job and their future employment opportunities were good.

Source: Based on J. Gatewood, "Proactive Partnership," *Human Resource Executive* (May 16, 2003): 36–38; C. Caggiano, "Insider Training," *Inc.* (May 1999): 63–64.

INTRODUCTION

The opening vignette illustrates that trainers are often forced to deal with a wide variety of important issues that fall outside the traditional discussion of the components of instructional system design. S&C Electric, Regence BlueShield, and Tucker Technology recognize that the economically disadvantaged can be talented employees if the company is willing to invest in training. Training not only benefits a company's bottom line but also benefits the community and the individuals who receive jobs. Such training programs are one example of how understanding the larger environment (e.g., the labor market) relates to successful training initiatives.

Other environmental pressures that influence companies include legal issues, globalization, and an increasingly diverse work force. Both trainers and managers who purchase training services must be aware of how legal issues relate to training practices, cross-cultural preparation, diversity training, and school-to-work and hard-core–unemployed training programs. These issues are covered in the first part of this chapter.

The second part of the chapter covers issues that result from pressures from the company's internal environment. These pressures include the need to train managerial talent, provide training and development opportunities for all employees (regardless of their personal characteristics), and motivate employees to learn through the company's compensation system. Specifically, the second half of the chapter covers melting the glass ceiling, joint union-management training programs, succession planning programs, training dysfunctional managers, and skill-based pay systems.

TABLE 10.1
Situations That May Result in Legal Action

- Failing to provide required training
- Incurring employee injury during a training activity
- Incurring injuries to employees or others outside the training session
- Incurring breach of confidentiality or defamation
- Reproducing and using copyrighted material in training classes without permission
- Excluding women, minorities, and older Americans from training programs
- Not ensuring equal treatment while in training
- Requiring employees to attend training programs they find offensive
- Revealing discriminatory information during a training session
- Not accommodating trainees with disabilities
- Incorrectly reporting training as an expense or failing to report training reimbursement as income

TRAINING ISSUES RESULTING FROM THE EXTERNAL ENVIRONMENT

Legal Issues

Table 10.1 shows potential training activities and situations that can make an employer vulnerable to legal actions. The following sections describe each situation and potential implications for training.[1]

Failing to Provide Training

Companies should provide training to reduce the potential for a hostile work environment for employees protected by Title VII of the Civil Rights Act (race, color, gender, religion, nationality, national origin), the Age Discrimination in Employment Act (age) , or the Americans with Disabilities Act (disability).[2] For example, the U.S. Supreme Court considers sexual harassment training to be an important factor for companies that wish to avoid punitive damages in sexual harassment cases. Employers must also train employees to comply with practices designed to prevent harassment of any class protected by Title VII.

Federal laws may require a certain number of training hours and types of training for employees. For example, initial training for flight attendants must include how to handle passengers, use galley equipment, and use the public address system. In several states, candidates interested in being hired as full-time police officers must complete approved police training. Legislation can also require training that is related to providing a drug-free workplace (e.g., training about drug abuse and making counseling available) and a safe work place (e.g., training about the handling of hazardous materials and the use of safety equipment as dictated by the Occupational Safety and Health Act).

Incurring Employee Injury during a Training Activity

On-the-job training and simulations often involve the use of work tools and equipment (e.g., welding machinery, printing press) that could cause injury if incorrectly used. Workers' compensation laws in many states make employers responsible for paying employees their salary and/or providing them with a financial settlement for injuries received during any employment-related activity such as training. Managers should ensure that (1) employees are warned of potential dangers from incorrectly using equipment and (2) safety equipment is used.

Incurring Injuries to Employees or Others Outside a Training Session

Managers should ensure that trainees have the necessary level of competence in knowledge, skills, and behaviors before they are allowed to operate equipment or interact with customers. Even if a company pays for training to be conducted by a vendor, it is still liable for injuries or damages resulting from the actions of poorly, incorrectly, or incompletely trained employees. A company that contracts out training to a vendor or consultant should ensure that it has liability insurance, be sure that the trainers are competent, and determine if there has been previous litigation against the trainer or the vendor providing the training. Also, trainers should be sure to keep copies of notes, activities, and training manuals that show that training procedures were correct and followed the steps provided by licensing or certification agencies (if appropriate).

Incurring Breach of Confidentiality or Defamation

Managers should ensure that information placed in employees' files regarding performance in training activities is accurate. Also, before discussing an employee's performance in training with other employees or using training performance information for promotion or salary decisions, managers should tell employees that training performance will be used in that manner.

Reproducing and Using Copyrighted Material in Training Classes without Permission

Copyrights protect the expression of an idea (e.g., a training manual for a software program) but not the ideas that the material contains (e.g., the use of help windows in the software program).[3] Copyrights also prohibit others from creating a product based on the original work and from copying, broadcasting, or publishing the product without permission.

The use of videotapes, learning aids, manuals, and other copyrighted materials in training classes without obtaining permission from the owner of the material is illegal. Managers should ensure that all training materials are purchased from the vendor or consultant who developed them or that permission to reproduce materials has been obtained. Material on Internet sites is not necessarily free from copyright law.[4] Many websites are governed by the fair use doctrine, which means that you can use small amounts of copyrighted material without asking permission or paying a fee as long as the use meets four standards. The standards include (1) the purpose for which the copyrighted materials are being used, (2) what the copyrighted work is, (3) the proportion of the copyrighted material you are using, and (4) how much money the copyright owner can lose as a result of the use. Republishing or repackaging under your own name material that you took from the Internet can be a violation of copyright law. For example, the CEO of Crisp Learning frequently finds his small company in court defending copyright issues. Crisp Learning develops and sells video and training courses that deal with skills such as business report writing and time management. The series of courses, known as the Fifty-Minute series, is popular because it is easily applied and can be completed in a short period of time. Crisp Learning has found that copyright violators have actually retyped its books and sold them as their own work. Violating copyright can be expensive. Copyright violators can end up paying expensive legal fees and paying damages that are more expensive than what it would have cost to legally purchase the training materials. To obtain copyright permission, you need to directly contact the owners of the material or visit the Copyright Clearance website *(www.copyright.com)*.

Excluding Women, Minorities, and Older Employees from Training Programs

Two pieces of legislation make it illegal for employers to exclude women, minorities, or older persons from training programs. Title VII of the Civil Rights Act of 1964 (amended in 1991) makes it illegal to deny access to employment or deprive a person employment because of the person's race, color, religion, gender, or national origin. The Age Discrimination in Employment Act (ADEA) prohibits discrimination against persons who are age 40 or older. The Equal Employment Opportunity Commission (EEOC) is responsible for enforcing both the Civil Rights Act and the ADEA.

Although these two pieces of legislation have existed for several years, a study by the U.S. Department of Labor found that training experiences necessary for promotion are not as available or accessible to women and minorities as they are to white males.[5] Women, minorities, and older employees can be illegally excluded from training programs either by not being made aware of opportunities for training or by purposeful exclusion from enrollment in training programs. Denial of training opportunities and better treatment of younger employees can support claims of age discrimination.[6] Older employees may bring lawsuits against companies based on a denied promotion or discharge. As evidence for age discrimination, the courts will investigate whether older workers were denied training opportunities that were provided to younger workers. To avoid age discrimination in training, managers and trainers need to ensure that the organization's culture and policies are age-neutral. Decisions about training and development opportunities should not be made on the basis of stereotypes about older workers and should take into account job-relevant factors such as performance. Managers should be held accountable for fair training and development practices and for ensuring that all employees have development plans. Finally, all employees should receive training on the ADEA and on how age stereotypes can affect treatment of older employees. Stereotypes such as "older workers are resistant to change" may result in exclusion of older workers from training and development programs.

Coca-Cola recently settled out of court a discrimination suit in which African American employees were excluded from programs needed to receive promotions in the company. In April 1999, four current and former Coke employees filed a lawsuit alleging race discrimination in pay, promotions, and performance evaluations within the Coca-Cola company.[7] Rather than face continued legal and public scrutiny and to move forward on initiatives to correct the perceived racial discrimination, Coca-Cola agreed to pay $113 million in cash to the plaintiffs, $3.5 million to adjust salaries of African American employees during the next 10 years, and $36 million to implement various diversity initiatives. The goal of the settlement is to change the company culture. Coke's employment practices have been reviewed by a task force consisting of experts in civil rights, diversity, labor, employment, and business. The task force also reviews Coke's human resource practices. The settlement required more oversight of managers' decisions on promotions, more mentoring programs, and regular diversity training for all employees. Coke has made progress in complying with the requirements of the settlement agreement.[8] Coke's external recruiting of minorities has increased, and the company has sent all its managers and half its employees to two-day diversity awareness training. However, according to employee surveys, Coke's African American employees were, on average, less positive about fairness within the company than were white employees, particularly about fairness related to advancement and career opportunities. The task force will continue to monitor Coke's policies over the next few years.

Not Ensuring Equal Treatment of All Employees While in Training

Equal treatment of all trainees means that conditions of the learning environment such as opportunities for practice, feedback, and role playing are available for all trainees regardless of their background. Also, trainers should avoid jokes, stories, and props that might create a hostile learning environment. For example, because of claims that women employees were being harassed at air traffic control centers, the Federal Aviation Administration (FAA) required employees to attend diversity training. The diversity training required male employees to experience what it felt like to be taunted and jeered at as you walked down the aisle in an air traffic control facility (known as "walking the gauntlet"). One of the male employees found the experience to be distasteful and psychologically stressful, sued the FAA, and won.

Requiring Employees to Attend Programs That Might Be Offensive

Allstate Insurance has been the focus of several religious discrimination lawsuits by insurance agents who found Scientology principles emphasized in agent training programs to be offensive and counter to their religious beliefs (e.g., employees who met their sales goals were not to be questioned no matter how they behaved, whereas persons who failed to meet their sales goals deserved to be harassed and treated poorly).[9]

Revealing Discriminatory Information during a Training Session

At Lucky Store Foods, a California supermarket chain, notes taken during a diversity training program were used as evidence of discrimination.[10] In the training session, supervisors were asked to verbalize their stereotypes. Some comments ("women cry more," "black women are aggressive") were derogatory toward women and minorities. The plaintiff in the case used the notes as evidence that the company conducted the training session to avoid an investigation by the Equal Employment Opportunity Commission. The case was settled out of court.

Not Accommodating Trainees with Disabilities

The **Americans with Disabilities Act (ADA)** of 1990 prohibits individuals with disabilities from being discriminated against in the workplace. The ADA prohibits discrimination based on disability in employment practices including hiring, firing, compensation, and training. The ADA defines a disability as a physical or mental impairment that substantially limits one or more major life activities, a record of having an impairment, or being regarded as having such an impairment. This includes serious disabilities such as epilepsy, blindness, or paralysis as well as persons who have a history of heart disease, mental illness, or cancer that is currently in remission.

The ADA requires companies to make "reasonable accommodation" to the physical or mental condition of a person with a disability who is otherwise qualified unless it would impose an "undue hardship" on the organization's operations. Determination of undue hardship is made by analyzing the type and cost of the accommodation in relation to the company's financial resources. Even if the undue hardship can be justified, the ADA requires that the person with the disability be provided the option of paying that part of the cost that causes the undue hardship.

In the context of training, **reasonable accommodation** refers to making training facilities readily accessible to and usable by individuals with disabilities. Reasonable accommodation may also include modifying instructional media, adjusting training policies, and providing trainees with readers or interpreters. Employers are not required to make reasonable accommodation if the person does not request them. Employers are also not required to make reasonable accommodation if persons are not qualified to participate in training programs (e.g., they lack the prerequisite certification or educational requirements).

One example of how the ADA might influence training activities involves adventure learning. Adventure learning experiences demand a high level of physical fitness. Employees who have a disability cannot be required to attend adventure learning training programs.[11] If it does not cause an undue hardship, employees should be offered an alternative program for developing the learned capabilities emphasized in the adventure learning program.

It is impossible to give specific guidelines regarding the type of accommodations that trainers and managers should make to avoid violating the ADA. It is important to identify if the training is related to "essential" job functions. That is, are the tasks or knowledge, skills, and abilities that are the focus of training fundamental to the position? Task analysis information (discussed in Chapter 3) can be used to identify essential job functions. For example, tasks that are frequently performed and critical for successful job performance would be considered essential job functions. If training relates to a function that may be performed in the job but does not have to be performed by all persons (a marginal job function), then a disability in relation to that function cannot be used to exclude that person from training. To the extent that the disability makes it difficult for the person to receive training necessary to complete essential job functions, the trainer must explore whether it is possible to make reasonable accommodations.

Incorrectly Reporting Training as an Expense or Failing to Report Training Reimbursement as Income

The cost of training is covered by Internal Revenue code. Companies can often deduct the cost of training provided to employees as a business expense. The Employer Assistance Program allows an employer to pay an employee up to $5,250 per year for certain educational expenses. This amount can be deducted by the employer as a business expense without adding the payment to the employee's yearly gross income. In other programs (e.g., the Educational Reimbursement Program), the employer can decide which training is paid for and how it is funded. Reimbursements for training expenses that employees incur may be considered part of the employees' taxable incomes. Employees may be able to deduct work-related educational expenses as itemized deductions on their income taxes. To be deductible, the expenses must be for training that maintains or improves skills required in the job or that serves a business purpose of the company and is required by the company, or by law or regulations, in order for employees to keep their present salary, status, or job. See *www.irs.org* for more information about business and individual reporting of educational expenses.

Cross-Cultural Preparation

As was mentioned in Chapter 1, companies today are challenged to expand globally. In a recent two-year period, for example, U.S. businesses doubled their annual investment in foreign operations.[12] Such expansion is good business sense, considering the growth potential of foreign markets. China's population is so large and its demand for products and services growing so fast that some observers predict that doing business there will turn regional companies into major global players. Hard Rock Café is an example of a U.S. company expanding into Asia and the Pacific region. It has restaurants in Bangkok, Kuala Lumpur, Djakarta, Taipei, Bali, and Beijing.[13]

Because of the increase in global operations, employees often work outside their country of origin or work with employees from other countries. Top managers who obtain experience through international assignments contribute to their global company's successful performance. Table 10.2 shows the different types of employees in global companies. **Expatriates** work in a country other than their country of origin. For example, Microsoft is headquartered in the United States but has facilities around the world. To be effective, expatriates in the Microsoft Mexico operations in Mexico City must understand the region's business and social culture. Because of a growing pool of talented labor around the world, greater use of host-country nationals is occurring.[14] (**Host-country nationals** are employees with citizenship in the country where the company is located.) A key reason is that a host-country national can more easily understand the values and customs of the work force than an expatriate can. Also, training and transporting U.S. employees and their families to a foreign assignment and housing them there tend to be more expensive than hiring a host-country national.

Cross-cultural preparation involves educating employees (expatriates) and their families who are to be sent to a foreign country. To successfully conduct business in the global marketplace, employees must understand the business practices and the cultural norms of different countries. Table 10.3's "impression shock" column shows the typical impressions that a Japanese manager may have of the U.S. culture. The "integration shock" column describes the typical American interpretation of Japanese managers' style. Clearly, for American and Japanese managers to have successful business discussions, they need to be prepared to deal with cultural differences!

Cross-cultural preparation is important for the success of the assignment, which can be very expensive. The annual cost of sending an employee overseas has been estimated to be three to seven times the employee's salary. Besides salary, expenses include taxation, housing, and education.[15] Most companies offer tax equalization to expatriates. That is, the company will either pay taxes, offer additional salary, or provide other goods and services, depending on tax laws, so that the employee does not incur additional tax expenses by living abroad. For example, expatriates in Germany may have twice the income tax they would have in the United States, and they are taxed on their housing and cost-of-living allowances. Most employees expect to duplicate their U.S. housing arrangements, and expatriates with families may expect that they will be able to send their children to English-speaking schools, which adds considerable expense. Unfortunately, U.S. companies lose more than $2 billion a year as a result of failed overseas assignments.[16]

TABLE 10.2 Types of Employees in Global Companies	*Parent-country national:* Employee whose country of origin is where the company has its headquarters *Host-country national:* Employee from the host country *Third-country national:* Employee who has a country of origin different from both the parent country and host country where he or she works

TABLE 10.3 Negative Surprises Facing the Newly Arrived Japanese Manager

	Impression Shock— Japanese Perceptions of American Ways	Integration Shock— American Responses to Japanese Ways
Community Life	Social diversity	Aloof/clannish community
	Violence and crime	Misunderstood customs
	Poverty and homelessness	Economic takeover
	Education problems	Lingering resentment
	Ignorance of foreign ways	Self-serving conduct
Business Practice	Different operations	Vagueness and delay
	Shortsightedness	Overworked employees
	Lackluster service	Unfair industrial groups
	Hasty dealmaking	Ethical violations
	Legal minefields	Influence peddling
Organizational Dynamics	No spiritual quality	Management inexperience
	Individual careerism	Avoided accountability
	Narrow job focus	Closed inner circle
	Political confrontation	Stifled employees
	Employee disloyalty	Discriminatory practices
Interpersonal Dealings	Assertiveness	Distrust/secrecy
	Frankness	Arrogance/hubris
	Egoism	Withheld sentiments
	Glibness	Cautious intimacy
	Impulsiveness	Excessive sensitivity

Note: The rows and tables are not symmetrical. They merely list the major surprises experienced by visitors.

Source: Richard G. Linowes, "The Japanese Manager's Traumatic Entry into the United States: Understanding the American-Japanese Cultural Divide," *Academy of Management Executive* 7, no. 4 (1993): 26.

Dimensions of Cultural Differences

Many cultural characteristics influence employee behavior. Keep in mind that there are national cultures as well as company cultures. A **culture** refers to the set of assumptions that group members share about the world and how it works and the ideals worth striving for.[17] Culture is important because it influences the effectiveness of different behaviors and management styles. A management style that seems friendly to some employees might offend others who would rather maintain distance and respect toward their bosses.

For example, consider how cultural differences affect European managers' perceptions of American managers.[18] European managers admire the financial results of many companies. But they also believe that American managers don't know how to eat and drink properly and don't understand European history. One German manager was embarrassed when managers from an Indiana company to whom he was recently introduced called him by his first name. In Germany, such informality occurs only after long-term relationships have been established. Other work style differences include the American emphasis on monthly and quarterly business results versus the European focus on yearly and longer-term profits.

Research conducted by G. Hofstede identified five dimensions of national culture: individualism-collectivism, uncertainty avoidance, masculinity-femininity, power distance, and time orientation.[19] Figure 10.1 shows the locations of selected countries on these dimensions.

FIGURE 10.1 Cultural dimensions with relative standing of selected countries

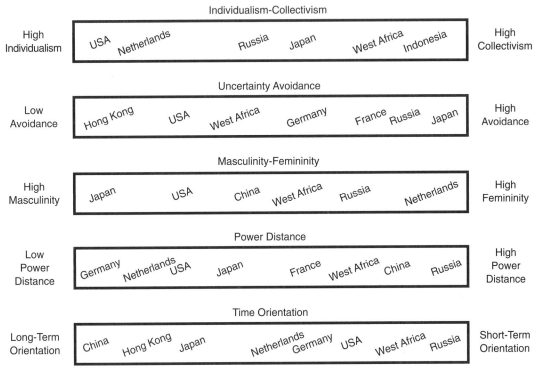

Source: From P. M. Wright and R. A. Noe, *Management of Organizations* (Burr Ridge, IL: Irwin/McGraw-Hill, 1996).

Awareness of these dimensions can help trainers develop cross-cultural preparation programs that include meaningful information regarding the culture the expatriates will find themselves working in. Awareness of these dimensions can also help trainers adapt their training styles to employees in non-U.S. locations. But note that individuals differ within any culture, so these generalizations describe some members of a culture better than others.

The degree to which people act as individuals rather than as members of a group is the cultural dimension known as **individualism-collectivism.** In an individualistic culture like the United States, employees expect to be hired, evaluated, and rewarded based on their personal skills and accomplishments. In a collectivist culture, employees are more likely to have a voice in decisions. As you saw in Table 10.3, Japanese managers, who tend to have a collectivist orientation, can be shocked by the apparent self-interest of their American colleagues!

Upjohn Company of Kalamazoo, Michigan, and Pharmacia AB of Sweden experienced a clash of cultures after the companies merged.[20] Because of the similarities between Swedes and Americans, the companies were not prepared for the cultural differences they encountered. For example, employees in both companies speak English and enjoy similar lifestyles. However, there were significant cultural differences in decision-making styles. Swedes are used to an open system, in which small teams are largely left on their own and executives prefer to get consensus before making a decision. Upjohn was used to more authoritarian, top-down decision making. This difference caused strain in the relationship between the companies.

Uncertainty avoidance refers to the degree to which people prefer structured rather than unstructured situations. Cultures with a strong uncertainty avoidance orientation (e.g., Japan, Russia) favor structured situations. Religion, law, or technology in these countries socialize people to seek security through clear rules on how to act. In a culture with weak uncertainty avoidance (e.g., Jamaica, Hong Kong), employees cope by not worrying too much about the future.

Masculinity-femininity refers to the extent to which the culture values behavior considered traditionally masculine (competitiveness) or feminine (helpfulness). Examples of "masculine" cultures include Japan, Germany, and the United States. Here assertiveness and competitiveness are valued. In contrast, in a culture such as the Netherlands, a higher value is likely placed on quality of life, helping others, and preserving the environment.

Power distance refers to expectations for the unequal distribution of power in a hierarchy. India, Mexico, and Russia, for example, have great power distance. This means that people attempt to maintain differences between various levels of the hierarchy. For example, because complaining about managers is unthinkable in Mexico, a U.S. manager of a steel conveyor plant failed in his effort to establish a system to handle employee complaints. Under the system, employees were to first discuss the problem with their manager. No one ever complained so the managers were caught by surprise when employees staged a plant walkout.[21]

Time orientation refers to the degree to which a culture focuses on the future rather than the past and present. In cultures with a short-term orientation, such as the United States, Russia, and West Africa, the orientation is toward the past and present. These cultures tend to emphasize respect for tradition and social obligations. A culture with a long-term orientation, such as Japan and China, values such traits as thrift and persistence, which pay off in the future rather than the present.

Implications for Expatriates and Their Families: Cross-Cultural Training

To prepare employees for cross-cultural assignments, companies need to provide cross-cultural training. To be successful in overseas assignments, expatriates (employees on foreign assignments) need to be

1. Competent in their area of expertise.
2. Able to communicate verbally and nonverbally in the host country.
3. Flexible, tolerant of ambiguity, and sensitive to cultural differences.
4. Motivated to succeed, able to enjoy the challenge of working in other countries, and willing to learn about the host country's culture, language, and customs.
5. Supported by their families.[22]

One study found that personality characteristics were related to expatriates' desire to terminate the assignment as well as to their performance in the assignment.[23] Expatriates who were extroverted (outgoing), agreeable (cooperative, tolerant), and conscientious (dependable, achievement-oriented) were more likely to want to stay on the assignment and perform well. This study suggests that cross-cultural training may be effective only when an expatriate's personality predisposes him or her to be successful in assignments in other cultures.

One reason for U.S. expatriates' high failure rate is that companies place more emphasis on developing employees' technical skills than on preparing them to work in other cultures. Research suggests that the comfort of an expatriate's spouse and family is the most important determinant of whether the employee will complete the assignment.[24]

One key to successful foreign assignment appears to be a combination of training and career management for employees and their families. Foreign assignments involve three phases: predeparture, on-site, and repatriation (preparing to return home). Training is necessary in all three phases.

Predeparture Phase In the predeparture phase, employees need to receive language training and an orientation in the new country's culture and customs. It is critical that the family be included in the orientation programs.[25] Expatriates and their families need information about housing, schools, recreation, shopping, and health care facilities in the area where they will live. Expatriates also must discuss with their managers how the foreign assignment fits into employees' career plans and what type of position expatriates can expect upon return.

Cross-cultural training methods range from presentational techniques, such as lectures that expatriates and their families attend on the customs and culture of the host country, to actual experiences in the home country in culturally diverse communities.[26] Experiential exercises, such as miniculture experiences, allow expatriates to spend time with a family in the United States from the ethnic group of the host country.

Research suggests that the degree of difference between the United States and the host country (cultural novelty), the amount of interaction with host country citizens and host nationals (interaction), and the familiarity with new job tasks and work environment (job novelty) all influence the "rigor" of the cross-cultural training method.

Rigor here refers to the degree to which the training program emphasizes knowledge about the culture as well as behavior and skills needed to effectively live in the culture. Less rigorous training methods such as lectures and briefings focus on communicating factual material about the country and culture to trainees. More rigorous methods include factual material and help expatriates and their families develop communication skills and behavior needs to interact in another country. Figure 10.2 shows the relationship between training rigor and training focus (characteristics that a training program needs to be effective).[27] Experiential training methods are most effective (and most needed) in assignments with a high level of cultural and job novelty that require a good deal of interpersonal interaction with host nationals.

On-Site Phase On-site training involves continued orientation to the host country and its customs and cultures through formal programs or through a mentoring relationship. Expatriates and their families may be paired with a mentor from the host country who helps them understand the new, unfamiliar work environment and community.[28]

A major reason that employees refuse expatriate assignments is that they can't afford to lose their spouse's income or are concerned that their spouse's career could be derailed by being out of the work force for a few years.[29] Some "trailing" spouses decide to use the time to pursue educational activities that could contribute to their long-term career goals. But it is difficult to find these opportunities in an unfamilar place. Pfizer, the pharmaceutical firm, is taking action to help trailing spouses. It provides a $10,000 allowance that the spouse can use in many different ways. A person at the expatriate location is assigned to help the spouse with professional development and locating educational or other resources. In countries where spouses are allowed to work, Pfizer tries to find them jobs within the company. Pfizer also provides cross-cultural counseling and language assistance. The company tries to connect the family with the expatriate community.

FIGURE 10.2
Relationship between training methods and training rigor

Source: Based on M. Mendenhall, E. Dunbar, and G. Oddou, "Expatriate Selection, Training, and Career-Pathing: A Review and Critique," *Human Resource Management* 26 (1987): 331–45.

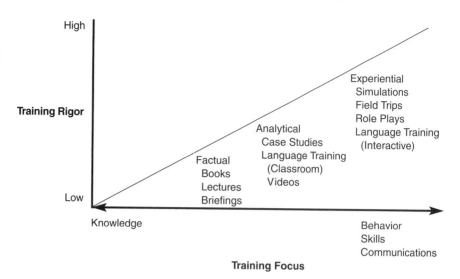

Research suggests that companies should offer support for expatriates.[30] Services such as career counseling for expatriates are important for reducing stress and anxiety. Support from the foreign facility (either one person or a department) is also important for work and interaction adjustment. Expatriates who had high-quality relationships with their supervisors were more effective in completing job responsibilities.

Repatriation Phase **Repatriation** prepares expatriates for return to the parent company and country from the foreign assignment. Expatriates and their families are likely to experience high levels of stress and anxiety when they return because of the changes that have occurred since their departure. This shock can be reduced by providing expatriates with company newsletters and community newspapers and by ensuring that they receive personal and work-related mail from the United States while they are on foreign assignment. It is also not uncommon for employees and their families to have to readjust to a lower standard of living in the United States than they had in the foreign country, where they may have enjoyed maid service, a limousine, private schools, and clubs. Salary and other compensation arrangements should be worked out well before employees return from overseas assignments.

Aside from reentry shock, many expatriates decide to leave the company because the assignment they are given upon returning to the United States has less responsibility, challenge, and status than the foreign assignment.[31] As noted earlier, career planning discussions need to be held before the employees leave the United States to ensure that they understand the positions they will be eligible for upon repatriation.

Employees should be encouraged to self-manage the repatriation process.[32] Before they go on the assignment, they need to consider what skills they want to develop and the types of jobs that might be available in the company for an employee with those skills. Because the company changes and because colleagues, peers, and managers may leave while the expatriate is on assignment, he or she needs to maintain contact with key company and industry people. Otherwise, the employee's reentry shock will be heightened from having to deal with new colleagues, a somewhat changed job, and a company culture that may have shifted.

Royal Dutch Shell, a joint Dutch and United Kingdom oil and gas company, has one of the world's largest expatriate work forces.[33] To avoid expatriates who feel undervalued and leave the company, Royal Dutch gets involved with expatriates and their career. Resource planners track workers abroad, helping to identify their next assignment. Most expatriates know their next assignment three to six months before the move, and all begin the next assignment with a clear job description. Expatriates who have the potential to reach top-level management positions are placed in the home office every third assignment to increase their visibility to company executives. Expatriates are also assigned technical mentors who evaluate their skills and help them improve their skills through training at Royal Dutch's training center.

Because of the difficulty in getting employees to accept foreign assignments and the low success rate of expatriate assignments, companies are creating "virtual" expatriate positions and using short-time assignments.[34] **Virtual expatriates** have an assignment to manage an operation abroad without being located permanently in that country. The employees periodically travel to the overseas location, return, and later use videoconferencing and communications technology to manage the operation. Virtual expatriates eliminate exposing the family to the culture shock of an overseas move. This setup also allows the employee to manage globally while keeping in close touch with the home office. Virtual expatriates are less expensive than traditional expatriates, who can cost companies over three times as much as a host national employee. One major disadvantage of virtual expatriates is that visiting a foreign operation on a sporadic basis may lengthen the time needed to build a local management team, so it will take longer to solve problems because of the lack of a strong personal relationship with local employees.

Because of family issues, poor economic times, and security issues, many companies are reducing the number of expatriates and relying more on short-time assignments, frequent business travel, and international commutes in which an employee lives in one country and works in another.[35] Companies such as Wal-Mart Stores and NCR have reduced the number of expatriate assignments, but they still believe that long-term expatriate assignments are necessary in order to develop key talent possessing global responsibilities and experience. One of the potential difficulties of short-term international assignments is that employees may be perceived as foreigners rather than colleagues because they haven't had the time to build relationships and develop trust among co-workers in their short-term location. Another is that traveling can take a physical and emotional toll on employees as they try to juggle business responsibilities with maintaining contact with family and friends. Procter & Gamble helps employees on short-term assignments by providing a trip fund that is based on the length of time an employee is on an extended business trip. For example, a U.S.-based employee working in western Europe for six months would get a fund containing the cost of five business-class round-trips. The employee can use money from the fund to take trips home or to cover family visits to the employee's location.

Implications of Cultural Differences for Training

Table 10.4 presents the implications of each of the cultural dimensions for training. In the United States, interaction between the trainer and the trainees is viewed as a positive characteristic of the learning environment. However, in other cultures, this type of learning environment may not be familiar to the trainee or may violate expected norms of good instruction. For example, in China, a culture high on power distance, trainees do not expect to be asked to question the trainer.[36] This means that the instructor must actively seek out

TABLE 10.4   **Implications of Cultural Dimensions for Training Design**

Cultural Dimension	Implications
Individualism	Culture high in individualism expects participation in exercises and questioning to be determined by status in the company or culture.
Uncertainty Avoidance	Culture high in uncertainty avoidance expects formal instructional environments; less tolerance for impromptu style.
Masculinity	Culture low in masculinity values relationships with fellow trainees; female trainers less likely to be resisted in low-masculinity cultures.
Power Distance	Culture high in power distance expects trainer to be expert; trainers expected to be authoritarian and controlling of session.
Time Orientation	Culture with a long-term orientation will have trainees who are likely to accept development plans and assignments.

Source: Based on B. Filipczak, "Think Locally, Act Globally," *Training* (January 1997): 41–48.

their participation. Also, when seeking audience participation in China, trainers may invite the senior member of the group to speak first; questions from other trainees may be forwarded to this person. This avoids embarrassing a senior executive by having an employee of lower status ask a better question.

Expectations regarding the environment in which training is to occur may also differ from U.S. culture. On-the-job training may be viewed skeptically by Russian employees because historically most workers were expected to have been formally trained by attending lectures at an institute or university.[37] Because Russian culture values family relationships (Russian culture is more "feminine" than American culture), the meaningfulness of training materials is likely to be enhanced by using examples from employees' work and life situations.

Besides cultural dimensions, trainers must consider language differences in preparing training materials. If an interpreter is used, it is important to conduct a practice session with the interpreter to evaluate pacing of the session and whether the amount of topics and material is appropriate. Training materials including videos and exercises need to be translated well in advance of the training session.

The key to success in a foreign training session is preparation! The needs assessment must include an evaluation of cultural dimensions and the characteristics of the audience (such as language ability, trainees' company, and cultural status).

Managing Work Force Diversity

Despite the efforts of many companies to embrace diversity, women and minorities continue to report many barriers to feeling valued and advancing in their careers.[38] A survey by the Society for Human Resource Management revealed barriers including stereotyping and preconceptions, corporate culture, exclusion from informal networks, and lack of mentors and role models. That is, anyone who is perceived as "different" is likely to have a difficult time contributing to company goals and experiencing personal growth.

What Is Diversity? Why Is It Important?

The goals of diversity training are (1) to eliminate values, stereotypes, and managerial practices that inhibit employees' personal development and (2) therefore to allow employees to contribute to organizational goals regardless of their race, age, physical condition, sexual orientation, gender, family status, religious orientation, or cultural background.[39] Because of equal opportunity employment laws, companies have been forced to ensure that women and minorities are adequately represented in their labor force. That is, companies are focused on ensuring equal access to jobs. Also, as was discussed in Chapter 1, the impact of culture on the workplace, and specifically on training and development, has received heightened attention. Cultural factors that companies need to consider include the terrorist attacks of 9/11; employees' fear of discussing cultural differences; more work being conducted in teams whose members have many different characteristics; the realization that people from diverse cultures represent an important customer market; and, especially for professional and technical jobs, the availability of highly trained employees that has many companies seeking workers from overseas. These new immigrants need diversity training to help them understand such facets of American culture as obsession with time, individualistic attitudes, and capitalistic ideas.[40]

Managing diversity involves creating an environment that allows all employees to contribute to organizational goals and experience personal growth. This environment includes access to jobs as well as fair and positive treatment of all employees. The company must develop employees who are comfortable working with people from a wide variety of ethnic, racial, and religious backgrounds. Managing diversity may require changing the company culture. It includes the company's standards and norms about how employees are treated, competitiveness, results orientation, innovation, and risk taking. The value placed on diversity is grounded in the company culture.

Table 10.5 shows how managing diversity can help companies gain a competitive advantage. Various customer groups appreciate doing business with employees like themselves. Also, diverse employees can contribute insights into customers and product markets. For example, Voice Processing Corporation benefits from having employees with different language skills and cultural orientations.[41] Diversity gives the firm an edge in producing and marketing software that enables computers to process voice commands. Companies also need creativity and innovation to cope with the rapid pace of change. Research supports the view that these traits are more likely to exist in a company whose employees come from a variety of backgrounds.[42]

Capitalizing on diversity also plays a major role in the success of work teams.[43] Diversity goes beyond differences in race, physical appearance, ethnicity, and sexual orientation to include differences in communication and problem-solving style and professional and functional expertise (e.g., marketing versus engineering). When teams don't capitalize on differences but instead get caught up in identifying differences, distrust and unproductive teams usually result. Many companies (e.g., IBM, Colgate-Palmolive) have used a strategy that focuses on awareness of differences and on providing the skills that successful team members need. Team mission statements should reflect not only what the team is supposed to accomplish but also how interpersonal conflict should be handled. Some companies even require rotation of responsibilities so each person has a chance to demonstrate his or her abilities (and show that stereotypes based on race or function are not valid).

Little research addresses the impact of diversity or diversity-management practices on financial success. Diversity may enhance performance when organizations have an environment that promotes learning from diversity. There is no evidence to support the direct relationship between diversity and business.[44] Rather, a company will see the success of its diversity efforts only if it makes a long-term commitment to managing diversity. Successful diversity requires that it be viewed as an opportunity for employees to (1) learn from

TABLE 10.5   **How Managing Diversity Can Provide Competitive Advantage**

Argument	Rationale
Cost	As organizations become more diverse, the cost of a poor job in integrating workers will increase. Those who handle integration well will thus create cost advantages over those who don't.
Resource Acquisition	Companies develop reputations on favorability as prospective employers for women and ethnic minorities. Those with the best reputations for managing diversity will win the competition for the best personnel. As the labor pool shrinks and changes composition, this edge will become increasingly important.
Marketing	For multinational organizations, the insight and cultural sensitivity that members with roots in other countries bring to the marketing effort should improve these efforts in important ways. The same rationale applies to marketing to subpopulations within domestic operations.
Creativity	Diversity of perspectives and less emphasis on conformity to norms of the past (which characterize the modern approach to management of diversity) should improve the level of creativity.
Problem Solving	Heterogeneity in decisions and problem-solving groups potentially produces better decisions through a wider range of perspectives and more thorough critical analysis of issues.
System Flexibility	An implication of the multicultural model for managing diversity is that the system will become less determinant, less standardized, and therefore more fluid. The increased fluidity should create greater flexibility to react to environmental changes (i.e., reactions should be faster and at less cost).

Source: T. H. Cox and S. Blake, "Managing Cultural Diversity: Implications for Organizational Competitiveness," *Academy of Management Executive* 5 (1991): 47. Reprinted with permission.

each other how to better accomplish their work, (2) be provided with a supportive and cooperative organizational culture, and (3) be taught leadership and process skills that can facilitate effective team functioning. Diversity is a reality in labor and customer markets and is a social expectation and value. Managers should focus on building an organizational environment, on human resource practices, and on managerial and team skills that all capitalize on diversity. As you will see in the discussion that follows, managing diversity requires difficult cultural change, not just slogans on the wall!

Managing Diversity through Adherence to Legislation

One approach to managing diversity is through affirmative action policies and human resource practices that meet standards of equal employment opportunity laws.[45] This approach rarely results in changes in employees' values, stereotypes, and behaviors that inhibit productivity and personal development. Figure 10.3 shows the cycle of disillusionment that results from managing diversity by relying solely on adherence to employment laws. The cycle begins when the company realizes that it must change policies regarding women and minorities because of legal pressure or a discrepancy between the number or percentage of women and minorities in the company's work force and the number available in the broader labor market. To address these concerns, a greater number of women and minorities are hired by the company. Managers see little need for additional action because women and minority employment rates reflect their availability in the labor

FIGURE 10.3

Cycle of disillusionment that results from managing diversity through adherence to legislation

Source: "Capitalizing on Global Diversity" by Cresencio Torres and Mary Bruxelles, *HR Magazine*, December 1992, pp. 30–33. Reprinted with the permission of *HR Magazine*. Published by the Society for Human Resource Management, Alexandria, VA.

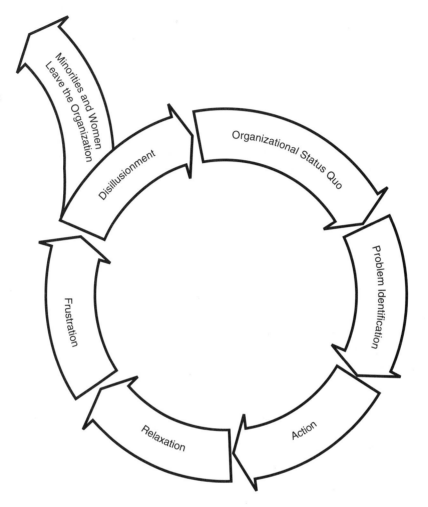

market. However, as women and minorities gain experience in the company, they likely become frustrated. Managers and co-workers may avoid providing coaching or performance feedback to women and minorities because they are uncomfortable interacting with individuals from different gender, ethnic, or racial backgrounds. Co-workers may express beliefs that women and minorities are employed only because they received special treatment (e.g., hiring standards were lowered).[46] As a result of their frustration, women and minorities may form support groups to voice their concerns to management. Because of the work atmosphere, women and minorities may fail to fully utilize their skills and may leave the company.

Managing Diversity through Diversity Training Programs

The preceding discussion is not to suggest that companies should be reluctant to engage in affirmative action or pursue equal opportunity employment practices. However, affirmative action without additional supporting strategies does not deal with issues of assimilating women and minorities into the work force. To successfully manage a diverse work force, companies need to ensure that

- Employees understand how their values and stereotypes influence their behavior toward people of a different gender, ethnicity, race, or religion.
- Employees gain an appreciation of cultural differences among themselves.
- Behaviors that isolate or intimidate minority group members improve.

These goals can be accomplished through diversity training programs. **Diversity training** refers to training designed to change employee attitudes about diversity and/or to help employees develop skills needed to work with a diverse work force. Diversity training programs differ according to whether attitude or behavior change is emphasized.[47] There is not a lot of research to guide the development of effective diversity training programs. Some research suggests that composition of the training group and prior experience with diversity training may affect attitudinal and behavior change.[48]

Attitude Awareness and Change Programs   **Attitude awareness and change programs** focus on increasing employees' awareness of differences in cultural and ethnic backgrounds, physical characteristics (e.g., disabilities), and personal characteristics that influence behavior toward others. The assumption underlying these programs is that by increasing their awareness of stereotypes and beliefs, employees will be able to avoid negative stereotypes when interacting with employees of different backgrounds. The programs help employees consider the similarities and differences between cultural groups, examine their attitudes toward affirmative action, or analyze their beliefs about why minority employees are successful or unsuccessful in their jobs. Many of these programs use videotapes and experiential exercises to increase employees' awareness of the negative emotional and performance effects of stereotypes, values, and behaviors on minority group members. For example, 3M conducts workshops in which managers are asked to assess their attitudes toward stereotypical statements about race, age, and gender.[49] The participants select two stereotypes they hold and consider how these stereotypes affect their ability to manage. One of the most popular video training packages, Copeland Griggs Productions' "Valuing Diversity Training Program," involves three days of training that focuses on managing differences, diversity in the workplace, and cross-cultural communications.

The attitude awareness and change approach has been criticized for several reasons.[50] First, by focusing on group differences, the program may communicate that certain stereotypes and attitudes are valid. For example, in diversity training a male manager may learn that women employees prefer to work by building consensus rather than by arguing until others agree with their point. He might conclude that the training has validated his stereotype. As a result, he will continue to fail to give women important job responsibilities that involve "heated" negotiations with customers or clients. Second, encouraging employees to share their attitudes, feelings, and stereotypes toward certain groups may cause employees to feel discriminated against, guilty, angry, and less likely to see the similarities among racial, ethnic, or gender groups and the advantages of working together. (Consider the discussion of Lucky Store Foods earlier in the chapter.)

Behavior-Based Programs   **Behavior-based programs** focus on changing the organizational policies and individual behaviors that inhibit employees' personal growth and productivity.

One approach of these programs is to identify incidents that discourage employees from working up to their potential. Groups of employees are asked to identify specific promotion opportunities, sponsorship, training opportunities, or performance management practices that they believe were handled unfairly. The program may collect employees' views regarding how well the work environment and management practices value employee differences and provide equal opportunity. Specific training programs may be developed to address the issues presented in the focus groups.

Another approach is to teach managers and employees basic rules of behavior in the workplace.[51] These lessons include behavior toward peers and managers as well as customers. For example, managers and employees should learn that it is inappropriate to use statements and engage in behaviors that have negative racial, sexual, or cultural content. Companies that have focused on teaching rules and behavior have found that employees react less negatively to this type of training than to other diversity training approaches. All 11,000 employees at Saks Fifth Avenue, the New York–based retailer, have received diversity training that focuses on providing customer service to a diverse customer base. The training is video-based and shows actual employees interacting with customers in various situations. Saks Fifth Avenue estimates that every customer interaction is worth about $250, so treating customers inappropriately can cost the company a lot of money.[52]

A third approach is cultural immersion. **Cultural immersion** refers to the process of sending employees directly into communities where they have to interact with persons from different cultures, races, and/or nationalities. The degree of interaction varies, but it may involve talking with community members, working in community organizations, or learning about religious, cultural, or historically significant events. For example, the United Parcel Service (UPS) Community Internship Program is a management development program designed to help UPS senior managers understand the needs of diverse customers and a diverse work force through exposure to poverty and inequality.[53] UPS is the world's largest package delivery company and a leading global provider of transportation and logistic services. Since 1968, over 1,200 senior managers have completed the program, an internship that typically lasts four weeks. The internships take the managers to cities throughout the United States, where they work on the problems facing local populations. UPS managers may find themselves serving meals to the homeless, working in AIDS centers, helping migrant farm workers, building temporary housing and schools, and managing children in a Head Start program. These experiences take the managers outside their comfort zones, and the problems that they encounter—from transportation to housing to education to health care— help them better understand the issues that many UPS employees face daily. This enlightenment is a business necessity for UPS because three out of four managers are white whereas 35 percent of the employees are minorities. UPS has not formally evaluated the program, but the company continues to invest $10,000 per intern. The company has invested a total of more than $13.5 billion in the program since its start in 1968. Despite the lack of hard evaluation data, UPS managers report that the program helps them look for unconventional solutions to problems. One manager who spent a month working at a halfway house in New York was impressed by the creative ideas of uneducated addicts for keeping teens away from drugs. The manager realized that she had failed to capitalize on the creativity of the employees she supervised. As a result, when she returned to her job and faced problems, she started brainstorming with her entire staff, not just senior managers. Other managers report that the experience helped them empathize with employees facing crises at home.

Characteristics of Successful Diversity Efforts

Which is most effective, a behavior-based program or an attitude awareness and change program? Increasing evidence shows that attitude awareness programs are ineffective and that one-time diversity training programs are unlikely to succeed. For example, R. R. Donnelley and Sons suspended its diversity awareness training program even though the company has spent more than $3 million on it as a result of a racial discrimination lawsuit.[54]

At various R. R. Donnelley training sessions, participants were encouraged to voice their concerns. Many said that they were experiencing difficulty in working effectively because of abuse and harassment. The managers who were attending the training disputed those concerns. Also, after training, an employee who applied for an open position was rejected because, she was told, she was too honest in expressing her concerns during the diversity training session. Although R. R. Donnelley held many diversity training sessions, little progress was made in increasing the employment and promotion rates of women and minorities. Because of the low ratio of black employees to white employees, many black employees were asked to attend multiple training sessions to ensure diverse groups, which they resented. The company declined to release to shareholders data that it provided to the Equal Employment Opportunity Commission regarding female and minority representation in jobs throughout the company. The firm also failed to act on recommendations made by company-approved employee "diversity councils."

More generally, a survey of diversity training efforts found that

- The most common area addressed through diversity is the pervasiveness of stereotypes, assumptions, and biases.
- Fewer than one-third of the companies do any kind of long-term evaluation or follow-up. The most common indicators of success were reduced number of grievances and lawsuits, increased diversity in promotions and hiring, increased self-awareness of biases, and increased consultation of human resource specialists on diversity-related issues.
- Most programs lasted only one day or less.
- Three-fourths of the survey respondents indicated that they believed the typical employee leaves diversity training with positive attitudes toward diversity. However, over 50 percent reported that the programs have no effect over the long term.[55]

Table 10.6 shows the characteristics associated with the long-term success of diversity programs. It is critical that the diversity program be tied to business objectives. For example, cultural differences affect the type of skin cream consumers believe they need or the fragrance they may be attracted to. Understanding cultural differences is part of understanding the consumer (which is critical to the success of companies such as Avon). Top management support can be demonstrated by creating a structure to support the initiative. Bank of America in San Francisco has a diversity department to handle day-to-day issues. The CEO of the bank created a corporate diversity task force involving 28 executives from different geographical locations and business functions whose goals were to gather employee feedback, review current programs, and suggest new ways to promote diversity. Diversity business councils were created to formulate strategies to ensure that the diversity effort was related to business needs. Diversity networks are available to assist white males, women, Hispanics, and African Americans in their personal and professional development.[56]

TABLE 10.6
Characteristics Associated with Diversity Programs' Long-Term Success

- Top management provides resources, personally intervenes, and publicly advocates diversity.
- The program is structured.
- Capitalizing on a diverse work force is defined as a business objective.
- Capitalizing on a diverse work force is seen as necessary to generate revenue and profits.
- The program is evaluated.
- Manager involvement is mandatory.
- The program is seen as a culture change, not a one-shot program.
- Managers and demographic groups are not blamed for problems.
- Behaviors and skills needed to successfully interact with others are taught.
- Managers are rewarded on progress toward meeting diversity goals.
- Management collects employee feedback and responds to it.

Source: S. Rynes and B. Rosen, "What Makes Diversity Programs Work?" *HR Magazine* (October 1994): 67–73; S. Rynes and B. Rosen, "A Field Survey of Factors Affecting the Adoption and Perceived Success of Diversity Training," *Personnel Psychology* 48 (1995): 247–70; J. Gordon, "Different from What? Diversity as a Performance Issue," *Training* (May 1995): 25–33; Corporate Leadership Council, *The Evolution of Corporate Diversity* (Washington, DC: Corporate Executive Board, 2002).

Another important characteristic of diversity programs is that managers are rewarded for progress toward meeting diversity goals.[57] Allstate Insurance Company surveys all 50,000 of its employees four times a year. The survey asks employees to evaluate how well the company is satisfying customers and employees. Several questions are used as a "diversity index." Employees are asked questions about the extent to which managers' racial or gender biases affect development opportunities, promotions, and service to customers. Twenty-five percent of a manager's yearly bonus is determined by how employees evaluate him or her on the diversity index.

Consider Texaco's diversity effort, shown in Table 10.7. Prior to becoming a subsidiary of Chevron Texaco, Texaco developed a state-of-the-art diversity program after the company had to pay more than $175 million to settle a racial discrimination lawsuit.[58] The lawsuit made public accusations that company executives were using racial slurs. As Table 10.7 shows, managing diversity at Texaco went far beyond workshop attendance. Managing diversity became part of a culture change. Texaco's diversity effort included programs designed to stop discrimination in hiring, retention, and promotion. Managers were held accountable for diversity goals in their performance evaluations. The company also realized that to capitalize on diversity from a business perspective, it needed to give more opportunities to minority vendors, suppliers, and customers.

There is considerable evidence that the program has transformed the culture. From 1996 to October 2001, Chevron and Texaco contracted $2.7 billion in products and services from women-owned or minority-owned suppliers.[59] Chevron Texaco also supports diversity networks, which are open to all employees. These formally structured organizations must show how they support the company's diversity objectives, vision, values, and strategy. Currently, there are nine groups with 3,360 members (approximately 5 percent of all employees). These groups include a Native American network, a lesbian and gay network, a women's network, a black employees network, and a Filipino-American network. These networks are more than social clubs. Their goals are to increase members' cultural awareness and leadership skills, to sponsor learning activities that help develop a more cross-culturally sensitive work force, and to communicate new ideas.

TABLE 10.7   Texaco's Diversity Effort

Recruitment and Hiring

- Ask search firms to identify wider arrays of candidates.
- Enhance the interviewing, selection, and hiring skills of managers.
- Expand college recruitment at historically minority colleges.

Identifying and Developing Talent

- Form a partnership with INROADS, a nationwide internship program that targets minority students for management careers.
- Establish a mentoring process.
- Refine the company's global succession planning system to improve identification of talent.
- Improve the selection and development of managers and leaders to help ensure that they are capable of maximizing team performance.

Ensuring Fair Treatment

- Conduct extensive diversity training.
- Implement an alternative dispute resolution process.
- Include women and minorities on all human resources committees throughout the company.

Holding Managers Accountable

- Link managers' compensation to their success in creating "openness and inclusion in the workplace."
- Implement 360-degree feedback for all managers and supervisors.
- Redesign the company's employee attitude survey and begin using it annually to monitor employee attitudes.

Improving Relationships with External Stakeholders

- Broaden the company's base of vendors and suppliers to incorporate more minority- and women-owned businesses.
- Increase banking, investment, and insurance business with minority- and women-owned firms.
- Add more independent, minority retailers and increase the number of minority managers in company-owned gas stations and Xpress Lube outlets.

Source: Don Hellriegel, Susan E. Jackson, and John W. Slocum, Jr., *Management*, 8th ed. (Cincinnati, OH: South-Western College Publishing, 1999). Originally adapted from V. C. Smith, "Texaco Outlines Comprehensive Initiatives," *Human Resource Executive* (February 1997): 13; A. Bryant, "How Much Has Texaco Changed? A Mixed Report Card on Anti-Bias Efforts," *The New York Times*, November 2, 1997: 3-1, 3-16, 3-17; and "Texaco's Worldforce Diversity Plan," as reprinted in *Workforce* (March 1997) supp. From D. Daft and R. Noe, *Organizational Behavior* (Fort Worth, TX: Dryden Press, 2001): 58.

Successful diversity programs involve more than just an effective training program. They require an ongoing process of culture change that includes top management support as well as diversity policies and practices in the areas of recruitment and hiring, training and development, and administrative structures, such as conducting diversity surveys and evaluating managers' progress on diversity goals.[60]

School-to-Work Transition

Industry and education experts agree that a system is needed for training students who do not attend college directly after high school. **School-to-work transition programs** combine classroom experiences with work experiences to prepare high school graduates for employment. Many school districts have changed their curriculum to include more work experience as part of the traditional classroom-based educational experience. The federal government, recognizing a need for this type of program, has helped fund local government efforts. The **School-to-Work Opportunities Act** is designed to assist the states in building school-to-work systems that prepare students for high-skill, high-wage jobs or future education. The act encourages partnerships between educational institutions, employers, and labor unions. The act requires that every school-to-work system include work-based learning, school-based learning, and connecting activities that match students with employers and bring classrooms and workplaces together. For example, a high school in Wisconsin has a program that combines engineering classes at school with paid, on-the-job engineering experience.[61] Wisconsin has one of the most fully developed school-to-work programs. Apprenticeships are offered in 13 fields ranging from tourism to engineering. Committees of employers and educators developed the skill sets to be covered and identified appropriate classroom and work experiences.

Although students are seeking to enroll in the program, less than 1 percent of all high school juniors and seniors in Wisconsin participate. The problem is that employer interest in the program cannot support the number of students who are interested. There is a shortage of workplace apprenticeship experiences. One reason for employers' lack of enthusiasm is that they don't understand what school-to-work programs involve. Another is that although apprenticeships provide the most intense, relevant experience, they are the most time consuming to develop and implement. The key is to identify how the student can benefit the company. The challenge is to make the program practical enough for employers, with a large payoff to educators to create students learning opportunities that are interesting and relevant to careers.

Approximately 20 percent of the production workers at Northrup Grumman Newport News, the Virginia shipbuilder, are required to do welding as part of their jobs.[62] Work force aging and retirements have led the company to recognize the need to develop a source of employees with welding skills. To do so, Northrup Grumman Newport News partners with five vocational schools in the Newport News, Virginia, area to improve their welding programs. The company pays student tuition, offers students paid work experiences, licenses its training software to the schools, and works to upgrade the schools' programs and facilities. Northrup Grumman Newport News believes that active involvement in the schools helps make both students and the school aware of the opportunities at the company and the skills that are required to be successful. This program helps ensure that the company is able to attract competent employees.

Company-sponsored mentoring programs are also used to link companies to students.[63] Leadership Connections matches mentors with female high school students who are recruited through churches, schools, and juvenile courts. The students come from poor, rural North Carolina. The volunteer mentors are women from more than 40 companies, including Sara Lee and Carolina Power and Light. The only requirement is that the women be willing to commit to improving the mentee's well-being. The mentoring program gives students an awareness of the expectations of the working world. The mentors help at-risk students develop self-esteem and confidence and stay out of trouble. Most of the students have improved their school grades since joining the program and many go on to college.

Training's Role in Welfare-to-Work and Other Public-Private Sector Programs

As the chapter opening vignette illustrated, companies are seeking to hire people from nontraditional sources (e.g., welfare roles) to meet labor needs. Also, the welfare reform act passed by Congress in 1996 (the Personal Responsibility and Work Opportunity Act) increased the pressure on welfare recipients to find jobs, through either public employment agencies or other ways. Under the law, most people have a five-year limit on benefits and must find jobs within two years. The law also gives employers incentives (tax credits) for each welfare recipient they hire. Training plays an important part in helping these employees succeed on the job.

TJX Companies, the parent of off-price clothing retailers T.J. Maxx and Marshalls, was desperate to fill jobs in its retail stores.[64] Turnover is typically a problem in retailing, and TJX was accustomed to 100 percent turnover of store jobs in a year. To find employees, TJX has taken people off the welfare rolls. The company pays CIC Enterprises to create and run a job hotline tied to agencies that help prepare welfare recipients for work. A store manager for a T.J. Maxx or Marshalls in any city can call a toll-free number at any time to request candidates for job openings. For every ten calls made to the hotline, eight have produced a job candidate who has been hired. TJX also started a program with Morgan Memorial Goodwill Industries in Boston. The program gives welfare recipients three weeks of class-room training followed by an internship at a store. Those who complete the internship are guaranteed jobs. A case manager follows up on program graduates for at least a year, help-ing solve child care and transportation problems that the employee might experience.

TJX has received many benefits from hiring former welfare recipients. The company reports that the retention rate for welfare-to-work hires is above the retention rate for tra-ditional hires. The welfare-to-work hires are looking for full-time jobs, whereas the typical retail employee is looking for short-term and part-time work.

Marriott International's welfare-to-work program has resulted in jobs for 700 people in the past five years. Marriott currently operates the program in several large cities such as New Orleans, Atlanta, and Los Angeles. Marriott helps find employment for persons who would otherwise be considered "hard-core unemployed." Now working for Marriott as hotel employ-ees are persons formerly on welfare who could not find and retain jobs because of problems ranging from dropping out of high school, drug addiction, and arrest records to emotional scarring from poor marital or family relationships. Marriott's Pathways to Independence pro-gram is considered a model of how corporate-sponsored training and employment efforts can move welfare recipients to work. The six-week program consists of classroom training and work sessions in Marriott properties (e.g., hotels).

To qualify for the program, applicants must have a sixth-grade reading level, pass a drug test, and demonstrate a desire to work. Less than 25 percent of the applicants are accepted into the program. Despite the rigorous selection process, program participants often need to develop both job skills and life management skills to succeed. Besides providing job skills, trainers have to build trainees' self-confidence and often help the employee deal with personal issues. For example, one Marriott trainer brought a pair of slacks and shoes to work for a trainee. She also made numerous phone calls to arrange child care for other trainees and spent an afternoon visiting shelters and driving trainees to government agen-cies. A key problem is how to prepare workers to budget their money and manage their first paycheck. Some participants were spending all the money they earned on entertain-ment and not leaving enough to pay rent and buy food. Trainers teach about checking accounts and budgeting.

Welfare recipients who complete the Pathways program become Marriott "associates" (employees). They are provided with a toll-free phone number where trained counselors answer questions about child care, finances, school systems, and domestic and substance abuse.

Training evaluation has helped Marriott modify the program to increase the success rate of Pathway trainees. Analysis revealed that unreliable child care and drug abuse were primary causes of Pathway trainees' failing to complete training or leaving the company. Marriott requires trainees to have child care, transportation, and housing arrangements. It runs background checks and requires participants to take drug tests before and during training.[65]

There are two methods for training welfare recipients.[66] In the first method, government agencies refer welfare recipients to a company-sponsored training program subsidized with money and tax credits from the government. An example is Marriott's Pathways to Independence program.

The second method is for state and local governments to provide life and skills training directly to welfare recipients. The skills developed are often based on the needs of local employers. For example, in Oregon, the Department of Human Resources' JOBS training program has helped 19,000 people find work. Participants attend training sessions on basic work habits and learn to interview, write résumés, and manage their personal lives. The welfare-to-work transition is facilitated by a state law that requires welfare recipients to find work or risk losing their benefits. Another program requires the state to reimburse companies for the wages of welfare recipients for six months, while the employers provide meaningful work experiences and training. In one program for clerical workers, 85 percent of those who stayed in the program for four months were hired by the employers and still had jobs even after the state subsidy ended.

One problem facing welfare-to-work programs is that as unemployment rises, welfare recipients face competition against an increased number of job seekers who have greater experience, fewer problems finding child care, and better access to transportation.[67] For example, Cleveland Track Material, which makes railroad track equipment, has 14 Center for Employment Training alumni in its work force of 220 employees. Cleveland Track Material would like to hire more workers from the employment center, but when business dropped, the company reduced all hiring.

The **Workforce Investment Act** of 1998 created a new, comprehensive work force investment system. The reformed system is intended to be customer focused, to help Americans manage their careers through information and high-quality services, and to help U.S. companies find skilled workers. The cornerstone of the new system is One-Stop service delivery, which unifies numerous training, education, and employment programs into a single, customer-friendly system in each community. The underlying notion of One-Stop is the coordination of programs, services, and governance structures so that the customer has access to a seamless system of work force investment services. It is envisioned that a variety of programs could utilize One-Stop's common intake, case management, and job development services in order to take full advantage of One-Stop's potential for efficiency and effectiveness. A wide range of services, including training and employment programs, will be available to meet the needs of employers and job seekers. The challenge in helping One-Stop live up to its potential is to make sure that the state and local boards can effectively coordinate and collaborate with the network of other service agencies, including Temporary Assistance for Needy Families agencies, transportation agencies and providers, metropolitan planning organizations, child care agencies, nonprofit and community partners, and the broad range of partners who work with youth.

O*NET, the Occupational Information Network, is a unique, comprehensive database and directory of occupational titles, worker competencies, and job requirements and resources.[68] O*NET, which supports One-Stop service delivery, is the primary source of occupational information in the United States. The O*NET database includes information on skills, abilities, knowledge, work activities, and interests associated with occupations.

O*NET information can be used to facilitate career exploration, vocational counseling, and a variety of human resources functions, such as developing job orders, creating position descriptions, and aligning training with current workplace needs. Job seekers can use O*NET to find out which jobs fit with their interests, skills, and experience, and can identify the skills, knowledge, and abilities needed for their dream job.

TRAINING ISSUES RELATED TO INTERNAL NEEDS OF THE COMPANY

Basic Skills Training

Chapter 1 highlighted employers' difficulty in finding competent entry-level job candidates—persons with appropriate reading, writing, and arithmetic skills. Chapter 3 emphasized the relationship between cognitive ability, reading skills, and training success. Also, Chapter 3 discussed how basic skills can be identified during needs assessment. Because employers have not been successful at finding job candidates with appropriate levels of basic skills (a recruiting and selection issue), employers are forced to develop basic skills training programs. Also, as companies move toward high-performance workplace systems, they may find that current employees lack the skills needed to realize these systems' benefits. Basic skills include the ability to read instructions, write reports, and do math at a level needed to perform job duties.

As explained in Chapter 3, basic skills programs involve several steps. First, the necessary skill level needs to be identified. That is, what level of basic skills do employees need to be successful in their jobs? Second, employees' current skill levels must be assessed. The training programs that are developed will be based on the gap between current skill level and desired skill level. Training programs need to include an emphasis on basic skills in the context of work problems to increase their meaningfulness to trainees. In 24-hour operations (such as manufacturing plants) that use several shifts of employees, basic skills training needs to be available to employees during their off-shift times. Finally, many employees who lack basic skills do not want their peers to be aware of these deficiencies. Participation in basic skills training needs to be as private as possible. If privacy cannot be guaranteed, those employees who most need basic skills training may not participate.

Chapter 3 discussed how Georgia-Pacific identified basic skills deficiencies and contracted with a local community college to offer basic skills training. Other companies are developing on-site learning centers to help employees develop basic skills.

For example, Smith and Wesson, the firearms manufacturer, reorganized its production department.[69] The reorganization made jobs more interesting and challenging by requiring employees to interpret process control statistics and operate in work teams. The reorganization revealed that some employees' basic skills deficiencies kept them from being successful in the new production environment. Smith and Wesson conducted an assessment of the skills that employees needed in the new production environment. This assessment identified three skills: higher math skills for understanding numerical control equipment, better reading and writing skills, and better oral communication skills for working in teams and interacting with other employees. A literacy audit showed that employees needed to have at least an eighth-grade reading level. To determine which employees needed training, Smith and Wesson used tests. To ensure employee confidentiality, the test results were sent to employees' home addresses. Thirty percent of employees scored below the eighth-grade level in either reading or math. These employees were told that they would not lose their jobs, but they were expected to take basic skills classes on company time, paid for by the company. Management presentations on the business benefits of the classes helped encourage employees who were reluctant to participate.

Evaluation of the first classes was very positive. Seventy percent of employees who attended the classes improved their reading skills to the eighth-grade level or higher. A company survey found that the program helped employees improve their writing and ability to read charts, graphs, and bulletin boards; increased their ability to use fractions and decimals; and improved their self-confidence.

Melting the Glass Ceiling

A major training and development issue facing companies today is how to get women and minorities into upper-level management positions—how to break the **glass ceiling.** The glass ceiling is a barrier to advancement to the higher levels of the organization. This barrier may be due to stereotypes or company systems that adversely affect the development of women or minorities.[70] The glass ceiling is likely caused by lack of access to training programs, to appropriate developmental job experiences, and to developmental relationships (such as mentoring).[71] Male managers' development experiences tend to be given to them; female managers have to be more proactive about getting development assignments. Research has found no gender differences in access to job experiences involving transitions such as handling new job responsibilities or creating change such as fixing business problems or making strategic changes in the business.[72] However, male managers received significantly more assignments involving high levels of responsibility (high stakes, international assignments managing business diversity, handling external pressure) than did female managers of similar ability and managerial level. Also, female managers reported experiencing more challenge because of lack of personal support (a type of job demand considered to be an obstacle that has been found to relate to harmful stress). Career encouragement from peers and senior managers does help women advance to the highest management levels.[73] Managers making developmental assignments must carefully consider whether gender biases or stereotypes are influencing the types of assignments given to women versus men.

Consider Deloitte and Touche's efforts to melt the glass ceiling. Deloitte and Touche is an accounting, tax, and consulting firm with offices throughout the United States. The company had been experiencing high turnover of talented women and set out to understand why this was occurring and what could be done to stop it.[74] Table 10.8 shows Deloitte and Touche's recommendations for melting the glass ceiling and for helping retain talented women. The recommendations involve first preparing for change and then providing operational steps ensuring that qualified women would be promoted and women's turnover rate would fall. Deloitte's Initiative for the Retention and Advancement of Women grew from a task force chaired by the company's chief executive officer. Deloitte and Touche made a business case for change by showing the senior partners of the company that half of the new hires were women and that half of them left the company before becoming candidates for upper-management positions (i.e., partners). Data on the problem were gathered by having every management professional in the company attend a workshop designed to explore how gender attitudes affected the work environment (and led to the loss of talented women). The workshops included discussions, videos, and case studies. For example, in one case scenario partners evaluated two promising employees (one male and one female) with identical

TABLE 10.8
Deloitte and Touche's Recommendations for Melting the Glass Ceiling

Source: Based on D. McCracken, "Winning the Talent War for Women," *Harvard Business Review* (November–December 2000): 159–67.

Make sure that senior management supports and is involved in the program.
Make a business case for change.
Make the change public.
Using task forces, focus groups, and questionnaires, gather data on problems causing the glass ceiling.
Create awareness of how gender attitudes affect the work environment.
Create accountability through reviews of promotion rates and assignment decisions.
Promote development for all employees.

skills. One issue raised through this case analysis was that men were evaluated on their potential, women on their performance. Discussion suggested that the male employee could be expected to grow into the position through mentoring and other types of development. The female employee's evaluation was based on performance in her current position. Her potential was not considered; for example, her past performance indicated that she was good in her current job but didn't have the necessary skills to move into executive management. The workshop also focused on how work assignments were allocated. High-profile, high-revenue assignments were important for advancement in the company. Discussion in the workshops showed that women were passed over for these desirable assignments because of false assumptions that male partners made about what women wanted, such as no travel. Also, women tended to get assigned to projects in nonprofit, health care, and retail—important segments but not as highly visible as areas such as manufacturing, financial services, and mergers and acquisitions.

As a result of the workshops, Deloitte and Touche began discussing assignment decisions to make sure that women had opportunities for highly visible assignments. Also, the company started formal career planning for both women and men. The company also sponsored networking events for women, where they had the opportunity to hear from successful women partners and meet other women at their level and higher in the company.

To measure the effectiveness of the program, Deloitte and Touche offices were given a menu of goals that they could choose from as evaluation criteria. These goals included recruiting more women and reducing their turnover. The compensation and promotability of office managers depended in part on their meeting these objectives. Top-level managers were given results on turnover and promotion rates for each office. Low-performing offices were visited by top-level managers to facilitate more progress.

Melting the glass ceiling takes time. Currently, 14 percent of Deloitte's partners and directors are women. Women's and men's turnover rates are comparable. Reducing the turnover rate for women has saved the company an estimated $250 million in hiring and training costs. Deloitte is still striving to make sure that more women are partners and directors. In a global business world, one challenge is to extend the values of the initiative while respecting local cultural norms that might view women as less desirable employees or business partners.

Women and minorities often have trouble finding mentors because of their lack of access to the "old boy network," managers' preference to interact with other managers of similar status rather than with line employees, and intentional exclusion by managers who have negative stereotypes about women's and minorities' abilities, motivation, and job preferences.[75] Potential mentors may view minorities and women as a threat to their job security because they believe affirmative action plans give those groups preferential treatment. Wal-Mart's strong corporate culture—emphasizing leadership, trust, willingness to relocate on short notice, and promotion from within—may have unintentionally created a glass ceiling.[76] Eighty-six percent of store manager positions are held by men. More than two-thirds of Wal-Mart managers started as hourly employees. Hourly job openings are posted at each store, but Wal-Mart never posted openings for management training positions that allowed hourly employees to move up into salaried, management positions. Part of the reason for this practice was that Wal-Mart values efficiency and never saw the need for job postings to fill open management positions. The other reason is that Wal-Mart trusts its managers to promote individuals who deserve promotion. However, women at Wal-Mart claim that it is difficult to find out about manager jobs. Traditionally, managers at Wal-Mart had to be willing to move with short notice. At Wal-Mart, this relocation requirement results in more opportunities for management jobs for men than for women. Male employees had more access to information about management job openings because they spent more time socializing and talking with management employees (who are primarily male). Wal-Mart is taking steps to ensure that the company remains a good place to work. For example, to give women more opportunities for management positions, Wal-Mart is developing a posting system for all management jobs. The company also plans on providing employees with a database that will notify them of job openings at stores across the country.

Many companies, as part of their approach to managing a diverse work force, are using mentoring programs to ensure that women and minorities gain the skills and visibility needed to move into managerial positions. Procter and Gamble (P&G) has a unique program called "Mentoring Up," which asks mid- and junior-level female managers to mentor senior-level managers to raise their awareness of work-related issues affecting women. The goals of the program are to reduce turnover of promising female managers, to give women managers greater exposure to P&G's top decision makers, and to improve cross-gender communications. Mentoring Up was developed because of turnover of high-potential female employees who in exit interviews cited not feeling valued (rather than money, promotions, or better assignments) as the reason why they were leaving the company. Although the program was designed to help upper-level managers better understand how to manage women, the program also includes five upper-level female managers who are participating as mentees.

How does the program work? It incorporates many characteristics of effective mentoring programs. All eligible female junior-level managers and male senior-level managers are expected to participate. The female managers must have at least one year of tenure and be good performers. Junior mentors are matched with senior mentors based on their responses to a questionnaire. Both mentors and protégés attend an orientation session that includes a panel discussion by past participants in the program and a series of exercises probing women's workplace issues and reasons for success at P&G. The mentor-mentee pairs are required to meet at least once every two months. Mentors and mentees receive discussion guides designed to help facilitate dialogue. For example, one guide asked the mentor-mentee pairs to explore the keys to success and failure for women and men in company leadership positions. The discussion guides also include questions designed to elicit feelings about when women feel valued. The mentor and mentee explore differences and similarities in responses to these questions to identify how people like to be recognized. Two issues have frequently been raised in the mentor–mentee relationships: first, the barriers that women face in achieving a balance between work and life and, second, differences in managerial and decision-making styles between men and women.

One of the biggest benefits of the program has been that mentors and mentees have shared advice and perspectives and feel comfortable using each other to test out new ideas. Junior female managers also get exposure to the top executives who make promotion and succession-planning decisions. The program has reduced the turnover rate of female managers. Turnover of female managers whom the company wanted to retain is down 25 percent and is now at the same rate as male manager turnover.[77]

Joint Union–Management Programs

To be more competitive, U.S. industries that have lost considerable market share to foreign competition (e.g., the auto industry) have developed joint union–management training. Both labor and management have been forced to accept new roles. Employees need to become involved in business planning and strategic decision making, and management needs to learn how to share power and allow worker participation in decision making.

The initial goal of these programs was to help displaced employees find new jobs by providing skill training and outplacement assistance. Currently, **joint union–management training programs** provide a wide range of services designed to help employees learn skills that are directly related to their job and also develop skills that are "portable"—that is, valuable to employers in other companies or industries.[78] Both employers and unions contribute money to run the programs, and both oversee their operation. Major joint efforts include the International Association of Machinists and Aerospace Workers (IAM) with the Boeing Company; the United Auto Workers (UAW) with Ford and General Motors; and the Communications Workers of America with Qwest Communications, SBC Communications, and Verizon Communications. Boeing and the IAM have been working together on educational programs since 1989.[79] The IAM–Boeing Company joint program offers educational opportunities to IAM-represented employees, training to improve personal and work skills, and programs related to safety and wellness at work, at home, and in the community. Recently, the joint programs have helped laid-off Boeing employees gain reemployment through job search assistance and retraining.

The National Coalition for Telecommunications Education and Learning (NACTEL) is a partnership between telecommunications companies and labor unions that have developed online education programs.[80] NACTEL includes courses that allow employees to work toward associate degrees (e.g., Telecommunications) and certificate programs (e.g., Introduction to Telecommunications). The NACTEL programs are offered by Pace University's School of Computer Science and Information Systems. The curriculum is based on training programs offered by SBC, Qwest, and Verizon.

The UAW–Ford joint effort offers a number of programs, including a technical skills program that helps employees gain skills needed to function in the high-performance workplace and including UAW–Ford University, which offers online courses from accredited universities that can be taken by employees for credit toward certificate programs and toward associate, bachelor's, master's, and even doctoral degrees.[81] A negotiated central fund and local training funds support the joint training efforts. Program administration is provided by the first national training center ever negotiated in a labor contract in the United States and by a network of local committees at each UAW–Ford location in the United States. At both the national and local levels, the programs address issues in product quality, education and development, team structures, health and safety, and employee assistance (e.g., counseling, help with care of elders). For example, the UAW–Ford "Best in Class" Quality Program established a new certification training for quality representatives, established a review process for quality concerns, and helped employees work together to improve quality.

Yes, these programs are costly (General Motors has spent over $1.6 billion jointly with the UAW), and employees may get trained in skills that are not directly related to their current jobs. But both labor and management believe that these programs improve the literacy levels of the work force and contribute to productivity. Both parties believe that encouraging lifelong learning is a key aspect of a work force that can adapt to new technologies and global competition.

Succession Planning

Many companies are losing a sizable number of upper-level managers because of retirement and company restructurings that reduce the number of potential upper-level managers. Companies are finding that their middle managers are not ready to move into upper management positions because of skill weaknesses or lack of experience. These problems create the need for succession planning.

Succession planning refers to the process of identifying and developing the future leadership of the company. Succession planning helps organizations in several different ways.[82] It requires senior management to systematically conduct a review of leadership talent in the company. It ensures that top-level managerial talent is available. It provides a set of development experiences that managers must complete to be considered for top management positions, which avoids premature promotion of managers who are not ready for upper-management ranks. Succession planning systems also help attract and retain managerial employees by providing them with development opportunities that they can complete if upper-level management is a career goal for them.

High-potential employees are employees that the company believes are capable of being successful in higher-level managerial positions such as general manager of a strategic business unit, functional director (e.g., director of marketing), or chief executive officer (CEO).[83] The activities discussed in Chapter 9 are used to develop high-potential employees. High-potential employees typically complete an individualized development program that involves education, executive mentoring and coaching, and rotation through job assignments.[84] Job assignments are based on the successful career paths of the managers that the high-potential employees are being prepared to replace. High-potential employees may also receive special assignments, such as making presentations and serving on committees and task forces. The group is the talent pool from which to choose replacements for top-level managers.

Research suggests that the development of high-potential employees involves three stages.[85] A large pool of employees may initially be identified as high-potential employees, but the numbers are reduced over time because of turnover, poor performance, or a personal choice not to strive for a higher-level position. In stage 1, high-potential employees are selected. Those who have completed elite academic programs (e.g., an MBA at Stanford) or who have been outstanding performers are identified. Psychological tests—such as those done at assessment centers—may also be used.

In stage 2, high-potential employees receive development experiences. Those who succeed are the ones who continue to demonstrate good performance. A willingness to make sacrifices for the company is also necessary (e.g., accepting new assignments or relocating to a new location). Good oral and written communication skills, ease in interpersonal relationships, and talent for leadership are a must. In what is known as a tournament model of

TABLE 10.9
The Succession Planning Process

Source: Based on B. Dowell, "Succession Planning," in *Implementing Organizational Interventions*, ed. J. Hedge & E. Pulaskos (San Francisco: Jossey Bass, 2002): 78–109.

1. Identify what positions are included in the plan.
2. Identify the employees who are included in the plan.
3. Develop standards to evaluate positions (e.g., competencies, desired experiences, desired knowledge, developmental value).
4. Determine how employee potential will be measured (e.g., current performance and potential performance).
5. Develop the succession planning review.
6. Link the succession planning system with other human resource systems, including training and development, compensation, and staffing systems.
7. Determine what feedback is provided to employees.

job transitions, high-potential employees who meet the expectations of their senior managers in this stage are given the opportunity to advance into the next stage of the process.[86] Employees who do not meet the expectations are ineligible for higher-level managerial positions in the company.

To reach stage 3, high-potential employees usually have to be viewed by top management as fitting into the company's culture and having the personality characteristics needed to successfully represent the company. These employees have the potential to occupy the company's top positions. In stage 3, the CEO becomes actively involved in developing the employees, who are exposed to the company's key personnel and given a greater understanding of the company's culture. Note that the development of high-potential employees is a slow process. Reaching stage 3 may take 15 to 20 years.

Table 10.9 shows the steps that a company takes to develop a succession planning system. The first step is to identify what positions are included in the succession plan, such as all management positions or only certain levels of management. The second step is to identify which employees are part of the succession planning system. For example, in some companies only high-potential employees are included in the succession plan. Third, the company needs to identify how positions will be evaluated. For example, will the emphasis be on competencies needed for each position or on the experiences an individual needs to have before moving into the position? Fourth, the company should identify how employee potential will be measured. That is, will employees' performance in their current jobs as well as ratings of potential be used? Will employees' position interests and career goals be considered? Fifth, the succession planning review process needs to be developed. Typically, succession planning reviews first involve employees' managers and human resources. A talent review could also include an overall assessment of leadership talent in the company, an identification of high-potential employees, and a discussion of plans to keep key managers from leaving the company. Sixth, succession planning is dependent on other human resource systems, including compensation, training and development, and staffing. Incentives and bonuses may be linked to completion of development opportunities. Activities such as training courses, job experiences, mentors, and 360-degree feedback can be used to meet development needs. Companies need to make decisions such as will they fill an open management position internally with a less-experienced employee who will improve in the role over time, or will they hire a manager from outside the company who can immediately deliver results. Finally, employees need to be provided with feedback on future moves, expected career paths, and development goals and experiences.

A good example of succession planning is the system at WellPoint, a health care company headquartered in Thousand Oaks, California.[87] WellPoint has a Web-based corporate database that identifies employees for management jobs throughout the company and tracks the development of employee talent. WellPoint has operations across the United States, including locations in California and Georgia. The succession planning system includes 600 managers and executives across five levels of the company. The Human Resource Planning System (HRPS) has detailed information on possible candidates, including performance evaluations, summaries of the candidates' accomplishments at the company, self-evaluations, information about career goals, and personal data such as the candidates' willingness to relocate to another part of the company. Part of the development of HRPS involved identifying the company's strength and weaknesses at each position. Senior management team members developed standards, or benchmarks, to use to identify the best candidates for promotion. The HRPS system allows managers and the human resource team to identify and evaluate candidates for every management position in the company. It helps identify and track the development of promising internal candidates and also identifies areas where internal candidates are weak, so that (1) external candidates can be recruited, (2) a special development program can be initiated to develop employee talent, and (3) the company can place more emphasis on developing the missing skills and competencies in internal candidates. For example, because WellPoint lacked candidates for two levels of management, the company created a special training program that used business case simulations for 24 managers and executives who had been identified as high-potential candidates for upper-level management positions.

WellPoint's process of succession planning includes several steps. First, each employee who is eligible for succession planning completes a self-evaluation that is sent to his or her manager. The manager adds a performance appraisal, a rating on the employee's core competencies, and a promotion assessment, that is, an assessment of the employee's potential for promotion. The promotion assessment includes the manager's opinion regarding what positions the employee might be ready for and when the employee should be moved. It also includes the manager's view on who could fill the open position if the employee is promoted. The information from the employee and the manager is used to create an online résumé for each eligible employee. The system has benefited the company's bottom line. WellPoint realized a 86 percent internal promotion rate, which exceeded its goal of filling 75 percent of management positions from within. By improving employees' opportunities for promotion, WellPoint has reduced its turnover rate by 6 percent since 1997 and has saved $21 million on recruitment and training expenses. The time to fill open management positions has been reduced from 60 days to 35 days.

Developing Managers with Dysfunctional Behaviors

A number of studies have identified managerial behaviors that can cause an otherwise competent manager to be a "toxic" or ineffective manager. These behaviors include insensitivity to others, inability to be a team player, arrogance, poor conflict-management skills, inability to meet business objectives, and inability to change or adapt during a transition.[88] For example, a skilled manager who is interpersonally abrasive, aggressive, and autocratic may find it difficult to motivate subordinates, may alienate internal and external customers, and may have trouble getting ideas accepted by superiors. These managers are in jeopardy of losing their jobs and have little chance of future advancement because of their dysfunctional behaviors. Typically, a combination of assessment, training, and counseling is used to help managers change dysfunctional behavior.

One example of a program designed specifically to help managers with dysfunctional behavior is the Individual Coaching for Effectiveness (ICE) program.[89] Although the effectiveness of these types of programs needs to be further investigated, initial research suggests that managers' participation in these programs results in skill improvement and reduced likelihood of termination.[90] The ICE program includes diagnosis, coaching, and support activities. The program is tailored to the manager's needs. Clinical, counseling, or industrial/organizational psychologists are involved in all phases of the ICE program. They conduct the diagnosis, coach and counsel the manager, and develop action plans for implementing new skills on the job.

The first step in the ICE program, diagnosis, involves collecting information about the manager's personality, skills, and interests. Interviews with the manager and the manager's supervisor and colleagues plus psychological tests are used to determine whether the manager can actually change the dysfunctional behavior. For example, personality traits such as extreme defensiveness may make it difficult for the manager to change the problem behavior. If it is determined that the manager can benefit from the program, then typically the manager and the manager's supervisor set specific developmental objectives tailored to the manager's needs.

In the coaching phase of the program, the manager is first presented with information about the targeted skills or behavior. This information may be about principles of effective communication or teamwork, tolerance of individual differences in the workplace, or methods for conducting effective meetings. The second step is for the manager to participate in behavior-modeling training, which was discussed in Chapter 7. The manager also receives psychological counseling to overcome beliefs that may inhibit learning the desired behavior.

The support phase of the program involves creating conditions to ensure that on the job the manager is able to use the new behaviors and skills acquired in the ICE program. The supervisor provides feedback to the manager and the psychologist about progress the manager has made in using the new skills and behavior. The psychologist and manager identify situations in which the manager may tend to rely on dysfunctional behavior. The coach and manager also develop action plans that outline how the manager should try to use new behavior in daily work activities.

Training and Pay Systems

Compensation refers to pay and benefits that companies give to employees in exchange for performing their jobs. Companies use compensation systems to achieve many objectives, including attracting talented employees to join the company, motivating employees, and retaining employees by paying wages and benefits that meet or exceed those the employee might receive from other companies in the labor market (local as well as national or even international companies). As was discussed in Chapter 1, to remain competitive, companies need employees who possess a wide range of skills and are willing and able to learn new skills to meet changing customer service and product requirements.

Training is increasingly linked to employees' compensation through the use of skill-based pay systems. In **skill-based** or **knowledge-based pay systems,** employees' pay is based primarily on the knowledge and skills they possess rather than the knowledge or skills necessary to successfully perform their current job.[91] The basic idea is that to motivate employees to learn, pay is based on the skills that employees possess. Why would a company do this?

TABLE 10.10   **Example of a Skill-Based Pay System**

Skill Block	Description	Pay Rate
A	*Molding:* Operates molding machines and performs machine setup	$15 per hour
B	*Finishing:* Operates finishing machine and performs finishing machine setup function	$20 per hour
	Inspection: Operates both inspection machines and makes scrap/rework decisions	
	Packaging: Operates packaging equipment and performs inventory and shipping functions	
C	*Quality control:* Performs quality control functions	$25 per hour

Source: Based on R. L. Bunning, "Models for Skill-Based Pay Plans," *HR Magazine* (February 1992): 62–64.

The rationale is that this type of system ensures that employees are learning and gives the company additional flexibility in using employees to provide products and services. Skill-based pay systems are often used to facilitate cross-training. Cross-training involves training employees to learn the skills of one or several jobs. This system is especially critical for work teams where employees need to be able to rotate between jobs or substitute for employees who are absent.

The skill-based pay approach contributes to better use of employees' skills and ideas. It also provides the opportunity for leaner staffing levels because employee turnover or absenteeism can be covered by employees who are multiskilled. Multiskilled employees are important where different products require different manufacturing processes or where supply shortages call for adaptive or flexible responses. These are characteristics typical of many so-called advanced manufacturing environments (e.g., flexible manufacturing or just-in-time systems).[92]

Table 10.10 shows a skill-based pay system. In this example, skills are grouped into skill blocks. Employees' compensation increases as they master each skill block. Entry-level employees begin at $15 per hour and can progress to $25 per hour by mastering other skill blocks.

Skill-based pay systems have implications for needs assessment, delivery method, and evaluation of training.[93] Since pay is directly tied to the amount of knowledge or skill employees have obtained, employees will be motivated to attend training programs. This means that the volume of training conducted as well as training costs will increase. Although employee motivation to attend training may be high, it is important to conduct a thorough needs assessment (e.g., using testing) to ensure that employees have the prerequisite knowledge needed to master the new skills.

Training must also be accessible to all employees. For example, if the company manufactures products and provides services on a 24-hour basis, training must be available for employees working all shifts. Computer-assisted instruction or intranet-based training are ideal for skill-based pay systems. Training can be easily offered at all hours on an as-needed basis—employees only need access to a computer! Also, computer-based instruction can automatically track an employee's progress in training.

In skill-based pay systems, managers and/or peers usually serve as trainers. Training involves a combination of on-the-job training and use of presentation techniques such as lectures or videos. As a result, employees need to be trained to be trainers.

Finally, a key issue in skill-based pay systems is skill perishability—ensuring that employees have not forgotten the skills when it comes time to use them. Skill-based pay systems require periodic evaluation of employees' skills and knowledge using behavior and learning outcomes. Although employees may be certified that they have mastered skills, many skill-based pay programs require them to attend refresher sessions on a periodic basis to remain certified (and receive the higher wage).

Summary

This chapter explored special training and development issues relating to pressures that companies face from the external and internal company environments. External environmental pressures include the need to comply with laws, globalization, an increasingly diverse work force, and lack of skills in the labor market. The chapter addressed these environmental pressures by presenting information on legal issues in training, cross-cultural preparation, diversity training, school-to-work transition, and hard-core–unemployed training programs.

Internal issues that companies face relate to preparing the company's current work force for the future, helping dysfunctional managers, and motivating employees to learn. The chapter discussed succession planning systems, basic skills training, joint union–management training programs, and methods to ensure that women and minorities can receive training and development opportunities (melting the glass ceiling). The chapter also covered skill-based pay systems that directly link training to employees' wage rates to encourage employees to learn.

Note that for many issues discussed in this chapter, training is one part of the solution. For example, trainers and managers can take steps to ensure that women and minorities are not excluded from training programs, but this action alone will not solve the broader issue of discrimination in our society. Similarly, companies like Marriott are using training to provide welfare recipients with employment. However, training cannot overcome broader societal ills that have resulted in persons being overly dependent on the welfare system. Only through partnerships among education, private sector training practices, and government legislation can societal problems of discrimination and hard-core unemployment be resolved.

Key Terms

copyrights, *306*
Americans with Disabilities Act (ADA), *308*
reasonable accommodation, *309*
expatriate, *310*
host-country nationals, *310*
cross-cultural preparation, *310*
culture, *311*
individualism-collectivism, *312*
uncertainty avoidance, *313*
masculinity-femininity, *313*

power distance, *313*
time orientation, *313*
rigor, *314*
repatriation, *315*
virtual expatriate, *316*
managing diversity, *318*
diversity training, *321*
attitude awareness and change programs, *321*
behavior-based programs, *321*
cultural immersion, *322*
school-to-work transition programs, *325*

School-to-Work Opportunities Act, *326*
Workforce Investment Act, *328*
glass ceiling, *330*
joint union–management training programs, *333*
succession planning, *334*
high-potential employee, *334*
skill-based pay systems, *337*
knowledge-based pay systems, *337*

Discussion Questions

1. What are some potential legal issues that a trainer should consider before deciding to run an adventure learning program?

2. Discuss the steps in preparing a manager to go overseas.

3. List the five dimensions of culture. How does each of the dimensions affect employee behavior?

4. What does the "rigor" of a cross-cultural training program refer to? What factors influence the level of training rigor needed?

5. What are virtual expatriates? What are their advantages and disadvantages for the company and the manager?

6. What does "managing diversity" mean to you? Assume you are in charge of developing a diversity training program. Who would be involved? What would you include as the content of the program?

7. What are school-to-work transition programs? Why are they needed?

8. What are some potential advantages and disadvantages of attitude-awareness–based diversity training programs?

9. Discuss the implications of a skill-based pay system for training practices.

10. List and discuss the steps involved in developing a succession planning system. How might a succession planning system differ between high-potential employees and employees with midlevel managerial talent?

Application Assignments

1. Go to *www.succession-planning.com,* the home page for a consulting firm that specializes in developing succession planning systems. What is the company's process for succession planning? What development activities are included in the process? What differentiates effective succession planning systems from ineffective ones?

2. Go to the website for Hewlett-Packard (HP) at *www.hp.com.* Hewlett-Packard is known for its commitment to diversity. How does HP demonstrate this commitment? What is the diversity "value chain"?

3. The Big Brothers/Big Sisters of America is the oldest teen mentor organization in the country. Go to its website at *www.bbbsa.org.* Read about the corporate partners and the news stories. Identify the benefits that a company receives by working with this organization.

4. You are in charge of preparing a team of three managers from the United States to go to Ciudad Juarez, Mexico, where you have recently acquired an auto assembly plant. The managers will be in charge of reviewing current plant operations and managing the plant for the next three years. You have one month to prepare them to leave on assignment. What will you do? Use the following resources to help develop your plan: M. Gowan, S. Ibarreche, and C. Lackey, "Doing the Right Things in Mexico," *Academy of Management Executive* 10, no. 1 (1996): 74–81; and M. de Forest, "Thinking of a Plant in Mexico?" *Academy of Management Executive* 8, no. 1 (1994): 33–40.

5. Go to *http://fairuse.stanford.edu,* a website called Copyright and Fair Use created by Stanford University Libraries. How does work fall into the public domain? That is, how can you use someone else's work for free without having to obtain permission to use it?

6. In 2000, Coca-Cola agreed to a $192 million settlement in a race discrimination lawsuit. As part of the settlement, Coke agreed to review its human resource systems to promote a diverse environment and ensure fairness and equal employment opportunity. Go to *www.coke.com,* the website for Coca-Cola. Click on Our Company, and in the pull-down menu, click on Diversity. Review Coca-Cola's diversity effort. What has Coca-Cola done to strengthen its diversity effort? Use the following categories to group Coca-Cola's diversity efforts: Recruitment and Hiring, Identifying and Developing Talent, Ensuring Fair Treatment, Holding Managers Accountable, and Improving Relationships with External Shareholders. What other recommendations would you make to Coca-Cola for improving its diversity efforts? Be as specific as possible.

7. Go to *www.uawford.com* the website for the UAW–Ford National Programs Center. Choose one of the joint programs to investigate. Search the website to find out information about the program. What is the purpose of the program? What activities does the program include? Who participates in the program?

Endnotes

1. J. K. McAfee and L. S. Cote, "Avoid Having Your Day in Court," *Training and Development Journal* (April 1985): 56–60; A. Cardy, "The Legal Framework of Human Resource Development: Overview, Mandates, Strictures, and Financial Implications," *Human Resource Development Review* 2 (2003): 26–53; A. Cardy, "The Legal Framework of Human Resource Development, Part II: Fair Employment, Negligence, and Implications for Scholars and Practitioners," *Human Resource Development Review* 2 (2003): 130–54.

2. W. Turner and C. Thrutchley, "Employment Law and Practices Training: No Longer the Exception—It's the Rule," in *Legal Report* (Alexandria, VA: Society for Human Resources Management, July–August 2003): 1–4.

3. G. Kimmerling, "A Licensing Primer for Trainers," *Training and Development* (January 1997): 30–35.

4. R. Ganzel, "Copyright or Copywrong?" *Training* (2002): 36–44.

5. U.S. Department of Labor, *A Report on the Glass Ceiling Initiative* (Washington, DC: U.S. Government Printing Office, 1991); C. Petrini, "Raising the Ceiling for Women," *Training and Development* (November 1995): 12.

6. T. Maurer and N. Rafuse, "Learning, Not Litigating: Managing Employee Development and Avoiding Claims of Age Discrimination," *Academy of Management Executive* 15 (2001): 110–21.

7. B. McKay, "Coke Settles Bias Suit for $192.5 Million," *The Wall Street Journal,* November 17, 2000: A3, A8.

8. D. Morse, "Coke Rated 'Acceptable' on Diversity," *The Wall Street Journal,* September 26, 2002: A6.

9. R. Sharpe, "In Whose Hands? Allstate and Scientology," *The Wall Street Journal,* March 22, 1995: A1, A4.

10. Bureau of National Affairs, "Female Grocery Store Employees Prevail in Sex-Bias Suit against Lucky Stores," *BNAs Employee Relations Weekly* 10 (1992): 927–38; *Stender v. Lucky Store Inc.,* DCN California, No. C-88-1467, 8/18/92.

11. J. Sample and R. Hylton, "Falling Off a Log—and Landing in Court," *Training* (May 1996): 67–69.

12. M. J. Mandel, "Business Rolls the Dice," *Business Week* (October 17, 1994): 88–90.

13. "It's Only Rock 'n' Rice," *The Economist* (April 9, 1994): 71.

14. B. Ettorre, "Let's Hear It for Local Talent," *Management Review* (October 1994): 9; S. Franklin, "A New World Order for Business Strategy," *Chicago Tribune,* May 15, 1994: 19-7 to 19-8.

15. S. Gale, "Taxing Situations for Expatriates," *Workforce* (June 2003): 100–104.

16. R. L. Tung, "Selection and Training of Personnel for Overseas Assignments," *Columbia Journal of World Business* 16 (1981): 18–78.

17. V. Sathe, *Culture and Related Corporate Realities* (Homewood, IL: Richard D. Irwin, 1985); M. Rokeach, *Beliefs, Attitudes, and Values* (San Francisco: Jossey-Bass, 1968).

18. C. Hymowitz, "Companies Go Global, but Many Managers Just Don't Travel Well," *The Wall Street Journal,* August 15, 2000: B1.

19. G. Hofstede, "Dimensions of National Cultures in Fifty Countries and Three Regions," in *Expectations in Cross-Cultural Psychology,* eds. J. Deregowski, S. Dziurawiec, and R. C. Annis (Lisse, Netherlands: Swet and Zeitlinger, 1983); G. Hofstede, "Cultural Constraints in Management Theories," *Academy of Management Executive* 7, no.1 (1993): 81–94.

20. R. Frank and T. M. Burton, "Cross-Border Merger Results in Headaches for a Drug Company," *The Wall Street Journal,* February 4, 1997: A1, A12.

21. M. E. de Forest, "Thinking of a Plant in Mexico?" *Academy of Management Executive* 8, no. 1 (1994): 33–50.

22. W. A. Arthur, Jr., and W. Bennett, Jr., "The International Assignee: The Relative Importance of Factors Perceived to Contribute to Success," *Personnel Psychology* 48, (1995): 99–114; G. M. Spreitzer, M. W. McCall, Jr., and Joan D. Mahoney, "Early Identification of International Executive Potential," *Journal of Applied Psychology* 82 (1997): 6–29; R. Garonzik, J. Brockner, and P. Siegel, "Identifying International Assignees at Risk for Premature Departure: The Interactive Effect of Outcome Favorability and Procedural Fairness," *Journal of Applied Psychology* 85 (2000): 13–20.

23. P. Caligiuri, "The Big Five Personality Characteristics as Predictors of Expatriates' Desire to Terminate the Assignment and Supervisor-Rated Performance," *Personnel Psychology* 53 (2000): 67–88.

24. J. S. Black and J. K. Stephens, "The Influence of the Spouse on American Expatriate Adjustment and Intent to Stay in Pacific Rim Overseas Assignments," *Journal of Management* 15 (1989): 529–44.

25. E. Dunbar and A. Katcher, "Preparing Managers for Foreign Assignments," *Training and Development Journal* (September 1990): 45–47.

26. J. S. Black and M. Mendenhall, "A Practical but Theory-Based Framework for Selecting Cross-Cultural Training Methods," in *Readings and Cases in International Human Resource Management,* eds. M. Mendenhall and G. Oddou (Boston: PWS-Kent, 1991): 177–204.

27. S. Ronen, "Training the International Assignee," in *Training and Development in Organizations,* ed. I. L. Goldstein (San Francisco: Jossey-Bass, 1989): 417–53.

28. P. R. Harris and R. T. Moran, *Managing Cultural Differences* (Houston: Gulf Publishing, 1991).

29. C. Solomon, "Unhappy Trails," *Workforce* (August 2000): 36–41.

30. M. Kraimer, S. Wayne, and R. Jaworski, "Sources of Support and Expatriate Performance: The Mediating Role of Expatriate Adjustment," *Personnel Psychology* 54 (2001): 71–99.

31. Solomon, "Unhappy Trails."

32. H. Lancaster, "Before Going Overseas, Smart Managers Plan Their Homecoming," *The Wall Street Journal,* September 28, 1999: B1; A. Halcrow, "Expats: The Squandered Resource," *Workforce* (April 1999): 42–48.

33. J. Barbian, "Return to Sender," *Training* (January 2002): 40–43.

34. J. Flynn, "E-Mail, Cellphones, and Frequent-Flier Miles Let 'Virtual' Expats Work Abroad but Live at Home," *The Wall Street Journal,* October 25, 1999: A26; J. Flynn, "Multinationals Help Career Couples Deal with Strains Affecting Expatriates," *The Wall Street Journal,* August 8, 2000: A19; C. Solomon, "The World Stops Shrinking," *Workforce* (January 2000): 48–51.

35. J. Cook, "Rethinking Relocation," *Human Resources Executive* (June 2, 2003): 23–26.

36. B. Filipczak, "Think Locally, Train Globally," *Training* (January 1997): 41–48.

37. L. Thach, "Training in Russia," *Training and Development* (July 1996): 34–37.

38. P. Sappal, "Women and Minorities Continue to Take a Backseat in Business," *The Wall Street Journal,* October 17, 2000: B22.

39. S. E. Jackson and Associates, *Diversity in the Workplace: Human Resource Initiatives* (New York: Guilford Press, 1992); A. Wellner, "How Do You Spell Diversity?" *Training* (April 2000): 34–38.

40. M. Lee, "Post-9/11 Training," *T&D* (September 2002): 33–35.

41. M. Selz, "Small Company Goes Global with Diverse Workforce," *The Wall Street Journal,* October 12, 1994: B2.

42. R. M. Kanter, "When a Thousand Flowers Bloom: Structural, Collective, and Social Conditions for Innovations in Organizations," in *Research in Organizational Behavior,* vol. 10, eds. L. L. Cummings and B. M. Staw (Greenwich, CT: JAI Press, 1988): 169–211; W. Watson, Kamalesh Kumar, and L. K. Michaelsen, "Cultural Diversity's Impact on Interaction Process and Performance: Comparing Homogeneous and Diverse Task Groups," *Academy of Management Journal* 36 (1993): 590–602.

43. S. Caudron, "Diversity Ignites Effective Work Teams," *Personnel Journal* (September 1994): 54–63.

44 T. Kochan, K. Bezrukova, R. Ely, S. Jackson, A. Joshi, K. Jehn, J. Leonard, D. Levine, and D. Thomas, "The Effects of Diversity on Business Performance: Report of the Diversity Research Network," *Human Resource Management* 42 (2003): 3–21; F. Hansen, "Diversity's Business Case Just Doesn't Add Up," *Workforce* (June 2003): 29–32.

45. R. R. Thomas, "Managing Diversity: A Conceptual Framework," in S. Jackson and Associates (eds.), *Diversity in the Workplace* (New York: Guilford Press, 1992): 306–18.

46. M. E. Heilman, C. J. Block, and J. A. Lucas, "Presumed Incompetent? Stigmatization and Affirmative Action Efforts," *Journal of Applied Psychology* 77 (1992): 536–44.

47. B. Gerber, "Managing Diversity," *Training* (July 1990): 23–30; T. Diamante, C. L. Reid, and L. Ciylo, "Making the Right Training Moves," *HR Magazine* (March 1995): 60–65.

48. L. Roberson, C. Kulik, and M. Pepper, "Designing Effective Diversity Training: Influence of Group Composition and Trainee Experience," *Journal of Organizational Behavior* 22 (2001): 871–85.

49. C. M. Solomon, "The Corporate Response to Workforce Diversity," *Personnel Journal* (August 1989): 43–53; A. Morrison, *The New Leaders: Guidelines on Leadership Diversity in America* (San Francisco: Jossey-Bass, 1992).

50. S. M. Paskoff, "Ending the Workplace Diversity Wars," *Training* (August 1996): 43–47; H. B. Karp and N. Sutton, "Where Diversity Training Goes Wrong," *Training* (July 1993): 30–34.

51. Paskoff, "Ending the Workplace Diversity Wars."

52. J. Barbian, "Moving toward Diversity," *Training* (February 2003): 44–48.

53. L. Lavelle, "For UPS Managers, a School of Hard Knocks," *Business Week* (July 22, 2002): 58–59; M. Berkley, "UPS Community Internship Program (CIP) Fact Sheet" (Atlanta, GA: United Parcel Service, 2003).

54. A. Markels, "Diversity Program Can Prove Divisive," *The Wall Street Journal,* January 30, 1997: B1–B2; "R. R. Donnelley Curtails Diversity Training Moves," *The Wall Street Journal,* February 13, 1997: B3.

55. S. Rynes and B. Rosen, "What Makes Diversity Programs Work?" *HR Magazine* (October 1994): 67–73; S. Rynes and B. Rosen, "A Field Survey of Factors Affecting the Adoption and Perceived Success of Diversity Training," *Personnel Psychology* 48 (1995): 247–70.

56. G. Flynn, "Do You Have the Right Approach to Diversity?" *Personnel Journal* (October 1995): 68–72; M. Galen and A. T. Palmer, "Diversity: Beyond the Numbers Game," *Business Week* (August 14, 1995): 60–61.

57. L. E. Wynter, "Allstate Rates Managers on Handling Diversity," *The Wall Street Journal,* November 1, 1997: B1.

58. H. Rosin, "Cultural Revolution at Texaco," *The New Republic* (February 2, 1998): 15–18; K. Labich, "No More Crude at Texaco," *Fortune* (September 6, 1999): 205–12.

59. See Social Responsibility section of *www.chevrontexaco.com,* website for Chevron Texaco.

60. C. T. Schreiber, K. F. Price, and A. Morrison, "Workforce Diversity and the Glass Ceiling: Practices, Barriers, Possibilities," *Human Resource Planning* 16 (1994): 51–69.

61. D. Stamps, "Will School-to-Work Transition Work?" *Training* (June 1996): 72–81.

62. ASTD Public Policy Council, *The Human Capital Challenge* (Alexandria, VA: ASTD, 2003).

63. R. Ganzel, "Reaching Out to Tomorrow's Workers," *Training* (June 2000): 71–75.

64. A. Harrington, "How Welfare Worked for T.J. Maxx," *Fortune* (November 13, 2000): 453–56.

65. F. Jossi, "From Welfare to Work," *Training* (April 1997): 45–50; D. Milbank, "Hiring Welfare People, Hotel Chain Finds Is Tough but Rewarding," *The Wall Street Journal,* October 31, 1996: A1, A14; D. Milbank, "Marriott Tightens Job Program Screening," *The Wall Street Journal,* July 15, 1997: A2, A12.

66. F. Jossi, "From Welfare to Work," *Training* (April 1997): 45–50.

67. C. Tejada, "Lack of Jobs Is Complicating Welfare Rules," *The Wall Street Journal,* March 11, 2003: B1, B10.

68. See *http//online.onetcenter.org/*.

69. D. Baynton, "America's 60 Billion Dollar Problem," *Training* (May 2001): 50–52, 54, 56.

70. U.S. Department of Labor, *A Report on the Glass Ceiling Initiative*.

71. P. J. Ohlott, M. N. Ruderman, and C. D. McCauley, "Gender Differences in Managers' Developmental Job Experiences," *Academy of Management Journal* 37 (1994): 46–67; K. Lyness and D. Thompson, "Climbing the Corporate Ladder: Do Female and Male Executives Follow the Same Route?" *Journal of Applied Psychology* 85 (2000): 86–101.

72. L. A. Mainiero, "Getting Anointed for Advancement: The Case of Executive Women," *Academy of Management Executive* 8 (1994): 53–67; J. S. Lublin, "Women at Top Still Are Distant from CEO Jobs," *The Wall Street Journal,* February 28, 1995: B1, B5; P. Tharenov, S. Latimer, and D. Conroy, "How Do You Make It to the Top? An Examination of Influences on Women's and Men's Managerial Advancement," *Academy of Management Journal* 37 (1994): 899–931.

73. P. Tharenou, (2001). "Going Up? Do Traits and Informal Social Processes Predict Advancing in Management?" *Academy of Management Journal* 44 (2001): 1005–17.

74. D. McCracken, "Winning the Talent War for Women," *Harvard Business Review* (November–December 2000): 159–67.

75. U.S. Department of Labor, *A Report on the Glass Ceiling Initiative;* R. A. Noe, "Women and Mentoring: A Review and Research Agenda," *Academy of Management Review* 13 (1988): 65–78; B. R. Ragins and J. L. Cotton, "Easier Said Than Done: Gender Differences in Perceived Barriers to Gaining a Mentor," *Academy of Management Journal* 34 (1991): 939–51.

76. C. Daniels, "Women vs. Wal-Mart," *Fortune* (July 21, 2003): 78–82.

77. D. Zielinski, "Mentoring Up," *Training* (October 2000): 136–40.

78. M. Hequet, "The Union Push for Lifelong Learning," *Training* (March 1994): 26–31; S. J. Schurman, M. K. Hugentoble, and H. Stack, "Lessons from the UAW-GM Paid Education Leave Program," in *Joint Training Programs,* eds. L. A. Ferman, M. Hoyman, J. Cutcher-Gershenfeld, and E. J. Savoie (Ithaca, NY: ILR Press, 1991): 71–94.

79. See *www.iamboeing.com,* website for IAM–Boeing Joint Programs.

80. See *www.nactel.org,* website for the National Coalition for Telecommunications Education and Learning.

81. See *www.uawford.com,* website for UAW–Ford National Programs Center.

82. W. J. Rothwell, *Effective Success in Planning,* 2d ed. (New York: Amacom, 2001).

83. C. B. Derr, C. Jones, and E. L. Toomey, "Managing High-Potential Employees: Current Practices in Thirty-Three U.S. Corporations," *Human Resource Management* 27 (1988): 273–90.

84. H. S. Feild and S. G. Harris, "Entry-Level, Fast-Track Management Development Programs: Developmental Tactics and Perceived Program Effectiveness," *Human Resource Planning* 14 (1991): 261–73.

85. Derr, Jones, and Toomey, "Managing High-Potential Employees"; K. M. Nowack, "The Secrets of Succession," *Training and Development* 48 (1994): 49–54; J. S. Lublin, "An Overseas Stint Can Be a Ticket to the Top," *The Wall Street Journal,* January 29, 1996: B1–B2.

86. Ibid.

87. P. Kiger, "Succession Planning Keeps WellPoint Competitive," *Workforce* (April 2002): 50–54.

88. M. W. McCall, Jr., and M. M. Lombardo, *Off the Track: Why and How Successful Executives Get Derailed,* Technical Report no. 21 (Greensboro, NC: Center for Creative Leadership, 1983); E. V. Veslor and J. B. Leslie, "Why Executives Derail: Perspectives across Time and Cultures," *Academy of Management Executive* 9 (1995): 62–72.

89. L. W. Hellervik, J. F. Hazucha, and R. J. Schneider, "Behavior Change: Models, Methods, and a Review of Evidence," in *Handbook of Industrial and Organizational Psychology,* 2d ed., eds. M. D. Dunnette and L. M. Hough (Palo Alto, CA: Consulting Psychologists Press, 1992), 3: 823–99.

90. D. B. Peterson, "Measuring and Evaluating Change in Executive and Managerial Development." Paper presented at the annual conference of the Society for Industrial and Organizational Psychology, Miami, FL, 1990.

91. G. E. Ledford, "Paying for the Skills, Knowledge, Competencies of Knowledge Workers," *Compensation and Benefits Review* (July–August 1995): 55.

92. E. E. Lawler III, *Strategic Pay* (San Francisco: Jossey-Bass, 1990).

93. D. Feuer, "Paying for Knowledge," *Training* (May 1987): 57–66.

Chapter **Eleven**

Careers and Career Management

Objectives

After reading this chapter, you should be able to

1. Identify the reasons why companies should help employees manage their careers.
2. Discuss the protean career and how it differs from the traditional career.
3. Explain the development tasks and activities in the career development process.
4. Design a career management system.
5. Discuss the role of the Web in career management.
6. Effectively perform the manager's role in career management.

Career Management Is a Long-Term Investment

Ohio Savings Bank, with headquarters in Cleveland, Ohio, provides ongoing opportunities for employees' personal growth and the fulfillment of career aspirations. Ohio Savings Bank prides itself on promoting a continuous learning environment, offering many possibilities for employees to learn and grow. These possibilities include formal education available outside the bank through a tuition assistance program as well as classes offered internally at no cost to employees.

Ohio Savings Bank developed a formal career counseling program to identify and develop employee talent and to give employees the tools and training they need to direct their own careers. Career development counselors play an important role in the program. Employees can meet with a career development counselor to discuss career paths and training requirements for positions within Ohio Savings Bank. Information sessions are available for employees who are thinking about changing divisions within the company. During these sessions, managers from different divisions provide information about current or future job openings. The career development counselor also meets with managers to discuss employees' career plans. Managers and counselors might discuss high-potential employees or action plans for employees to reach their career goals. Ohio Savings Bank also has a Career Development Services Web page that employees can access. This Web page has more hits than any other internal Web page!

Source: Based on T. Galvin, "Ohio Savings Bank," *Training* (March 2003): 60–61; Ohio Savings Bank website, *www.ohiosavings.com*.

INTRODUCTION

Career development is important for companies to create and sustain a continuous learning environment. A study conducted by PricewaterhouseCoopers of companies in finance, online services, hospitality, real estate, and high-tech industries suggests that companies that are successful at managing the employee growth that accompanies business expansion and increased demand for their products and services focus on recruitment, career development, culture orientation, and communications.[1] These companies emphasize that employees are to be responsible for career management. But they also provide company resources that support careers, such as career counselors, development opportunities, mentoring, and managerial training in how to coach employees. The biggest challenge companies face is how to balance advancing current employees' careers with simultaneously attracting and acquiring employees with new skills. For example, T. Rowe Price created task forces and councils across the company that were charged with looking at the role of career management in employee attraction and retention. One program focused on a career path for new phone representatives. The program helped identify and quickly bring development opportunities to promising new employees by offering them financial incentives and advancement opportunities directly related to training and job experiences.[2]

Another factor influencing the concept of careers is the growing use of teams to produce products and provide services. Teams give companies the flexibility to bring talented persons both inside the company (full-time employees) and outside the company (temporary and contract employees) to work on services and products on an as-needed basis. In some cases, careers are viewed as project careers. **Project careers** are a series of projects that may not be in the same company. These changes are altering the career concept and increasing the importance of career management from both the employee's and the company's perspective.

Because many persons spend a large amount of their lives working, work provides a place where employees look to satisfy a number of needs, such as affiliation, achievement, power, and growth. Career management can help employees satisfy these needs. Career management is becoming important also because the workplace is an area where social equality, workplace diversity, and personal liberation can be achieved.[3] To melt the glass ceiling and to manage diversity, companies have to pay more attention to the career experiences provided to all employees. With the increased use of contingent employees such as independent contractors and temporary employees (recall the discussions in Chapter 1), career management has become more of a challenge. A related issue is that some employees (especially independent contractors and temporary employees) choose to frequently change jobs and careers for personal interests or to avoid becoming obsolete or expendable by specializing in one job as technology, the economy, or business changes. For example, a senior consultant at New York's Health and Human Services Department has worked on many different jobs, some of which she designed.[4] She also networks with professionals outside the agency. She says the contacts and exposure keep her "thinking about new ideas and different approaches." Many employees do not want to sacrifice personal lives and their family lives for their careers. For example, some employees are seeking jobs that provide shorter and more flexible work hours, attractive work environments, relaxed dress codes, and benefits such as child care, elder care, and concierge services, which help employees better balance their work and nonwork lives.

You may wonder why a training book covers career and career management. It is important to recognize that employees' motivation to attend training programs, the outcomes they expect to gain from attendance, their choice of programs, and how and what they need to know have been affected by changes in the concept of a "career." For example, an employee's career may not entirely be with one company. Career management is not something that companies do for employees. Rather, employees have to take the initiative to manage their career by identifying the type of work they want, their long-term work interests, and the skills they would like to develop. As you will learn in this chapter, changing expectations that employers and employees have for one another (referred to as the psychological contract) have caused more emphasis to be placed on using job experiences and relationships for learning rather than formal training courses and seminars. Also, trainers may be responsible for designing programs to help managers play an effective role in career management systems.

This chapter begins with a discussion of why career management is important. The second part of the chapter introduces changes in the concept of a career. The implications of these changes for career management are emphasized. The chapter presents a model of career development that is based on the new career concept and that highlights the developmental challenges employees face and how companies can help employees meet these challenges. The chapter concludes by examining the specific components of career management systems and by discussing the roles played by employees, managers, and companies in successful career management systems.

WHY IS CAREER MANAGEMENT IMPORTANT?

Career management is the process through which employees

- Become aware of their own interests, values, strengths, and weaknesses.
- Obtain information about job opportunities within the company.
- Identify career goals.
- Establish action plans to achieve career goals.[5]

Career management is important from both the employees' perspective and the company's perspective.[6] From the company's perspective, the failure to motivate employees to plan their careers can result in a shortage of employees to fill open positions, in lower employee commitment, and in inappropriate use of monies allocated for training and development programs. From the employees' perspective, lack of career management can result in frustration, feelings of not being valued in the company, and being unable to find suitable employment should a job change (internal or with another company) be necessary due to mergers, acquisitions, restructuring, or downsizing.

Career Management's Influence on Career Motivation

Companies need to help employees manage their careers to maximize their career motivation. **Career motivation** refers to employees' energy to invest in their careers, their awareness of the direction they want their careers to take, and their ability to maintain energy and direction despite barriers they may encounter. Career motivation has three aspects: career resilience, career insight, and career identity.[7] **Career resilience** is the extent to which employees are

FIGURE 11.1

The value
of career
motivation

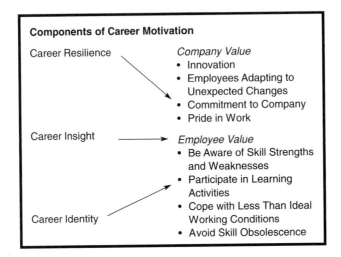

able to cope with problems that affect their work. **Career insight** involves (1) how much employees know about their interests and their skill strengths and weaknesses and (2) the awareness of how these perceptions relate to their career goals. **Career identity** is the degree to which employees define their personal values according to their work.

Figure 11.1 shows how career motivation can create value for both the company and employees. Career motivation likely has a significant relationship to the extent to which a company is innovative and adaptable to change. Employees who have high career resilience are able to respond to obstacles in the work environment and adapt to unexpected events (such as changes in work processes or customer demands). They are dedicated to continuous learning, they are willing to develop new ways to use their skills, they take responsibility for career management, and they are committed to the company's success.[8] Research suggests that low career motivation may be especially detrimental for older, more experienced employees.[9]

Employees with high career insight set career goals and participate in development activities that help them reach those goals. They tend to take actions that keep their skills from becoming obsolete. Employees with high career identity are committed to the company; they are willing to do whatever it takes (e.g., work long hours) to complete projects and meet customer demands. They also take pride in working for the company and are active in professional and trade organizations. Research suggests that both career identity and career insight are related to career success.[10]

Career motivation is positively influenced by the extent to which companies provide opportunities for achievement, encouragement for development, and information about career opportunities. Career management systems help identify these opportunities and provide career information. Sears Credit's experience with career management is a good example of (1) how career management can help a company cope with competitive challenges and (2) the positive outcomes that can result from career management.[11] Sears Credit, responsible for all credit transactions in the retail stores of Sears Merchandise Group, underwent a major reorganization. The company's strategic plan caused nine units to expand, closed 50 small units, offered a major voluntary retirement program, and accepted third-party charge cards in competition with the Sears charge card. As a result of the reorganization, the company lost 3,000 associates (employees), going from 13,000 to 10,000 associates.

The reorganization created a career development nightmare. Virtually all jobs were redefined or newly created. Career paths were obsolete. There was a need to develop succession plans so associates were prepared to fill future positions. As a result, a major career development initiative was launched to align employees' skills and work loads. Senior management wanted the company to have more open communications about career opportunities and to redefine career success in terms of what was important to the associate rather than in terms of training and preparing employees for promotion opportunities. Senior management also emphasized the need to have employees take more personal responsibility for managing their careers and for managers to accept their role as career coaches.

A key element of the career development process was identifying the competencies needed for success in the restructured jobs. Five major categories of competencies were identified, based on surveys of associates and managers: business knowledge and contribution to financial results, leadership, customer focus, individual effectiveness, and associate development. Sears Credit also decided to implement an assessment system involving manager, self, and peer evaluations to help employees identify growth areas. To ensure that associates understood the system, Sears Credit developed workshops. All exempt employees were expected to participate in a two-day workshop explaining the self-assessment activities and the development planning process. Managers also participated in a workshop to help them develop career coaching skills and provide advice on how they could manage their own careers. Technology was utilized to make new job descriptions available to all employees on the electronic mail system. Also, a data bank of employees' career goals was developed. The data bank was available to match employees' needs and interests with specific jobs and to assist in the planning of training activities. Because career development is impacted by a company's incentive system, Sears Credit introduced a new compensation program. The program, known as broadbanding, expanded pay grades and allowed salary increases for lateral job moves that traditionally were not entitled to increased compensation. The hope was that the broadbanding system would motivate employees to develop a broader range of skills.

Preliminary evaluations of the program have been positive. Most associates report taking responsibility for their own career, developing specific career plans and goals, and being more aware and realistic about their interests, strengths, and development needs. As Tom Cataruzolo, director of human resources and training, explains, "The career-development process was the catalyst that changed personal career planning from passive participation of each manager to a very active role in individual career growth. It heightened the awareness of self-assessments, job competencies, and performance. More importantly, it helped foster an environment of openness."

WHAT IS A CAREER?

Four different meanings can be applied to the concept of careers.[12] First, careers have been described as advancement. That is, careers are described as a sequence of promotions or upward moves in a company during the person's work life. Second, careers have been described as a profession. This definition suggests that careers occur only in certain occupations in which there is a clear pattern of advancement. For example, doctors, professors, businesspersons, lawyers, and other professionals have a path of career movement. University faculty members can hold positions as assistant, associate, and full professor. Managers can start in management trainee jobs, become supervisors, and then move to positions as managers and executives. Employees in jobs that do not lead to a series of related positions, such as waiters and maintenance employees, are not considered to have careers. Third, careers can be considered a lifelong sequence of jobs. A person's career is the series of jobs held during the course of that person's life, regardless of occupation or job level. According to this description, all persons have careers. Fourth, careers can be described as a lifelong sequence of role-related experiences. Careers represent how persons experience the sequence of jobs and assignments in their work history. This definition includes positions held and job moves as well as a person's feelings and attitudes about their jobs and their life.

This book uses Hall's definition of careers.[13] A **career** refers to the individual sequence of attitudes and behavior associated with work-related experiences and activities over the span of the person's life This definition does not imply career success or failure based on promotion or advancement, and it recognizes that a career is a process, that is, a series of work-related experiences that all persons have, not just employees in professional careers. Work experiences, which include the employee's position, job experiences, and tasks, are influenced by the employee's values, needs, and feelings. Employees' values, needs, and feelings vary, depending on their stage of career development and biological age. As a result, managers and human resource development professionals must understand the career development process and the differences in employee needs and interests at each stage of development.

The Protean Career

Today's careers are known as protean careers.[14] A **protean career** is based on self-direction with the goal of psychological success in one's work. Protean employees take major responsibility for managing their careers. For example, an engineering employee may take a sabbatical from her engineering position to work at the United Way Agency for a year in a management position. The purpose of this assignment is to develop her managerial skills as well as to enable her to personally evaluate whether she likes managerial work more than engineering.

Traditional Career versus Protean Career

Table 11.1 compares the traditional organizational career to the protean career on several dimensions. Changes in the psychological contract between employees and company have influenced the career concept.[15] A **psychological contract** is the expectations that employers and employees have about each other. Traditionally, the psychological contract emphasized that the company would provide continued employment and advancement opportunities if the employee remained with the company and maintained a high level of job performance. Pay increases and status were linked directly to vertical movement in the company (promotions).

However, the psychological contract between employees and employers has changed. Why? One reason is the change in companies' organizational structures. Because companies' structures tend to be "flat" (meaning the structure has fewer layers of management), authority is decentralized, and more of employees' responsibilities are organized on a project or customer basis rather on a functional basis. Flat structures are found especially in

TABLE 11.1 **Comparison of Traditional Career and Protean Career**

Dimension	Traditional Career	Protean Career
Goal	Promotions Salary increase	Psychological success
Psychological Contract	Security for commitment	Employability for flexibility
Mobility	Vertical	Lateral
Responsibility for Management	Company	Employee
Pattern	Linear and expert	Spiral and transitory
Expertise	Know how	Learn how
Development	Heavy reliance on formal training	Greater reliance on relationships and job experiences

Source: Based on D. T. Hall, "Protean Careers of the 21st Century," *Academy of Management Executive* 10 (1996): 8–16; N. Nicholson, "Career Systems in Crisis: Change and Opportunity in the Information Age," *Academy of Management Executive* 10 (1996): 40–51; K. Brousseau, M. J. Driver, K. Eneroth, and R. Larsson, "Career Pandemonium: Realigning Organizations and Individuals," *Academy of Management Executive* 10 (1996): 52–66; D. Hall, *Careers In and Out of Organizations* (Thousand Oaks, CA: Sage, 2002).

small and mid-size organizations such as e-businesses. As a result, employees are expected to develop a wide variety of skills (recall the forces that affect work and learning discussed in Chapter 1). Another reason the psychological contract has changed is that due to increased domestic and global competition as well as mergers and acquisitions, companies can't offer job security and may have to downsize. Instead of offering job security, companies can offer employees opportunities to attend training programs and participate in work experiences that can increase their employability with their current and future employers.

For example, the term *blue-collar work* has always meant manufacturing work, but technology has transformed the meaning dramatically.[16] Traditional assembly-line jobs that required little skill and less education have been sent overseas. Today's blue-collar workers are more involved in customized manufacturing. At U.S. Steel employees make more than 700 different kinds of steel, requiring greater familiarity with additives and more understanding of customers and markets. Jobs once considered as lifetime employment are now more temporary, forcing employees to adapt by moving from one factory to another or by changing work shifts. Employees are taking classes to keep up with the latest developments in steelmaking, such as lathes and resins. Despite the lack of guaranteed lifetime employment, many blue-collar jobs are safer and better paying than they were 10 years ago.

The goal of the protean career is psychological success. **Psychological success** is the feeling of pride and accomplishment that comes from achieving life goals that are not limited to achievements at work (e.g., raising a family, good physical health). Psychological success is more under the control of the employee than were traditional career goals, which were not only influenced by employee effort but controlled by the availability of positions in the company. Psychological success is self-determined rather than determined solely through signals the employee receives from the company (e.g., salary increase, promotion). Psychological success appears to be especially prevalent among the new generation of persons entering the work force.

Different generations of employees (or employee cohorts) likely have different career needs and interests. Table 11.2 shows some of the personal characteristics of so-called millenniums, Generation X (Gen Xers), baby boomers, and traditionalists. Some traits, such as health consciousness, may be present in all cohorts but are more important to some cohorts

TABLE 11.2   Suggested Characteristics of Different Generations of Employees

Generation	Age	Traits
Millennium	0 to early 20s	Are independent spenders Are globally concerned Are health conscious Accept nontraditional families Accept constant change Understand need for training to remain employable Are cyber-savvy Have high expectations Want challenging work
Generation X	Mid-20s to early 40s	Are experienced and confident using new technologies Are diverse Are independent Are entrepreneurial Are flexible Are team players Expect more feedback than older workers do Have a hard time accepting authority Don't want to have to hold people accountable Bring personal concerns into the workplace
Baby Boomers	Mid-40s to mid-50s	Are idealistic Are competitive Question authority Are members of the "me" generation
Traditionalists	Late 50s to early 80s	Are patriotic Are loyal Are fiscally conservative Have faith in institutions Want their experience to be valued Respect previous generations, business leaders

Source: Based on J. Salopek, "The Young and the Rest of Us," *Training and Development* (February 2000): 26–29; M. Alch, "Get Ready for the Net Generation," *Training and Development* (February 2000): 32–34; N. Woodward, "The Coming of the Managers," *HR Magazine* (March 1999): 75–80; C. Solomon, "Ready or Not, Here Come the Net Kids," *Workforce* (February 2000): 62–68.

than others. Millenniums and Gen Xers are more used to change and job insecurity than are baby boomers and traditionalists. For example, Gen Xers are loyal to their own skills, and they change jobs to develop them.[17] They seek achievement of their own goals and value personal relationships. Gen Xers tend to perform several tasks quickly and often have to balance competing work demands. They respond best to short-deadline, multifaceted projects. Gen Xers are looking for meaning in their work. They want to see the company commit resources for career management. They do not believe the company is responsible for their careers. An important difference between Gen Xers and baby boomers is that many baby boomers worked during a time when companies tended to reward years of service with promotions, job security, and benefits. Gen Xers work in a still-turbulent business environment characterized by swings between business growth and downsizing. Despite the turbulent nature of business today, many baby boomers and traditionalists expect companies to provide clearly defined career paths and reward good performance with promotions. Given the changes in the business environment and psychological contract, today's companies need to communicate to all employees, especially baby boomers and traditionalists, about the need to self-manage their careers and to reconsider linking their personal career success to promotions and salary increases.

An important difference between the traditional career and the protean career is the need for employees to be motivated and able to learn rather than relying on a static knowledge base. This difference has resulted from companies' need to be more responsive to customers' service and product demands. The types of knowledge that an employee needs to be successful have changed.[18] In the traditional career, "knowing how"—having the appropriate skills and knowledge to provide a service or produce a product—was critical. Although knowing how remains important, employees need to "know why" and "know whom." Knowing why refers to understanding the company's business and culture so that the employee can develop and apply knowledge and skills that can contribute to the business. Knowing whom refers to relationships that the employee may develop to contribute to company success. These relationships may include networking with vendors, suppliers, community members, customers, or industry experts. To learn to know whom and know why requires more than formal courses and training programs.

Consider the growing use of consultants in the information services area.[19] Internal information processing staffs have been downsized as companies have decided that they don't need internal staffs and can find talented employees on an as-needed basis. Many companies have an overabundance of experienced information systems staff who are solid performers but don't bring to the job the ambition, experience, and ideas that consultants have developed by working with different clients.

Learning and development in the protean career are increasingly likely to involve relationships and job experiences rather than formal courses. For example, as was mentioned in Chapter 9, through mentoring relationships employees can gain exposure and visibility to a wide range of persons inside and outside the company. Job experiences involving project assignments and job rotation can improve employees' understanding of the business strategy, functions, and divisions of the company as well as help them develop valuable contacts.

The emphasis on continuous learning and learning beyond knowing how as well as changes in the psychological contract are resulting in changes in direction and frequency of movement within careers (career pattern).[20] Traditional career patterns consisted of a series of steps arranged in a linear hierarchy, with higher steps in the hierarchy related to increased authority, responsibility, and compensation. Expert career patterns involve a life-long commitment to a field or specialization (e.g., law, medicine, management). These types of career patterns will not disappear. Rather, career patterns involving movement across specializations or disciplines (spiral career patterns) will become more prevalent. Also, careers in which the person moves from job to job every three to five years (transitory career patterns) are likely to become more common. For many employees, changing jobs can be satisfying because it offers them opportunity for new challenges and skill development.

The most appropriate view of a career is that it is "boundaryless."[21] It may include movement across several employers or even different occupations. Statistics indicate that the average employment tenure for all U.S. workers is only five years.[22] For example, Craig Matison, 33 years old, took a job with Cincinnati Bell Information System, a unit of Cincinnati Bell Corporation that manages billing for phone and cable companies.[23] Although he has been on the job for only six months, he is already looking to make his next career move. He does not want to stay on the technical career path and regularly explores company databases for job postings, looking for sales and marketing opportunities within the company. A career may also involve identifying more with a job or profession than with the present employer. A career can also be considered boundaryless in the sense that career plans or goals are influenced by personal or family demands and values. Finally, *boundaryless* refers to the fact that career success may not be tied to promotions. Rather, career success is related to achieving goals that are personally meaningful to the employee rather than those set by parents, peers, or the company.

A MODEL OF CAREER DEVELOPMENT

Career development is the process by which employees progress through a series of stages, each characterized by a different set of developmental tasks, activities, and relationships.[24] There are several career development models. Although it is widely accepted that the concept of a career has changed, the research literature does not agree on which career development model is best.[25]

Table 11.3 presents a model that incorporates the important contributions that the life-cycle, organization-based, and directional pattern models make to understanding career development. The **life-cycle models** suggest that employees face certain developmental tasks over the course of their careers and that they move through distinct life or career stages. The **organization-based models** also suggest that careers proceed through a series of stages, but these models propose that career development involves employees' learning to perform certain activities. Each stage involves changes in activities and relationships with peers and managers. The **directional pattern model** describes the form or shape of careers.[26] As noted in the discussion of the changing career concept, these models suggest that employees make decisions about how quickly they want to progress through the career stages and at what point they want to return to an earlier career stage. For example, some employees plan on staying in a job or occupation their entire lives and have well-thought-out plans for moving within the occupation (this career has a linear shape). Other employees view their careers as having a spiral shape. The spiral career form is increasing as many employees work on projects or in jobs for a specific period of time and then take a different job or project within or outside their current employer. As discussed in Chapter 9, employees may actually accept a job in another functional area that is lower in status than their current job (known as a downward move) in order to learn the basic skills and get the experiences needed to be successful in this new function.

Career Stages

Table 11.3 shows the four career stages: exploration, establishment, maintenance, and disengagement. Each career stage is characterized by developmental tasks, activities, and relationships. Employee retention, motivation, and performance are affected by how well the company addresses the development tasks at each career stage.

Research suggests that employees' current career stage influences their needs, attitudes, and job behaviors. For example, one study found that salespersons in the exploration career stage tended to change jobs and accept promotions more frequently than did salespersons

TABLE 11.3 **A Model of Career Development**

	Career Stage			
	Exploration	**Establishment**	**Maintenance**	**Disengagement**
Developmental Tasks	Identify interests, skills, fit between self and work	Advancement, growth, security, develop lifestyle	Hold on to accomplishments, update skills	Retirement planning, change balance between work and nonwork
Activities	Helping Learning Following directions	Making independent contributions	Training Sponsoring Policy making	Phasing out of work
Relationships to Other Employees	Apprentice	Colleague	Mentor	Sponsor
Typical Age	Less than 30	30–45	45–60	61+
Years on Job	Less than 2 years	2–10 years	More than 10 years	More than 10 years

in other career stages.[27] Another study found that the degree to which employees identify with their job is affected more by the job's characteristics (e.g., variety of tasks, responsibility for task completion) in early career stages than in later career stages.[28]

Exploration Stage

In the **exploration stage,** individuals attempt to identify the type of work that interests them. They consider their interests, values, and work preferences, and they seek information about jobs, careers, and occupations from co-workers, friends, and family members. Once they identify the type of work or occupation that interests them, individuals can begin pursuing the needed education or training. Typically, exploration occurs in the midteens to early-to-late twenties (while the individual is still a student in high school, college, or technical school). Exploration continues when the individual starts a new job. In most cases, employees who are new to a job are not prepared to take on work tasks and roles without help and direction from others. In many jobs, the new employee is considered an apprentice. An **apprentice** is an employee who works under the supervision and direction of a more experienced colleague or manager. From the company's perspective, orientation and socialization activities are necessary to help new employees get as comfortable as possible with their new jobs and co-workers so they can begin to contribute to the company's goals.

Establishment Stage

In the **establishment stage,** individuals find their place in the company, make an independent contribution, achieve more responsibility and financial success, and establish a desirable lifestyle. Employees at this stage are interested in being viewed as contributors to the company's success. Employees who have reached the establishment stage are considered to be colleagues. **Colleagues** are employees who can work independently and produce results. They are less dependent or more experienced employees than those in the exploration stage.

They learn how the company views their contributions from informal interactions with peers and managers and from formal feedback received through the performance-appraisal system. For employees in this stage, the company needs to develop policies that help balance work and nonwork roles. Also, employees in this stage need to become more actively involved in career-planning activities.

Maintenance Stage

In the **maintenance stage,** the individual is concerned with keeping skills up to date and being perceived by others as someone who is still contributing to the company. Individuals in the maintenance stage have many years of job experience, much job knowledge, and an in-depth understanding of how the company expects business to be conducted. Employees in the maintenance stage can be valuable trainers or mentors for new employees. A **mentor** is an experienced employee who teaches or helps less experienced employees.

Maintenance-stage employees may be asked to review or develop company policies or goals. Their opinions about work processes, problems, and important issues that the work unit is facing may be solicited. From the company's perspective, a major issue is how to keep employees in the maintenance stage from plateauing. Also, the company needs to ensure that employees' skills do not become obsolete.

To keep its employees from plateauing, General Electric emphasizes career development during its annual performance reviews.[29] During the reviews, employees discuss their goals with their managers. Those discussions are reviewed by operations and human resources personnel, who try to match employees' career goals (e.g., seeking job changes) with job openings. For example, older and more experienced managers who have knowledge about General Electric and about the people in the business may change jobs to help integrate newly acquired businesses into General Electric. Other managers who have new mobility when their children leave home may be encouraged to take advantage of overseas assignments.

Disengagement Stage

In the **disengagement stage,** individuals prepare for a change in the balance between work and nonwork activities. They may take on the role of sponsor. A **sponsor** provides direction to other employees, represents the company to customers, initiates actions, and makes decisions.

Disengagement typically refers to older employees electing to retire and concentrate entirely on nonwork activities such as sports, hobbies, traveling, or volunteer work. However, a survey conducted by Watson Wyatt, an international human resources consulting company, found that three out of four older employees preferred to reduce their work hours gradually rather than face the traditional all-work or no-work type of retirement.[30] For many employees, the disengagement phase means a gradual reduction in work hours. Phased retirement programs help both the employee and the company. The company gets to take advantage of the experienced employees' knowledge and specialized skills while reducing the costs related to hiring and training a new employee. These benefits are especially important in times when the unemployment rate is low. During these times, companies are concerned with attracting and retaining qualified employees. For employees, phased retirement means that they have the opportunity to choose retirement in a way that meets their financial and emotional needs. To capitalize on older employees' talents, companies need to be flexible—for example, they might offer part-time and consulting work.

Also, keep in mind that regardless of age, employees may elect to leave a company to change occupations or jobs. Some may be forced to leave the company because of downsizing or mergers. Others may leave because of their interests, values, or abilities.

Employees who leave the company often recycle back to the exploration stage. They need information about potential new career areas, and they have to reconsider their career interests and skill strengths. From the company's perspective, the major career management activities in the disengagement stage are retirement planning and outplacement. Downsizing, outplacement, and retirement are discussed more in Chapter 12.

As Table 11.3 shows, an employee's age and length of time on the job are believed to be good signals of his or her career stage. However, relying strictly on these two characteristics could lead to erroneous conclusions about the employee's career needs. For example, many changes that older employees make in their careers involve "recycling" back to an earlier career stage.[31] **Recycling** involves changing one's major work activity after having been established in a specific field. Recycling is accompanied by a reexploration of values, skills, interests, and potential employment opportunities.

Recycling is not just limited to older employees who are nearing retirement. Many companies that face a serious shortage of qualified employees are developing retraining programs in hopes of filling labor shortages with employees from other fields.[32] Companies are using these training programs to help recycle employees into new jobs and careers. For example, in the computer-help-desk field, companies face a shortage of qualified staff for internal help desks and customer service. Also, many persons with computer skills who seek these positions lack the interpersonal skills needed to give counsel and advice to users of software, databases, and company intranets. The computer consulting industry is training former stockbrokers, flight attendants, and bank tellers to work at help desks. These training programs are referred to as "boot camps" because the training emphasizes total immersion in the job, one-on-one supervision, and cramming into a short training program what knowledge and skills the employee needs to know.

It is also not uncommon for employees who are considering recycling to conduct informational interviews with managers and other employees who hold jobs in functional areas they believe may be congruent with their interests and abilities. Employees conduct **informational interviews** with a manager or other employees to gather information about the skills, job demands, and benefits of their jobs. Employees may also "try out" new jobs. Nancy Handley, a Wal-Mart employee who oversees the men's department, is trying out management work to see if it matches her interests. She is not sure that she is willing to work the longer hours and live with the possibility of having to transfer to an out-of-state store if she takes a managerial position. Regardless, she is handling personnel issues and spends time at the customer service desk (both managerial responsibilities) one day a week.[33]

Stan Alger provides a good example of the concept of recycling in the career stage model. For 30 years, Alger worked as a factory sales representative for a bicycle company in the San Francisco area.[34] However, Alger often thought about working for Home Depot, the home improvement retailer. Alger enjoyed looking at the gadgets in the Home Depot store in his area and finding materials for his home projects. After his employer changed ownership, Alger quit his job. At age 59, he now works part-time at Home Depot. He enjoys helping people learn to use tools. "When you tell them how, and you see that light click on in their eyes, it's kind of fun," he says.

FIGURE 11.2
The career
management
process

Self-Assessment ⟶ Reality Check ⟶ Goal Setting ⟶ Action Planning

Employees bring a range of career development issues to the workplace. Specific career development issues (e.g., orientation, outplacement, work, and family) are discussed in Chapter 12. Besides developing policies and programs that will help employees deal with their specific career development issues (in order to maximize their level of career motivation), companies need to provide a career management system to identify employees' career development needs. A **career management system** helps employees, managers, and the company identify career development needs.

CAREER MANAGEMENT SYSTEMS

Companies' career management systems vary in the level of sophistication and the emphasis they place on the different components of the process. However, all career management systems include the components shown in Figure 11.2: self-assessment, reality check, goal setting, and action planning.

The four steps in the career management process use the development activities (assessment, job experiences, formal courses, relationships) that were discussed in Chapter 9. The career management process is similar to the development planning process. Assessment information from psychological tests, performance evaluations, assessment centers, or 360-degree feedback can be used as part of the self-assessment or reality check steps. Employees engaged in action planning may use job experiences, relationships (mentoring or coaching), or formal courses to reach their short- and long-term career goals.

Self-Assessment

Self-assessment refers to the use of information by employees to determine their career interests, values, aptitudes, and behavioral tendencies. It often involves psychological tests such as the Strong-Campbell Interest Inventory and the Self-Directed Search. The former helps employees identify their occupational and job interests; the latter identifies employees' preferences for working in different types of environments (e.g., sales, counseling, landscaping). Tests may also help employees identify the relative value they place on work and leisure activities. Self-assessment can also involve exercises such as the one in Table 11.4. This type of exercise helps employees consider where they are now in their careers, identify future plans, and assess how their career fits with their current situation and available resources. Career counselors are often used to assist employees in the self-assessment process and interpret the results of psychological tests.

For example, a man who had served as a branch manager at Wells Fargo Bank for 14 years enjoyed both working with computers and researching program development issues.[35] He was experiencing difficulty in choosing whether to pursue further work experiences with computers or enter a new career in developing software applications. Psychological tests that he completed as part of the company's career assessment program confirmed that he had strong interests in research and development. As a result, he began his own software design company.

TABLE 11.4   **Example of a Self-Assessment Exercise**

Activity   (Purpose)

Step 1:   *Where am I?* (Examine current position of life and career.)
Think about your life from past and present to the future. Draw a time line to represent important events.

Step 2:   *Who am I?* (Examine different roles.)
Using 3 × 5 cards, write down one answer per card to the question "Who am I?"

**Step 3:   *Where would I like to be and what would I like to happen?*
(This helps in future goal setting.)**
Consider your life from present to future. Write an autobiography answering three questions: What do you want to have accomplished? What milestones do you want to achieve? What do you want to be remembered for?

Step 4:   *An ideal year in the future* (Identify resources needed.)
Consider a one-year period in the future. If you had unlimited resources, what would you do? What would the ideal environment look like? Does the ideal environment match step 3?

Step 5:   *An ideal job* (Create current goal.)
In the present, think about an ideal job for you with your available resources. Consider your role, resources, and type of training or education needed.

Step 6:   *Career by objective inventory* (Summarize current situation.)
- What gets you excited each day?
- What do you do well? What are you known for?
- What do you need to achieve your goals?
- What could interfere with reaching your goals?
- What should you do now to move toward reaching your goals?
- What is your long-term career objective?

Source: Based on J. E. McMahon and S. K. Merman, "Career Development," in *The ASTD Training and Development Handbook*, 4th ed., ed. R. L. Craig (New York: McGraw-Hill, 1996): 679–97.

Reality Check

Reality check refers to the information employees receive about how the company evaluates their skills and knowledge and where they fit into the company's plans (e.g., potential promotion opportunities, lateral moves). Usually, this information is provided by the employee's manager as part of the performance appraisal process. It is not uncommon in well-developed career planning systems for the manager to hold separate performance appraisals and career development discussions. For example, in Coca-Cola USA's career planning system, employees and managers have a separate meeting after the annual performance review to discuss the employee's career interests, strengths, and possible development activities.[36]

Goal Setting

In **goal setting,** employees develop short- and long-term career objectives. These goals usually relate to desired positions (e.g., to become sales manager within three years), level of skill application (e.g., to use one's budgeting skills to improve the unit's cash flow problems), work setting (e.g., to move to corporate marketing within two years), or skill acquisition (e.g., to learn how to use the company's human resource information system). These goals are usually discussed with the manager and written into a development plan. Figure 11.3 shows a

FIGURE 11.3 Career development plan

Name: **Title:** Project Manager   **Immediate Manager:**

Competencies
Please identify your three greatest strengths and areas for improvement.
Strengths:
Strategic thinking and execution (confidence, command skills, action orientation)
Results orientation (competence, motivating others, perseverance)
Spirit for winning (building team spirit, customer focus, respect for colleagues)

Areas for Improvement
Patience (tolerance of people or processes and sensitivity to pacing)
Written communications (ability to write clearly and succinctly)
Overly ambitious (too much focus on successful completion of projects rather than developing relationships
  with individuals involved in the projects)

Career Goals
Please describe your overall career goals.
Long-term: Accept positions of increased responsibility to a level of general manager (or beyond). The areas of specific interest include but are not limited to product and brand management, technology and development, strategic planning, and marketing.
Short-term: Continue to improve my skills in marketing and brand management while utilizing my skills in product management, strategic planning, and global relations.

Next Assignments
Identify potential next assignments (including timing) that would help you develop toward your career goals.
Manager or director level in planning, development, product, or brand management. Timing estimated to be spring 2006.

Training and Development Needs
List both training and development activities that will either help you to develop in your current assignment or provide overall career development.
Master's degree classes will allow me to practice and improve my written communications skills. The dynamics of my current position, teamwork, and reliance on other individuals allow me to practice patience and to focus on individual team members' needs along with the success of the projects.

Employee _____   **Date** _____
Immediate Manager _____   **Date** _____
Mentor _____   **Date** _____

---

development plan for a product manager. Development plans usually include descriptions of strengths and weaknesses, career goals, and development activities (assignments, training) for reaching the career goals.

Action Planning

In **action planning,** employees determine how they will achieve their short- and long-term career goals. Action plans may involve enrolling in training courses and seminars, conducting informational interviews, or applying for job openings within the company.

**TABLE 11.5
Design Factors
of Effective
Career
Management
Systems**

Source: Based on
B. Baumann, J. Duncan, S. E. Former, and
Z. Leibowitz, "Amoco
Primes the Talent
Pump," *Personnel Journal* (February 1996):
79–84; D. Hall,
*Careers In and Out of
Organizations* (Thousand Oaks, CA: Sage,
2002).

1. System is positioned as a response to a business need or supports a business strategy.
2. Employees and managers participate in development of the system.
3. Employees are encouraged to take active roles in career management.
4. Evaluation is ongoing and used to improve the system.
5. Business units can customize the system for their own purposes (with some constraints).
6. Employees need access to career information sources (including advisors and positions available).
7. Senior management supports the career system.
8. Career management is linked to other human resource practices such as performance management, training, and recruiting systems.
9. System creates a large, diverse talent pool.
10. Information about career plans and talent evaluation is accessible to all managers.

The career development system established by United Parcel Service (UPS) illustrates the career planning process and the strategic role it can play in ensuring that staffing needs are met.[37] UPS has 285,000 employees in 185 nations and territories who are responsible for making sure that packages are picked up and delivered in a timely fashion. UPS wanted to put together a management development system that would ensure that managers' skills were up-to-date and that would link the system to selection and training activities. As a result, UPS designed a career management process. The manager starts the process by identifying the skills, knowledge, and experience required by the work team to meet current and anticipated business needs. Gaps between needs and relevant qualifications of the team are pinpointed. The manager then identifies the development needs of each team member. Next, the team members complete a series of exercises that help them with self-assessment, goal setting, and development planning (self-assessment). The manager and each employee work together to create an individual development plan. In the discussion, the manager shares performance appraisal information and analysis of team needs with the employee (reality check). The plan includes the employee's career goals and development actions during the next year (goal setting and action planning). To ensure that the career management process helps with future staffing decisions, divisionwide career development meetings are held. At these meetings managers report on the development needs and plans as well as capabilities of their work teams. Training and development managers attend to ensure that a realistic training plan is created. The process is repeated at higher levels of management. The ultimate result is a master plan with training activities and development plans that are coordinated among the functional areas.

The UPS system includes all the steps in the career planning process. The most important feature of the system is the sharing of information about individual employees, districts, and functional development and training needs and capabilities. This use of information at all three levels allows UPS to be better prepared to meet changing staffing needs and customer demands.

Table 11.5 shows several important design factors that should be considered in the process of developing a career management system. Tying development of the system to business needs and strategy, top management support (as in the Sears Credit example), and having managers and employees participate in building the system are especially important factors in overcoming resistance to the system.

TABLE 11.6
Elements of Career Management Websites

User Access	Website Features
Self-assessment tools	Jobs database
Training resources	Employee profile database
Job data	Matching engine
Salary information	Tools and services such as assessment, online training programs, development resources
Career management advice	

Career Management Websites

Many companies are developing career management websites that provide employees with self-assessment tools, salary information for jobs within the company, career management advice, and training resources. Similarly, many companies in the employee recruitment business (such as monster.com) provide similar resources for job seekers and employers. Table 11.6 presents the elements of career management websites. As the left side of Table 11.6 shows, users or employees need access to self-assessment tools, training resources, job data, salary information, and career management advice. The right side of Table 11.6 shows the features the company needs to include in the website design (e.g., job database, tools, and services). Users may include employees, managers, recruiters, or human resource managers. Both the users and the company gain valuable information from these systems—information that is useful for ensuring that employees' abilities, skills, and interests match their jobs. If there is a mismatch, these sites provide links to assessment tools so employees can determine what type of work best suits them as well as training and development resources for them to develop their skills. The company benefits from such systems in several ways. First, it can quickly post job openings and reach a large number of potential job seekers. Second, such websites provide detailed accessible information about jobs and careers within the company, which facilitates employee development. Employees are aware of what knowledge and skills are needed for jobs and careers in the company. Third, online systems encourage employees to be responsible for and take an active role in career management. This benefit is congruent with the new psychological contract and protean career discussed earlier in this chapter.

For example, Ford Motor Company's "Personal Development Roadmap" (PDR), a Web-based resource available on the company intranet, gives marketing, sales, and service employees control of their career development.[38] The PDR helps employees answer three questions: What skills do I have? What skills should I have? How do I enhance my skills? Annually, employees are asked to self-assess their current skills levels by completing an online profile. The PDR compares each employee's profile to the expected skill levels for that employee's job group. After the self-assessment, the employee identifies areas for development. The PDR recommends education and training (within Ford Motor), exploration (outside Ford Motor), and/or experiences to help meet the employee's needs. Employees can directly enroll in suggested training courses through the website. The PDR also helps employees create an annual development plan. The PDR is focused on helping employees develop specific leadership competencies (e.g., drive for results, innovation, desire to serve) that the company believes are needed for it to become the leading marketing, sales, and service company.

Thompson Corporation is a leader in the information sectors of the legal and regulatory, financial services, scientific, reference, health care, education, and corporate training markets on a global basis.[39] In your college classes you may have used textbooks published by Thomson. The company has offices in Stamford, Connecticut, as well as Toronto, Ontario, and London, England. Thomson's goal is to become the dominant global e-information and solutions business.

For its growth strategy to be successful, Thomson has to retain key employees. The company believes that the essence to employee retention is to create a satisfying and challenging work environment, maintain the right fit between employees and their jobs, and make sure that employees have the right tools to successfully perform their jobs. One of Thomson's goals is to facilitate employees' career development. To do so, Thomson had to educate employees on possible career opportunities within the company and make it easier for employees to move within the company.

In a company with 40,000 employees working in several divisions of five major groups, there were many promotion and transfer opportunities that employees didn't find out about. The company needed a means of educating the employees about Thomson's businesses, increasing employees' awareness of job openings across the company, and convincing employees that transferring to different businesses within the company was not only acceptable but encouraged.

Thomson developed an online career center to meet its needs. The *www.thomsoncareers. com* website includes 700 to 900 job listings per month. Employees can specify preferred locations and full- or part-time work. A personal search agent notifies employees automatically whenever a new opening related to their job or career interests is posted. The site is being developed to include self-assessments so that employees can determine if they have the skills required for open positions. If employees decide that they need education or training to qualify for a position, the site will link them to courses in Thomson University, the company's corporate university, which includes online courses.

ROLES OF EMPLOYEES, MANAGERS, HUMAN RESOURCE MANAGERS, AND COMPANY IN CAREER MANAGEMENT

Employees, their managers, human resource managers, and the company share the responsibility for career planning.[40] Figure 11.4 shows the roles of employees, managers, human resource managers, and the company in career management.

Employee's Role

The new psychological contract mentioned earlier in the chapter suggests that employees can increase their value to their current employer (and increase their employment opportunities) by taking responsibility for career planning. Companies with effective career management systems (such as Sears Credit and UPS) expect employees to take responsibility for their own career management. British Petroleum Exploration's employees are provided with a personal development planning guidebook that leads them through assessment, goal setting, development planning, and action planning.[41] Participation in the program is voluntary. The employees must also approach their manager to initiate career-related discussion as part of the personal development planning process.

FIGURE 11.4

Shared responsibility: Roles in career management

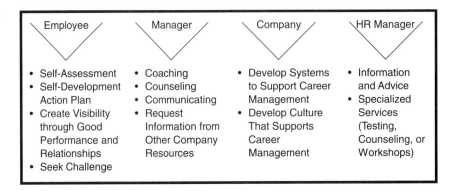

Employee	Manager	Company	HR Manager
• Self-Assessment • Self-Development Action Plan • Create Visibility through Good Performance and Relationships • Seek Challenge	• Coaching • Counseling • Communicating • Request Information from Other Company Resources	• Develop Systems to Support Career Management • Develop Culture That Supports Career Management	• Information and Advice • Specialized Services (Testing, Counseling, or Workshops)

Regardless of how sophisticated the company's career planning system is, employees should take several career management actions:[42]

- Take the initiative to ask for feedback from managers and peers regarding their skill strengths and weaknesses.
- Identify their stage of career development and development needs.
- Seek challenges by gaining exposure to a range of learning opportunities (e.g., sales assignments, product design assignments, administrative assignments).
- Interact with employees from different work groups inside and outside the company (e.g., professional associations, task forces).
- Create visibility through good performance.

Manager's Role

Regardless of the type of formal career planning system in place at the company, managers play a key role in the career management process. In most cases, employees look to their managers for career advice. Why? Because managers typically evaluate employees' readiness for job mobility (e.g., promotions). Also, managers are often the primary source of information about position openings, training courses, and other developmental opportunities. Unfortunately, many managers avoid becoming involved in career planning activities with employees because they do not feel qualified to answer employees' career-related questions, they have limited time for helping employees deal with career issues, and they lack the interpersonal skills needed to fully understand career issues.[43]

To help employees deal with career issues, managers need to be effective in four roles: coach, appraiser, advisor, and referral agent.[44] The responsibilities of each of these roles is shown in Table 11.7. Managers are responsible for helping employees manage their career through meeting personal needs as well as company needs. Coaching, appraising, advising, and serving as a referral agent are important roles for managers to play for employees in all stages of their careers. Employees early in their career may need information related to how well their performance is meeting customer expectations. Employees in both establishment and maintenance stages may use the manager as a sounding board for ideas and perspectives on job changes and career paths. Managers need to understand employees' interests by discussing with employees their job likes and dislikes.[45] One way to initiate this

TABLE 11.7
Managers' Role in Career Management

Source: Based on Z. B. Leibowitz, C. Farren, and B. L. Kaye, *Designing Career Development Systems* (San Francisco: Jossey-Bass, 1986).

Roles	Responsibilities
Coach	Probe problems, interests, values, needs.
	Listen.
	Clarify concerns.
	Define concerns.
Appraiser	Give feedback.
	Clarify company standards.
	Clarify job responsibilities.
	Clarify company needs.
Advisor	Generate options, experiences, and relationships.
	Assist in goal setting.
	Provide recommendations.
Referral Agent	Link to career management resources.
	Follow up on career management plan.

discussion is to ask employees to write up the characteristics of a satisfying career. This exercise helps employees better understand what they want from work in both the short term and long term. Only after understanding employees' interests can managers match employees to job experiences related to their interests.

To understand the manager's role in career management, consider the case of José, who works in the oil and chemical industry. José is an industrial hygienist at a chemical plant, where safety is critical. He is unhappy about what he thinks is a lack of career development at the company. As a result, he is considering leaving the company. José has been at a refinery in Texas the past year, but he wants to move back to Utah for family reasons. He was denied a lateral move to a plant in Utah. He made the request at a time when the company was downsizing and seeking voluntary retirements. The company understands that José wants to return to Utah, but it does not feel he is ready for another move. José considers his career stunted, and he thinks that the company does not care about him. Although he is unhappy, his performance is acceptable.

How can José's manager help him deal with this career issue to avoid losing a solid performer? José and his manager need to sit down and discuss his career. Table 11.8 presents the results that a manager should try to achieve in a career discussion. José's manager needs to clarify José's career concerns (coaching role). The manager also needs to make sure that José understands that although his job performance is acceptable, the company believes he needs to gain more experience at the Texas facility (appraiser role). Third, José's manager needs to discuss with José what can be done now to help him feel better about his job and the company and also help him understand how the company's need for a hygienist with his qualifications at the Texas refinery fits into the larger picture of his career development (advisor role). José and his manager should discuss and agree on a timetable for his next possible move (which could be to a position in Utah). The manager may give José advice concerning the correct timing for requesting a transfer, given the company's financial situation. Finally, José's manager should let him know about career counseling or other career management resources available within the company (role of referral agent).

TABLE 11.8
Characteristics of Successful Career Discussions

Source: Adapted from F. L. Otte and P. G. Hutcheson, *Helping Employees Manage Careers* (Englewood Cliffs, NJ: Prentice-Hall, 1992): 57–58.

Manager gains an awareness of employee's work-related goals and interests.
Manager and employee agree on the next developmental steps.
Employee understands how the manager views his or her performance, developmental needs, and options.
Manager and employee agree on how the employee's needs can be met on the current job.
Manager identifies resources to help the employee accomplish the goals agreed on in the career discussion.

Human Resource Manager's Role

Human resource managers should provide information or advice about training and development opportunities. Also, human resource managers may provide specialized services such as testing to determine employees' values, interests, and skills; preparing employees for job searches; and offering counseling on career-related problems.

Company's Role

Companies are responsible for providing employees with the resources needed to be successful in career planning. These resources include specific programs as well as processes for career management:

- Career workshops (seminars on such topics as how the career management system works, self-assessment, goal setting, and helping managers understand and perform their roles in career management).
- Information on career and job opportunities (places such as a career center or newsletters, electronic databases, or websites where employees can find information about job openings and training programs).
- Career planning workbooks (printed guides that direct employees through a series of exercises, discussions, and guidelines related to career planning).
- Career counseling (advice from a professionally trained counselor who specializes in working with employees seeking assistance with career issues).
- Career paths (planning job sequences and identifying skills needed for advancement within and across job families, such as moving from technical jobs to management jobs).

The company also needs to monitor the career planning system to (1) ensure that managers and employees are using the system as intended and (2) evaluate whether the system is helping the company meet its objectives (e.g., shortening the time it takes to fill positions).

For example, banking conglomerate First USA created its Opportunity Knocks program in response to employee dissatisfaction with professional growth opportunities following the company's merger with Bank One.[46] The Opportunity Knocks program offered a series of career management skill workshops and developed career resource centers at each bank. The career resource centers provided business publications, career management literature, and computers for updating résumés. The program also included development advisers to help employees with career issues. Evaluation of Opportunity Knocks found that employee satisfaction with career development improved 25 percent. Turnover rates for employees who participated in the program were 65 percent lower than for those who did not participate, saving the company an estimated $2.2 million in employee replacement costs.

At 3M, career management is supported by a network of resources throughout the company.[47] Activities include a performance appraisal and development process designed to facilitate communication between employees and managers, who work together to develop plans for performance and career development. The company also has a career resources center, which provides reference materials, publications, and books regarding career planning issues and development opportunities within the company. Employees can discuss career issues with trained counselors and explore interests, values, and work environment preferences through psychological testing. The Career Resources Department at 3M offers seminars on topics such as self-assessment, interviewing techniques, and managers' roles in career development. The company also provides help in placing employees who have lost their jobs because of transfers, downsizing, health problems, or disabilities. Finally, 3M has two information bases devoted to career issues. The computer-based Job Information System allows employees to nominate themselves for job openings. Managers can use the Internal Search System to identify employees who match job requirements. The Internal Search System contains data regarding employees' job history, location, performance rating, and career interests.

EVALUATING CAREER MANAGEMENT SYSTEMS

Career management systems need to be evaluated to ensure that they are meeting the needs of employees and the business. The outcomes, methods, and evaluation study designs that were discussed in Chapter 6 relating to training evaluation are relevant for career management system evaluation.

Several types of outcomes can be used to evaluate career management systems. First, the *reactions* of the customers (employees and managers) who use the career management system can be determined through surveys. For example, employees who use the services (planning, counseling, etc.) can be asked to evaluate the information's timeliness, helpfulness, and quality. Managers can provide information regarding how the system affected the time needed to fill open positions in their department as well as the quality of the job candidates and the employees selected for the positions. Second, more objective information related to *results* of the career management system can be tracked, such as actual time to fill open positions, employee use of the system (including contact with career counselors, use of career libraries, or inquiries on job postings), or number of employees identified as ready for management positions. If the goals of the system relate to diversity, the number of women and minorities promoted into management positions may be an appropriate measure.

Evaluation of a career management system should be based on its objectives. If improving employee morale is the system's goal, then attitudes should be measured. If the system objectives are more concrete and measurable (as with a system designed to retain employees with high potential for management), then appropriate data (turnover rates) should be collected.

Summary

This chapter explained the concept of a career and career management. It began by discussing career management's importance for the company and employees. The chapter described the changing nature of the career concept. Today, careers are more flexible and more likely to be evaluated on psychological success than on salary increases or promotions. The chapter introduced a career development model based on the new career concept and on life-cycle, organizational, and directional pattern perspectives of careers. It suggested that employees face different developmental tasks, depending on their career stage (exploration, establishment, maintenance, disengagement). The actions that companies can take to help employees deal with these developmental tasks were highlighted. The career management process consists of assessment, reality check, goal setting, and action planning. For career management to be successful, employees, managers, and the company must all be actively involved.

Key Terms

project career, *348*
career management, *349*
career motivation, *349*
career resilience, *349*
career insight, *350*
career identity, *350*
career, *352*
protean career, *352*
psychological contract, *352*
psychological success, *353*
career development, *356*

life-cycle models, *356*
organization-based
model, *356*
directional pattern
model, *356*
exploration stage, *357*
apprentice, *357*
establishment stage, *357*
colleague, *357*
maintenance stage, *358*
mentor, *358*

disengagement stage, *358*
sponsor, *358*
recycling, *359*
informational
interview, *359*
career management
system, *360*
self-assessment, *360*
reality check, *361*
goal setting, *361*
action planning, *362*

Discussion Questions

1. What stage of career development are you in? What career concerns are most important to you? Are these concerns consistent with any one of the development models presented in the chapter?

2. Discuss the implications that the career development model presented in this chapter may have for training and development activities.

3. Why should companies be interested in helping employees plan their careers? What benefits can companies gain? What are the risks?

4. What are the three components of career motivation? Which is most important? Which is least important? Why?

5. How does the protean career concept differ from traditional career concept on the following dimensions: pattern, development sources, goal, responsibility for management?

6. What is a psychological contract? How does the psychological contract influence career management?

7. What are the manager's roles in a career management system? Which role do you think is most difficult for the typical manager? Which is easiest? List the reasons why managers might resist involvement in career management.

8. How has the Web influenced career management for employees? For companies?

9. If you were asked to develop a career management system, what would it look like? How might you evaluate whether it was effective? What information would you use to develop the system?

Application Assignments

1. Go to *www.thomsoncareers.com,* the part of the website for the Thomson Corporation that provides career assistance for current Thomson employees and job seekers. What does Thomson Corporation provide on the site that helps prospective and current employees? Be specific and explain how each part of the site helps in career management.

2. Go to *www.monster.com.* Click on Get Career Advice. Click on Career Changers. Under Career Changers Resources, click on Self-Assessment. Complete one of the assessments found on the self-assessment page. How is the assessment useful for career development? What is the purpose of the assessment? What did it tell you about yourself?

3. Go to *www.monster.com.* Click on Career Center. In the Career Center, click on General Resources. Under the category Work Smarter, click on Quizzes and Tools. Find the Self-Directed Search (SDS). What is the SDS? How can it be useful for career management from the employee's perspective? The company's perspective?

4. Go to *www.ncsu.edu/careerkey/,* the website for Career Key, an assessment tool that can be used for self-assessment and career management. Click on You. Next, sign in. Take the Career Key measure. What information does it provide? What assumptions does it make about careers?

5. Go to *www.2h.com.* This website contains links to assessment tools and tests available on the Web. From the list provided, choose a test and complete it. What does it tell you? How would it be useful for career management?

6. The World Wide Web is increasingly being used by companies to list job openings and by individuals to find jobs. Using the websites listed here (or sites you find yourself by surfing the Web), find two job openings that you may be qualified for. The websites include

   www.careermosaic.com

   www.hire.com

   www.jobtrak.com

   www.monster.com

   www.jobcenter.com

   www.careerexchange.com

   www.ajb.dni.us/

   Choose one of these websites and describe the career resources it provides. From the company's perspective, what are the advantages of using the Web to recruit new employees? What are the advantages from the job searcher's perspective?

7. Complete the self-assessment exercise in Table 11.4. What changes would you make in the exercise to improve it?

Endnotes

1. P. Weber, "Getting a Grip on Employee Growth," *Training and Development* (May 1999): 87–94.

2. Ibid.

3. D. Hall, *Careers In and Out of Organizations* (Thousand Oaks, CA: Sage, 2002).

4. C. Hymowitz, "Baby Boomers Seek New Ways to Escape Career Claustrophobia," *The Wall Street Journal,* June 24, 2003: B1.

5. D. C. Feldman, *Managing Careers in Organizations* (Glenview, IL: Scott-Foresman, 1988).

6. J. E. Russell, "Career Development Interventions in Organizations," *Journal of Vocational Behavior* 38 (1991): 237–87; T. C. Gutteridge, "Organizational Career Development Systems: The State of the Practice," in *Career Development in Organizations,* ed. D. T. Hall and Associates (San Francisco: Jossey-Bass, 1986): 50–94.

7. M. London and E. M. Mane, *Career Management and Survival in the Workplace* (San Francisco: Jossey-Bass, 1987); M. London, "Toward a Theory of Career Motivation," *Academy of Management Review* 8 (1983): 620–30.

8. R. H. Waterman, Jr., J. A. Waterman, and B. A. Collard, "Toward a Career-Resilient Workforce," *Harvard Business Review* (July–August 1994): 87–95.

9. G. Wolf, M. London, J. Casey, and J. Pufahl, "Career Experience and Motivation as Predictors of Training Behaviors and Outcomes for Displaced Engineers," *Journal of Vocational Behavior* 47 (1995): 316–31.

10. L. Eby, M. Butts, and A. Lockwood, "Predictors of Success in the Era of the Boundaryless Career," *Journal of Organizational Behavior* 24 (2003): 689–708.

11. P. O'Herron and P. Simonsen, "Career Development Gets a Charge at Sears Credit," *Personnel Journal* (May 1995): 103–6.

12. Hall, *Careers In and Out of Organizations.*

13. Ibid.

14. D. T. Hall, "Protean Careers of the 21st Century," *Academy of Management Executive* 10 (1996): 8–16; Hall, *Careers In and Out of Organizations.*

15. D. M. Rousseau, "Changing the Deal While Keeping the People," *Academy of Management Executive* 10 (1996): 50–61; D. M. Rousseau and J. M. Parks, "The Contracts of Individuals and Organizations," in *Research in Organizational Behavior* 15, eds. L. L. Cummings and B. M. Staw (Greenwich, CT: JAI Press, 1992): 1–47.

16. C. Ansberry, "A New Blue-Collar World," *The Wall Street Journal,* June 30, 2003: B1.

17. P. Sellers, "Don't Call Me a Slacker," *Fortune* (December 12, 1994): 181–96.

18. M. B. Arthur, P. H. Claman, and R. J. DeFillippi, "Intelligent Enterprise, Intelligent Careers," *Academy of Management Executive* 9 (1995): 7–20.

19. B. Wysocki, Jr., "High Tech Nomads Write New Program for Future Work," *The Wall Street Journal,* August 19, 1996: A1, A6.

20. K. R. Brousseau, M. J. Driver, K. Eneroth, and R. Larsson, "Career Pandemonium: Realigning Organizations and Individuals," *Academy of Management Executive* 10 (1996): 52–66.

21. M. B. Arthur, "The Boundaryless Career: A New Perspective of Organizational Inquiry," *Journal of Organization Behavior* 15 (1994): 295–309; P. H. Mirvis and D. T. Hall, "Psychological Success and the Boundaryless Career," *Journal of Organization Behavior* 15 (1994): 365–80.

22. B. P. Grossman and R. S. Blitzer, "Choreographing Careers," *Training and Development* (January 1992): 67–69.

23. J. S. Lubin and J. B. White, "Throwing Off Angst, Workers Are Feeling in Control of Their Careers," *The Wall Street Journal,* (1997): A1, A6.

24. J. H. Greenhaus and G. A. Callanan, *Career Management,* 2d ed. (Fort Worth, TX: Dryden Press, 1994).

25. D. Brown, L. Brooks, and Associates, *Career Choice and Development,* 3d ed. (San Francisco: Jossey-Bass, 1996).

26. D. E. Super, *The Psychology of Careers* (New York: Harper and Row, 1957); G. Dalton, P. Thompson, and R. Price, "The Four Stages of Professional Careers," *Organizational Dynamics* (Summer 1972): 19–42; M. J. Driver, "Career Concepts—A New Approach to Career Research," in *Career Issues in Human Resource Management,* ed. R. Katz (Englewood Cliffs, NJ: Prentice-Hall, 1982): 23–34; D. T. Hall, *Careers in Organizations* (Pacific Palisades, CA: Goodyear, 1976); M. B. Arthur, D. T. Hall, and B. S. Lawrence, *Handbook of Career Theory* (New York: Cambridge University Press, 1989).

27. J. W. Slocum and W. L. Cron, "Job Attitudes and Performance during Three Career Stages," *Journal of Vocational Behavior* 26 (1985): 126–45.

28. S. Rabinowitz and D. T. Hall, "Changing Correlates of Job Involvement," *Journal of Vocational Behavior* 18 (1981): 138–44.

29. Hymowitz, "Baby Boomers Seek New Ways."

30. D. Fandray, "Gray Matters," *Workforce* (July 2000): 26–32.

31. F. L. Otte and P. G. Hutcheson, *Helping Employees Manage Careers* (Englewood Cliffs, NJ: Prentice-Hall, 1992).

32. A. Karr, "Boot Camp for Job Hoppers," *The Wall Street Journal,* July 11, 2000: B1, B14.

33. L. Lee, "I'm Proud of What I've Made Myself Into—What I've Created," *The Wall Street Journal,* August 28, 1997: B1, B5.

34. S. Shellenbarger, "Seeking Part-Time Work: 60-Something Former Exec Will File, Answer Phones," *The Wall Street Journal,* August 14, 2003: D1.

35. Consulting Psychologists Press, "Wells Fargo Helps Employees Change Careers," *Strong Forum* 8, no. 1 (1991): 1.

36. L. Slavenski, "Career Development: A Systems Approach," *Training and Development Journal* (February 1987): 56–60.

37. Z. Leibowitz, C. Schultz, H. D. Lea, and S. E. Forrer, "Shape Up and Ship Out," *Training and Development* (August 1995): 39–42.

38. "Personal Development Roadmap," 1998. Brochure from Ford Motor Company.

39. J. Salopek, "Career Centered," *Training and Development* (April 2000): 24–26; and Thomson Corporation website, *www.thomson.com.*

40. D. T. Jaffe and C. D. Scott, "Career Development for Empowerment in a Changing Work World," in *New Directions in Career Planning and the Workplace,* ed. J. M. Kumerow (Palo Alto, CA: Consulting Psychologists Press, 1991): 33–59; F. J. Miner, "Computer Applications in Career Development Planning," in Hall, *Career Development in Organizations:* 202–35.

41. K. Labich, "Take Control of Your Career," *Fortune* (November 18, 1991): 87–96; R. Tucker and M. Moravec, "Do-It-Yourself Career Development," *Training* (February 1992): 48–52.

42. S. Sherman, "A Brave New Darwinian Workplace," *Fortune* (January 25, 1993): 50–56.

43. B. M. Moses and B. J. Chakins, "The Manager as Career Counselor," *Training and Development Journal* (July 1989): 60–65.

44. Z. B. Leibowitz, C. Farren, and B. L. Kaye, *Designing Career Development Systems* (San Francisco: Jossey-Bass, 1986).

45. T. Butler and J. Waldrop, "Job Sculpting: The Art of Retaining Your Best People," *Harvard Business Review* (September–October 1999): 144–52.

46. J. Barbian, "jeff brown," *Training* (November 1, 2001):

47. "Personal Career Management." Brochure provided by Susan Runkel, management resource planning specialist, 3M, December 1991.

Chapter Twelve

Special Challenges in Career Management

Objectives

After reading this chapter, you should be able to

1. Design an effective socialization program for employees.
2. Discuss why a dual-career path is necessary for professional and managerial employees.
3. Provide advice on how to help a plateaued employee.
4. Develop policies to help employees and the company avoid technical obsolescence.
5. Develop policies to help employees deal with work-and-life conflict.
6. Select and design outplacement strategies that minimize the negative effects on displaced employees and "survivors."
7. Explain why retirees may be valuable as part-time employees.

Nonwork Lives Are Important Food for Thought

General Mills markets consumer brands across a wide range of food categories, including cereals, meals, baking products, snacks, and yogurt. The General Mills work environment is dynamic and high-energy. Expectations for employees' performance are high. But General Mills does not ignore employees' lives outside work. The company wants employees to be challenged and to succeed, but also wants them to have time for family and hobbies. General Mills CEO Steve Sanger believes that flexible work arrangements and family leaves contribute positively to the cereal maker's bottom line by reducing expensive turnover. In poor economic times, it might seem surprising to see a company dedicate time and money to helping employees balance their work and nonwork lives. But Sanger believes that these programs will benefit the company in the future. He believes it is better to allow someone to take a leave of absence and keep that person with the company in order to be making contributions 15 or 20 years from now for General Mills and not a competitor.

General Mills's family-friendly workplace initiatives include flexible work arrangements, on-site child care and health care, backup child care, and one week of paid leave for new fathers. Also included are services that make it easier to balance work and nonwork life, including a dry cleaner. Many employees consider the best benefit of all to be a 12:30 P.M. quitting time on Fridays between Memorial Day and Labor Day. Sanger says, "We try to do what we can do to take care of people's stress. Are we perfect? Of course not. But I would like to think that, more often than not we hit the mark."

For example, the company's marketing director took an 18-month leave of absence for travel and volunteer work. She started a book club for African American professional women and middle-school girls. When she was ready to return to the company, she learned she was pregnant. The company brought her back into a newly created position exploring cereal growth opportunities and held the job open while she took a three-month maternity leave. Two years later, she took an eight-month leave with her second child. In the meantime, she was promoted to vice president of marketing for Cheerios and Wheaties. She believes the company understands that having to devote time to nonwork issues does not mean employees are not committed. She says, "No one ever asked, Are you committed? After ten years with the company this was a given."

Source: Based on B. Rubin, "Think outside the (Cereal) Box," from the website for *Working Mother,* *www.workingmother.com;* and the website for General Mills, lifestyle and benefits section, *www.generalmills.com.*

INTRODUCTION

As the chapter opening vignette highlights, many companies believe that helping employees balance work and life benefits the business and employees' personal lives. Work-life balance from the employee's perspective means trying to manage work obligations as well as family and life responsibilities. From the company's perspective, work-life balance is the challenge of creating a supportive company culture where employees can focus on their jobs while at work. A **supportive work-life culture** is a company culture that acknowledges and respects family and life responsibilities and obligations and encourages managers and employees to work together to meet personal and work needs.[1] Work-life initiatives such as those at General Mills have been shown to have a positive relationship to shareholder returns, low absenteeism, motivation, decreased health care costs and stress-related illnesses, and retention.[2]

This chapter discusses a wide range of companies' special challenges in career management, including emphasizing work-life balance, socializing and orienting new employees, developing dual-career paths, avoiding skill obsolescence, helping employees cope with job loss, and preparing employees for retirement. These issues are considered career challenges because they tend to be challenges that employees and companies face at one point in employees' careers (e.g., retirement), throughout their careers (e.g., work-life balance), or at different points in their careers (e.g., socialization and orientation to new jobs). These challenges also affect a company's ability to attract, retain, and motivate talented employees. As this chapter explains, training programs and development activities are usually part of a company's solution to the career challenges of socialization, orientation, and skill obsolescence. It is important to emphasize that solving all the challenges discussed in this chapter requires a collaborative effort among trainers, line managers, human resource managers, and counselors as well as support from the company's top level.

TABLE 12.1   **What Employees Should Learn and Develop through Socialization**

History	The company's goals, values, traditions, customs, and myths; background of members
Company Goals	Rules or principles directing the company
Language	Slang and jargon unique to the company; professional technical language
Politics	How to gain information regarding the formal and informal work relationships and power structures in the company
People	Successful and satisfying work relationships with other employees
Performance Proficiency	What needs to be learned; effectiveness in using and acquiring the knowledge, skills, and abilities needed for the job

Source: Based on G. T. Chao, A. M. O'Leary-Kelly, S. Wolf, H. Klein, and P. D. Gardner, "Organizational Socialization: Its Content and Consequences," *Journal of Applied Psychology* 79 (1994): 730–43.

SOCIALIZATION AND ORIENTATION

Organizational socialization is the process by which new employees are transformed into effective members of the company. As Table 12.1 shows, the purpose of orientation is to prepare employees to perform their jobs effectively, learn about the organization, and establish work relationships. The three phases of the socialization process are anticipatory socialization, encounter, and settling in.[3]

Anticipatory Socialization

Anticipatory socialization occurs before the individual joins the company. Through **anticipatory socialization,** employees develop expectations about the company, job, working conditions, and interpersonal relationships. These expectations are developed through interactions with representatives of the company (e.g., recruiters, prospective peers, and managers) during the recruitment and selection process. The expectations are also based on prior work experiences in similar jobs.

Potential employees need to be provided with realistic job information. A **realistic job preview** provides accurate information about the attractive and unattractive aspects of the job, working conditions, company, and location to ensure that employees develop appropriate expectations. This information needs to be provided early in the recruiting and selection process. It is usually given in brochures, in videos, or by the company recruiter during an interview. Although research specifically investigating the influence of realistic job previews on employee turnover is weak and inconsistent, we do know that unmet expectations resulting from the recruitment and selection process have been shown to relate to dissatisfaction and turnover.[4] Employees' expectations about a job and a company may be formed by interactions with managers, peers, and recruiters rather than from specific messages about the job.

Encounter

The **encounter phase** occurs when the employee begins a new job. No matter how realistic the information was that they were provided during interviews and site visits, individuals beginning new jobs will experience shock and surprise.[5] Employees need to become familiar with job tasks, receive appropriate training, and understand company practices and procedures.

Challenging work plus cooperative and helpful managers and peers have been shown to enhance employees' learning a new job.[6] New employees view managers as an important source of information about their job and the company. Research evidence suggests that the nature and quality of new employees' relationship with the manager has a significant impact on socialization.[7] In fact, the negative effects of unmet expectations can be reduced if new employees have a high-quality relationship with the manager! Managers can help create a high-quality work relationship by helping new employees understand their role, by providing information about the company, and by being understanding regarding the stresses and issues that new employees are experiencing.

Settling In

In the **settling-in phase,** employees begin to feel comfortable with their job demands and social relationships. They begin to work on resolving work conflicts (e.g., too much work to do, conflicting demands of the job) and conflicts between work and nonwork activities. Employees are interested in the company's evaluation of their performance and in learning about potential career opportunities within the company.

Employees need to complete all three phases of the socialization process to fully contribute to the company. For example, employees who do not feel that they have established good working relationships with co-workers will likely spend time and energy worrying about relationships with other employees rather than worrying about product development or customer service. Employees who experience successful socialization are more motivated, more committed to the company, and more satisfied with their jobs.[8]

Socialization and Orientation Programs

Socialization and orientation programs play an important role in socializing employees. As shown in Table 12.1, effective socialization and orientation programs focus on providing the employee with a broad understanding of the history of the company, the company goals, and day-to-day interpersonal relationships as well as performance requirements. Effective socialization programs result in employees who have strong commitment and loyalty to the company, which reduces turnover.[9] Orientation involves familiarizing new employees with company rules, policies, and procedures. Table 12.2 shows the content of orientation programs. Typically, a program includes information about the company, the department in which the employee will be working, and the community.

While the content of orientation programs is important, the process of orientation cannot be ignored. Too often, orientation programs consist of completing payroll forms and reviewing personnel policies with managers or human resource representatives. The new employee is a passive recipient of information. New employees have little opportunity to ask questions or interact with peers and their managers.

Effective orientation programs include active involvement of the new employee. To learn the orientation content shown in Table 12.2, new employees need social networks that provide information as well as the feeling that the new employee is an important part of the company.[10] Social networks can be established through company orientation programs that provide new employees with opportunities to meet other new employees as well as employees in different parts of the company, with social events that allow new employees to meet other people and develop networks, and with mentors who can help new employees develop relationships with managers and other higher-level employees. Table 12.3 shows the characteristics of effective orientation programs.

TABLE 12.2
Content of Orientation Programs

Source: J. L. Schwarz and M. A. Weslowski, "Employee Orientation: What Employers Should Know," *The Journal of Contemporary Business Issues* (Fall 1995): 48.

I. Company-Level Information
Company overview (e.g., values, history, mission)
Key policies and procedures
Compensation
Employee benefits and services
Safety and accident prevention
Employee and union relations
Physical facilities
Economic factors
Customer relations

II. Department-Level Information
Department functions and philosophy
Job duties and responsibilities
Policies, procedures, rules, and regulations
Performance expectations
Tour of department
Introduction to department employees

III. Miscellaneous
Community
Housing
Family adjustment

TABLE 12.3
Characteristics of Effective Orientation Programs

Employees are encouraged to ask questions.
Program includes information on both technical and social aspects of the job.
Orientation is the responsibility of the new employee's manager.
New employees are not debased or embarrassed.
Formal and informal interactions with managers and peers occur.
Programs involve relocation assistance (e.g., house hunting, information session on the community for employees and their spouses).
Employees are provided with information about the company's products, services, and customers.

Several companies offer programs that include the characteristics shown in Table 12.3.[11] For example, Mission Bell Winery exposes new hires to every department for up to five days. New hires see how each department works and meet that department's employees. An online scavenger hunt as well as a Lunch and Learn program in which new hires visit with the leaders of the company are part of StorageTek's orientation program. Inter-tel pairs new hires with mentors to develop a career plan during their first week on the job. Prior to their first day on the job, new Inter-tel employees receive a phone call from a fellow worker and a welcome packet providing information on parking suggestions, dress guidelines, the on-site cafeteria menu, and automatic bank machine locations. The Mayo Clinic awards employees with movie tickets and coupons for free food in the cafeteria for answering questions correctly during a game show exercise that reviews orientation materials. The Verizon Wireless orientation program includes three "tours": an online virtual tour that includes information such as the code of conduct and benefits; a team tour that helps new employees become comfortable with peers and bosses; and a classroom visit that highlights the company history, mission, and values.

At Eddie Bauer, a needs analysis revealed that most employees did not remember what was discussed during the second day of the company's two-day orientation program. The company developed a new orientation program that starts with an initial presentation that lasts four hours. The program includes a guided tour through the associates resource guide, two hours of technical training to learn desktop skills, and a campus tour. The resource guide includes an initial performance plan for the associate to follow and an introduction to online material. New employees are required to attend four seminars during their first 90 days at work. The seminars cover topics such as corporate history and products overview. Eddie Bauer managers are also involved in the orientation. An online course that managers complete explains their responsibility to each new associate. E-mail reminders are sent to new associates about resources available in the human resource department and to ask the employees if they have the information they need. Once the 90-day orientation period is complete, associates are surveyed and feedback is provided to all corporate directors and managers.

An example of how orientation and socialization can reduce turnover and contribute to business is National City Corporation's Early Success program. National City Corporation, a bank and financial services company based in Cleveland, Ohio, was challenged by the high level of turnover that occurred among new employees within 90 days of being hired.[12] Turnover was 51 percent. Because it is difficult to provide excellent service and retain customers if customers are always dealing with a new employee, National City developed the National City Institute. Within the institute, the Early Success program provides a comfortable environment, a support network, and a series of classes where new hires learn product knowledge and customer service skills. For example, one course called Plus provides an overview of National City's corporate objectives, employee benefits, and information about the brand.

Another course, called People, Policies, and Practices, complements the employee handbook. Top-Notch Customer Care focuses on how to provide service and work in teams. New employees are matched with a peer (known as a buddy). The buddies are a support network for new hires that provides someone to answer their questions. The peer mentor is trained in coaching skills. The hiring managers also attend training designed to help them select buddy mentors, create a supportive work environment, communicate clearly, understand how to allow the new hire to gradually take on more responsibility, and help new hires achieve career goals. With the new program, new employees are 50 percent less likely to quit in the first three months on the job, resulting in a savings of approximately $1.35 million per year.

Onboarding refers to the orientation process for newly hired managers. Onboarding gives new managers an introduction to the work they will be supervising and an understanding of the culture and operations of the entire company. For example, at Pella Corporation, an Iowa-based manufacturer of windows and doors, new managers are sent on a tour of production plants, meeting and observing employees and department heads. These tours ensure that the managers will get a better sense of the market and how the company's products are designed, built, and distributed.[13] At The Limited, the Columbus, Ohio, retail clothing company, new vice presidents and regional directors spend their days talking to customers, reading company history, working the floor of retail stores, investigating the competition, and studying the company's current and past operations. They spend a month with no responsibilities for the tasks related to their new positions. Limited's philosophy is that managers are better able to perform their job by first taking time to understand the people, customers, company, and operations they will be working with.

FIGURE 12.1
Traditional
career path for
scientists and
managers

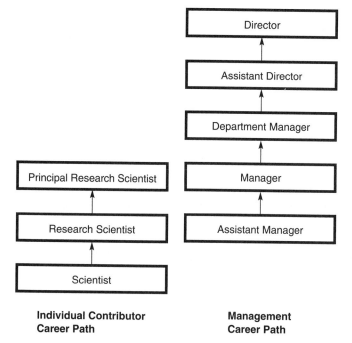

DUAL-CAREER PATHS

A **career path** is a sequence of job positions involving similar types of work and skills that employees move through in the company.[14] For companies with professional employees such as engineers and scientists, an important issue is how to ensure that they feel valued. Many companies' career paths are structured so that the only way engineers and scientists (individual contributors) can advance and receive certain financial rewards (such as stock options) is by moving into managerial positions. Figure 12.1 shows an example of a traditional career path for scientists and managers. Advancement opportunities within a technical career path are limited. Individual contributors who move directly into management may lack the experience and/or competencies needed to be successful. Managerial career paths may be more highly compensated than technical career paths. A career path system such as the one in Figure 12.1 can have negative consequences for the company. Scientists may elect to leave the company because of lower status, less salary, and fewer advancement opportunities than managers enjoy. Also, if scientists want to gain status and additional salary, they must choose to become managers. Scientists who cannot meet the challenges of a managerial position may leave the company.

Many companies are developing multiple- or dual-career-path systems to give scientists and other individual contributors additional career opportunities. Developing career paths involves analyzing work and information flows, the types of tasks performed across jobs, similarities and differences in working environments, and the historical movement patterns of employees into and out of jobs (i.e., where in the company employees come from and what positions they take after leaving the job).[15]

FIGURE 12.2

Example of
dual-career-
path system

Source: Z. B. Leibowitz,
B. L. Kaye, and
C. Farren, "Multiple
Career Paths,"
*Training and
Development Journal*
(October 1992):
31–35.

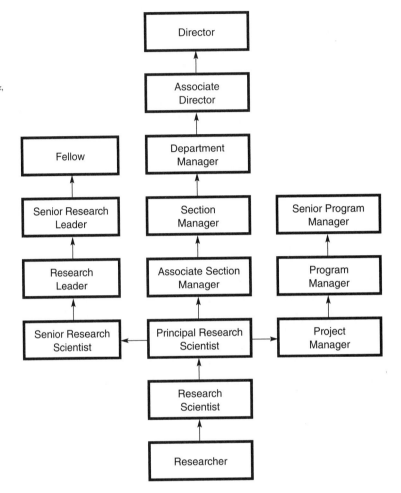

A **dual-career-path system** enables employees to remain in a technical career path or move into a management career path.[16] Figure 12.2 shows a dual-career-path system. Research scientists have the opportunity to move into three different career paths: a scientific path and two management paths. It is assumed that because employees can earn comparable salaries and have similar advancement opportunities in all three paths, they will choose the path that best matches their interests and skills.

Effective career paths have several characteristics:[17]

- Salary, status, and incentives for technical employees compare favorably with those of managers.
- Individual contributors' base salary may be lower than managers', but they are given opportunities to increase their total compensation through bonuses (e.g., for patents and developing new products).
- The individual contributor career path is not used to satisfy poor performers who have no managerial potential. The career path is for employees with outstanding technical skills.

- Individual contributors are given the opportunity to choose their career path. The company provides assessment resources (such as psychological tests and developmental feedback, as discussed in Chapters 9 and 11). Assessment information enables employees to see how similar their interests, work values, and skill strengths are to those of employees in technical and managerial positions.

A good example of the process used to develop an effective dual-career-path system is found at British Petroleum Exploration (BPX).[18] BPX created a dual-career-path system because individual contributors (nonmanagerial employees such as engineers and scientists who are directly involved in the development of a product or service) could not move to higher positions in the company without assuming managerial responsibility. After individual contributors reached the top job in the career path, their choices were to stop progressing upward or leave the company.

BPX decided to develop a dual-career-path system similar to that in Figure 12.2. One path was for managers, the other for individual contributors. The paths were comparable in terms of responsibility, rewards, and influence.

Managers, individual contributors, and human resource staff all contributed to the development of the career path system. The first step in the process was the development of descriptions of skills and performance levels that applied to managerial and individual contributor positions. Skill matrices were constructed for the two career paths. Each skill matrix described the skills needed for each position within each career path. The skills matrices were distributed to all employees so that they were aware of the skills they needed in their current jobs and the skills they needed to develop to change jobs. The skill matrices were integrated with other human resource systems including performance management, reward, and training systems. For example, the skills matrices served as a source of information for BPX's development program. The matrices were used to determine what performance improvement, training, or experience the employee needed to meet current job responsibilities and to prepare for their next job experience. Employees could move from the individual contributor to the management career path based on their performance, their qualifications, and business need (e.g., turnover).

BPX believes that innovation is enhanced by providing employees with career paths that reward individual contributors as well as management contributors. Also, BPX believes that it will be easier to recruit and keep talented scientists and engineers because the dual-career-path system demonstrates the company's interests in satisfying employees' career interests.

Skill-based pay systems (discussed in Chapter 10) are also used by companies to reward employees who are unlikely to move into managerial positions. In these systems, part of employees' pay is based on their level of knowledge or skills rather than the requirements of their current job. These systems (1) motivate employees to broaden their skill base and (2) reduce the differential in pay rates between managerial and nonmanagerial positions.

PLATEAUING

Plateauing means that the likelihood of the employee receiving future job assignments with increased responsibility is low. Compared to employees in other career stages, midcareer employees are most likely to plateau. For example, a 54-year-old manager once specialized in marketing production. He has had to learn finance, marketing, and purchasing.

He works 12 hours a day doing the same job he did 10 years ago. The salary and status of his job have not changed much. But the knowledge and skills needed and the time demands have increased dramatically. He used to manage people, but now he spends most of his time managing information. He is given fewer resources to accomplish more work. He once had his own secretary to manage his schedule and handle phone calls, but not any more. His phone is constantly ringing, his e-mail box is filled with messages. Plateauing is not necessarily bad for the employee or the company. A plateaued employee may not desire increased job responsibilities. Job performance may meet the minimum acceptable standards. Plateauing becomes dysfunctional when the employee feels stuck in a job that offers no potential for personal growth. Such frustration results in poor job attitude, increased absenteeism, and poor job performance.[19]

Employees can plateau for several reasons:[20]

- Discrimination based on, for example, age, gender, or race.
- Lack of ability.
- Lack of training.
- Low need for achievement.
- Unfair pay decisions or dissatisfaction with pay raises.
- Confusion about job responsibilities.
- Slow company growth resulting in reduced development opportunities.

Table 12.4 provides several means to help plateaued employees. Employees need to understand why they are plateaued. Being stuck in a position is not necessarily the employee's fault. Plateauing may be due to restructuring of the company that has eliminated many potential positions. (This situation is known as structural plateauing.) If plateauing is due to a performance problem, employees need to be aware of this so they correct the problem.

Plateaued employees should be encouraged to become involved in developmental opportunities, including training courses, job exchanges, and short-term assignments in which they can use their expertise outside their departments. Participating in developmental opportunities may prepare employees for more challenging assignments in their current job or may qualify them for new positions within the company. Plateaued employees may need career counseling to help them understand why they are plateaued and their options for dealing with the problem. For example, to cope with stress the 54-year-old manager mentioned earlier meets with a group of middle-aged men twice a month. Discussions often revolve around the difficulty of keeping up with new products and the relentless pressure to produce. Many discussions focus on retirement or finding new careers such as consulting or working with the needy. The group's underlying feelings are clear. They feel they have peaked in their careers but not in life. They have been caught unexpectedly by the erosion of the relationship between natural talent, hard work, good morals, job security, and stability.[21] Employees

TABLE 12.4 **Possible** **Remedies for** **Plateaued** **Employees**	Employee understands the reasons for plateauing. Employee is encouraged to participate in development activities. Employee is encouraged to seek career counseling. Employee does a reality check on his or her solutions.

should be encouraged to do a reality check on their plateauing solutions through discussions with their manager, co-workers, and human resource manager. A reality check is necessary to ensure that their solutions are realistic given the resources available in the company. At times it may be in the best interest of the employee and the company if the employee is encouraged to leave the company.

SKILLS OBSOLESCENCE

Obsolescence is a reduction in an employee's competence resulting from a lack of knowledge of new work processes, techniques, and technologies that have developed since the employee completed his or her education.[22] Avoiding skills obsolescence has traditionally been a concern of employees in technical and professional occupations such as engineering and medicine. However, rapid technological change affects all aspects of business from manufacturing to administration, so all employees are at risk of becoming obsolete. Also, obsolescence needs to be avoided if companies are trying to become learning organizations. If employees' skills become obsolete, both the employee and the company suffer. The company will be unable to provide new products and services to customers, losing its competitive advantage. As was mentioned in the discussion on plateauing, lack of up-to-date skills is one reason why employees become plateaued. For example, a secretary who fails to keep up with developments in word processing software (e.g., merging text with figures, tables, charts, and pictures) will soon be unable to produce state-of-the-art documents for the secretary's internal customer, the advertising manager. The advertising manager's clients may view the company's material as outdated and therefore give their advertising business to a competitor. The secretary will likely be given more mundane and uninteresting work and will likely be an outplacement candidate.

What can be done to avoid skills obsolescence? Examine Figure 12.3. As was mentioned in Chapter 5, the company culture plays an important role in encouraging employees to develop their skills. Through implementing a climate for continuous learning, many companies combat skills obsolescence by encouraging employees to attend courses, seminars, and programs and to consider how to do their jobs better on a daily basis. Obsolescence can also be avoided by[23]

FIGURE 12.3

Factors related to updating skills

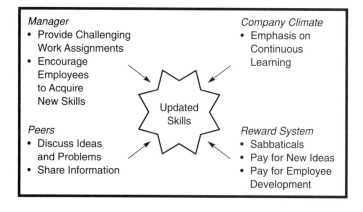

- Providing employees with the opportunity to exchange information and ideas.

- Giving employees challenging job assignments early in their careers.

- Providing job assignments that challenge employees and require them to "stretch" their skills.

- Providing rewards for updating behaviors (such as taking courses), suggestions, and customer service and product innovations.

- Allowing employees to attend professional conferences, subscribe to professional journals and magazines, or enroll in university, technical school, or community center courses at low or no cost.

- Encouraging employees to interact in person or electronically to discuss problems and new ideas.

Sabbaticals are one of companies' methods to help employees avoid obsolescence. A **sabbatical** refers to a leave of absence from the company to renew or develop skills. Employees on sabbatical often receive full pay and benefits. Sabbaticals allow employees to get away from their day-to-day job stresses and acquire new skills and perspectives. Sabbaticals also allow employees more time for personal pursuits such as writing a book or raising young children. Sabbaticals are common in a variety of industries ranging from consulting firms to the fast-food industry. Fallon Worldwide, an advertising agency, offers a program called Dreamcatchers to staff members who want to work on a project or travel.[24] Dreamcatchers was developed to help the agency avoid having employees burn out and lose their creative edge. Employees have taken time off to write novels, kayak, and motorcycle through the Alps. Fallon Worldwide matches employee contributions of up to $1,000 annually for two years and offers up to two extra weeks of paid vacation. The agency partners believe that the program has helped in the retention of key employees and the recruiting of new ones. The partners also believe that the program helps recharge employees' creativity, which is key for employees to do their best work for customers.

Morningstar, the mutual fund tracking company, provides a six-week paid sabbatical every four years for all employees.[25] A Morningstar manager who had recently been promoted to the role of exhibit/conference manager worked an extra year before taking his sabbatical. He spent half his sabbatical on the beach in California and another three weeks pursuing his passion for modern dance. At first, he was worried about phone calls, messages, deadlines, faxes, and mail back at the office. He was also nervous about temporarily giving up his job to someone else. But soon, being totally separated from work was pleasing to him. He returned to Morningstar tan and reenergized. This is exactly what Morningstar intended with the program. Morningstar CEO Don Phillips believes that employees reach points in their careers where they are so concerned about getting day-to-day tasks completed that they forget the larger perspective. Sabbaticals allow employees to gain a clearer perspective of their jobs, careers, and company, and help them avoid burnout. While some employees leave Morningstar after the sabbatical, Phillips believes that both the company and the person are better off being separated if the employee is dissatisfied. Key issues that need to be addressed for a sabbatical program to work include employees' worries about their financial security; concerns that clients, contacts, and subordinates will be well taken care of; and helping employees adjust to a slower lifestyle while still staying stimulated.

BALANCING WORK AND LIFE

Families with a working husband, homemaker wife, and two or more children account for only 7 percent of American families. Typically, work and family research and practice has focused on men and women who are married or living with a partner and who have children.[26] But work-life balance is also a concern of single-earner mothers and fathers, single and childless employees, blended families with children from both marriages, families with shared custody of children, grandparents raising their grandchildren, and employees with responsibility for elder care. One way that companies can help employees balance work and life is to provide support for employees who are concerned with simultaneously meeting the needs of work and family. Work and family roles are likely to conflict because employees are forced to take several different roles (e.g., parent, spouse, employee) in a number of different environments (e.g., workplace, home, community). Many working moms feel that they are failures both at home and at work. To fit into the "ideal worker" mold (an employee who works at least eight hours a day, 40 hours a week and longer), women often feel that they have to sacrifice being good mothers. One study even suggested that to reach high-level managerial jobs, women must sacrifice having children![27] Research suggests that dual-career families, single-parent families, and families with children under age five are likely to experience the most work and family conflict.[28]

Social legislation has been approved to help employees balance work and family. The **Family and Medical Leave Act (FMLA)** is a federal law that provides for up to 12 weeks of unpaid leave for parents with new infants or newly adopted children. The FMLA also covers employees who must take a leave of absence from work to care for a family member who is ill or to deal with a personal illness. Companies are required to provide the employee with health care benefits during their leave of absence. The U.S. Senate has considered including paid leave as part of the FMLA.[29] California will be the first state to offer a paid family leave to both mothers and fathers. Canada's family leave policy—which allows parents to take leave for up to one year while collecting as much as 55 percent of their weekly pay, up to a maximum of $308 (U.S.)—has been considered a model for the new U.S. policy.

Maintaining a healthy work-life balance is a concern for all employees, even those without families or dependents. Flexibility in when and where work is performed, and support services are valuable for helping all employees deal with the stresses and strains related to work and nonwork conflicts. Employees with dependents struggle with child care and elder care. All employees struggle with finding time to participate in nonwork activities when they have increasing work demands.

Training can play two roles in balancing work and nonwork. First, trainers and managers may be responsible for developing policies and procedures. Second, trainers may be responsible for developing training programs to teach managers their role in administering and overseeing the use of work-life policies.

Types of Work-Life Conflict

Employees often feel that their work and life are out of balance because of conflicts between the two. Feelings of frustration are only one outcome of work and nonwork conflict. Work-life conflict has also been found to be related to increased health risks, decreased productivity, tardiness, turnover, and poor mental health.[30] All employees have nonwork roles and activities that may conflict with work. Three types of work-family conflict have been identified: time-based conflict, strain-based conflict, and behavior-based conflict.[31]

Time-based conflict occurs when the demands of work and nonwork interfere with each other. For example, jobs that demand late evenings at the office, overtime work, or out-of-town travel conflict with family activities and team-sport schedules. **Strain-based conflict** results from the stress of work and nonwork roles. For example, a newborn child deprives parents of sleep; as a result, it is difficult for them to concentrate at work. **Behavior-based conflict** occurs when employees' behavior in work roles is not appropriate for their behavior in nonwork roles. For example, managers' work demands that they be logical, impartial, and authoritarian. At the same time, these same managers are expected to be warm, emotional, and friendly in their relationships with their family members or friends.

Employees who work on nonstandard shifts are especially vulnerable to these types of conflict.[32] One estimate is that 20 percent of the U.S. work force does not have the traditional dayshift (9 to 5) work schedule. These employees may suffer from lack of sleep (making them irritable). Nonstandard shifts also cause them to miss special events and meals. Family life can be disrupted as the shiftworker, spouse, and children all lead separate lives. For example, a data processing supervisor for an insurance company spent 10 years rotating every 12 to 18 months among day, evening, and overnight shifts. Communication with her husband, who worked a day shift, was difficult, and she missed her children's after-school events. The stress affected her ability to sleep. She would wake up and not know what time of day it was. Working nonstandard shifts, however, sometimes enables parents to be part of their kids' lives in situations where they couldn't with a 9 to 5 work schedule.

COMPANY POLICIES TO ACCOMMODATE WORK AND NONWORK

Besides following the FMLA, many companies are beginning to respond to work and nonwork issues by developing policies designed to reduce the potential for work-life conflict. These policies emphasize the communication of realistic information about the demands of jobs and careers, flexibility in where and when work is performed, job redesign, and support services such as child care and elder care programs. Research suggests that company policies that help employees manage work and nonwork conflicts enhance employees' job performance, lower costs associated with disability leave, and reduce turnover and absenteeism.[33] Bank of America, one of the world's leading financial services companies, has earned the distinction of being recognized by *Working Mother* magazine as one of the top 10 companies for working mothers. Table 12.5 shows some of the work-life programs at Bank of America. Note that the programs shown in Table 12.5 are relevant and accessible for all employees, not just those with children.

Consider the actions taken by the National Association of Insurance Commissioners, a Kansas City–based nonprofit group that supports the 50 state insurance commissioners, to help employees balance work and life. The company was losing employees to competitors who were offering 50 percent salary increases.[34] Turnover had reached 30 percent. Unable to offer higher salaries, the company began to offer benefits that would give employees more flexibility and a higher quality of life. The benefits included a infants-in-the-workplace program

TABLE 12.5 Some Work-Life Programs at Bank of America

Child Care Plus	Pays for child care expenses up to $175 per month per child.
Adoption Reimbursement	Pays up to $4,000 in financial assistance per adopted child.
Tuition Reimbursement	Pays for college tuition and tuition-related expenses, up to $2,000 per calendar year for undergraduate courses and $4,000 for graduate courses.
Flexible Work Arrangements	Allows employee and manager to define when and where the employee works; includes flextime, job sharing, part-time work, and telecommuting.
Time Off and Leaves	Provides employees with both paid and unpaid leave time for personal reasons or illness; includes adoption leave, family leave, and maternity or paternity leave.
Employee Assistance Program	Provides confidential, short-term counseling for problems involving stress, family, mental health, and substance abuse.
LifeWorks©	Is a confidential resource and referral program that provides practical advice, consultations, and seminars from experts who can help employees manage work and personal responsibilities.

Source: B. Russell, "Bank of America Named as One of Top 10 Companies for Working Mothers by *Working Mother* magazine (September 24, 2002)," (from Bank of America website, *www.bankofamerica.com/newsroom*).

that allowed employees to bring babies up to the age of six months to their offices. Parents had to sign a liability release and designate a co-worker to serve as a care provider when the employee was in meetings. Changing tables were installed in all restrooms, and a quiet room with soft lights, crib, and rocking chair were available for parents. The company established a grievance procedure for other employees to complain about distractions as a result of infants in the workplace (no one has ever used the process). Other benefits included a four-day compressed work week, flextime, telecommuting, a sick-leave pool that enables employees to donate unused sick days to a peer with a serious illness, a zero-interest computer purchase program for employees to buy a home personal computer, and one day off each year to participate in Habitat for Humanity. The program has been successful— turnover has been reduced to 7 percent.

Identifying Work and Life Needs and Communicating Information about Work and Nonwork Policies and Job Demands

Companies have to understand employees' needs, solicit their input, and make work-life benefits accessible to everyone. To do so, companies need to comprehend the diversity, complexity, and reality of employees' lives. Programs should be designed with the idea to provide as many benefits as possible to meet the needs of as many people as possible. For example, at Hartford Insurance, employees could take time off for vacation, personal time, or sick days. But these options did not relate to employees' lives. Through surveys and focus groups, the company learned that employees with families, especially single parents, wanted a more liberal unscheduled-absence policy. As a result, the company designed a paid-time-off program that provides a specific number of days for employees to use as they wish.

Work-life program benefits need to be communicated and available to all employees whether they are married or single, parents or childless.[35] At Deloitte and Touche, benefits are not dependent on parental status. Employees who request a flexible work arrangement are not asked for their marital or family status or to explain why they are making the request. The employees only need to prove they can meet the job requirements. Intel makes sure that benefits are publicized in as many ways as possible, including the intranet and in-house newsletters, and the company shares stories of how various benefits are being used. For example, an employee who loves to paint as a hobby does his best work in the early morning, and he was able to rearrange his schedule to arrive at work a few hours late. Kodak has a program known as Unique Personal Opportunity Leave, which allows employees to take up to 52 weeks for personal, humanitarian, or educational needs. This program helps parents, but it also allows nonparents opportunities to travel, go on a mission, sail, or whatever they feel would benefit them. For both parents and nonparents, the manager has to approve the leave request.[36]

Employees need to be made aware of the time demands and the stress related to jobs within the company. This information should be part of a realistic job preview that employees receive during the recruitment process (both when they first join the company and for jobs within the company). This information helps employees choose career opportunities that match the importance they place on work.

Flexibility in Work Arrangements and Work Schedules

There are two ways to deal with work-life conflicts. One is to provide employees with more flexibility about when work is performed (work schedules) and where it is performed (work arrangements). To help employees with their work schedules, companies should educate them about the positives and negatives of various schedules, allow them to participate in choosing their schedules, and train them in handling the physical, family, and social effects of their work schedule. For example, when Sawtek, a producer of microelectronic filters, expanded operations from five days a week to 24 hours a day, seven days a week, focus groups of employees met to design different scheduling choices (e.g., 8- and 12-hour shifts).[37] Some employees chose the 12-hour shift, which caused severe changes to their life schedules, but they accepted those changes because they had an active role in choosing their own schedule. The company also hired consultants to train employees (and their spouses) in how to deal with sleep problems. Other companies (such as Cinergy, an energy company) allow employees to swap shifts, with the manager's approval, to accommodate personal needs.

The second method is to reduce the pressure that many employees face to work long hours. Work-family conflict can be reduced by increasing employees' control over work and family demands.[38] One way many companies have provided employees with additional control is through alternative work schedules involving flextime or part-time work. Table 12.6 presents examples of alternative work arrangements and work schedules. These work arrangements provide employees with some control over their work schedule, giving them time to deal with family demands (e.g., paying bills, caring for infants and small children) and avoid the difficulties of commuting. Alternative work arrangements reduce stress and absenteeism.[39] Home-based work is dominated by individuals in educational, professional, business, repair, and social service occupations.

Technology can both help and interfere with the work-life balance. The explosion of data capabilities related to increased use of e-mail, the Web, beepers, and cellular phones has bombarded employees with demands and information in both their work and nonwork lives. In the car, at home, on vacation, and even in the bathroom, employees can be reached and asked to respond to work demands. However, technology can also provide employees with flexibility to balance work and life. It can remove the need for face-time with peers or customers.

TABLE 12.6   Alternative Work Schedules and Work Arrangements

	Where	**When**
Traditional	Place of employment	5 days, 40 hours per week
Flextime	Place of employment	40 hours per week but have choice of when to start and end work; may require work during certain core hours
Compressed Workweek	Place of employment	4 days, 10-hour workdays
Temporary Work	Place of employment	On as-needed basis
Job Sharing	Place of employment	Split 5-day, 40-hour workweek with another employee
Part-Time Work	Place of employment	Less than 8 hours a day or 5 days a week
Shift Work	Place of employment	Morning, afternoon, or overnight shifts sometimes on a rotating basis
Telecommuting	Home	Varies; could be one or more days during normal business hours
Reduced Work Hours	Place of employment; home	Varies; could include reduced number of meetings, no weekend work, work maximum of 8 hours per day
Hoteling	Shared office space in a company location designed for use on a drop-in basis	Varies

Being in the office as a demonstration that an employee is working hard was once the accepted norm—it is now outdated. Employees do not have to be in the office to be responsive to peers, managers, and customers. Office computers can be operated by remote control and e-mail timers let employees send e-mails at any time of the day. For example, the manager of a trucking company took a cruise to Acapulco, but his clients never knew he left the office.[40] He used software to manipulate his computer by remote control. He could even check on the position of each of his trucks by using global positioning maps. If an employee was not on the correct route, he could send a text message to the truck. The flexibility that technology provides can also be misused by workers who are shirking their duties. Technology allows employees to make it look like they are working when they are not. One technology worker was fired because he manipulated his computer from a diner so he could take three-hour lunches.

Many companies are trying new work schedules that give employees more control over their jobs. For example, at Johnson and Johnson in Racine, Wisconsin, twice a month the company that makes floor waxes, window cleaner, and storage bags bans meetings by its 3,500 U.S. employees. Meeting-Free Fridays help employees avoid taking work home on weekends.[41] Employees often were in meetings the entire workday, forcing them to work on a weekend that they needed for rest. Intel Corporation encourages employees to tell managers to stop calling them at home or at night. Both Radio Shack and iVillage have policies that employees should not call the office while on vacation. Consulting firm Deloitte and Touche eliminated Sunday business trips for its consultants. Consultants leave Monday to spend three nights and four days at clients' offices and return to work the fifth day back at their office at Deloitte and Touche.

The major difficulties posed by alternative work schedules and work arrangements include communication problems (employees may be at different locations and on different work schedules), a lack of necessary supplies and equipment, and family interruptions.[42] To try to avoid these difficulties, companies are allowing flexible schedules only if certain conditions are met. For example, Kodak believes that employees whose work schedules meet their needs will be better able to meet their work obligations. At Kodak, flexible work arrangements can involve working at any location, at any hour, or on any schedule as long as two conditions are met.[43] First, the flexible arrangement cannot have a negative impact on business operations. Second, the manager must approve the plan. Managers are trained in how to work with flexible work arrangements without having them adversely affect business operations. It is the employee's responsibility to make the business case for the flexible arrangement and convince the manager that it can work. Employees use a booklet provided by Kodak to create their proposals for flexible arrangements. The manager and employee discuss the proposal and identify advantages and disadvantages of different work arrangements.

Job sharing might be the most challenging work option.[44] **Job sharing** refers to having two employees divide the hours, the responsibilities, and the benefits of a full-time job. For example, two consulting systems engineers at Bank of America in San Francisco have shared one job for eight years. They are an invaluable source of information for many inexperienced employees. Their experience and expertise are valuable assets that the company could not have received from a series of temporary employees. Companies may also use two job-sharing part-time employees to fill a full-time position. The company gains the expertise of two employees (rather than one) and can save substantial costs because part-time employees may not be eligible for health care and retirement benefits.

For job sharing to be effective,

- The impact of job sharing on clients and customers must be determined. If satisfying client and customer needs is compromised (if customers want one consistent contact person, for example), job sharing is likely to be an unattractive option.
- The employee interested in job sharing must find another employee performing the same job who wants reduced work hours.
- The two people sharing the job need to have similar work values and motivations. Otherwise, interpersonal conflicts will interfere with completing assignments.
- The manager must actively communicate with the job-sharing employees and accept the fact that they might not be immediately available for consultation.
- Meeting schedules, work assignments, and vacation schedules need to be carefully coordinated. Employees need to plan to overlap some of their time to meet.
- Performance evaluation of job sharers needs to include both an individual and team appraisal.

J&A Corporate Financial has capitalized on the increasing number of corporations seeking outside help with projects and the large number of professionals looking for flexible, part-time work. J&A employs seven consultants who average 10 years of experience. All are certified public accountants, and most have MBAs. Six employees are mothers. J&A is a serious rival for larger companies because the staff are paid high wages, which attracts well-qualified candidates, but at the same time they are paid only for the hours they work. Also, because the consultants are independent contractors and work at home, the company does not have to pay Social Security taxes or provide benefits. As a result, they undercut the competition by charging about $100 per hour compared to $250 for larger consulting firms.

Margaret Johnsson, owner of the company, set up a contingency plan to avoid problems with the availability of her work force. For each consulting project, she assigns a primary consultant and a backup. If home obligations (such as having to spend all night in an emergency room with a sick child) force the primary consultant to miss work, the backup takes over. Ms. Johnsson also tries to assign projects based on both skills and schedules. She stresses to clients that even though staff may not be immediately reached, they will return calls within two hours. She insists that staff leave the kids at home and avoid taking excessive breaks to deal with personal problems at clients' offices.[45]

Redesigning Jobs

As companies move away from traditional job descriptions and toward cross-functional teams and more contingent employees (e.g., consultants, temporary employees), it becomes less clear who is responsible for work. As a result, work assignments can be given to anyone, including those people who are already overworked. Companies need to review employees' work loads and identify what work is necessary and what work is not.[46] For example, at Merck, a pharmaceutical company, employees were complaining about work schedules and overwork. Merck assigned groups of employees to teams who analyzed work and reorganized so that employees had more control over their work loads and schedules. In one area, employees were not happy with the large number of overtime hours they had to work. The employee teams realized that much of their work was most critical early in the week. Solutions included reducing employees' commute time by allowing them to work at home more often, and providing compressed workweeks. Some of the work load was adjusted by outsourcing (giving the work to other companies). Recall the discussion of competencies in Chapter 3. Another approach to redesigning work is to focus on identifying core competencies. For example, the Massachusetts Housing Finance Agency identified eight core competencies that relate to what employees in each of five roles (e.g., business leader, individual contributor) are expected to accomplish at work. By focusing on competencies, the company is eliminating extraneous work.

Managerial Support for Work-Life Policies

Many employees are concerned about using flexible work arrangements and schedules because they fear that managers will view them as uninterested in their careers and accuse them of shirking their job responsibilities. They fear that managers may not provide them with development opportunities and will evaluate their performance less favorably. Companies need to train managers to understand that employees' use of work-family policies should not be punished. The more supportive the manager is (e.g., willing to listen to employees' family-related work problems and offer solutions based on the company's program), the less work-family conflict employees will experience.[47]

By supporting work-life policies, top-level managers can reduce employees' anxiety. For example, General Mills CEO Steve Sanger, as the chapter opening vignette showed, is an avid supporter of work-life policies. Kenneth Lewis, CEO of Bank of America, believes that the company's work-life policies help make the company the best place to work, which means that customers have the best place to do business.

Dependent Care Support: Child and Elder Care

Companies can help employees deal with child care demands in a number of ways. The child care services that companies most frequently provide include help in identifying child care resources and flexible benefit plans that allow employees to pay for child care with pre-tax dollars.

Child care services need to be flexible to meet the needs of a diverse work force. A single parent may need more assistance than an employee with a spouse who works part-time. Employees with infants may want to choose parental leave or work part-time or at home. Although more than half of companies offer flextime, less than one-third offer telecommuting on a part-time or regular basis, compressed workweeks, child-care referral services, or parental leave beyond that allowed by the FMLA.[48] The lack of child care likely has the greatest impact on low-income parents, who cannot afford to pay for child-care services. These parents face the difficult decision of working (and leaving children unattended) or not working and staying home with their children.

Two companies in Boulder, Colorado—Exabyte Corporation, which manufactures high-storing computerized information, and Synergen, a biopharmaceutical development company—discovered through conversations between their human resources managers that employees at both companies had child-care concerns.[49] As a result, these two companies, along with nine others, created a nonprofit organization, the Boulder Business Dependent Care Association, to develop more and higher quality local child care. The nonprofit organization compiled a directory of day-care program discounts, provided direct subsidies for some child-care needs such as sick-child care, and negotiated with a local YMCA for a school vacation program. The fee to join the organization is based on number of employees.

A growing concern for many employees is elder care—how to care for aging parents. At least 20 percent of all employees currently care for a parent. The care of elderly persons will only increase in importance in the United States because 13 percent of Americans are age 65 or older, and by 2030, 20 percent of Americans will be more than 65 years old. The population age 85 and older is the fastest-growing segment of the older population, growing by 274 percent over the past 25 years.[50] The stresses of elder care result in problems similar to working parents' difficulties: absenteeism, work interruptions, negative attitudes toward work, and lack of energy.[51] Elder care may be even more demanding than child care if the elder person has a debilitating disease such as Alzheimer's.

The Bon Secours Richmond Health System found that the costs for helping employees with elder care so employees can remain on the job are less than what the company would pay for temporary workers to fill in while the caregivers were absent.[52] Bon Secours Richmond provides half the cost of in-home care, up to 10 days per year for employees' elderly relatives. If the employee's obligations take him or her away from the elderly relative, the company will place the elder in one of the company's assisted-living facilities. Fannie Mae, a mortgage financing company, offers elder care benefits that include flexible work options, employee assistance program consultations, and reimbursement for a portion of backup dependent care costs (e.g., when a scheduled caregiver is not available). A counselor is available at the company's Washington, D.C., headquarters to help employees find resources, arrange consultations, and help with other caregiving needs. Fannie Mae also offers employees a discount on long-term care insurance.

TABLE 12.7
**Recommenda-
tions for the
Development
of Dependent
Care
Assistance
Programs**

Source: Based on
E. E. Kossek,
B. J. DeMarr, K. Back-
man, and M. Kollar,
"Assessing Employees'
Emerging Eldercare
Needs and Reactions
to Dependent Care
Benefits," *Public Per-
sonnel Management*
(Winter 1993):
617–38.

Use surveys and focus groups to determine need.
Develop a philosophy or rationale related to business objectives.
Solicit employees' participation in designing and implementing the program.
Allocate resources for communicating the program to employees and managers.
Request feedback from users to make adjustments to the program.

Table 12.7 provides recommendations for companies that want to develop dependent care (elder or child care) assistance programs. The first step is to determine if employees perceive a need for assistance and in what form they need assistance (e.g., on-site child care, referrals for elder care, flexible schedules). Communication of dependent care benefits is critical to ensure that employees are aware of the types of assistance available. As mentioned earlier, managers need to be trained as to the purpose and use of the program. Finally, ongoing evaluation is needed to ensure that the program is satisfying employees' and the company's needs.

Dependent programs will fail if the needs assessment is not accurate. Consider what happened to Marriott International.[53] Five hotels in the Atlanta area worked together to build a child-care facility that would be available to employees at all work hours. The center is open 24 hours a day, seven days a week. Tuition is tied to the family's income. The center is within walking distance of several downtown hotels. Although the center is a valuable asset to the community, it doesn't meet hotel employees' needs. Only about one-third of the center's enrollees are children of hotel employees. Many hotel employees are uncomfortable about going outside their families and neighborhoods to find child care. Although the cost of care is tied to income, the tuition is still too high for many hotel employees.

COPING WITH JOB LOSS

Coping with job loss is an important career development issue because of the increased use of downsizing to deal with excess staff resulting from corporate restructuring, mergers, acquisitions, and takeovers. Research suggests that layoffs do not result in improved profits, they have mixed effects on productivity, and they have adverse effects on the morale, work load, and commitment of employees who remain with the company.[54] Job loss also causes stress and disrupts the personal lives of laid-off employees.[55] Because of the potential damaging effects of downsizing, companies should first seek alternative ways to reduce head count (the number of employees) and lower labor costs. These alternatives may include asking employees to work fewer hours, offering early retirement plans, delaying wage increases, and deciding not to fill position openings created by turnover and retirements. Job loss may be inevitable because of mergers or acquisitions (which may create redundant positions and an excess of employees with similar skills) or downturns in business, forcing the company to reduce labor costs by eliminating employees in order to survive.

Job loss is especially traumatic for older workers. They may find it difficult to find a job because of their age. A middle manager who had been making $65,000 a year was laid off from his job at Boston Mutual Life Insurance Company.[56] He and his wife are down to their last $2,500 after using up all his unemployment benefits. He finds himself standing on a street corner with a sign that says "I need a job . . . 36 yrs exper; Insur/mngmnt" and includes his phone number. He has no pension, and he cannot live on the $1,200 per month that

Social Security would pay. Pillowtex Corporation, a North Carolina–based textile company, recently laid off 5,500 employees.[57] Ruth Jones, an 83-year-old employee with over 50 years of service, doesn't know how she will meet her expenses. She gets unemployment benefits and Social Security benefits, but she is unlikely to get severance pay from Pillowtex. She does get two small pensions from two companies that preceded Pillowtex (Cannon Mills and Fieldcrest Cannon), and her home is paid off. She plans to seek other jobs at the local grocery store or the gas station.

From a career management standpoint, companies and managers have two major responsibilities. First, they are responsible for helping employees who will lose their jobs. Second, steps must be taken to ensure that the "survivors" of the layoff (the remaining employees) remain productive and committed to the organization.

To prepare employees for layoffs and reduce the potential negative effects, companies need to provide outplacement services. Outplacement services should include[58]

- Advance warning and explanation for a layoff.
- Psychological, financial, and career counseling.
- Assessment of skills and interests.
- Job campaign services such as résumé-writing assistance and interview training.
- Job banks where job leads are posted and where out-of-town newspapers, phones, and books regarding different occupations and geographic areas are available.
- Electronic delivery of job openings, self-directed career management guides, and values and interest inventories.

Many companies are teaming with the public sector to assist outplaced employees. For example, Boeing Company, the aircraft manufacturer in Washington, is working with the state of Washington and local business and government officials to offer a small business training program to outplaced employees.[59] Selection for the program—which involves classes, reviews of business plans, and consultation—is rigorous. Applicants must have a viable business idea, identify competitors and customers, and indicate how they will support themselves until the business is making a profit. Since the course was first offered in 1994, 61 laid-off workers have started businesses, including restaurants, book stores, and accounting offices. Besides helping former employees, the program allows Boeing to hold down its unemployment insurance contributions and improve its image in the community. Also, many laid-off workers, frustrated by long job searches and craving independence, have started their own businesses despite high odds against success.[60] For example, Michele Free, a technical writer, was laid off last year. Unable to find a job, she started an online literary agency. Her agency helps writers find publishers. She has nine clients on contract and has sold a fantasy trilogy and a Civil War history book. Free is much happier, although to make ends meet she has to sell food grown on her property and cash in stock that she received from her last job.

Employees in upper-level managerial and professional positions typically receive more personalized outplacement services (e.g., office space, private secretary) than do lower-level employees.[61] Outplacement also involves training managers in how to conduct termination meetings with employees. Table 12.8 presents guidelines for such meetings. Providing counseling for laid-off employees is critical because employees first have to deal with the shock of the layoff and their feelings of anger, guilt, disbelief, and blame. Many outplaced employees

TABLE 12.8   Guidelines for Termination Meetings with Employees

1. Planning
- Alert outplacement firm that termination will occur (if appropriate).
- Prepare severance and benefit packages.
- Prepare public statement regarding terminations.
- Prepare statement for employees affected by terminations.
- Have telephone numbers available for medical or security emergencies.
- Consider security issues (software, documents, facility access, badges).

2. Timing
- Terminations should not occur on Friday afternoon, very late on any day, or before a holiday.
- Terminate employees early in the week so employees can receive counseling and outplacement assistance.

3. Place
- The termination meeting usually occurs in the employee's office.
- A human resources representative may need to be present to explain severance and outplacement package.
- In sensitive cases where severe emotional reaction is expected, a third party is needed.

4. Length
- Meeting should be short and to the point. Termination should occur within the first two minutes. Remainder of time should be spent on explaining separation benefits and allowing employee to express feelings.

5. Approach
- Provide straightforward explanation, stating reasons for termination.
- Statement should be made that the decision to terminate was made by management and is irreversible.
- Do not discuss your feelings, needs, or problems.

6. Benefits
- A written statement of salary continuation, benefits continuation, outplacement support (e.g., office arrangements, counseling), and other terms and conditions should be provided and discussed with the employee.

Source: Adapted from R. D. Sommer, "How to Implement Organizational Resizing," in *Resizing the Organization*, ed. K. De Meuse and M. Marks (San Francisco: Jossey-Bass, 2003): 246–74; R. J. Lee, "Outplacement Counseling for the Terminated Manager," in *Applying Psychology in Business*, eds. J. W. Jones, B. D. Steffy, and D. W. Bray (Lexington, MA: Lexington Books, 1991): 489–508.

also experience mood swings, question their self-worth, experience mild depression, and may be indecisive and pessimistic about the future.[62] Trained counselors can help employees work through these concerns so that they can focus full attention on conducting a campaign to find a new job.

Typically, companies devote more resources to outplacing employees who have lost their jobs than to employees who remain. Although losing a job causes grief and denial in employees, once employees have worked through their emotions, they are capable of carrying on a campaign to find a new job. Laid-off employees are certain of their future in that they know that they need to seek alternative employment. However, for the **survivors** (employees who remain with the company following a downsizing), uncertainty about their future remains. Survivors feel some sense of gratification because they have kept their jobs. However, they do not know how safe their current job is nor do they know in what direction the company is heading. Also, in many cases, survivors are expected to perform the work of the laid-off employees as well as their own. As a result, survivors experience considerable anxiety, anger toward top-level managers, cynicism toward reorganization and new business plans, resentment, and resignation.[63]

Research suggests that survivors' attitudes and productivity are influenced by their beliefs regarding the fairness of the layoffs and the changes in working conditions.[64] Survivors are more likely to view layoffs as fair if employees are asked to cut costs to avoid layoffs, if the factors used to decide whom to lay off (e.g., performance, seniority) are applied equally to line and staff employees, if advance notice is provided, and if clear and adequate explanations are given for the layoffs. Survivors need to be trained to deal with increased work loads and job responsibilities due to the consolidation and loss of jobs. The company also needs to provide survivors with realistic information about their future with the company.

DEALING WITH OLDER WORKERS

A survey of 150 Fortune 500 companies found that one-third expect some of their executives to leave within the next five years, and the companies lack confidence that they will be able to find talented people to replace them.[65] This shortage of talented employees goes beyond the managerial ranks. Because of the shortage of skilled and experienced employees in many industries, companies are likely to try to keep talented older employees working. To do this, companies are offering alternative work schedules and arrangements including part-time work, rehiring retirees, and phased retirement programs in which employees gradually reduce their work hours. Although many companies see the value of older workers, some do not. As was mentioned in Chapter 10, the **Age Discrimination in Employment Act** is a federal law that prohibits discrimination against individuals 40 years of age or older. This includes denying access to training programs and forcing the retirement of employees covered by the act.

Consider what the Tennessee Valley Authority (TVA) is doing to reduce the impact of retirements. TVA, located in Knoxville, Tennessee, has a highly skilled and experienced work force, but the average age of the work force is nearly 47, and almost one-third of the employees plan to retire in the next five years.[66] TVA is concerned that these workers will take with them knowledge that is critical to the future of the company. TVA is developing a process to identify this critical knowledge and retain it. TVA's problem is a special situation of knowledge management that was discussed in Chapters 2 and 5. To identify the potential for lost knowledge through retirements, TVA interviews line managers each year to identify what knowledge will be lost, what the consequences are of losing knowledge, and the line managers' suggestions of how to retain the knowledge. Employees who are planning to retire and who have important knowledge are asked to take on roles as consultants, instructors, and mentors as ways to pass on their knowledge to other employees. In other cases, the employee knowledge is based on a process and a procedure that is written down. TVA also looks at whether a retired employee's knowledge is based on technology or equipment that needs to be updated. If so, the retirement is regarded by TVA as an opportunity to update systems or reengineer processes.

Meeting the Needs of Older Workers

Companies can take several actions to meet the needs of older employees.[67] First, flexibility in scheduling allows older employees to take care of sick spouses, go back to school, travel, or work fewer hours. GlaxoSmithKline, for example, allows employees to retire with their pensions and then return to work part time. In their part-time job, the retirees can start working toward a new pension.[68] Second, research suggests that the probability of receiving company-sponsored training peaks at age 40 and declines as an employee's age increases.[69] Companies need to ensure that older employees receive the training they need to avoid obsolescence and to be prepared to use new technology. Third, older employees need resources and referral help that addresses long-term health care and elder care. Fourth, assessment and counseling are necessary to help older employees recycle to new jobs or careers, or transition to less secure positions whose responsibilities are not as clearly outlined. Finally, companies need to ensure that employees do not hold inappropriate stereotypes about older employees (e.g., that they fear new technology or cannot learn new skills).

Preretirement Socialization

Preretirement socialization is the process of helping employees prepare for exit from work. It encourages employees to learn about retirement life; plan for adequate financial, housing, and health care resources; and form accurate expectations about retirement. Employees' satisfaction with life after retirement is influenced by their health, their feelings about their jobs, and their level of optimism. Employees who attend preretirement socialization programs have fewer financial and psychological problems and experience greater satisfaction with retirement compared to employees who do not attend these programs. These programs typically address the following topics:[70]

- Psychological aspects of retirement, such as developing personal interests and activities.
- Housing, including a consideration of transportation, living costs, and proximity to medical care.
- Health during retirement, including nutrition and exercise.
- Financial planning, insurance, and investments.
- Health care plans.
- Estate planning.
- The collection of benefits from company pension plans and Social Security.

Preretirement socialization or retirement planning can help employees avoid being forced to return to work because of poor financial planning. For example, a 58-year-old retiree took an early retirement package from GTE, the telecommunications company.[71] He accepted a buyout from GTE after its merger talks with Bell Atlantic. Stock market losses and his decision to withdraw $2,000 from his retirement account each month have made it necessary for him to seek employment again. He now works for $10.50 per hour at a car dealership chain, loading and delivering car parts. After paying his bills, he is able to save $100 per week in a savings account. He is considering retirement again at age 60 when he will begin collecting his military pension. But the turbulence in the stock market and rising health insurance expenses (which have increased between $150 and $450 per quarter) may make it difficult for him to retire until he reaches age 62, when he can collect Social Security benefits.

Many companies also use alternative work arrangements to help employees make the transition into retirement while at the same time continuing to utilize their talents. Monsanto Corporation has developed its own in-house temporary employment agency, the Retiree Resource Corporation (RRC), to utilize retirees' talents.[72] Through RRC, retired employees who want to work part-time may do so on a temporary basis. Monsanto's retirees return to work for a number of reasons, but most retirees focus on quality of life. The retirees want time for bridge, golf, and grandchildren, but also to enjoy work. Managers submit specific requests to the business leader of the Retiree Resource Corporation, who recruits the best person for the job. Managers tend to be flexible about working with a retiree's work schedule preferences because they would rather work with a retired Monsanto worker (who knows the company and its systems) than with someone from an outside employment agency.

Monsanto's program is successful because (1) senior management encourages the full use of older workers; (2) more than 2,500 retirees live within commuting distance of company headquarters, so there is a large labor pool; (3) detailed information about the program is made available as part of the career management process for employees nearing retirement; and (4) feedback is provided on a retiree's performance on the temporary job.

Monsanto has gained a number of benefits from rehiring its retirees: These employees are dependable and mature, able to handle responsibilities, and familiar with how the company operates. Returning retirees can get to work on the task faster than would inexperienced new employees who are unfamiliar with the company culture and policies.

Formal preretirement socialization programs are primarily for employees who are considering retirement, but financial planning, estate planning, and purchasing insurance need to be done much earlier in their career to ensure that employees will have the financial resources necessary to live comfortably during retirement.

Retirement

Retirement involves leaving a job and a work role and making a transition into life without work. For some employees, retirement involves making a transition out of their current job and company and seeking full- or part-time employment elsewhere. This concept of recycling was discussed in Chapter 11.

Research suggests that issues regarding retirement will increase in importance in the near future. By the year 2008, over 47 percent of the U.S. labor force will be over 40 years of age. Recent changes in the Social Security system no mandatory retirement age for most jobs, and financial needs suggest that employees may elect to work longer.[73] However, over half of all employees retire before age 63, and 80 percent leave by the time they are 70. This may be because employees accept companies' offers of early retirement packages, which usually include generous financial benefits. Also, employees may find work less satisfying and be interested in pursuing primarily nonwork activities as a source of satisfaction.

The aging work force and the use of early retirement programs to shrink companies' work forces have three implications. First, companies must meet the needs of older employees. Second, companies must take steps to prepare employees for retirement. Third, companies must be careful that early retirement programs do not unfairly discriminate against older employees.

Early Retirement Programs

Early retirement programs offer employees financial benefits to leave the company. These programs are usually part of the company's strategy to reduce labor costs without having to lay off employees. Financial benefits usually include a lump sum of money and a percentage of salary based on years of service. These benefits can be quite attractive to employees, particularly those with long tenure with the company. Eligibility for early retirement is usually based on age and years of service. For example, GTE Telephone Operations–North Area invites employees to consider retirement when the sum of their age and years of service approaches 76.[74] Early retirement programs have two major problems. First, employees who would be difficult to replace elect to leave the company. Second, older employees may believe that early retirement programs are discriminatory because they feel they are forced to retire. To avoid costly litigation, companies need to make sure that their early retirement programs contain the following features:[75]

- The program is part of the employee benefit plan.
- The company can justify age-related distinctions for eligibility for early retirement.
- Employees are allowed to voluntarily choose early retirement.

Eligibility requirements should not be based on stereotypes about ability and skill decrements that occur with age. Research suggests that age-related declines in specific abilities and skills have little effect on job performance.[76] Employees' decisions are considered voluntary if they can refuse to participate, if they are given complete information about the plan, and if they receive a reasonable amount of time to make their decisions.

Training plays an important role in early retirement programs. Companies teach employees to understand the financial implications of early retirement. Training programs are also used to help employees understand when and in what forms health benefits and retirement savings can be received. For example, retirement savings can often be distributed to retirees either as a one-time lump sum of money or as a payout of a specific amount of money each month, quarter, or year.

Summary

This chapter presented several career management challenges that trainers and managers need to be prepared to deal with. The challenges include new employee orientation and socialization, dual-career paths, plateauing, obsolescence, balance of work and nonwork, job loss, and retirement. The chapter includes specific practices of companies that have successfully dealt with these issues.

Key Terms

supportive work-life culture, *376*

organizational socialization, *377*

anticipatory socialization, *377*

realistic job preview, *377*

encounter phase, *377*

settling-in phase, *378*

onboarding, *380*

career path, *381*

dual-career-path system, *382*

plateauing, *383*

obsolescence, *385*

sabbatical, *386*

Family and Medical Leave Act (FMLA), *387*

time-based conflict, *388*

strain-based conflict, *388*

behavior-based conflict, *388*

job sharing, *392*

survivors, *397*

Age Discrimination in Employment Act, *398*

preretirement socialization, *399*

retirement, *400*

early retirement programs, *400*

Discussion Questions

1. Describe the stages of socialization. What are the employees' needs at each stage?

2. Why are content and process important in the design of employee orientation programs? What content should an effective orientation program include? What process should be used?

3. What is a dual-career path? What are the characteristics of an effective dual-career path?

4. Why do employees plateau? How could you help a plateaued employee? Discuss the characteristics of a plateaued employee who might resist your help.

5. Why should managers be trained as part of establishing supportive work-life policies?

6. How could you help downsized survivors remain motivated and productive? Rank your recommendations in order of importance. Provide a rationale for your ranking.

7. What advantages and disadvantages might a company gain by rehiring retired employees?

8. Are work-family programs the same as work-life programs? Explain.

Application Assignments

1. Interview a relative or friend who is currently employed. The interview should
   a. Identify her current career development stage.
   b. Identify a special career management challenge she faces.
   c. Find out how her current employer is helping her deal with the career management challenge.
   d. Evaluate her employer's response to the career management issue.
   e. Suggest how the company might better help her deal with the issue.
   Write a paper summarizing your interview.

2. Go to *www.abbott.com,* the website for Abbott Laboratories. Abbott Labs was recognized as one of the top 10 of the 100 Best Companies for Working Mothers by *Working Mother* magazine. Review the website, identify Abbott Labs' work-life programs, and describe the programs. Which of the programs would be most useful to you? What programs should they offer? Do the programs only help employees with children? Why or why not?

3. Visit the website *www.careerjournal.com.* This *Wall Street Journal* website has articles related to career issues.
   a. Look at the menu under Manage Your Career. Choose an article to read.
   b. Write a one-page paper or send an e-mail to your professor (per your professor's preference) summarizing the article and your evaluation of its implications for companies.

4. Several websites provide guidance to working and nonworking parents. They include *www.en-parent.com* (for the entrepreneurial parent), *www.wahm.com* (for work-at-home moms), *www.ivillage.com/work* (for stay-at-home parents), and *www.slowlane.com* for stay-at-home dads. Visit one of these sites. Summarize the resources available at the site. Evaluate the recommendations provided. Are they realistic? Explain.

5. Go to *www.att.com,* the website for AT&T. In the A-to-Z index, Click on T, then click on Teleworking. Click on Getting Started. Review the site to answer the following questions: What is teleworking? What are the benefits of teleworking? What are the different types of telework? What characteristics do teleworkers need to have to be successful?

6. Go to *www.fanniemae.com/aboutfm/responsibility/eldercare/index.jhtml,* the website about Fannie Mae's elder care benefits. Review the Best Practices Report, and summarize the best practices. Why are they considered "best practices"? Why are elder care programs important for businesses? Explain.

Endnotes

1. N. Lockwood, *Work/Life Balance: Challenges and Solutions* (Alexandria, VA: SHRM Research Quarterly, 2003).

2. J. Landauer, "Bottom Line Benefits of Work/Life Programs," *HR Focus* 74 (1997): 3–4.; M. Arthur, "Share Price Reactions to Work Family Initiatives: An Institutional Perspective," *Academy of Management Journal* 46 (2003): 497–505.

3. D. C. Feldman, "A Contingency Theory of Socialization," *Administrative Science Quarterly* 21 (1976): 433–52; D. C. Feldman, "A Socialization Process That Helps New Recruits Succeed," *Personnel* 57 (1980): 11–23; J. P. Wanous, A. E. Reichers, and S. D. Malik, "Organizational Socialization and Group Development: Toward an Integrative Perspective," *Academy of Management Review* 9 (1984): 670–83; C. L. Adkins, "Previous Work Experience and Organizational Socialization: A Longitudinal Examination," *Academy of Management Journal* 38 (1995): 839–62; E. W. Morrison, "Longitudinal Study of the Effects of Information Seeking on Newcomer Socialization," *Journal of Applied Psychology* 78 (1993): 173–83.

4. G. M. McEnvoy and W. F. Cascio, "Strategies for Reducing Employee Turnover: A Meta-Analysis," *Journal of Applied Psychology* 70 (1985): 342–53.

5. M. R. Louis, "Surprise and Sense Making: What Newcomers Experience in Entering Unfamiliar Organizational Settings," *Administrative Science Quarterly* 25 (1980): 226–51.

6. R. F. Morrison and T. M. Brantner, "What Enhances or Inhibits Learning a New Job? A Basic Career Issue," *Journal of Applied Psychology* 77 (1992): 926–40.

7. D. A. Major, S. W. J. Kozlowski, G. T. Chao, and P. D. Gardner, " A Longitudinal Investigation of Newcomer Expectations, Early Socialization Outcomes, and the Moderating Effect of Role Development Factors," *Journal of Applied Psychology* 80 (1995): 418–31.

8. D. C. Feldman, *Managing Careers in Organizations* (Glenview, IL: Scott-Foresman, 1988).

9. H. Klein and N. Weaver, "The Effectiveness of an Organizational-Level Orientation Program in the Socialization of New Hires," *Personnel Psychology* 53 (2000): 47–66.

10. Feldman, *Managing Careers in Organizations;* D. Reed-Mendenhall and C. W. Millard, "Orientation: A Training and Development Tool," *Personnel Administrator* 25, no. 8 (1980): 42–44; M. R. Louis, B. Z. Posner, and G. H. Powell, "The Availability and Helpfulness of Socialization Practices," *Personnel Psychology* 36 (1983): 857–66; C. Ostroff and S. W. J. Kozlowski, Jr., "Organizational Socialization as a Learning Process: The Role of Information Acquisition," *Personnel Psychology* 45 (1992): 849–74; D. R. France and R. L. Jarvis, "Quick Starts for New Employees," *Training and Development* (October 1996): 47–50; E. Morrison, "Newcomers' Relationships: The Role of Social Network Ties During Socialization," *Academy of Management Journal* 45 (2002): 1149–60.

11. J. Schettler, "Welcome to ACME Inc." *Training* (August 2002): 36–43.

12. M. Hammers, "Quashing Quick Quits," *Workforce* (May 2003): 50.

13. K. Rhodes, "Breaking in the Top Dogs," *Training* (February 2000): 67–71.

14. J. Greenhaus and G. Callanan, *Career Management,* 2nd ed. (Fort Worth, TX: Dryden Press, 1994).

15. R. H. Vaughn and M. C. Wilson, "Career Management Using Job Trees: Charting a Path through the Changing Organization," *Human Resource Planning* 17 (1995): 43–55.

16. H. D. Dewirst, "Career Patterns: Mobility, Specialization, and Related Career Issues," in *Contemporary Career Development Issues,* eds. R. F. Morrison and J. Adams (Hillsdale, NJ: Lawrence Erlbaum, 1991): 73–107.

17. Z. B. Leibowitz, B. L. Kaye, and C. Farren, "Multiple Career Paths," *Training and Development Journal* (October 1992): 31–35.

18. M. Moravec and R. Tucker, "Transforming Organizations for Good," *HR Magazine* (October 1991): 74–76; R. Tucker, M. Moravec, and K. Ideus, "Designing a Dual Career Track System," *Training and Development Journal* (June 1991): 55–58.

19. D. C. Feldman and B. A. Weitz, "Career Plateaus Reconsidered," *Journal of Management* 14 (1988): 69–80; Feldman, *Managing Careers in Organizations;* J. P. Near, "A Discriminant Analysis of Plateaued versus Nonplateaued Employees," *Journal of Vocational Behavior* 26 (1985): 177–88; S. K. Stout, J. Slocum, Jr., and W. L. Cron, "Dynamics of the Career Plateauing Process," *Journal of Vocational Behavior* 22 (1988): 74–91.

20. Feldman and Weitz, "Career Plateaus Reconsidered"; B. Rosen and T. H. Jerdee, "Managing Older Working Careers," in *Research in Personnel and Human Resource Management,* vol. 6, eds. F. R. Ferris and F. M. Rowland (Greenwich, CT: JAI Press, 1988): 37–74.

21. J. Kaufman, "A Middle Manager, 54 and Insecure, Struggles to Adapt to the Times," *The Wall Street Journal* (May 5, 1997): A1, A6.

22. S. S. Dubin, "Maintaining Competence through Updating," in *Maintaining Professional Competence,* eds. S. L. Willis and S. S. Dubin (San Francisco: Jossey-Bass, 1990): 9–43.

23. J. A. Fossum, R. D. Arvey, C. A. Paradise, and N. E. Robbins, "Modeling the Skills Obsolescence Process: A Psychological/Economic Integration," *Academy of Management Review* 11 (1986): 362–74; S. W. J. Kozlowski and B. M. Hults, "An Exploration of Climates for Technical Updating and Performance," *Personnel Psychology* 40 (1988): 539–64.

24. F. Jossi, "Taking Time Off from Advertising," *Workforce* (April 2002): 15.

25. W. Bounds, "Give Me a Break," *The Wall Street Journal,* May 5, 2000: W1, W4.

26. S. Parasuraman and J. Greenhaus, "Toward Reducing Some Critical Gaps in Work-Family Research," *Human Resource Management Review* 12 (2002): 299–312.

27. S. Garland, "The New Debate over Working Moms," *Business Week* (September 18, 2000): 102–16.

28. C. Lee, "Balancing Work and Family," *Training* (September 1991): 23–28; D. E. Super, "Life Career Roles: Self-Realization in Work and Leisure," in *Career Development in Organizations,* ed. D. T. Hall (San Francisco: Jossey-Bass, 1986): 95–119; P. Voydanoff, "Work Role Characteristics, Family Structure Demands, and Work/Family Conflict," *Journal of Marriage and the Family* 50 (1988): 749–62; R. F.

Kelly and P. Voydanoff, "Work/Family Role Strain among Employed Parents," *Family Relations* 34 (1985): 367–74.

29. E. Cherney, "Family-Leave Advocates Look to Canada for Generous Model," *The Wall Street Journal,* September 16, 2003: B12.

30. J. H. Greenhaus and N. Beutell, "Sources of Conflict between Work and Family Roles," *Academy of Management Review* 10 (1985): 76–88; J. H. Pleck, *Working Wives/Working Husbands* (Newbury Park, CA: Sage, 1985); Kelly and Voydanoff, "Work/Family Role Strain."

31. Greenhaus and Beutell, "Sources of Conflict between Work and Family Roles"; R. G. Netemeyer, J. S. Boles, and R. McMurrian, "Development and Validation of Work-Family Conflict and Family-Work Conflict Scales," *Journal of Applied Psychology* 81 (1996): 401–10.

32. S. Shellenberger, "Some Employees Begin to Find What Helps Shiftworker Families," *The Wall Street Journal,* September 20, 2000: B1.

33. J. H. Greenhaus, "The Intersection of Work and Family Roles: Individual, Interpersonal, and Organizational Issues," in *Work and Family,* ed. E. B. Godsmith (Newbury Park, CA: Sage, 1987): 23–44; Bureau of National Affairs, "Measuring Results: Cost-Benefit Analyses of Work and Family Programs," *Employee Relations Weekly* (Washington, DC: Bureau of National Affairs, 1993); L. T. Thomas and D. C. Ganster, "Impact of Family-Supportive Work Variables on Work-Family Conflict and Strain: A Control Perspective," *Journal of Applied Psychology* 80 (1995): 6–15; New York Times News Service, " Many Americans Shelve Job Success to Be with Family, Study Says," *Chicago Tribune,* Sunday, October 29, 1995: section 1, 17; S. Hand and R. A. Zawacki, "Family Friendly Benefits: More Than a Frill," *HR Magazine* (October 1994): 79–84.

34. M. Hammers, "Babies Deliver a Loyal Workforce," *Workforce* (April 2003): 52.

35. M. Hammers, "A 'Family Friendly' Backlash," *Workforce Management* (August 2003): 77–79.

36. J. Spencer, "Shirk Ethic: How to Fake a Hard Day at the Office," *The Wall Street Journal,* May 15, 2003: D1, D3.

37. Shellenberger, "Some Employees Begin to Find."

38. L. E. Duxbury and C. A. Higgins, "Gender Differences in Work-Family Conflict," *Journal of Applied Psychology* 76 (1991): 60–74.

39. B. Baltes, T. Briggs, J. Huff, J. Wright, and G. Neuman, "Flexible and Compressed Workweek Schedules: A Meta-analysis of Their Effects on Work-Related Criteria," *Journal of Applied Psychology* 84 (2000): 496–513.

40. Spencer, "Shirk Ethic."

41. J. S. Lublin, "Memo to Staff: Stop Working," *The Wall Street Journal,* July 6, 2000: B1, B4.

42. J. L. Pierce, J. W. Newstrom, R. B. Dunham, and P. E. Barber, *Alternative Work Schedules* (Boston: Allyn and Bacon, 1989); F. W. Horvath, "Work at Home: New Findings from the Current Population Survey," *Monthly Labor Review* 109, no. 11 (1986): 31–35; J. R. King, "Working at Home Has Yet to Work Out," *The Wall Street Journal,* December 22, 1989: B1–B2.

43. C. Solomon, "Workers Want a Life! Do Managers Care?" *Workforce* (August 1999): 58–67; J. Cook, "No Kidding," *Human Resource Executive* (May 6, 2002): 32–36; F. Hansen, "Truth and Myths about Work/Life Balance," *Workforce* (December 2002): 34–39.

44. C. M. Solomon, "Job Sharing: One Job, Double Headache?" *Personnel Journal* (September 1994): 88–96.

45. B. Marsh, "A Consulting Business Thrives by Hiring Mothers Part-Time," *The Wall Street Journal,* February 24, 1994: 428.

46. J. Laabs, "Overload," *Workforce* (January 1999): 30–37.

47. F. S. Rodgers and C. Rodgers, "Business and the Facts of Family Life," *Harvard Business Review* (November–December 1989): 121–29; S. J. Goff, M. K. Mount, and R. L. Jamison, "Employer Support Child Care, Work/Family Conflict, and Absenteeism: A Field Study," *Personnel Psychology* 43 (1990): 793–809.

48. M. Burke, E. Esen, and J. Collison, *SHRM Fondation 2003 Benefits Survey* (Alexandria, VA: Society for Human Resource Management, 2003).

49. J. Haupt, "Training Today—Joining Forces to Provide Child Care," *Training* (March 1993).

50. Society for Human Resource Management, "Work-Life Balance," *Workplace Visions* 4 (2002): 1–8.

51. E. E. Kossek, B. J. DeMarr, K. Backman, and M. Kollar, "Assessing Employees' Emerging Elder Care Needs and Reactions to Dependent Care Benefits," *Public Personnel Management* 22 (1993): 617–37.

52. T. Shea, "Help with Elder Care," *HR Magazine* (September 2003): 113–18.

53. E. Graham, "Marriott's Bid to Patch the Child Care Gap Gets a Reality Check," *The Wall Street Journal,* February 2, 2000: B1.

54. W. Cascio, *Responsible Restructuring: Creative and Profitable Alternatives to Layoffs* (San Francisco: Berrett-Koehler, 2002).

55. J. Brockner, "The Effects of Work Layoffs on Survivors: Research, Theory, and Practice," in *Research in Organizational Behavior,* vol. 10, eds. B. M. Staw and L. L. Cummings (Hillsdale, NJ: Lawrence Erlbaum, 1988): 45–95; L. Greenhalgh, A. T. Lawrence, and R. I. Sutton, "Determinants of Workforce Reduction Strategies in Declining Organizations," *Academy of Management Review* 13 (1988): 241–54; J. Nocera, "Living with Layoffs," *Fortune* (April 1, 1996): 69–71; J. Martin, "Where Are They Now?" *Fortune* (April 1, 1996): 100–8.

56. J. Pereira, "A Worker's Quest for a Job Lands on a Street Corner," *The Wall Street Journal,* March 5, 2003: A1, A7.

57. D. Morse, "Older Workers in the Lurch," *The Wall Street Journal,* August 20, 2003: B1, B10.

58. J. C. Latack and J. B. Dozier, "After the Ax Falls: Job Loss as Career Transition," *Academy of Management Review* 11 (1986): 375–92; J. Brockner, "Managing the Effects of Layoffs on Survivors," *California Management Review* (Winter 1992): 9–28; S. L. Guinn, "Outplacement Programs: Separating Myth from Reality," *Training and Development Journal* 42 (1988): 48–49; D. R. Simon, "Outplacement: Matching Needs,

Matching Services," *Training and Development Journal* 42 (1988): 52–57; S. Rosen and C. Paul, "Learn the Inner Workings of Outplacement," *The Wall Street Journal,* July 31, 1995: editorial page; S. Spera, E. D. Buhrfeind, and J. P. Pennebaker, "Expressive Writing and Coping with Job Loss," *Academy of Management Journal* 37 (1994): 722–33.

59. J. Cole, "Boeing Teaches Employees How to Run Small Business," *The Wall Street Journal,* November 7, 1995: B1–B2.

60. K. Dunham, "Frustrated Laid-Off Workers Take Risk of Entrepreneurship," *The Wall Street Journal,* July 8, 2003: B10.

61. E. B. Picolino, "Outplacement: The View from HR," *Personnel* (March 1988): 24–27.

62. B. Z. Locker, "Job Loss and Organization Change: Psychological Perspectives," in *Special Challenges in Career Management,* ed. A. J. Pickman (Mahwah, NJ: Lawrence Erlbaum, 1997): 13–24.

63. H. M. O'Neill and D. J. Lenn, "Voices of Survivors: Words That Downsizing CEOs Should Hear," *Academy of Management Executive* 9 (1995): 23–34.

64. Brockner, "Managing the Effects of Layoffs on Survivors"; J. Brockner, M. Konovsky, R. Cooper-Schneider, R. Folger, C. Martin, and R. J. Bies, "Interactive Effects of Procedural Justice and Outcome Negativity on Victims and Survivors of Job Loss," *Academy of Management Journal* 37 (1994): 397–409.

65. W. Byham, "Grooming Next-Millennium Leaders," *HR Magazine* (February 1999): 46–53.

66. B. Leonard, "Taking HR to the Next Level," *HR Magazine* (July 2003): 57–63.

67. L. Thornburg, "The Age Wave Hits," *HR Magazine* (February 1995): 40–45.

68. K. Greene, "Companies Could Lure Older Workers to Stay On," *The Wall Street Journal,* November 20, 2002: D2.

69. C. A. Olson, "Who Receives Formal Firm-Sponsored Training in the U.S.?" October 15, 1996, National Center for the Workplace, Institute of Industrial Relations, University of California (Berkeley). Document at *http://violet.lib.berkeley.edu/~iir/.*

70. A. L. Kamouri and J. C. Cavanaugh, "The Impact of Preretirement Education Programs on Workers' Preretirement Socialization," *Journal of Occupational Behavior* 7 (1986): 245–56; N. Schmitt and J. T. McCune, "The Relationship between Job Attitudes and the Decision to Retire," *Academy of Management Review* 24 (1981): 795–802; N. Schmitt, B. W. Coyle, J. Rauschenberger, and J. K. White, "Comparison of Early Retirees and Non-retirees," *Personnel Psychology* 32 (1981): 327–40; T. A. Beehr, "The Process of Retirement," *Personnel Psychology* 39 (1986): 31–55; S. M. Comrie, "Teach Employees to Approach Retirement as a New Career," *Personnel Journal* 64, no. 8 (1985): 106–8; L. Grensing-Pophal, "Departure Plans," *HR Magazine* (July 2003): 83–86.

71. K. Greene, "Back on an Early Shift, But at Half the Pay," *The Wall Street Journal,* March 5, 2003: B1, B2.

72. L. Phillon and J. Brugger, "Encore! Retirees Give Top Performance as Temporaries," *HR Magazine* (October 1994): 74–77; B. Gerber, "Who Will Replace Those Vanishing Execs," *Training* (July 2000): 49–53.

73. K. Greene, "Many Older Workers to Delay Retirement Until After Age 70," *The Wall Street Journal,* September 23, 2003: D2.

74. R. E. Hill and P. C. Dwyer, "Grooming Workers for Early Retirement," *HR Magazine* (September 1990): 59–63.

75. M. L. Colusi, P. B. Rosen, and S. J. Herrin, "Is Your Early Retirement Package Courting Disaster?" *Personnel Journal* (August 1988): 60–67.

76. B. Rosen and T. Jerdee, "Managing Older Workers' Careers," In G. Ferris and K. Rowland (eds.) *Research in Personel and Human Resources Management vol. 6* (Greenwich, CT: JAI Press, 1998): 37–74.

Chapter **Thirteen**

The Future of Training and Development

Objectives

After reading this chapter, you should be able to

1. Identify the future trends that are likely to influence training departments and trainers.

2. Discuss how these future trends may impact training delivery and administration as well as the strategic role of the training department.

3. Discuss the features of a learning management system and why it is important.

4. Describe the components of the change model and how they can be used to introduce a new training method.

5. Benchmark current training practices.

6. Discuss how process reengineering can be used to review and redesign training administration practices (e.g., enrollment in training).

Training Helps Create New Business

United Parcel Services (UPS) created E-Commerce University, a week-long sales training program, because the UPS sales force lacked the knowledge of new shipping technology that they needed to increase sales. UPS wanted the sales force to have a conversational comfort level with the different technologies and to understand what technology can do for customers. UPS plans to have its entire sales force complete the training. The company sends between 30 and 40 salespeople to Atlanta for each session. Although this training is costly, it helps the attendees meet other salespeople from different parts of the country and different backgrounds. Students are divided into two groups, and they train for 9 to 10 hours every day. The training includes lectures, discussions, groupwork, role plays, roundtables, and presentations. One topic is online tools such as XML, HTML, and flat-file billing. The sales force needs to comprehend the new technologies' capabilities and processes to communicate to customers. When salespeople can talk the language with customers and talk about process improvement, they can be consultants to customers rather than just salespeople, and UPS becomes a long-term provider of services rather than a one-stop shop for shipping packages. The training also includes subject-matter experts who answer questions. To ensure transfer of training, salespersons identify one of their accounts and think of ways that they can apply their new learning to that customer. At the end of the week of training, each salesperson discusses with the training group the customer he or she has chosen. Subject-matter experts and other trainees provide input on how to apply the new technology for that customer. Since the start of E-Commerce University, the sales performance of those UPS salespeople who have attended training has ranged from 2 to 7 percent better than the sales force as a whole. More than 69 percent of the salespeople who were surveyed report that the training had an impact on their revenue-generating success.

Source: H. Johnson, "Postmarked for Growth," *Training* (September 2003): 20–23.

INTRODUCTION

The UPS approach to training its sales force relates to one of several trends affecting training. Companies are providing training as a means to increase demand for their products and services in the competitive marketplace. The previous 12 chapters discussed training design and delivery as well as employee development and career management. This chapter looks toward the future by discussing trends that are likely to influence the future of training and development and your future as a trainer. Table 13.1 presents the future trends affecting training.

NEW TECHNOLOGIES FOR TRAINING DELIVERY

The use of multimedia, the World Wide Web, and other new technologies will likely increase in the future for several reasons. First, the cost of these technologies will decrease. Second, as the chapter opening vignette illustrates, companies can use technology to better prepare employees to service customers and generate new business. Third, use of these new technologies can substantially reduce training costs (e.g., travel, food, housing) related to bringing geographically dispersed employees to one central training location. Fourth, these technologies allow trainers to build into training many of the desirable features of a learning environment (e.g., practice, feedback, reinforcement). Fifth, as companies employ more contingent employees (e.g., part-timers, consultants) who may not work in a central geographic area, technology will allow training to be delivered to these employees in a timely, effective manner.

TABLE 13.1
Future Trends
That Will
Affect Training

1. The use of new technologies for training delivery will increase.
2. Demand for training for virtual work arrangements will rise.
3. Emphasis on capture and storage and use of intellectual capital will increase.
4. Companies will rely on learning management systems, integration with business processes, and real-time learning.
5. Training will focus on business needs and performance.
6. Training departments will develop partnerships and will outsource.
7. Training and development will be viewed more from a change model perspective.

New technology also makes it possible to create "smart" products.[1] For example, packages sent by UPS leave an electronic trail that can be used to improve shipping and delivery processes. In the future, training products may also leave an electronic trail that will enable trainers and managers to better understand how these products are being used. New technologies that combine computer science, instructional design, and graphic interfaces have the potential to increase our ability to learn.[2] Employees may soon learn in their sleep. One device detects when a person is dreaming, which is a good time to acquire new skills. Tele-immersion is a technology that provides realistic, life-sized holographic projections in which employees can hear and see collaborators as if they were physically present in the office. Tele-immersion can be used to create a holographic training room in the office with virtual trainees beamed in from other locations. Virtual retinal display is a technology that projects images directly on the retina of the eye. Virtual retinal display allows real-time, on-site performance support. The technology takes what is shown on a computer monitor and reduces it through special glasses directly onto the retina in full color. The image looks like it is floating in air about two feet away. Digital Avatar is an animated virtual teacher. With this technology, corporate trainers can create animated version of themselves for online instruction.

VIRTUAL WORK ARRANGEMENTS

Virtual work arrangements include virtual teams as well as **teleworking,** work that is conducted in a remote location (distant from central offices), where the employee has limited contact with peers but is able to communicate electronically. The critical feature of virtual work arrangements is that location, organization structure, and employment relationships are not limiting factors.[3] For example, employees from two or three organizations may work together on projects designed to meet the strategic and operational needs of their organizations. Similarly, employees within a single organization may work with peers from different units or functions on a project team. Virtual knowledge teams have members that are distributed across multiple time zones, countries, and or companies. They are more diverse than other knowledge teams, with team members representing different specialties and perhaps different cultures, languages, and organizational allegiances. These teams do not have constant membership. Team members may move onto and off the team at different points in a project. Some members may participate in all team tasks, whereas others may only work on some. Successful virtual knowledge teams need structure (e.g., reporting relationships, membership), leadership (empowered, shared leadership, integration with other teams), shared values (what do we value as a team, how will we run meetings, make decisions, and solve problems?), and rewarded goals (e.g., what are our key goals, what do customers need from us, and how will we reward goal accomplishment?). If team members are from different cultures, working from a distance can make language and cultural differences even more difficult to deal with. For example, teams responsible for evaluating business opportunities for Shell Technology Ventures, a subsidiary of Royal Dutch/Shell found that it was challenging to create a team process structured so that team members who prefer structure can move forward without creating so much bureaucracy that it inhibits team members who do best in an unstructured environment. Dutch team members prefer more details about how a process works, who will make a decision, and what the next steps are than do their colleagues from the United States.

There are two training challenges for virtual work arrangements. First, companies will have to invest in training delivery methods that facilitate digital collaboration.[4] **Digital collaboration** refers to an interaction between two or more people mediated by a computer. The Web, intranet, and learning portals enable employees to access training from their desktops and to collaborate with others on an as-needed basis. Virtual work arrangements will rely on digital collaboration. Training will need to be provided in team work skills and understanding cultural differences as well as technical skills and competencies needed to perform their jobs. Second, for companies with virtual work arrangements, having knowledge, knowing which employees possess it, and sharing knowledge within and across functions, teams, and individuals are critical for effectiveness. Teams and employees must be provided with tools that they need for finding knowledge—knowledge that can be used to provide a service, develop or manufacture a product, or refine a process.

INTELLECTUAL CAPITAL

Software such as Lotus Notes and intranets (a company's own Internet system) as well as a growing emphasis on creating a learning organization (recall Chapter 5's discussion of learning organizations) mean that companies will increasingly seek ways to turn employees' knowledge (intellectual capital) into a shared company asset. Trainers and the training department likely will be charged with managing knowledge and coordinating organizational learning. For example, Cigna Corporation, a property and casualty insurer, gave its home-office managers the job of building a knowledge base that is contained in the same software that every underwriter uses to process applications.[5] When new information comes in (such as feedback from the claims department or insights from the underwriters), the manager evaluates the information and adds it to the database. Hewlett-Packard has an internal consulting group (Product Process Organization) that provides services to the business units. The Product Process Organization is in charge of collecting case histories, "war stories," and best practices and putting them on the company's website. How might the knowledge network be used? A manager who is, for example, looking for information about outsourcing practices can learn how others have done it as well as who has done it.

The increasing use of new technologies to deliver training and to store and communicate knowledge means that trainers must be technologically literate. That is, they must understand the strengths and weaknesses of new technologies and implementation issues such as overcoming users' resistance to change (which is discussed later in this chapter). Also, many companies have created new positions, such as knowledge manager, whose job it is to identify reliable knowledge and make sure it is accessible to employees.

LEARNING MANAGEMENT SYSTEMS

The direction in training is away from learning as the primary outcome and more toward learning as a way to enhance business performance. This trend has resulted in the development of learning analytics, analysis tools that come with learning management software.[6] The software allows the tracking of learning activity and costs, and can relate learning results to product revenues or sales goals. Companies are also starting to use learning management systems. A **learning management system (LMS)** is used to automate the administration of online training programs. An LMS can help companies reduce travel costs related to training, reduce time for program completion, increase employees' accessibility to training across the business, and provide administrative capabilities to track program completion and course enrollments. An LMS gives a company the opportunity to understand the competencies of its work force very quickly so that it can respond with the right employees to meet a business need.[7] The LMS may also interface with other human resource systems such as performance management and development. An LMS is important for human capital management. **Human capital management** integrates training with the human resource function to determine how training dollars are spent and how that expense relates to business dollars for the company. Human capital management is accomplished through a software system that integrates all human resource management activities with each other (e.g., performance evaluation, training, career management). A recent survey found that the two major reasons that companies adopted an LMS were the need to report learning activities and the need to reduce administrative costs.[8] Thirty-eight percent of the companies integrated the LMS with human resource information systems.

For example, Accenture's LMS, known as myLearning, is linked to applications that run payroll, billing, and facilities management. The integration helps the company track training dollars and the return on investment. Employees can also use myLearning to set their annual goals. Turner Construction has a competency model that divides all the jobs into nine job families and divides the families into job levels (e.g., senior management, administrative/clerical, and management). When employees at Turner receive an online performance evaluation, they are evaluated on their skills and attributes based on their job family and level. The performance management system links to the company's LMS. The LMS analyzes employees for skill weaknesses and then links each employee to courses that can improve those skills. The LMS system allows Turner Construction to identify skill gaps for entire levels, job families, or business units. The results can be used to identify where to spend the training budget. For example, if most employees in the construction family have a communications skill gap, communications training can be included in the training and development plans.

How should an LMS be developed? First, senior management needs to be convinced that an LMS will benefit employees, improve business functions, and contribute to overall business strategy and goals. Second, the company must have an e-learning culture that supports online learning and encourages employee participation. Third, the online learning environment needs to be under the control of the learner. Learners need not only choices in what and when to learn but also involvement in learning (practice, feedback, appeals to multiple senses).[9] To develop the LMS for the Internal Revenue Service (IRS), a group known as Strategic Human Resource, which is responsible for establishing human resource policy across the IRS, has developed a partnership with IRS business units and information technology staff.[10] The Strategic Human Resources unit has begun meeting with the business units to identify their training needs. The LMS has to support content from different sources but also has to integrate with the IRS's existing information technology structure. The IRS already had many e-learning courses from different vendors and had also developed products internally. The e-learning courses as well as classroom instruction have to be managed through a single system. Strategic Human Resource has had to implement specific requirements, standards, and specifications for e-learning administration, scheduling, enrollment, and product development and design. The LMS must also be integrated with human resource

FIGURE 13.1

Functional areas and applications of real-time extended business

Source: Based on S. Adkins, "The Brave New World of Learning," T&D (June 2003): 28–37.

Resource Management	Collaborator Management
• Human Capital Development • Enterprise Resource Management • Employee Resource Management • Learning Management Systems	• Structured Knowledge Management • Instant Messaging • Collaborative Web-Conferencing
Product Management	Process Management
• Product Life-Cycle Management • Supply Chain Management • Work Force Management • Customer Relations Management	• Work Flow Management • Customer Analytics • Work Force Analytics • Business Process Management

systems. The interfaces between the systems will provide basic employee information such as business unit, geographic location, and job title. For employees who are attending training, information about course titles and completion dates will also be stored in the LMS. The Strategic Human Resource unit is developing standards, providing assistance to the business units, and setting up the technology architecture. The LMS is being implemented in three phases. Phase 1 involves building the technology infrastructure, establishing product development standards and policies, and developing policies. Phase 2 requires the organization of learning and knowledge content for accessibility by the LMS. In Phase 3 the IRS will integrate learning with actual work performance, enabling employees to get training on an as-needed basis on the job.

Companies are moving away from courseware and classes as a performance improvement method and are instead adopting true performance support that is available during the work process.[11] Such products include task-specific, real-time content and simulation that are accessible during work as well as real-time collaboration in virtual workspaces. Recent and rapid adoption of wireless technology is connecting employees directly to business processes. For example, radio frequency identification chips are implanted in products such as clothing, tires, and mechanical parts. These chips contain information that is beamed via radio waves to employees processing handheld wireless devices. The device, the task context, and the performance environment are not compatible with classroom or courseware-based learning but with performance support. Learning is a business process that is integrated with several other business processes. Learning is expected as a result of collaboration with employees and machines in the work process. Employees can be provided with real-time performance support through communications with experts and through automated coaching.

Figure 13.1 shows the four functional areas and applications of real-time extended business, in which employees and systems work together in a process to produce products and services. The four areas are resource management, collaboration management, product management, and process management. Resource management includes applications designed to create inventories and map resources. Resources include people, property, machines, systems, and learning content. Collaboration management includes events, processes, and experiences that characterize work. Collaboration involves the exchange of information and knowledge. Process management includes analysis of the work flow and of people and systems in the work flow. Product management includes the link between employees, products, partners, and customers. E-learning can be used to integrate the four quadrants.

BUSINESS NEEDS AND PERFORMANCE

Because of an increasing focus on contributing to the company's competitive advantage, training departments will have to ensure that they are seen as helping the business functions (e.g., marketing, finance, production) meet their needs. This requires a shift from training as *the* solution to business problems to a performance analysis approach. A **performance analysis approach** involves identifying performance gaps or deficiencies and examining training as one possible solution for the business units (the customers). Two ways that training departments will need to be involved are (1) focusing on interventions related to performance improvement and (2) providing support for high-performance work systems.

Training departments' responsibilities will likely include a greater focus on systems that employees can use for information (such as expert systems or electronic performance support systems) on an as-needed basis. This need is driven by the use of contingent employees and the increased flexibility necessary to adapt products and services to meet customers' needs. For example, companies do not want to spend money to train employees who may be with the company only a few weeks. Instead, through temporary employment agencies, companies can select employees with the exact skill set needed. Training departments need to provide mechanisms to support the temporary employees once they are on the job and encounter situations, problems, rules, and policies they are unfamiliar with because they are not yet knowledgeable about the company.

As was discussed in Chapter 1, more companies are striving to create high-performance workplaces because of the productivity gains that can be realized through this type of design. High-performance work requires that employees have interpersonal skills necessary to work in teams. High-performance work systems also require employees to have high levels of technical skills. Employees need to understand statistical process control and the Total Quality Management philosophy. Employees also must understand the entire production and service system so they can better serve both internal and external customers. As more companies move to high-performance work systems, training departments will need to be prepared to provide effective training in interpersonal, quality, and technical skills as well as to help employees understand all aspects of the customer-service or production system.

Business competitiveness can be realized by quick change, speed in delivery, and reductions in costs and time constraints. Cypress Semiconductors, a supplier of integrated circuits for network equipment that is based in San Jose, California, utilizes competency models that are linked to success profiles that detail employees' roles, activities, responsibilities, career development initiatives, and training options.[12] The profiles are used for employee performance evaluations, and they are also used in the hiring process. For example, a training plan can be developed for new hires as soon as they are on the job so that they can be successful as quickly as possible.

Just-in-time learning is many companies' answer to quick learning and quick application of learning to the business.[13] Memorial Sloan Kettering Cancer Center developed a set of simulation tools that are integrated with the implementation of several clinical support systems (order management, electronic medical records, picture archival and communications, and disease management) available to the entire medical center. IBM Global Services has moved its training from three days in the classroom to just-in-time on the Web. E-business consultants can now access a website that provides them with the training they need or with information or case studies from which the training was built. They can also collaborate with other consultants to share knowledge.

PARTNERSHIPS AND OUTSOURCING

Because downsizing has caused reductions in training staffs, because employees are needing to learn specialized new knowledge, because demand for training services is fluctuating, companies are now turning to external suppliers for their training services. External suppliers may include consultants, academics, graduate students, and companies in the entertainment and mass communications industries. External suppliers can be used as partners or as sole providers of training services.

BellSouth developed a new training program on the basics of wireless communications for its own employees. Members of the training team believed that if employees within BellSouth could benefit from knowing more about how wireless communications work, wouldn't key suppliers, end-user customers, and companies that sell the wireless products also benefit? This type of training might give BellSouth an advantage over its competitors. As a result, BellSouth's Intro to Wireless Communications training is being offered both within the company and to companies that sell BellSouth's products, such as Best Buy and Circuit City. Best Buy and Circuit City are making the training available to their customers. BellSouth is also providing training that can help make its networks of suppliers and customers more knowledgeable in other areas, such as basic personal computer skills for managing computer networks. BellSouth offers courses from training suppliers on its company website. The company charges a fee for the training.

Why train suppliers, customers, and vendors? The intent is to build a broad understanding of what wireless technology does, how it works, where it works, why it works, its strengths and weaknesses, and its potential applications. Providing training also enhances the value of BellSouth's services. That customers, vendors, and suppliers are learning more about BellSouth's products and services translates into higher sales. For example, the more that salespeople understand the products and the technology they are selling, the better they can match customer needs and product capabilities. This knowledge increases customer satisfaction and word-of-mouth advertising, and it lowers the number of returns and complaints—thus cutting the costs of doing business.[14]

Training departments will be increasing their partnerships with academic institutions (e.g., community colleges, universities) to provide basic skills training and to develop customized programs. For example, in school-to-work transition programs (which were discussed in Chapter 10), companies are actively involved in designing curricula and providing experiences for students to help ensure they are competent to enter the work force. Another use of academic partners is as subject-matter experts. The academics evaluate current training practices and modify training programs to increase their effectiveness. Academic partners may also work with training departments to develop specialized programs for employees at all levels in the company. For example, Westcott Communication is working with eight business schools to provide executive education for several companies including Kodak, Disney, and Texas Instruments.[15] Sematech, the semiconductor industry association, is working with community colleges in the Phoenix, Arizona, area to develop a curriculum for training entry-level manufacturing technicians.[16]

The reliance on external suppliers to provide training services is known as **outsourcing.** As the role of external suppliers of training increases, trainers will need to become more savvy in contract negotiations and make-versus-buy analysis.[17] Trainers will need to know how to identify and select training vendors. Trainers may be called on to support managers and employees who will actually conduct the training. For example, rather than developing training programs, trainers increasingly are likely to need competency in designing train-the-trainer programs.

For example, Motorola outsourced its training to ACS to create ACS Global HR Solutions, which manages all human resource and training activities worldwide for the company.[18] Motorola transferred 650 key human resources and learning employees to ACS. Motorola decided it wanted world-class management of administrative and transactional human resource functions, including training and development. Outsourcing also allowed Motorola to reduce costs during a downsizing. ACS gained Motorola's service center, employee portal, and employees. Motorola will retain control over strategic areas, assessment, and customer interface. It will also have the final decision on whether to design training or buy it from an outside supplier. Motorola believes that the careers of its former employees will be enhanced, because training is a primary business of ACS whereas it was only a support function at Motorola.

One type of training outsourcing is use of an application service provider. An **application service provider (ASP)** is a company that rents out access to software for a specific application.[19] Some ASPs have relationships with courseware developers that provide online learning. These relationships allow the ASP to offer structured courses as well as custom options. The major benefit is that company resources are not used to purchase or maintain an internal network or intranet. Also, companies save the costs associated with building, renting, or maintaining a training facility. Typically, the company pays for a license along with a maintenance contract. Training delivery and administration programs are run on the ASP's computers. The ASP can track how many employees use the software contracted for, which areas are accessed the most, and how employees perform on posttraining tests. The ASP also provides technical support, including software upgrades. The company pays the ASP a fee. For example, KPMG Consulting challenged its e-learning department to develop a program that would train 8,500 employees worldwide in e-business.[20] The national director of e-learning recognized that he had to ensure that the program didn't overload KPMG's computer system. The solution was to use an ASP to host the company's computer-based training program, providing access to employees worldwide while using none of KPMG's computer resources. The use of an ASP allowed KPMG to quickly develop and make the training available to its work force.

TRAINING AND DEVELOPMENT FROM A CHANGE MODEL PERSPECTIVE

Although the concept of change is usually addressed in an organizational behavior course, the reality is that for new training or development practices to be successfully implemented, they must be accepted by the customer (manager, upper management, employees). For managers

FIGURE 13.2

A change model

Source: David A. Nadler and Michael L. Tushman, "A Congruence Model for Diagnosing Organizational Behavior," in *Organizational Psychology: A Book of Readings*, eds. D. Rabin and J. McIntyre (Englewood Cliffs, NJ: Prentice Hall, 1979), as reprinted in David A. Nadler, "Concepts for the Management of Organizational Change," in *Readings in the Management of Innovation*, 2d ed., eds. M. L. Tushman and N. Moore (Cambridge, MA: Ballinger Publishing Co., 1988): 722.

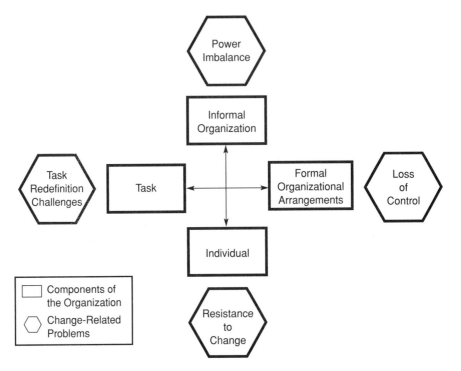

and employees, change is not easy. Even when employees know a practice or program could be better, they have learned to adapt to its inadequacies. Therefore, resistance to new training and development practices is likely. As a result, prior to implementing a new training or development practice, trainers should consider how they can increase the likelihood of its acceptance.

Figure 13.2 provides a model of change. The process of change is based on the interaction among four components of the organization: task, employees, formal organizational arrangements (structures, processes, systems), and informal organization (communications patterns, values, norms).[21] As shown in the figure, different types of change-related problems occur depending on the organizational component that is influenced by the change. These change-related problems include power imbalance, loss of control, resistance to change, and task redefinition.

For example, introducing new technology for training into a company (such as multimedia training using the Internet) might cause changes in the organization's power structure. With the new technology, managers may have less control over access to training programs than they had with traditional methods of training. The result is tension related to the power imbalance created by the new system. If these issues are not dealt with, the managers will not accept the new technology or provide support for transfer of training.

Four change-related problems need to be considered for any new training practice: resistance to change, control, power, and task redefinition. **Resistance to change** refers to managers' and employees' unwillingness to change. Managers and employees may be anxious about change, feel they will be unable to cope, value the current training practice, or not understand the value of the new practice. **Control** relates change to managers' and employees' ability to obtain and distribute valuable resources such as data, information, or money. Changes can cause managers and employees to have less control over resources. Change can also give managers and employees control over processes that they have not previously been involved in (e.g., choosing which training programs to attend). **Power** refers to the ability to influence others. Managers may lose the ability to influence employees as employees gain access to databases and other information, thus getting more autonomy to deliver products and services. Employees may be held accountable for learning in self-directed training. Web-based training methods such as **task redefinition** refer to changes in managers' and employees' roles and job responsibilities. Employees may be asked not only to participate in training but also to consider how to improve its quality. Managers may be asked to become facilitators and coaches.

METHODS TO DETERMINE WHETHER CHANGE IS NECESSARY

Viewing training from a systems perspective means that companies and trainers need to understand both internal and external environments.[22] Specifically, they need to understand the effectiveness and efficiency of current training practices. They also need to be aware of other companies' practices to ensure that their training practices are the best possible. Benchmarking provides information about other companies' practices. Process reengineering provides information about the effectiveness and efficiency of training systems within the company.

Benchmarking

As was mentioned in Chapter 3, benchmarking is the practice of finding examples of excellent products, services, or systems (i.e., best practices). Benchmarking is an important component of a company's quality strategy. Benchmarking training practices are useful for several reasons.[23] By looking at how excellent companies conduct training, a company can identify how its training practices compare to the best practices. Benchmarking also helps a company learn from others. A company can see what types of training practices work and how they were successfully implemented. Use of this information can increase the chances that new training practices will be accepted and effective. Learning what other successful companies are doing can help managers create a case for changing current training and development practices in the company (i.e., overcoming resistance to change). Benchmarking can also be used to help establish a training strategy and set priorities for training practices.

What does the benchmarking process involve? Xerox's well-known benchmarking process features the 10 steps shown in Table 13.2. Besides collecting its own benchmarking information, a company may want to subscribe to a service that collects data regarding human resource practices from several companies. For example, the American Society for Training and Development sponsors a benchmarking forum. The 62 companies that belong to the forum are generally large companies such as Xerox. They report information regarding training expenditures, structure of training programs, training design, and delivery practices. This information is shared among forum members; a report summarizing the results is sold to other interested parties. Some estimate that as many as 70 percent of Fortune 500 companies use benchmarking on a regular basis.[24]

Trainers need to take several factors into account when benchmarking.[25] Trainers must gather information about internal processes to serve as a comparison for best practices. It is important to clearly identify the purpose of benchmarking and the practice to be benchmarked.

TABLE 13.2
Xerox's
Benchmarking
Practices

Source: Based on
S. Greengard,
"Discover Best
Pictures through
Benchmarking,"
Personnel Journal
(November 1995):
62–73.

1.	Identify what is to be benchmarked.
2.	Identify comparable companies.
3.	Determine data collection methods and collect data.
4.	Determine current performance levels.
5.	Project future performance levels.
6.	Communicate benchmark results and gain acceptance.
7.	Establish functional goals.
8.	Develop action plans.
9.	Implement action plans and monitor progress.
10.	Recalibrate benchmarks.

Upper-level management needs to be committed to the project. Both quantitative (numbers) and qualitative data should be collected. Descriptions of programs and how they operate are as valuable as knowing how best practices contributed to the bottom line. Trainers must be careful to gather data from companies both within and outside their industry. Benchmarking may actually limit a company's performance if the goal is only to learn and copy what other companies have done and not consider how to improve on the process. Trainers should be careful not to view human resource practices in isolation from each other. For example, examining training practices also requires consideration of the company's staffing strategy (use of internal labor market versus the external labor market to fill positions). Benchmarking will not provide a "right" answer. The information collected needs to be considered in terms of the context of the companies. Finally, benchmarking is one part of an improvement process. As a result, use of the information gathered from benchmarking needs to be considered in the broader framework of organization change, which was discussed in the previous section.

Process Reengineering

Trainers need to understand their current training practices and processes and evaluate them to determine what should be changed. **Reengineering** is a complete review of critical processes and redesign of those processes to make them more efficient and able to deliver higher quality. Reengineering is critical to ensuring that the benefits of new training and development programs can be realized. Reengineering is especially important when trainers attempt to deliver training using new technology. Reengineering is also important when training departments try to streamline administrative processes and improve the services they offer to their "customers." This streamlining can apply to course enrollment processes, processes related to issuing tuition reimbursement, and processes related to employees reviewing their training records. Applying new technology (e.g., interactive voice technology) to a course enrollment process burdened with too many steps will not result in improvements in efficiency or effectiveness. What it will result in is increased product or service costs related to the introduction of the new technology.

Reengineering can be used to review the training department functions and processes or it can be used to review a specific training program or development program practice such as a career management system. The reengineering process involves the four steps shown in Figure 13.3: Identify the process to be reengineered, understand the process, redesign the process, and implement the new process.[26]

FIGURE 13.3
The reengineering process

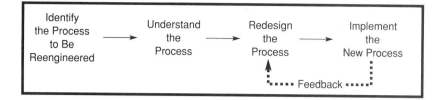

Identify the Process

Managers and trainers who control the process or are responsible for functions within the process ("process owners") should be identified and asked to participate on the reengineering team. Team members should include employees involved in the process (to provide expertise) and outside the process, as well as internal or external customers who see the outcome of the process.

Understand the Process

Several factors need to be considered when evaluating a process:

- Can tasks (e.g., course enrollment and pretraining assessment) be combined?
- Can we provide employees with more autonomy? Can we build decision making and control into the process through streamlining it?
- Are all of the steps necessary in the process?
- Are data redundancy or unnecessary checks and controls built into the process?
- How many special cases and exceptions have to be dealt with?
- Are the steps in the process arranged in their natural order?
- What is the desired outcome? Are all of the tasks necessary? What is the value of the process?

A number of techniques are used to understand processes. **Data-flow diagrams** show the flow of data between departments. For example, to investigate why tuition reimbursement checks take too long to reach employees, trainers may want to investigate the relationship between the training department (where tuition reimbursement is approved) and accounting (where checks are issued). **Data-entity relationship diagrams** show the types of data used within a business function and the relationship among the different types of data. These diagrams would be especially useful for investigating, for example, the time and people within the training department involved in filling employees' requests for their training records. In **scenario analysis,** simulations of real-world issues are presented to data end users. The end users are asked to indicate how a new technology could help address their particular situations and what data should be maintained to deal with those situations. Surveys and focus groups collect information about the data collected, used, and stored in a functional area as well as information about time and data processing requirements. Users may be asked to evaluate the importance, frequency, and criticality of automating specific tasks within a functional area. (For example, how critical is it to have an employee tracking system that maintains data on employees' fluency in foreign languages?) Cost-benefit analyses compare the costs of completing tasks with and without an automated system or software application. For example, the analysis should include (1) the costs in terms of people, time, materials, and dollars, (2) the anticipated costs of software and hardware, and (3) labor, time, and material expenses.[27]

Redesign the Process

The team develops models, tests them, chooses a prototype, and determines how to integrate the prototype into the organization.

Implement the Process

The company tries out the process by testing it in a limited, controlled setting before expanding companywide.

STEPS IN IMPLEMENTING CHANGE

As noted in Chapter 1, companies face many forces—including new technologies, globalization, and a diverse work force—that mean they have to change to be successful. **Organization development** is a planned, systematic change process that uses behavioral science knowledge and techniques to improve companies' effectiveness by improving relationships and increasing learning and problem-solving capabilities.[28] Organization development helps create a learning environment through increased trust, confrontation of problems, employee empowerment and participation, knowledge sharing, work design, and cooperation between groups, and through allowing employees to maximize their skills and grow.

Change Management

Change management is the process of ensuring that new interventions such as training practices are accepted and used by employees and managers. The change management process involves four steps: overcoming resistance to change, managing the transition to the new practice, shaping political dynamics, and using training to understand new tasks.

Overcoming Resistance to Change

Resistance to change can be overcome by involving the affected people in planning the change and rewarding them for desired behavior. It is also critical for managers to divide the implementation of the new practice into steps that are understandable and that employees believe they can accomplish. Employees need to understand how new training practices help them to meet their needs.[29] These needs may include better-quality training, faster access to descriptions of training programs, a link between training and compensation, and more meaningful training or access to training programs from their personal computers.

For example, 20 different departments within the Pepsi Bottling Group's shared services division had been accustomed to operating independently.[30] They performed the same functions at different Pepsi Groups, but they each had their own practices and procedures for getting work done. A small team of employees tried to create one set of shared practices and procedures, but the departments did not accept them. The next step to persuade the departments to accept the change was to involve as many employees as possible. This larger group of employees came up with a common set of procedures and documented them online. Similarly, Detroit Edison used involvement of as many employees as possible to help determine ways to cut costs. One-third of the entire organization participated in the process. The changes were accepted by employees, and Detroit Edison saved millions of dollars.

TABLE 13.3
**Managers'
Misconceptions
about Training**

Source: Based on
R. F. Mager, "Morph-
ing into a . . . 21st
Century Trainer,"
Training (June 1996):
47–54.

- Training is not valuable.
- Training is an expense, not an investment.
- Anybody can be a trainer.
- The training department is a good place to put poor performers.
- Training is the responsibility of trainers.

Managing the Transition

Tactics for managing the transition include communicating a clear picture of the future and creating organizational arrangements for the transition (e.g., contact person, help line). It might be good to allow an old practice and a new practice to exist simultaneously (run parallel) so that employees can see the benefits and advantages of the new practice. Then, any problems that are identified can be worked out. This parallel process is commonly done when new technology is introduced in companies.

Shaping Political Dynamics

Managers need to seek the support of key power groups including formal and informal leaders. For example, as was mentioned in Chapter 10, successful diversity efforts are characterized by active involvement and endorsement by top managers. Not only do top managers talk about the need to manage diversity, but they also get actively involved through mentoring programs, setting up formal committees and positions to promote diversity, and rewarding managers for their diversity efforts.

Managers of support functions such as human resources that are not directly involved in the design, manufacturing, or delivery of a product or service to the marketplace can shape political dynamics by becoming business partners. The steps to becoming a business partner relate to the discussion of strategic training in Chapter 2. First, the trainer identifies and understands the business problems that the manager is facing. Second, the trainer explains to the manager how training can help solve the problem. Third, the trainer works with the manager to develop the best training solution that meets the manager's needs. The manager should be treated as a customer. Finally, the trainer measures how training has helped overcome or solve the business problem.

Table 13.3 shows several misconceptions that some managers hold about training. These misconceptions are likely due to a lack of understanding of the function and value of the training department.

To counter these misconceptions and gain political alliances with managers in the business functions, trainers need to take several actions. As mentioned in Chapter 1 and 2, trainers need to ensure that the training department adds value to the business, builds relationships with functional business managers, and establishes credibility in the company.[31] This reassurance is accomplished through helping functional managers deal with training-related problems, evaluating the effectiveness of training practices, and providing excellent service to the function managers (e.g., providing information and finishing projects in a timely manner, committing only to projects that can be realistically delivered).

Using Training to Explain New Tasks

Because many practices involve changes not only in the way the service or process is going to be provided, but also in employees' and managers' roles, training is critical. Managers and employees need to be trained to deal with new systems whether they involve job redesign (e.g., teams), performance management (e.g., use of 360-degree feedback systems), selection systems (e.g., a structured interview), or new technology (e.g., a new computer-based manufacturing system).

For example, these principles helped with the introduction of a computerized flexible manufacturing system at a manufacturer of diesel engines.[32] The computers were to be used to provide instructions for customized orders and to give the order center updates on production status. The production workers were reluctant to use the computers. Their objections included that they did not know how to type and that their jobs made their hands too greasy. To ensure that the production workers would use the new system, the company took several steps. First, an electronic performance support system was placed in the cafeteria to answer employees' questions about the system. Second, the company asked workers for suggestions as they tested prototypes of the system. Third, the touch screen system was modified so that employees could use foot controls, thus alleviating concerns about greasy hands when typing. Twenty months after the process for introducing the new manufacturing system began, the system was in place.

Consider how Boeing used change management principles and training to revive its failing Boeing 717 airplane. Boeing was losing millions of dollars on every 100-seat 717 commercial jet that was sold.[33] The manufacturing process was inefficient; employees, union workers, and suppliers were not cooperating; and the merger with McDonnell Douglas had resulted in layoffs that created a negative attitude at the facility where the 717 was built. The company considered shutting down the 717 program, but team-based management and training gave the 717 program a chance. To start the transformation of the 717 and gain support, a five-day off-site training event was held for four key groups who affected the 717: employees, union workers, support organizations, and stakeholders in the supply chain. The groups agreed that their goal was to reduce costs and sell more planes. This goal would benefit each group. Employees would gain job security, earnings would increase for shareholders, and suppliers would obtain financial gains. The group also identified seven areas in which change was required to meet their goal: leadership, team-based culture, supplier alignment, overhead costs, relationship with labor, strategies, and customer focus. Teams were formed for each of the seven areas to make changes and communicate them to the rest of the company.

With the help of a consultant, Boeing's director of employee involvement created an entrepreneurial team-based manufacturing environment. Self-managing work teams were formed. Employees were grouped by function, not title. For example, instead of housing engineers in separate buildings, they were grouped in teams around specific tasks. Employees in all functions of the organization were grouped according to tasks such as interior design, final assembly, propulsion, and product delivery. The work flow process was redesigned so employees worked side by side. Teams were equipped with everything they needed to keep airplanes moving, including easy access to inspectors, a parts fabrication shop, rapid response to equipment requests, and a parts receiving and inventory area.

Boeing decided to focus on what the company does best: designing, developing, integrating, and assembling airplanes. They did this by outsourcing the manufacturing of the planes' parts to a few key manufacturers, and in exchange, those suppliers cut their prices by 20 to 30 percent.

Training was used to help employees understand business concepts such as return on investment and shareholder value. This knowledge raised their awareness of how their performance affected overall costs and could create a competitive advantage in the marketplace. The teams became more efficient and cost-focused, which saved money. Also, understanding how they affect the bottom line served to increase employees' pride in the products they build. To overcome employee skepticism of the program, managers received leadership training and mentoring that taught them how to model the behaviors and attitudes they expected of employees. Because employees were working in teams, managers had to learn how to align teams with the company goals and provide them with the resources they needed to reach those goals. In the training program, managers learned how to coach employees and motivate them. They also gained a better understanding of how they could help teams contribute to the company's profitability.

The redesign of the work increased efficiency, and the training reduced costs and delivery time. It takes one-third less time to manufacture a 717 plane (one every four days) than it once did. Boeing has outsold companies such as Airbus Industries that manufacture similar-sized airplanes. Executives at Boeing support the 717 program and are looking to implement the lessons learned in the 717 turnaround in other airplane manufacturing programs.

Change Interventions

Besides training, there are several interventions that companies have used successfully to bring about change. These include survey feedback, process consultation, and group interventions.

Survey Feedback

Survey feedback refers to the process of collecting information about employees' attitudes and perceptions using a survey, summarizing the results, and providing employees with feedback to stimulate discussion, identify problems, and plan actions to solve problems. The goal of survey feedback is to identify issues, solve problems, and improve relationships among work group members through discussion of shared problems.

Process Consultation

In **process consultation,** a consultant works with managers or other employees to help them understand and take action to improve specific events that occur at work. Process consultation may involve analysis of relationships between employees, the work flow, how decisions are made, communication patterns, or other behaviors. The consultant helps employees diagnose what processes need to be improved.

Group Interventions

Large group interventions involve employees from different parts of the organization. They may also involve customers and other important stakeholders from outside the company. The interventions bring together the participants in an off-site setting to discuss problems and opportunities or to plan change. For example, the Work Out program within General Electric (GE) includes six steps:[34]

1. A process or problem for discussion is chosen.
2. A cross-functional team, including customers and others outside GE (e.g., suppliers), is selected.
3. A "champion" is assigned to follow through on recommendations made by the team.
4. Team meetings generate recommendations to improve processes or solve problems.

5. Top managers meet with the teams to review recommendations and evaluate them.

6. Additional meetings are held to pursue the recommendations.

The program grew out of former CEO Jack Welch's desire to motivate the more than 300,000 employees at GE. Welch believed that employees have to be involved in creating change for it to occur.

Large group interventions seek to bring about radical change in the entire company by involving the entire company system (managers, employees, customers) in the change effort. Intergroup activities occur on a much smaller scale. **Intergroup activities** attempt to improve relationships between different teams, departments, or groups. These interventions have been used for labor–management conflicts, to smooth mergers and acquisitions, and to alleviate differences between staff and line functions. One intergroup activity has the involved groups meet separately and list the beliefs they have about themselves and the other group.[35] The groups discuss their similarities and differences and how misperceptions have developed. The groups then discuss possible solutions to their conflict and misperceptions.

Summary

This chapter discussed future trends that are likely to influence training and development. These trends relate to training delivery and structure of the training function. New technology will have a growing impact on training delivery in the future. Also, new technology allows training departments to store and share intellectual capital throughout the company. Learning management systems will be developed as a way to automate the administration of available online training programs. There will be an increased emphasis on integrating training with other human resource functions and showing how training helps the business. Training departments are more likely to develop partnerships with vendors and other companies in the future. The chapter discussed the importance of viewing training from a change perspective. Benchmarking training practices and reengineering training processes are important prerequisites for creating a need for change. For new training practices to be accepted by employees and managers, trainers need to overcome resistance to change, manage the transition, shape the political dynamics, and use training to redefine the task. Organization development interventions involving consultants, groups, and survey feedback can be used to create change.

Key Terms

virtual work arrangement, *411*

teleworking, *411*

digital collaboration, *412*

learning management systems (LMS), *412*

human capital management, *413*

performance analysis approach, *415*

outsourcing, *417*

application service provider (ASP), *417*

resistance to change, *418*

control, *418*

power, *419*

task redefinition, *419*

reengineering, *420*

data-flow diagrams, *421*

data-entity relationship diagrams, *421*

scenario analysis, *421*

organization development, *422*

change management, *422*

survey feedback, *425*

process consultation, *425*

large group intervention, *425*

intergroup activity, *426*

Discussion Questions

1. Discuss how new technologies are likely to impact training in the future.
2. What new skills will trainers need to be successful in the future?
3. How does the use of a learning management system better link training to business strategy and goals?
4. What is benchmarking? Explain the process you would use to benchmark a company's safety training programs.
5. What is process reengineering? Why is it relevant to training?
6. Discuss the steps necessary to introduce a new training practice from a change model perspective.
7. What misconceptions do managers have about training? How could you change those misconceptions?
8. Explain what you believe are the advantages and disadvantages of creating a training consortium or partnership with other companies.
9. What is organization development? Describe the interventions used to create change.
10. What are the implications of virtual work arrangements for training?

Application Assignments

1. Interview a manager. Ask him to evaluate his company's training department in terms of training delivery, service, expertise, and contribution to the business. Ask him to explain the rationale for his evaluation. Summarize this information. Based on the information you gathered, make recommendations regarding how the training department can be improved.
2. This chapter discussed several trends that will influence the future of training. Based on future social, economic, political, or technological factors, identify one or two additional trends that you think will influence training. Write a two- to three-page paper summarizing your ideas. Make sure you provide a rationale for your trends. Many organizations are moving from a training perspective to a performance perspective. That is, they are interested in performance improvement, not training just for the sake of training.
3. GeoLearning is an application service provider (ASP). Visit *www.geolearning.com*. What services and products does this ASP provide?
4. Go to *www.knowledge.base.net*. Review the Knowledge Base. What features does it have to help capture knowledge? What are its benefits?

Endnotes

1. C. E. Plott and J. Humphrey, "Preparing for 2020," *Training and Development* (November 1996): 46–49.
2. J. Barbian, "The Future Training Room," *Training* (September 2001): 40–45.
3. N. Crandall and M. Wallace, Jr., *Work and Rewards in the Virtual Workplace* (New York: AMACOM, 1998).
4. J. Salopek, "Digital Collaboration," *Training and Development* (June 2000): 38–43.

5. T. A. Stewart, "Getting Real about Brainpower," *Fortune* (November 27, 1995): 201–3; P. Stamps, "Managing Corporate Smarts," *Training* (August 1997): 40–46; K. Vander Linde, N. Horney, and R. Koonce, "Seven Ways to Make Your Training Department One of the Best," *Training and Development* (August 1997): 20–28.

6. M. Hequet, "The State of the E-Learning Market," *Training* (September 2003): 24–29.

7. J. Barbian, "Great Expectations," *Training* (September 2002): 102–12.

8. E. Cohen, "At the Ready," *Human Resource Executive* (August 2003): 40–42.

9. K. Dobbs, "Take the Gamble Out of an LMS," *Workforce* (November 2002): 52–58.

10. M. Gold, "IRS Goes E," *TD* (May 2003): 76–82.

11. S. Adkins, "The Brave New World of Learning," *T&D* (June 2003): 28–37.

12. H. Dolezalek, "Mining for Gold," *Training* (September 2003): 36–42.

13. R. Weintraub and J. Martineau, "The Just-in-Time Imperative," *T&D* (June 2002): 50–58.

14. D. Garrett, "Crossing the Channel," *Training* (September 1999): OL14–OL20.

15. L. J. Bassi, G. Benson, and S. Cheney, "The Top Ten Trends," *Training and Development* (November 1996): 28–42.

16. S. Jackson, "Your Local Campus: Training Ground Zero," *Business Week* (September 30, 1996): 68.

17. C. J. Bachler, "Trainers," *Workforce* (June 1997): 93–105; Bassi, Benson, and Cheney, "The Top Ten Trends."

18. P. Harris, "A New Market Emerges," *T&D* (September 2003): 30–38.

19. D. Schaaf, "ERP or Oops?" *Training* (May 2000): S4–S12.

20. M. Kaeter, "Training for Rent," *Training* (May 2000): S14–S22.

21. D. A. Nadler, "Concepts for the Management of Organizational Change," in *Readings in the Management of Innovation,* 2d ed., ed. M. L. Tushman and N. L. Moore (Cambridge, MA: Ballinger, 1988): 722.

22. A. P. Brache and G. A. Rummler, "Managing an Organization as a System," *Training* (February 1997): 68–74.

23. E. F. Glanz and L. K. Dailey, "Benchmarking," *Human Resource Management,* 31 (1992): 9–20; C. E. Schneier and C. Johnson, "Benchmarking: A Tool for Improving Performance Management and Reward Systems," *American Compensation Association Journal* (Spring/Summer 1993): 14–31.

24. S. Greengard, "Discover Best Practices through Benchmarking," *Personnel Journal* (November 1995): 62–73; J. D. Weatherly, "Dare to Compare for Better Productivity," *HR Magazine* (September 1992): 42–46.

25. C. E. Bogan and M. J. English, "Benchmarking for Best Practices," in *The ASTD Handbook for Training and Development,* 4th ed., ed. R. L. Craig (New York: McGraw-Hill, 1996): 394–412.

26. T. B. Kinni, "A Reengineering Primer," *Quality Digest* (January 1994): 26–30; "Reengineering Is Helping Health of Hospitals and Its Patients," *Total Quality Newsletter* (February 1994): 5; R. Recardo, "Process Reengineering in a Finance Division," *Journal for Quality and Participation* (June 1994): 70–73.

27. S. E. O'Connell, "New Technologies Bring New Tools, New Rules," *HR Magazine* (December 1995): 43–48; S. F. O'Connell, "The Virtual Workplace Works at Warp Speed," *HR Magazine* (March 1996): 51–57.

28. "What Is Organization Development?" in *Organizational Development and Transformation: Managing Effective Change,* ed. W. French, C. Bell, Jr., and R. Zawacki (Burr Ridge, IL: Irwin/McGraw-Hill, 2000): 16–19.

29. E. Kossek, "The Acceptance of Human Resource Innovation by Multiple Constituencies," *Personnel Psychology* 42 (1989): 263–81.

30. W. Webb, "Winds of Change," *Training* (July 2002): 40–43.

31. J. J. Laabs, "Put Your Job on the Line," *Personnel Journal* (June 1995): 74–88.

32. M. Samuel, "Managing Change: Safety, Accountability, and Some Discomfort Needed," *Total Quality Newsletter* (September 1994).

33. S. Gale, "The Little Airplane That Could," *Training* (December 2000): 60–67.

34. J. Quinn, "What a Work Out!" *Performance* (November 1994): 58–63; R. Ashkenas and T. Jick, "From Dialogue to Action in GE Work-Out: Developmental Learning in a Change Process." In *Research in Organizational Change and Development,* ed. R. Woodman and W. Pasmore (Greenwich, CT: JAI Press, 1992): 267–87.

35. D. Daft and R. Noe, *Organizational Behavior* (Fort Worth, TX: Harcourt College Publishers, 2001).

Glossary

360-degree feedback A special case of the upward feedback system. Here employees' behaviors or skills are evaluated not only by subordinates but also by peers, customers, bosses, and employees themselves via a questionnaire rating them on a number of dimensions.

ability The physical and mental capacity to perform a task.

action learning Training method that involves giving teams or work groups a problem, having them work on solving it and committing to an action plan, and then holding them accountable for carrying out the plan.

action plan A written document detailing steps that a trainee and the manager will take to ensure that training transfers to the job.

action planning An employee's process of determining how the employee will achieve short- and long-term career goals.

advance organizers Outlines, texts, diagrams, and graphs that help trainees organize information that will be presented and practiced.

adventure learning Training method focusing on developing teamwork and leadership skills using structured outdoor activities.

affective outcomes Outcomes including attitudes and motivation.

Age Discrimination in Employment Act A federal law that prohibits discrimination against individuals 40 years of age or older.

Americans with Disabilities Act (ADA) A 1990 act prohibiting workplace discrimination against people with disabilities.

andragogy The theory of adult learning.

anticipatory socialization Initial phase in organizational socialization involving the development of an employee's expectations about the company, job, working conditions, and interpersonal relationships.

application assignments Work problems or situations that trainees are asked to apply training content to solve.

application planning The preparing of trainees to use key behaviors on the job.

application service provider (ASP) A company that rents out access to software for specific applications.

apprentice An employee in the exploration stage of his or her career who works under the supervision and direction of a more experienced colleague or manager.

apprenticeship A work-study training method with both on-the-job and classroom training.

assessment The collecting of information and providing of feedback to employees about their behavior, communication style, or skills.

assessment center A process in which multiple raters or evaluators (also known as assessors) evaluate employees' performances on a number of exercises.

asynchronous communication Non–real-time interactions in which people cannot communicate with each other without a time delay.

attitude Combination of beliefs and feelings that predispose a person to behave in a certain way.

attitude awareness and change program Program focusing on increasing employees' awareness of their attitudes toward differences in cultural and ethnic backgrounds, physical characteristics (e.g., disabilities), and personal characteristics that influence behavior toward others.

audiovisual instruction Media-based training that is both watched and heard.

auditing As regards training, the providing of information related to the frequency of training within a company.

automatization Making performance of a task, recall of knowledge, or demonstration of a skill so automatic that it requires little thought or attention.

baby boomers People born between 1945 and 1960.

balanced scorecard A means of performance measurement that allows managers to view the overall company performance or the performance of departments or functions (such as training) from the perspective of internal and external customers, employees, and shareholders.

bandwidth The number of bytes and bits (information) that can travel between computers per second.

basic skills Skills necessary for employees to perform their jobs and learn the content of training programs.

behavior-based conflict Conflict occurring when an employee's behavior in work roles is not appropriate in nonwork roles.

behavior-based program   Program focusing on changing the organizational policies and individual behaviors that inhibit employees' personal growth and productivity.

behavior modeling   A training method in which trainees are presented with a model who demonstrates key behaviors to replicate and provides them with the opportunity to practice those key behaviors.

benchmarking   The use of information about other companies' training practices to help determine the appropriate type, level, and frequency of training.

Benchmarks©   A research instrument designed to measure important factors in being a successful manager.

benefits   What of value the company gains from a training program.

blended learning   Learning involving a combination of online learning, face-to-face instruction, and other methods.

business game   A training method in which trainees gather information, analyze it, and make decisions.

business strategy   A plan that integrates a company's goals, policies, and actions.

career   The pattern of work-related experiences that span the course of a person's life.

career development   The process by which employees progress through a series of stages, each characterized by a different set of developmental tasks, activities, and relationships.

career identity   The degree to which employees define their personal value according to their work.

career insight   The degree to which employees know about their interests as well as their skill strengths and weaknesses; the awareness of how these perceptions relate to their career goals.

career management   The process through which employees (1) become aware of their own interests, values, strengths, and weaknesses, (2) get information about job opportunities within a company, (3) identify career goals, and (4) establish action plans to achieve career goals.

career management system   System that helps employees, managers, and the company identify career development needs; includes self-assessment, reality check, goal setting, and action planning.

career motivation   Employees' energy to invest in their careers, their awareness of the direction they want their careers to take, and their ability to maintain energy and direction despite any barriers that they may encounter.

career path   A sequence of job positions involving similar types of work and skills that employees move through in a company.

career resilience   Employees' ability to cope with problems that affect their work.

career support   Coaching, protection, sponsorship, and provision of challenging assignments, exposure, and visibility to an employee.

case study   A description of how employees or an organization dealt with a situation.

CD-ROM   An aluminum disc from which a laser reads text, graphics, audio, and video.

change   The adoption of a new idea or behavior by a company.

change management   The process of ensuring that new interventions such as training practices are accepted and used by employees and managers.

chief learning officer (CLO), or knowledge officer   A leader of a company's knowledge management efforts.

climate for transfer   Trainees' perceptions about a wide variety of characteristics of the work environment; these perceptions facilitate or inhibit use of trained skills or behavior.

coach   A peer or manager who works with employees to motivate them, help them develop skills, and provide reinforcement and feedback.

cognitive ability   Verbal comprehension, quantitative ability, and reasoning ability.

cognitive outcomes   Outcomes used to measure what knowledge trainees learned in a training program.

cognitive strategies   Strategies that regulate the learning processes; they relate to the learner's decision regarding what information to attend to, how to remember, and how to solve problems.

cognitive theory of transfer   Theory asserting that the likelihood of transfer depends on the trainee's ability to retrieve learned capabilities.

colleague   Employees, generally in the establishment stage of their career, who can work independently and produce results.

combination   Systematizing explicit concepts into a knowledge system by analyzing, categorizing, and repurposing information.

community of practice   A group of employees who work together, learn from each other, and develop a common understanding of how to get work accomplished.

comparison group A group of employees who participate in an evaluation study but do not attend a training program.

competency An area of personal capability that enables employees to perform their job.

competency model A model identifying the competencies necessary for each job as well as the knowledge, skills, behavior, and personal characteristics underlying each competency.

competitive advantage An upper hand over other firms in an industry.

competitiveness A company's ability to maintain and gain market share in an industry.

computer-based training (CBT) An interactive training experience in which the computer provides the learning stimulus, the trainee must respond, and the computer analyzes responses and provides feedback to the trainee.

concentration strategy Business strategy focusing on increasing market share, reducing costs, or creating a market niche for products and services.

consequences Incentives employees receive for performing well.

contingent work force Independent contractors, on-call workers, temporary workers, and contract workers.

continuous learning A learning system in which employees are required to understand the entire work system including the relationships among their jobs, their work units, and the company. Also, employees are expected to acquire new skills and knowledge, apply them on the job, and share this information with fellow workers.

control A manager's or employee's ability to obtain and distribute valuable resources.

coordination training Training a team in how to share information and decision making responsibilities to maximize team performance.

copyright Legal protection for the expression of an idea.

corporate university model A training model in which the client group includes not only company employees and managers but also stakeholders outside the company.

cost-benefit analysis The process of determining the economic benefits of a training program using accounting methods.

course objectives (lesson objectives) The expected behaviors, content, conditions, and standards of a training course or lesson; more specific than program objectives.

course parameters General information about a training program including course title, audience, purpose, goals, location, time, prerequisites, and name of trainer.

criteria relevance The extent to which training outcomes relate to the learned capabilities emphasized in training.

criterion contamination A training program's outcomes measuring inappropriate capabilities or being affected by extraneous conditions.

criterion deficiency The failure to measure training outcomes that were emphasized in training objectives.

cross-cultural preparation The education of employees (expatriates) and their families who are to be sent to a foreign country.

cross training Training method in which team members understand and practice each other's skills so that members are prepared to step in and take another member's place should someone temporarily or permanently leave the team; also, more simply, training employees to learn the skills of one or several additional jobs.

cultural immersion Used to prepare employees for overseas assignments; involves sending employees directly into a community where they have to interact with persons from different cultures, races, and/or nationalities.

culture A set of assumptions group members share about the world and how it works as well as ideals worth striving for.

customer model A training model in which a training department is responsible for the training needs of one division or function of the company.

data-entity relationship diagram An illustration of the types of data used within a business function and the relationships among the different types of data.

data-flow diagram An illustration of the flow of data between departments.

detailed lesson plan The translation of the content and sequence of training activities into a guide used by the trainer to help deliver training.

development Formal education, job experiences, relationships, and assessments of personality and abilities that help employees prepare for the future.

development planning process Process of identifying development needs, choosing a development goal, identifying actions the employee and company need to take to achieve the goal, determining how progress toward goal attainment will be measured, and establishing a timetable for development.

digital collaboration   An interaction between two or more people mediated by a computer; the use of technology to enhance and extend employees' ability to work together regardless of their geographic proximity.

direct costs   Training costs including salaries and benefits of all employees involved, program supplies, equipment and classroom rental or purchase, and travel costs.

directional pattern model   A model describing the form or shape of careers.

discrimination   The degree to which trainees' performances on an outcome actually reflect true differences in performance.

disengagement stage   Career stage in which an individual prepares for a change in the balance between work and nonwork activities.

disinvestment strategy   Business strategy emphasizing liquidation and divestiture of businesses.

distance learning   Training method in which geographically dispersed companies provide information about new products, policies, or procedures as well as skills training and expert lectures to field locations.

diversity training   Training programs designed to change employees' attitudes about diversity and/or to develop skills needed to work with a diverse work force.

downward move   Reduction of an employee's responsibility and authority.

dual-career-path system   A career path system that enables technical employees to either remain in a technical career path or move into a management career path.

DVD (digital video disc)   A technology in which a laser reads text, graphics, audio, and video off an aluminum disc.

early retirement program   A system of offering employees financial benefits to leave the company.

e-commerce   A technology enabling business transactions and relationships to be handled electronically.

elaboration   A learning strategy requiring the trainee to relate the training material to other more familiar knowledge, skills, or behavior.

e-learning   Instruction and delivery of training by computer online through the Internet or Web.

electronic performance support system (EPSS)   Computer application that can provide, as requested, skills training, information access, and expert advice.

empowerment   Giving employees responsibility and authority to make decisions regarding product development or customer service.

encounter phase   Middle phase in organizational socialization in which an employee begins a new job.

establishment stage   Career stage in which an individual finds his or her place in a company, makes an independent contribution, achieves more responsibility and financial success, and establishes a desirable life style.

evaluation design   Designation of what information is to be collected, from whom, when, and how to determine training's effectiveness.

expatriate   A person working in a country other than his or her nation of origin.

expectancy   Belief about the link between trying to perform a behavior (or effort) and actually performing well; the mental state that the learner brings to the instructional process.

experiential learning   A training method in which participants (1) are presented with conceptual knowledge and theory, (2) take part in a behavioral simulation, (3) analyze the activity, and (4) connect the theory and activity with on-the-job or real-life situations.

expert systems   Technology (usually software) that organizes and applies human experts' knowledge to specific problems.

explicit knowledge   Knowledge that can be formalized, codified, and communicated.

exploration stage   Career stage in which individuals attempt to identify the type of work that interests them.

external conditions   Processes in the learning environment that facilitate learning.

external growth strategy   Business strategy emphasizing acquiring vendors and suppliers or buying businesses that allow the company to expand into new markets.

external validity   The generalizability of study results to other groups and situations.

externalization   Translating tacit knowledge into explicit knowledge.

externship   Situation in which a company allows an employee to take a full-time, temporary operational role at another company.

faculty model   A training model that resembles the structure of a college. The training department is headed by director with a staff of experts having specialized knowledge of a particular topic or skill area.

Family and Medical Leave Act (FMLA) A federal law that provides for up to 12 weeks of unpaid leave for parents with new infants or newly adopted children; also covers employees who must take a leave of absence from work to care for a family member who is ill or to deal with a personal illness.

far transfer Trainees' ability to apply learned capabilities to the work environment even though it is not identical to the training session environment.

feedback Information employees receive while they are performing about how well they are meeting objectives.

fidelity The extent to which a training environment is similar to a work environment.

focus group A face-to-face meeting with subject-matter experts in which specific training needs are addressed.

formal education program Off-site or on-site program designed for a company's employees, short course offered by a consultant or school, an executive MBA program, or university program in which students live at the university while taking classes.

formative evaluation Evaluation conducted to improve the training process; usually conducted before and during the training process.

Gen Xers People born between 1961 and 1980.

generalization A trainee's ability to apply learned capabilities to on-the-job work problems and situations that are similar but not identical to problems and situations encountered in the learning environment.

generalizing Adapting learning for use in similar but not identical situations.

glass ceiling A barrier to advancement to an organization's higher levels.

goal What a company hopes to achieve in the medium- to long-term future.

goal orientation A trainee's goals in a learning situation.

goal setting An employee's process of developing short- and long-term career objectives.

goal setting theory A theory assuming that behavior results from a person's conscious goals and intentions.

gratifying The feedback that a learner receives from using learning content.

group building methods Training methods designed to improve team or group effectiveness.

group mentoring program Program in which a successful senior employee is paired with a group of four to six less experienced protégés to help them understand the organization, guide them in analyzing their experiences, and help them clarify career directions.

groupware (electronic meeting software) A special type of software application that enables multiple users to track, share, and organize information, and to work on the same document simultaneously.

hands-on method Training method in which the trainee is actively involved in learning.

Hawthorne effect A situation in which employees in an evaluation study perform at a high level simply because of the attention they are receiving.

high-leverage training Training that uses an instructional design process to ensure that it is effective and that compares or benchmarks the company's training programs against other companies'.

high-potential employee An employee whom the company believes is capable of succeeding in a higher-level managerial position.

host-country national An employee with citizenship in the country where the company is located.

human capital management The integration of training with other human resource functions so as to track how training benefits the company.

human resource development The integrated use of training and development, organizational development, and career development to improve individual, group, and organizational effectiveness.

human resource management The policies, practices, and systems that influence employees' behavior, attitudes, and performance.

human resource management (HRM) practices Management activities relating to investments in staffing, performance management, training, and compensation and benefits.

human resource planning The identification, analysis, forecasting, and planning of changes needed in a company's human resources area.

hyperlinks Links that allow a user to easily move from one Web page to another.

imaging Scanning documents, storing them electronically, and retrieving them.

in-basket A training exercise involving simulation of the administrative tasks of the manager's job.

indirect costs   Costs not related directly to a training program's design, development, or delivery.

individualism-collectivism   The cultural dimension reflecting the degree to which people act as individuals rather than members of a group.

informational interview   An interview an employee conducts with a manager or other employee to gather information about the skills, job demands, and benefits of that person's job.

input   Instructions that tell employees what, how, and when to perform; also, the resources employees are given to help them perform their jobs.

instruction   The characteristics of the environment in which learning is to occur.

Instructional Systems Design (ISD)   A process for designing and developing training programs.

instructor evaluation   A measurement of a trainer's or instructor's success.

instrumentality   In expectancy theory, a belief that performing a given behavior is associated with a particular outcome.

intellectual capital   Cognitive knowledge, advanced skills, system understanding and creativity, and self-motivated creativity.

intellectual skills   Mastery of concepts and rules.

intelligent tutoring system (ITS)   An instructional system using artificial intelligence.

interactive video   Training medium combining video and computer-based instruction, with the trainee interacting with the program.

interactive voice technology   Technology using a conventional PC to create a phone-response system.

intergroup activity   A change intervention that attempts to improve relationships between different teams, departments, or groups.

internal conditions   Processes within the learner that must be present for learning to occur.

internal growth strategy   Business strategy focusing on new market and product development, innovation, and joint ventures.

internal validity   Establishing that the treatment (training) made a difference.

internalization   Converting explicit knowledge to tacit knowledge.

Internet   A global collection of computer networks that allows users to exchange data and information; a communications tool for sending and receiving messages quickly and inexpensively; a means of locating and gathering resources.

Internet-based training   Training delivered on public or private computer networks and displayed by a Web browser.

intranet-based training   Training delivered using a company's own computer network or server.

ISO 9000:2000   A family of standards developed by the International Organization for Standardization that includes 20 requirements for dealing with such issues as how to establish quality standards and document work processes.

job   A specific position requiring completion of certain tasks.

job analysis   The process of developing a description of the job (duties, tasks, and responsibilities) and the specifications (knowledge, skills, and abilities) that an employee must have to perform it.

job enlargement   The adding of challenges or new responsibilities to an employee's current job.

job experience   The relationships, problems, demands, tasks, and other features that an employee faces on the job.

job incumbent   An employee currently holding the job.

job rotation   Assigning employees a series of jobs in various functional areas of a company or movement among jobs in a single functional area or department.

job sharing   Work situation in which two employees divide the hours, responsibilities, and benefits of a full-time job.

joint union–management training program   Program created, funded, and supported by both union and management to provide a range of services to help employees learn skills that are directly related to their jobs and that are "portable" (valuable to employers in other companies or industries).

key behavior   One of a set of behaviors that is necessary to complete a task. Important part of behavior modeling training.

knowledge   Facts or procedures. hat individuals or teams of employees know or know how to do (human and social knowledge); also a company's rules, processes, tools, and routines (structured knowledge).

knowledge-based pay system   Pay system based primarily on an employee's knowledge rather than on the job he or she is performing (also called skill-based pay system).

knowledge management The process of enhancing company performance by designing and implementing tools, processes, systems, structures, and cultures to improve the creating, sharing, and use of knowledge.

knowledge officer (or chief learning officer) A leader of a company's knowledge management efforts.

knowledge workers Employees who own the means of producing a product or service. These employees have a specialized body of knowledge or expertise which they use to perform their jobs and contribute to company effectiveness.

lapse Situation in which a trainee uses previously learned, less effective capabilities instead of trying to apply capabilities emphasized in a training program.

large group intervention A change intervention that brings together employees from different parts of an organization (and perhaps customers and other stake-holders) in an off-site setting to discuss problems and opportunities or to plan change.

laser disc A disc that uses a laser to provide video and sound.

leaderless group discussion A training exercise in which a team of five to seven employees must work together to solve an assigned problem within a certain time period.

learner control A trainee's ability to actively learn through self-pacing, exercises, exploring links to other material, and conversations with other trainees and experts.

learning The acquisition of knowledge by individual employees or group of employees who are willing to apply that knowledge in their jobs in making decisions and accomplishing tasks for the company; a relatively permanent change in human capabilities that does not result from growth processes.

learning management systems (LMS) A system for automating the administration of online training programs.

learning organization A company that has an enhanced capacity to learn, adapt, and change; an organization whose employees continuously attempt to learn new things and then apply what they have learned to improve product or service quality.

learning portal Website that provides, via e-commerce transactions, access to training courses, services, and online learning communities from many sources.

lecture Training method in which the trainer communicates through spoken words what trainees are supposed to learn.

lesson plan overview A plan matching a training program's major activities to specific times or time intervals.

life-cycle model A model suggesting that employees face certain developmental tasks over the course of their careers and that they move through distinct life or career stages.

logical verification Perceiving a relationship between a new task and a task already mastered.

maintenance The process of continuing to use newly acquired capabilities over time.

maintenance stage Career stage in which an individual is concerned about keeping skills up to date and being perceived by others as someone who is still contributing to the company.

Malcolm Baldrige National Quality Award National award created in 1987 to recognize U.S. companies' quality achievements and to publicize quality strategies.

manager support Trainees' managers (1) emphasizing the importance of attending training programs and (2) stressing the application of training content on the job.

managing diversity The creation of an environment that allows all employees (regardless of their demographic group) to contribute to organizational goals and experience personal growth.

masculinity-femininity The cultural dimension reflecting the degree to which a culture values behavior that is considered traditionally masculine (competitiveness) or feminine (helpfulness).

massed practice Training approach in which trainees practice a task continuously without rest.

mastery orientation An effort to increase ability or competence in a task.

matrix model A training model in which trainers report to both a manager in the training department and a manager in a particular function.

mental requirements The degree to which a person must use or demonstrate mental skills or cognitive skills or abilities to perform a task.

mentor An experienced, productive senior employee who helps develop a less experienced employee (a protégé).

metacognition A learning strategy whereby trainees direct their attention to their own learning process.

millenniums (or nexters) People born after 1980.

mission A company's long-term reason for existing.

modeling   Having employees who have mastered the desired learning outcomes demonstrate them for trainees.

modeling display   Often done via videotape or computer, a training method in which trainees are shown key behaviors, which they then practice.

motivation to learn   A trainee's desire to learn the content of a training program.

motor skills   Coordination of physical movements.

multimedia training   Training that combines audio-visual training methods with computer-based training.

Myers-Briggs Type Indicator (MBTI)   A psychological test for employee development consisting of over 100 questions about how the person feels or prefers to behave in different situations.

near transfer   A trainee's ability to apply learned capabilities exactly to the work situation.

need   A deficiency that a person is experiencing at any point in time.

needs assessment   The process used to determine if training is necessary. The first step in the instructional system design model.

nexters (or millenniums)   People born after 1980.

norms   Accepted standards of behavior for work-group members.

objective   The purpose and expected outcome of training activities.

obsolescence   A reduction in an employee's competence resulting from a lack of knowledge of new work processes, techniques, and technologies that have developed since the employee completed his or her education.

offshoring   The process of moving jobs from the United States to other locations in the world.

onboarding   The orientation process for newly hired managers.

online learning   Instruction and delivery of training by computer online through the Internet or Web.

on-the-job training (OJT)   Training in which new or inexperienced employees learn through first observing peers or managers performing the job and then trying to imitate their behavior.

opportunity to perform   The chance to use learned capabilities.

organization development   A planned, systematic change process that uses behavioral science knowledge and techniques to improve a company's effectiveness by improving relationships and increasing learning and problem-solving capabilities.

organization-based model   A model suggesting that careers proceed through a series of stages with each stage involving changes in activities and relationships with peers and managers.

organizational analysis   Training analysis that determines the appropriateness of training, considering the context in which training will occur.

organizational socialization   The process of transforming new employees into effective company members. Its phases are anticipatory socialization, encounter, and settling in.

organizing   A learning strategy that requires the learner to find similarities and themes in the training materials.

other   In task analysis, a term referring to the conditions under which tasks are performed, for example, physical condition of the work environment or psychological conditions, such as pressure or stress.

output   A job's performance standards.

outsourcing   The acquisition of training and development activities from outside the company.

overall task complexity   The degree to which a task requires a number of distinct behaviors, the number of choices involved in performing the task, and the degree of uncertainty in performing the task.

overlearning   Employees' continuing to practice even if they have been able to perform the objective several times.

part practice   Training approach in which each objective or task is practiced individually as soon as it is introduced in a training program.

past accomplishments   System of allowing employees to build a history of successful accomplishments.

perception   The ability to organize a message from the environment so that it can be processed and acted upon.

performance analysis approach   An approach to solving business problems that identifies performance gaps or deficiencies and examines training as a possible solution.

performance appraisal   The process of measuring an employee's performance.

performance orientation   A learner's focus on task performance and how the learner compares to others.

person analysis   Training analysis involving (1) determining whether performance deficiencies result from lack of knowledge, skill, or ability or else from a motivational or work-design problem, (2) identifying who needs training, and (3) determining employees' readiness for training.

person characteristics An employee's knowledge, skill, ability, behavior, or attitudes.

physical requirements The degree to which a person must use or demonstrate physical skills and abilities to perform and complete a task.

pilot testing The process of previewing a training program with potential trainees and managers or other customers.

plateauing A workplace situation with little likelihood of the employee receiving future job assignments with increased responsibility.

plug-in Extra software that needs to be loaded on a computer, for example, to listen to sound or watch video.

posttest only An evaluation design in which only posttraining outcomes are collected.

posttraining measure A measure of outcomes taken after training.

power The ability to influence others.

power distance Expectations for the unequal distribution of power in a hierarchy.

practicality The ease with which outcome measures can be collected.

practice An employee's demonstration of a learned capability; the physical or mental rehearsal of a task, knowledge, or skill to achieve proficiency in performing the task or skill or demonstrating the knowledge.

preretirement socialization The process of helping employees prepare for exit from work.

presence In training, the perception of actually being in a particular environment.

presentation methods Training methods in which trainees are passive recipients of information.

pretest/posttest An evaluation design in which both pretraining and posttraining outcomes measures are collected.

pretest/posttest with comparison group An evaluation design that includes trainees and a comparison group. Both pretraining and posttraining outcome measures are collected.

pretraining measure A baseline measure of outcomes.

process consultation The use of a consultant to work with managers or other employees to help them to understand and take action to improve specific events that take place at work.

program design The organization and coordination of the training program.

program objectives Broad summary statements of a program's purpose.

project career A career based on a series of projects that may or may not be in the same company.

promotion An advancement into a position with greater challenges, more responsibility, and more authority than the previous job provided; usually includes a pay increase.

protean career A career that is frequently changing based on changes in the person's interests, abilities, and values as well as changes in the work environment.

psychological contract The expectations that employers and employees have about each other, and the employment relationship.

psychological success A feeling of pride and accomplishment that comes from achieving life goals.

psychosocial support Serving as a friend and role model to an employee; also includes providing positive regard, acceptance, and an outlet for the protégé to talk about anxieties and fears.

random assignment The assignment of employees to training or a comparison group on the basis of chance.

reaction outcomes A trainee's perceptions of a training program, including perceptions of the facilities, trainers, and content.

readability Written materials' level of difficulty.

readiness for training The condition of (1) employees having the personal characteristics necessary to learn program content and apply it on the job and (2) the work environment facilitating learning and not interfering with performance.

realistic job preview Stage in which a prospective employee is provided accurate information about attractive and unattractive aspects of a job, working conditions, company, and location to be sure that the employee develops appropriate expectations.

reality check Information an employee receives about how the company values that employee's skills and knowledge as well as where that employee fits into the company's plans.

reasonable accommodation In terms of the Americans with Disabilities Act and training, making training facilities readily accessible to and usable by individuals with disabilities; may also include modifying instructional media, adjusting training policies, and providing trainees with readers or interpreters.

recycling Changing one's major work activity after having been established in a particular field.

reengineering   A complete review and redesign of critical processes to make them more efficient and able to deliver higher quality.

rehearsal   A learning strategy focusing on learning through repetition (memorization).

reinforcement theory   Theory emphasizing that people are motivated to perform or avoid certain behaviors because of past outcomes that have resulted from those behaviors.

reliability   The degree to which outcomes can be measured consistently over time.

repatriation   Preparing expatriates for return to the parent company and country from a foreign assignment.

repurposing   Directly translating a training program that uses a traditional training method onto the Web.

request for proposal (RFP)   A document that outlines for potential vendors and consultants the requirements for winning and fulfilling a contract with a company.

resistance to change   Managers' and/or employees' unwillingness to change.

results   Outcomes used to determine a training program's payoff.

retirement   The leaving of a job and work role to make the transition into life without work.

retrieval   The identification of learned material in long-term memory and use of it to influence performance.

return on investment (ROI)   A comparison of a training program's monetary benefits and costs.

reversal   A time period in which training participants no longer receive training intervention.

rigor   The degree to which a training program emphasizes behavior and skills needed to effectively accomplish the training's goals.

role play   A training exercise in which the participant takes the part or role of a manager or some other employee; training method in which trainees are given information about a situation and act out characters assigned to them.

sabbatical   A leave of absence from the company to renew or develop skills.

scenario analysis   Simulation of real-world issues presented to data end-users.

School-to-Work Opportunities Act (1994)   Federal act designed to assist the states in building school-to-work systems that prepare students for high-skill, high-wage jobs or future education.

school-to-work transition program   Program combining classroom experience with work experience to prepare high school students for employment after graduation.

self-assessment   An employee's use of information to determine career interests, values, aptitudes, and behavioral tendencies.

self-directed learning   Training in which employees take responsibility for all aspects of their learning (e.g., when it occurs, who is involved).

self-efficacy   Employees' belief that they can successfully perform their job or learn the content of a training program.

self-management   Person's attempt to control certain aspects of his or her decision making and behavior.

semantic encoding   The actual coding process of incoming memory.

settling-in phase   A phase in the job socialization process in which employees begin to feel comfortable with their job demands and social relationships.

simulation   A training method that represents a real-life situation, with trainees' decisions resulting in outcomes that mirror what would happen if they were on the job.

situational constraints   Work environment characteristics including lack of proper equipment, materials, supplies, budgetary support, and time.

Six Sigma process   A process of measuring, analyzing, improving, and then controlling processes once they have been brought within the Six Sigma quality tolerances or standards.

skill   Competency in performing a task.

skill-based outcomes   Outcomes used to assess the level of technical or motor skills or behavior; include skill acquisition or learning and on-the-job use of skills.

skill-based pay system   Pay system based primarily on an employee's skills rather than on the job the employee is performing (also called knowledge-based pay system).

social learning theory   Theory emphasizing that people learn by observing other persons (models) who they believe are credible and knowledgeable.

social support   Feedback and reinforcement from managers and peers.

socialization   Sharing tacit knowledge by sharing experiences.

Solomon four-group   An evaluation design combining the pretest/posttest comparison group and the posttest-only control group designs.

spaced practice   Training approach in which trainees are given rest intervals within the practice session.

sponsor   A staff member who provides direction to other employees, represents the company to customers, initiates actions, and makes decisions.

staffing strategy   A company's decisions regarding where to find employees, how to select them, and the mix of employee skills and statuses.

stakeholders   The parties with an interest in a company's success (include shareholders, employees, customers, and the community).

stimulus generalization approach   The construction of training to emphasize the most important features or general principles.

strain-based conflict   Conflict resulting from the stress of work and nonwork roles.

strategic training and development initiatives   Learning-related actions that a company takes to achieve its business strategy.

subject-matter expert (SME)   Person who is knowledgeable of (1) training issues, (2) knowledge, skills, and abilities required for task performance, (3) necessary equipment, and (4) conditions under which tasks have to be performed.

succession planning   The process of identifying and tracking high-potential employees for advancement in a company.

summative evaluation   Evaluation of the extent that trainees have changed as a result of participating in a training program.

support network   A group of two or more trainees who agree to meet and discuss their progress in using learned capabilities on the job.

supportive work-life culture   A company culture that acknowledges and respects family and life responsibilities and obligations and encourages managers and employees to work together to meet personal and work needs.

survey feedback   The process of collecting information about employees' attitudes and perceptions using a survey, summarizing the results, and providing employees with feedback to stimulate discussion, identify problems, and plan actions to solve problems.

survivor   An employee remaining with a company after downsizing.

SWOT analysis   An identification of a company's operating environment as well as an internal analysis of its strengths and weaknesses. SWOT is an acronym for strengths, weaknesses, opportunities, and threats.

synchronous communication   Communication in which trainers, experts, and learners interact with each other live and in real time in the same way as they would in face-to-face classroom instruction.

tacit knowledge   Personal knowledge that is based on individual experience and that is difficult to explain to others.

task   A statement of an employee's work activity in a specific job.

task analysis   Training analysis involving identifying the tasks and knowledge, skills, and behaviors that need to be emphasized in training for employees to complete their tasks.

task redefinition   Changes in managers' and/or employees' roles and methods.

team leader training   Training that a team manager or facilitator receives.

team training   Training method that involves coordinating the performances of individuals who work together to achieve a common goal.

teleconferencing   Synchronous exchange of audio, video, and/or text between two or more individuals or groups at two or more locations.

teleworking   Working in a remote location (distant from a central office), where the employee has limited contact with peers but can communicate electronically.

theory of identical elements   A theory that transfer of learning occurs when what is learned in training is identical to what the trainee has to perform on the job.

threats to validity   Factors that will lead one to question either (1) study results' believability or (2) the extent to which evaluation results are generalizable to other groups of trainees and situations.

time-based conflict   Situation in which the demands of work and nonwork interfere with each other.

time orientation   The degree to which a culture focuses on the future rather than the past and present.

time series   An evaluation design in which training outcomes are collected at periodic intervals pre- and posttraining.

Total Quality Management (TQM)   A style of doing business that relies on the talents and capabilities of both labor and management to build and provide high-quality products and services and continuously improve them.

traditionalists   People born between 1920 and 1944.

trainee characteristics   The abilities and motivation that affect learning.

training   A company's planned effort to facilitate employees' learning of job-related competencies.

training administration   Coordination of activities before, during, and after a training program.

training context   The physical, intellectual, and emotional environment in which training occurs.

training design   Characteristics of the learning environment.

training design process   A systematic approach to developing training programs. Its six steps include conducting needs assessment, ensuring employees' readiness for training, creating a learning environment, ensuring transfer of training, selecting training methods, and evaluating training programs.

training effectiveness   Benefits that a company and its trainees receive from training.

training evaluation   The process of collecting the outcomes needed to determine if training has been effective.

training outcomes (criteria)   Measures that a company and its trainer use to evaluate training programs.

training site   The place where training is conducted.

transfer   Giving an employee a different job assignment in a different area of the company.

transfer of training   Trainees' applying learned capabilities gained in training to their jobs.

uncertainty avoidance   A preference for structured rather than unstructured situations.

upward feedback   An appraisal process involving collection of subordinates' evaluations of managers' behaviors or skills.

utility analysis   A cost-benefit analysis method that involves assessing the dollar value of training based on estimates of the difference in job performance between trained and untrained employees, the number of individuals trained, the length of time a training program is expected to influence performance, and the variability in job performance in the untrained group of employees.

valence   The value that a person places on an outcome.

values   Principles and virtues that symbolize the company's beliefs.

verbal information   Names or labels, facts, and bodies of knowledge.

verbal persuasion   Offering words of encouragement to convince others that they can learn.

vicarious reinforcement   Situation in which a trainee sees a model being reinforced for using certain behaviors.

virtual expatriate   An employee assigned to work on an operation in another country without being located permanently in it.

virtual reality   A computer-based technology that provides trainees with a three-dimensional learning experience.

virtual team   A team that is separated by time, geographic distance, culture, and/or organizational boundaries and that relies almost exclusively on technology to interact and complete projects.

virtual training organization   A training organization operating on four principles: (1) employees, rather than the company, have primary responsibility for learning, (2) training needs to be developed to meet customer needs, (3) the most effective learning occurs on the job, and (4) the manager-employee relationship is critical for training to be translated into improved job performance.

virtual work arrangement   Work arrangement (including virtual teams as well as teleworking) in which location, organization structure, and employment relationship are not limiting factors.

vision   The picture of the future that the company wants to achieve.

webcasting   Classroom instructions that are provided online through live broadcasts.

whole practice   Training approach in which all tasks or objectives are practiced at the same time.

work environment: On-the-job factors that influence transfer of training.

work team   A group of employees with various skills who interact to assemble a product or produce a service.

Workforce Investment Act   A 1998 federal act that created a new, comprehensive work force investment system that is customer focused, that provides Americans with career management information and high-quality services, and that helps U.S. companies find skilled workers.

working storage   The rehearsal and repetition of information, allowing it to be coded for memory.

World Wide Web (WWW)   A user-friendly service on the Internet; provides browser software enabling users to explore the Web.

Name Index

Company Index

Index